A Reference Publication in Literature

Everett Emerson, *Editor*

An Annotated Bibliography of American Literary Periodicals, 1741-1850

Compiled and Edited
Jayne K. Kribbs

G. K. HALL & CO., 70 LINCOLN STREET, BOSTON, MASS.

Library of Congress Cataloging in Publication Data

Kribbs, Jayne K
    An annotated bibliography of American literary peri-
odicals, 1741-1850.

    (Reference guides in literature)
    Includes indexes.
    1. American literature--Periodicals--Bibliography.
I. Title.
Z1219.K75   [PS1]   016.81'05   77-7487
ISBN 0-8161-7970-0

This publication is printed on permanent/durable acid-free paper
MANUFACTURED IN THE UNITED STATES OF AMERICA

I dedicate this volume to
Professor Harrison T. Meserole, of course

"Among the various causes that have contributed to the general diffusion of knowledge in the present age, nothing seems to have been of more importance than the circulation of so many different periodical papers."

--The Literary Miscellany, or Monthly Review
    May 1811, p. 39.

--The Olio, a Literary and Miscellaneous
    Paper 13 Feb. 1813, p. 19.

"We may venture to assert there are few things which have a more direct tendency to enlighten the general mind, and to refine the sentiments of the general community, than the species of literature which is known under the title of Periodical."

--The American Monthly Magazine
    March 1833, p. 2.

Contents

Introduction

In the April 1831 issue of The Illinois Monthly Magazine, the author of an article entitled "Periodicals" exclaimed: "I love periodicals, for the same reason that I like oysters, because they are palatable, and easy of digestion. They may not satisfy the craving appetite of the student who hungers and thirsts after knowledge, and prowls through libraries, like a gaunt wolf, seeking whom he may devour. The philosopher may set them down as naught, because they are not apt to contain anything very abstruse, or unintelligible. But for one who, like myself, is blessed with very moderate propensities: never indifferent, yet never absolutely craving for literary food, they are the very things--and especially as they may be taken at any moment with perfect ease and pleasure" (p. 302).

These sentiments were echoed by editors and readers across the country and across the decades between 1741 and 1850--wherever and whenever periodicals were being published. And rightly so, for after some early sputtering successes and discouraging failures, literary periodicals began to capture the imagination of the American reading public. These magazines, journals, miscellanies, and reviews became entertaining and instructive repositories for established and aspiring authors of the eighteenth and nineteenth centuries.

However, what might legitimately be called a periodical publication was issued in the colonies a full fifty years before the first magazines in 1741. On September 25, 1690 the first number of Benjamin Harris's newspaper Publick Occurrences Both Foreign and Domestick appeared. Although it lasted only four days and contained little of what might be called "literary," it became important as the herald of what was to become a major industry in America. No other attempt at publishing a newspaper was made until 1704, when John Campbell published the Boston News-Letter. Later James Franklin began the New-England Courant which, in addition to foreign and domestic news, included a number of poems and entertaining and instructive essays. It was here that the editor's apprenticed printer brother, Benjamin, published his first prose writing under the name of Silence Dogood. Gradually, others began to follow these early leads, so that by 1741, most of the colonies were printing weekly newspapers, many of which contained literary departments filled with poetry and Addison-like essays. Among the more widely circulated of these were the Virginia Gazette, Pennsylvania Gazette, South Carolina Gazette, and the Boston Evening-Post.

But the literary periodical as a form was born in January 1741 with the publication of two rival Philadelphia magazines--Andrew Bradford's The American Magazine, or a Monthly View of the Political State of the British Colonies and Benjamin Franklin's The General Magazine, and Historical Chronicle, for All the British Plantations in America. These and many other journals which followed for the next thirty years openly acknowledged their imitation of such highly successful British models as the London Magazine, the Edinburgh Review, and the Gentleman's Magazine.

With the coming of the Revolutionary War, however, the character of periodicals began to change. It was an age in which many of the young country's writers turned to the business of promoting independence, democracy, and patriotism, and with this patriotic fervor and democratic zeal came the desire for a national literature. There were a number of difficulties in its creation, though. Established or current literary modes in England and Europe contended with this often unruly spirit of nationalism in creating an American literary tradition and a truly American periodical. On one hand, the reading public eagerly sought out such writers as Scott, Johnson, Byron, Lytton-Bulwer, Sheridan, and on the other called for a uniquely American literature. To succeed at publishing a literary periodical in late eighteenth- and early nineteenth-century America, then, proved difficult indeed. The editor and publisher had to reconcile these sometimes confusing demands, and the aspiring American writer had to imitate the English masters by giving his "imitation" an American setting. Thus, many works appearing in American periodicals were re-workings of popular English models. But because editors accepted for publication or pirated from other journals the "imitations" which were certain to increase their journals' subscription lists, they encouraged for a time a kind of literary mediocrity that attracted such "secondary" American writers as Mrs. Seba Smith, Alfred B. Street, Emma C. Embury, and Catharine Maria Sedgwick—along with the droves of known and pseudonymous authors whose work appeared in the periodicals across the country. So, except for Joseph Dennie's early recognition of Freneau and Franklin in the Port Folio, critics acknowledged almost no outstanding, enduring figures in American literary periodicals until the successes of Cooper, Bryant, and Irving.

Yet in the period 1741-1850, poetry was highly regarded. It was the rare periodical without a poets' corner or a section devoted to original domestic or selected foreign poetry, especially the ode, pastoral, elegy, and satire. Editors rarely paid for poetry because the quantity was so vast; everyone wrote it, and in forms and language that were thoroughly familiar, following Pope, Swift, Cowper, Goldsmith, and Gray—and later such romantic poets as Wordsworth, Coleridge, Byron, and Shelley. The English masters again provided ready molds into which many poetasters poured their Della Cruscan or overwritten "effusions."

American periodicals also became the best source for accounts of travels, histories, and biographies of religious, political, and literary persons. In the Port Folio for February 12, 1808, Dennie remarked that "Next to the periodical essays, and the biography of the learned, for which not only ourselves but the great majority of our readers have a strong and just partiality, we have always admitted tours and travels" (p. 96).

Respectability of the periodical press seemed to grow in direct proportion to the development and maturity of the United States in the 1830s and '40s. Attitudes began to change toward the legitimacy of American authors and the press. Now writers were searching out the magazines as vehicles for their creative energies. Editor John Inman understood the immense value and the new spirit of periodical publications: "The magazine is the true channel into which talent should direct itself for the acquisition of literary fame. . . . Magazine publishers can and do more efficiently promote the development of talent than any other class of purveyors for the intellectual appetite of the country" (from The Columbian Lady's and Gentleman's Magazine, January 1844, pp. 2-3).

Any large-scale study of American literary periodicals inevitably yields some interesting statistical results. For example, of the three major population centers, New York City published 172 literary periodicals between 1741 and 1850; Boston was second with 142, and Philadelphia third with 124. From here, there is a dramatic dropping off, with Baltimore publishing only 30; Cincinnati ("the Rose of the West") 28; Albany 18, New Haven 17, and Washington, D.C., Richmond, and Charleston each recording 11. A number of out-of-the-way cities issued periodicals as well. Portland, Oregon, had one journal, The Christian Intelligencer, Gallatin, Texas, had Southron; Natchez, Mississippi, the South-Western Journal; and New Orleans could boast of four: The Monthly Miscellany, Parley's Magazine for Children and Youth, The New Orleans Miscellany, and The Southern Quarterly Review.

The states with the most literary periodicals published follows closely in line with their cities: New York with 236, Massachusetts with 185, Pennsylvania with 144, Ohio with 47, and Connecticut and Maryland each with 32. Illinois published 4 journals, Michigan 3, and Indiana and Wisconsin each had 2.

As might be expected, the number of literary periodicals issued rose sharply with each passing decade. The years 1781 to 1790 saw the publication of 22 journals; 1791-1800, 60 journals; 1801-1810, 97 journals; 1811-1820, 101 journals; 1821-1830, 144 journals; 1831-1840, 167 journals; and 1841-1850, 170+ journals. 1841 and 1842 led all other years with 29 journals beginning each year; 1834 was second with 25; 1828 third with 23, and 1833 fourth with 22. Most editors and publishers decided to establish their periodicals at the beginning of each new year. An impressive 167 journals sprang into existence in January alone. July was a distant second with only 65. The month with the fewest periodicals beginning was March with 29, then December with 34.

A study of the literary figures represented by pieces by or about them in these periodicals also yields some expected and unexpected results. Topping the list are both Byron and Franklin with pieces by or about them appearing in 153 periodicals. Samuel Johnson is next, appearing in 137. Third is William Cowper, 126; then, Lydia H. Sigourney, 124; Thomas Moore, 122; Felicia Hemans, 119, Sir Walter Scott, 115; Nathaniel Parker Willis, 112; William Cullen Bryant, 100; and Robert Southey rounding out the top ten with 95. Only four from this list are American; only two are women.

The ten most frequently published poets include: Lydia H. Sigourney, whose work appears in 111 journals; next is Thomas Moore, in 107; then, Felicia Hemans, 105; Byron, 101; Bryant, 89; James Montgomery, 88; William Cowper, 79; Thomas Campbell, 72; Nathaniel Parker Willis, 72; and Hannah F. Gould, 67. From this list, only four are American; only three are women.

Twenty eight journals carried biographies of Franklin; 20 journals noticed Washington; 18 recounted the life of Benjamin West; 17 noticed Scott. Other figures whose biographies appeared often include: Napoleon Buonaparte, in 16; William Cowper, in 14; Byron, in 13; and Burns, LaFayette, and Penn, in 12. Of this group, only five are American.

Tales by Washington Irving appeared in at least 23 periodicals, followed by Nathaniel Parker Willis in at least 16; Hawthorne, 13. E. Lytton Bulwer, James Hogg, and Mary Russell Mitford each appeared in at least 8; T.S. Arthur in 7; Emma C. Embury in 6.

It must be emphasized that these statistics, however interesting they might be, should be viewed only as by-products of the indexes from which they were culled. The purpose of the indexes is to offer a key into the large and diverse body of information found in the main body of this bibliography. Ultimately, of course, the entire bibliography becomes a key which opens to the user the complex and extensive mass of material found in American literary periodicals.

One final note: In the first issue of The Monthly Magazine, and American Review (April 1799), "Candidus" warned editor Charles Brockden Brown of the critics who would inevitably find fault with his brave undertaking. After having gathered, organized, and codified such a large and complex body of information, I am as consciously aware of my would-be detractors as was Candidus when he wrote: "Your efforts to please will be frustrated by some unlucky difference of opinion between you and your reader. . . . Your merits will be rigorously scanned, your defects eagerly blazoned, and your pretensions reluctantly admitted. Each one will look for discussions connected with his favourite pursuit-- . . . and, ten to one but each will find you trite, brief, or superficial, and consign you to cobwebs and dust" (p. 2).

Explanatory Notes

A. Purpose, Scope, and Criteria for Inclusion and Exclusion

This bibliography presents, in alphabetical arrangement of titles, the literary periodicals published in the United States between 1741 and 1850. The decision to use these dates has been made on four bases. They complement volume I of Frank Luther Mott's unsurpassed five-volume study, A History of American Magazines, and round out the compilation to a fairly neat 100-year span. After 1850, the character of the literary periodical began to change; the publishing industry fairly exploded with a great many long-lived, machine-produced works. Finally, after that date periodicals become more accessible for direct study.

The purpose of this bibliography is to provide material for research into our vast literary, historical, and cultural heritage from a relatively unexplored source. It makes available for the first time valuable information on the literary figures and literary genres which attracted the eighteenth- and nineteenth-century reading audiences in America. It forms the largest, most comprehensive annotated bibliography of American literary periodicals ever to be assembled for this time span, and as such, provides a useful source of reference for the scholar and librarian alike.

This bibliography is the result of a careful search of three major sources: the microfilmed American Periodical Series, the fifth edition of the Union List of Serials, and Mott's A History of American Magazines, 1741-1850. In addition, the periodicals collections of eight east-coast libraries have been searched: The Pennsylvania State University, Temple University, The University of Pennsylvania, the American Philosophical Society, the Historical Society of Pennsylvania, the Library Company of Philadelphia, the Library of Congress, and the American Antiquarian Society.

Of the 940 total entries, approximately 100 are not annotated. More than half of this number represents periodicals which survive in only one or two scattered issues and are held in libraries which were not easily accessible. The others, though they experienced longer runs, were not available for direct examination in any of the above libraries or on the APS. Information on them has been extracted from the Union List of Serials.

To define the terms "literary" and "periodical" exactly in relationship to this bibliography is difficult. There are no sufficiently clear definitions of "newspaper" and "periodical"* to explain why some publications were omitted or included. Some periodicals have characteristics of newspapers--format, amount of foreign and domestic occurrences, advertisements, periodicity--yet contain, for instance, a significant number of poems, biographies, essays, tales, extracts, and anecdotes. (See The Rhode-Island Cadet and Statesman, for example.) In the first issue of The Columbian Lady's and Gentleman's Magazine (January 1844), editor John Inman recognizes these problematic distinctions: "All literature approximates to the magazine, either in form or character; books are so printed and bound as to resemble monthly periodicals; and newspapers, unable to emulate them in appearance, strive to do so in the variety and nature of their contents. In fact, the word newspaper has come to be almost a misnomer, for the purveying of news has ceased to be their characteristic vocation and object. What is the 'leading article' but an essay? What are nine-tenths of the narrative paragraphs but short tales, either of fact or fiction?" (p. 1).

---

*See the introduction to volume I of Mott's study for his definitions of such terms as "magazine," "journal," "review," and "periodical."

Explanatory Notes

Periodicals are included if they contain a "significant" amount of literature, or if, for whatever reason, they are of distinctly literary interest. Selection has been made on the basis of content rather than on periodicity, although no dailies, almanacs, gift or emblem books are included, and with perhaps two or three exceptions, annuals are also not included. No consistent attempt has been made to search all religious and juvenile periodicals, but a number of these are listed because of their high literature content. A number of publications which have "literary"-sounding titles but which, in fact, contain very little or no literature are not included. Thus, although the United States Literary Advertiser, and Journal of Politics, Religion, Health, Economy, and the Arts (June-November 1830) prints some poetry by Felicia Hemans and extracts from Benjamin Franklin's prose, it is almost exclusively a newspaper in content and intent and, as such, not listed. The Repository of Knowledge, Historical, Literary, Miscellaneous, and Theological (April-May 1801) has been omitted because of its religious content, although it contains a poem by Phillis Wheatley. And despite the fact that William Cobbett is considered a literary figure, Cobbett's American Political Register (1816-1818) has not been indexed because of its almost complete political/ historical focus.

Periodicals are not included in this compilation if they began publishing one or two years before 1850 and extended far beyond this date. Yet Godey's Lady's Magazine, first issued in 1830, and The National Aegis in 1801, which both continued far beyond the 1850 cut-off date are listed but examined only through 1850. In some few cases when entire runs of a periodical could not be searched, annotations were made on the basis of direct examination of all available issues.

Finally, this bibliography does not pretend to be exhaustive. Inevitably there are publications which have been overlooked or omitted. Further, a work of this scope can never be viewed as complete as long as there are missing issues of journals which could supplement the information found here.

B. The Periodical Entry

Unlike the Union List of Serials which indexes the last title of the periodical first, followed by a brief statement of its publishing history, this bibliography indexes by the first title and sub-title (when present) followed by subsequent titles and sub-titles. Those titles which differ significantly from the original are cross-referenced.

Occasionally only year designations are given for the first or last issue of periodicals when more precise information has not been supplied either by the periodical itself or by the ULS.

When available, two locations are noted for each periodical. Most frequently cited are the APS (American Periodical Series) and one library. The asterisk (*) following a library location indicates that, according to the ULS, holdings for that journal are complete. If a periodical is discussed in Mott's A History of American Magazines, "Mott" is inserted after the library locations, and if the periodical is indexed in Poole's Index to Periodical Literature, "Poole" is inserted.

This bibliography silently corrects errors in Mott and the ULS.

At first glance the content analysis of some publications may seem to be uneven. Only original and selected poetry that is signed by the author is listed; this bibliography makes no attempt to identify the authors of anonymous and pseudonymous verse. The categories in the "Prose" section—Biography, Travel, Essay, Familiar Essay, Criticism, Letters, and Book Reviews—remain, for the most part, unannotated. Only the Biography category is consistently annotated if the names are of significant literary interest.

All names and titles in the annotations are listed here in the order in which they initially appeared in the periodicals—this to facilitate the user's search into the original source. Additional information on authors and titles can be found by consulting the indexes following the main body of the bibliography.

While this bibliography cannot claim to have indexed all the tales, novels, and drama in eighteenth- and nineteenth-century American literary periodicals, it does approach a fairly complete survey of approximately 5,000 titles.

It is not the purpose of this bibliography to attribute authorship for all tales, novels, and drama. That is a task which must await a future study. For the most part, I have supplied authorship when the periodical has provided it or when attribution is positively identifiable without further search.

Acknowledgments

A research project such as this inevitably incurs a great many debts over the years. I am grateful, first, to The Pennsylvania State University for a 1974-75 Research Initiation Grant and to Temple University for a 1976 Summer Research Fellowship Award. I had the full support and cooperation of Charles W. Mann, Curator of the Rare Book Collection at The Pennsylvania State University, as well as the staffs of the American Philosophical Society, the Historical Society of Pennsylvania, the Library Company of Philadelphia, the Van Pelt Library of the University of Pennsylvania, and the Rare Books Division of the Library of Congress, who freely opened their periodical holdings to me. To Professor Joseph Katz I owe thanks for his advice and encouragement in the early stages of the research; to Professor Everett Emerson for his careful reading of the text; to my Penn State research assistants, Miss Candice Stover, who searched the Union List of Serials and Charles Evans' American Bibliography for early American literary periodicals, and Mrs. Effie Siegel, who helped to search titles in the American Periodical Series; to Mrs. Sheila Jacobs and the secretarial staff of the English Department at Temple University who hand sorted literally thousands of items for the title and name indexes; and to my Temple research assistant Miss Estar Jones who cooperated enthusiastically in every phase of index preparation. In particular, I wish to acknowledge the generous and courteous assistance of Mr. William Sartain, Director of the Stack and Reader Division of the Library of Congress, who tracked down a number of long neglected early American periodicals for me. Particular recognition is also due to a number of persons at the American Antiquarian Society: Associate Librarian, Mr. Frederick E. Bauer, Jr., Miss Mary E. Brown, Head of Readers' Service, and her assistants Marie Lamoreau and Alan Degustis, who made my stint at the Society pleasant and productive. Finally, with something of reverence, I acknowledge my indebtedness to Professor Harrison T. Meserole, mentor and friend, who generously offered his vast store of wisdom and sound advice at every stage of this project.

An Annotated Bibliography of American Literary Periodicals, 1741-1850

1 TITLE: L'Abeille américaine, journal,
   historique, politique et littéraire.

   Place of Publication: Philadelphia
   First Issue: 15 April 1815
   Last Issue: 9 July 1818//
   Periodicity: Weekly
   Editor: A.J. Blocquerst
   Publisher: S. Chaudron
   Available From: Lib. of Congress*; Amer.
                   Philosophical Soc.*
   Contents:
     Poetry: Original. Selected: Pope,
       Selleck Osborne, Béranger.
     Prose: Biography. Travel. Essay.
       Familiar Essay. Criticism. Letters.
     Fiction: Sketches.
     Miscellaneous: Extracts: from other
       journals; by various authors; Goldsmith.
       Anecdotes: on various subjects;
       Franklin, Buonaparte. Literary Notices.
       News: Foreign and Domestic.

2 TITLE: Abracadabra; or the Conceits of A,
   B & C.

   Place of Publication: Portland, Me.
   First Issue: 16 June 1808
   Last Issue: ?
   Available From: N.Y. Pub. Lib.; Boston Pub.
                   Lib.

3 TITLE: Academic Pioneer and Guardian of
   Education.

   Place of Publication: Cincinnati
   First Issue: July 1831
   Last Issue: Dec 1832//
   Available From: Hist. and Philosophical Soc.
                   of Ohio, Cincinnati;
                   Harvard Univ.

4 TITLE: The Academician, Containing the
   Elements of Scholastic Science, and the
   Outlines of Philosophic Education, Predi-
   cated on the Analysis of the Human Mind,
   and Exhibiting the Improved Methods of
   Instruction.

   Place of Publication: New York
   First Issue: 7 Feb 1818
   Last Issue: 29 Jan 1820//
   Periodicity: Semi-monthly
   Editors: Albert Picket; John W. Picket
   Publishers: Charles N. Baldwin
   Available From: APS; Lib. of Congress.*
                   Mott.
   Contents:
     Poetry: Original.
     Prose: Familiar Essay. Criticism. Book
       Reviews.
     Fiction: Essay Serials: "The Academician";
       "The Gleaner."
     Miscellaneous: Extracts: from other
       journals.

5 TITLES: (1) The Aeronaut: A Periodical
   Paper: By an Association of Gentlemen
   (2) The Aeronaut: A Periodical Paper, by
   a Literary Association (3) The Aeronaut.
   By a Literary Association (4) The
   Aeronaut.

   Place of Publication: New York
   First Issue: 18 May 1816
   Last Issue: 1822//
   Periodicity: Weekly
   Editors: ?
   Publishers: ?
   Available From: APS; Columbia Univ.
   Contents:
     Poetry: Original. Selected.
     Prose: Biography: Byron, Scott, W. Irving.
       Travel. Familiar Essay. Criticism.
       Letters.
     Fiction: Essay Serials: "Quidoniana";
       "Alcandriana." Tales: "The Princess of
       Madagascar. A Tale"; "Story of an
       Englishwoman."
   Note: Some articles of interest include:
     "Causes of the Dearth of Literary Genius
     in the United States"; "On the Metre &
     Phraseology of Poetry"; "On Scheming--The
     Pleasures and Toils of a Literary Life";
     "Peculiarites of American Manners"; "State
     of American Literature and Education--
     Female Education"; "Quibblers About
     Terms--Miseries and Subserviency of Poor
     Authors."

6   TITLE: Albany Bouquet: And Literary Spectator.

Place of Publication: Albany
First Issue: 18 April 1835
Last Issue: 19 Sept 1835//?
Periodicity: Weekly
Editor: George Trumbull
Publisher: George Trumbull
Available From: APS; N.Y. Hist. Soc.*
Contents:
    Poetry: Original: J.W. Goodrich.
        Selected: Hannah F. Gould, Bryant,
        Goldsmith, L.W. Trask, Hannah More.
    Prose: Biography: Franklin, Washington,
        Charles Brockden Brown.
    Fiction: Sketches. Tales: "The Storm";
        "The Leper of the City of Aosta"; "The
        Two Sisters.--A Tale"; "The Misfortunes
        of Annette---, a Tale of the French
        Revolution"; "The Indian Spy."
    Miscellaneous: Extracts: from other
        journals. News: Domestic.

7   TITLE: Albany Literary Gazette; a Repository
     of Literature and the Arts.

Place of Publication: Albany
First Issue: 3 Sept 1831
Last Issue: 7 April 1832//
Available From: N.Y. State Lib., Albany*;
                 Lib. of Congress

8   TITLE: Albany Religious Spectator. A Family
     Paper, Devoted to Religion and General
     Intelligence.

Place of Publication: Albany
First Issue: 2 Nov 1844
Last Issue: 25 Oct 1845//
Periodicity: Weekly
Editors: Erastus H. Pease; J. Munsell
Publishers: Erastus H. Pease; J. Munsell
Available From: Amer. Antiquarian Soc.*;
                 N.Y. State Lib., Albany*
Contents:
    Poetry: Original: Sarah M'Donald, Kate
        Rivington. Selected: Joseph H. Butler,
        Caroline F. Orne, Lydia H. Sigourney,
        E.G. Squier, L.E. Landon, Thomas Hood,
        Mary L. Gardiner, William Cowper, Joseph
        Harris, Schiller, Nathaniel P. Willis,
        Hannah F. Gould, William Leggett,
        Thomas L. Harris, William Motherwell,
        Frederick W. Cole, Mary Howitt, B.F.
        Romaine.
    Prose: Biography. Travel. Essay.
        Letters.
    Fiction: Essay Serial: "Notes by the Way."
        Sketches.
    Miscellaneous: Extracts: from other
        journals. Anecdotes: on various sub-
        jects. Literary Notices. News: Foreign
        and Domestic.

9   TITLES: (1) The Albion, or British, Colonial,
     and Foreign Weekly Gazette (2) The Albion;
     a Journal of News, Politics and Literature.

Place of Publication: New York
First Issue: 22 June 1822
Last Issue: 31 Dec 1876//?
Periodicity: Weekly
Editor: John S. Bartlett
Publisher: John S. Bartlett
Available From: APS; Yale Univ. Mott.
Contents:
    Poetry: Original. Selected: Byron, George
        Colman, Thomas Campbell, Burns, Scott,
        William Jones, Thomas Moore, Sidney,
        Joanna Baillie, J.G. Lockhart, Shakespeare.
    Prose: Biography. Travel. Letters. Book
        Reviews.
    Fiction: Essay Serials: "Literary Glean-
        ings." Drama: "Werner" [Byron]; "The
        Bride's Tragedy" [Thomas Lovell Beddoes].
    Miscellaneous: Extracts: from the other
        journals. Anecdotes: on various
        authors. Literary Notices. News: Foreign
        and Domestic.

10   TITLES: (1) The Album. And Ladies' Weekly
     Gazette (2) Philadelphia Album, and Ladies'
     Literary Gazette (3) The Philadelphia Album
     and Ladies' Literary Port Folio. [In 1828,
     it absorbed The Ladies' Literary Port Folio
     q.v. Merged into The Pennsylvania Inquirer,
     later The Philadelphia Inquirer.]

Place of Publication: Philadelphia
First Issue: 7 June 1826
Last Issue: 27 Dec 1834//
Periodicity: Weekly
Editors: Thomas Cottrell Clarke; Robert
         Morris
Publishers: Morris & Kenney; Jesper Harding
Available From: APS; Hist. Soc. of Pa.*
                 Mott.
Contents:
    Poetry: Original: James M'Henry, Richard
        Emmons, Harriet Muzzy, Nathaniel P. Willis,
        Whittier, Elizabeth Bogart, Bryant, Robert
        Morris. Selected: Felicia Hemans, William
        B. Tappan, Scott, Gray, Henry, Neele,
        Nathaniel P. Willis, W.G. Crosby, Sumner
        Lincoln Fairfield, William Leggette, Robert
        Montgomery, Lydia H. Sigourney, Robert
        Morris, Amelia Opie, Whittier, Shelley,
        Coleridge, Byron, J.O. Rockwell, Mary Anne
        Brown, Thomas Haynes Bayly, John G.
        Brainard, Fitz-Greene Halleck, Longfellow,
        James G. Percival, Mary Howitt, Barry
        Cornwall, Hannah More, Leigh Hunt.
    Prose: Biography: Goldsmith, Southey,
        Scott. Essay. Familiar Essay. Criti-
        cism. Letters. Book Reviews.
    Fiction: Essay Serials: "The Common Place
        Book"; "Sketches of Roseville"; "Specula-
        tions of Scriblerus Secundus, Esq.";
        "Hours of Leisure"; "The Traveller";
        "Desultory Scraps"; "My Scrap Book";
        "Notes of a Bookworm." Sketches. Tales:
        "The Lovers' Quarrel"; "Edward and Susan,
        or the Fatal Excursion"; "Lucy of the
        Fold"; "The Rival Brothers, a Tale of the
        Revolution"; "The Barber of Gottingen";
        "Osman and Fatima: A Turkish Story";
        "The Martyr, an Historical Tale"; "The
        Twin Sisters"; "The Orphan of the

Frontier"; "The Sister Victims"; "Ellen
Stanley, or the Victim of Vanity"; "The
Man with the Mouth"; "Reuben Melville";
"The Carib Cacique; or, the Chief in
Chains"; "The Ruse" [Nathaniel P. Willis];
"The Second Wife"; "The History of Sir
Reginald Granville"; "Azim; an Oriental
Tale"; "Francis Riordan"; "Everard
Graham" [Willis Gaylord Clark]; "The
Black Ferry"; "The Triple Marriage"; "A
'Man About Town'"; "The History of Uncle
Sam and His Boys. A Tale for Politi-
cians"; "The Spectre'Smitten"; "The
Pirate"; "Grace Kennedy--A Tale"; "Allan
M'Tavish"; "The Ruined Laird"; "Laura
Lovell"; "The Baronet's Bride"; "The
Forsaken Child"; "Gertrude Beverly";
"Tahmiroo, the Indian Wife."
  Miscellaneous: Extracts: from other
journals; Jefferson, W. Irving.
Anecdotes: Byron, Franklin, Thomas
Paine. Literary Notices.

11   TITLE: Alleghanian.

Place of Publication: New York
First Issue: 24 May 1845
Last Issue: 28 June 1845//?
Available From: N.Y. Pub. Lib.; Yale Univ.

12   TITLE: The Alleghany Magazine, or Repository
of Useful Knowledge.

Place of Publication: Meadville, Pa.
First Issue: July 1816
Last Issue: June 1817//
Periodicity: Monthly
Editor: Timothy Alden
Publisher: Thomas Atkinson
Available From: Hist. Soc. of Pa.*; Yale
                  Univ.
Contents:
  Poetry: Original. Selected.
  Prose: Biography. Letters.
  Fiction: Essay Serials: "The Aboriginal";
    "The Dead Languages."
  Miscellaneous: Extracts: from other
    journals; by various authors. Anecdotes:
    on various subjects. News: Domestic.
Note: Primarily a religious journal.

13   TITLE: Alter et idem, a New Review. For a
Summer Month in 1794.

Place of Publication: Reading, Pa.
First Issue: [Only one issue published]
            1794//
Available From: N.Y. Pub. Lib.; Yale Univ.

14   TITLE: Amaranth; a Monthly Magazine of New
and Popular Tales, Poetry, History,
Biography.

Place of Publication: New Brunswick, N.J.
First Issue: Jan 1841
Last Issue: Dec 1843//
Available From: N.Y. Hist. Soc.*; Brown
                  Univ., Providence, R.I.

15   TITLE: The Amaranth. A Semi-Monthly Publication, Devoted to Polite Literature,
Science, Poetry and Amusement.

Place of Publication: Ashland, Ohio
First Issue: 20 Feb 1847
Last Issue: 11 Dec 1847//
Periodicity: Semi-monthly
Editor: Robert V. Kennedy
Publisher: Robert V. Kennedy
Available From: APS; Lib. of Congress*
Contents:
  Poetry: Original: Marietta V. Fuller,
    L. Granger. Selected: Thomas Haynes
    Bayly, Coleridge, Erasmus Darwin, Lydia
    H. Sigourney, Byron, George W. Cutter.
  Prose: Biography: Pocahontas. Travel.
    Familiar Essay. Letters.
  Fiction: Sketches. Tales: "Lillie
    Lelford"; "Rena di Albuli--A Tale";
    "Temper"; "The Carnival; or, the Mock
    Marriage"; "Kate Darlington. A Tale of
    Merry England"; "The Princess of Chios;
    a Legend of the Greek Isles"; "Flirtation.
    A Story of the Opera"; "The Belle of the
    Ball Room."
  Miscellaneous: Extracts: from other
    journals. Anecdotes: on various sub-
    jects.

16   TITLE: The Amaranth and Literary Journal.
A Metropolitan Magazine of Literature and
the Fine Arts. [See The Amaranth, or
Literary Port Folio. A Semi-Monthly
Journal Devoted to Polite Literature and
the Arts.]

17   TITLE: Amaranth, Devoted to Literature, and
to the Interests of Literary Societies.

Place of Publication: New York
First Issue: 6 Nov 1841
Last Issue: ?
Available From: Duke Univ., Durham; Univ. of
                Fla., Gainesville

18   TITLES: (1) The Amaranth, or Literary Port
Folio. A Semi-Monthly Journal Devoted to
Polite Literature and the Arts (2) The
Amaranth and Literary Journal. A Metro-
politan Magazine of Literature and the Fine
Arts.

Place of Publication: East Bridgwater, Mass.;
                  Boston
First Issue: 14 July 1832
Last Issue: 13 Feb 1836//?
Periodicity: Semi-monthly
Editors: B. Brown; George H. Brown; William
        H. Burleigh; E. Porter Dyer
Publishers: George H. Brown; E.R. Broaders
Available From: Amer. Antiquarian Soc.; N.Y.
              State Lib.
Contents:
  Poetry: Original: Jane E. Locke, E.H.
    Chapin, Louisa Simes, Lucy Hooper,
    Vincent C. Allyn, John C. M'Cabe, E.
    Porter Dyer. Selected: William D.
    Gallagher, William Leggett, J.O. Rockwell,

L.E. Landon, Byron, Hannah F. Gould, Whittier, Emma C. Embury, George W. Thompson, Sumner Lincoln Fairfield, James Montgomery, Lydia H. Sigourney.
Prose: Biography. Letters.
Fiction: Essay Serials: "My Love Adventures"; "Scraps from My Port-Folio." Sketches. Tales: "Anna Morison"; "William Leslie"; "The Rattlesnake Hunter" [Whittier]; "The Circle of Human Wishes" [James Kirke Paulding]; "The Keeper of the Prison-Ship Jersey"; "The Forsaken Girl" [Whittier]; "The Basket-Maker, or, Virtue Rewarded"; "Isabella and the Moor"; "The Iron Shroud, or--Italian Vengeance"; "Two Yards of Jaconet, or a Husband. A Virginia Tale"; "The Deformed Girl" [Whittier]; "The Captain's Lady"; "The Pilgrim's Bride. A Tale of Olden Times"; "The Twice Wedded"; "Leavenworth Green. An Occidental Tale"; "The Oxford Students"; "Mary Bell"; "Tarpeia. A Historical Tale"; "Poor Dummy"; "Cassanova's Escape."
Miscellaneous: Extracts: from other journals; by various authors; Theodore Sedgwick Fay, Nathaniel P. Willis, Leigh Hunt. Anecdotes: on various subjects. News: Domestic.

19   TITLE: The Amaranth; or Masonic Garland.

Place of Publication: Boston
First Issue: April 1828
Last Issue: Oct 1829//
Periodicity: Monthly
Editor: C.W. Moore
Publisher: C.W. Moore
Available From: APS; Boston Pub. Lib.*
Contents:
  Poetry: Original: James Grahame. Selected: Felicia Hemans, Robert Montgomery, Thomas Haynes Bayly.
  Prose: Letters: John Locke.
  Fiction: Sketches.
  Miscellaneous: Extracts: by various authors. Anecdotes: on various subjects.

20   TITLE: Amateur. A Cabinet of Science, Literature and the Fine Arts. [See the Amateur, a Journal of Literature and the Fine Arts.]

21   TITLES: (1) Amateur, a Journal of Literature and the Fine Arts (2) Amateur. A Cabinet of Science, Literature and the Fine Arts.

Place of Publication: Boston
First Issue: 15 June 1830
Last Issue: Dec 1831//
Available From: N.Y. State Lib., Albany; Newberry Lib., Chicago

22   TITLES: (1) The American (2) The Rhode-Island American, and General Advertiser.

Place of Publication: Providence, R.I.
First Issue: 21 Oct 1808
Last Issue: 29 Dec 1820//?
Periodicity: Semi-weekly
Editors: William W. Dunham; David Hawkins, Jr.
Publishers: William W. Dunham; David Hawkins, Jr.
Available From: Amer. Antiquarian Soc.*
Contents:
  Poetry: Original. Selected: Thomas Campbell.
  Prose: Essay. Familiar Essay.
  Fiction: Sketches.
  Miscellaneous: Extracts: from other journals; by various authors. Literary Notices. News: Foreign and Domestic.

23   TITLE: American Academy of Language and Belles Lettres.

Place of Publication: New York
First Issue: 1 Oct 1820
Last Issue: Jan 1822//
Available From: Yale Univ.; Boston Athenaeum

24   TITLES: (1) The American Apollo, Containing the Publications of the Historical Society (2) The American Apollo, Containing Essays, Moral, Political and Poetical, and the Daily Occurrences in the Natural, Civil, and Commercial World.

Place of Publication: Boston
First Issue: 6 Jan 1792
Last Issue: 25 Dec 1794//
Periodicity: Weekly
Editors: ?
Publishers: Belknap and Hall
Available From: APS; Amer. Antiquarian Soc.* Mott.
Contents:
  Poetry: Original: William Morrell, Robert Treat Paine.
  Prose: Biography: Fernando Cortes, Cervantes, Voltaire. Travel: William Bartram. Essay. Familiar Essay. Letters.
  Fiction: Sketches. Tales.
  Miscellaneous: News: Foreign and Domestic.
Note: Includes many accounts of Indian uprisings, as well as articles on Indian customs, manners, religion, etc.

25   TITLES: (1) The American Athenaeum, a Repository of Belles Lettres, Science and the Arts (2) The American Athenaeum; Repository of the Arts, Sciences, and Belles Lettres [Merged into The New York Literary Gazette q.v., later The Literary Gazette and American Athenaeum.]

Place of Publication: New York
First Issue: 21 April 1825
Last Issue: 2 March 1826//
Periodicity: Semi-monthly; weekly
Editor: George Bond

Publisher: Geroge Bond & Co.
Available From: APS; N.Y. Pub. Lib.*
Contents:
  Poetry: <u>Original</u>. <u>Selected</u>: Shakespeare,
    Wordsworth, James Hogg.
  Prose: <u>Biography</u>. <u>Travel</u>. <u>Familiar Essay</u>.
    <u>Letters</u>. <u>Book Reviews</u>.
  Fiction: <u>Essay Serials</u>: "Le Moulinet";
    "The Gossip"; "The Itinerant"; "Essays
    by Hookey Walker, Gent." <u>Tales</u>: "The
    Discovery; or Characteristics"; "Forgive
    Me Not. A Tale"; "The Locket"; "The
    Involuntary Miracle"; "Slander"; "Ad-
    ventures of a Poet."
  Miscellaneous: <u>Extracts</u>: from other
    journals. <u>Anecdotes</u>: on various authors.
    <u>Literary Notices</u>.

26 TITLE: <u>American Biblical Repository</u>. [See
    <u>Biblical Repository and Classical Review</u>.]

27 TITLE: <u>The American Critic, and General
    Review</u>.

    Place of Publication: Washington, D.C.
    First Issue: 1 April 1820
    Last Issue: 29 April 1820//?
    Periodicity: Intended to be weekly, but
                 issue ii appeared 29 April.
    Editor: John Wright
    Publisher: John Wright
    Available From: APS; Lib. of Congress*
    Contents
      Poetry: <u>Original</u>. <u>Selected</u>: Byron.
      Miscellaneous: <u>Anecdotes</u>: on various
        subjects. <u>News</u>: Foreign and Domestic.

28 TITLE: <u>The American Eagle Magazine: A
    Journal, Dedicated to Science, Literature,
    and Art</u>.

    Place of Publication: New York
    First Issue: June 1847
    Last Issue: July 1847//?
    Periodicity: Monthly
    Editors: John J. Schoolcraft; Thomas C.
             Dudley; DeWitt Clinton Morris
    Publishers: John J. Schoolcraft; Thomas C.
                Dudley; DeWitt Clinton Morris
    Available From: APS; N.Y. Hist. Soc.
    Contents:
      Poetry: <u>Original</u>.
      Prose: <u>Familiar Essay</u>.
      Fiction: <u>Essay Serials</u>: "AEgyptia."
        <u>Tales</u>: "The Bird of Alton."
      Miscellaneous: <u>Anecdotes</u>: on various sub-
        jects. <u>Literary Notices</u>.

29 TITLE: <u>The American Eclectic: Or Selections
    from the Periodical Literature of All
    Foreign Countries</u> [Combined with <u>The Museum
    of Foreign Literature and Science</u> q.v. to
    form <u>The Eclectic Museum</u> q.v.]

    Place of Publication: Boston; New York
    First Issue: Jan 1841
    Last Issue: Nov 1842//

Periodicity: Bi-monthly
Editors: Absalom Peters; Selah B. Treat;
         John Holmes Agnew
Publishers: William R. Peters; Whipple &
            Damrell; Platt & Peters; Saxton
            & Pierce
Available From: APS; Boston Athenaeum*
                Mott. <u>Poole</u>.
Contents:
  Prose: <u>Essay</u>. <u>Familiar Essay</u>. <u>Criticism</u>.
    <u>Book Reviews</u>.
  Miscellaneous: <u>Extracts</u>: from other
    journals. <u>Literary Notices</u>.
Note: 32 British, German, French, and
  Netherlandic journals were used as
  sources.

30 TITLE: <u>The American Expositor</u>.

    Place of Publication: Mount Vernon, Ohio
    First Issue: [Only one issue published?]
                 May 1850//?
    Periodicity: Monthly?
    Editor: John A. Reed
    Publisher: John A. Reed
    Available From: APS; Ohio State Archaeo-
                    logical and Hist. Soc.
    Contents:
      Poetry: <u>Selected</u>.
      Prose: <u>Essay</u>. <u>Familiar Essay</u>.
      Miscellaneous: <u>Extracts</u>: William Ellery
        Channing. <u>Anecdotes</u>: on various subjects.

31 TITLE: <u>American Gleanor and Virginia Magazine</u>.

    Place of Publication: Richmond
    First Issue: 24 Jan 1807
    Last Issue: 26 Dec 1807//
    Periodicity: Irregular. Intended to be
                 semi-monthly.
    Editors: ?
    Publishers: ?
    Available From: APS; Va. State Lib.,
                    Richmond*
    Contents:
      Poetry: <u>Original</u>. <u>Selected</u>: Peter Pindar,
        Hugh Henry Brackenridge.
      Prose: <u>Biography</u>: Washington, William
        Jones, George Wythe. <u>Letters</u>.
      Miscellaneous: <u>Extracts</u>: from other
        journals; by various authors; Franklin,
        William Godwin. <u>Anecdotes</u>: on various
        subjects.

32 TITLE: <u>The American Herald; and the General
    Advertiser</u>. [See <u>The Boston Evening-Post;
    and the General Advertiser</u>.]

33 TITLE: <u>The American Herald; and the Worcester
    Recorder</u>. [See <u>The Boston Evening-Post;
    and the General Advertiser</u>.]

34 TITLE: <u>American Ladies' Magazine; Containing
    Tales, Essays, Literary and Historical
    Sketches, Poetry, Criticism, Music, and a
    Great Variety of Matter Connected with Many</u>

Subjects of Importance and Interest. [See
The Ladies' Magazine.]

35   TITLES: (1) American Lady's Album and
     Gentlemen's Parlor Miscellany (2) The
     Ladies' Magazine and Album (3) The Ladies'
     Magazine and Album. Devoted to the Arts,
     Science, Music, Painting, Religion and
     Literature (4) The Ladies' Album.

     Place of Publication: Boston
     First Issue: Jan 1843
     Last Issue: June 1853//?
     Periodicity: Monthly
     Editor: A.H. Davis
     Publishers: A.H. Davis; Davis & Prentiss
     Available From: Lib. of Congress; Boston
                     Pub. Lib.
     Contents:
       Poetry: Original: Lorina D. Leland, Henry
         J. Bogue, J.H. Hanaford, A.E. Remington,
         Charlotte Allen, Caroline Linwood, J.T.
         Crooker, Kate Capella, Amos Walton.
         Selected: Eliza Cook, John Quincy Adams,
         Schiller, Charlotte Holt.
       Prose: Biography: Coleridge, Jenny Lind.
         Essay. Familiar Essay. Letters. Book
         Reviews.
       Fiction: Essay Serial: "The Ladies'
         Mirror." Sketches. Tales: "Bernice,--
         A Tale of the Early Christians"; "The
         Mechanic's Wife; or, the Gold Watch";
         "A Loss of the Last Shilling"; "Fun with
         the Doctor" [T.S. Arthur]; "Respectably
         Married"; "The Shipwreck; or, Effie
         Melville"; "Marrying Blindfolded"; "The
         Step-Mother: A Tale of Home"; "The
         Golden Locket: A Tale of the Nineteenth
         Century. Founded on Facts"; "Mary
         Ackerman: Or the Advantages of a
         Boarding School Instruction"; "'Our
         Carrie'"; "The Frontier House" [Sarah J.
         Hale]; "Asmolan: A Tale of Persia";
         "The Martial Fairy: A German Tale";
         "The Search for Honor."
       Miscellaneous: Extracts: from other
         journals; by various authors. Anecdotes:
         on various subjects; Daniel Webster,
         Fenelon. Literary Notices.

36   TITLE: The American Literary Gazette and
     New York Weekly Mirror. [See The New Mirror,
     of Literature, Amusement, and Instruction:
     Containing Original Papers; Tales of
     Romance; Sketches of Society, Manners, and
     Every-day Life; Domestic and Foreign Cor-
     respondence; Wit and Humour; Fashion and
     Gossip; the Fine Arts, and Literary,
     Musical and Dramatic Criticism; Extracts
     from New Works; Poetry Original and
     Selected; the Spirit of the Public Jour-
     nals; etc. etc. etc.]

37   TITLE: The American Literary Magazine.

     Place of Publication: Albany; Hartford
     First Issue: July 1847
     Last Issue: Aug 1849//

     Periodicity: Monthly
     Editor: Timothy Dwight Sprague
     Publisher: Timothy Dwight Sprague
     Available From: Univ. of Pa.*; Lib. of
                     Congress.* Mott. Poole.
     Contents:
       Poetry: Original: Elizabeth G. Barber,
         H.A. Rodman, C.C. Van Arsdale, Myron
         L. Mason, Lily Graham, S.W. Perry, A.F.
         Olmstead. Selected: Thomas Moore,
         Longfellow, Tennyson, Schiller, Alfred B.
         Street, William Falconer, Lydia H.
         Sigourney, Lamartine, W.H.C. Hosmer.
       Prose: Biography: Sir Walter Raleigh,
         Noah Webster, John Quincy Adams, Timothy
         Dwight, Ann S. Stephens, Chateaubriand,
         Richard Hooker, Petrarch, Lydia H.
         Sigourney, W. Irving, Alfred B. Street,
         Washington. Travel. Essay. Familiar
         Essay. Criticism. Letters. Book Reviews.
       Fiction: Essay Serials: "Classic Vagaries";
         "Musings in Ferrara." Sketches. Tales:
         "The Blue Stocking"; "A Novel Writ, a
         True Story"; "The Old Minister of Sche-
         nectady"; "A Stray Leaf from the Papers
         of a Solitary Man"; "Fanny Richmond. A
         Tale"; "The Gold Pen"; "The Lawyer's
         Dream"; "Marschalk Manor"; "Cousin Ned";
         "The New Year Bells of Gotham"; "Smiles
         and Tears, or the Cousins"; "The Old
         Mathematician"; "A Case of Resuscitation."
       Miscellaneous: Literary Notices.

38   TITLE: American Lyceum. [Proceedings]

     Place of Publication: Boston
     First Issue: July 1832
     Last Issue: July 1833//
     Available From: Watkinson Lib., Trinity Coll.,
                     Hartford; U.S. Office of
                     Educ. Lib.

39   TITLE: The American Magazine, a Monthly
     Miscellany, Devoted to Literature, Science,
     History, Biography, and the Arts; Including
     also State Papers and Public Documents,
     with Intelligence, Domestic, Foreign, and
     Literary, Public News, and Passing Events;
     Being an Attempt to Form a Useful Repository
     for Every Description of American Readers.

     Place of Publication: Albany
     First Issue: June 1815
     Last Issue: May 1816//
     Periodicity: Monthly
     Editor: Horatio Gates Spafford
     Publishers: E. & E. Hosford
     Available From: APS; Boston Pub. Lib.*
     Contents:
       Poetry: Original. Selected.
       Prose: Biography. Travel. Essay.
         Familiar Essay. Letters. Book Reviews.
       Fiction: Tale: "Claudine. A Swiss Tale."
       Miscellaneous: Extracts: from various
         authors; Franklin. Anecdotes: on
         various subjects. News: Foreign and
         Domestic.

40 TITLE: <u>The American Magazine and Historical
Chronicle</u>.

Place of Publication: Boston
First Issue: Sept 1743
Last Issue: Dec 1746//
Periodicity: Monthly
Editor: Jeremiah Gridley
Publishers: Rogers and Fowle
Available From: APS; Amer. Antiquarian Soc.
        Mott.
Contents:
  Poetry: <u>Original</u>. <u>Selected</u>.
  Prose: <u>Biography</u>: Pope, Robert Boyle,
    John Locke. <u>Travel</u>. <u>Essay</u>. <u>Familiar
    Essay</u>. <u>Letters</u>.
  Miscellaneous: <u>Extracts</u>: from other
    journals. <u>Literary Notices</u>. <u>News</u>:
    Foreign and Domestic.
Note: Contains several interesting accounts
    of the North American Indians.

41 TITLE: <u>The American Magazine and Monthly
Chronicle for the British Colonies</u>.

Place of Publication: Philadelphia
First Issue: Oct 1757
Last Issue: Oct 1758//
Periodicity: Monthly
Editor: William Smith
Publisher: William Bradford
Available From: APS; Hist. Soc. of Pa.*
        Mott.
Contents:
  Poetry: <u>Original</u>: Francis Hopkinson,
    Thomas Godfrey, Jr., James Sterling,
    Joseph Shippen.
  Prose: <u>Familiar Essay</u>. <u>Letters</u>: by
    "Timothy Timbertoe."
  Fiction: <u>Essay Serials</u>: "The Pratler";
    "The Planter"; "The Hermit."
  Miscellaneous: <u>News</u>: Foreign and Domestic.
Note: Contains several accounts of the North
    American Indians, as well as "History of
    the War in North America."

42 TITLE: <u>The American Magazine, and Repository
of Useful Literature, Devoted to Science,
Literature, and Arts, and Embellished with
Numerous Engravings</u>.

Place of Publication: Albany
First Issue: July 1841
Last Issue: April 1842//
Periodicity: Monthly
Editors: John S. Wood; Barnabas Wood
Publisher: Barnabas Wood
Available From: APS; Lib. of Congress*
Contents:
  Poetry: <u>Original</u>: M.L. Gardiner, Alfred
    B. Street, E.M. Sheldon, Joseph H. Butler,
    Lydia H. Sigourney. <u>Selected</u>: William
    H. Burleigh, Charles Lamb, James Mont-
    gomery, Bryant, William H. Cranston,
    Park Benjamin, Mary E. Hewitt, Mary Anne
    Browne.
  Prose: <u>Biography</u>. <u>Essay</u>. <u>Familiar Essay</u>.
    <u>Book Reviews</u>.
  Fiction: <u>Tale</u>: "The Eldest Daughter."

Miscellaneous: <u>Extracts</u>: from other
    journals; W. Irving. <u>Anecdotes</u>: on
    various subjects. <u>Literary Notices</u>.
    <u>News</u>: Foreign and Domestic.

43 TITLE: <u>The American Magazine Containing a
Miscellaneous Collection of Original and
Other Valuable Essays, in Prose and Verse,
and Calculated Both for Instruction and
Amusement</u>.

Place of Publication: New York
First Issue: Dec 1787
Last Issue: Nov 1788//
Periodicity: Monthly
Editor: Noah Webster
Publishers: Samuel Loudon; S. and J. Loudon
Available From: APS; Amer. Antiquarian Soc.*
        Mott.
Contents:
  Poetry: <u>Original</u>: John Trumbull, Timothy
    Dwight. <u>Selected</u>: Joel Barlow.
  Prose: <u>Biography</u>: R. B. Sheridan, Edmund
    Burke, Edward Gibbon, Captain John Smith.
    <u>Essay</u>. <u>Familiar Essay</u>. <u>Criticism</u>.
    <u>Letters</u>: by S. Johnson, Hester L. Thrale
    Piozzi, Captain John Smith. <u>Book Reviews</u>.
  Fiction: <u>Essay Serials</u>: "The Life and
    Amusements of Isaac Bickerstaff, Junior."
    <u>Sketches</u>. <u>Tales</u>.
  Miscellaneous: <u>Extracts</u>: from other
    journals. <u>News</u>: Foreign and Domestic.
Note: Contains abridgments of Captain John
    Smith's <u>General History of Virginia</u> and
    Jefferson's <u>Notes on the State of Vir-
    ginia</u>. This journal is New York's first
    attempt at a monthly.

44 TITLE: <u>The American Magazine of Useful and
Entertaining Knowledge</u>.

Place of Publication: Boston
First Issue: Sept 1834
Last Issue: Sept 1837//
Periodicity: Monthly
Editors: Freeman Hunt; John L. Sibley
Publishers: Boston Bewick Company; John L.
        Sibley; William D. Ticknor
Available From: APS; Yale Univ. Mott.
Contents:
  Poetry: <u>Original</u>: Lydia H. Sigourney.
    <u>Selected</u>: Wordsworth, Felicia Hemans,
    Lydia H. Sigourney, Hannah F. Gould,
    William Cowper, Byron, Thomas Moore,
    Matthew Prior, Coleridge, James Mont-
    gomery, John G. Brainard, E. Lytton
    Bulwer, Nathaniel P. Willis, James
    Shirley, Bryant, Hannah More, John
    Bowering, Albert Pike, Thomas Hood,
    Thomas Carew, Charles Lamb, James G.
    Percival, Thomas Pringle, Richard Howitt,
    George Pope Morris, C.A. Goodrich,
    Charles Sprague, Mary Anne Browne,
    Alfred B. Street.
  Prose: <u>Biography</u>: Daniel Boone, Benjamin
    West, Franklin, LaFayette, Captain John
    Smith, James Fenimore Cooper, Benjamin
    Rush, Fisher Ames, Hannah More, Benjamin

Church. Travel. Essay. Familiar Essay.
Criticism. Letters. Book Reviews.
Fiction: Sketches.
Miscellaneous: Extracts: from other
journals; by various authors; Frances
Trollope. Anecdotes: on various sub-
jects; Washington, Milton. Literary
Notices.
Note: Contains the early work of Hawthorne.
He and his sister anonymously wrote or
revised almost all of the March through
August issues, 1836. Contains over 500
woodcuts.

45 TITLE: The American Magazine of Wonders, and
Marvellous Chronicle, Intended as a Record
of Accounts of the Most Extraordinary
Productions, Events, and Occurrences, in
Providence, Nature, Consisting Principally
of such Curious Articles as Come Under the
Denomination of Miraculous! Queer!
Strange! Marvellous! Whimsical! Absurd!
Out of the Way! and Unaccountable!

Place of Publication: New York
First Issue: [Only 2 volumes published]
1809//
Periodicity: Semi-annual?
Editor: Donald Fraser
Publishers: Southwick and Pelsue
Available From: APS; Lib. of Congress*
Contents:
Fiction: Sketches. Tales: "Monster,"
horror, gothic, and science fiction
stories; strange phenomena.
Miscellaneous: Anecdotes: on various
subjects; Oliver Cromwell.
Note: Additional information on the title
page reads: Including genuine accounts
of the most surprising escapes from
death and dangers--strange and unaccountable accidents--discoveries of long
concealed murders--absurd and ridiculous
customs, peculiar to different nations--
dreadful shipwrecks--heroic adventures--
uncommon instances of strength and
longevity--memorable exploits--and whatever else is calculated to promote
entertainment and improvement--Collected
from the writings of the most approved
Historians, Travellers, Philosophers, &c.
of all ages and countries. . . .

46 TITLE: The American Magazine, or a Monthly
View of the Political State of the British
Colonies.

Place of Publication: Philadelphia
First Issue: Jan 1741
Last Issue: March 1741//
Periodicity: Monthly
Editor: John Webbe
Publisher: Andrew Bradford
Available From: APS; N.Y. Hist. Soc.* Mott.
Contents:
Prose: Essay.
Miscellaneous: Extracts: from The London
Magazine. News: Foreign and Domestic.

Note: The first issue, dated January 1740/1,
precedes by three days the first issue of
Franklin's The General Magazine [q.v.]
and thus is the first magazine published
in America. It contains proceedings of
the Pennsylvania, New Jersey, New York,
and Maryland assemblies. Its focus is
primarily historical and political.

47 TITLE: The American Magazine or General
Repository.

Place of Publication: Philadelphia
First Issue: Jan 1769
Last Issue: Sept 1769//
Periodicity: Monthly
Editor: Lewis Nicola
Publishers: William and Thomas Bradford
Available From: APS; Univ. of Mich., Ann
Arbor.* Mott.
Contents:
Poetry: Original. Selected.
Miscellaneous: Literary Notices. News:
Foreign and Domestic.

48 TITLES: (1) American Masonic Record, and
Albany Saturday Magazine (2) American
Masonick Record, and Albany Saturday Maga-
zine: Being a Periodical Journal, Devoted
to Masonry, Arts and Sciences, Biography,
Sketches of Character, Manners and Customs,
Popular Tales, Miscellany, Poetry, Literary
and Political News, &c. &c. (3) American
Masonick Record and Albany Literary Journal.
[Supersedes The Escritor.]

Place of Publication: Albany
First Issue: 3 Feb 1827
Last Issue: 1832//
Periodicity: Weekly
Editors: C. Child; E.B. Child
Publisher: E.B. Child
Available From: Lib. of Congress*; N.Y. Hist.
Soc.
Contents:
Poetry: Original. Selected: Shelley,
Sarah J. Hale, Felicia Hemans, L.E.
Landon, Thomas Hood, John Bowring, Fitz-
Greene Halleck, James G. Percival,
Nathaniel P. Willis, Thomas Green
Fessenden, Bernard Barton, Walter
Raleigh, Thomas Moore, Henry Neele, Allan
Cunningham, Lydia H. Sigourney, Bryant,
Mary Anne Browne, Thomas Carew, Barry
Cornwall, Byron, Grenville Mellen, Scott,
Edmund Reade, Edward C. Pinckney, John
G. Brainard, James Montgomery, B. Johson,
Goethe, Robert Montgomery, S.G. Goodrich,
William Howitt, William Kennedy, E. Lytton
Bulwer, James Hogg, Whittier, Willis
Gaylord Clark, George Lunt, G.A. Gamage,
Hannah F. Gould, Mary Howitt, Charles
Swain, Jane Taylor, Thomas Campbell,
William Cowper, Thomas Haynes Bayly,
Wordsworth, Francis Beaumont, Alfred B.
Street, William Roscoe, Fanny Burney,
J.O. Rockwell, Caroline Lamb, George D.
Prentice, W.J. Snelling, Alaric Watts.

Prose: Biography: Shelley, Buonaparte. Travel. Essay. Familiar Essay. Criticism. Letters.
Fiction: Essay Serial: "On the Passions." Sketches. Tales: "Ugolino, the Bandit; or, the Revenge"; "The Condemned Cell"; "The Elopement"; "The Conjuror's Apprentice. A Fairy Tale"; "The Traitor's Grave"; "The Persecutions of Jack Edy"; "The Smuggler's Daughter"; "Ebony and Topaz"; "The Lone Indian"; "The Blind Boy"; "Auld Robin Gray. The Original Story"; "The Spectre's Voyage" [Henry Neele]; "The Mysterious Mansion. A Legend of the North End"; "The Hypocondriack"; "The Ghost of Granny Hogins"; "The Curate of Suverdsio"; "The Magick Mirror"; "The Phantom Hand"; "Too Handsome for Anything" [E. Lytton Bulwer]; "The Voluptuary Cured"; "Mike Wild. A Legend of the North End"; "The Spectre Smitten"; "The Devil's Mill"; "The Gridiron; or, Paddy Mullowney's Travels in France"; "The Faithful Servant"; "The Necromancer's Noviciate"; "The Dominie of Kilwoody"; "Benito de Soto, the Pirate of the Morning Star"; "The Goldsmith of Padua."
Miscellaneous: Extracts: from other journals; by various authors; Washington, William Temple, Swift, Hartley Coleridge. Anecdotes: on various subjects; Swift, R.B. Sheridan. News: Foreign and Domestic.

49   TITLE: The American Masonic Register, and Ladies' and Gentlemen's Magazine.

Place of Publication: New York
First Issue: Sept 1820
Last Issue: June 1823//
Periodicity: Monthly
Editor: Luther Pratt
Publisher: Benedict Bolmore
Available From: APS; Enoch Pratt Lib., Baltimore
Contents:
    Poetry: Original. Selected: Thomas Moore, William Ray.
    Prose: Biography. Travel. Familiar Essay.
    Fiction: Sketches. Tales: "Eugenia de Mirande, an Interesting Story"; "An Interesting Oriental Tale"; "Claudine. An Interesting Swiss Tale"; "Sophia, or the Girl of the Pine Woods."
    Miscellaneous: Extracts: from other journals. Anecdotes: on various subjects and authors; Franklin. Literary Notices.

50   TITLES: (1) The American Masonic Register. And Literary Companion, Being a Periodical Journal [Running title: American Masonic Register. Devoted to Masonry, Literature, and Useful Knowledge] (2) The American Masonic Register, and Literary Companion, Being a Periodical Journal. Devoted to Masonry, Literature, &c. &c.

Place of Publication: Albany
First Issue: Aug 1839
Last Issue: Oct 1847//
Periodicity: Monthly
Editor: Lewis G. Hoffman
Publisher: Lewis G. Hoffman
Available From: APS; N.Y. Hist. Soc.*
Contents:
    Poetry: Original. Selected: Miss Pardoe, James Russell Lowell, James Hogg, Longfellow, D.C. Colesworthy, J.O. Rockwell, Lydia J. Pierson, Schiller, William Leggett, Charles Swain.
    Prose: Biography. Travel. Essay. Familiar Essay. Letters.
    Fiction: Sketches. Tales: "Maria Schoning, a Tale of Truth" [Coleridge]; "Zillah--The Only Child"; "Het Kruys"; "A Race for a Wife. Or Pegot Magrath, the Irish Coquette"; "Lanah, a Tale of the Flood"; "Bible lesson of the Wissahikon" [George Lippard]; "The Talisman"; "The Juryman Mason"; "The Left-Handed Glove; or Circumstantial Testimony."
    Miscellaneous: Extracts: from other journals. Anecdotes: on various subjects; Scott, Franklin, Washington. News: Domestic.

51   TITLE: American Masonick Record and Albany Literary Journal. [See American Masonic Record, and Albany Saturday Magazine.]

52   TITLE: The American Mercury.

Place of Publication: Hartford
First Issue: 12 July 1784
Last Issue: 26 Dec 1820//
Periodicity: Weekly
Editor: Elisha Babcock
Publishers: Barlow and Babcock; Elisha Babcock
Available From: Amer. Antiquarian Soc.*
Contents:
    Poetry: Original. Selected.
    Prose: Travel. Essay.
    Fiction: Essay Serial: "Cook's Last Voyage."
    Miscellaneous: Literary Notices. News: Foreign and Domestic.

53   TITLE: The American Metropolitan Magazine.

Place of Publication: New York
First Issue: Jan 1849
Last Issue: Feb 1849//?
Periodicity: Monthly
Editor: William Landon
Publisher: Israel Post
Available From: APS; N.Y. Hist. Soc.*
Contents:
    Poetry: Original: Ralph Hoyt, R.H. Stoddard, Henry Bradfield, George Canning Hill, Hannah F. Gould, Frances S. Osgood, Sarah Helen Whitman, Park Benjamin.
    Prose: Biography: Washington. Familiar Essay.

Fiction: Sketches. Tales: "Holy-Eve: A Bit of a Love Story"; "Rural Life" [Catharine Maria Sedgwick]; "Saville Grey: Or, a Glimpse at Life's Romance"; "Jacob Jones; or, the Juvenile Delinquent"; "The Golden Speculation"; "The Old Love, and the New; or, the Sequel to a Bachelor's Vow"; "The Egyptian Masque; a Tale of the Crescent City" [William Gilmore Simms]; "The Headsman of Antwerp."

54 TITLE: The American Monitor: Or, the Republican Magazine, Containing the Greatest Variety of the Most Useful, Entertaining and Agreeable Matter, Both in Prose and Poetry.

Place of Publication: Boston
First Issue: [Only one issue published] Oct 1785//
Periodicity: Intended to publish at least once a month.
Editor: Ezekiel Russell
Publisher: Ezekiel Russell
Available From: APS; Amer. Antiquarian Soc.* Mott.
Contents:
Note: Although this journal intended to publish familiar essays and poetry, the first issue contains primarily advertisements and domestic news, as well as the bookseller's preface and prologue to The Pantheon, a Comedy, in Three Acts.

55 TITLE: American Monthly Knicker-bocker. Devoted to Literature, Art, Society and Politics. [See The Knickerbocker: Or, New-York Monthly Magazine.]

56 TITLE: The American Monthly Magazine [Merged into The New-York Mirror q.v.]

Place of Publication: Boston
First Issue: April 1829
Last Issue: July 1831//
Periodicity: Monthly
Editor: Nathaniel P. Willis
Publishers: Peirce and Williams
Available From: APS; Cornell Univ.* Mott.
Contents:
Poetry: Original: Rufus Dawes, George Lunt, Lydia H. Sigourney, Albert Pike, Park Benjamin. Selected: Shelley.
Prose: Biography. Travel. Essay. Familiar Essay. Criticism. Letters: Nathaniel P. Willis. Book Reviews.
Fiction: Essay Serials: "Letters of Horace Fritz, Esq."; "The Editor's Table." Sketches. Tales: "The Fancy Ball"; "The Elopement"; "Albina M'Lush"; "The Exile"; "The Rival Pilots"; "A Mystery of the Sea"; "Confessions of a Disliked Man"; "The Downer's Banner"; "Tete-a-tete Confessions"; "Quit-Claim"; "Salathiel: A Tale of the Past, the Present, and the Future"; "The Ghost-Seer" [Schiller]; "A Morning in the library."

Miscellaneous: Extracts: by various authors; Penn, Edmund Burke. Literary Notices. News: Foreign and Domestic.
Note: Modelled after Thomas Campbell's New Monthly Magazine, London.

57 TITLE: The American Monthly Magazine [Absorbed by The New-England Magazine q.v.]

Place of Publication: New York
First Issue: March 1833
Last Issue: Oct 1838//
Periodicity: Monthly; Semi-annual
Editors: Henry William Herbert; A.D. Patterson; Robert M. Bird; Charles Fenno Hoffman; Park Benjamin; Robert M. Walsh, Jr.
Publishers: Monson Bancroft; J. Wiley; Peter Hill; George Dearborn; G. and G. and H. Carvill; D.K. Minor, and T. & C. Wood; Otis Broaders and Company; Thomas Cottrell Clarke
Available From: APS; N.Y. Pub. Lib.* Mott. Poole.
Contents:
Poetry: Original: Park Benjamin, Albert Pike, Alfred B. Street, Grenville Mellen, Cleveland Coxe. Selected: Shelley, Wordsworth, Byron, Oliver Wendell Holmes, Washington Allston, Nathaniel P. Willis, Barry Cornwall, William Gilmore Simms, Bryant, Lydia H. Sigourney, G.B. Singleton, Scott, Lamartine, James Montgomery, Victor Hugo.
Prose: Biography: Nicholas Biddle, LaFayette, Thomas Green Fessenden. Travel. Essay. Familiar Essay. Criticism. Letters: Albert Pike. Book Reviews.
Fiction: Essay Serials: "Essays from the Fireside"; "The Analyst"; "Glances at Life." Tales: "The Wanderer's Return"; "The Exile"; "Couleur de Rose"; "Recollections of a Nautical Life"; "Laura Hungerford. A Tale of the Forty Five"; "The Fall of Murray, or, the Bride of Bothwelhaugh"; "Von Jung, the Mystific" [Poe]; "Chepstow Castle"; "The Eve of St. Bartholomew"; "The Reefer's First Cruise"; "The Haunted Hof"; "The Merchant's Daughter"; "The Brothers"; "Elsie Gray, a Tale of the Southwest"; "The Fortunes of the Maid of Arc"; "The Gallery of a Misanthrope"; "Fire Island Ana"; "A Night Adventure in the Alleghanies"; "The Sciote; a Tale of the Greek Revolution"; "Confessions of Jeremiah Dibbs, Histrion [sic]"; "Pauline, or Diplomacy Eighty Years Ago"; "'Squire Jock"; "Letters from Arkansas"; "Horae Germanicae"; "Mohegan-ana: Or Scenes and Stories of the Hudson" [Charles Fenno Hoffman]; "Lazy Jake, or the Devil Nonplussed"; "The Highest Prize. A Tale of Truth"; "Little White Hat"; "Barbito. A Spanish Nouvellette"; "Alice Vere"; "Vanderlyn, a Novel" [Charles Fenno Hoffman]; "An Octogenary, Fifty Years Since"; "Scenes in the Life of Joanna of Sicily"; "The Brothers, a Tale of the Fronde" [Henry William Herbert].

Miscellaneous: Anecdotes: on various subjects; Scott, Goethe. Literary Notices.
Note: Horace Greeley, Henry Clay, and
Nathaniel Hawthorne also contributed to
this journal.

58   TITLE: The American Monthly Magazine.

Place of Publication: Philadelphia
First Issue: Jan 1824
Last Issue: Dec 1824//
Periodicity: Monthly
Editor: James M'Henry
Publishers: Job Palmer; J. Mortimer
Available From: APS; Lib. of Congress.*
                Mott.
Contents:
   Poetry: Original: James M'Henry, Long-
   fellow, Sumner Lincoln Fairfield.
   Selected: James G. Percival.
   Prose: Biography: Andrew Jackson, Henry
   Clay. Travel. Familiar Essay. Criti-
   cism. Letters. Book Reviews.
   Fiction: Essay Serials: "Domestic
   Sketches"; "Extracts from a Bachelor's
   Chronicle"; "Adventures of a Rambler";
   "Voyages on Wings." Sketches. Tales:
   "The Jewels of Cornelia"; "O'Halloran,
   or the Insurgent Chief. An Irish His-
   torical Tale of 1798"; "Banca . . . A
   Tale"; "The Woodlands. A Tale . . . by
   a Recluse"; "Tales in the West, or a
   Week in the Prairies"; "The Scotchman's
   Story, or the Tale of Sandie M'Farland";
   "The German's Story, or the Tale of Hiram
   Heltzenpacker"; "The Victim Bride . . . A
   Tale of Monadnock"; "The Jerseyman's
   Story, or the Tale of Isaac Donne, of
   Brunswick"; "The Happy Return, or the
   Songster's Tale"; "Tales of a Traveller.
   By Geoffrey Crayon, Gent." [W. Irving].
   Miscellaneous: Anecdotes: on various sub-
   jects. Literary Notices.

59   TITLE: The American Monthly Magazine and
      Critical Review.

Place of Publication: New York
First Issue: May 1817
Last Issue: April 1819//
Periodicity: Monthly
Editors: Horatio Biglow; Orville Luther
         Holley
Publishers: Kirk & Mercein
Available From: APS; Lib. of Congress.*
                Mott.
Contents:
   Poetry: Original. Selected: George
   Frederic Busby.
   Prose: Biography: Benjamin Rush. Travel.
   Criticism: on Byron, Coleridge, Thomas
   Moore, Maria Edgeworth, Mandeville,
   Scott, Horace Walpole, Samuel Woodworth,
   James Hogg. Letters. Book Reviews.
   Miscellaneous: Extracts: from other
   journals. Anecdotes: on various sub-
   jects; Hogarth, Fenelon. Literary
   Notices. News: Foreign and Domestic.

Note: Among the leading contributors were
James Kirke Pauling, DeWitt Clinton.

60   TITLE: The American Monthly Review. [Merged
      into The New-England Magazine q.v.]

Place of Publication: Boston
First Issue: Jan 1832
Last Issue: Dec 1833//
Periodicity: Monthly
Editor: Sidney Willard
Publishers: Hilliard and Brown; Brown,
            Shattuck, and Co.; Hilliard,
            Gray, and Co.; Russell, Odiorne
            & Co.; Russell, Odiorne, and
            Metcalf; James Munroe and Co.
Available From: Amer. Antiquarian Soc.*;
                N.Y. State Lib., Albany.*
                Mott. Poole.
Contents:
   Poetry: Selected: Alonzo Lewis, Nathaniel
   P. Willis, Bryant, Hannah F. Gould,
   Sumner Lincoln Fairfield, Park Benjamin,
   Richard Henry Dana, Grenville Mellen,
   Caroline Norton.
   Prose: Biography: Madame de Staël,
   Franklin, Donne, William Roscoe. Travel.
   Essay. Book Reviews.
   Miscellaneous: Extracts: from other jour-
   nals; by various authors; W. Irving,
   James Fenimore Cooper, Harriet Martineau,
   William Ellery Channing, Scott, Marie
   Edgeworth, Richard Hooker, Franklin,
   Sarah J. Hale. Literary Notices.
Note: Primarily a Harvard publication.

61   TITLE: The American Monthly Review; or,
      Literary Journal.

Place of Publication: Philadelphia
First Issue: Jan 1795
Last Issue: Dec 1795//
Periodicity: Monthly
Editor: Samuel Harrison Smith
Publisher: Samuel Harrison Smith
Available From: APS; N.Y. Hist. Soc.*
Contents:
   Poetry: Original.
   Prose: Biography: Franklin. Travel.
   Essay: "Mrs. Woolstonecraft's View of
   the French Revolution." Familiar Essay.
   Letters. Book Reviews: of Goethe's
   Iphigenia in Tauris, David Hume's History
   of England, and B. D'Israeli's Curiosities
   of Literature.
   Fiction: Tales: "Mrs. Morton's Quabi; an
   Indian Tale" [Sarah Wentworth Morton];
   "The Count de Hoensdern: A German Tale";
   "The Farmer's Daughter: A Poetical Tale."
   Miscellaneous: Extracts: from various
   authors; Erasmus Darwin. News: Foreign.

62   TITLE: The American Moral & Sentimental
      Magazine, Consisting of a Collection of
      Select Pieces, in Prose and Verse, from
      the Best Authors, on Religious, Moral, and
      Sentimental Subjects, Calculated to Form
      the Understanding, and Improve the Heart.

Place of Publication: New York
First Issue: 3 July 1797
Last Issue: 21 May 1798//
Periodicity: Semi-monthly
Editor: Thomas Kirk
Publisher: Thomas Kirk
Available From: APS; Univ. of Mich., Ann
        Arbor.* Mott.
Contents:
  Poetry: Original.
  Prose: Biography: S. Johnson, Isaac New-
    ton. Travel: William Bartram. Essay.
    Familiar Essay. Letters. Book Reviews:
    three by Charles Brockden Brown.
  Fiction: Sketches.
  Miscellaneous: Anecdotes: on various sub-
    jects; Hogarth.
  Note: Contains a number of conversion nar-
    ratives, as well as several accounts of
    the customs and manners of the North
    American Indians.

63   TITLE: The American Museum of Literature and
     the Arts. [See The American Museum of
     Science, Literature, and the Arts. A
     Monthly Magazine.]

64   TITLES: (1) The American Museum of Science,
     Literature, and the Arts. A Monthly
     Magazine (2) The American Museum of
     Literature and the Arts.

Place of Publication: Baltimore
First Issue: Sept 1838
Last Issue: June 1839//
Periodicity: Monthly
Editors: Nathan C. Brooks; J. Evans
        Snodgrass
Publishers: Nathan C. Brooks; J. Evans
        Snodgrass; John Murphy & Co.
Available From: Lib. of Congress*; Amer.
        Antiquarian Soc.* Mott.
Contents:
  Poetry: Original: Nathan C. Brooks, J.
    Evans Snodgrass. Selected: George Pope
    Morris, Poe, Grenville Mellen, Rufus
    Dawes, William H. Carpenter, Isaac C.
    Pray, Jr., William B. Tappan, William
    Gilmore Simms, Hannah F. Gould, Thomas
    R. Hofland, William T. Bacon, Lydia H.
    Sigourney, J.H. Clinch, Charles West
    Thomson, H.T. Tuckerman, John Pierpont,
    Anna H. Dorsey.
  Prose: Biography: W. Irving, James
    Fenimore Cooper, L.E. Landon. Essay.
    Criticism. Book Reviews.
  Fiction: Tales: "Ligeia" [Poe]; "The
    Atlantis"; "The Royal Professor"; "The
    Psyche Zenobia"; "The Gamester's
    Daughter"; "The Young Sizer; or the
    Generous Revenge"; "The Grotto: An
    Extravaganza"; "The Handsome Stranger.
    An Old Gentleman's Story" [Emma C.
    Embury]; "Mutual Sympathy; or Changes in
    Human Feelings"; "The Pioneer of Penn-
    sylvania"; "Handel. A Novelette"; "The
    Philosophical Eater"; "Gaspar Scriblerus";
    "Count Otto Harpsburg [sic]: A Romance
    of the Rhine."

Miscellaneous: Anecdotes: on various sub-
    jects. Literary Notices.

65   TITLES: (1) The American Museum, or Repository
     of Ancient and Modern Fugitive Pieces,
     Prose and Poetical (2) The American Museum,
     or, Universal Magazine: Containing Essays
     on Agriculture--Commerce--Manufactures--
     Politics--Morals--and Manners. Sketches of
     National Characters--Natural and Civil
     History--and Biography. Law Information--
     Public Papers--Intelligence. Moral Tales--
     Ancient and Modern Poetry, &c. &c.

Place of Publication: Philadelphia
First Issue: Jan 1787
Last Issue: Dec 1792//
Periodicity: Monthly
Editor: Mathew Carey
Publishers: Mathew Carey; Carey, Stewart,
        and Co.
Available From: APS; Amer. Antiquarian Soc.*
        Mott.
Contents:
  Poetry: Original. Selected: Francis
    Hopkinson, Timothy Dwight, Dryden,
    Mathew Carey, Philip Freneau, John
    Trumbull, David Humphreys, Joseph Brown
    Ladd, Mather Byles.
  Prose: Biography: Thomas Paine, Washing-
    ton, Franklin, Benjamin Rush, Mathew
    Carey, Joseph Brown Ladd. Essay: Thomas
    Paine's Common Sense. Familiar Essay.
    Letters.
  Fiction: Essay Serials: "The Visitant";
    "The Worcester Speculator"; "The Colum-
    bian Observer." Sketches. Tales:
    "Azakia, a Canadian Story"; "Love and
    Joy. A Tale"; "Farmer and His Thirteen
    Sons, an Allegorical Tale"; "Peter, a
    German Tale"; "Zimeo, a West-India Tale";
    "Julia, or the Penitent Daughter."
  Miscellaneous: News: Foreign and Domestic.
  Note: Along with The Columbian Magazine
    [q.v.], The American Museum shares the
    distinction of being the first successful
    American magazine. Subscribers included
    Washington, Franklin, Hamilton, Jefferson,
    Madison, Edmond Randolph, Thomas Allibone,
    Francis Hopkinson, Jared Ingersoll, and
    Benjamin Rush.

66   TITLE: The American Museum, or, Universal
     Magazine. [See The American Museum, or
     Repository of Ancient and Modern Fugitive
     Pieces, Prose and Poetical.]

67   TITLE: American People's Journal of Science,
     Literature, and Art.

Place of Publication: New York
First Issue: June 1849
Last Issue: Feb 1850//?
Periodicity: Monthly
Editors: S.B. Brittan; Thomas L. Harris;
       Fanny Green; C.D. Stuart
Publisher: S.B. Brittan
Available From: APS; N.Y. Hist. Soc.

Contents:
  Poetry: <u>Original</u>: Fanny Green, Thomas L.
    Harris, Ralph Hoyt, Edgar Hyde. <u>Selected</u>:
    George Shepard Burleigh.
  Prose: <u>Essay</u>. <u>Familiar Essay</u>.
  Fiction: <u>Sketches</u>. <u>Tales</u>: "Ethelda";
    "Orfeo."

68   TITLE: <u>The American Pioneer, a Monthly</u>
     <u>Periodical, Devoted to the Objects of the</u>
     <u>Logan Historical Society; or, to Collecting</u>
     <u>and Publishing Sketches Relative to the</u>
     <u>Early Settlement and Successive Improve-</u>
     <u>ment of the Country</u>.

     Place of Publication: Chillicothe, Ohio;
                              Cincinnati
     First Issue: Jan 1842
     Last Issue: Oct 1843//
     Periodicity: Monthly
     Editor: John S. Williams
     Publisher: John S. Williams
     Available From: APS; Univ. of Mich., Ann
                        Arbor.* Mott.
     Contents:
       Poetry: <u>Original</u>: Joseph D. Cumming,
         Joseph Strong, Benjamin Sharp. <u>Selected</u>:
         J.E. Dow, Eliezer Williamson.
       Prose: <u>Biography</u>. <u>Travel</u>. <u>Essay</u>. <u>Letters</u>.
       Fiction: <u>Sketches</u>. <u>Tale</u>: "Our Cabin; or,
         Life in the Woods."
       Miscellaneous: <u>Extracts</u>: from other
         journals; by various authors; Franklin.
         <u>Anecdotes</u>: on various subjects.

69   TITLE: <u>The American Quarterly Observer</u>.

     Place of Publication: Boston
     First Issue: July 1833
     Last Issue: Oct 1834//
     Periodicity: Quarterly
     Editor: Bela B. Edwards
     Publishers: Perkins & Marvin
     Available From: APS; Univ. of Mich., Ann
                        Arbor.* Mott. <u>Poole</u>.
     Contents:
       Poetry: <u>Selected</u>: George Herbert, John
         Keble, Richard Henry Dana, Byron,
         Bryant.
       Prose: <u>Biography</u>: Milton, Byron. <u>Travel</u>.
         <u>Essay</u>. <u>Familiar Essay</u>. <u>Criticism</u>.
         <u>Book Reviews</u>.
       Miscellaneous: <u>Literary Notices</u>. <u>News</u>:
         Foreign and Domestic.

70   TITLE: <u>The American Quarterly Review</u>.

     Place of Publication: Philadelphia
     First Issue: March 1827
     Last Issue: Dec 1837//
     Periodicity: Quarterly
     Editor: Robert S. Walsh
     Publishers: Carey, Lea & Carey; Carey &
                    Lea; Carey, Lea & Blanchard;
                    Key & Biddle; Lydia R. Bailey;
                    Adam Waldie
     Available From: APS; Hist. Soc. of Pa.*
                        <u>Poole</u>.

Contents:
  Poetry: <u>Selected</u>: Whittier, James Kirke
    Paulding, Felicia Hemans, James G. Per-
    cival, Richard Henry Dana, Bryant,
    Nathaniel P. Willis, Joanna Baillie,
    Lydia H. Sigourney, Fitz-Greene Halleck,
    Joseph Rodman Drake, Wordsworth, Gren-
    ville Mellen, Willis Gaylord Clark, Poe,
    W. Irving, Byron, Scott, James M'Henry.
  Prose: <u>Biography</u>. <u>Travel</u>. <u>Essay</u>.
    <u>Familiar Essay</u>. <u>Criticism</u>. <u>Book Reviews</u>.
  Miscellaneous: <u>Literary Notices</u>.

71   TITLE: <u>The American Register, or General</u>
     <u>Repository of History, Politics and Science</u>.

     Place of Publication: Philadelphia
     First Issue: 1807
     Last Issue: 1810//
     Periodicity: Semi-annual
     Editors: Charles Brockden Brown; Robert S.
                 Walsh
     Publishers: C. & A. Conrad & Co.
     Available From: APS; Lib. of Congress.*
                        Mott.
     Contents:
       Prose: <u>Essay</u>. <u>Familiar Essay</u>. <u>Criticism</u>.
         <u>Book Reviews</u>.
       Fiction: <u>Sketches</u>.
       Note: Each issue contained at least one
         review essay and one article on litera-
         ture or criticism.

72   TITLE: <u>The American Register; or Summary</u>
     <u>Review of History, Politics, and Literature</u>.

     Place of Publication: Philadelphia
     First Issue: [Only two issues published]
                     1817//
     Periodicity: Semi-annual
     Editor: Robert S. Walsh
     Publishers: Thomas Dobson and Son
     Available From: APS; Boston Athenaeum.*
                        Mott.
     Contents:
       Prose: <u>Travel</u>. <u>Essay</u>. <u>Book Reviews</u>.
       Miscellaneous: <u>Extracts</u>: from other
         journals. <u>Literary Notices</u>.

73   TITLES: (1) <u>The American Review: A Whig</u>
     <u>Journal of Politics, Literature, Art and</u>
     <u>Science</u> (2) <u>The American Review: A Whig</u>
     <u>Journal Devoted to Politics and Literature</u>
     (3) <u>The American Whig Review</u>.

     Place of Publication: New York
     First Issue: Jan 1845
     Last Issue: Dec 1852//
     Periodicity: Monthly
     Editors: James D. Whelpley; George W. Peck;
                 George H. Colton
     Publishers: Wiley and Putnam; George H.
                    Colton
     Available From: APS; Hist. Soc. of Pa.*
                        Mott. <u>Poole</u>.
     Contents:
       Poetry: <u>Original</u>: J.S. Babcock, George H.
         Colton, W.T. Bacon, James D. Whelpley,

Hugh Bridgesson, A.M. Ide, William
Barber, Mary M. Chase, George W. Peck,
C.A. Bristed, Henry W. Colton, Anna Maria
Wells, Joseph Hartwell Barrett, H.W.
Parker, H.M. Goodwin, James Russell
Lowell, Philip Pendleton Cooke, Louis L.
Noble, J.H. Collier, William Gilmore
Simms, Poe, William Wallace, H.H.
Clements, William Butler Allen.
Selected: Ralph Hoyt, Tennyson, Barry
Cornwall, Macaulay, Frances S. Osgood,
Thomas Campbell, Alfred B. Street,
Thomas Hood, John Westall, William
Cowper, Richard Henry Dana, Ludwig Uhland,
Longfellow.
Prose: Biography. Travel. Essay.
Criticism. Book Reviews.
Fiction: Tales: "Jack Long; or, Lynch-
Law and Vengeance" [Charles Wilkins
Webber]; "The Boy-Lover" [Whitman]; "The
Mocking Bird--An Indian Legend"; "The
Ghostly Funeral"; "The Rejected Treasure";
"My First and Last Chamois Hunt"; "Von
Blixum's Heroic Experiment"; "The Picture
Gallery"; "Modest Assurance; or, Some
Passages in the Life of a Lawyer";
"Julietta; or, the Beautiful Head";
"Zadec's Story. The Magician"; "Diotima
the Prophetess; an Anthenian Tale"; "The
Adventures of a Night on the Banks of
the Devron"; "The Hack-Horse Wot Wouldn't
Go; or, How the Yankee Did the Yorkshire-
man"; "A Fantasy Piece"; "Ghost Stories";
"Cheese of Vif"; "Zephyr's Fancy"; "The
Drover's Carpet-Bag"; "A Dream"; "Ander-
port Records"; "St. Pierre's Story";
"Everstone"; "The Cabriolet: From Un-
published Memoranda of Mountain-Land [Ik.
Marvel]; "Dona Paula; or, the Convent and
the World. A Tale of Peru"; "The Rival
Painters."
Miscellaneous: Literary Notices.

74   TITLE: The American Review and Literary
      Journal [A Continuation of The Monthly
      Magazine, and American Review q.v.]

      Place of Publication: New York
      First Issue: Jan 1801
      Last Issue: Oct, Nov, Dec 1802//
      Periodicity: Quarterly
      Editor: Charles Brockden Brown
      Publishers: T. & J. Swords
      Available From: APS; Lib. of Congress.*
                     Mott.
      Contents:
      Prose: Essay. Familiar Essay. Letters.
      Book Reviews: of original American works
      on all subjects, as well as on republished
      foreign works.
      Miscellaneous: Literary Notices. News:
      Domestic.
      Note: The journal contains an interesting
      section entitled "New Patents, Inventions,
      and Discoveries."

75   TITLE: The American Review of History and
      Politics, and General Repository of
      Literature and State Papers. [Sometimes
      called Walsh's American Review.]

Place of Publication: Philadelphia
First Issue: Jan 1811
Last Issue: Oct 1812//
Periodicity: Quarterly
Editor: Robert Walsh, Jr.
Publishers: Farrand and Nicholas
Available From: Hist. Soc. of Pa.; Lib. Co.
               of Phila.
Contents:
Poetry: Selected: Lucius M. Sargent,
James Thomson, William Sotheby.
Prose: Biography: Buonaparte. Travel.
Essay. Familiar Essay. Criticism:
Goethe. Letters. Book Reviews.
Miscellaneous: Extracts: by various
authors. Anecdotes: on various subjects.

76   TITLE: The American Universal Magazine.

Place of Publication: Philadelphia
First Issue: 2 Jan 1797
Last Issue: 7 March 1798//
Periodicity: Weekly; Bi-weekly
Editor: Richard Lee
Publishers: Samuel H. Smith; Budd & Bartram;
            Snowden & M'Corkie
Available From: APS; Hist. Soc. of Pa.* Mott.
Contents:
Poetry: Original. Selected: Southey,
Dryden, Burns, Robert Lovell, Charlotte
Smith, Erasmus Darwin.
Prose: Biography: Molière, Burns, Frank-
lin, Penn, Benjamin Rush, Washington,
Bolingbroke, Andrew Marvell. Travel.
Letters.
Fiction: Essay Serials: "Literary
Curiosities"; "The Enquirer." Sketches.
Tales: "Tales of an Evening"; "Penetra-
tion and Advice. (A Chinese Story)";
"Almoran and Selima. An Oriental Tale";
"The Old Man and His Dog. A Tale"; "The
Prudent Judge. An Eastern Tale";
"Selico; an African Tale."
Miscellaneous: Extracts: by various
authors; Rousseau. Literary Notices.
News: Foreign and Domestic.

77   TITLES: (1) The American Watchman; and,
      Delaware Republican (2) The American
      Watchman.

Place of Publication: Wilmington, Del.
First Issue: 2 Aug 1809
Last Issue: 21 July 1820//
Periodicity: Bi-weekly
Editors: James Wilson; Selleck Osborne
Publishers: James Wilson; Selleck Osborne
Available From: Amer. Antiquarian Soc.*
Contents:
Poetry: Original. Selected: Thomas Paine,
William Ray, Thomas Campbell, Byron,
William Cowper, Scott, Southey, Thomas
Moore, Chatterton, Bryant, Goldsmith,
Allan Cunningham, Peter Pindar, Luis de
Camoens.
Prose: Biography. Travel. Essay.
Letters.

Fiction: Sketches.
Miscellaneous: Extracts: from other
   journals; by various authors; W. Irving,
   Franklin. Anecdotes: on various sub-
   jects; Franklin, Washington, Buonaparte.
   Literary Notices. News: Foreign and
   Domestic.

78   TITLE: The American Whig Review. [See The
      American Review: A Whig Journal of
      Politics, Literature, Art and Science.]

79   TITLES: (1) The Analectic Magazine, Con-
      taining Selections from Foreign Reviews
      and Magazines, of Such Articles as Are
      Most Valuable, Curious, or Entertaining
      (2) The Analectic Magazine, Containing
      Selections from Foreign Reviews and Maga-
      zines, Together with Original Miscellaneous
      Compositions (3) The Analectic Magazine
      and Naval Chronicle (4) The Analectic
      Magazine (5) The Analectic Magazine. Com-
      prising Original Reviews, Biography,
      Analytical Abstracts of New Publications,
      Translations from French Journals, and
      Selections from the Most Esteemed British
      Reviews.

Place of Publication: Philadelphia
First Issue: Jan 1813
Last Issue: Dec 1821//
Periodicity: Monthly
Editors: Washington Irving; Thomas Isaac
           Wharton
Publisher: Moses Thomas
Available From: APS; Amer. Antiquarian Soc.*
                Mott. Poole.
Contents:
   Poetry: Original: James Kirke Paulding.
      Selected: Byron, Scott, William Ingram,
      Southey, Thomas Campbell, Joanna Baillie,
      R.B. Sheridan.
   Prose: Biography: Hester L. Thrale Piozzi,
      Garrick, James Hogg, Hannah More, Timothy
      Dwight, Patrick Henry, Edward Jenner,
      Thomas Campbell, David Hume, Goldsmith,
      William Cliffton. Travel. Essay.
      Familiar Essay. Criticism. Letters.
      Book Reviews.
   Fiction: Tales: "Tales of Fashionable
      Life"; "Two Viziers"; "Tales of My Land-
      lord."
   Miscellaneous: Extracts: by various
      authors; W. Irving. Anecdotes: on
      various subjects; Buonaparte, Confucius,
      Montesquieu, Joshua Reynolds, Xerxes,
      Smollett, Racine, Franklin. Literary
      Notices.
   Note: Reviews or criticism of Maria Edge-
      worth, Thomas Moore, George Frederic
      Busby, Robert Treat Paine, M. de Staël,
      Chateaubriand, Byron, Southey, Burns,
      Junius, Scott, Hogarth, Gibbon, Words-
      worth, Hugh Henry Brackenridge, Shake-
      speare, B. Jonson, B. D'Israeli, Defoe,
      Kotzebue, Horace Walpole, John Trumbull.

80   TITLE: The Anglo-American. A Journal of
      Literature, News, Politics, the Drama,
      Fine Arts, etc. [Merged into The Albion
      q.v.]

Place of Publication: New York
First Issue: 29 April 1843
Last Issue: 13 Nov 1847//
Periodicity: Weekly
Editor: A.D. Paterson
Publisher: E. L. Garvin & Co.
Available From: APS; N.Y. Pub. Lib.*
Contents:
   Poetry: Original. Selected: Barry
      Cornwall, Thomas Hood, Allan Cunningham,
      Beranger, James E. Carpenter, Charles
      Swain.
   Prose: Biography: William Prescott, De
      Tocqueville, Felicia Hemans, Hans
      Christian Andersen. Travel. Essay.
      Familiar Essay. Criticism. Letters.
      Book Reviews.
   Fiction: Essay Serial: "A Trip to the
      South." Sketches. Tales: "Recollections
      of the Early Life of a Sailor"; "The Old
      Judge; or, Life in a Colony"; "The
      Guerilla's Leap; a True Tale of Portugal";
      "The Two Homes. A Story for Wives"; "Joe
      Oldoak's Revenge"; "A Tale of the
      Masorcha Club"; "The Outlaw of Sacra-
      mento"; "Norman's Bridge; or, the Modern
      Midas"; "Mabel Earnley."
   Miscellaneous: Extracts: by various
      authors; De Quincey, Melville. Anecdotes:
      on various subjects; Coleridge, Dickens,
      Isaac Newton, Goldsmith, Buonaparte.
      Literary Notices. News. Foreign and
      Domestic.

81   TITLE: Anglo-American Magazine.

Place of Publication: Boston
First Issue: Feb 1843
Last Issue: July 1843//
Periodicity: Monthly
Editors: ?
Publishers: ?
Available From: APS; Lib. of Congress
Contents:
   Poetry: Selected.
   Prose: Biography. Essay.
   Fiction: Sketches. Tales: "Jerome
      Chabert. Or, a Night in the Adriatic";
      "The Heart and the Key. A Tale of the
      Fens"; "The Galanti-Show; or, Laughter
      and Learning All the Year Round"; "Two
      Hours of Mystery"; "The Lady's Maid";
      "The Fairy Surprised"; "The Jeweller's
      Wife"; "Life in Hanover"; "A Maltese
      Ghost Story"; "The Last of the Shepherds";
      "The Sea-Lawyer"; "The Goal Chaplain:
      Or a Dark Page from Life's Volume."
   Miscellaneous: Extracts: from other
      journals.

82   TITLE: Annales philosophiques, politiques et
      littéraires. Ouvrage utile aux amateurs de
      la vérité.

Place of Publication: Philadelphia
First Issue: [Only one issue published?]
1807//?
Periodicity: Intended to be monthly
Editors: ?
Publishers: ?
Available From: APS; Newberry Lib.
Contents:
  Poetry: <u>Essay</u>: on history, the North
    American Indians, geography. <u>Familiar
    Essay</u>.
  Miscellaneous: <u>Anecdotes</u>: "Les trois
    docteurs."

83   TITLE: <u>The Antiquarian, and General Review</u>.

Place of Publication: Schenectady, N.Y.;
                     Lansingburgh, N.Y.
First Issue: March 1845
Last Issue: Feb 1849//
Periodicity: Monthly
Editors: ?
Publishers: ?
Available From: Lib. Co. of Philadelphia*;
               Lib. of Congress
Contents:
  Poetry: <u>Selected</u>.
  Prose: <u>Biography</u>. <u>Essay</u>. <u>Familiar Essay</u>.
  Fiction: <u>Sketches</u>: of the presidents.
    <u>Tales</u>: "The Fleet Prison Marriage";
    "Story of Wi-Jun-Jon [The Pigeon's Egg
    Head]"; "'Royal Charlie'"; "The Court-
    ship of Miles Standish."
  Miscellaneous: <u>Extracts</u>: from other
    journals; by various authors. <u>Anecdotes</u>:
    on various subjects; Cromwell, B. Jonson,
    Buonaparte. <u>News</u>: Foreign and Domestic.

84   TITLE: <u>The Aonidean Magazine and Review</u>.

Place of Publication: New York
First Issue: [Only one issue published?]
April 1849//?
Periodicity: Intended to be quarterly
Editors: ?
Publishers: ?
Available From: Lib. of Congress
Contents:
  Poetry: <u>Original</u>.
  Prose: <u>Book Reviews</u>.
  Fiction: <u>Tale</u>: "A Christmas Story."

85   TITLE: <u>The Apollo: Or, Weekly Literary
     Magazine</u>.

Place of Publication: Wilmington, Del.
First Issue: 16 Feb 1805
Last Issue: 24 Aug 1805//?
Periodicity: Weekly
Editor: H. Niles
Publisher: H. Niles
Available From: Lib. of Congress
Contents:
  Poetry: <u>Original</u>. <u>Selected</u>: Shakespeare,
    William Cowper, Peter Pindar.
  Prose: <u>Essay</u>. <u>Familiar Essay</u>. <u>Letters</u>.

Fiction: <u>Essay Serial</u>: "Quil Driving, by
  Capt. Jeffery Thickneck." <u>Sketches</u>.
  <u>Tales</u>: "The Cavern of Strozzi"; "History
  of Robert Jackson. An Original Tale";
  "Nicolas Pedrosa"; "The Confidant: Or,
  History of Henry and Delia. A Tale
  Founded on Fact"; "Tarempou and Serinda.
  A Tale"; "Appearances Deceitful. A Tale"
  [Kotzebue].
Miscellaneous: <u>Extracts</u>: by various
  authors; S. Johnson. <u>Anecdotes</u>: on
  various subjects.

86   TITLE: <u>Arcturus, a Journal of Books and
     Opinions</u>. [Merged with <u>The Boston
     Miscellany</u> q.v. in June 1842.]

Place of Publication: New York
First Issue: Dec 1840
Last Issue: May 1842//
Periodicity: Monthly
Editors: Cornelius Mathews; Evert A.
               Duyckinck
Publishers: Benjamin G. Trevett; George L.
                Curry and Company
Available From: Yale Univ.*; Lib. of
                Congress.* Mott.
Contents:
  Poetry: <u>Original</u>: James Russell Lowell,
    Longfellow.
  Prose: <u>Criticism</u>.
  Fiction: <u>Essay Serial</u>: "The City Article."
    <u>Sketches</u>. <u>Tales</u>: "The Career of Puffer
    Hopkins" [Cornelius Mathews. Illus. by
    "Phiz" (H.K. Browne)]; "The Old Maid in
    the Winding Sheet" [Hawthorne]; "The Man
    of Adamant" [Hawthorne]; "The Canterbury
    Pilgrims" [Hawthorne].

87   TITLE: <u>The Argus</u>. [See <u>The Herald of Free-
     dom, and the Federal Advertiser</u>.]

88   TITLES: (1) <u>The Ariel. And Ladies' Literary
     Gazette</u> (2) <u>The Ariel. A Literary and
     Critical Gazette</u> [Running title: <u>The Ariel.
     A Literary Gazette</u>] (3) <u>The Ariel, a
     Semi-Monthly Literary and Miscellaneous
     Gazette. Devoted to Literature and the
     Fine Arts. Containing Original and
     Selected Tales, Essays, Biographies of
     Distinguished Females, and of Eminent
     Individuals, Reviews of New Books, Literary
     Notices, Poetry, Original and Selected,
     Anecdotes, and a Choice Selection of
     Miscellaneous Reading, Calculated 'To
     Raise the Genius and to Mend the Heart.'</u>

Place of Publication: Philadelphia
First Issue: 14 April 1827
Last Issue: 24 Nov 1832//?
Periodicity: Semi-monthly
Editor: Edmund Morris
Publishers: Ellwood Walter; Edmund Morris
Available From: APS; Lib. Co. of Phila.*
Contents:
  Poetry: <u>Original</u>. <u>Selected</u>: Bernard
    Barton, Felicia Hemans, Fitz-Greene

Halleck, Nathaniel P. Willis, Addison, Shakespeare, Charles Churchill, Edward Reade, L.E. Landon, James Montgomery, John G. Brainard, Thomas Hood, Sir Walter Raleigh, James Hogg, Thomas Haynes Bayly, Thomas Moore, Mary Howitt, Henry Neele, T.K. Hervey, Joanna Baillie, Dryden, Alaric Watts, J.O. Rockwell, Hannah More, Whittier, William Leggett, William Roscoe, John Bowering, Coleridge, Caroline Bowles, Sumner Lincoln Fairfield, Henry Vaughan, Thomas Campbell, Charles Sprague, Hannah F. Gould, Leigh Hunt, B.B. Thatcher.
Prose: Biography: James Fenimore Cooper, Scott. Travel. Familiar Essay. Letters. Book Reviews.
Fiction: Essay Serials: "The Town Tatler"; "Life in Philadelphia." Sketches. Tales: "Blanche d'Albi"; "Lucy of the Fold"; "Hay-Carrying"; "The Smoking Dutchman"; "Emma, the Foundling, a Tale of the Eleventh Century"; "The Count de St. Germain's Tale"; "Jemima O'Keefy. A Sentimental Tale"; "Jesse of Dumblane"; "The Murderer's Last Night"; "Mateo Falcone . . . A Tale of Corsica"; "The Wild Rose of Langollen. A Tale"; "Sigilmon Dumps"; "The Grave by the Adriatic, and He That Made it"; "Esther Wharncliff. A Tale of the Reign of Mary"; "Tales of a Grandfather" [Scott]; "The Bell of St. Regis"; "The Hurons.--A Tale"; "Henry St. Clair" [Whittier]; "The Prison-Breaker"; "The Fraternal Executioner"; "The Haunted Hogshead. A Yankee Legend"; "The Iron Shroud. Or Italian Vengeance"; "The Merchant's Clerk"; "Body Snatching"; "The Forewarning"; "The Magdalen"; "Margaret Sunderland"; "The Cork Leg"; "Ali's Bride"; "Blannerhassett's Island."
Miscellaneous: Extracts: from other journals; by various authors; Goethe, W. Irving. Anecdotes: on various subjects; Washington, James Montgomery, Byron, Buonaparte, Garrick, Addison. Literary Notices. News: Foreign and Domestic.

89   TITLE: The Aristidean, a Magazine of Reviews, Politics and Light Literature.

Place of Publication: New York
First Issue: March 1845
Last Issue: Dec 1845//
Periodicity: Bi-monthly
Editor: Thomas Dunn English
Publisher: Lane & Co.
Available From: APS; N.Y. Pub. Lib.* Mott.
Contents:
  Poetry: Selected: Longfellow, Henry B. Hirst, John Pierpont, Bryant, Charles J. Peterson, Poe, George Pope Morris, Whittier.
  Prose: Travel. Familiar Essay. Criticism. Book Reviews.

Fiction: Tales: "Arrow-Tip"; "Shood-Swing A Tale of the Pigtails"; "Leaves from a Log Book"; "Jack Fallon, and Jack's Pet"; "The Fair Insensible."
Miscellaneous: Literary Notices.

90   TITLE: Arthur's Ladies' Magazine of Elegant Literature and the Fine Arts. [See Miss Leslie's Magazine; Home Book of Fashion, Literature and Domestic Economy.]

91   TITLE: The Artist; a Monthly Lady's Book.

Place of Publication: New York
First Issue: Sept 1842
Last Issue: May 1843//
Periodicity: Monthly
Editors: Park Benjamin; Thomas Williams
Publisher: F. Quarré
Available From: APS; Lib. of Congress*
Contents:
  Poetry: Original: David Lester Richardson, Anna Cora Mowatt, William H. Cranston, James Aldrich, Washington Allston, Park Benjamin. Selected: Tennyson, Catharine Parr, Lydia H. Sigourney, Jane T. Lomax, Mrs. Seba Smith.
  Prose: Criticims.
  Fiction: Tales: "Angelo; a Tale"; "The Rajhpoot's Daughter"; "The Out-Door Artist"; "Grounds for a Divorce" [Epes Sargent]; "The Haunted Fountain. A Story of the Rhine"; "The Two Victorines. A Tale of La Vendée"; "Debby Wilder, or, the Farmer's Daughter" [Mrs. Seba Smith]; "The Mother's Heart; or, the True History of Mademoiselle de la Faille"; "The Student of Göttingen"; "Justine, A French Tale"; "The Rescue; a Tale of Chivalry"; "Christmas at Solomon Briggs" [Seba Smith]; "The Polish Countess"; "The Knickerbocker Down East" [Seba Smith]; "The Indian Sachem, Squando" [Seba Smith].

92   TITLE: The Athenaeum.

Place of Publication: New Haven, Conn.
First Issue: 12 Feb 1814
Last Issue: 6 Aug 1814//
Periodicity: Semi-monthly
Editors: Students of Yale
Publisher: Oliver Steele
Available From: APS; Lib. of Congress*
Contents:
  Poetry: Original.
  Prose: Familiar Essay. Criticism. Letters.
  Fiction: Essay Serial: "The Vagrant." Tale: "The Art of Friendship; a Persian Story."
  Miscellaneous: Anecdotes: on various subjects.

93   TITLE: The Atheneum; Or, Spirit of the English Magazines.

Place of Publication: Boston
First Issue: Jan 1817
Last Issue: March 1833//
Periodicity: Semi-monthly
Editors: ?
Publishers: Munroe and Francis; John Cotton
Available From: APS; Yale Univ.* Mott.
Contents:
  Poetry: Original. Selected: Byron,
    Thomas Moore, James Montgomery, Scott,
    Chatterton, Thomas Campbell, James Hogg,
    Wordsworth, Charles Dibdin, Southey,
    Coleridge, Christopher Smart.
  Prose: Biography: Charles Brockden Brown,
    R.B. Sheridan, Southey, Madame de Staël.
    Travel. Criticism: Byron, Scott, Cole-
    ridge, Shakespeare, Wordsworth, Burns.
    Letters. Book Reviews.
  Fiction: Essay Serial: "The Gleaner."
    Sketches. Tales: "Tales of My Landlord"
    [Scott]; "The Maiden and the Rose. A
    Pastoral Tale"; "Martin Guerre, or, the
    Mysterious Husband"; "Unsuccessful
    Machinations; or, the Castle of Dunanachy";
    "Padilla: A Tale of Palestine"; "Rachel.
    A Tale"; "Zuma. A Tale by de Genlis";
    "Christmas Eve; or, the Conversion";
    "The Cypress Crown. A Tale"; "A Tale of
    Vavoo"; "The Cavalier in France"; "Death
    of a Miser, a Tale"; "The Dean of San-
    tiago."
  Miscellaneous: Extracts: from other
    journals; by various authors. Anecdotes:
    Buonaparte, Franklin, R.B. Sheridan,
    S. Johnson, Hannah More, Byron, Joel
    Barlow. Literary Notices.

94   TITLE: Atkinson's Casket. Gems of Literature,
      Wit and Sentiment. [See The Casket, or
      Flowers of Literature, Wit & Sentiment.]

95   TITLE: Atkinson's Evening Post, and Phila-
      delphia Saturday News. [See The Saturday
      Evening Post, an Illustrated Weekly Maga-
      zine.]

96   TITLE: Atkinson's Saturday Evening Post.
      [See The Saturday Evening Post, an
      Illustrated Weekly Magazine.]

97   TITLE: The Atlantic Magazine. [Superseded
      by The New-York Review, and Atheneum
      Magazine q.v.]

Place of Publication: New York
First Issue: May 1824
Last Issue: April 1825//
Periodicity: Monthly
Editors: Robert C. Sands; Henry J. Anderson
Publishers: Elam Bliss & E. White
Available From: APS; Lib. of Congress.*
           Mott.
Contents:
  Poetry: Original. Selected: Bryant,
    Southey, Wordsworth, John G. Brainard.
  Prose: Biography. Travel. Criticism.
    Wordsworth, Southey. Letters. Book Re-
    views.

Fiction: Tales: "Tales of a Traveller"
    [W. Irving]; "A Tale of Midnight"; "The
    Man Who Burnt John Rogers."
Miscellaneous: Literary Notices.

98   TITLE: The Atlas. A Select Literary and
      Historical Journal.

Place of Publication: New York
First Issue: 20 Sept 1828
Last Issue: 26 Oct 1833//?
Periodicity: Weekly
Editors: T.D. Porter; E. Prescott
Publishers: T.D. Porter; E. Prescott
Available From: Lib. of Congress; Brown
           Univ., Providence*

Contents:
  Poetry: Original. Selected: E. Lytton
    Bulwer, Felicia Hemans, Bryant, Charles
    Swain, James Hogg, L.E. Landon, Lydia H.
    Sigourney, William Gilmore Simms, Byron,
    Thomas Campbell, Nathaniel P. Willis,
    Hannah F. Gould, Scott, Thomas Haynes
    Bayly, James Montgomery, John Bowering,
    Caroline Norton, Thomas Moore, Barry
    Cornwall, Mary Howitt, Uhland, Tennyson,
    William Motherwell, Beranger.
  Prose: Biography: James Hogg, Scott.
    Travel. Essay. Familiar Essay. Criti-
    cism. Letters. Book Reviews.
  Fiction: Sketches. Tales: "The Martyr-
    Philosopher"; "The Coffin-Maker"; "The
    Wet Wooing"; "Tom Cringle's Log" [Michael
    Scott]; "The Soldier's Bride"; "Calaspo,
    a Tale of the French Republic"; "The
    Chase of the Smuggler"; "Life of Sir
    Frizzle Pumpkin"; "Mother and Son--
    Gaming"; "The Usurer's Daughter"; "The
    Bracelets. A Tale of Mystery"; "The
    Match-Maker, or the Snowing-Up of
    Strath Lugas"; "Paddy Fooshane's
    Fricassee"; "The Thunder-Struck"; "The
    Tale of the Green Taper" [Blanco White];
    "Old Rosy Posy"; "The Count Chabert";
    "The Promise of Marriage. Story of the
    Half-Pay Lieutenant."
  Miscellaneous: Extracts: from other jour-
    nals; by various authors. Anecdotes: On
    various subjects. News: Foreign and
    Domestic.

99   TITLE: Augusta Mirror. A Semi-Monthly
      Journal, Devoted to Polite Literature,
      Useful Intelligence, and the Arts.
      [Running title: The Augusta Mirror:
      Devoted to Polite Literature and Useful
      Intelligence.]

Place of Publication: Augusta, Ga.
First Issue: 5 May 1838
Last Issue: 18 Dec 1841//?
Periodicity: Semi-monthly
Editors: ?
Publishers: ?
Available From: Lib. of Congress
Contents:
  Poetry: Original: Mary S.B. Dana, Henry
    R. Jackson, Margaret Martin, William C.
    Richards, John Pierpont, R.H. Wilde,
    Samuel C. Oliver. Selected: T.K. Hervey,

Felicia Hemans, Robert M. Charlton, Lamartine, Mrs. Seba Smith, George W. Patten, H.T. Tuckerman, John Quincy Adams, Mary Anne Browne, Bryant.
Prose: Travel. Familiar Essay. Criticism. Letters.
Fiction: Essay Serial: "Extracts from My Journal." Sketches. Tales: "The Orphan Julia"; "The Botanist"; "Ellen, a Tale of the Frontier Settlements"; "The First and Last Victim"; "The Rencontre"; "John's Alive! Or the Bride of a Ghost. Being a True History of True Love"; "The Orphan"; "The Widow Won"; "The Sybil's Ban. A Tale of 1799"; "'Too Smart to Be Raised.' A Tale That Nobody Will Dispute"; "The Overseer's Daughter"; "Fanaticism, or the Family of Dutartre"; "The Senator of Bremen"; "Aunt Emily"; "The Fall of Pride" [J.N. M'Jilton]; "The Midnight Enemy"; "The Ring. A Story of the Stuarts."
Miscellaneous: Extracts: from other journals. Anecdotes: on various subjects. Literary Notices.

100 TITLE: The Bachelors' Journal. [Merged into The Yankee, and Boston Literary Gazette q.v.]

Place of Publication: Boston
First Issue: 24 April 1828
Last Issue: 18 Sept 1828//
Periodicity: Weekly
Editor: Samuel G. Andrews
Publisher: Samuel G. Andrews
Available From: Boston Pub. Lib.; Amer. Antiquarian Soc.

Contents:
Poetry: Original: John Miller, Peter Wilkins. Selected: Henry Pickering, Thomas Hood, John Bowring.
Prose: Familiar Essay. Letters.
Fiction: Essay Serial: "Confessions of a Fatalist." Sketches. Tales: "The Heir"; "The Leaguer Monk"; "The Fever Ship"; "The Phantom Players"; "The Mystic Messenger"; "Salathiel. A Story of the Past, the Present and the Future"; "The Indian Wife"; "The Student, or the Evils of Love"; "The Scotchman Bewitched, or Sawney and the Devils"; "The Sorcerer. A Venetian Story"; "Misanthrope. A Tale"; "The German Gibbet"; "Hallidon Hall"; "The Traitor's Grave"; "Hualpha. A Tale of Mexico."
Miscellaneous: Extracts: from other journals; by various authors. Anecdotes: on various subjects; Scott, Byron, William Cowper. Literary Notices.

101 TITLES: (1) The Balance, and Columbian Repository (2) The Balance [Supplemented by Balance Advertiser] (3) The Balance, and New-York State Journal.

Place of Publication: Hudson, N.Y.; Albany
First Issue: 5 Jan 1802
Last Issue: 29 Dec 1809//

Periodicity: Weekly; By-weekly
Editors: ?
Publishers: Ezra Sampson; George Chittenden; Harry Croswell; Croswell & Frary
Available From: APS; Amer. Antiquarian Soc.*
Contents:
Poetry: Original. Selected: William Cowper, Timothy Dwight, Erasmus Darwin, Peter Pindar, Hannah More, Thomas Paine, S. Johnson, Burns, James Pye, Southey, Charlotte Smith, Abraham Cowley.
Prose: Biography: Shakespeare, Thomas Paine. Essay. Familiar Essay. Letters: Jefferson, Penn.
Fiction: Essay Serials: "To the People"; "Maxims and Thoughts"; "Thoughts, by Mentor"; "The Egoist"; "Editor's Closet."
Miscellaneous: Extracts: by various authors; Mason Locke Weems, Sterne. Anecdotes: on various subjects. Literary Notices. News: Foreign and Domestic.

102 TITLE: The Balance, and New-York State Journal. [See The Balance, and Columbian Repository.]

103 TITLES: (1) Ballou's Dollar Monthly Magazine (2) The Dollar Monthly Magazine (3) Ballou's Monthly Magazine.

Place of Publication: Boston
First Issue: 1841
Last Issue: 1893//?
Editor: M.M. Ballou
Available From: Boston Pub. Lib.; Lib. of Congress

104 TITLE: Baltimore Athenaeum, and Young Men's Paper. A Weekly Journal--Devoted to Polite Literature, Science, and the Fine Arts. [Running title: The Baltimore Athenaeum, a Journal of Literature.]

Place of Publication: Baltimore
First Issue: 7 June 1834
Last Issue: 18 June 1836//?
Periodicity: Weekly
Editors: J.N. M'Jilton; W.T. Leonard; J.L. Carey; T.S. Arthur
Publishers: J.N. M'Jilton; W.T. Leonard; J.L. Carey; T.S. Arthur
Available From: Lib. of Congress; Enoch Pratt Lib., Baltimore
Contents:
Poetry: Original: John C. M'Cabe, T.S. Arthur. Selected: Lydia H. Sigourney, Lady Mary Wortley Montagu.
Prose: Familiar Essay. Letters: Schiller, Goethe. Book Reviews.
Fiction: Essay Serials: "The Misogynist"; "Reveries and Reminiscences"; "The Mysterious Visiter." Sketches. Tales: "The Fate of Pompey"; "Bachelor Plummer"; "Mohegan-Ana. Or, Scenes and Stories of the Hudson" [Charles Fenno Hoffman]; "The Old Man's Story."
Miscellaneous: Extracts: from other journals; by various authors; Charles Lamb.

Anecdotes: on various subjects.
Literary Notices.

105 TITLE: The Baltimore Literary Monument.
A Weekly Journal Devoted to Literature,
Science and the Fine Arts. [Supersedes
The Baltimore Monument q.v.]

Place of Publication: Baltimore
First Issue: Oct 1838
Last Issue: Oct 1839//
Periodicity: Monthly
Editors: T.S. Arthur; John N. M'Jilton
Publisher: T.S. Arthur
Available From: APS; Lib. of Congress.*
    Mott.
Contents:
  Poetry: Original: William H. Carpenter,
  Lucy Seymour, James Hungerford, John
  Newland Moffet, T.S. Arthur, John N.
  M'Jilton. Selected: B. Jonson, Thomas
  Carew, Lydia H. Sigourney, Hannh F.
  Gould, Anna Maria Wells, Sarah J. Hale,
  Park Benjamin, Byron, Thomas Moore,
  James Hogg, James Montgomery, Felicia
  Hemans.
  Prose: Biography. Familiar Essay. Book
  Reviews.
  Fiction: Essay Serials: "The Naturalist";
  "Village Annals." Sketches. Tales:
  "Yanasa. A Tale of the Early Settlers";
  "Romance of American History"; "The Or-
  phan"; "Parnassian Pastimes"; "The Art
  of Shining"; "Home, or the Iron Rule";
  "The Old Henley House"; "The Little
  Pilgrim. A Simple Story"; "The Adven-
  tures of the Last Abencerage"; "Grizel
  Cochrane. A Tale of Tweedmouth Moor";
  "The Last Arrow"; "Wuhloma"; "Theodore
  Kerner."
  Miscellaneous: Extracts: by various
  authors. Anecdotes: on various sub-
  jects; Swift. Literary Notices.

106 TITLE: The Baltimore Magazine.

Place of Publication: Baltimore
First Issue: [Only one issue published?]
    July 1807//?
Periodicity: Intended to be monthly
Editors: ?
Publishers: ?
Available From: APS; N.Y. Psychiatric Inst.
Contents:
  Poetry: Original.
  Prose: Familiar Essay.
  Fiction: Novel: "The Starling. A Novel
  in Miniature." Tales: "Remarkable
  Suicide"; "Melancholy."
  Miscellaneous: Extracts: from other
  journals.

107 TITLE: Baltimore Magazine and Literary
Repository. [See the Orphan's Friend and
Literary Repository.]

108 TITLE: The Baltimore Monthly Visitor.

Place of Publication: Baltimore
First Issue: [Only one issue published?]
    April 1842//?
Periodicity: Intended to be monthly
Editors: ?
Publishers: ?
Available From: APS; Enoch Pratt Free Lib.,
    Baltimore
Contents:
  Poetry: Original: E. Tudor Horton.
  Selected: D.C. Colesworthy.
  Prose: Essay. Familiar Essay.
  Fiction: Tales: "The Timing of the Shrew:
  A Shakespearean Tale"; "The Two Gamblers:
  A Tale of Crime"; "Love and Jealousy."
  Miscellaneous: Anecdotes: on various sub-
  jects. Literary Notices.

109 TITLES: (1) The Baltimore Monument. A
Weekly Journal, Devoted to Polite Litera-
ture, Science, and the Fine Arts (2) The
Monument. A Volume Devoted to Polite
Literature, Science, and the Fine Arts
[Superseded by The Baltimore Literary
Monument q.v.]

Place of Publication: Baltimore
First Issue: 8 Oct 1836
Last Issue: 29 Sept 1838//
Periodicity: Weekly
Editors: T.S. Arthur; John N. M'Jilton;
    David Creamer
Publisher: David Creamer
Available From: APS; Peabody Inst.,
    Baltimore.* Mott.
Contents:
  Poetry: Original: John N. M'Jilton, T.S.
  Arthur, Nathan C. Brooks, C.C. Cox, Giles
  M'Quiggin, James Hungerford, Thomas
  Holley Chivers, J.H. Hewitt, Lucy Sey-
  mour, Lydia J. Pierson, William Carey,
  M.S. Lovett, N.M. Knapp. Selected:
  Boston Bard, Goethe, William Cowper,
  Charles Swain, Henry Kirke White, Hannah
  F. Gould, George D. Prentice, Goldsmith.
  Prose: Biography: R.B. Sheridan. Travel.
  Essay. Familiar Essay.
  Fiction: Essay Serials: "Errantries";
  "Marble for the Monument"; "Leaves from
  a Journal"; "The Examiner"; "College
  Reminiscences"; "Sketches of Character";
  "Scenes of the Revolution." Sketches.
  Tales: "Herbert Harris"; "Florinda's
  Vow"; "The Water Spout. A Tale of the
  Sea"; "Eveline Torrance"; "The Bride of
  the Barrens"; "Willard Gray, the Girl of
  the Conewago"; "Mariamne; or, the Last
  of the Asmoneans. A Hebrew Tale"; "The
  Midnight Meeting. A Tale of Terror";
  "The Flower Tokens"; "The Wild Man of
  the Rocks"; "The Fatalist"; "Shah Ghebal.
  An Eastern Story"; "Winona--The Indian's
  First Love"; "Sister Ellen"; "Luck's All;

or, the History of Obed Brown"; "Ellen
Peircy. A Legend of the Revolution";
"Love in a Cottage"; "A Watch in the
Main-Top"; "Glenorran: Or, the Picture
Gallery"; "The Village Churchyard";
"Little Lilly Hands"; "Alice Howard";
"Philip, the Wampanoag"; "The Divorce";
"The Fancy Ball"; "Gunilda's Prophecy";
"Joe Hodges"; "Truth by Mistake."
  Miscellaneous: Extracts: from other jour-
    nals; by various authors. Anecdotes:
    on various subjects; Washington, Frank-
    lin, Jefferson. Literary Notices.
Note: This periodical is considered to be
  one of the best of its time.

110   TITLE: The Baltimore Repertory, of Papers
       on Literary and Other Topics.

Place of Publication: Baltimore
First Issue: Jan 1811
Last Issue: June 1811//?
Periodicity: Monthly
Editors: "By a Society of Gentlemen"
Publisher: Joseph Robinson
Available From: APS; N.Y. Pub. Lib.*
Contents:
  Poetry: Original. Selected: Charlotte
    Smith, William Jones, Byron.
  Prose: Biography: Charlotte Smith,
    Madame de Sévigné. Travel. Essay.
    Familiar Essay. Criticism: Scott, N.G.
    Dufief. Letters. Book Reviews.
  Fiction: Essay Serials: "The Vigil";
    "Evening Recreations, by a Desultory
    Reader." Sketches. Tale: "Agrarius
    Denterville, or the Victim of Discontent:
    A Tale" Drama: "Wild Oats, or the
    Strolling Gentlemen" [John O'Keefe];
    "The Devil to Pay; or, the Wives Metamor-
    phos'd" [Charles Coffey]; "The Liar"
    [Samuel Foote]; "The Doubtful Son; or,
    Secrets of a Palace" [William Dimond].
  Miscellaneous: Extracts: from other
    journals; Sir Thomas More. Anecdotes:
    on various subjects. Literary Notices.
    News: Foreign and Domestic.

111   TITLE: The Baltimore Weekly Magazine,
       Complete in One Volume.--Containing--A
       Variety of Entertaining, Instructive, and
       Useful Productions,--Original and
       Selected--. . . Suited to the Palates of
       the Moralist, Lovers of Sentiment, Poetry
       or Anecdote.

Place of Publication: Baltimore
First Issue: 26 April 1800
Last Issue: 27 May 1801//
Periodicity: Weekly
Editor: John B. Colvin
Publisher: John B. Colvin
Available From: APS; Lib. of Congress.*
                Mott.
Contents:
  Poetry: Original: John Davis. Selected:
    Thomas Campbell, Peter Pindar, Erasmus
    Darwin
  Prose: Biography. Letters.

Fiction: Sketches. Tales: "History of
  Jack Smith"; "Edric of the Forest";
  "Adventures of a Louse"; "Character of a
  Gentlemen"; "The Sorrows of Amelia. Or
  Deluded Innocence--Founded on Fact";
  "History of Pauline de Rivieres"; "The
  Cruel Jealousy of an Arab of the Desert";
  "Schabraco. A Romance"; "Feodor &
  Alexowin-a. A Russian Tale"; "The
  History of Jack Martin"; "Lorenzo and
  Violetta, a Matrimonial Tale"; "The Maid's
  Husband"; "Cottager"; "Ildegerte";
  "Leonora."
Miscellaneous: Extracts: from other
  journals. Anecdotes: on various sub-
  jects. News: Domestic.

112   TITLE: The Bangor Journal of Literature,
       Science, Morals, and Religion.

Place of Publication: Bangor, Me.
First Issue: 1 June 1837
Last Issue: 24 May 1838//
Periodicity: Weekly
Editor: Thomas Curtis
Publisher: S.S. Smith
Available From: Coll. of Wooster, Wooster,
                Ohio*; Bowdoin Coll., Bruns-
                wick, Me.*
Contents:
  Poetry: Original. Selected: Thomas
    Carew, Thomas Hood, George Crabbe, Anna
    Maria Paine.
  Prose: Essay: Amos Bronson Alcott.
    Familiar Essay. Letters: Franklin,
    Coleridge. Book Reviews.
  Fiction: Sketches. Tale: "Precepts and
    Practice."
  Miscellaneous: Extracts: from other
    journals; by various authors; Scott,
    Coleridge. Literary Notices. News:
    Domestic.

113   TITLE: The Barber's Shop Kept by Sir David
       Razor.

Place of Publication: Salem, Mass.
First Issue: [Only four issues published]
             1807-08//
Periodicity: ?
Editors: ?
Publishers: ?
Available From: APS; N.Y. Pub. Lib.*
Contents:
  Poetry: Original.
  Prose: Sketches: Whimsical Chit-chat.
Note: Razor styles himself: "Grand Secret-
  ary to the Worshipful Association of
  Free and Accepted Barbers; Shaver to his
  Venerability the Deputy, Scribe of the
  Ancient and Honourable Roustigouche
  Society, Branch No. 174; Weatherwise-
  General to his own family and neighbor-
  hood; Story-Teller; 'Guesser'; Observer
  of Men and Manners; Joke-Cracker; Sleeve-
  Laugher, &c. &c. &c."

114 TITLES: (1) <u>The Belles-Lettres Repository,
and Monthly Magazine</u> (2) <u>The Belles-
Lettres Repository, a Monthly Literary
Gazette, and Magazine of Amusement</u>
(3) <u>The New-York Literary Journal, and
Belles-Lettres Repository.</u>

Place of Publication: New York
First Issue: May 1819
Last Issue: April 1821//
Periodicity: Monthly
Editors: ?
Publishers: A.T. Goodrich & Co.
Available From: APS; Lib. of Congress*
Contents:
  Poetry: <u>Original</u>. <u>Selected</u>: Thomas
    Moore, Byron, Barry Cornwall, Charles
    Lloyd, Wordsworth, Joanna Baillie,
    Thomas Campbell, Schiller.
  Prose: <u>Biography</u>: Kotzebue, Luis de
    Camoens, LaFayette, Maturin, W. Irving,
    Benjamin West, Matthew Gregory [Monk]
    Lewis. <u>Travel</u>. <u>Familiar Essay</u>.
    <u>Letters</u>. <u>Book Reviews</u>.
  Fiction: <u>Essay Serials</u>: "Omniana";
    "Moschus." <u>Sketches</u>. <u>Tales</u>: "Tooti
    Nameh"; "The Power of Love and Honour";
    "Story of an Apparition"; "Peter (a
    German Tale)"; "Halfpenny Geordie"; "The
    Wife of a Genius. A True Tale"; "The
    Pinch of Snuff"; "The Village Maid";
    "Salem Witchcraft, an Eastern Tale";
    "Tales of Passaic"; "The Old Maid's
    Story"; "The Recollections of an Old
    Soldier"; "The Young Lady's Story"; "The
    Hermit of Drooninggarde"; "The Proof-
    Sheet."
  Miscellaneous: <u>Extracts</u>: from other jour-
    nals; by various authors; Maturin,
    Madame de Staël, W. Irving, Washington
    Allston, Thomas Campbell. <u>Anecdotes</u>:
    Scott, Franklin, Byron, Buonaparte, Sir
    Thomas More. <u>Literary Notices</u>. <u>News</u>:
    Foreign and Domestic.

115 TITLES: (1) <u>Biblical Repertory. A Col-
lection of Tracts in Biblical Literature</u>
(2) <u>Biblical Repertory. A Journal of
Biblical Literature and Theological
Science</u> (3) <u>The Biblical Repertory and
Theological Review</u> (4) <u>The Biblical
Repertory and Princeton Review for the
Year --</u> (5) <u>The Presbyterian Quarterly and
Princeton Review</u> (6) <u>The Princeton Review</u>
(7) <u>The New Princeton Review.</u>

Place of Publication: New York; Princeton;
                 Philadelphia; Pitts-
                 burgh
First Issue: Jan 1825
Last Issue: Nov-Dec 1888//
Periodicity: Quarterly
Editors: Charles Hodge; James A. Peabody;
       M.B. Hope; Lyman H. Atwater; Henry
       B. Smith; John M. Libbey; William
       M. Sloane

Publishers: G. and C. Carvill; James Kay,
           Jun. & Co.; John I. Kay & Co.;
           Russell & Martien; Henry
           Perkins; William H. Mitchell
Available From: APS; Yale Univ.* Mott.
               Poole.
Contents:
  Prose: <u>Biography</u>. <u>Essay</u>. <u>Familiar Essay</u>.
    <u>Criticism</u>: Emerson, MacCaulay. <u>Book
    Reviews</u>.
  Miscellaneous: <u>Literary Notices</u>.

116 TITLES: (1) <u>Biblical Repository and
Classical Review</u> (2) <u>American Biblical
Repository</u> (3) <u>The American Biblical
Repository, Devoted to Biblical and
General Literature, Theological Discussion,
the History of Theological Opinions, etc.</u>
(4) <u>The Biblical Repository and Classical
Review.</u> [Absorbed <u>The American Quarterly
Observer</u> in Jan 1835 and <u>The Quarterly
Christian Spectator</u> in Jan 1839. Merged
into <u>Bibliotheca Sacra</u> q.v. in Jan 1851.]

Place of Publication: New York
First Issue: 1831
Last Issue: 1850//
Editors: Edward Robinson; Bela B. Edwards;
       Absalom Peters; Selah B. Treat;
       John Holmes Agnew; Walter Hilliard
       Bidwell; James Manning Sherwood
Publishers: Edward Robinson; Bela B. Ed-
           wards; Absalom Peters; Selah B.
           Treat; John Holmes Agnew;
           Walter Hilliard Bidwell; James
           Manning Sherwood
Available From: Lib. of Congress*; Amer.
               Antiquarian Soc.*
Contents:
  Prose: <u>Biography</u>: religious figures.
    <u>Essay</u>: Exegesis. <u>Criticism</u>: on Words-
    worth, Shelley, Coleridge, William
    Cowper, Felician Hemans. <u>Book Reviews</u>:
    on Jonathan Edwards, Nathaniel Ward,
    Melville, Southey, Carlyle.
  Miscellaneous: <u>Literary Notices</u>.

117 TITLES: (1) <u>Bibliotheca Sacra; or, Tracts
and Essays on Topics Connected with Biblical
Literature and Theology</u> (2) <u>Bibliotheca
Sacra and Theological Review</u> (3) <u>Bibli-
otheca Sacra</u> (4) <u>Bibliotheca Sacra and
Theological Eclectic</u> (5) <u>Bibliotheca
Sacra. A Religious and Sociological
Quarterly.</u>

Place of Publication: New York; Andover,
               Mass.; Oberlin, Ohio
First Issue: Feb 1843
Last Issue: ?
Periodicity: Quarterly
Editors: Edward Robinson; Bela B. Edwards;
       Edwards A. Park; Samuel H. Taylor;
       George E. Day

Publishers: Wiley and Putnam; Warren F.
Draper; Allen, Merrill and Ward-
well; E.J. Goodrich
Available From: APS; Lib. of Congress.*
Mott. Poole.
Contents:
Poetry: Original. Selected: Shakespeare.
Prose: Biography: Chrysostom, Origen,
Confucius, Coleridge. Essay: Exegesis.
Criticism: N. Machiavelli, Virgil,
Homer; "German Literature in America";
"Shakespeare--The Old and the New Criti-
cism on Him"; "Coleridge and His American
Disciples" [On Jonathan Edwards and
others]. Letters. Book Reviews.
Miscellaneous: Literary Notices.

118   TITLE: Boston Book; Being Specimens of
Metropolitan Literature.

Place of Publication: Boston
First Issue: 1836
Last Issue: 1850//
Available From: N.Y. State Lib., Albany*;
Bowdoin Coll., Brunswick,
Me.*

119   TITLE: The Boston Chronicle.

Place of Publication: Boston
First Issue: 21 Dec 1767
Last Issue: 21 June 1770//
Periodicity: Bi-weekly
Editors: ?
Publishers: Mein and Fleeming
Available From: Amer. Antiquarian Soc.*
Contents:
Prose: Travel. Familiar Essay. Book
Reviews.
Miscellaneous: Literary Notices. News:
Foreign and Domestic.

120   TITLES: (1) The Boston Evening-Post; and the
General Advertiser (2) The American
Herald; and the General Advertiser
(3) The American Herald (4) The American
Herald; and the Worcester Recorder.

Place of Publication: Boston; Worcester,
Mass.
First Issue: 20 Oct 1781
Last Issue: 8 Oct 1789//
Periodicity: Weekly
Editor: Edward E. Powars
Publisher: Edward E. Powars
Available From: Amer. Antiquarian Soc.*
Contents:
Poetry: Original. Selected.
Prose: Travel. Essay. Familiar Essay.
Letters. Book Reviews.
Miscellaneous: Extracts: by various
authors. Anecdotes: on various sub-
jects. Literary Notices. News: Foreign
and Domestic.

121   TITLES: (1) The Boston Gazette (2) The
Boston Gazette, or, Weekly Journal
(3) The Boston Gazette, or, Weekly Advertiser (4) The Boston Gazette, or
Country Journal (5) The Boston Gazette,
and Weekly Republican Journal.

Place of Publication: Boston
First Issue: 21 Dec 1719
Last Issue: 17 Sept 1798//
Periodicity: Weekly
Editors: James Franklin; S. Kneeland;
T. Green; Benjamin Edes
Publishers: James Franklin; S. Kneeland and
T. Green; Benjamin Edes & Son
Available From: Amer. Antiquarian Soc.
Contents:
Poetry: Original. Selected.
Prose: Essay. Familiar Essay: Franklin.
Miscellaneous: Literary Notices. News:
Foreign and Domestic.

122   TITLE: Boston Kaleidoscope and Literary
Rambler. [See The Kaleidoscope.]

123   TITLE: Boston Literary Gazette.

Place of Publication: Boston
First Issue: 16 Feb 1828
Last Issue: 9 Aug 1828//?
Periodicity: Weekly
Editor: James William Miller
Publisher: S.G. Goodrich
Available From: Amer. Antiquarian Soc.*
Contents:
Poetry: Original. Selected: Shelley,
Thomas Moore, Henry Neele, Keats,
Charles Wolfe, L.E. Landon, Bryant,
Charles Lamb, Rufus Dawes, Allan Cunning-
ham, Felicia Hemans.
Prose: Biography: James Hogg, Scott,
Coleridge. Book Reviews.
Fiction: Essay Serials: "A Rambler's
Reminiscences"; "Gossipiana"; "An
Angler's Reminiscences"; "Literary
Recreations." Sketches. Tales: "Hyde
Nugent. A Tale of Fashionable Life";
"The Last of the Dog-Days"; "Insurance
and Assurance."
Miscellaneous: Anecdotes: on various sub-
jects. Literary Notices.

124   TITLE: The Boston Literary Magazine.

Place of Publication: Boston
First Issue: 1 May 1832
Last Issue: April 1833//
Periodicity: Monthly
Editors: W.G. Danaford; D. Bourne
Publishers: Clapp and Hull
Available From: APS; N.Y. Pub. Lib.*
Contents:
Poetry: Original. Selected: Felicia
Hemans, Bryant, Lydia H. Sigourney,
Hannah F. Gould, Sarah J. Hale.

Prose: Biography. Essay. Familiar Essay. Book Reviews.
Fiction: Essay Serial: "The Fine Arts." Sketches. Tales: "The Red Man. A Tale of Truth"; "The Mountain Sibyl"; "The Loved and Lost One. A Jewish Story"; "The Ruins. A New England Tale"; "The Pilot Boat"; "The First Foot.--A Tale"; "The Shakeress"; "Mowheena. A Tale of the Sandwich Islands."
Miscellaneous: Extracts: from other journals. Anecdotes: on various subjects. Literary Notices.

125   TITLE: The Boston Lyceum.

Place of Publication: Boston
First Issue: 15 Jan 1827
Last Issue: Nov 1827//
Periodicity: Monthly
Editors: ?
Publishers: ?
Available From: APS; Lib. of Congress*
Contents:
    Poetry: Original. Selected: George Lunt, Sumner Lincoln Fairfield, Scott, Byron, Sarah J. Hale.
    Prose: Biography. Essay. Familiar Essay. Criticism. Letters. Book Reviews.
    Fiction: Sketches. Tales: "The Revellers"; "The Deserter"; "Thersites and Eudora. A Tale of Modern Greece"; "The Man in the Moon. A Boston Story"; "Libussa. A Tale from the German"; "Caramura. A Tale of Brazil"; "The Coterie"; "The Lottery Bubble"; "Ebony and Topaz."
    Miscellaneous: Anecdotes: Buonaparte, Thomas Campbell, W. Irving. News: Foreign and Domestic.

126   TITLE: The Boston Magazine . . . Containing a Collection of Instructive & Entertaining Essays, in the Various Branches of Useful and Polite Literature; Together with, Foreign & Domestic Occurrences, Anecdotes, Observations on the Weather, &c. &c.

Place of Publication: Boston
First Issue: Oct 1783
Last Issue: Nov-Dec 1786//
Periodicity: Monthly
Editors: John Eliot; James Freeman; George R. Minot
Publishers: Greenleaf and Freeman; Normal & White
Available From: APS; Lib. of Congress.* Mott.
Contents:
    Poetry: Original. Selected.
    Prose: Biography: Voltaire, S. Johnson, Franklin, John Adams. Essay. Familiar Essay. Letters.
    Fiction: Essay Serials: "The Competitor"; "Remarks Concerning the Savages of North America." Sketches: Swift, Tillotson, Temple, Shaftesbury, Addison. Tales: "Narrative of a Shipwreck"; "The Prince of Brittany, a New Historical Novel."

Miscellaneous: Anecdotes: on various subjects. News: Foreign and Domestic.

127   TITLE: Boston Masonic Mirror. [See Masonic Mirror: And Mechanics' Intelligencer.]

128   TITLE: Boston Mirror.

Place of Publication: Boston
First Issue: 22 Oct 1808
Last Issue: 21 July 1810//
Periodicity: Weekly
Editor: Edward Oliver
Publishers: Oliver & Munroe; Edward Oliver
Available From: Amer. Antiquarian Soc.*; Boston Pub. Lib.*
Contents:
    Poetry: Original: Thomas Paine, Thomas Dermo, C.M. Warren. Selected: Thomas Moore, Amelia Opie.
    Prose: Biography. Familiar Essay. Criticism. Book Reviews.
    Fiction: Essay Serial: "The Touchstone, or Theatrical Register." Sketches. Tales: "Liberty and Equality"; "The Consolations"; "Diana and Endymion"; "The Wandering Friar"; "Nicolas Pedrosa"; "The History of Hypasia" [Goldsmith]; "A Love Stratagem."
    Miscellaneous: Extracts: by various authors; M. de Staël. Anecdotes: on various subjects; Handel. Literary Notices.

129   TITLE: Boston Mirror and Literary Chronicle.

Place of Publication: Boston
First Issue: [undated] 1835
Last Issue: [undated] 1835//?
Available From: Boston Pub. Lib.

130   TITLE: The Boston Miscellany of Literature and Fashion. [Combined with the Arcturus q.v.]

Place of Publication: Boston; New York
First Issue: Jan 1842
Last Issue: Feb 1843//
Periodicity: Monthly
Editors: Nathan Hale, Jr.; H.T. tuckerman
Publishers: Bradbury, Soden & Co.
Available From: APS; Yale Univ.* Mott.
Contents:
    Poetry: Original: H.T. Tuckerman, Park Benjamin, George H. Colton, Bryant, Mrs. Seba Smith, William Cutter, J.H. Ingraham, T.W. Parsons, Alexander H. Everett, James T. Fields, Lewis L. Noble, Charles T. Congdon, Henry Peterson, Charles C. Eastman, George Lunt, Mary E. Hewitt, Charles Fenno Hoffman, James Russell Lowell, Lewis J. Cist, W.W. Story.
    Prose: Essay. Familiar Essay. Book Reviews: Poe's review of Griswold's Poets and Poetry in America.
    Fiction: Tales: "Silent Love: Or, Leah for Rachel"; "A Tale of a Salamander";

"The Canary"; "The King's Bride. A Story Drawn from Nature"; "The Three Sleigh Rides"; "A Virtuoso's Collection" [Hawthorne]; "The Tourists: A Tale of Naples"; "'Beauty and the Beast': Or, Handsome Mrs. Titton and Her Plain Husband"; "Brown's Day with the Mimpsons" [Nathaniel P. Willis]; "Master John Wacht"; "Sympathy and Antipathy"; "Those Ungrateful Blidgimses" [Nathaniel P. Willis]; "Tales of the Knights of Seven Lands"; "The Schoolmaster Abroad, or Who Was the Victim?"; "The Maniac Maid. A Tale of the Tyrol"; "Nahwista: A Story of the Colonies"; "Bitter Fruits from Chance Sown Seeds"; "The Story of John Dobs and His Cantelope"; "The Phrisee and the Barber" [Nathaniel P. Willis]; "The Haunted Wreck: Or, the Mystery of the Old Hulk off South Boston Bridge"; [Other stories and tales by Edward Everett Hale and Edward Everett.]
  Miscellaneous: Literary Notices.

131   TITLE: Boston Monthly Magazine.

Place of Publication: Boston
First Issue: June 1825
Last Issue: July 1826//
Periodicity: Monthly
Editor: Samuel L. Knapp
Publisher: Samuel L. Knapp
Available From: APS; Lib. of Congress.*
                Mott. Poole.
Contents:
  Poetry: Original. Selected.
  Prose: Biography: Tasso. Familiar Essay.
    Criticism. Book Reviews.
  Fiction: Sketches. Tales: "The Lost
    Child"; "The Jubilee of Genius"; "The
    Blank Nuns"; "Sketches Among the Tombs";
    "A Legend of Mount Nebo"; "Night
    Horrors."
  Miscellaneous: Extracts: by various
    authors; Milton, Petrarch. Literary
    Notices.

132   TITLE: Boston Notion, or Roberts' Weekly
      Journal of American and Foreign Literature,
      Fine Arts, and General News.

Place of Publication: Boston
First Issue: 9 Oct 1841
Last Issue: 9 March 1844//?
Periodicity: Weekly
Available From: Boston Pub. Lib.; U.C.L.A.

133   TITLE: The Boston Pearl. A Gazette of
      Polite Literature. [See The Bouquet:
      Flowers of Polite Literature.]

134   TITLE: The Boston Pearl and Galaxy. [See
      New-England Galaxy & Masonic Magazine.]

135   TITLE: The Boston Pearl and Literary Gazette.
      [See The Bouquet: Flowers of Polite
      Literature.]

136   TITLE: The Boston Quarterly Review. [Merged
      with the Democratic Review; superseded by
      Brownson's Quarterly Review q.v.]

Place of Publication: Boston
First Issue: Jan 1838
Last Issue: Oct 1842//
Periodicity: Quarterly
Editor: Orestes A. Brownson
Publisher: Benjamin H. Greene
Available From: APS; Lib. of Congress.*
                Mott. Poole.
Contents:
  Poetry: Original. Selected: Whittier,
    William Thompson Bacon, Wordsworth,
    Shelley.
  Prose: Essay. Criticism. Book Reviews.
  Fiction: Essay Serial: "Chat in Boston
    Bookstores."
  Miscellaneous: Literary Notices.
  Note: Addresses and orations by Ralph Waldo
    Emerson, John Quincy Adams. Articles by
    Alexander H. Everett, George Bancroft,
    Amos Bronson Alcott, Margaret Fuller,
    Elizabeth Peabody.

137   TITLE: The Boston Satirist; or Weekly Museum.
      [See The Satirist. By Lodowick Lash'em.]

138   TITLE: The Boston Spectator, and Ladies'
      Album. [Superseded by The Bower of Taste
      q.v.]

Place of Publication: Boston
First Issue: 7 Jan 1826
Last Issue: 29 Dec 1827//
Periodicity: Weekly
Editors: ?
Publishers: Ingraham and Hewes
Available From: Lib. of Congress*; Boston
                Pub. Lib.*
Contents:
  Poetry: Original. Selected: William
    Roscoe, Bernard Barton, James G. Percival,
    R.B. Sheridan, Felicia Hemans, Boston
    Bard [R.S. Coffin], James Montgomery,
    Sarah J. Hale, Lamartine, Walter Raleigh,
    Anna Letitia Barbauld, Bryant, William
    Blackstone, Nathaniel P. Willis, Harriet
    Muzzy, Chaucer, Thomas Campbell, L.E.
    Landon, Allan Cunningham, R.H. Wilde,
    Coleridge, John Bowring, Richard Henry
    Dana.
  Prose: Biography: Burns, Goethe. Travel.
    Essay. Familiar Essay. Letters. Book
    Reviews.
  Fiction: Sketches. Tales: "Maria Mait-
    land. An English Story"; "The Lottery
    Ticket"; "The Switzer's Wife" [Felicia
    Hemans]; "Gertrude de Wart, or, Fidelity

Until Death"; "Yankee Hospitality"; "Os-
car, the Greek Patriot"; "The English
Orphan"; "Opium versus Toothache"; "The
Fountain"; "The Unknown"; "Humble Life'
or, the Sycamore Tree"; "Tradition--Or
Saint Kevin's Bed"; "The Major and the
Farmer"; "Carol More O'Daly; or . . .
The Constant Lover"; "The Emigrants, or,
Aspasia de Nemours . . . Founded Upon
Facts"; "Night Horrors"; "Ambition, or
the Story of William and Catharine";
"The Family Mansion"; "The Mysterious
Mansion. A Legend of the North End."
  Miscellaneous: Extracts: from other jour-
    nals; by various authors; Franklin,
    Benjamin Rush, W. Irving. Anecdotes:
    on various subjects; Goldsmith, William
    Cowper, Voltaire, Swift, Franklin.
    News: Domestic.

139   TITLE: The Boston Spectator; Devoted to
      Politicks and Belles-Lettres.

      Place of Publication: Boston
      First Issue: 1 Jan 1814
      Last Issue: 25 Feb 1815//
      Periodicity: Weekly
      Editor: John Park
      Publishers: Munroe & Francis
      Available From: APS; Lib. of Congress.*
                     Mott.
      Contents:
        Poetry: Original. Selected: Thomas
          Moore, Thomas Dodsley, Henry Kirke White,
          Byron, Mary Russell Mitford, Scott,
          Southey, William Pitt, James Montgomery,
          Washington Allston, R.H. Wood, William
          Jones, B. Jonson, Erasmus Darwin.
        Prose: Essay. Familiar Essay. Criticism:
          on Maria Edgeworth, Shakespeare, Gold-
          smith, James Thomson, Byron. Letters.
        Fiction: Essay Serials: "The Confidant";
          "The Writer." Sketches.
        Miscellaneous: Extracts: by various
          authors. Anecdotes: on various sub-
          jects; George Whitefield, S. Johnson,
          John Locke, Edward Gibbon, Milton,
          Voltaire, B. D'Israeli. News: Foreign
          and Domestic.

140   TITLE: The Boston Weekly Magazine.

      Place of Publication: Boston
      First Issue: 2 March 1743
      Last Issue: 16 March 1743//
      Periodicity: Weekly
      Editor: ?
      Publishers: Rogers and Fowle
      Available From: APS; Mass. Hist. Soc.*
                     Mott.
      Contents:
        Poetry: Original. Selected: Addison.
        Fiction: Sketches.
        Miscellaneous: News: Domestic.

141   TITLE: Boston Weekly Magazine and Ladies'
      Miscellany. [See The Boston Weekly Maga-
      zine, Devoted to Polite Literature . . . . .
      Useful Science . . . . . Biography . . . . .
      and Dramatic and General Criticism.]

142   TITLE: Boston Weekly Magazine. Devoted to
      Moral and Entertaining Literature, Science,
      and the Fine Arts: Containing Original and
      Selected Tales, Moral and Humorous Essays,
      Sketches of Nature and Society, Elegant
      Extracts, Poetry, Criticism, and Selections
      from Works of History and Adventure: Em-
      bellished with Music, Arranged for the
      Piano Forte, Flute, &c.

      Place of Publication: Boston
      First Issue: 8 Sept 1838
      Last Issue: 11 Sept 1841//
      Periodicity: Weekly
      Editors: David H. Ela; John B. Hall
      Publishers: David H. Ela; John B. Hall
      Available From: APS; Amer. Antiquarian Soc.*
                     Mott.
      Contents:
        Poetry: Original: William Thompson Bacon,
          Mary H. Mann, William B. Tappan, Wilson
          Flagg, Isaac F. Shepard. Selected:
          James T. Fields, Lydia H. Sigourney,
          Byron, Herrick, Felicia Hemans, Joshua
          Sylvester, James G. Percival, Nathaniel
          P. Willis.
        Prose: Biography: Franklin, William
          Caxton. Essay. Familiar Essay. Criti-
          cism.
        Fiction: Essay Serials: "Rural Sketches--
          By a Rambler"; "The Oglio"; "Collectanea
          Minorae"; "Collectanea Majora"; "Trifles
          from My Escritoire." Sketches. Tales:
          "The Apparition"; "The Sultana of the
          Desert"; "Cousin William"; "Ferdinand,
          the Broken-Hearted, or, the Point of
          Pines"; "The Unexpected"; "The Cousins";
          "The Prisoner's Last Dream"; "The Legend
          of Merry the Miner"; "The Lakes of Lynn";
          "The Canadian Patriot. A Tale of the
          Times"; "The Gamester's Daughter"; "Tales
          of the Province House" [Hawthorne]; "The
          Belle; or, My Aunt Martha"; "Pride of the
          Village" [W. Irving]; "The Suspicious
          Stranger. A Tale Founded on Fact"
          [Amelia Opie]; "The Devoted Wife"; "The
          Sisters"; "The Unrevealed"; "Ruth Deane;
          or, the Collegian's Sister"; "The Cross";
          "The Merchant's Daughter"; "The Wife of
          Seven Husbands. A Legend of London";
          "The Politician"; "The Ruined Laird";
          "Grace Falkiner"; "Henry Clifton. A
          Tale, Founded on Fact."
        Miscellaneous: Extracts: from other jour-
          nals. Anecdotes: Shakespeare, Boswell,
          S. Johnson, Park Benjamin, Erasmus
          Darwin, George Cruikshank. Literary
          Notices. News: Foreign and Domestic.

143   TITLES: (1) The Boston Weekly Magazine;
Devoted to Morality, Literature, Biography,
History, the Fine Arts, Agriculture, &c. &c.
(2) Boston Weekly Magazine: or, Ladies'
and Gentlemen's Miscellany. [Continued as
The Emerald, or, Miscellany of Literature
q.v.]

Place of Publication: Boston
First Issue: 30 Oct 1802
Last Issue: 26 April 1806//
Periodicity: Weekly
Editors: Samuel Gilbert; Thomas Dean;
          Joshua Belcher; Samuel T. Armstrong
Publishers: Gilbert & Dean; Belcher &
             Armstrong
Available From: APS; Univ. of Mich.* Mott.
Contents:
  Poetry: Original. Selected: Erasmus
  Darwin, Goldsmith, William Cowper,
  Thomas Paine.
  Prose: Biography. Travel. Essay.
  Familiar Essay. Criticism: on Dryden,
  Pope, S. Johnson, Kotzebue. Letters.
  Fiction: Essay Serials: "The Moralist";
  "The Gossip"; "The Itinerant"; "The
  Passenger." Sketches.
  Miscellaneous: Extracts: by various
  authors. Anecdotes: on various subjects.
  News: Domestic.

144   TITLES: (1) The Boston Weekly Magazine,
Devoted to Polite Literature . . . . .
Useful Science . . . . Biography . . . . .
and Dramatic and General Criticism
(2) Boston Weekly Magazine and Ladies'
Miscellany.

Place of Publication: Boston
First Issue: 12 Oct 1816
Last Issue: 25 Dec 1824//
Periodicity: Weekly
Editors: ?
Publishers: Parmenter and Norton; Tileston
             & Parmenter; Henry Bowen
Available From: APS; Lib. of Congress.*
Contents:
  Poetry: Original. Selected: Edmund
  Waller, Swift, Milton, James Hogg,
  Charles Chruchill, Chatterton, James
  Montgomery.
  Prose: Biography: Jane Shore, Rousseau,
  R.B. Sheridan, Scott, Benjamin West.
  Travel. Familiar Essay. Criticism: on
  Voltaire, Scott. Letters. Book Reviews.
  Fiction: Essay Serials: "The Contributor";
  "The Reflector"; "The Thinker"; "The
  Pedlar"; "The Poetical Moralist." Tales:
  "The Indians. A Tale"; "The Hermit of
  the Mountains, an Eastern Tale"; "Sir
  Reginald de Cuthbert"; "Claudine. A
  Swiss Tale"; "The Shepherdess of the
  Alps"; "Frederick and Louisa"; "The
  Balance of Comfort; or . . . the Old
  Maid and the Married Woman."
  Miscellaneous: Extracts: from other jour-
  nals; Swift. Anecdotes: on various
  subjects; S. Johnson, Nathaniel Lee,
  Franklin, Buonaparte, Addison, Sterne,
  Burke, Savage, R.B. Sheridan. News:
  Foreign and Domestic.

145   TITLE: Boston Weekly Magazine: or, Ladies'
and Gentlemen's Miscellany. [See The
Boston Weekly Magazine; Devoted to Morality,
Literature, Biography, History, the Fine
Arts, Agriculture, &c. &c.]

146   TITLES: (1) The Bouquet: Flowers of Polite
Literature; Consisting of Original and
Selected Tales, Legends, Essays, Traveling
[sic] and Historical Sketches, American
Biography, General Miscellany, and Poetry
(2) The Pearl and Literary Gazette. Devoted
to Original and Selected Tales, Legends,
Essays, Travelling, Literary, and Historical
Sketches, Biography, Poetry, etc. (3) The
Boston Pearl and Literary Gazette. Devoted
to Original and Selected Tales, Legends,
Essays, Travelling, Literary and Historical
Sketches, Biography, Poetry, Criticism,
etc. [Title page reads: The Hartford
Pearl and Literary Gazette, later The
Boston Pearl and Literary Gazette] (4) The
Boston Pearl. A Gazette of Polite Litera-
ture. Devoted to Original Tales, Legends,
Essays, Translations, Travelling, Literary
and Historical Sketches, Biography, Poetry,
Criticisms, Music, etc. And Containing a
Variety of Matter Connected with Many Sub-
jects of Importance and Interest.

Place of Publication: Hartford; Boston
First Issue: 11 June 1831
Last Issue: 14 Sept 1836//
Periodicity: Semi-monthly; Weekly
Editors: Melzar Gardner; Isaac C. Pray, Jr.
Publishers: Joseph Hurlbut; William A.
             Hawley
Available From: APS; Enoch Pratt Lib.,
                 Baltimore.
Contents:
  Poetry: Original. Selected: Lydia H.
  Sigourney, George D. Prentice, Whittier,
  Nathaniel P. Willis, Bryant, Grenville
  Mellen, Joseph Rodman Drake, Felicia
  Hemans, James G. Percival, S.G. Goodrich,
  Fitz-Greene Halleck, Hannah F. Gould,
  Edward Coote Pinckney, Bernard Barton,
  Robert Morris, Henry Kirke White, Thomas
  Haynes Bayly, Shelley, William Leggett,
  Park Benjamin, Byron, Charles Sprague,
  Edward Morton, James G. Brooks, Coleridge,
  Keats, John G. Brainard, Francis Hop-
  kinson, Sumner Lincoln Fairfield, John
  Bowering, Albert Pike, E. Lytton Bulwer,
  Washington Allston, Isaac C. Pray, Jr.
  Prose: Biography: John Trumbull, James G.
  Percival, John Neal, Bryant, Scott,
  Shakespeare, James Macpherson, Joel
  Barlow, John G. Brainard, James Fenimore
  Cooper, E. Lytton Bulwer, William Cowper,
  William Collins, Washington, Jefferson.
  Travel. Essay. Familiar Essay. Criti-
  cism.
  Fiction: Essay Serials: "Musings"; "Genius
  of the Past"; "Reminiscences of a Rambler";
  "Bachelor's Reveries"; "Looker On"; "The
  Pearl Fisher"; "Reveries and Sketches";
  "Strings of Paragraphs"; "Tavern Lounger".
  Sketches. Tales: "The Indian Fighter";
  "Timothy Weasel" [James Kirke Paulding];
  "Albina McLush" [Nathaniel P. Willis];

"The Forsaken Girl" [Whittier]; "The
Utilitarian" [John Neal]; "Yankee Court-
ship" [John Neal]; "The Sleigh Ride"
[John Neal]; "Death of the Gentle Usher"
[Nathaniel P. Willis]; "A Profligate's
Last Month"; "The Deformed Girl" [Whit-
tier]; "Mark Gherrit's Ring"; "Mizzarro,
a Tale of Venice"; "Ashton Grey"; "Mrs.
Washington Potts"; "Emma Grandison";
"Asem, the Man-Hater" [Goldsmith]; "The
Outlaw of the Pines"; "Captain Thomson"
[Nathaniel P. Willis]; "The Doale. A
Tale of the Revolution"; "P. Calamus,
Esq!" [Nathaniel P. Willis]; "Maleena.
A Story of the Indians"; "Story of Eliza
Wickliff"; "The Monk. A Tale of the
Crusades"; "Monedo--The Daughter of
Snow"; "Catuca, or the Female Hermit";
"Mad Rosalie"; "The Maniac Bride"; "A
Tale of Tweeddale"; "Almira, or the
Victim of Indulgence"; "The Diamond
Necklace"; "The Man Mole. A True Tale";
"A Tale of the Wissahickon."
  Miscellaneous: Extracts: from other jour-
  nals; W. Irving, Coleridge, Charles Lamb,
  Schiller, Sterne. Anecdotes: on various
  subjects; Buonaparte, Franklin, Washing-
  ton. Literary Notices.

147 TITLE: The Bower of Taste. [Supersedes
     The Boston Spectator, and Ladies' Album
     q.v.]

Place of Publication: Boston
First Issue: 5 Jan 1828
Last Issue: 24 May 1830//
Periodicity: Weekly
Editor: Katharine A. Ware
Publishers: Ingraham & Andrews; Samuel G.
            Andrews; Dutton & Wentworth
Available From: Amer. Antiquarian Soc.*;
               Boston Pub. Lib.*
Contents:
  Poetry: Original. Selected: Nathaniel P.
  Willis, Sumner Lincoln Fairfield, William
  Cowper, James G. Percival, Barry Corn-
  wall, Thomas Moore, Scott, L.E. Landon,
  Felicia Hemans, William Leggett, Lydia
  H. Sigourney, George W. Doane, S.G.
  Goodrich, Rufus Dawes, Byron, Frederic S.
  Hill.
  Prose: Biography. Essay. Familiar Essay.
  Letters.
  Fiction: Essay Serials: "Omnium Gatherum";
  "Native Sketches"; "Scraps from a Port-
  Folio"; "Reminiscences." Sketches.
  Tales: "The Mysterious Bridal, Founded
  on Fact"; "The Queen of the Rose"; "The
  Brothers"; "Ingratitude. An American
  Story"; "Antonio--Or, Three Weeks' Hap-
  piness"; "The Emigrant"; "Claudine Mig-
  not, Surnamed La Lhauda"; "The Felon's
  Son"; "The Ice Ship. From an Old Sea-
  Captain's Manuscript"; "The Exile of the
  Alleghany"; "Picture of a Young Parson";
  "The Sexton of Cologne"; "The Legend of
  Bethel Rock"; "Travelling by Night. The
  Young Soldier's Furlough"; "The Pirates,
  or . . . Errors of Public Justice"; "A
  Legend of the White Mountains"; "The

Mysterious Fireman"; "D'Lamet; a Tale of
the French Revolution"; "The Maniac, or
the Effects of Jealousy"; "Edwin and
Ophelia: A Native Tale"; "The Poor
Artist"; "The Yankee Ghost"; "Eustace de
Santerre"; "The Mournful Bridal"; "In-
gratitude.--(A True Story)"; "The Fruits
of Ambition"; "Louise . . . A Convent
Story"; "A Tale of the Deserted Isle";
"Alfred and Almira"; "Stolen Matches";
"First and Last Ticket, from the Manu-
script of a Condemned Criminal."
  Miscellaneous: Extracts: from other jour-
  nals; by various authors; John Neal.
  Anecdotes: on various subjects; Buona-
  parte, Scott. Literary Notices. News:
  Domestic.

148 TITLE: Boys' and Girls' Journal, a Magazine
     for the People and Their Children. [See
     Boys' and Girls' Penny Journal.]

149 TITLE: Boys' and Girls' Journal, a Miscellany
     of Choice and Useful Reading for the Young,
     in the Varied Departments of Literature.
     With a Collection of Original Articles by
     Pupils of the Philadelphia Schools and
     Other Youth. [See Boys' and Girls' Penny
     Journal.]

150 TITLES: (1) Boys' and Girls' Literary
     Boquet [sic] (2) Boys' and Girls' Bouquet
     (3) Boys' and Girls' Monthly Bouquet.

Place of Publication: Philadelphia
First Issue: Nov 1842
Last Issue: June 1846//
Periodicity: Monthly
Editor: James C. Catlin
Publisher: James C. Catlin
Available From: Lib. of Congress
Contents:
  Poetry: Original. Selected: Felicia
  Hemans.
  Prose: Biography. Travel. Essay.
  Fiction: Tales: "Ellen Stanley"; "The
  Hated Task"; "Troublesome Tom. A Tale
  for Little Folks, Showing That Duty Is
  Safety"; "Mary Woodley, or the Children's
  Party" [Caroline F. Orne]; "Anne Bell;
  or the Faults" [T.S. Arthur].
  Miscellaneous: Anecdotes: on various sub-
  jects; William Cowper.

151 TITLE: Brown's Literary Omnibus. News,
     Books Entire, Sketches, Reviews, Tales
     Miscellaneous Intelligence. [See Waldie's
     Literary Omnibus. News, Books Entire,
     Sketches, Reviews, and Miscellaneous In-
     telligence.]

152 TITLE: Boys' and Girls' Magazine.

Place of Publication: Boston
First Issue: Jan 1843
Last Issue: Dec 1843//?

Periodicity: Monthly
Editor: Mrs. S. Colman
Publishers: T. Harrington Carter & Co.
Available From: Amer. Antiquarian Soc.*;
N.Y. State Lib., Albany*
Contents:
Poetry: Original: Grenville Mellen, T.S.
Arthur, Susan Jewett, Jane Roscoe, Han-
nah F. Gould, Lydia H. Sigourney, Frances
S. Osgood, James T. Fields, Solyman
Brown, G.M. Bussey.‘ Selected: Tennyson,
Blake, Rufus Dawes, Mary Howitt, Leigh
Hunt, Sarah Coleridge, Barry Cornwall.
Prose: Biography: Franklin. Familiar
Essay. Letters.
Fiction: Essay Serial: "Pastimes at Home."
Sketches. Tales: "Ann and Louisa, or
the Law Case"; "The Baby-House" [Catha-
rine M. Sedgwick]; "Faithfulness; or the
Story of the Bird's Nest"; "The Story of
Edward Lyon; or Confessing a Fault" [T.S.
Arthur]; "Susan Howe's Dream"; "Story of
the Knocker; or, Antonio and the Judge";
"The Captive Children"; "The Morning
Walk" [T.S. Arthur]; "Presence of Mind"
[Catharine M. Sedgwick]; "Little Daffy-
downdilly" [Hawthorne]; "Anselmo's Es-
cape; or, the Dog Saint Bernard"; "Little
Margaret Seaton"; "The Yount Light-
Keeper"; "Little Mary"; "Lizzy, a Fairy
Tale"; "Story of Narina.--A Fairy Tale";
"An Old-Fashioned Pic-Nic."
Miscellaneous: Extracts: from other jour-
nals. Anecdotes: on various subjects.

153   TITLE: The Boys' and Girls' Magazine, and
Fireside Companion.

Place of Publication: Boston
First Issue: Jan 1848
Last Issue: Dec 1857//
Periodicity: Monthly
Editor: Mark Forrester
Publishers: Bradbury & Guild
Available From: APS; Boston Pub. Lib.
Contents:
Poetry: Original. Selected: Herrick, A
Wallace Thaxter, Oneida Seaton, John
Quincy Adams, Nilla Forrester, Mary
Howitt, William J. Hamersley.
Prose: Travel. Essay. Familiar Essay.
Fiction: Essay Serial: "Life of the
Editor." Sketches. Tales: "Wishy and
Worky.--A Good Story"; "Life and Ad-
ventures of William Wander"; "Maurice
Wilkins, the Shetland Adventurer";
"Honesty Is the Best Policy"; "Wishes";
"Malay Village"; "Little Frank and the
Boat"; "The Newfoundland Dog"; "Filial
Piety"; "Laura Bridgman"; "Adolphus and
James"; "The Clever Boy"; "The Lost
Child"; "Old Ponto"; "The Basket of
Cherries"; "Billy Egg"; "Johnny Leonard
and His Mother"; "The Seven-Shilling
Piece"; "The Coronation"; "Mischievous
Theodore"; "The Rabbit"; "The Farmer's
Boy."
Miscellaneous: Anecdotes: on various
subjects.

154   TITLES: (1) Boys' and Girls' Penny Journal
(2) Boys' and Girls' Penny Journal, a
Miscellany of Entertaining and Instructive
Knowledge (3) Boys' and Girls' Journal, a
Miscellany of Choice and Useful Reading for
the Young, in the Varied Departments of
Literature. With a Collection of Original
Articles by Pupils of the Philadelphia
Schools and Other Youth (4) Boys' and
Girls' Journal, a Magazine for the People
and Their Children. [Running title:
Fithian's Magazine for Boys and Girls.]

Place of Publication: Philadelphia
First Issue: Jan 1848
Last Issue: 1853//?
Periodicity: Weekly; Semi-monthly
Editors: Charles Fithian; Lydia J. Pierson
Publisher: Aaron F. Cox
Available From: Lib. of Congress; Amer.
Antiquarian Soc.
Contents:
Poetry: Original: Maria Mifflin, James M.
Small, Martin F. Tupper, W.H. Luckenbach.
Selected: D.C. Colesworthy, Mary Howitt,
T.S. Arthur, Lydia H. Sigourney, Caroline
Norton, Thomas Haynes Bayly, Edward
Young, Frances S. Osgood, Felicia Hemans,
Hannah F. Gould, Barry Cornwall, Catha-
rine M. Sedgwick, Eliza Cook, Charles
Swain, H.T. Tuckerman, W.H.C. Hosmer,
Charles Fithian, Nathaniel P. Willis, John
G. Brainard, James Montgomery, Emma C.
Embury, Joseph Rodman Drake, Charles
Lester, Sarah J. Hale, William Jones,
Oliver Wendell Holmes, George W. Patten,
Anna Cora Mowatt, P.M. Wetmore, George
D. Prentice, William Leggett, Whittier,
Alice Carey.
Prose: Biography. Travel. Essay.
Familiar Essay.
Fiction: Sketches. Tales: "Teacher's
Mite, and Rich Man's Thousands"; "Abby's
Year in Lowell"; "The Shipwrecked Or-
phans: Said to Be a True Narrative of
Four Years' Suffering"; "The Little Mill
Dam"; "The Cousins"; "The Little Men of
Gold. A French Fairy Tale"; "Mark Max-
well: Or, I Can and I Will"; "The Lucky
Mishap; or, Truth and Honesty Always the
Best Policy"; "Never Be Rash--Or the
Cockpit Duel"; "Harry Harvey; or, 'Never
Say You Can't Until You Try'"; "The Tale
of a Triangle" [Mary Howitt]; "The Stu-
dent and the Apprentice; or Never Teach
One Thing and Do Another"; "The Idle
Schoolboy; or, the Utility of Knowledge";
"Try" [T.S. Arthur]; "The Ruined Son.
A Tale of Truth for Parents"; "Lazy Jake,
the Trout-Fisher"; "The Little Sick
Brother; a Lesson on Personal Kindness."
Miscellaneous: Extracts: from other jour-
nals. Anecdotes: on various subjects;
Washington, Buonaparte, Edmund Burke,
William Pitt, Penn, Scott, Maria Edge-
worth, S. Johnson. Literary Notices.

155   TITLE: The Broadway Journal.

Place of Publication: New York
First Issue: 4 Jan 1845
Last Issue: 3 Jan 1846//
Periodicity: Weekly
Editors: Charles F. Briggs; Edgar Allan Poe;
      Henry O. Watson
Publishers: John Bisco; Edgar Allan Poe
Available From: APS; Boston Athenaeum.*
      Mott.
Contents:
  Poetry: Original: Park Benjamin, James
    Russell Lowell, Poe, William Wallace,
    Thomas Dunn English, Mary E. Hewitt,
    Maria White Lowell, William Gilmore
    Simms, Philip Pendleton Cooke, Frances
    S. Osgood, Richard Henry Dana, Mary G.
    Wells, Henry B. Hirst, A.B. Meek.
    Selected: Thomas Hood, James Aldrich,
    Thomas Holley Chivers, Sarah J. Hale,
    William D. Gallagher.
  Prose: Essay. Familiar Essay. Criticism.
    Letters. Book Reviews.
  Fiction: Essay Serials: "Thoughts of a
    Silent Man"; "The Living Artists of
    Europe"; "Glimpses of Broadway";
    "Desultory Thoughts"; "Correspondence
    with a Governess." Sketches: "Sketches
    of American Prose Writers" [William
    Jones, Nathaniel P. Willis, John Waters,
    Richard Henry Dana, H.T. Tuckerman.]
    Tales: "The Great Tower of Tarudant";
    "Berenice" [Poe]; "Bon-Bon"; "Law and
    Waltzing"; "The Grateful Clerk, a Tale
    Founded on Facts"; "Three Sundays in a
    Week" [Poe]; "The Pit and the Pendulum"
    [Poe]; "The Assignation" [Poe]; "The
    Premature Burial" [Poe]; "The Adventures
    of a Gentleman in Search of a Dinner";
    "The Masque of the Red Death" [Poe];
    "The Literary Life of Chingum Bob, Esq.
    Late Editor of the 'Goosetherumfoodle'"
    [Poe]; "The Business Man" [Poe]; "The
    Man That Was Used Up. A Tale of the Late
    Bugaboo and Kickapoo Campaign" [Poe];
    "Never Bet the Devil Your Head: A Tale
    with a Moral" [Poe]; "The Tell-Tale
    Heart" [Poe]; "William Wilson" [Poe];
    "The Landscape Garden" [Poe]; "Ligeia"
    [Poe]; "Ms. Found in a Bottle" [Poe];
    "King Pest. A Tale Containing an
    Allegory" [Poe]; "The Thousand-and-
    Second Tale of Scheherazade" [Poe];
    "The Devil in the Belfry" [Poe]; "The
    Spectacles" [Poe]; "A Tale of Ragged
    Mountain" [Poe]; "The Oblong Box" [Poe].
    Drama: "The Magnetizer; or, Ready for
    Any Body."
  Miscellaneous: Anecdotes: on various sub-
    jects; Thomas Hood. Literary Notices.

156   TITLE: Brother Jonathan. A Weekly Compend
    of Belles Lettres and the Fine Arts,
    Standard Literature, and General Intel-
    ligence.

Place of Publication: New York
First Issue: 1 Jan 1842
Last Issue: 23 Dec 1843//

Periodicity: Weekly
Editors: Park Benjamin; Rufus Wilmot Gris-
      wold; H. Hastings Weld; John Neal
Publishers: Wilson & Company
Available From: APS; Lib. of Congress.*
      Mott.
Contents:
  Poetry: Original: Whitman, Thompson
    Westcott, Thomas Dunn English, Eliza
    Cook, William Howitt, Henry Morford,
    H. Hastings Weld, C. Donald MacLeod,
    George Pope Morris. Selected: McDonald
    Clarke, Charles Swain, Thomas Ingoldsby,
    George Cruikshank, Nathaniel P. Willis,
    Thomas Hood, Thomas Campbell, John Neal,
    Mrs. Seba Smith, Tennyson, Frances S.
    Osgood, John Oxenford, Leigh Hunt, Victor
    Hugo, Schiller, Hannah F. Gould, James
    Kirke Paulding, E.B. Hale.
  Prose: Essay. Familiar Essay. Criticism.
    Letters. Book Reviews.
  Fiction: Sketches. Tales: "The Adventures
    of Tom Stapleton"; from "Home as Found"
    [James Fenimore Cooper]; "The Storming
    of Badajoz"; "The Lieutenant's Story";
    "The Legend of the Dead Bridgegroom";
    "Story of Krusenstern and Avensleben";
    "Misadventures at Margate. An O'er True
    Tale"; "Jack Hinton, the Guardsman";
    "Timothy Bushnell, Esq. or, Day's Market-
    ing"; "Matthew Scrawler, the Charity Boy";
    "Lucy Gray"; "Know Your Man. A Tale of
    the Last Century"; "Little Joe Junk and
    the Fisherman's Daughter" [John Neal];
    "'Mum O' the Marsh.' A Legend of
    Connecticut"; "The Commissioner; or, de
    Lunatico Inquirendo"; "Ho-Fi of the
    Yellow Girdle"; "Fluffy Jack"; "The
    Dancing Feather, or the Amateur Free-
    booters" [J.H. Ingraham]; "Hector
    O'Halloran and His Man"; "The Thunder
    Storm. A Tale of Scotland"; "The Mercer's
    Wife"; "The Charcoal-Burners. A Tale";
    "Marriage in a Mask; or, the Cunning
    Shaver, Chin"; "The Widow by Brevet; or,
    That Sad Affair of Miss Picklin"
    [Nathaniel P. Willis]; "The Alderman. A
    Legend of the Ward of Cheap"; "Lady
    Florinda Bellayse. A Tale of the Dead";
    "The Palfrey; a Love-Story of Olden
    Times" [Leigh Hunt]; "The Grimsby Ghost"
    [Thomas Hood]; "The Miser's Daughter"
    [William Harrison Ainsworth]; "The Mayor
    of Hole-Cum-Corner" [Douglas Jerrold];
    "'Hans Myer's Dream.' A Legend of New
    York"; "The Hunchback. A Pennsylvania
    Story"; "The Minister's Daughter. A
    Tale for Wine Drinkers--Being the Sad
    History of Emma Harrington--Related by
    Herself"; "The Hadjee of Ameenabad. A
    Tale of Persia"; "Two Hours of Mystery";
    "The Belle of the Belfry; or the Daring
    Lover" [Nathaniel P. Willis]. Novels:
    "The Career of Puffer Hopkins"; "Zanoni:
    Or, the Secret Order" [E. Lytton Bulwer];
    "The Tempter and the Tempted"; "Phineas
    Quiddy"; "The Life and Adventures of
    Martin Chuzzlewit" [Dickens]; "The Last
    of the Barons" [E. Lytton Bulwer];
    "Forest Days." Drama: "Patrick O'Flynn;
    or, the Man in the Moon."

Miscellaneous: <u>Extracts</u>: from other jour-
nals; by various authors; James Fenimore
Cooper, Frances Trollope, Charles Lamb,
Dickens. <u>Anecdotes</u>: on various subjects;
H. Greeley, S. Johnson. <u>Literary Notices</u>.
<u>News</u>: Domestic.

157 TITLE: <u>Brownson's Quarterly Review</u>.
[Supersedes <u>The Boston Quarterly Review</u>
q.v.]

Place of Publication: Boston
First Issue: Jan 1844
Last Issue: Oct 1875//
Periodicity: Quarterly
Editor: Orestes A. Brownson
Publishers: Benjamin H. Greene; E. Dunigan
& Bro.; D. & J. Sadler; Fr.
Pustet & Co.
Available From: APS; Yale Univ.* Mott.
Poole.
Contents:
Poetry: <u>Original</u>: George W. Thompson.
<u>Selected</u>.
Prose: <u>Essay</u>. <u>Familiar Essay</u>. <u>Criticism</u>.
<u>Book Reviews</u>.
Fiction: <u>Tale</u>: "Edward Morton."
Miscellaneous: <u>Extracts</u>: from other jour-
nals; Emerson, Longfellow. <u>Literary
Notices</u>.

158 TITLE: <u>Burton's Gentleman's Magazine, and
Monthly American Review</u>. [See <u>The Gentleman's Magazine</u>.]

159 TITLE: <u>The Cabinet</u>.

Place of Publication: Taunton, Mass.
First Issue: 12 Dec 1829
Last Issue: 3 Dec 1831//
Periodicity: Weekly
Editor: William S. Tisdale
Publisher: William S. Tisdale
Available From: Amer. Antiquarian Soc.; N.Y.
Pub. Lib.
Contents:
Poetry: <u>Original</u>. <u>Selected</u>: Mary Anne
Browne, Joseph Rodman Drake, Harriet
Muzzy, George W. Doane.
Prose: <u>Letters</u>.
Fiction: <u>Sketches</u>. <u>Tales</u>: "The Indolent
Fairy"; "The Palace of Beauty. A Fairy
Tale"; "The Lonely Inn"; "Maternal
Ingenuity. Or, Trying to Hook a
Bachelor"; "Cousin Nancy, or the Virgin
of '76"; "The Turkey's Leg."
Miscellaneous: <u>Extracts</u>: from other jour-
nals. <u>Anecdotes</u>: on various subjects;
Isaac Newton. <u>News</u>: Domestic.

160 TITLE: <u>The Cabinet; a Repository of Polite
Literature</u>.

Place of Publication: Boston
First Issue: 5 Jan 1811
Last Issue: 23 March 1811//
Periodicity: Weekly

Editors: ?
Publishers: ?
Available From: APS; Amer. Antiquarian Soc.*
Contents:
Poetry: <u>Original</u>. <u>Selected</u>: Joseph
Warton, George Crabbe.
Prose: <u>Biography</u>: George Frederick Cooke.
<u>Familiar Essay</u>. <u>Criticism</u>. <u>Letters</u>.
Fiction: <u>Essay Serial</u>: "The Peripatetic."
<u>Tales</u>: "Retribution—An Oriental Tale";
"Hann and Gulphenha. An Oriental Tale by
Wieland."
Miscellaneous: <u>Extracts</u>: from other jour-
nals; by various authors; Kotzebue.
<u>Anecdotes</u>: on various subjects; S. John-
son, Isaac Newton, Garrick.

161 TITLE: <u>The Cabinet of Entertainment, and
Weekly Visiter. Interesting Tales, Legends,
and Adventures, History, Voyages, Travels,
Poetry, Music, &c</u>.

Place of Publication: Boston; Salem, Mass.
First Issue: 23 Aug 1834
Last Issue: 1835//?
Periodicity: Weekly
Editors: John Emmes Dill; Daniel D. Smith
Publishers: John Emmes Dill; Daniel D.
Smith; Dill & Sanborn
Available From: Amer. Antiquarian Soc.;
Boston Pub. Lib.
Contents:
Poetry: <u>Original</u>. <u>Selected</u>: Felicia
Hemans, Joanna Baillie, L.E. Landon,
William Howitt, Barry Cornwall, Selleck
Osborne, Ann S. Stephens, Charles Swain.
Prose: <u>Travel</u>. <u>Familiar Essay</u>.
Fiction: <u>Sketches</u>. <u>Tales</u>: "The Black
Mask. A Legend of Hungary"; "The Wife
of Seven Husbands. A Legend of Ancient
London"; "The Mountain Sibyl"; "Orsino
and Ellen"; "The Skull House"; "The Loved
and Lost One—A Jewish Story"; "Margaret
Campbell"; "The Boatswain's Tale"; "The
Sexton of Cologne"; "The Trademan's
Daughter" [Ann S. Stephens]; "The
Podesta's Daughter"; "The Stern Father—
A Tale"; "The Idiot"; "Mad Rosalie";
"Fire Island-Ana"; "Kellingham House.
A Tale of the Suburbs of London"; "The
Villi Dance. A Tale of Hungary."
Miscellaneous: <u>Anecdotes</u>: on various sub-
jects; Franklin, S. Johnson, James Hogg.

162 TITLE: <u>The Cabinet of Instruction, Literature,
and Amusement</u>. [See <u>The Cabinet of Literature, Instruction, and Amusement</u>.]

163 TITLE: <u>The Cabinet of Literature, and Monthly
Miscellany, Containing History, Biography,
Voyages, Travels, Curiosities of Nature and
Art, Poetry, Music, Elegant Extracts, Select
Anecdotes, Passing Events, etc. etc</u>.

Place of Publication: New York
First Issue: [Only one issue published]
1 Sept 1833//
Periodicity: Intended to be monthly

Editors: ?
Publishers: A.R. Crain & Co.
Available From: Lib. of Congress; Chicago
                Pub. Lib.
Contents:
  Poetry: Original. Selected.
  Prose: Biography. Travel. Familiar Essay.
  Fiction: Sketches.
  Miscellaneous: Extracts: from other jour-
    nals; by various authors; Addison.
    Anecdotes: on various subjects;
    Washington, Scott.

164   TITLES: (1) The Cabinet of Literature,
      Instruction, and Amusement (2) The Cabinet
      of Instruction, Literature, and Amusement
      (3) The Cabinet of Religion, Education,
      Literature, Science, and Intelligence.
      [Running title: The New-York Cabinet.]

      Place of Publication: New York
      First Issue: 16 Sept 1828
      Last Issue: June 1831//
      Periodicity: Semi-monthly; Weekly
      Editors: Ralph Hoyt; John Newland Maffitt
      Publishers: Piercy & Burling; Theodore
                  Burling; Henry R. Piercy
      Available From: Lib. of Congress*; Amer.
                      Antiquarian Soc.
      Contents:
        Poetry: Original. Selected: Byron,
          Nathaniel P. Willis, Hannah More, Herrick,
          Thomas Moore, John W. Stebbins, Keats,
          Sumner Lincoln Fairfield, Southey, L.E.
          Landon, Fitz-Greene Halleck, Thomas
          Haynes Bayly, Henry Neele, Jane Taylor,
          William Howitt, Elizabeth Bogart,
          William Kennedy, Felicia Hemans, Bernard
          Barton, Wordsworth, James Hogg, William
          L. Bowles, Robert Montgomery, S.G. Good-
          rich, Willis Gaylord Clark, Charles
          Sprague.
        Prose: Biography: John Ledyard, Scott,
          John Quincy Adams, Coleridge, Voltaire.
          Travel. Familiar Essay. Letters.
        Fiction: Sketches. Tales: "The Fisher-
          man's Daughter"; "The Curate of Suverd-
          sio"; "The Castle of Costanzo, an
          Italian Tale"; "The Green Taper"; "Mary
          Harvey. A Tale of the Other Times";
          "Blighted Affection"; "The Tiger's Cave";
          "Blanche d'Albi"; "The Iron Mask"; "The
          Eloquent Thief"; "A Blue Stocking Party";
          "The House on the Moors. A Tale"; "The
          Man Mountain"; "The Mysterious Wedding";
          "A Tale of Vavoo"; "Jack the Shrimp";
          "The Barber of Göttingen"; "The Iron
          Shroud"; "The Broken Hearted."
        Miscellaneous: Extracts: from other jour-
          nals; by various authors; Coleridge,
          Sumner Lincoln Fairfield, Scott.
          Anecdotes: on various subjects;
          Buonaparte, S. Johnson, Washington,
          Milton. Literary Notices.

165   TITLE: The Cabinet of Religion. Education,
      Literature, Science, and Intelligence.
      [See The Cabinet of Literature, Instruction,
      and Amusement.]

166   TITLE: Cadet and Statesman. [See Literary
      Cadet, and Saturday Evening Bulletin.]

167   TITLE: The Calvary Token and Literary
      Souvenir.

      Place of Publication: Auburn, N.Y.
      First Issue: Jan 1846
      Last Issue: Dec 1846//?
      Available From: Univ. of Minn.*

168   TITLES: (1) Campbell's Foreign Monthly
      Magazine; or, Select Miscellany of the
      Periodical Literature of Great Britain
      (2) Campbell's Foreign Semi-Monthly Maga-
      zine, or Select Miscellany of European
      Literature and Art.

      Place of Publication: Philadelphia
      First Issue: Sept 1842
      Last Issue: Aug 1844//
      Periodicity: Monthly; Semi-monthly
      Editor: James M. Campbell
      Publisher: James M. Campbell
      Available From: APS; Lib. of Congress.*
                      Mott.
      Contents:
        Poetry: Selected: Thomas Moore, Robert
          C. Welsh, Tennyson, Thomas Hood, Schiller,
          Wordsworth, W.H. Fisk, Charles Wolfe,
          Charles Hervey, Charles Swain, Victor
          Hugo, James Sheridan Knowles, T.B.
          Macaulay, Lamartine, James Hogg, Eliza
          Cook.
        Prose: Biography: Buonaparte, Addison,
          Jeremy Bentham. Essay. Familiar Essay.
          Criticism. Letters. Book Reviews.
        Fiction: Essay Serial: "Reminiscences
          of Men and Things." Sketches. Tales:
          "Abednego the Money-Lender"; "The
          Inconveniences of Being Like Somebody
          Else"; "The Student's Bride"; "A Short
          Story of a Cow and a Sow"; "A Fleet Mar-
          riage"; "Young Scotland; or, an Evening
          at Treport"; "A Jar of Honey from Mount
          Hybla" [Leigh Hunt].
        Miscellaneous: Extracts: from other jour-
          nals. Anecdotes: on various subjects.

169   TITLE: The Canal of Intelligence.

      Place of Publication: Norwich, Conn.
      First Issue: 2 June 1826
      Last Issue: 18 Nov 1829//
      Available From: Yale Univ.; Western Reserve
                      Hist. Soc., Cleveland

170   TITLE: The Candid Examiner.

      Place of Publication: Montrose, Pa.
      First Issue: 19 June 1826
      Last Issue: 18 June 1827//
      Periodicity: Bi-monthly
      Editor: C.R. Marsh
      Publisher: Dimock & Fuller
      Available From: APS; Amer. Antiquarian Soc.

Contents:
  Poetry: <u>Original</u>: Felicia Hemans, William
    Ray. <u>Selected</u>: Thomas Moore, Southey.
  Prose: <u>Familiar Essay</u>.
  Fiction: <u>Essay Serial</u>: "Sketches of Indian
    History."
  Miscellaneous: <u>Anecdotes</u>: on various sub-
    jects. <u>Literary Notices</u>.

171   TITLE: <u>Carey's Library, of Choice Literature.
    Containing the Best Works of the Day, in
    Biography, History, Travels, Novels, Poetry,
    &c. &c.</u>

Place of Publication: Philadelphia
First Issue: 1 Oct 1835
Last Issue: 26 March 1836//
Periodicity: Weekly
Editor: E.L. Carey
Publishers: E.L. Carey & A. Hart
Available From: APS; Univ. of Pa.*
Contents:
  Prose: <u>Biography</u>. <u>Travel</u>.
  Fiction: <u>Tales</u>: "Adventures in the Rifle
    Brigade, in the Peninsula, France, and
    the Netherlands, from 1809 to 1815";
    "One in a Thousand; or the Days of Henry
    Quatre"; "Rienzi, the Last of the
    Tribunes"; "Confessions and Crimes; or
    Posthumous Records of a London Clergyman";
    "The Tin Trumpet; or Heads and Tales.
    For the Wise and Waggish"; "Village
    Sayings and Doings; or My Village, versus
    'Our Village.'" <u>Drama</u>: "Henriquez: A
    Tragedy" [Joanna Baillie]"; "The Martyr:
    A Drama"; "The Separation: A Tragedy";
    "The Phantom: A Musical Drama."

172   TITLES: (1) <u>The Carlisle Gazette, and the
    Western Repository of Knowledge</u> (2) <u>The
    Carlisle Gazette</u> (3) <u>Kline's Carlisle
    Weekly Gazette</u> (4) <u>Kline's Weekly Carlisle
    Gazette</u>.

Place of Publication: Carlisle, Pa.
First Issue: 10 Aug 1785
Last Issue: 23 Oct 1817//
Periodicity: Weekly
Editor: George Kline
Publisher: George Kline
Available From: Amer. Antiquarian Soc.*
Contents:
  Poetry: <u>Original</u>. <u>Selected</u>.
  Prose: <u>Essay</u>.
  Fiction: <u>Sketches</u>.
  Miscellaneous: <u>Anecdotes</u>: on various sub-
    jects. <u>News</u>: Foreign and Domestic.

173   TITLE: <u>The Casket: And Philadelphia
    Monthly Magazine</u>. [See <u>The Casket, or,
    Flowers of Literature, Wit & Sentiment</u>.]

174   TITLE: <u>The Casket. By Charles Candid</u>.

Place of Publication: Hudson, N.Y.
First Issue: 7 Dec 1811
Last Issue: 30 May 1812//?

Periodicity: Weekly
Editor: C.N. Bement
Publisher: C.N. Bement
Available From: APS; Amer. Antiquarian Soc.
Contents:
  Poetry: <u>Original</u>. <u>Selected</u>: James Mont-
    gomery, Southey, Peter Pindar, Thomas
    Moore, William Cowper, Goldsmith, Amelia
    Opie.
  Prose: <u>Biography</u>: Lord Nelson, Pocahontas.
    <u>Travel</u>. <u>Familiar Essay</u>. <u>Letters</u>.
  Fiction: <u>Essay Serials</u>: "The Essayist";
    "Rover." <u>Tale</u>: "Perourou; or the Bellows
    Mender."
  Miscellaneous: <u>Extracts</u>: from other jour-
    nals; by various authors; Franklin, Gold-
    smith. <u>Anecdotes</u>: on various subjects.

175   TITLE: <u>The Casket. Devoted to Literature,
    Science, the Arts, News, &c.</u>

Place of Publication: Cincinnati
First Issue: 15 April 1846
Last Issue: 7 Oct 1846//
Periodicity: Weekly
Editor: Emerson Bennett
Publisher: Baillie & Co.
Available From: APS; Lib. of Congress*
Contents:
  Poetry: <u>Original</u>: Sophia H. Oliver, C.B.
    Gillespie, Emerson Bennett, Alice Carey,
    S.C. Kinney, Phoebe Carey. <u>Selected</u>:
    Thomas Moore, Longfellow, Hannah F. Gould,
    Charles Fenno Hoffman, Burns.
  Prose: <u>Essay</u>. <u>Familiar Essay</u>.
  Fiction: <u>Essay Serials</u>: "Self-Command";
    "American Sketches." <u>Sketches</u>. <u>Tales</u>:
    "Hellena Ashton"; "The Lieutenant's
    Story; or, the Condemned Soldier's Last
    Hour. A Tale of the Florida War"; "The
    Merchant's Son"; "The Benefactor"; "The
    Betrothed. A Tale of the Santee"; "The
    Silver Lute; or, the Gypsey Singer"; "The
    Poor Student, or the Linwood Family";
    "Astounding Disclosure"; "Edith Warren.
    A Tale of the Revolution"; "The Young
    Artist"; "Idalene"; "The Unknown Countess:
    Or Crime and Its Results"; "Retribution;
    or, the Three Chimneys"; "The Creole's
    Daughter."
  Miscellaneous: <u>Extracts</u>: from other jour-
    nals; by various authors. <u>Anecdotes</u>:
    Pope, Thomas Moore. <u>Literary Notices</u>.
    <u>News</u>: Foreign and Domestic.

176   TITLES: (1) <u>The Casket, or, Flowers of
    Literature, Wit & Sentiment</u> (2) <u>Atkinson's
    Casket. Gems of Literature, Wit and Senti-
    ment</u> (3) <u>The Casket: And Philadelphia
    Monthly Magazine</u> (4) <u>Graham's Lady's and
    Gentleman's Magazine</u> (5) <u>Graham's Magazine
    of Literature and Art</u> (6) <u>Graham's Ameri-
    can Monthly Magazine of Literature and Art</u>
    (7) <u>Graham's Illustrated Magazine of
    Literature, Romance, Art, and Fashion</u>.

Place of Publication: Philadelphia
First Issue: Jan 1826
Last Issue: Dec 1858//

Periodicity: Monthly
Editors: Samuel C. Atkinson; George R. Graham; Rufus Wilmot Griswold; Charles H. Peterson; Edgar Allan Poe; Emma C. Embury; Ann S. Stephens; Robert T. Conrad; Charles Godfrey Leland
Publishers: Atkinson & Alexander; George R. Graham; Samuel D. Patterson & Co.; R.H. See & Co.; Watson & Co.
Available From: APS; Harvard Univ.* Mott.
Contents:
  Poetry: Original: L.W. Trask, J.N. M'Jilton, Jane E. Locke, W.F. Marvin, Agnes Strickland, L.A. Wilmer, L.E. Landon, William Ball, Grenville Mellen, John Neal, John B. Dillon, Samuel W. Stockton, Robert Hamilton, Charles Bird Barrett, Thomas Dunn English, Howard Draper, T. Westcott, Emily Taylor, William Wood, Mary Anne Browne, Catharine H. Waterman, Felicia Hemans, Hannah F. Gould, Ann S. Stephens, Emma C. Embury, Poe. Selected: Park Benjamin, Willis Gaylord Clark, B.F. Chatham, Thomas G. Spear, Henry B. Hirst, H. Percival, James Russell Lowell, Bryant, Goethe, Thomas Campbell, William B. Tappan, Nathaniel P. Willis, Thomas Hood, William Fraser, John Bowering, Thomas Roscoe, Lydia H. Sigourney, William Roscoe, Longfellow, Erasmus Darwin, Thomas Moore, Robert Montgomery, James Montgomery, Felicia Hemans, Bernard Barton, V.V. Ellis, Alaric Watts, James G. Percival, E. Lytton Bulwer, Henry Pickering, James Sheridan Knowles, William Falconer, Mrs. Seba Smith, H.T. Tuckerman, Elizabeth Barrett, James Aldrich, Charles Fenno Hoffman, Henry William Herbert, Louis L. Noble, C.P. Cranch, Richard Henry Dana, Lydia J. Pierson, Elizabeth Oakes Smith, Charles W. Baird, Frances S. Osgood, Walter Golton, Catharine Maria Sedgwick, Bayard Taylor, T.B. Read, L.J. Cist, Caroline F. Orne, J.E. Dow, W.H.C. Hosmer, J.R. Chandler, Thomas Paine, Jeremy Taylor, Thomas Haynes Bayly, Fanny Kemble, Barry Cornwall, William Howitt, Byron, Luis de Camoens, W.W. Story, Alfred B. Street, Grenville Mellen, Mary Anne Browne, Poe.
  Prose: Biography: Penn, Jefferson, Franklin, John Quincy Adams. Essay. Familiar Essay. Criticism: "The Philosophy of Composition" [Poe]; "Thomas Carlyle and His Works [Thoreau]; "Fifty Suggestions" [Poe]. Letters. Book Reviews.
  Fiction: Essay Serials: "Rambles to the Booksellers' Counters"; "Cruizing in the Last War"; "Leaves from a Lawyer's Port-Folio" [Poe]. Sketches. Tales: "The Thunder-Struck"; "Seven Marriages and Never a Husband"; "Mrs. Washington Potts"; "The Outlaw of the Pines. A Tale of the Revolution"; "Opposite Neighbors, or the Peeping Lodger"; "The Condemned"; "Crogan, or the Hero of Sandusky"; "The Martyrs, a Tale of the Revolution"; "The Sister of Charity"; "Moravian Indians: A Tale"; "The Deserter"; "The Italian Bride"; "Remorse--A Tale"; "Sachem's Head; a Story of the Seventeenth Century"; "The Moderate Drinker: Or the Unhappy Marriage"; "Washaloo, the Indian Sachem: Or, Faith Unbroken"; "Los Musicos: Or, the Spanish Exquisite"; "The Mother and Daughter"; "Ellery Truman and Emily Raymond, or the Soldier's Tale"; "Rosina Vangorden, or the Off-spring of a Daughter"; "The Pursuit of Happiness"; "A Persian Legend"; "The Lovers"; "Fashionable Watering Places"; "The Wedding"; "Cousin Mary"; "Neal Gordon, or Indian Love. A Tale of the Revolution"; "The Buried Alive"; "Romance of Real Life"; "Albert, or the Feeling Brother"; "A Wedding at College"; "The Coquette"; "Annette"; "The Contrast"; "The Pride of Inverhale"; "The Burial"; "The Ghost. A Village Story"; "The Sea Voyage"; "The Volunteer, a Tale of the Revolution"; "The Way to Rise"; "The Quaker. A Tale"; "The Twin Flowers"; "Reverses. A Tale of the Past Season"; "The Vacation"; "The Generous Stranger"; "Catherine of Lancaster, or the Tournament of Toledo"; "The Exile of Florence"; "The Surgeon's Daughter" [Scott]; "The Felon's Son"; "The Vicar's Daughter"; "The Soldier of the Revolution"; "Wedding Under Ground"; "The Story of the Lady Olivia de Castro"; "The Brownie of the Black Haggs"; "The Phantom Hand"; "Too Handsome for Anything"; "The Spider Caught in His Own Web"; "The Indian Trader; or, James Holton of Orange"; "The Delusion of Three Days"; "Ann Dillon. A Tale"; "The Breast Pin"; "The Guard"; "The False Rhyme" [Mary Godwin Shelley]; "The Fugitive. A Tale"; "The Bride of Lammermoor" [Scott]; "A Scholar's Death-Bed"; "Camden. A Tale of the South"; "The Buccaneer"; "The Reclaimed"; "Ellen Howe, or, Deception"; "Eafitte, the Baratarian Chief"; "The Village Cricle"; "The Portrait"; "The Broken Heart"; "The Italian Bride"; "The Rejected One!"; "Laura Lovel"; "Tale of Error"; "The Ladies' Ball"; "The Suicide"; "The Ring. Or Lovers' Mistakes"; "The Unknown"; "The Merchant's Clerk"; "Thubber-Na-Shie; or, the Fairy Well"; "The Tempter. A Tale of Jerusalem"; "David Swan" [Hawthorne]; "Blue-Stockings"; "The Conspiracy. A Tale of West Point"; "Isabel de Vere"; "The Harem Queen"; "The Murders in the Rue Morgue" [Poe]; "A Descent into the Maelström" [Poe]; "The Island of the Fay" [Poe]; "The Colloquy of Monos and Una" [Poe]; "The King's Bride" [Richard Henry Dana]; "Life in Death" [Poe]; "The Masque of the Red Death" [Poe]; "Bainbridge" [James Fenimore Cooper]; "Autobiography of a Pocket Handkerchief" [James Fenimore Cooper]; "Count Potts' Strategy" [Nathaniel P. Willis]; "Born to Love Pigs & Chickens" [Nathaniel P. Willis]; "Meena Dimity" [Nathaniel P. Willis]; "Love and Pistols" [Nathaniel P. Willis]; "Nora Mehidy" [Nathaniel P. Willis]; "The Imp

of the Perverse" [Poe]; "The System of
Dr. Tarr and Prof. Fether" [Poe]; "The
Icy Veil" [Nathaniel P. Willis]; "The
Islets of the Gulf; or, Rose Budd" [James
Fenimore Cooper]; "Matthew Mizzle, of the
Inquiring Mind" [Joseph C. Neal].
Miscellaneous: Extracts: from other jour-
nals; by various authors; Goldsmith.
Anecdotes: on various subjects; Garrick,
Byron, Horace Walpole, Franklin, Edmund
Burke. Literary Notices.

177   TITLE: The Centinel of Freedom.

Place of Publication: Newark, N.J.
First Issue: 5 Oct 1796
Last Issue: 1909//?
Periodicity: Weekly
Editors: Daniel Dodge; Aaron Pennington;
      Jabez Parkhurst; Samuel Pennington;
      Stephen Gould
Publishers: Daniel Dodge; Aaron Pennington
      & Daniel Dodge; Jabez Parkhurst
      & Samuel Pennington; Samuel
      Pennington & Stephen Gould;
      Tuttle & Pike; W. Tuttle & Co.;
      John Tuttle & Co.
Available From: Amer. Antiquarian Soc.*
Contents:
  Poetry: Original: Edward Sharman,
    Nathaniel Gott. Selected: Bernard Barton.
  Prose: Familiar Essay.
  Fiction: Sketches.
  Miscellaneous: Anecdotes: on various sub-
    jects. News: Foreign and Domestic.

178   TITLE: The Champagne Club. A Chronicle of
Military and Fashionable Events and Things,
and Criminal Record of Literary and Other
Misdoings--By Ebenezer Lovemuch & Capt.
Marcius Mucklewrath. Aided and Abetted by
a Secret Society of Gentlemen.

Place of Publication: Washington, D.C.
First Issue: 6 Dec 1834
Last Issue: 7 March 1835//
Periodicity: Weekly
Editors: ?
Publishers: ?
Available From: Lib. of Congress*; Hist.
                Soc. of Pa.

Contents:
  Poetry: Original. Selected.
  Prose: Familiar Essay. Letters.
  Fiction: Sketches.
  Miscellaneous: Anecdotes: on various sub-
    jects.
Note: Whimsical.

179   TITLE: The Chandelier. Devoted to Literature
and the Arts.

Place of Publication: Boston
First Issue: 1 May 1850
Last Issue: 18 May 1850//?
Available From: Lib. of Congress

180   TITLE: The Charleston Spectator, and Ladies'
Literary Port Folio. By Google, Spectacles,
& Co.

Place of Publication: Charleston, S.C.
First Issue: 9 Aug 1806
Last Issue: 5 Dec 1806//?
Periodicity: Weekly
Editor: J. Hoff
Publisher: J. Hoff
Available From: APS; Amer. Antiquarian Soc.*
Contents:
  Poetry: Original. Selected: Robert
    Bloomfield, William Cowper, Thomas Moore,
    Benjamin Tompson.
  Prose: Familiar Essay. Letters.
  Fiction: Tales: "Julius and Maria"; "The
    Worn Soldier"; "Ivar and Matilda."
  Miscellaneous: Anecdotes: on various sub-
    jects: Addison, Dryden. News: Domestic.

181   TITLE: Cheap Repository.

Place of Publication: Philadelphia
First Issue: [Undated. nos. 1-42] 1799-1800//
Periodicity: Weekly
Editors: ?
Publishers: ?
Available From: APS; Hist. Soc. of Pa.*
Contents:
  Poetry: Original.
  Prose: Biography. Familiar Essay.
  Fiction: Tales: "The Shepherd of Salis-
    bury-Plain"; "The Two Wealthy Farmers'
    or, the History of Mr. Bragwell"; "The
    Two Blacksmiths"; "The Cheapside Ap-
    prentice; or, the History of Mr. Francis
    H***"; "True Examples of the Interposition
    of Providence, in the Discovery and
    Punishment of Murder"; "Husbandry
    Moralized"; "Black Giles the Poacher";
    "Tawny Rachel"; "The History of the Two
    Shoemakers"; "The Harvest Home"; "The
    History of Diligent Dick; or, Truth Will
    Out Though It Be Hid in a Well"; "The
    Gamester"; "History of Mr. George
    Wisheart, Another Martyr"; "The History
    of the Beggerly Boy"; "The Shopkeeper
    Turned Sailor"; "A True Story of a Good
    Negro Woman"; "The Troubles of Life, or
    the Guinea and the Shilling"; "The History
    of Mary Wood, the Housemaid; or, the
    Danger of False Excuses"; "The Hubbub; or,
    the History of Farmer Russel, the Hard-
    Hearted Overseer"; "The Black Prince, a
    True Story"; "Betty Brown, the St. Gile's
    Orange Girl"; "The Cock-Fighter. A True
    History"; "Onesimus; or, the Run-Away
    Servant Converted. A True Story"; "The
    History of Charles Jones, the Footman."

182   TITLE: Chicora; or, Messenger of the South.
A Journal of Belles-Lettres and the Fine
Arts, and a Weekly Gazette of Science,
Education and General Intelligence. [Merged
into The Magnolia; or, Southern Apalachian
q.v.]

Place of Publication: Charleston, S.C.
First Issue: 9 July 1842
Last Issue: 24 Sept 1842//?
Available From: Duke Univ., Durham

183   TITLE: Child of Pallas: Devoted Mostly to the Belles-Lettres.

Place of Publication: Baltimore
First Issue: Nov 1800
Last Issue: Jan 1801//
Periodicity: Weekly
Editor: Charles Prentiss
Publishers: Warner & Hanna
Available From: APS; Lib. of Congress.*
                Mott.
Contents:
   Poetry: Original. Selected.
   Prose: Biography. Familiar Essay. Letters.
   Fiction: Essay Serials: "The Jumper"; "The
      Crites"; "Spangles and Ribbons" [anecdotes,
      quips, riddles, etc.]. Sketches.
   Miscellaneous: Extracts: from other jour-
      nals; by various authors; Boswell.
      Anecdotes: on various subjects; Garrick,
      S. Johnson, Goldsmith, Voltaire, Handel,
      Milton, Dryden, Addison. News: Foreign
      and Domestic.

184   TITLE: The Child's Cabinet.

Place of Publication: New Haven, Conn.
First Issue: [Only one issue published?]
            1832//?
Periodicity: ?
Editor: Jeremy L. Cross
Publisher: Jeremy L. Cross
Available From: Lib. of Congress; Yale Univ.
Contents:
   Poetry: Original: Lydia H. Sigourney.
      Selected: Mary Howitt, Lydia H. Sigour-
      ney, Hamilton Buchanan, James Montgomery.
   Prose: Biography: Franklin. Essay.
   Fiction: Sketches. Tale: "The Early Wed
      and the Early Dead."
   Miscellaneous: Anecdotes: on various sub-
      jects; Washington.

185   TITLE: The Child's Companion.

Place of Publication: Skaneateles, N.Y.
First Issue: 1838
Last Issue: 1839//?
Available From: N.Y. State Lib.*

186   TITLES: (1) The Child's Friend; Designed for
       Families and Sunday Schools (2) The
       Child's Friend.

Place of Publication: Boston
First Issue: Oct 1843
Last Issue: Dec 1858//
Periodicity: Monthly
Editors: Eliza L. Follen; Lee Cabot
Publisher: Leonard C. Bowles
Available From: APS; Harvard Univ.*

Contents:
   Poetry: Original: D.M. Moir, Eliza L.
      Follen, Robert Nicol, James Aldrich,
      William Nicholson, Maria White Lowell,
      Lydia Maria Child, Elizabeth Carter, J.
      Clement. Selected: Harriet Martineau,
      A.J. Moultrie, Schiller, Goethe, F.
      Ruckert, Browning, W.C. Bennett, William
      Leggett, Leigh Hunt, Nathaniel P. Willis,
      Jones Very, Eliza Cook.
   Prose: Biography. Familiar Essay.
   Fiction: Tales: "Pic-Nic at Dedham";
      "Methuselah and Arak"; "Green Spots in
      This Golden World"; "The Toll-Man's
      Family. A True Story"; "The Invalid
      Boy"; "The Caterpillar's Nest"; "New
      Year's Eve"; "John the Leper. A Tale";
      "The Return Home"; "The Orange Gatherers";
      "Conrad, the Beggar Boy"; "The Quaker
      Shawl"; "The Lost Child"; "The Necklace";
      "The Party of Pleasure"; "Good Little
      Violet"; "Playing Tricks"; "Ferdinand, or
      the Temptation" [Goethe]; "The Three
      Brothers"; "Grace Mills"; "The Two Little
      Friends"; "Princess Alderia; or, the Five
      Wishes. A Fairy Tale"; "The Mother's
      Tale"; "The Story of Caliph Stork"; "The
      Little Expecter, or, Fairy Music"; "Janet
      Melville; or, too Late"; "The Twin
      Sisters"; "May Morning"; "The Shipwreck";
      "The Cousins"; "The Doves"; "Ellen
      Sevard"; "The Bunch of Flowers"; "Little
      Laura"; "Lois, the Schoolmate Ridiculed";
      "Hyacinth and Viola"; "Little Harry";
      "The White Lady"; "Mary Anne, or the
      Cloister Maiden"; "Merlin. A Minstrel's
      Tale"; "Ruth Brown"; "How Saint Elroy Was
      Cured of Vanity"; "The Canary Bird"; "A
      Vision of Christmas"; "It Is only a
      Trifle"; "Frank and Harry; or Penitence
      and Peace"; "Clara Howard's New Year's
      Dream"; "Charlotte and Rebecca"; "The
      Nightingale"; "The Grateful Scholars";
      "The Wishing-Cap"; "The Affrighted Ass"
      [Dumas]; "Minnie"; "The Poor Girl and
      Her Dog"; "Tapioca Pudding."

187   TITLE: The Child's Newspaper.

Place of Publication: Cincinnati
First Issue: 7 Jan 1834
Last Issue: 2 Sept 1834//?
Periodicity: Semi-monthly
Editors: Thomas Brainerd; B.P. Aydelotte
Publishers: Corey & Fairbank; Eli Taylor;
            Taylor & Tracy
Available From: APS; Western Reserve Hist.
                Soc.*
Contents:
   Poetry: Original. Selected: Mary Howitt,
      George Crabbe, Hannah F. Gould, Bernard
      Barton.
   Prose: Letters.
   Fiction: Essay Serial: "The Fire Side."
      Sketches.
   Miscellaneous: Anecdotes: on various sub-
      jects.

188   TITLE: The Christian, and Literary Register.

Place of Publication: New York
First Issue: 15 Aug 1827
Last Issue: 1 Sept 1827//
Available From: N.Y. Pub. Lib.*

189   TITLE: The Christian Family Magazine,
      Devoted to Religion, Literature, Science,
      and General Intelligencer.

Place of Publication: Cincinnati
First Issue: [Only one issue published]
              1845//
Available From: Iowa State Traveling Lib.,
                 Des Moines*; Drake Univ.,
                 Des Moines*

190   TITLE: The Christian History, Containing
      Accounts of the Revival and Propogation of
      Religion in Great-Britain & America.

Place of Publication: Boston
First Issue: 5 March 1743
Last Issue: 25 Feb 1745//
Periodicity: Weekly
Editor: Thomas Prince, Jr.
Publishers: S. Kneeland and T. Green
Available From: APS; Amer. Antiquarian Soc.*
                 Mott.
Contents:
  Poetry: Original.
  Prose: Letters.
  Miscellaneous: Extracts: by various
    authors. Literary Notices.
Note: Of particular interest are extracts
    from works by Jonathan Edwards, Samuel
    Stoddard, Samuel Sewall, Cotton Mather,
    Jonathan Dickinson, and others, as well
    as some of their sermons. There are
    also extensive accounts of the Reverend
    Mr. George Whitefield.

191   TITLES: (1) The Christian Intelligencer
      (2) The Christian Intelligencer and Eastern
      Chronicle (3) Christian Intelligencer.

Place of Publication: Portland; Gardiner, Me.
First Issue: Sept 1821
Last Issue: 30 Dec 1836//?
Periodicity: Semi-monthly; Weekly
Editors: Russell Streeter; William A. Drew;
          Cleaveland Fletcher
Publishers: P. Sheldon; Sheldon & Dickman;
             John Ramsey
Available From: APS; Amer. Antiquarian Soc.
Contents:
  Poetry: Original: Joss Malcom, Samuel
    Woodworth, A. Haslet. Selected: Thomas
    Hood, D.J. Mandell, Erasmus Darwin,
    Grenville Mellen, Thomas Campbell,
    Felicia Hemans, Thomas Moore, J. Frieze,
    Alaric Watts, Henry Neele, John Holmes,
    William Wood, Richard Henry Dana, Byron,
    Charles Sprague, Bryant, George D.
    Prentice, James Hogg, Lydia H. Sigourney,
    Rufus Darby, James W. Eastburn, John C.
    Park, Willis Gaylord Clark, Whittier,
    J.H. Kinney, Hannah More, John Pierpont.

Prose: Essay. Familiar Essay. Book Re-
    views.
Fiction: Essay Serial: "New-England Wars."
    Sketches. Tales: "Fire at Sea"; "The
    Plague in Gibralter"; "The Witch of
    Endor"; "The Mysterious Bell"; "The Castle
    of Erasmus, or, Bertrand and Eliza";
    "Scenes of Childhood"; "The Shell"; "The
    Unlucky Present"; "A Tale of Wo"; "The
    Schoolmaster" [Whittier]; "The Triumph
    of Truth.--A Tale"; "Edward and Cornelia";
    "The Contrast--or, Which Is the Chris-
    tian"; "The Two Millers"; "The Story of
    Le Fevre."
Miscellaneous: Extracts: by various
    authors; Franklin. Anecdotes: on various
    subjects; Jefferson, John Quincy Adams,
    Patrick Henry, Isaac Newton. Literary
    Notices. News: Foreign and Domestic.

192   TITLE: The Christian Journal, and Literary
      Register.

Place of Publication: New York
First Issue: 22 Jan 1817
Last Issue: Dec 1830//
Periodicity: Semi-monthly; Monthly
Editors: John Henry Hobart; Benjamin T.
          Onderdonk
Publishers: T. and J. Swords
Available From: APS; N.Y. Pub. Lib.* Mott.
Contents:
  Poetry: Original. Selected: Wordsworth,
    Southey, William Cowper, James Hogg,
    William Jones, James Montgomery, Anna
    Letitia Barbauld.
  Prose: Biography: R.B. Sheridan, William
    Cowper, Richard Hooker; Saints and
    religious figures. Travel. Criticism:
    on Byron, Scott, William Cowper, Southey,
    James Hogg. Letters. Book Reviews.
  Fiction: Essay Serial: "The Country
    Clergyman."
  Miscellaneous: Extracts: from other jour-
    nals. Anecdotes: on various subjects;
    Byron, Buonaparte, S. Johnson, William
    Jones, William Cowper, Pope, Abraham
    Cowley. Literary Notices.

193   TITLE: The Christian Observatory: A
      Religious and Literary Magazine.

Place of Publication: Boston
First Issue: Jan 1847
Last Issue: April 1850//
Periodicity: Monthly
Editors: A.W. McClure; N. Adams; J.A. Albro;
          E. Beecher; E.N. Kirk; W.A. Stearns;
          A.C. Thompson
Publishers: J.V. Beane & Co.; Woodbridge,
             Moore & Co.
Available From: APS; Amer. Antiquarian Soc.*
Contents:
  Prose: Biography: William Bradford,
    Roger Williams, William Brewster,
    Thomas Hooker, Penn. Essay. Criticism.
    Letters. Book Reviews: on Melville's
    Typee.
  Fiction: Tale: "Conrad: An Allegory."
  Miscellaneous: Literary Notices.

194   TITLE: Christian Philanthropist. Devoted
       to Literature and Religion.

       Place of Publication: New Bedford, Mass.
       First Issue: 14 May 1822
       Last Issue: 13 May 1823//
       Periodicity: Weekly
       Editor: Daniel K. Whitaker
       Publisher: Daniel K. Whitaker
       Available From: APS; Amer. Antiquarian Soc.
       Contents:
         Poetry: Original. Selected: Selleck
           Osborne, Thomas Moore, Samuel Woodworth,
           Joanna Baillie.
         Prose: Biography: S. Johnson. Familiar
           Essay. Criticism: on Scott, Milton,
           Thomas Moore. Letters. Book Reviews.
         Fiction: Essay Serials: "The Ladies'
           Friend"; "The Correspondent"; "Fugacity";
           "Remarker." Sketches. Tales: "Ade-
           laide: Or the Lovely Rustic"; from "The
           Spy--a Tale of the Neutral Ground"
           [James Fenimore Cooper]; "An Arabian
           Tale."
         Miscellaneous: Extracts: from other jour-
           nals. Anecdotes: on various subjects;
           John Locke, Boswell, Lavater, Franklin.
           Literary Notices. News: Foreign and
           Domestic.

195   TITLE: The Christian's, Scholar's, and
       Farmer's Magazine; Calculated, in an Eminent
       Degree, to promote Religion; to Disseminate
       Useful Knowledge; to Afford Literary
       Pleasure and Amusement, and to Advance the
       Interests of Agriculture.

       Place of Publication: Elizabethtown, N.J.
       First Issue: April-May 1789
       Last Issue: Feb-March 1791//
       Periodicity: Bi-monthly
       Editor: Shepard Kollock
       Publisher: Shepard Kollock
       Available From: APS; Amer. Antiquarian Soc.
       Contents:
         Poetry: Original. Selected: Dryden,
           Milton.
         Prose: Biography: Sterne, Steele, Frank-
           lin, Hogarth, Addison, Isaac Newton,
           Francis Bacon, John Calvin, John Locke,
           Chrysostom. Travel. Familiar Essay.
           Letters.
         Miscellaneous: News: Foreign and Domestic.

196   TITLE: The Cincinnati Literary Gazette.

       Place of Publication: Cincinnati
       First Issue: 1 Jan 1824
       Last Issue: 29 Oct 1825//
       Periodicity: Weekly
       Editor: John P. Foote
       Publisher: John P. Foote
       Available From: APS; Lib. of Congress.*
                        Mott.
       Contents:
         Poetry: Original. Selected: Byron,
           William Cowper, James G. Percival,
           Lorenzo De Medici, J. Zeyden, Selleck
           Osborne, Garrick, Luis de Camoens,

       William Jones, William Falconer, Tasso,
       Wordsworth, Charlotte Smith, Southey,
       Schiller, Bryant, James Montgomery,
       Thomas Moore, James Hogg.
         Prose: Biography. Travel. Criticism.
           Letters. Book Reviews.
         Fiction: Essay Serials: "The Plagiarist";
           "Clio"; "From the Couch of a Valetudi-
           narian." Tales: "Bass-Island Cottage";
           "The Antiquaries, in the West"; "Arthur
           Fitzroy"; "The Maniac"; "The Victim of
           Gaming"; "The Lovers' Political Race, or,
           a Kentucky Election"; "The Romance of
           Real Life"; "Which Gift Was the Best.
           An Eastern Tale"; "The Shipwreck. A
           Tale Founded on Fact"; "Theodore Roland";
           "The Little Antiquary"; "The Rational
           Lunatic."
         Miscellaneous: Extracts: from other jour-
           nals; by various authors; William Cowper,
           Amelia Opie. Anecdotes: on various sub-
           jects. Literary Notices. News: Foreign
           and Domestic.

197   TITLES: (1) The Cincinnati Mirror and Ladies'
       Parterre. Devoted to Polite Literature
       [Title page reads: The Cincinnati Mirror,
       and Ladies' Parterre, and Museum] (2) The
       Cincinnati Mirror, and Western Gazette of
       Literature and Science (3) The Cincinnati
       Mirror, and Western Gazette of Literature,
       Science, and the Arts.

       Place of Publication: Cincinnati
       First Issue: 1 Oct 1831
       Last Issue: 17 Sept 1836//?
       Periodicity: Semi-monthly; Weekly
       Editors: William D. Gallagher; Thomas H.
                 Shreve; James H. Perkins
       Publishers: Wood and Stratton; Shreve and
                    Gallagher; T.H. Shreve & Co.;
                    Flash, Ryder, & Co.
       Available From: APS; Lib. Co. of Philadelphia
       Contents:
         Poetry: Original: William D. Gallagher.
           Harvey D. Little, W.B. Oaks, Lewis Foulk
           Thomas. Selected: Nathaniel P. Willis,
           George D. Prentice, Fitz-Greene Halleck,
           Whittier, Hannah F. Gould, J.B. Gardner,
           Sarah J. Hale, Barry Cornwall, J.N.
           M'Jilton, Otway Curry, Bernard Barton,
           Charles Swain, Thomas Campbell, Robert
           Nicol, Felician Hemans, Byron, E. Lytton
           Bulwer, Emma C. Embury.
         Prose: Biography: William Ellery Channing,
           R.B. Sheridan, James Fenimore Cooper,
           Byron, Scott, Edward Gibbon, Franklin.
           Travel. Essay. Familiar Essay. Criti-
           cism. Letters. Book Reviews.
         Fiction: Essay Serials: "The Paragraphist";
           "Sketches from My Note Book"; "Desk of a
           Reformed Coquette"; "Reminiscences of a
           Sea Captain"; "Papers from My Attic";
           "Facts and Fancies." Sketches. Tales:
           "The Stormed Port.--A Tale of 1756"; "My
           Cousin Lucy"; "The Painter.--A Sicilian
           Tale"; "Ellen Landon; or the Sacrificed.
           A Tale"; "The Brothers; or, the Unnatural
           Meeting"; "Ashton Grey"; "Mizzarro. A
           Tale of Venice"; "The Rattlesnake Hunter"

[Whittier]; "Mrs. Washington Potts"; "Boonesborough"; "Salmos Brandt"; "Big Isam, A Tale of the South"; "The Blind Grandfather"; "Mary Gray and Bessy Bell"; "The Heiress of Rock-Hollow"; "Gertrude Beverly"; "Calum Dhu. A Highland Tale"; "Harlaem House, a Tale of the Times of Old"; "The Girl of the Cane Brake"; "The Brigand's Daughter"; "The Broken Ring"; "The Temptation of Rachel Morrison"; "AB and CD, or the Susceptible Gentleman"; "The Chaplet of Pearls"; "The Last in the Lease"; "Marion Godfrey"; "Sir Dowling O'Hartigan."
Miscellaneous: Extracts: from other journals; by various authors; Coleridge. Anecdotes: on various subjects; Buonaparte, Byron, William Cobbett, Burns. Literary Notices. News: Domestic.

198 TITLE: The Cincinnati Mirror, and Western Gazette of Literature, Science, and the Arts. [See The Cincinnati Mirror and Ladies' Parterre.]

199 TITLE: The City Firefly and Humorous Repository.

Place of Publication: Boston
First Issue: 19 Oct 1822
Last Issue: 25 Feb 1823//?
Available From: Boston Pub. Lib; Mass. State Lib., Boston

200 TITLE: Classical Journal, and Scholars' Review.

Place of Publication: Boston
First Issue: Jan 1830
Last Issue: Dec 1830//
Periodicity: Monthly
Editors: ?
Publishers: ?
Available From: Amer. Antiquarian Soc.*; Boston Pub. Lib.*
Contents:
Poetry: Original. Selected: Hannah F. Gould.
Prose: Biography: Chatterton. Essay. Familiar Essay. Book Reviews.
Fiction: Essay Serial: "The Album." Sketches.
Miscellaneous: Extracts: from other journals. Anecdotes: on various subjects; Buonaparte.

201 TITLE: The Club-Room.

Place of Publication: Boston
First Issue: Feb 1820
Last Issue: July 1820//
Periodicity: Irregular
Editor: Timothy Swan
Publisher: Timothy Swan
Available From: APS; Amer. Antiquarian Soc.*

Contents:
Poetry: Original. Selected: William Cowper, Spenser, George Crabbe, Byron, Herrick.
Prose: Familiar Essay: "Happiness. A Vision"; "Recollections"; "Castle Building"; "Ennui"; "The Village Grave-Yard"; "The Sea of the Poets"; "The Memorial: Of Sundry Aggrieved English Words"; "Ruins of Rome."

202 TITLES: (1) Collections, Topographical, Historical and Biographical, Relating Principally to New-Hampshire (2) Collections, Historical and Miscellaneous; and Monthly Literary Journal.

Place of Publication: Concord, N.H.
First Issue: Jan 1822
Last Issue: 1824//
Periodicity: Bi-monthly; Monthly
Editors: J. Farmer; Jacob B. Moore
Publishers: Hill & Moore; Jacob B. Moore
Available From: Lib. of Congress*; Univ. of Pa.*
Contents:
Poetry: Original: Thomas C. Upham. Selected: Robert Treat Paine.
Prose: Biography: Jeremy Belknap, Timothy Dwight, Robert Montgomery, Benjamin Church, Urian Oakes. Essay. Familiar Essay. Letters. Book Reviews.
Fiction: Essay Serials: "Miscellanies"; "Cincinnatus"; "Tales of the Revolution." Sketches. Tale: "Captivity of Mrs. Johnson."
Miscellaneous: Anecdotes: on various subjects. Literary Notices. News: Foreign and Domestic.

203 TITLE: The Collegian, or American Students' Magazine.

Place of Publication: New York
First Issue: Jan 1819
Last Issue: Feb 1819//?
Periodicity: Monthly
Editors: ?
Publishers: ?
Available From: APS; Lib. of Congress*
Contents:
Poetry: Original. Selected: Samuel Woodworth.
Prose: Biography. Familiar Essay. Letters. Book Reviews.
Fiction: Essay Serial: "The Essayist."
Miscellaneous: Anecdotes: on various subjects.

204 TITLE: The Columbian Lady's and Gentleman's Magazine, Embracing Literature in Every Department; Embellished with the Finest Steel and Mezzotint Engravings, Music and Colored Fashions.

Place of Publication: New York
First Issue: Jan 1844

Last Issue: Feb 1849//
Periodicity: Monthly
Editors: John Inman; Robert A. West;
      Stephen M. Chester
Publishers: Israel Post; Ormsby & Hackett;
      John S. Taylor; Darius Mead
Available From: APS; Amer. Antiquarian Soc.*
      Mott.
Contents:
  Poetry: Original: Isaac Fitzgerald
  Shepard, Mathilda P. Hunt, Richard
  Grant White, H.T. Tuckerman, Augustus
  Snodgrass, William Russell, Jr., Henry
  B. Hirst, Anna Blackwell, Isabel Jocelyn,
  James P. Jett, D. Ellen Goodman.
  Selected: Jane C. Hopkins, Edwin Heriot,
  H.P. Grattan, Joseph H. Butler, Francis
  C. Woodworth, Fitz-Greene Halleck,
  Theodore Sedgwick Fay, Robert A. West,
  Frances S. Osgood, Lydia H. Sigourney,
  Henry A. Clark, Bryant, Mrs. Seba Smith,
  Park Benjamin.
  Prose: Essay. Familiar Essay. Criticism.
  Book Reviews.
  Fiction: Tales: "Clevenger" [H.T. Tucker-
  man]; "The Lady's Shadow"; "The Trans-
  planted Flower, or the Florentine Bride";
  "Lead Us Not into Temptation"; "The
  Fountain of Youth--A Vision" [James
  Kirke Paulding]; "Honor O'Neil; or the
  Days of the Armada"; "The Bells of
  Etherington"; "Lucy Maynard"; "The
  Mysterious Neighbor"; "The Solitary";
  "Vincent Hervey, or the Man of Impulse";
  "The Demon of the Bush: A Tale of
  Albany in Its Cradle Days"; "The Angel
  of the Old--An Extravaganza" [Poe];
  "Adam Baker--The Renegade. A Tale of the
  Texas Frontier"; "The Adopted Daughter";
  "Marrying in Haste to Repent at Leisure";
  "The Knight of Lori"; "Edith Fairlie";
  "The Children of Mount Ida"; "The Double
  Ruse"; "The Youthful Emigrant. A True
  Story of the Early Settlement of New
  Jersey"; "Grace Linden. Four Ages in
  the Life of an American"; "The School-
  master"; "Hilda Silfverling. A Fantasy";
  "Nelly, the Rag-Gatherer"; "The Quiet
  Home" [James Kirke Paulding]; "Rug Raf-
  fles"; "Vulgar Relations"; "The Elder's
  Daughter. A Tale of Fairfield County
  in 1707"; "Willfulness and Weakness"; "The
  Father and Child."
  Miscellaneous: Literary Notices.

205   TITLE: The Columbian Magazine or Monthly
       Miscellany Containing a View of the History,
       Literature, Manners & Characteristics of
       the Year. [Continued as The Universal
       Asylum, and Columbian Magazine q.v.]

       Place of Publication: Philadelphia
       First Issue: Sept 1786
       Last Issue: Feb 1790//
       Periodicity: Monthly
       Editors: Emollit Mores; Mathew Carey;
          William Spotswood; James Trenchard;
          Francis Hopkinson; Alexander
          James Dallas; Charles Cist

Publishers: Mathew Carey; James Trenchard;
      T. Seddon; William Spotswood;
      Charles Cist; Emoleit Mores
Available From: APS; Amer. Antiquarian Soc.*
      Mott.
Contents:
  Poetry: Original: Francis Hopkinson.
    Selected: Gray, Robert Bolling, David
    Humphreys, Joel Barlow.
  Prose: Biography: Nathaniel Greene, Penn,
    John Winthrop, Jefferson, Washington,
    S. Johnson. Travel. Familiar Essay.
    Criticism. Letters. Book Reviews.
  Fiction: Essay Serials: "The Trifler";
    "The Rhapsodist" [Charles Brockden Brown].
    Sketches. Tales: "The Foresters, an
    American Tale" [Jeremy Belknap]; "Amelia:
    Or the Faithless Briton. An Original
    Novel, Founded upon Recent Facts";
    "Memoirs of Captain John Smith"; "Ela;
    or the Delusion of the Heart, a Tale
    Founded on Facts"; "A Pretty Story"
    [Francis Hopkinson]; "The Contemplant:
    An Eastern Tale"; "Ishmael Couloski--A
    Turkish Tale"; "The Danger of Sporting
    with Innocent Credulity: Exemplified in
    the History of Miss Hariot Aspin."
  Miscellaneous: Extracts: from other jour-
    nals. Anecdotes: on various subjects;
    Pocahontas. Literary Notices. News:
    Foreign and Domestic.
Note: Considered the most handsome magazine
  of the eighteenth century.

206   TITLE: The Columbian Museum, or, Universal
       Asylum: Containing Essays on Agriculture--
       Commerce--Manufactures--Politics--Morals--
       and Manners. Sketches of National Char-
       acters--Natural and Civil History--and
       Biography. Law Information--Public Papers--
       Intelligence. Moral Tales--Ancient and
       Modern Poetry, &c. &c.

       Place of Publication: Philadelphia
       First Issue: [Only one issue published]
          Jan 1793//
       Periodicity: Intended to be monthly
       Editor: John Parker
       Publisher: John Parker
       Available From: APS; N.Y. Pub. Lib. Mott.
       Contents:
         Poetry: Original. Selected: Thomas Paine.
         Miscellaneous: News: Domestic.

207   TITLE: The Columbian Observer. A Journal of
       Literature and Politics.

       Place of Publication: Philadelphia
       First Issue: 6 April 1822
       Last Issue: 8 Aug 1825//?
       Available From: Boston Athenaeum; N.Y. State
          Lib.

208   TITLE: The Columbian Phenix and Boston
       Review. Containing Useful Information on
       Literature, Religion, Morality, Politics
       and Philosophy; with Many Interesting

Particulars in History and Biography,
Forming a Compendium of the Present State
of Society.

Place of Publication: Boston
First Issue: Jan 1800
Last Issue: July 1800//
Periodicity: Monthly
Editors: Joseph Hawkins; Daniel Tillotsen
Publishers: Joseph Hawkins; Daniel Tillotsen
Available From: APS; Lib. of Congress.*
            Mott.
Contents:
  Poetry: Original. Selected: Franklin,
    Erasmus Darwin, Thomas Paine, Anthony
    Pasquin, Joseph Story.
  Prose: Biography. Travel. Familiar Essay.
    Criticism. Letters.
  Fiction: Essay Serials: "The Eagle";
    "Literary Review"; "The Laugher"; "The
    Gentleman at Large"; "The Hermit of
    Virginia"; "Common Sense in Dishabile."
  Miscellaneous: Extracts: from other jour-
    nals; Edmund Burke, Horace Walpole,
    Mrs. Inchbald. Anecdotes: on various
    subjects; Handel, Arbuthnot, S. Johnson,
    Diderot. Literary Notices. News:
    Foreign and Domestic.

209   TITLE: The Columbian Star.

Place of Publication: Washington, D.C.
First Issue: 2 Feb 1822
Last Issue: 2 May 1829//?
Periodicity: Weekly
Editor: James D. Knowles
Publishers: Anderson & Meehan
Available From: APS; Lib. of Congress. Mott.
Contents:
  Poetry: Original. Selected: William
    Cowper, Thomas Campbell, James Mont-
    gomery, Coleridge, Southey, Allan Cun-
    ningham, Bryant, Charles Churchill,
    Anna Letitia Barbauld, Thomas Moore.
  Prose: Biography: religious figures;
    LaFayette. Familiar Essay. Criticism:
    on W. Irving, Byron. Letters. Book
    Reviews.
  Miscellaneous: Extracts: from other jour-
    nals; by various authors; Hannah More,
    S. Johnson. Anecdotes: Isaac Newton,
    S. Johnson, Garrick. Literary Notices.
    News: Foreign and Domestic.
Note: Deals primarily with religion and
    literature.

210   TITLE: Columbian Telescope & Literary
    Compiler.

Place of Publication: Alexandria, D.C.
First Issue: 16 June 1819
Last Issue: 20 May 1820//
Periodicity: Weekly
Editors: ?
Publishers: Samuel H. Davis
Available From: Hist. Soc. of Pa.*; Lib. of
            Congress*

Contents:
  Poetry: Original. Selected: Hannah More,
    Byron, William Cowper, Chesterfield.
  Prose: Biography: Goldsmith. Familiar
    Essay. Criticism.
  Fiction: Sketches.
  Miscellaneous: Extracts: from other jour-
    nals; by various authors, W. Irving.
    Anecdotes: on various subjects; Voltaire,
    B. Jonson, Fennell. Literary Notices.
    News: Domestic.
Note: Primarily light sketches and anecdotes.

211   TITLE: The Comet.

Place of Publication: Boston
First Issue: 19 Oct 1811
Last Issue: 11 Jan 1812//
Periodicity: Weekly
Editor: Joseph T. Buckingham
Publisher: Joseph T. Buckingham
Available From: APS; Lib. of Congress*
Contents:
  Poetry: Original. Selected: William
    Congreve, Francis Quarles, Royall Tyler,
    Mary Russell Mitford, Richard Cumberland,
    George Colman, Dryden, Donne, William
    Browne, B. Jonson.
  Prose: Biography: George Psalmanazar,
    Schiller, Richard Cumberland, Robert
    Treat Paine. Travel. Familiar Essay.
    Criticism: on William Congreve. Letters.
    Book Reviews.
  Fiction: Essay Serials: "The Trifler";
    "Theatrical Recorder." Tale: "An
    Eastern Tale, No Man Is Born for Himself."
  Miscellaneous: Anecdotes: on various sub-
    jects; Joshua Reynolds.

212   TITLE: The Comet.

Place of Publication: New York
First Issue: 19 April 1832
Last Issue: 28 July 1833//
Periodicity: Weekly
Editor: H.M. Duhecquet [pseud. of H.D.
            Robinson]
Publisher: H.M. Duhecquet
Available From: Lib. of Congress*; Amer.
            Antiquarian Soc.*
Contents:
  Poetry: Original. Selected: Byron,
    Shelley, Shakespeare, William Cowper,
    Goldsmith, Charles Churchill.
  Prose: Essay. Letters.
  Fiction: Essay Serials: "The Devil's
    Pulpit"; "Silvarum Liber"; "The Lady at
    the Rotunda." Sketches.
  Miscellaneous: Extracts: from other jour-
    nals; by various authors. Anecdotes:
    on various subjects; Voltaire, Buonaparte,
    Isaac Newton, S. Johnson.
Note: Contains many sermons and lectures on
    religious matters.

213   TITLE: The Comet.

Place of Publication: Washington City
First Issue: 1 Feb 1842
Last Issue: 15 Aug 1842//
Periodicity: Semi-monthly
Editors: A.W. Machen; W.L. Childs
Publishers: A.W. Machen; W.L. Childs
Available From: Lib. of Congress*; Univ. of
                 Wash., Seattle*
Contents:
  Poetry: Original. Selected.
  Prose: Essay. Familiar Essay. Letters.
  Fiction: Sketches. Tales: "A Legend of
    Madiera"; "The Franciscan. A Tale of
    Spain."
  Miscellaneous: Anecdotes: on various sub-
    jects; Franklin, George Whitefield.

214   TITLE: The Companion and Weekly Miscellany.
       By Edward Easy, Esquire. [Superseded by
       The Observer (Baltimore) q.v.]

Place of Publication: Baltimore
First Issue: 3 Nov 1804
Last Issue: 25 Oct 1806//
Periodicity: Weekly
Editor: ?
Publishers: Cole & Hewes
Available From: APS; Amer. Antiquarian Soc.*
                 Mott.
Contents:
  Poetry: Original. Selected: Peter Pindar,
    William Shenstone, Amelia Opie, Thomas
    Moore, Erasmus Darwin, Smollett.
  Prose: Biography. Familiar Essay. Letters.
  Fiction: Essay Serials: "The Trifler";
    "On Calumny"; "The Pedestrian"; "Common
    Sense"; "The By-Stander"; "The Observer";
    "The Spy"; "The Sylph." Tales: "Seduc-
    duction"; "The Singular Adventure of
    Count Beaumont."
  Miscellaneous: Extracts: by various
    authors; Burton, Franklin. Anecdotes:
    on various subjects; Dryden, Swift,
    Sterne. Literary Notices.
Note: Motto: "A Safe Companion, and an Easy
  Friend" [Pope].

215   TITLE: Companion for Youth.

Place of Publication: New Haven, Conn.
First Issue: 17 Nov 1838
Last Issue: 11 May 1839//
Periodicity: Weekly
Editor: S.A. Thomas
Publishers: L.H. Young; Young & Uhlborn
Available From: Amer. Antiquarian Soc.*;
                 Yale Univ.*
Contents:
  Poetry: Original. Selected: Mary Howitt.
  Prose: Familiar Essay.
  Fiction: Sketches. Tale: "Elm Tree Hall."
  Miscellaneous: Extracts: from other jour-
    nals. Anecdotes: on various subjects.

216   TITLES: (1) The Concord Herald, and New
       Hampshire Intelligencer (2) Concord
       Herald (3) Courier of New Hampshire.

Place of Publication: Concord, N.H.
First Issue: 6 Jan 1790
Last Issue: 30 Oct 1805//
Periodicity: Weekly
Editor: George Hough
Publisher: George Hough
Available From: Amer. Antiquarian Soc.*
Contents:
  Poetry: Original. Selected: Peter Pindar,
    Freneau.
  Prose: Essay. Familiar Essay.
  Fiction: Sketches.
  Miscellaneous: Literary Notices. News:
    Foreign and Domestic.

217   TITLE: The Connecticut Magazine, or
       Gentleman's and Lady's Monthly Museum of
       Knowledge & Rational Entertainment.

Place of Publication: Bridgeport, Conn.
First Issue: Jan 1801
Last Issue: June 1801//
Periodicity: Monthly
Editors: ?
Publishers: L. Beach & S. Thompson
Available From: APS; Yale Univ.*
Contents:
  Poetry: Original. Selected: S. Johnson,
    Chatterton, William Cowper, Burns.
  Prose: Biography: Edward Cave, John
    Quincy Adams, John Trumbull, James Cook.
    Travel. Familiar Essay. Letters.
  Fiction: Essay Serials: "Walpoliana"
    sketches and sayings of Horace Walpole.
    Sketches. Tale: "The Ruins of St. Os-
    wald. A Romance."
  Miscellaneous: Anecdotes: on various sub-
    jects; Horace Walpole. News: Domestic.

218   TITLE: Connecticut Republican Magazine.

Place of Publication: Suffield, Conn.
First Issue: [Only 5 issues published?]
              July 1802-03//?
Periodicity: ?
Editor: Luther Pratt
Publisher: Luther Pratt
Available From: APS; Case Western Reserve
                 Univ., Cleveland
Contents:
  Poetry: Original. Selected: Peter Pindar.
  Prose: Biography: Jefferson, Burr,
    Nathaniel Greene [By Mathew Carey]. Essay.
    Letters.
  Fiction: Tales.
  Miscellaneous: Extracts: from other jour-
    nals; by various authors; Thomas Paine
    [from Common Sense].
Note: Like so many journals of its day, the
  Connecticut Republican reprinted the
  Declaration of Independence and the Con-
  stitution. Several interesting articles
  include: "Intrigue of Aaron Burr"; "Of
  Alexander Hamilton's Proposed Monarchy."

219 TITLES: (1) The Constitutionalist (2) Constitutionalist and Weekly Magazine.

Place of Publication: Exeter, N.H.
First Issue: 21 May 1810
Last Issue: 14 June 1814//
Periodicity: Weekly
Editor: E.C. Beals
Publisher: E.C. Beals
Available From: Amer. Antiquarian Soc.*
Contents:
  Poetry: Original. Selected: Burns, Scott.
  Prose: Essay. Book Reviews.
  Fiction: Sketches.
  Miscellaneous: Extracts: from other journals; by various authors. Anecdotes: on various subjects. Literary Notices.
  News: Foreign and Domestic.

220 TITLE: The Corrector. By Toby Tickler, Esq.

Place of Publication: New York
First Issue: 28 March 1804
Last Issue: 26 April 1804//
Periodicity: Semi-weekly
Editors: ?
Publishers: S. Gould & Co.
Available From: APS; Boston Athenaeum. Mott.
Contents:
  Poetry: Selected.
  Prose: Letters.
  Fiction: Essay Serials: "Brutus"; Coelius"; "Procius." Sketches. Tale: "Major Purdy's Obsequies. A War Story Founded on Fact. 'Who Killed Cock Robin?'"
  Miscellaneous: Anecdotes: on various subjects.
Note: Motto: "I Fear No Frowns, and Seek No Blind Applause."

221 TITLE: The Corsair. A Gazette of Literature, Art, Dramatic Criticism, Fashion and Novelty.

Place of Publication: New York
First Issue: 16 March 1839
Last Issue: 7 March 1840//
Periodicity: Weekly
Editors: Nathaniel P. Willis; T.O. Porter
Publishers: Nathaniel P. Willis; T.O. Porter
Available From: APS; Yale Univ.* Mott.
Contents:
  Poetry: Original. Selected. Goethe, Herrick, Alfred B. Street, Nathaniel P. Willis, Charles Fenno Hoffman, Joseph Rodman Drake, Carew, William Thompson Bacon, Shelley, Lamartine, Alfred Domett, E. Lytton Bulwer, Longfellow.
  Prose: Biography: LaFayette, Buonaparte, R.B. Sheridan, Franklin, Matthew Gregory [Monk] Lewis. Familiar Essay. Criticism. Letters. Book Reviews.
  Fiction: Essay Serial: "Jottings Down." Sketches. Tales: "The Fugitive of the Jura"; "A Story Writ for the Beautiful"; "A Tale of True Love"; "The Lovers' Quarrel. A Tale of the English Chronicles"; "Falkenstein. A Tale of

Germany"; "The Mayor of Hole-Cum Corner"; "The Father"; "A Stir in the Household"; "Adventures of a Maintop-Crosstree-Man"; "A Week in the Woodlands"; "The Datura Fastuosa.--A Botanical Tale"; "Mr. Singleton Slipslop's Great-Go Party"; "A Romance in the Forest"; "The Green Stockings: A Story of Domestic Life"; "The Youth of Julia Howard, or, First Love"; "The Grisette"; "Madelina: A Roman Story"; "Jack Waller's Story"; "The Compact. A Tale Founded on Fact"; "A Tale of the Morgue."
  Miscellaneous: Extracts: from other journals; Nathaniel P. Willis, James Hogg, Chateaubriand. Anecdotes: on various subjects; Buonaparte, Dickens, Swift, Byron. Literary Notices. News: Foreign and Domestic.

222 TITLE: The Country Courier. [Supersedes The Examiner.]

Place of Publication: New York
First Issue: 3 June 1816
Last Issue: 24 March 1817//?
Periodicity: Semi-weekly
Editors: Barent Gardenier; Abraham Vosburgh
Publishers: Barent Gardenier; Abraham Vosburgh
Available From: APS; Boston Pub. Lib.
Contents:
  Poetry: Original. Selected: Thomas Dibdin, Selleck Osborne, Byron, Burns, Thomas Campbell.
  Prose: Familiar Essay. Criticism: on Byron. Letters.
  Fiction: Essay Serial: "The Critic." Sketches.
  Miscellaneous: Extracts: from other journals; by various authors; Franklin. Anecdotes: on various subjects. Literary Notices. News: Foreign and Domestic.

223 TITLES: (1) The Courier (2) The Courier. Boston Evening Gazette and Universal Advertiser.

Place of Publication: Boston
First Issue: 1 July 1795
Last Issue: 30 Dec 1795//
Periodicity: Semi-weekly
Editor: Benjamin Sweetser
Publishers: Sweetser and Burdick; Benjamin Sweetser
Available From: Amer. Antiquarian Soc.*
Contents:
  Poetry: Original.
  Prose: Biography. Essay.
  Miscellaneous: Literary Notices. News: Foreign and Domestic.

224 TITLE: Courier of New Hampshire. [See The Concord Herald, and New Hampshire Intelligencer.]

225   TITLE: The Critic. A Weekly Review of
       Literature, Fine Arts, and the Drama.
       [Merged into The New-York Mirror: A Weekly
       Gazette of Literature and the Fine Arts.
       See The New-York Mirror, and Ladies'
       Literary Gazette.]

       Place of Publication: New York
       First Issue: 1 Nov 1828
       Last Issue: 20 June 1829//
       Periodicity: Weekly
       Editor: William Leggett
       Publisher: William Leggett
       Available From: APS; N.Y. Pub. Lib.* Mott.
       Contents:
         Poetry: Original: William Leggett, P.M.
           Wetmore. Selected: James Nack,
           Nathaniel P. Willis, James Montgomery,
           Felicia Hemans, Lydia H. Sigourney,
           William B. Tappan, Fitz-Greene Halleck,
           Sumner Lincoln Fairfield, William L.
           Stone, Lucretia Maria Davidson.
         Prose: Biography: Bryant, James G. Per-
           cival, W. Irving, Fitz-Greene Halleck,
           Samuel Woodworth, Cotton Mather. Travel.
           Essay. Familiar Essay. Criticism.
           Book Reviews.
         Fiction: Sketches. Tales: "The Steel
           Clasp"; "Recollections of a Revolutionary
           Soldier"; "The Stanton Ghost; or, Mistake
           of the Press"; "A Watch in the Main-Top";
           "White Hands; or Not Quite in Character";
           "Tom Wilson, and His Burnt Portfolio";
           "The Squatter. A Tale, by a Country
           Schoolmaster"; "Ignatius Loyola."
         Miscellaneous: Anecdotes: on various sub-
           jects. Literary Notices.

226   TITLE: The Critic. By Geoffrey Juvenal,
       Esq.

       Place of Publication: Philadelphia
       First Issue: 29 Jan 1820
       Last Issue: 10 May 1820//
       Periodicity: Irregular
       Editors: ?
       Publishers: ?
       Available From: APS; Lib. of Congress*
       Contents:
         Prose: Essay. Familiar Essay. Criticism:
           on Cervantes, Coleridge, James Kirke
           Paulding. Letters.

227   TITLE: The Crystal Fount, a Monthly Maga-
       zine, Devoted to the Order Sons of
       Temperance, Temperance, and Literature.

       Place of Publication: Baltimore
       First Issue: 1 Feb 1847
       Last Issue: 1 Aug 1848//
       Periodicity: Monthly
       Editor: E.D. Williams
       Publisher: E.D. Williams
       Available From: Amer. Antiquarian Soc.*;
                        Enoch Pratt Lib., Baltimore*
       Contents:
         Poetry: Original: E.D. Williams, L.M.
           Smith, J.E. Snodgrass, William L. Shoe-
           maker, John S. Moore, A.J. Cleaveland,

E.O. Sampson. Selected: Lydia H. Sigourney, G.L. Beckett, Wordsworth, Barry
Cornwall.
         Prose: Biography. Essay. Familiar Essay.
           Criticism: on Wordsworth, Shelley.
         Fiction: Sketches. Tales: "An Indian
           Romance; or the War-Eagle and the White-
           Swan"; "A Manuscript of Olden Time; or
           Von Lopez the Miser"; "The Clock-Pedler
           at Home"; "The Mountain Rose: An Indian
           Romance"; "Emma Glent"; "The Deserter";
           "The Death of the Artist"; "From the
           Dardanelles"; "The True Reformer, or the
           Way the Wife Reclaimed Her Husband";
           "Arthur Granville, or the Stranger's
           Confession"; "Ruin's Flowery Fields, Her
           Desert Waste and Marsh of Death. A
           Dramatic Tale"; "Harrington's Escape. A
           Tale of Indian Adventure."
         Miscellaneous: Anecdotes: on various sub-
           jects; Franklin. Literary Notices.

228   TITLE: The Cynick. By Growler Gruff,
       Esquire, Aided by a Confederacy of Lettered
       Dogs.

       Place of Publication: Philadelphia
       First Issue: 21 Sept 1811
       Last Issue: 12 Dec 1811//
       Periodicity: Weekly
       Editors: ?
       Publishers: ?
       Available From: APS; Lib. Co. of Philadel-
                        phia*
       Contents:
         Poetry: Original.
         Prose: Essay. Familiar Essay. Criticism:
           on Pope, Swift, Thomas Paine, Robert
           Walsh.
         Fiction: Essay Serials: "Groans of the
           Town"; "By the Manager's Dog."

229   TITLES: (1) The Daguerreotype: A Magazine
       of Foreign Literature and Science; Compiled
       Chiefly from the Periodical Publications
       of England, France, and Germany (2) Museum
       of Literature; Being a Selection of Choice
       Articles from the English Reviews and
       Magazines.

       Place of Publication: Boston
       First Issue: 7 Aug 1847
       Last Issue: 14 April 1849//
       Periodicity: Bi-monthly
       Editor: J.M. Whittemore
       Publishers: J.M. Whittemore; Crosby and
                    Nichols
       Available From: APS; Amer. Antiquarian Soc.*
       Contents:
         Poetry: Selected: Wordsworth, Tennyson,
           Thomas Campbell, Longfellow.
         Prose: Biography. Travel. Essay.
           Familiar Essay. Criticism. Book Reviews.
         Fiction: Essay Serial: "Collectanea."
           Sketches. Tales: "The Keeping-Room of
           an Inn; or, Judge Beler's Ghost"; "A
           Long Night and a Long Story"; "A Lawyer's
           Reminiscences"; "The Bachelor of the
           Albany"; "The Apothecary's Wife.--A

Russian Story"; "A Visit to Santona. An
Adventure of the Late War"; "Aunt Brid-
get's Story"; "A Day's Gunning in New
Jersey."
Miscellaneous: Extracts: from other jour-
nals; by various authors; Franklin,
Lamartine, Goethe. Literary Notices.
News: Foreign.

230 TITLE: The Dawn, a Semi-Monthly Magazine:
Containing Original and Selected Essays,
Anecdotes, &c. in Prose and Poetry. Devoted to the Instruction and Amusement of
the Rising Generation.

Place of Publication: Wilmington, Del.
First Issue: 1 May 1822
Last Issue: 1 Nov 1822//
Periodicity: Semi-monthly
Editor: Lewis Wilson
Publisher: Lewis Wilson
Available From: APS; Wilmington Inst. Free
Lib.*
Contents:
Poetry: Original. Selected: Samuel
Woodworth.
Prose: Familiar Essay. Letters.
Fiction: Sketches.
Miscellaneous: Extracts: from other jour-
nals. Anecdotes: on various subjects.
Note: In issue one: "We wish our readers
to bear in mind that the original matter
in our paper is written by youths, whose
compositions seldom, if ever before ap-
peared in print. . . ."

231 TITLE: The Democrat.

Place of Publication: Boston
First Issue: 4 Jan 1804
Last Issue: 2 June 1809//
Periodicity: Semi-weekly
Editor: Benjamin Parks
Publishers: True & Parks; Benjamin Parks
Available From: Amer. Antiquarian Soc.*
Contents:
Poetry: Original. Selected: William
Cowper, Thomas Moore.
Prose: Essay. Familiar Essay. Letters:
Jefferson, John Quincy Adams.
Fiction: Sketches.
Miscellaneous: Extracts: from other jour-
nals; by various authors. Literary
Notices. News: Foreign and Domestic.

232 TITLE: The Dessert to the True American.

Place of Publication: Philadelphia
First Issue: 14 July 1798
Last Issue: 19 Aug 1799//
Periodicity: Weekly
Editor: Samuel F. Bradford
Publisher: Samuel F. Gradford
Available From: APS; Lib. Co. of
Philadelphia

Contents:
Poetry: Original: John Trumbull, David
Humphreys, Timothy Dwight, John Davis.
Selected.
Prose: Biography. Familiar Essay. Criti-
cism.
Fiction: Sketches. Tales: "Azakia: A
Canadian Story"; "The Horrors of Okendale
Abbey. A Romance"; "Zimeo; a Tale";
"Retribution; a Tale"; "Abu-Casem's
Slippers; an Arabian Tale"; "The Fair
Recluse. A Tale"; "Innocence Avenged, a
Tale"; "The Triumph of Fraternal Friend-
ship; a Tale"; "Valeria; an Italian Tale";
"Colville. A West Indian Tale."
Miscellaneous: Extracts: from other jour-
nals; by various authors; Anthony Pasquin.
Anecdotes: on various subjects.
Literary Notices.

233 TITLE: The Dial: A Magazine for Literature,
Philosophy, and Religion.

Place of Publication: Boston
First Issue: July 1840
Last Issue: April 1844//
Periodicity: Quarterly
Editors: Ralph Waldo Emerson; Henry David
Thoreau; Amos Bronson Alcott;
Margaret Fuller
Publishers: Metcalf, Torry and Ballou;
Elizabeth Peabody; James Munroe
& Co.; Weeks, Jordan & Co.;
Jordan & Co.
Available From: APS; Lib. of Congress.*
Mott. Poole.
Contents:
Poetry: Original: Jones Very, Thoreau,
Emerson, J.F. Clarke, Ellen Hooper,
Caroline S. Tappan, Timothy Dwight,
Margaret Fuller, C.P. Cranch, William
Ellery Channing, E.J. Clapp, Theodore
Parker, James Russell Lowell. Selected:
Samuel Ward, Henry More, Keats, Shake-
speare.
Prose: Essay. Familiar Essay. Criticism.
Letters. Book Reviews.
Fiction: Essay Serials: "Record of the
Months"; "Youth of the Poet and the
Painter." Sketches. Tales: "Ernest the
Seeker"; "Marie Van Oosterwich."
Miscellaneous: Extracts: by various
authors; Goethe, William Pickering, Amos
Bronson Alcott, Thomas More, Dante.
Anecdotes: Edmund Burke, Goethe, Sweden-
borg. Literary Notices.
Note: Among the leading contributors were
Elizabeth Peabody, Margaret Fuller,
Theodore Parker, Emerson, Thoreau, George
Ripley, C.P. Cranch, Timothy Dwight,
William Ellery Channing, Charles Lane.

234 TITLE: The Diana, and Ladies' Spectator.

Place of Publication: Boston
First Issue: 1 Oct 1822

Last Issue: 26 Oct 1822//?
Periodicity: Weekly
Editor: M.L. Rainsford
Publisher: M.L. Rainsford
Available From: APS; Boston Athenaeum
Contents:
  Poetry: <u>Original</u>. <u>Selected</u>: W.L. Bowles,
    Charlotte Smith.
  Prose: <u>Biography</u>: Abigail Adams, Queen
    Charlotte. <u>Familiar Essay</u>. <u>Letters</u>.
  Fiction: <u>Tales</u>: "Glicera"; "Almerine and
    Shelimah."
  Miscellaneous: <u>Extracts</u>: from other jour-
    nals; by various authors. <u>Anecdotes</u>:
    on various subjects.

235   TITLE: <u>The Dollar Magazine</u>. [See <u>Holden's
    Dollar Magazine, of Criticisms, Biographies,
    Sketches, Essays, Tales, Reviews, Poetry,
    etc., etc.</u>]

236   TITLE: <u>The Dollar Magazine; a Literary,
    Political, Advertising, and Miscellaneous
    Newspaper</u>. [A new series of <u>The Museum
    of Foreign Literature, Science, and Art</u>.
    See <u>The Museum of Foreign Literature and
    Science</u>.]

Place of Publication: Philadelphia
First Issue: Jan 1833
Last Issue: Dec 1833//
Periodicity: Monthly
Editor: Eliakim Littell
Publishers: E. Littell and T. Holden
Available From: APS; Lib. of Congress.*
        Mott.
Contents:
  Poetry: <u>Selected</u>: Mary Howitt.
  Prose: <u>Essay</u>. <u>Familiar Essay</u>. <u>Letters</u>.
  Fiction: <u>Sketches</u>. <u>Tales</u>: "Life in the
    Wilds. A Tale"; "The Hill and the
    Valley. A Tale"; "Brooke and Brooke
    Farm. A Tale"; "Demerara. A Tale";
    "Ella of Garveloch. A Tale"; "Weal and
    Woe in Garveloch. A Tale"; "A Manchester
    Strike. A Tale"; "Cousin Marshall";
    "Ireland. A Tale"; "Grace Kennedy. A
    Tale"; "The Carpenter's Daughter. A
    Country Tale."
  Miscellaneous: <u>Extracts</u>: from other jour-
    nals. <u>Literary Notices</u>. <u>News</u>: Foreign.

237   TITLES: (1) <u>The Dollar Magazine. A Monthly
    Gazette of Current American and Foreign
    Literature, Fashion, Music, and Novelty</u>
    (2) <u>The Dollar Magazine, a Gazette of Cur-
    rent American and Foreign Literature,
    Music, the Arts, Fashion and Novelty</u>
    (3) <u>The Dollar Magazine. A Monthly
    Gazette of Current Literature, Music and
    Art</u>.

Place of Publication: New York
First Issue: Jan 1841
Last Issue: Dec 1842//
Periodicity: Monthly
Editors: Nathaniel P. Willis; H. Hastings
    Weld

Publishers: Wilson & Company
Available From: APS: Yale Univ.* Mott.
Contents:
  Poetry: <u>Original</u>: Nathaniel P. Willis,
    H. Hastings Weld. <u>Selected</u>: Thomas
    Moore, Barry Cornwall, Rufus Dawes,
    Whittier, George Lunt, John Anster, H.T.
    Tuckerman, Nathaniel P. Willis, Thomas
    Hood, Lydia H. Sigourney, Mary Anne
    Browne, Bernard Barton, George Crabbe,
    George Withers, Longfellow.
  Prose: <u>Familiar Essay</u>. <u>Letters</u>.
  Fiction: <u>Sketches</u>. <u>Tales</u>: "Beau Nash,
    the Monarch of Bath"; "Manuel el Rayo.
    A Tale of the Contrabandists"; "The
    Banker's Daughter"; "The Three Rings.
    An Eastern Tale"; "The Maiden's Adventure.
    A Tale of the Early Settlers of Virginia";
    "The Story of William Saxbury"; "Kitty
    Kirby. A Tale of Real Life"; "The
    Member's Lady"; "Poor Bridget: Or the
    Narrative of an Emigrant Family";
    "Grandmother's Grave: A Sequel to 'Poor
    Bridget'"; "Rooshkulum, or the Wise
    Simpleton"; "The Last Arrow"; "Haroun;
    the Lonely Man of Shiraz"; "The Foster
    Brother. A Tale of Ninety-Eight";
    "The Fatherless and Motherless";
    "Florence Willesden: A Tale of Real
    Life"; "The Chamois Hunter"; "MacKenna's
    Ghost"; "The Glenroys"; "Marian Marshall.
    A Tale of a Constant Heart"; "The
    Switch-Tail Pacer. A Tale of Other Days";
    "The Night Key: Or Matrimonial Reserva-
    tions"; "The Belle of Belleville";
    "Alonzo de Ulloa, el maestro del campo";
    "The Doomed Father"; "Emeline, the In-
    constant."
  Miscellaneous: <u>Extracts</u>: from other jour-
    nals; by various authors; W. Irving,
    James Fenimore Cooper. <u>Anecdotes</u>: on
    various subjects; Byron. <u>Literary
    Notices</u>.

238   TITLE: <u>The Dollar Monthly Magazine</u>. [See
    <u>Ballou's Dollar Monthly Magazine</u>.]

239   TITLE: <u>The Dramatic Mirror and Literary
    Companion</u>.

Place of Publication: New York; Philadelphia
First Issue: 14 Aug 1841
Last Issue: 7 May 1842//
Periodicity: Weekly
Editor: James Rees
Publisher: Turner & Fisher
Available From: APS; Lib. of Congress.*
        Mott.
Contents:
  Poetry: <u>Original</u>: S.S. Steele. <u>Selected</u>:
    Eliza Cook.
  Prose: <u>Biography</u>. <u>Essay</u>. <u>Familiar Essay</u>.
    <u>Criticism</u>.
  Fiction: <u>Essay Serial</u>: "Old Maids."
    <u>Sketches</u>. <u>Tales</u>: "The Forsaken Girl";
    "The Aspirant"; "The Adventures of
    Simpey"; "Muggs and His Lady Love."
  Miscellaneous: <u>Anecdotes</u>: on various
    subjects. <u>Literary Notices</u>.

240 TITLE: The Dramatic Mirror, Containing
     Critical Remarks upon the Theatrical Per-
     formance of Every Night, in the City of
     Boston.

     Place of Publication: Boston
     First Issue: 24 Jan 1829
     Last Issue: 8 Dec 1829//?
     Available From: Boston Pub. Lib.

241 TITLES: (1) Dwight's American Magazine, and
     Family Newspaper: With Numerous Illus-
     trative and Ornamental Wood Engravings for
     the Diffusion of Useful Knowledge, and
     Moral and Religious Principles [Caption
     title: American Penny Magazine, and Family
     Newspaper] (2) Dwight's American Maga-
     zine, and Family Newspaper.

     Place of Publication: New York
     First Issue: 8 Feb 1845
     Last Issue: July 1851//
     Periodicity: Weekly
     Editor: Theodore Dwight, Jr.
     Publisher: Theodore Dwight, Jr.
     Available From: APS; Yale Univ.
     Contents:
       Poetry: Original: John G. Brainard,
         Eliza Cook, W.H.C. Hosmer, Lydia H.
         Sigourney. Selected: Scott, Spenser,
         Thomas Otway, Hannah F. Gould, Byron,
         Lady Mary Wortley Montagu, George Chap-
         man, Whittier, William Leggett, William
         H. Tappan, Lydia H. Sigourney.
       Prose: Biography: Fisher Ames, John
         Bunyan, Thomas Hooker, Washington,
         Buonaparte. Travel. Essay. Familiar
         Essay. Letters.
       Fiction: Essay Serials: "Foreign Travels";
         "Living Sketches of Italy." Sketches.
         Tale: "The Last Imprecation."
       Miscellaneous: Extracts: from other jour-
         nals; by various authors. Anecdotes:
         on various subjects. Literary Notices.
         News: Foreign and Domestic.
     Note: Contains a great deal of information
       on printing presses and book binding.

242 TITLE: The Eastern Argus.

     Place of Publication: Portland, Me.
     First Issue: 8 Sept 1803
     Last Issue: 1921//
     Periodicity: Weekly
     Editors: Nathaniel Willis; Calvin Day;
         Francis Douglas
     Publishers: Day & Willis; Nathaniel Willis;
         Willis and Francis Doublas;
         Thomas Todd & Co.
     Available From: Amer. Antiquarian Soc.
     Contents:
       Poetry: Original: Selleck Osborne,
         Robert Bloomfield. Selected: Burns,
         Shakespeare, William Cowper.
       Prose: Essay.
       Fiction: Sketches. Tales.
       Miscellaneous: Anecdotes: on various
         subjects. Literary Notices. News:
         Foreign and Domestic.

243 TITLE: The Eastern Magazine; A Monthly
     Periodical. [Merged with the Portland
     Magazine q.v. to form The Main Monthly
     Magazine q.v.]

     Place of Publication: Bangor, Me.
     First Issue: July 1835
     Last Issue: June 1836//
     Periodicity: Monthly
     Editor: Matilda P. Carter
     Publisher: John S. Carter
     Available From: APS; Amer. Antiquarian Soc.*
                      Mott.
     Contents:
       Poetry: Original. Selected: Lydia H.
         Sigourney, B.B. Thatcher, Hannah F. Gould,
         George W. Patten, Shelley, Isaac C. Pray,
         Jr., Grenville Mellen.
       Prose: Essay. Familiar Essay. Book Re-
         views.
       Fiction: Essay Serial: "Matters and
         Things." Sketches. Tales: "The Sacri-
         fice, a Tale of the War of 1814"; "The
         Lumberman"; "The Rivals"; "Laura De'
         Esperville"; "The Weird Woman. A Tale
         of Olden Times."
       Miscellaneous: Extracts: from other jour-
         nals. Anecdotes: on various subjects.
         Literary Notices.

244 TITLE: Eccentricities of Literature and Life;
     or the Recreative Magazine. [American
     edition of the London Recreative Review.]

     Place of Publication: Boston
     First Issue: [Only six issues published]
                   1822//
     Periodicity: Bi-monthly
     Editors: ?
     Publishers: Reprinted by Munroe and Francis
     Available From: APS; Lib. of Congress*
     Contents:
       Poetry: Original.
       Prose: Essay: on newspapers, false
         prophets, letter writing, satire,
         plagiarism, "Demons--Incubi--Vampyres--
         Empusae--Pawwawing, or Witchcraft."
         Familiar Essay: on "Chewing the Cud,"
         hats, duelling, etiquette, wigs, cour-
         tiers, clowns and fools. Letters.
       Fiction: Sketches.
       Miscellaneous: Extracts: from other jour-
         nals; by various authors; Hester L.
         Thrale Piozzi. Anecdotes: on various
         subjects; Horace Walpole, Garrick, S.
         Johnson, Swift, Dryden.

245 TITLES: (1) The Eclectic Magazine of Foreign
     Literature, Science and Art (2) The
     Eclectic Magazine and Monthly Edition of
     The Living Age (3) The Eclectic Magazine
     of Foreign Literature.

     Place of Publication: New York
     First Issue: Jan 1844
     Last Issue: June 1907//
     Periodicity: Monthly
     Editors: John Holmes Agnew; Walter Hilliard
         Bidwell

Publishers: Leavitt, Trow & Co.; Walter
Hilliard Bidwell; E.R. Pelton
Available From: APS; Lib. of Congress.*
Mott. Poole.
Contents:
Poetry: Selected: Eleanor Darby, Keats,
James Henderson, H.S. Brooks, Lamartine,
J.B. Manson, E.H. Barrington, William
Kennedy, Robert Story, Elizabeth
Barrett, Mary Howitt, Ebenezer Elliott,
Hans Christian Andersen, S.W. Partridge,
Charles MacKay, Anne Savage, Eliza Cook,
Frances Brown, T. Westwood, Hannah F.
Gould, Samuel Rogers, Southey, James
Kenney, Barry Cornwall, Robert Gilfillan,
J. Walker Ord, Charles Swain, Horace
Smith, Thomas Hood, Camilla Toulmin.
Prose: Biography. Essay. Familiar Essay.
Criticism. Book Reviews.
Fiction: Essay Serials: "Reminiscences of
Men and Things"; "The Robertses on Their
Travels"; "Travelling Letters Written on
the Road" [Dickens]. Sketches. Tales:
"The Rajpoot Bride; a Tale of the
Nerbudda"; "Adventures in Texas"; "No
Concealments!"; "Behind the Scenes.
(Confessions of a Keyhole)"; "The
Chieftain's Daughter; a Tale of Raj-
pootana"; "Confessions of an Illegible
Writer"; "The Meria Grove; a Tale of
Sacrifice"; "The Frog and the Fox"; "The
Wandering Jew. A Tale"; "My Doctor's
Degree"; "The Belle's Choice"; "The
Orphan Girls"; "The Lady of Elm-Wood";
"The Chamber of the Bell"; "Behind the
Scenes"; "The Ecrivain Public"; "The
Rector's Daughter"; "Husband-Catching";
"Gossip and Mischief"; "The Little
Match-Girl" [Hans Christian Andersen];
"The Rosicrucian.--A Tale of Cologne";
"The Cradle of Gold and Wicker"; "The
Two Millionaires"; "Philip Armytage; or
the Blind Girl's Love"; "The Two Sisters";
"A Story of Ways and Means"; "Visit to
Edgeworthstown"; "Sick-Calls"; "It Is
Possible: Or, the Value of 'Self-
Dependence'"; "Saying and Doing"; "The
Chamber of Refuge"; "Recollections of a
Police-Officer."
Miscellaneous: Extracts: from other jour-
nals; by various authors; Tennyson,
Victor Hugo, Schiller, Henry Taylor,
Henry Vaughan, Browning. Literary
Notices.

246   TITLE: The Eclectic Museum of Foreign
Literature, Science and Art. [Superseded
by The Eclectic Magazine of Foreign
Literature, Science and Art q.v.]

Place of Publication: New York; Philadelphia
First Issue: Jan 1843
Last Issue: Jan 1844//
Periodicity: Monthly
Editors: John Holmes Agnew; Eliakim Littell
Publisher: Eliakim Littell
Available From: APS; Lib. of Congress.*
Mott. Poole.

Contents:
Poetry: Selected: Schiller, Charles
MacKay, C.F. Gellert, Thomas Hood,
Wordsworth, Elizabeth Auchinleck,
Frances Brown, Lamartine, Thomas Campbell,
Miss Pardoe, William Thom, Felicia
Hemans, Lydia H. Sigourney.
Prose: Biography. Travel. Essay.
Familiar Essay. Criticism. Book
Reviews.
Fiction: Tales: "The Monomaniac. A Tale";
"Cleverness"; "Keeping Secrets"; "A
Sleigh Ride in Canada West"; "A Fight in
the Dark"; "The Repeal of the Union."
Miscellaneous: Extracts: by various
authors; Wordsworth, Lydia H. Sigourney,
Felicia Hemans.

247   TITLE: Eclectic Recorder.

Place of Publication: New York
First Issue: 21 Sept 1827
Last Issue: 29 March 1828//
Periodicity: Weekly
Editor: Orson Kellogg
Publishers: Kellogg & Rice; Orson Kellogg;
Kellogg & Davis; Kellogg &
Anderson
Available From: Lib. of Congress*; N.Y.
State Lib., Albany
Contents:
Poetry: Original. Selected: Michael
Bruce, James Montgomery, Bernard Barton,
Felicia Hemans, John Bowring, Selleck
Osborne.
Prose: Biography. Travel. Essay.
Letters.
Fiction: Sketches.
Miscellaneous: Extracts: from other jour-
nals; by various authors; S. Johnson,
William Cobbett. Anecdotes: on various
subjects; Washington, Buonaparte,
Franklin. Literary Notices.

248   TITLE: The Eglantine. Devoted to Original
and Select Literature.

Place of Publication: Boston
First Issue: 7 Jan 1837
Last Issue: 23 Sept 1837//?
Periodicity: Weekly
Editor: William Comstock
Publisher: John E. Dill
Available From: Lib. of Congress; Boston
Athenaeum
Contents:
Poetry: Original. Selected: George W.
Patten, Mary L. Horton, Alaric Watts,
Mary Comstock, Albert Pike, Oliver
Wendell Holmes, Isaac C. Pray, Jr.
Prose: Essay. Familiar Essay. Letters.
Fiction: Essay Serial: "The Riddler."
Sketches. Tales: "The Haunted Cobbler";
"Terence O'Flaherty. A Story of
Kilrandy"; "The Convicted Judge.--
Founded on Fact"; "Love and Law, or a
Lawyer's Revenge"; "The Husband's Revenge";

"Gonzalez the Fated One, or the Gipsey's Prediction"; "An Adventure on the Isle of Women"; "The German Jew"; "The Heir of Baliol, a Scottish Tale"; "Woman's Wit, or the Young Merchant of Bagdad"; "Adele and Camille, or Love-Breezes"; "Bianca of Pisa, a Venetian Tale" [Thomas Roscoe]; "The Barber of Gottingen College"; "The Rival Belles"; "Love and Inconsistency, or the Story of Walter and Katherine Trevor."
Miscellaneous: Extracts: from other journals; by various authors; Franklin, Scott. Anecdotes: on various subjects. Literary Notices. News: Domestic.

249 TITLE: The Emerald and Baltimore Literary Gazette. [Merged with The Baltimore Minerva.]

Place of Publication: Baltimore
First Issue: 29 March 1828
Last Issue: 11 April 1829//
Periodicity: Weekly
Editor: Rufus Dawes
Publisher: Benjamin Edes
Available From: APS; Yale Univ. Mott.
Contents:
    Poetry: Original: Rufus Dawes. Selected: Wordsworth, Shakespeare, James Hogg, Thomas Moore, Nathaniel P. Willis, Edmund Waller, Coleridge, Charles Sprague, R.H. Wilde, Edward Young, Bryant, Washington Allston, Felicia Hemans.
    Prose: Biography. Familiar Essay. Criticism. Book Reviews.
    Fiction: Sketches. Tales: "The Gambler"; "The Log Hut in the Forest"; "The Bath of Beauty"; "The Venetian Girl"; "Melancholy Fate of a Peasant"; "Mademoiselle Henrietta Sontag"; "An Adventure in the South Seas"; "The Murderer's Grave"; "The Widow Bewitched"; "The Fortune Teller"; "From the Roué"; "The Disinterment"; "The Natchez Bride"; "The White Cottage"; "The Funeral"; "The Broken Vow"; "The Retribution"; "The Kiss"; "No Man Is Born for Himself"; "A False Alarm"; "The Shipwrecked Wanderer"; "The Young Soldier"; "A Sea Trip"; "The Seer of the Pyramid."
    Miscellaneous: Extracts: by various authors; Nathaniel P. Willis. Anecdotes: on various subjects.

250 TITLE: The Emerald. By Peter Pleasant, & Co.

Place of Publication: Baltimore
First Issue: 3 Nov 1810
Last Issue: 2 March 1811//?
Periodicity: Weekly
Editor: ?
Publisher: Benjamin Edes
Available From: APS; Peabody Inst., Baltimore
Contents:
    Poetry: Original. Selected: Selleck Osborne.

Prose: Biography: George Frederick Cooke. Travel. Familiar Essay. Letters.
Fiction: Essay Serials: "The Monitor"; "The Old Bachelor"; "The Times." Tales: "Mary, a True Story"; "The False Prince of Modena"; "The Wizard. A Tale of the 14th Century."
Miscellaneous: Anecdotes: on various subjects; Hester Lynch Thrale Piozzi, George Whitefield.

251 TITLE: The Emerald, or, Miscellany of Literature, Containing Sketches of the Manners, Principles and Amusements of the Age. [A continuation of The Boston Weekly Magazine q.v.]

Place of Publication: Boston
First Issue: 3 May 1806
Last Issue: 15 Oct 1808//?
Periodicity: Weekly
Editors: Oliver C. Greenleaf; Joshua Belcher; Samuel T. Armstrong
Publishers: Belcher & Armstrong
Available From: APS; Amer. Antiquarian Soc.* Mott.
Contents:
    Poetry: Original. Selected: Peter Pindar, William Cowper, William Jones.
    Prose: Biography: R.B. Sheridan, Washington, Edmund Burke, William Pitt, Schiller, James Beattie, Boileau, Boethius. Travel. Familiar Essay. Criticism. Letters. Book Reviews.
    Fiction: Essay Serials: "The Wanderer"; "The Ordeal." Sketches. Tales: "Amaryllis. A Tale"; "Carazan, an Oriental Tale"; "Selico. A Tale."
    Miscellaneous: Anecdotes: Goldsmith, S. Johnson, Thomas Moore, Rabelais, Sterne, Smollett, Voltaire. Literary Notices.
    Note: Contains reviews or criticism on: As You Like It, Coriolanus, Hamlet, King Lear, King John, Othello, Romeo and Juliet, The Belle's Strategem, Jane Shore, Emerson's sermons, Robert Treat Paine's poems, Madoc, The Provok'd Husband.

252 TITLE: The Episcopal Family Monitor, Devoted to Religion, Literature, and the Fine Arts.

Place of Publication: New York
First Issue: 20 July 1842
Last Issue: 6 Nov 1843//?
Periodicity: Monthly
Editors: ?
Publisher: J.D. Lockwood
Available From: Conn. State Lib., Hartford; Amer. Antiquarian Soc.
Contents:
    Poetry: Original: Emma C. Embury.
    Prose: Essay. Familiar Essay.
    Fiction: Tale: "The Merchant's Clerk. An Original Temperance Tale."
    Miscellaneous: Anecdotes: on various subjects.

253 TITLE: The Essayist: A Young Men's Magazine.

Place of Publication: Boston
First Issue: 14 Nov 1829
Last Issue: Sept 1833//
Periodicity: Monthly [Irregular]
Editor: George Washington Light
Publishers: George Washington Light & Co.
Available From: Lib. of Congress; Yale Univ.*
Contents:
   Poetry: Original: George Washington Light.
      Selected: B.B. Thatcher, Francis Quarles,
      John Pierpont, Shelley, Coleridge,
      I. M'Lellan, Jr., Hannah F. Gould,
      Nathaniel P. Willis, H.T. Tuckerman, John
      G. Brainard, L.E. Landon.
   Prose: Travel. Essay. Familiar Essay.
      Criticism: on John Pierpont, Charles
      Sprague, Francis Quarles, Nathaniel P.
      Willis, William Ellery Channing. Book
      Reviews.
   Fiction: Essay Serials: "Sketches by a
      Looker-On"; "Spectator"; "The Cobbler's
      Genius"; "The Observer." Sketches.
      Tale: "Romance of Real Life."
   Miscellaneous: Anecdotes: on various sub-
      jects.

254 TITLES: (1) The Essex Gazette (2) The New
      England Chronicle: Or, the Essex Gazette.

Place of Publication: Salem, Mass.
First Issue: 2 Aug 1768
Last Issue: 28 March 1776//
Periodicity: Weekly
Editor: Samuel Hall
Publisher: Samuel Hall
Available From: Amer. Antiquarian Soc.
Contents:
   Poetry: Original. Selected.
   Prose: Essay. Familiar Essay. Letters.
   Miscellaneous: Extracts: by various
      authors. Anecdotes: on various sub-
      jects. Literary Notices. News: Foreign
      and Domestic.

255 TITLES: (1) The Essex Journal and Merrimack
      Packet: Or, the Massachusetts and New-
      Hampshire General Advertiser (2) The
      Essex Journal, or, the Massachusetts and
      New-Hampshire General Advertiser (3) The
      Essex Journal or, New-Hampshire Packet
      (4) The Essex Journal: Or the New-
      Hampshire Packet, and the Weekly Advertiser
      (5) The Essex Journal (6) The Essex
      Journal and the Massachusetts and New-
      Hampshire General Advertiser (7) The
      Essex Journal & New-Hampshire Packet.

Place of Publication: Newbury-Port, Mass.
First Issue: 4 Dec 1773
Last Issue: 2 April 1794//
Periodicity: Weekly
Editors: Isaiah Thomas; Henry W. Tinges;
      E. Lunt; John Mycall
Publishers: Isaiah Thomas; Henry W. Tinges;
      E. Lunt; John Mycall
Available From: Amer. Antiquarian Soc.

Contents:
   Poetry: Original. Selected.
   Prose: Essay. Letters.
   Miscellaneous: Anecdotes: on various sub-
      jects. Literary Notices. News: Foreign
      and Domestic.

256 TITLE: Essex Register. [See The Impartial
      Register.]

257 TITLE: The Euterpeiad: An Album of Music,
      Poetry, and Prose.

Place of Publication: New York
First Issue: 15 April 1830
Last Issue: 1 Nov 1831//
Periodicity: Semi-monthly
Editors: Charles Dingley; John Thomas;
      James Boardman
Publisher: George W. Bleecker
Available From: Boston Pub. Lib.*; Lib. of
      Congress
Contents:
   Poetry: Original. Selected: L.E. Landon,
      Wordsworth, Erasmus Darwin, William
      Leggett, Felicia Hemans, Emma C. Embury,
      Leigh Hunt, Bernard Barton, Lydia H.
      Sigourney, Hannah F. Gould, James G.
      Percival, James Montgomery, Byron,
      Sumner Lincoln Fairfield, Thomas Moore,
      William Roscoe.
   Prose: Biography. Letters.
   Fiction: Sketches. Tales: "A Sea Bath,
      on the Banks of Newfoundland"; "The Fatal
      Shot"; "Pietro Boni, the Burgher of
      Sienna"; "The Hermit of Sion."
   Miscellaneous: Anecdotes: on various sub-
      jects. Literary Notices. News: Foreign.

258 TITLES: (1) Euterpeiad or, Musical Intelli-
      gencer. Devoted to the Diffusion of
      Musical Information and Belles Lettres
      (2) The Euterpeiad: Or, Musical Intelli-
      gencer, and Ladies' Gazette. Devoted to
      the Diffusion of Musical Information, Po-
      lite Literature, and Belles Lettres
      (3) The Euterpeiad, or Musical Intelligencer;
      and Select Repository of Classic and
      Polite Literature. [Beginning 30 March
      1822, published in conjunction with The
      Minerviad q.v.]

Place of Publication: Boston
First Issue: 1 April 1820
Last Issue: June 1823//
Periodicity: Weekly; Semi-monthly; Monthly
Editors: John R. Parker; Charles Dignley
Publisher: Thomas Badger, Jr.
Available From: APS; Lib. of Congress
Contents:
   Poetry: Original. Selected: Thomas
      Moore, Scott, William B. Tappan, Thomas
      Campbell, Sellect Osborne.
   Prose: Biography. Essay. Familiar Essay.
      Criticism. Letters.
   Fiction: Essay Serials: "Musical Pleiades";
      "The Monitress." Tales: "Justina, or

the Will; a Domestic Story"; "Perseverance: Or, the Infallible Method."
Miscellaneous: Extracts: by various
authors. Anecdotes: on various subjects; Chesterfield, Voltaire. Literary
Notices.

259   TITLE: The Evangelical Repertory.

Place of Publication: Boston
First Issue: 15 July 1823
Last Issue: 15 June 1824//?
Available From: Mass. Hist. Soc.*; Tufts
                 Univ., Medford, Mass.*

260   TITLE: The Evening Fire-Side; or Weekly
       Intelligence in the Civil, Natural, Moral,
       Literary and Religious Worlds. Calculated
       Particularly for the Perusal of the Young,
       and Those of Retired Habits of Life.
       Published Independently of Any Interested
       Party Attachment, and with Special Refer-
       ence to the Principles of Truth and Purity.
       [Supersedes The Weekly Monitor q.v.]

Place of Publication: Philadelphia
First Issue: 15 Dec 1804
Last Issue: 27 Dec 1806//
Periodicity: Weekly
Editors: ?
Publishers: Joseph M. Rakestraw & Co.
Available From: APS; Hist. Soc. of Pa.*
                 Mott.
Contents:
    Poetry: Original. Selected: William
    Cowper.
    Prose: Biography: Lindley Murray, James
    H. Beattie, S. Johnson, John Calvin.
    Familiar Essay. Letters: Jefferson,
    S. Johnson, Penn, Buonaparte, Phillis
    Wheatley, Lady Mary Wortley Montagu.
    Miscellaneous: Extracts: from other jour-
    nals. Anecdotes: Addison, William
    Cowper, Pope, Voltaire, Chesterfield.
    News: Foreign and Domestic.

261   TITLE: The Evergreen: A Monthly Magazine
       of New and Popular Tales and Poetry.

Place of Publication: New York
First Issue: Jan 1840
Last Issue: June 1841//
Periodicity: Monthly
Editor: J. Winchester
Publisher: J. Winchester
Available From: APS; Yale Univ.*
Contents:
    Poetry: Original: R.M. Milnes, T.K.
    Hervey. Selected: Longfellow, Park
    Benjamin, Thomas Haynes Bayly, Bryant,
    Thomas Moore, Macaulay, Douglas Jerrold,
    E.M. Fitzgerald, Winthrop M. Praed, John
    Neal, Alfred B. Street.
    Prose: Biography: Handel. Essay.
    Familiar Essay. Criticism.
    Fiction: Sketches. Tales: "The Wood-
    cutter"; "The Roundhead's Daughter";
    "The Beacon"; "An Adventure in Havana.

A Story of the Yellow Fever"; "Pic-Nic on
the Hudson"; "Crossed in Love"; "The
Signal"; "Emily, or the Unexpected
Meeting"; "The Inquest"; "The Money-
Lender"; "The Miser Outwitted: An Ori-
ginal Tale of a Man About Town"; "Pelayo
and the Merchant's Daughter" [W. Irving];
"The Tragedy of Errors; or, Facts
Stranger than Fiction"; "The Narrow
Escape. A Tale of Truth"; "The Red
Seal"; "The Knight of Malta" [W. Irving];
"Lady Ravelgold" [Nathaniel P. Willis];
"Ixion in Heaven" [B. D'Israeli]; "The
Daguerreotype in the Harem"; "The Spectre
of Tappington"; "The Eighteen Girls of
Nidwalden. A Legend of 1798"; "The
Dead Man of St. Anne's Chapel. A
Criminal Story"; "Beatrice di Tenda";
"The Conspiracy of Neamatha. An Au-
thentic Sketch" [W. Irving]; "The
Boarwolf"; "The Goblet." Novels: "Poor
Jack"; "The Tower of London. A Historical
Romance" [William Harrison Ainsworth];
"Master Humphrey's Clock" [Dickens];
"Stanley Thorn"; "George St. George
Julian"; "The Prince."
Miscellaneous: Extracts: by various
authors; Oliver Wendell Holmes, Leigh
Hunt.

262   TITLE: The Every Body's Album: A Humorous
       Collection of Tales, Quips, Quirks, Anec-
       dotes, and Facetiae.

Place of Publication: Philadelphia
First Issue: July 1836
Last Issue: June 1837//
Periodicity: Monthly
Editor: Charles Alexander
Publisher: Charles Alexander
Available From: APS; Lib. of Congress*
Contents:
    Poetry: Selected: Thomas Campbell,
    Robert Beresford, Thomas Hood, James
    Sheridan Knowles, Caroline Norton,
    Tennyson, Felicia Hemans.
    Prose: Biography: Washington.
    Fiction: Sketches. Tales: "Humorous
    Adventures of Fra Pasqual"; "Avarice
    Chastised; or, the Miser Punished";
    "Falsehood Punished; or, Innocence
    Rewarded and Restored"; "The Fantastic
    Contract"; "Rubens and His Scholars"
    [Theodore Sedgwick Fay]; "Murder of
    Miss Jane M'Crea"; "The Temptation of
    Rachel Morisson"; "The Murderer's
    Pardon"; "The Ring; or, the Merry Wives
    of Madrid"; "The Alibi; or, Trial of a
    Highwayman"; "The Gridiron; or Paddy
    Moloney's Adventures in France"; "Alice
    Ford; or, the Last Days of Queen Mary";
    "The Counterfeiter's Daughter"; "The
    Turners: A Tale of the Old Country"
    [James Hogg]; "Jimmy Charcoal.--Fall of
    the Carbonari"; "Leniter Salix, the Best-
    natured Man in the World"; "The Hair
    Market of Evreux"; "Nina Dalgarooki";
    "The Merchant's Clerk"; "Timor Timpkins:
    Or, the Errors of Education"; "The Mail
    Robber"; "Wee Watty: A Surgeon Student's

Tale"; "Julian and Leonor"; "The Hunch-back of Notre Dame"; "The Wine Cellar" [Douglas Jerrold]; "The Miser of Padua. A Tale."
Miscellaneous: <u>Anecdotes</u>: on various subjects; Voltaire, S. Johnson, Boswell, Washington, Timothy Dwight, Joseph Dennie, Chateaubriand, Shakespeare.

263 TITLE: <u>Every Body's Book; or, Something for All.</u>

Place of Publication: New York
First Issue: 1841
Last Issue: ?
Available From: Yale Univ.

264 TITLE: <u>Every Youth's Gazette.</u>

Place of Publication: New York
First Issue: 22 Jan 1842
Last Issue: 31 Dec 1842//
Periodicity: Weekly; Semi-monthly
Editor: Park Benjamin [?]
Publisher: J. Winchester
Available From: APS; Amer. Antiquarian Soc.*
Contents:
  Poetry: <u>Original</u>: Frances S. Osgood, Henry G. Watson. <u>Selected</u>: Mary Howitt, George Herbert, Park Benjamin, Long-fellow, L.E. Landon, Lydia H. Sigourney, Wordsworth, Southey, Sarah J. Hale, Felicia Hemans, Colley Cibber, James Aldrich, Alaric Watts, Charles Sprague, William Cowper, Allan Cunningham, Charles MacKay, John Wilson, Richard Howitt, Thomas Campbell, Mary Russell Mitford, Epes Sargent, Tennyson, Bryant, James G. Percival, Thomas Hood, James Hogg, Schiller, E. Lytton Bulwer, John Quincy Adams, Nathaniel P. Willis, Jones Very, James Montgomery, Al Willmott, William Leggett, A.J. Moultrie, Cole-ridge.
  Prose: <u>Biography</u>: S. Johnson, Benjamin West, Chatterton, John Quincy Adams. <u>Travel</u>. <u>Essay</u>. <u>Familiar Essay</u>. <u>Letters</u>.
  Fiction: <u>Essay Serials</u>: "Letters from Sister Jane"; "Charlie's Discoveries." <u>Sketches</u>. <u>Tales</u>: "Little Red Riding Hood"; "The Three Wishes" [Mary Howitt]; "Mary and Martha"; "The Lost One"; "The Lion"; "The Stolen Boy"; "The Snow-Bird"; "Amy Ross, and Her Blind Grand-father"; "The Inchcape Rock, and the Story of Ralph the Rover"; "Dialogue Between Emma and Her Mother"; "Pretty Bobby"; "The Perils of Paul Percival; or, the Young Adventurer"; "The Beggar"; "Susan Yates, on First Going to Church"; "History of Old Ready"; "The Magical Watch"; "Ali Bey in the Desert of Morocco"; "The Story of Mr. Bull and the Giant Atmodes"; "The Diving Bell"; Guolownin's Captivity"; "Old Pedro"; "The Ivy-Leafed Crowfoot"; "The Ad-ventures of a Bee"; "The Happy Boy"; "The Highland Fairies"; "The Lily"; "Adventures in an Egyptian Catacomb";

"Story of the Farmer and the Soldier"; "The Ambitious Primrose"; "Camgno, or the Tame Roe"; "The Two Beggar Boys: A Story for the Young"; "Adventures in the Arctic Ocean"; "A Visit to the Esquimaux"; "The Love of Home"; "A Winter in Charlton Island"; "The Lost Children"; "The Foolish Porter and the Wise Old Man"; "A Bull Fight in Madrid"; "The Escape of Capt. Bligh."
  Miscellaneous: <u>Extracts</u>: from other jour-nals; by various authors; Charles Lamb. <u>Anecdotes</u>: on various subjects.

265 TITLE: <u>The Examiner and Hesperian.</u> [See <u>The Literary Examiner, and Western Monthly Review.</u>]

266 TITLE: <u>The Expositor. A Weekly Journal of Foreign and Domestic Intelligence, Literature, Science, and the Fine Arts.</u>

Place of Publication: New York
First Issue: 8 Dec 1838
Last Issue: 20 July 1839//?
Periodicity: Weekly
Editor: Louis Fitzgerald Tasistro
Publisher: Louis Fitzgerald Tasistro
Available From: APS; N.Y. Pub. Lib.*
Contents:
  Poetry: <u>Original</u>. <u>Selected</u>: Lamartine, Rufus Dawes, L.E. Landon.
  Prose: <u>Essay</u>. <u>Familiar Essay</u>. <u>Criticism</u>. <u>Letters</u>. <u>Book Reviews</u>.
  Fiction: <u>Sketches</u>. <u>Tales</u>: "Confessions of a Man of Fiction"; "The Day of Trial"; "The Medeans"; "The Maidschenstein"; "Laudanum and Rum: A Vision of Negro-Head and Havannah"; "The Spoilt Child"; "The Atonement"; "The Monthly Nurse" [Leigh Hunt]; "The Tatar's Tale"; "The Parisian at Sea"; "The Factory Child" [Douglas Jerrold]; "The Chimney Sweep"; "The Undertaker" [Douglas Jerrold]; "Bonny Bell"; "The Blighted One."
  Miscellaneous: <u>Anecdotes</u>: on various subjects. <u>Literary Notices</u>. <u>News</u>: Foreign and Domestic.

267 TITLE: <u>The Eye: by Obadiah Optic.</u>

Place of Publication: Philadelphia
First Issue: 7 Jan 1808
Last Issue: 29 Dec 1808//
Periodicity: Weekly
Editor: John W. Scott
Publisher: John W. Scott
Available From: APS; Lib. of Congress*
Contents:
  Prose: <u>Biography</u>. <u>Familiar Essay</u>. <u>Letters</u>.
  Fiction: <u>Essay Serials</u>: "The American Idler" [On egotism, old age, weakness of men]; "Mushroom" [The author's account of himself, shopping adventures]; "The Spectacles" [On idleness, novel reading, solitude, slander, fashion]; "The Tor-toise" [On friendship, domestic happi-ness, a beggar, pickpocket, avarice];

"The Eye-Lash" [On education, electioneer-
ing, pride, a lady of fashion]; "The
Expatiator" [On Justice, matrimony,
motives and objects of writers]; "Robert
Rustic" [Letters to Jeremiah Listless
and others on various subjects].
Sketches. Tales.
Miscellaneous: Anecdotes: on various
subjects.
Note: Accounts, conversations, letters concerning members of the Optic family.

268 TITLE: Extra Equator: evoted [sic] to the
Interests of Science and Literature in the
West.

Place of Publication: Bloomington, Ind.
First Issue: Nov 1840
Last Issue: March 1841//?
Available From: Ind. State Lib., Indianapolis;
N.Y. Pub. Lib.

269 TITLE: The Family Favorite and Temperance
Journal. Gems of the Press--An Offering
to Religion, Temperance and Pure Literature.

Place of Publication: Adrian, Mich.
First Issue: Dec 1849
Last Issue: Sept 1850//?
Periodicity: Monthly
Editor: J.V. Watson
Publisher: E.Q. Fuller
Available From: APS; Univ. of Mich., Ann
Arbor
Contents:
Poetry: Original. Selected: Bryant,
James T. Fields, Whittier, Charles
MacKay.
Prose: Essay. Familiar Essay. Letters.
Fiction: Sketches. Tales: "The Beggar
Ship"; "The Poor Student's Dream; or,
the Golden Rule"; "The Orphan Crime."
Miscellaneous: Extracts: from other jour-
nals; by various authors; W. Irving.
Anecdotes: on various subjects;
Jefferson.

270 TITLES: (1) The Family Magazine, or Weekly
Abstract of General Knowledge (2) The
Family Magazine; or, Monthly Abstract of
General Knowledge.

Place of Publication: New York
First Issue: 20 April 1833
Last Issue: May 1841//
Periodicity: Weekly; Monthly
Editors: Origen Bacheler; Benson J. Lossing
Publishers: J.S. Redfield; Origen Bacheler;
Redfield & Lindsay
Available From: APS; Amer. Antiquarian Soc.*
Mott.
Contents:
Poetry: Original: Carlos Wilcox, Louisa
P. Smith, J.O. Rockwell, Timothy Flint.
Selected: Joseph Rodman Drake, John G.
Brainard, James G. Percival, Charles
Edwards, William Cowper, Béranger,
Charles Fenno Hoffman, Bryant, Nathaniel

P. Willis, Grenville Mellen, Longfellow,
James W. Eastburn, Lydia H. Sigourney,
H. Greeley, Samuel Woodworth, Joseph
Chester, John Quincy Adams, Mary Howitt,
M.K. Townsend, James Beattie, Alonzo
Lewis, E. Lytton Bulwer, Sarah J. Hale,
R.H. Wilde, Fitz-Greene Halleck, James
Montgomery, Charles Sprague, James Kirke
Paulding, Park Benjamin, George W. Patten,
Hannah F. Gould, George D. Prentice, J.O.
Rockwell, Wordsworth, Barry Cornwall.
Prose: Biography. Essay. Familiar Essay.
Fiction: Sketches.
Miscellaneous: Extracts: by various
authors; Goethe. Anecdotes: on various
subjects; Washington. Literary Notices.

271 TITLE: The Family Minstrel: A Musical and
Literary Journal. [Running title: The
Family Minstrel. A Repository of Music
and Poetry.]

Place of Publication: New York
First Issue: 15 Jan 1835
Last Issue: 15 Jan 1836//
Periodicity: Semi-monthly
Editor: Charles Dingley
Publisher: James De Voe
Available From: APS; Hist. Soc. of Pa.*
Contents:
Poetry: Original: Cleveland Coxe.
Selected: T.K. Hervey, Park Benjamin,
Mrs. Abdy, Bernard Barton, Thomas Gray,
James G. Percival, Felicia Hemans, Lydia
H. Sigourney.
Prose: Biography: Handel, Haydn.
Familiar Essay. Book Reviews.
Fiction: Sketches.
Miscellaneous: Extracts: from other jour-
nals. Anecdotes: on various subjects.
Note: The focus is primarily musical,
although this journal is of literary
interest.

272 TITLE: Family Pioneer & Juvenile Key.

Place of Publication: Brunswick, Me.
First Issue: [?] 1831
Last Issue: 7 May 1836//
Periodicity: Weekly
Editor: Joseph Griffin
Publisher: Joseph Griffin
Available From: Lib. of Congress; Western
Reserve Hist. Soc., Cleve-
land*
Contents:
Poetry: Original. Selected: Harriet
Muzzy, Lucius M. Sargent, James Mont-
gomery, Lydia H. Sigourney.
Prose: Biography: Burns. Travel.
Familiar Essay.
Fiction: Sketches. Tales: "The Orphan
Family"; "The Trial. Founded on Fact";
"Sky Leapers"; "The Orphan. A Country
Tale" [Caroline Norton]; "The Soldier's
Wife"; "The Wandering Minstrels. A
Tale. Founded on Fact"; "The Black
Linn"; "The Wedding and the First Cup"
[Grenville Mellen]; "The Show Girl.

Founded on Fact"; "Crizel Cochrane.--An
Historical Fragment"; "The Soldier's
Return"; "My Brother Bob"; "Out of Debt
Out of Danger"; "The Stolen Boy"; "The
Buccaneers"; "Jumbo and Zairee"; "The
Poor Man's House Repaired. Or the
Wretched Made Happy"; "Malem-Boo. The
Brazilian Slave"; "The Fool's Pence. Or
Transmutation"; "The Wondrous Tale; or
the Little Man in Gosling Green"; "The
Wedding" [Whittier]; "The Chimney Sweep-
er"; "The Lost Son"; "The Idle School-
boy" [John Inman]; "The White Horse";
"Whaling in the Pacific"; "The Power of
Imagination" [Thomas Haynes Bayly]; "The
Gipsy's Ride" [Nathaniel P. Willis];
"The Blind Widow and Her Family"; "The
Spoiled Child."
  Miscellaneous: Extracts: from other jour-
    nals; by various authors; W. Irving.
    Anecdotes: on various subjects;
    Nathaniel P. Willis, Franklin. Literary
    Notices. News: Foreign and Domestic.

273 TITLE: Farmer's Museum, or Lay Preacher's
     Gazette. [See The New Hampshire Journal:
     Or, the Farmer's Weekly Museum.]

274 TITLE: Federal Orrery.

     Place of Publication: Boston
     First Issue: 20 Oct 1794
     Last Issue: 31 Oct 1796//
     Periodicity: Bi-weekly
     Editor: Thomas Paine
     Publisher: Benjamin Sweetser
     Available From: Amer. Antiquarian Soc.
     Contents:
       Poetry: Original. Selected.
       Prose: Biography. Essay. Familiar Essay.
       Fiction: Tale: "The Pig and the Pot."
       Miscellaneous: Anecdotes: on various
         subjects. Literary Notices. News:
         Foreign and Domestic.

275 TITLE: Fithian's Magazine for Boys and
     Girls. [See Boys' and Girls' Penny
     Journal.]

276 TITLE: Flag of Our Union; a Literary and
     Miscellaneous Family Journal, Containing
     News, Wit, Humor and Romance . . . Inde-
     pendent of Party or Sect.

     Place of Publication: Philadelphia
     First Issue: [?] 1842
     Last Issue: [?] 1853//?
     Available From: Lib. of Congress. Mott.

277 TITLE: The Floriad.

     Place of Publication: Schenectady, N.Y.
     First Issue: 24 May 1811
     Last Issue: 6 Dec 1811//
     Periodicity: Semi-monthly
     Editors: ?

Publisher: William S. Buell
Available From: APS; N.Y. Pub. Lib.*
Contents:
  Poetry: Original. Selected: William
    Cowper, Byron.
  Prose: Biography: William Linn. Essay.
    Familiar Essay. Criticism. Book Reviews.
  Fiction: Essay Serials: "The Rambler";
    "The Literary Spy." Tales: "Edwin; or,
    Moral and Religious Thoughts Exemplified";
    "Gertrude of Wyoming" [Thomas Campbell].
  Miscellaneous: Extracts: by various
    authors; Kotzebue, Thomas Campbell.
    Anecdotes: on various subjects; Joel
    Barlow, Hume. Literary Notices.
Note: Published under the direction of two
  literary societies at Union College.
  The journal is devoted solely to liter-
  ature.

278 TITLE: The Fly; or Juvenile Miscellany. By
     Simon Scribble & Co.

     Place of Publication: Boston
     First Issue: 16 Oct 1805
     Last Issue: 2 April 1806//?
     Periodicity: Semi-monthly
     Editor: Josiah Ball
     Publisher: Josiah Ball
     Available From: APS; Amer. Antiquarian Soc.*
     Contents:
       Poetry: Original. Selected: Pope,
         William Cowper, Mary Robinson.
       Prose: Biography.
       Fiction: Essay Serials: "The Scribbler";
         "The Speculator"; "The Inspector General";
         "The Enquirer." Tale: "Eastern Tale.
         The Contending Brothers."

279 TITLE: Foederal American Monthly. [See The
     Knickerbocker: Or, New-York Monthly
     Magazine.]

280 TITLE: The Fool. By Thomas Brainless, Esq.
     LL.D. Jester to His Majesty the Public.

     Place of Publication: Salem, Mass.
     First Issue: Feb 1807
     Last Issue: April 1807//?
     Periodicity: Irregular
     Editors: ?
     Publishers: ?
     Available From: APS; Harvard Univ.*
     Contents:
       Poetry: Original.
       Prose: Familiar Essay.
       Fiction: Sketches.
     Note: A whimsical journal devoted to every-
       thing except serious discussion. "A
       Conspicuous place will be reserved for
       conundrums, rebusses, acrostics,
       (especially if mis-spelt), enigmatical
       lists, charades, and other articles of
       no stamp. Unfinished impromptus, with
       various readings of the same, we shall
       always be happy to insert. Fantastical
       combinations of letters of the alphabet,
       without any signification, shall always
       grace the first page of The Fool."

281 TITLE: The Franklin Minerva.

Place of Publication: Chambersburg, Pa.
First Issue: 2 Feb 1799
Last Issue: 18 Jan 1800//?
Periodicity: Bi-weekly
Editor: G.K. Harper
Publisher: G.K. Harper
Available From: APS; Lib. of Congress
Contents:
  Poetry: Original: J.H. Wynne. Selected:
    Thomas Paine, Peter Pindar.
  Prose: Essay. Familiar Essay.
  Fiction: Sketches. Tales: "Marcus and
    Monimia. A True Story"; "Angelinde, or
    the Fatal Effects of Precipitancy. A
    Tale"; "Florio and Angelica. A Tale";
    "The History of the Duchess"; "The Life
    of St. André."
  Miscellaneous: Extracts: by various
    authors. Anecdotes: on various subjects.

282 TITLE: Free-Masons Magazine and General
    Miscellany.

Place of Publication: Philadelphia
First Issue: April 1811
Last Issue: March 1823//?
Periodicity: Monthly
Editor: George Richards
Publishers: Levis & Weaver
Available From: APS; Amer. Antiquarian Soc.*
Contents:
  Poetry: Original. Selected: James
    Thomson, John Gay, Edward Young,
    Shakespeare, S. Johnson.
  Prose: Biography. Familiar Essay. Letters.
  Fiction: Essay Serial: "The Scrapiad."
    Sketches. Tales: "The Pilgrim's Story";
    "Madelina: A Female Portrait"; "Story
    of Lucy Watson"; "Adelisa and Leander";
    "The Traveller: A Pathetic Fragment";
    "The Combat of Amadis and Dardan";
    "Clementina: A Narrative"; "Hassan and
    Ibarand: An Eastern Tale"; "Claudine.
    A Charming Swiss Tale"; "The Abbey of
    Santo Pieta; or, a Father's Vengeance.
    An Original Romance."
  Miscellaneous: Extracts: by various
    authors. Anecdotes: on various subjects;
    S. Johnson, Sterne, Garrick, Franklin.

283 TITLES: (1) The Friend, a Periodical Work,
    Devoted to Religion, Literature, and Useful
    Miscellany (2) The Friend, a Monthly
    Magazine, Devoted to Religion, Literature,
    and Useful Miscellany.

Place of Publication: Albany
First Issue: July 1815
Last Issue: June 1816//?
Periodicity: Monthly
Editors: ?
Publishers: D. & S.A. Abbey; Churchill &
    Abbey
Available From: APS; N.Y. State Lib.,
    Albany

Contents:
  Poetry: Original. Selected: Chatterton,
    Scott, Byron.
  Prose: Travel. Familiar Essay. Book
    Reviews.
  Fiction: Sketches. Tales: "Story of
    Fernando"; "The Bashful Man."
  Miscellaneous: Extracts: by various
    authors; Kotzebue, Montesquieu.
    Anecdotes: Goldsmith, Thomas More,
    Fenelon, S. Johnson, Cromwell, Thomas
    Aquinas, Voltaire. Literary Notices.
    News: Foreign and Domestic.

284 TITLE: The Friend. A Religious and
    Literary Journal. [Merged with Friends'
    Intelligencer to form Friends Journal.]

Place of Publication: Philadelphia
First Issue: 13 Oct 1827
Last Issue: June 1955//
Periodicity: Weekly
Editors: Robert Smith; Charles Evans;
    Joseph Walton
Publishers: John Richardson; William Salter;
    George W. Taylor; John S. Stokes
Available From: APS; Lib. of Congress.*
    Mott.
Contents:
  Poetry: Original: Emma C. Embury, Charles
    West Thomson, Miss Jewsbury, Harvey D.
    Little. Selected: Nathaniel P. Willis,
    Felicia Hemans, George Croly, Josiah
    Conder, William Collins, Jane Taylor,
    Bryant, William D. Gallagher, James M.
    Latta, Benjamin Gough, Wordsworth, C.I.
    Webb, Bernard Barton, Park Benjamin,
    Hannah F. Gould, Southey, Lydia H.
    Sigourney, John Bowering, William Cowper,
    James Montgomery, Avis Howland, Jose M.
    Heredia, E.M. Chandler, Henry Ware,
    Grenville Mellen, Charles Sprague, John
    G. Brainard, Longfellow, Whittier, S.G.
    Arnold, James Aldrich, Barry Cornwall,
    R.C. French, William H. Burleigh, Allan
    Cunningham, James Wallis Eastburn, J.T.
    Calder, Charles West Thomson, Coleridge,
    J.W. Alexander, Thomas Hood, Caroline F.
    Orne, Thomas Ragg, William Croswell,
    Alaric Watts, George D. Prentice, E.P.
    Hood, J. Craig, Mary Howitt.
  Prose: Essay. Familiar Essay. Criticism.
    Letters. Book Reviews.
  Fiction: Essay Serial: "Adventures in the
    Pacific Ocean." Sketches. Tales: "The
    Bullock"; "The Confession."
  Miscellaneous: Extracts: by various
    authors; Milton, Spenser, Wordsworth,
    Penn. Anecdotes: on various subjects;
    Penn.

285 TITLE: The Friendly Visitor, Being a
    Collection of Select and Original Pieces.
    Instructive and Entertaining, Suitable to
    Be Read in All Families.

Place of Publication: New York
First Issue: 1 Jan 1825
Last Issue: 28 Dec 1825//
Periodicity: Weekly
Editor: William M. Stilwell
Publisher: William M. Stilwell
Available From: APS; Amer. Antiquarian Soc.*
Contents:
  Poetry: Original. Selected: James Mont-
    gomery, Robert Southwell.
  Prose: Biography. Familiar Essay. Letters.
  Fiction: Sketches. Tales: "A Murderer's
    Death Bed"; "The Mountain Cottage";
    "Widow Richmond and Her Son Peter."
  Miscellaneous: Extracts: from other jour-
    nals; by various authors; Swift, Frank-
    lin, John Wesley. Anecdotes: on various
    subjects; Hume, John Bunyan, William
    Cowper, S. Johnson, John Wesley. News:
    Foreign and Domestic.
Note: Contains a number of conversion nar-
  ratives.

286 TITLE: The Friends' Intelligencer: Devoted
     to Religion, Morals, Literature, the Arts,
     Sciences, &c.

     Place of Publication: New York
     First Issue: 2 April 1838
     Last Issue: 1 July 1839//
     Available From: N.Y. Pub. Lib.*; Harvard
                     Univ.*

287 TITLE: The Galaxy. [See New-England Galaxy
     & Masonic Magazine.]

288 TITLE: The Garland. Devoted to the Interests
     of the Young.

     Place of Publication: Union Mills, N.Y.
     First Issue: 23 Jan 1836
     Last Issue: 7 Jan 1837//
     Available From: Brown Univ., Providence*;
                     Huntington Lib., San Marino,
                     Calif.*

289 TITLE: Garland of the West, and Wisconsin
     Monthly Magazine. [Superseded by The
     Wisconsin Monthly Magazine.]

     Place of Publication: Southport, Wis.
     First Issue: June 1842
     Last Issue: Nov 1842//?
     Available From: State Hist. Soc. of Wis.,
                     Madison; N.Y. Pub. Lib.

290 TITLE: The Garland, or New General Repository
     of Fugitive Poetry Moral, Descriptive and
     Sentimental. Selected from the Periodical
     and Other Journals, American and Foreign.

     Place of Publication: Auburn, N.Y.
     First Issue: June 1825
     Last Issue: Aug 1825//?
     Periodicity: Monthly
     Editor: G.A. Gamage

Publisher: T.M. Skinner
Available From: APS; Harvard Univ.*
Contents:
  Poetry: Original. Selected: James Mont-
    gomery, Marvell, Henry Neele, Herrick,
    Alaric Watts, William B. Tappan.

291 TITLE: Garland's Lady's Magazine. [See The
     Southern Lady's Magazine. A Monthly Jour-
     nal, of Literature, Art and Science.]

292 TITLE: The Gavel: A Monthly Periodical
     Devoted to Odd Fellowship & General
     Literature.

     Place of Publication: Albany
     First Issue: Sept 1844
     Last Issue: 1848//?
     Periodicity: Monthly
     Editors: C.C. Burr; John Tanner; Thomas L.
              Harris
     Publisher: John Tanner
     Available From: N.Y. State Lib., Albany;
                     Amer. Antiquarian Soc.
     Contents:
       Poetry: Original: C.C. Burr, Thomas L.
         Harris, William Wrightson, William K.
         Cole, S. Anna Lewis, Sarah Broughton,
         M.L. Gardiner, E.H. Van Benschaten,
         Henry Channing, C. Theresa Clarke, B.
         Frank Palmer. Selected: Alfred B.
         Street, Barry Cornwall, Charles Swain.
       Prose: Biography. Essay. Familiar Essay.
         Criticism. Letters.
       Fiction: Essay Serial: "Romantic Sketches."
         Sketches. Tales: "The Promise"; "The
         Rivals"; "Lynch and Gomez"; "Claud
         Hamilton"; "The Jew of Hamah"; "Charles
         Arthur--A Tale"; "The Anderson Family--
         Or Life as We Find It"; "Helen Maxwell--
         A True Story"; "The Lone Dweller";
         "Rachel Budolph.--A Tale"; "Ill Temper--
         Domestic Clouds"; "The Blind Blacksmith."
       Miscellaneous: Anecdotes: on various sub-
         jects; S. Johnson. Literary Notices.
         News: Domestic.

293 TITLE: The General Magazine, and Historical
     Chronicle, for All the British Plantations
     in America.

     Place of Publication: Philadelphia
     First Issue: Jan 1741
     Last Issue: June 1741//
     Periodicity: Monthly
     Editor: Benjamin Franklin
     Publisher: Benjamin Franklin
     Available From: APS; N.Y. Pub. Lib.* Mott.
     Contents:
       Poetry: Original. Selected.
       Prose: Familiar Essay. Letters: George
         Whitefield.
       Fiction: Essay Serial: "Historical
         Chronicle." Sketches.
       Miscellaneous: Extracts: from other jour-
         nals. Literary Notices.
     Note: "Accounts of and Extracts from New
       Books, Pamphlets, &c. Published in the
       Plantations."

294 TITLE: <u>The General Magazine, and Impartial</u>
<u>Review, of Knowledge and Entertainment.</u>

Place of Publication: Baltimore
First Issue: June 1798
Last Issue: July 1798//
Periodicity: Monthly
Editors: ?
Publishers: A. Hanna & H. Greene
Available From: APS; Enoch Pratt Free Lib.,
Baltimore. Mott.
Contents:
Poetry: <u>Original</u>. <u>Selected</u>.
Prose: <u>Biography</u>: <u>William Cobbett</u>.
<u>Familiar Essay</u>: "Memoirs and Anecdotes
of Peter Pindar, Esqr."
Fiction: <u>Sketches</u>. <u>Tale</u>: "Charles and
Amelia; or, the Unfortunate Lovers. A
Tale."
Miscellaneous: <u>News</u>: Foreign and Domestic.

295 TITLE: <u>The General Repository and Review.</u>
[Supersedes <u>The Monthly Anthology, and</u>
<u>Boston Review</u> q.v.]

Place of Publication: Cambridge, Mass.
First Issue: Jan 1812
Last Issue: Oct 1813//
Periodicity: Quarterly
Editor: Andrews Norton
Publishers: Hilliard & Metcalf
Available From: APS; Amer. Antiquarian Soc.*
Mott. <u>Poole</u>.
Contents:
Poetry: <u>Original</u>. <u>Selected</u>: Anna Letitia
Barbauld, Milton.
Prose: <u>Biography</u>. <u>Essay</u>. <u>Criticism</u>: on
Thomas Moore, Milton, Michael Drayton,
Scott. <u>Book Reviews</u>.
Miscellaneous: <u>Extracts</u>: by various
authors; Madame de Staël. <u>Literary</u>
<u>Notices</u>.
Note: A Harvard periodical. Leading con-
tributors included: Edward Everett,
John Pickering.

296 TITLE: <u>The Genesee Olio; a Semi-Monthly</u>
<u>Journal Devoted to Miscellany and</u>
<u>Literature.</u>

Place of Publication: Rochester, N.Y.
First Issue: 9 Jan 1847
Last Issue: 27 Dec 1849//?
Available From: Rochester Pub. Lib.;
Buffalo and Erie County
Pub. Lib.

297 TITLE: <u>The Gentleman and Lady's Town and</u>
<u>Country Magazine; or, Repository of</u>
<u>Instruction and Entertainment.</u>

Place of Publication: Boston
First Issue: May 1784
Last Issue: Jan 1785//
Periodicity: Monthly
Editors: Job Weeden; William Barrett
Publishers: Weeden and Barrett

Available From: APS; Amer. Antiquarian Soc.*
Mott.
Contents:
Poetry: <u>Original</u>.
Prose: <u>Travel</u>. <u>Essay</u>. <u>Familiar Essay</u>.
<u>Letters</u>.
Fiction: <u>Tales</u>: "Story of La Roche";
"Fatima. A Moral Tale"; "Zaman: An
Oriental Tale"; "The Soldier. A Tale";
"The Merited Disappointment: A Tale";
"The Fair Recluse"; "The Precipitate
Lover. A Moral Tale"; "The Discontented
Man. An Eastern Tale"; "The Partial
Mother. A Moral Tale"; "The Way to
Reclaim Him. A Moral Tale."
Miscellaneous: <u>Extracts</u>: from other jour-
nals; by various authors. <u>Anecdotes</u>:
on various subjects. <u>News</u>: Foreign and
Domestic.

298 TITLES: (1) <u>The Gentleman's Magazine</u>
(2) <u>The Gentleman's Magazine, and Monthly</u>
<u>American Review</u> (3) <u>Burton's Gentleman's</u>
<u>Magazine, and Monthly American Review</u>
(4) <u>Burton's Gentleman's Magazine, and</u>
<u>American Monthly Review</u> (5) <u>Graham's</u>
<u>Magazine</u>.

Place of Publication: Philadelphia
First Issue: July 1837
Last Issue: Dec 1840//
Periodicity: Monthly
Editors: William E. Burton; George R. Graham;
Edgar Allan Poe
Publishers: Charles Alexander; William E.
Burton; George R. Graham
Available From: APS; Univ. of Mich., Ann
Arbor. Mott.
Contents:
Poetry: <u>Original</u>: Charles West Thomson,
Cornelius Webbe, J. Houston Mifflin,
Macworth Praed, I.P. Ives, Catharine H.
Waterman, Jane H. Williams, Park Ben-
jamin, Robert R. Raymond, Thomas Dunn
English, Richard Harrington, James Henry
Carlton, Thomas Dale, Joseph Sill, George
L. Curry, James F. Otis, Poe, Philip
Pendleton Cooke, Sarah J. Lambert,
Frederick West, Robert Morris, Helen
Mathews, Grenville Mellen. <u>Selected</u>:
James Montgomery, Leigh Hunt, J.H.
McIlvaine, Thomas Carew, Edmund Waller.
Prose: <u>Biography</u>: Dickens, Cruikshank.
<u>Travel</u>. <u>Essay</u>. <u>Familiar Essay</u>.
<u>Criticism</u>. <u>Letters</u>. <u>Book Reviews</u>.
Fiction: <u>Sketches</u>. <u>Tales</u>: "The Schuyl-
kill Pic Nic"; "The Negro Queen"; "The
Convict and His Wife"; "Life's Vagaries,
or, the Stage, the Army, and the Law";
"The Friar of Dillow. A Mono-Drame";
"Wild Water Pond"; "The Ladies in Black";
"The Picture. A Long-Ago Adventure";
"The Half Breed. A Tale of South
America"; "The Lovers' Quarrel. A Tale
of the English Chroniclers"; "The Secret
Cell"; "The Excommunicated. A Tale";
"Don Ricardo"; "The Man in the Big Boots.
A Road-Side Marvel"; "Henry Pulteney:
Or, the Adventures of a Wanderer"; "The

Physician's Fee"; "Love and Ambition. A Jewish Story"; "The Palisadoes"; "The Cork Leg"; "The Man-Mule. A Legend of Gallicia"; "The Last Abencerage. A Romance"; "The Kentucky Tragedy. A Tale Founded on Facts of Actual Occurrence"; "My First Cousin and My First Kiss"; "The Land Pirates"; "Charles. A Tale of the American Revolution"; "The Seven Adjutants: Or, My Grandmother's Will"; "The Indian Maid"; "The Massacre of the Jews at Lisbon in 1506. A Historical Tale"; "The Man of Many Hopes"; "The Jester and His Child"; "The Panorama of Life"; "The Unwedded Bride. A True Story of American Life"; "The Autobiography of Bob Stubbs. A Man About Town"; "The Waste Lands. A Tale"; "The Privateer. A Tale of the Late American War"; "Pontiac, the Ottawa. An Indian Tale"; "The Man That Was Used Up. A Tale of the Late Bugaboo and Kickapoo Campaign" [Poe]; "The Fall of the House of Usher" [Poe]; "William Wilson" [Poe]; "Morella. A Tale" [Poe]; "The Conversation of Eiros and Charmion" [Poe]; "The Last Shilling"; "Peter Pendulum, the Business Man"; "The Miami Valley"; "The Mail Robber. A Tale"; "A Sail in Sight; or, the Rescue"; "The Money Diggers. A Down-East Story" [Mrs. Seba Smith]; "The Young Merchant"; "The Fatal Belt. A Tale of the Mississippi Valley"; "Edmund and His Cousin"; "The Lover and the Poet"; "The Man of the Crowd" [Poe]; "The Journal of Julius Rodman, Being an Account of the First Passage Across the Rocky Mountains of North America Ever Achieved by a Civilized Man" [Poe].
Miscellaneous: Extracts: by various authors; from other journals. Anecdotes: on various subjects. Literary Notices.

299   TITLE: The Gentleman's Magazine, and Monthly American Review. [See The Gentleman's Magazine.]

300   TITLE: The Gentlemen and Ladies Town and Country Magazine: Consisting of Literature, History, Politics, Arts, Manners, and Amusements, with Various Other Matter.

Place of Publication: Boston
First Issue: Feb 1789
Last Issue: Aug 1790//
Periodicity: Monthly
Editors: Nathaniel Coverly; William Hoyt
Publishers: Nathaniel Coverly; William Hoyt
Available From: APS; Boston Pub. Lib.*
                 Mott.
Contents:
  Poetry: Original. Selected: Gray.
  Prose: Biography: LaFayette, Isaac Bickerstaff, Jr. Travel. Essay.
  Familiar Essay. Letters.
  Fiction: Sketches. Tales: "Matrimonial Infidelity. A Genuine Story"; "A Tale. No Woman Without Her Value"; "The Fatal

Discovery"; "The Friar's Tale"; "Louisa: An Elegiac Tale"; "On the Venality: An Italian Story."
Miscellaneous: Extracts: by various authors. Anecdotes: on various subjects. News: Foreign and Domestic.

301   TITLE: The Georgia Analytical Repository.

Place of Publication: Savannah
First Issue: May-June 1802
Last Issue: March-April 1803//?
Periodicity: Bi-monthly
Editor: Henry Holcombe
Publisher: Henry Holcombe
Available From: APS; Brown Univ.,
                 Providence*
Contents:
  Poetry: Original. Selected.
  Prose: Biography. Essay. Letters.
  Fiction: Sketches.
  Miscellaneous: Anecdotes: on various subjects. News: Foreign and Domestic.
Note: Although this journal is primarily religious, it is of literary interest in that it contains a number of conversion narratives.

302   TITLES: (1) The Gleanor; or, Monthly Magazine (2) The Monthly Magazine.

Place of Publication: Lancaster, Pa.
First Issue: Sept 1808
Last Issue: Nov 1809//?
Periodicity: Monthly
Editors: Stacy Potts, Jr.; Gervase Godard
Publishers: Gervase Godard & Co.
Available From: APS; Univ. of Chicago
Contents:
  Poetry: Original. Selected: James Montgomery, John Davis, Scott, Erasmus Darwin.
  Prose: Biography: Madison, Southey, Buonaparte. Travel. Familiar Essay.
  Criticism. Letters.
  Fiction: Essay Serials: "The Grumbler"; "The Moderator"; "The Ranger." Sketches.
  Tale: "Story of Eugenio and Lucinda."
  Miscellaneous: Extracts: from other journals; by various authors; Penn.
  Anecdotes: on various subjects. News: Foreign and Domestic.

303   TITLES: (1) Godey's Magazine (2) Lady's Book (3) Monthly Magazine of Belles-Lettres and Arts, the Lady's Book (4) Godey's Lady's Book, and Ladies American Magazine (5) Godey's Magazine and Lady's Book (6) Godey's Lady's Book.

Place of Publication: Philadelphia
First Issue: 1 July 1830
Last Issue: Aug 1898//
Periodicity: Monthly
Editors: Sarah J. Hale; Lydia H. Sigourney; Louis A. Godey; E. Leslie; Morton M'Michael; Grade Greenwood
Publisher: Louis A Godey

Available From: APS; Lib. of Congress.*
Mott. Poole.
Contents:
  Poetry: Original: Sarah J. Hale, Lydia
    H. Sigourney, John W. Overall, T.B.
    Read. Selected: Nathaniel P. Willis,
    Eliza Cook, Sarah J. Hale, Lydia H.
    Sigourney, Hannah F. Gould, Caroline F.
    Orne, E.M. Fitzgerald, Willis Gaylord
    Clark, Thomas Haynes Bayly, Scott,
    William Alexander, James M'Henry.
  Prose: Biography: Addison, Buonaparte,
    Fitz-Greene Halleck, James Sheridan
    Knowles, Penn. Essay. Familiar Essay.
  Fiction: Essay Serials: "The Gatherer";
    "The Toilet." Sketches. Tales: "The
    Suicide's Last Carouse: A Tale of
    Fashionable Life"; "The Little Black
    Porter"; "Anna and Eudosia, a Polish
    Story"; "The Lovers' Quarrel"; "Cain,
    an Antediluvian Tale"; "A Tale of Gal-
    way"; "A Tale of the Alhambra"; "The
    Merchant's Daughter"; "The Witch. A
    Tale, Related by an English Nobleman";
    "The Drover. A Tale"; "Thomas Weston--
    A Tale"; "Jeanie Stevenson. A Tale of
    the Dominie"; "Kascambo. A Tale of the
    Caucasus"; "The Snow Feather; a Tale";
    "The Veiled Picture. A Tale of the Fine
    Arts"; "A Sketch of Fashionable Life; a
    Tale"; "The Two Rings: A Tale of the
    Thirteenth Century"; "The Restored; a
    Tale"; "Retaliation. A Tale"; "The Old
    Gentleman. A Tale"; "The Marsh Maiden.
    A Tale of the Palatinate"; "The Villi
    Dance. A Tale of Hungary"; "John
    Tarleton. A Tale of New England"; "The
    Bandit's Confession. A Tale of Spain";
    "The Hungarian Princess. An Historical
    Tale"; "Very Mysterious, a Tale"; "The
    Two Light-Houses. A Tale of the Ocean";
    "The Murderer's Fate; or, the Effect of
    Conscience. A Tale"; "The Victims of
    Passion; a Tale of the East"; "The Tale
    of an Aeronaut"; "The Farmer's Return,
    a Tale"; "A Tale of the Richelieu";
    "Eliza--A Tale"; "Talent--A Tale";
    "Caballero Ladrone. A Tale"; "The
    Adopted Daughter. A Tale"; "The Moorish
    Father. A Tale of Malaga"; "Deaf and
    Dumb; a Tale."
  Miscellaneous: Extracts: from other jour-
    nals; by various authors; Washington.
    Anecdotes: on various subjects.
    Literary Notices.
  Note: In a special section labelled "Poetic-
    al Portraits" appeared brief extracts by
    such poets as: Shakespeare, Milton,
    Scott, Byron, Spenser, Wordsworth, John
    Wilson, Gray, Burns, Coleridge, William
    Cowper, Edward Young, W.L. Bowles,
    Shelley, James Montgomery, James Hogg,
    Thomas Haynes Bayly, Caroline Bowles,
    Felicia Hemans, L.E. Landon, Thomas
    Moore, Southey, James Thomson, Barry
    Cornwall, George Crabbe, Allan Cunning-
    ham, Keats, Robert Bloomfield, Thomas
    Hood.

304 TITLE: Graham's American Monthly Magazine of
     Literature and Art. [See The Casket, or,
     Flowers of Literature, Wit & Sentiment.]

305 TITLE: Graham's Illustrated Magazine of
     Literature, Romance, Art, and Fashion.
     [See The Casket, or, Flowers of Literature,
     Wit & Sentiment.]

306 TITLE: Graham's Lady's and Gentleman's
     Magazine. [See The Casket, or, Flowers
     of Literature, Wit & Sentiment.]

307 TITLE: Graham's Magazine. [See The
     Gentleman's Magazine.]

308 TITLE: Graham's Magazine of Literature and
     Art. [See The Casket, or, Flowers of
     Literature, Wit & Sentiment.]

309 TITLES: (1) The Green Mountain Gem. A
     Monthly Journal of Moral and Entertaining
     Literature (2) The Green Mountain Gem.
     A Semi-Monthly Journal of Moral and
     Entertaining Literature (3) The Green
     Mountain Gem: A Monthly Publication of
     Polite Literature, Science and the Arts.

     Place of Publication: Bradford, Vt.
     First Issue: Jan 1843
     Last Issue: 1849//
     Periodicity: Monthly; Semi-monthly; Monthly
     Editor: A.B.F. Hildreth
     Publisher: A.B.F. Hildreth
     Available From: APS; Univ. of Vt., Burlington
     Contents:
       Poetry: Original: A.B.F. Hildreth, James
         T. Fields, George W. Patten, Florence
         Percy, Emily R. Page. Selected: Bryant,
         H.W. Rockwell, Frances S. Osgood, Sarah
         J. Hale, Felicia Hemans, Mary L. Lawson,
         Hannah F. Gould, George Pope Morris,
         Whittier, William Jones, James Russell
         Lowell, Thomas Hood, Barry Cornwall,
         Oliver Wendell Holmes, Lydia H. Sigourney,
         Longfellow, William H. Cranston, Rufus
         Dawes, Charles Swain, Park Benjamin,
         William Leggett, Nathaniel P. Willis,
         Albert Pike, James G. Percival, Joseph
         T. Buckingham, Sumner Lincoln Fairfield.
       Prose: Biography: Burns, Shelley, Milton,
         LaFayette, Zachary Taylor, Samuel Wood-
         worth, Washington, Felicia Hemans, Byron,
         Horace Greeley. Travel. Essay. Familiar
         Essay. Criticism. Letters. Book Re-
         views.
       Fiction: Essay Serials: "Literary Snow-
         Flakes"; "School Reminiscences." Sketches.
         Tales: "Henry and Marie; or, the Faith-
         ful Ones"; "Ten Thousand Dollars; or,
         Who's the Lady?"; "The Raft; or, the
         Widow's Two Sons"; "Lallaree"; "Losing
         and Winning. A Deeply Interesting Tale";

"Pride; or, the Folly of Ambition"; "The Ventriloquist; or the Forged Will"; "The Lost Bride; a Legend of the White Mountains" [Sarah J. Hale]; "Lucy Gray"; "Amelia Livingston; or, the Lost Property Restored"; "Henri Wilmot; or, the Deceived"; "The Beautiful Country Girl; or, Benevolence Rewarded" [Lydia Maria Child]; "The Green Mountain Boy. A Tale of Ticonderoga"; "Ellen Carlton: Or, the Capricious Bride" [J.H. Ingraham]; "Florence Errington. 'An O'er True Tale'"; "The Earl of Montrose. A Tale of Modern Times"; "The Fatal Leap and Subsequent Revenge. A Tale of the Early Settlers"; "Henry Montford; or, the Discarded"; "The Purse. A Tale of the Green-Mountain State"; "Ellen Neville; or the Dangers of Infatuation. A Tale of Domestic Life"; "The Hero Woman" [George Lippard]; "Clement Westley. A Tale of the Colonies"; "William Harden. A Thrilling Tale of the Revolution"; "The Tulip-Poplar; or, the Poor Men Heroes of the Revolution" [George Lippard]; "Everett Dunstan. A Tale of the Black Hills"; "The Captive Maiden. A Tale of the Early Settlement of Maine"; "Mr. Merritt and His Family; or, Lending a Name."
  Miscellaneous: Extracts: from other journals; Edward Everett, Nathaniel P. Willis, Whittier, Carlyle, Burns. Anecdotes: on various subjects; Franklin, S. Johnson, John Quincy Adams, Hogarth, John Neal, Garrick, Byron, Isaac Newton, B. Jonson, Milton. Literary Notices. News: Domestic.

310   TITLE: The Green Mountain Patriot.

Place of Publication: Peacham, Vt.
First Issue: 23 Feb 1798
Last Issue: 27 Jan 1810//?
Periodicity: Weekly
Editors: ?
Publishers: Farley & Goss
Available From: Amer. Antiquarian Soc.
Contents:
  Poetry: Original. Selected: Peter Pindar, Samuel Butler, William Cowper, Hannah More, Selleck Osborne, James Montgomery, Southey, Burns.
  Prose: Biography: Buonaparte. Essay. Familiar Essay.
  Fiction: Sketches. Tales: "The Story of Celsus"; "The Tale of the Mahometan Hog; or Love of the World Detected"; "The Monkies--A Tale"; "The Parrot--A Fable"; "Little John.--A Christmas Tale"; "The Weeping Mother. A True Tale"; "The Bears.--A Tale"; "The Dog and the Elbow. A Metrical Tale"; "Dick Strype; or, the Force of Habit.--A Tale"; "The Best of Wives. A Tale"; "The Horrors of War. A Tale"; "The Orphan Boy's Tale."
  Miscellaneous: Anecdotes: on various subjects. News: Foreign and Domestic.

311   TITLE: The Green Mountain Repository.

Place of Publication: Burlington, Vt.
First Issue: Jan 1832
Last Issue: Dec 1832//
Periodicity: Monthly
Editors: ?
Publishers: ?
Available From: APS; Lib. of Congress*
Contents:
  Poetry: Original. Selected: Spenser, Bernard Barton, Wordsworth, Bryant.
  Prose: Biography: Nathan Hale, John Quincy Adams, Scott. Essay. Familiar Essay. Book Reviews.
  Fiction: Sketches.
  Miscellaneous: Extracts: from other journals; by various authors. Anecdotes: on various subjects; Buonaparte, Smollett. Literary Notices.

312   TITLE: The Gridiron.

Place of Publication: Dayton, Ohio
First Issue: 29 Aug 1822
Last Issue: 8 May 1823//
Periodicity: Weekly
Editor: John Anderson
Publisher: John Anderson
Available From: APS; Dayton Pub. Lib.
Contents:
  Poetry: Original. Selected: Hugh Henry Brackenridge, Peter Pindar, Matthew Prior.
  Prose: Essay. Letters.
  Fiction: Sketches. Tales: "George Harvest: Parson and Comedian"; "Bracebridge Hall" [W. Irving].
  Miscellaneous: Extracts: from other journals; by various authors; Kotzebue, Goldsmith, W. Irving. Anecdotes: on various subjects; Franklin, Garrick. News: Domestic.

313   TITLE: The Guardian.

Place of Publication: Albany
First Issue: 21 Nov 1807
Last Issue: 12 Nov 1808//
Periodicity: Weekly
Editors: ?
Publishers: Van Benthuysen & Wood
Available From: APS; Univ. of Mich., Ann Arbor
Contents:
  Poetry: Original. Selected: Peter Pindar, Burns, John Blair Linn, Southey, Timothy Dwight.
  Prose: Biography. Travel. Familiar Essay. Letters.
  Fiction: Essay Serials: "Tempus"; "The Knight-Errant." Sketches. Tales: "The Triumph of Truth"; "A Tale" [Kotzebue]; "Alcander and Monima, or the Folly of Excessive Affection"; "The Nutshell. A

Tale"; "The Witch of the Wold"; "Rolando and Lucilia. A Sabine Tale of the Times"; "The Castle of Erasmus, or Bertrand and Eliza. A Tale"; "The Death Bed."
Miscellaneous: Extracts: from other journals; by various authors; Sterne, Rousseau, Charlotte Smith. Anecdotes: on various subjects. Literary Notices. News: Foreign and Domestic.
Note: Motto: From Education, as the Leading Cause,/The Public character Its Colour Draws;/Hence the Prevailing Manners Take Their Cast,/Extravagant or Sober, Loose or Chaste.--Cowper.

314 TITLE: The Guardian, a Semi-Monthly Magazine, Dedicated to the Younger Members of Society.

Place of Publication: New York
First Issue: 1 Sept 1833
Last Issue: 15 Nov 1833//?
Available From: N.Y. Hist. Soc.

315 TITLE: The Guardian and Monitor. A Monthly Publication Devoted to the Moral Improvement of the Rising Generation. [See The Guardian, or, Youth's Religious Instructor: A Monthly Publication, Devoted to the Moral Improvement of the Rising Generation.]

316 TITLES: (1) The Guardian, or, Youth's Religious Instructor: A Monthly Publication, Devoted to the Moral Improvement of the Rising Generation (2) The Guardian and Monitor. A Monthly Publication Devoted to the Moral Improvement of the Rising Generation.

Place of Publication: New Haven, Conn.
First Issue: Jan 1819
Last Issue: Dec 1898//
Periodicity: Monthly
Editor: E.B. Coleman
Publishers: Stephen Dodge; N. Whiting
Available From: Amer. Antiquarian Soc.*; Lib. of Congress
Contents:
Poetry: Original. Selected: James Montgomery, Hannah More, B. Johnson, William Cowper, Thomas Hood, Felicia Hemans, Jane Taylor.
Prose: Biography: Benjamin West. Travel. Essay. Familiar Essay. Criticism. Letters.
Fiction: Essay Serials: "The Monitress"; "Evidences of Conversion"; "Recollections of a Childhood." Sketches. Tales: "The Aged Visitant of Ticonderoga"; "Jane Bond. A True Narrative"; "Daniel Rutherford: A True Tale"; "The Robber's Daughter"; "Memoir of Mary Ann Clap"; "A Family Scene"; "The Infant Preacher; or, the Story of Henrietta Smith"; "'I Can Do Without It'"; "The Sore Tongue"; "History of Dick Simmons"; "The Contrast"; "The Dying Orphan. A Narration of Facts";

"Temper, or the Two Old Ladies"; "The Little Shepherdess"; "Lucy and Her Dhaye"; "Charles Whiston. A Story"; "Little Robert"; "The Infidel Reclaimed"; "The Ploughboy"; "Liffy and Illy Cewen of Locklarene. A Scottish Story of Truth"; "Ellen and Sophia; or, the Broken Hyacinth"; "Illustrations of Lying. The Stage Coach."
Miscellaneous: Anecdotes: on various subjects. News: Domestic.

317 TITLE: The Halycon Luminary, and Theological Repository, a Monthly Magazine, Devoted to Religion and Polite Literature. Conducted by a Society of Gentlemen.

Place of Publication: New York
First Issue: Jan 1812
Last Issue: Dec 1812//?
Periodicity: Monthly
Editor: Samuel Woodworth
Publishers: Samuel Woodworth & Co., and E. Riley
Available From: APS; Yale Univ.*
Contents:
Poetry: Original. Selected: Luis de Camoens, James Montgomery, Scott, Allan Cunningham, Milton.
Prose: Biography: Handel. Travel. Essay. Letters.
Miscellaneous: Extracts: from other journals; by various authors; S. Johnson, Franklin. Anecdotes: on various subjects.

318 TITLE: The Hartford Pearl and Literary Gazette. [See The Bouquet: Flowers of Polite Literature.]

319 TITLE: The Harvard Lyceum.

Place of Publication: Cambridge, Mass.
First Issue: 14 July 1810
Last Issue: 9 March 1811//
Periodicity: Semi-monthly
Editors: Edward Everett; John Chipman Gray
Publishers: Hilliard and Metcalf
Available From: APS; Lib. of Congress.* Mott.
Contents:
Poetry: Original.
Prose: Biography. Essay. Criticism: on Dryden, Spenser, Scott, Holingshed. Letters.
Fiction: Tales: "Sociability and Ceremony. An Allegory"; "Emily."
Miscellaneous: Anecdotes: on various subjects; Voltaire, S. Johnson, William Cowper, Goldsmith.
Note: This is the first Harvard periodical, and contains primarily essays on many subjects.

320 TITLE: The Harvard Register.

Place of Publication: Cambridge, Mass.
First Issue: March 1827

Last Issue: Feb 1828//
Periodicity: Monthly
Editors: Students of Harvard
Publishers: Hilliard and Brown
Available From: APS; Harvard Univ.*
Contents:
  Poetry: Original.
  Prose: Biography: Mather Byles, Thomas
    Godfrey, Jr. Essay. Familiar Essay.
    Criticism: on W. Irving, R.B. Sheridan,
    James Fenimore Cooper, Thomas Moore.
    Book Reviews.
  Fiction: Essay Serials: "Notices of Amer-
    ican Poets"; "Journal of the Polyglot
    Clug." Sketches. Tales: "The Pre-
    sentiment. A Legend of the Den"; "A
    Confession."

321 TITLES: (1) L'hémisphère, journal français;
     Contenant des variétés littéraires et
     politique, dédié aux Americains, amateurs
     de la langue française [Running title:
     L'hémisphère, journal littéraire et
     politique] (2) L'hémisphère, journal
     français et anglais; (French and English
     Journal;) Contenant des variétés littéraires,
     biographiques, &c. dédié aux Américains
     amateurs de la langue française.

     Place of Publication: Philadelphia
     First Issue: 7 Oct 1809
     Last Issue: 28 Sept 1811//
     Periodicity: Weekly
     Editors: J.J. Negrin; J. Edwards
     Publishers: J.J. Negrin; William C. Keen;
               J. Edwards
     Available From: APS; Lib. Co. of Philadel-
               phia*
     Contents:
       Poetry: Original. Selected.
       Prose: Biography. Travel: Mungo Park.
         Essay: on Buonaparte, Washington,
         William Cobbett, Franklin, Jefferson,
         Victor Hugo. Familiar Essay. Criti-
         cism: on Goldsmith. Letters.
       Miscellaneous: Extracts: by various
         authors; William Shenstone. Anecdotes:
         on various subjects.
     Note: Issue one lists 47 French journals
       published in Paris in 1809.

322 TITLES: (1) The Herald of Freedom, and the
     Federal Advertiser (2) The Herald of
     Freedom (3) The Argus.

     Place of Publication: Boston
     First Issue: 15 Sept 1788
     Last Issue: 28 June 1793//
     Periodicity: Bi-Weekly
     Editors: Edmund Freeman; Loring Andrews;
               John Howel; Edward E. Powars
     Publishers: Edmund Freeman; Loring Andrews;
               John Howel; Edward E. Powars
     Available From: Amer. Antiquarian Soc.*
     Contents:
       Poetry: Original: Peter Pindar. Selected:
         Robert Merry.
       Prose: Essay. Familiar Essay.

Fiction: Essay Serial: "The Life and
  Amusements of Isaac Bickerstaffe."
  Sketches. Tales.
Miscellaneous: Anecdotes: on various sub-
  jects. Literary Notices. News: Foreign
  and Domestic.

323 TITLE: The Herald of Literature and Science.

     Place of Publication: Detroit
     First Issue: 14 May 1831
     Last Issue: Sept 1831//
     Publisher: Detroit Debating Soc.
     Available From: Detroit Pub. Lib.

324 TITLE: The Herald of Truth, a Monthly
     Periodical, Devoted to the Interests of
     Religion, Philosophy, Literature, Science
     and Art.

     Place of Publication: Cincinnati
     First Issue: Jan 1847
     Last Issue: July 1848//
     Periodicity: Monthly
     Editor: Lucius A. Hine
     Publisher: Lucius A. Hine
     Available From: APS; Wis. State Hist. Soc.,
               Madison.* Mott.
     Contents:
       Poetry: Original. Selected: Emerson
         Bennett, William D. GAllagher, Whittier,
         Frances S. Osgood, Sarah C. Edgerton,
         S.J. Howe, Thomas L. Boucher, Shelley,
         Bryant, Schiller, William D. Emerson,
         Longfellow, Frances D. Gage, Phoebe
         Carey, Alice Carey, C.A. Chamberlain.
       Prose: Essay. Familiar Essay. Letters.
         Book Reviews.
       Fiction: Tales: "Platonic Love"; "The
         Fatal Compact.--An Allegory."
       Miscellaneous: Literary Notices.

325 TITLES: (1) The Hesperian; or, Western
     Monthly Magazine (2) The Hesperian: A
     Monthly Miscellany of General Literature,
     Original and Select.

     Place of Publication: Columbus, Ohio;
                           Cincinnati
     First Issue: May 1838
     Last Issue: Nov 1839//
     Periodicity: Monthly
     Editors: William D. Gallagher; Otway Curry
     Publisher: John D. Nichols
     Available From: APS; Lib. of Congress.*
                     Mott. Poole.
     Contents:
       Poetry: Original: Otway Curry, William
         D. Gallagher, George Wallis, Lydia H.
         Sigourney, William Gilmore Simms, C.P.
         Cranch. Selected: Park Benjamin,
         Nathaniel P. Willis.
       Prose: Travel. Essay. Familiar Essay.
         Criticism. Book Reviews.
       Fiction: Essay Serials: "Reminiscences
         of a Lady." Sketches. Tales: "The
         First Kiss.--A Tale"; "The Mysterious

Passenger"; "Zeik Smith"; "The Wolf
Hunter"; "Howe's Masquerade. A Tale of
the Old Province House" [Hawthorne];
"Margaret Sunderland. A Story of One in
Ten Thousand"; "The Compact. A German
Story"; "The Young Inebriate. A Tale
of the Old Dominion"; "The Vow--A
Northern Tale"; "Boyhood; or, the Truant
Messenger--A Reminiscence of the Moun-
tains"; "Man Without Money"; "The Prison
of Life. An Allegory"; "The Chase";
"Old Polly Cary. A Tale of Every-Day
Life in America"; "The Coquette; or, a
Season at the Springs"; "The Lesson of
History"; "The White Scarf"; "Animal
Magnetism. A Tale"; "The Dutchman's
Daughter. A Tale of the Early Emigrants";
"Mr. Inklin; or the Man of Leisure";
"The Night-Watch"; "Aunt Esther. A Tale
of Humble Life."
Miscellaneous: Extracts: from other jour-
nals; by various authors; Carlyle,
Thomas Campbell, James Fenimore Cooper,
Rousseau, Southey, Dickens, Robert M.
Bird, Benjamin Drake, F.W. Thomas.
Anecdotes: on various subjects; Washing-
ton. Literary Notices.

326 TITLE: The Hive. [Superseded by The Lancaster True American.]

Place of Publication: Lancaster, Pa.
First Issue: 22 June 1803
Last Issue: 12 June 1805//
Periodicity: Weekly
Editors: Charles M'Dowell; William Greear
Publishers: M'Dowell & Greear
Available From: APS; Pa. Hist. Soc.
Contents:
  Poetry: Original. Selected: Swift,
  Erasmus Darwin, Shakespeare, Wordsworth,
  Thomas Moore, Southey, William Cowper.
  Prose: Biography: William Cowper, Mary
  Wollstonecraft Godwin, Lady Jane Grey,
  James Woodhouse, Robert Bloomfield,
  Burns. Familiar Essay. Letters.
  Fiction: Essay Serials: "The Gleaner";
  "The Passenger." Sketches. Tales:
  "History of Maria Arnold"; "The Chimney
  Sweeper; or, the School for Levity";
  "Jeannot and Colin. A Tale"; "The
  Village Curate; or As You Like It. A
  Tale"; "The Shrubbery. A Tale"; "The
  Wooden Leg"; "Zimeo.--A Tale"; "Amanda:--
  A Tale, Founded on Fact"; "The Starling.
  A Novel in Miniature."
  Miscellaneous: Anecdotes: on various
  subjects; Goldsmith, Garrick, Penn,
  Shenstone, Swift, Burns.

327 TITLE: The Hive. [Supersedes The Monthly
Magazine (Lancaster, Pa.).]

Place of Publication: Lancaster, Pa.
First Issue: 19 May 1810
Last Issue: 11 Dec 1810//?
Periodicity: Weekly
Editor: William Hamilton
Publisher: William Greear

Available From: APS; Lib. of Congress
Contents:
  Poetry: Original. Selected: James
  Beattie.
  Prose: Biography. Familiar Essay.
  Letters.
  Fiction: Essay Serial: "Onesimus."
  Miscellaneous: Extracts: from other jour-
  nals. Anecdotes: on various subjects.

328 TITLE: The Hive.

Place of Publication: Northampton, Mass.
First Issue: 30 Aug 1803
Last Issue: 25 Dec 1804//?
Periodicity: Weekly
Editor: Thomas M. Pomroy
Publisher: Thomas M. Pomroy
Available From: Lib. of Congress; Boston
                Athenaeum
Contents:
  Poetry: Original. Selected: Peter Pindar,
  Wordsworth, Robert Bloomfield, Coleridge.
  Prose: Biography: William Cowper, Edmund
  Burke. Familiar Essay. Letters.
  Fiction: Essay Serial: "The Sylph."
  Sketches. Tales: "Ingratitude Punished.
  An Eastern Tale"; "The Diary of Chaubert,
  the Misanthropist"; "Vision of Almet, the
  Dervise"; "The Pilgrim's Story."
  Miscellaneous: Extracts: from other jour-
  nals; by various authors; Jefferson,
  B. D'Israeli, John Winthrop. Anecdotes:
  on various subjects; George Whitefield,
  Kotzebue, Garrick, Swift. Literary
  Notices. News: Foreign and Domestic.

329 TITLE: The Hive.

Place of Publication: Salem, Mass.
First Issue: 27 Sept 1828
Last Issue: 20 Sept 1830//
Periodicity: Weekly
Editors: W. Ives; S.B. Ives
Publishers: W. & S.B. Ives
Available From: Boston Pub. Lib.*; N.Y.
                State Lib., Albany*
Contents:
  Poetry: Original: N.A. Haven. Selected:
  Felicia Hemans.
  Prose: Biography: Chatterton, Franklin,
  Captain John Smith, Benjamin West, Penn,
  John Eliot. Familiar Essay.
  Fiction: Sketches. Tale: "The Dead
  Alive."
  Miscellaneous: Extracts: from other jour-
  nals. Anecdotes: on various subjects;
  Franklin, George Whitefield, Gray,
  Christopher Smart, James Thomson.
  Literary Notices. News: Foreign and
  Domestic.
  Note: Motto: Hither may youth direct its
  curious mind,/And in our Hive a golden
  treasure find.

330 TITLE: The Hive. A Semi-Monthly Magazine;
Devoted to Literature, and Amusing Miscellany.

Place of Publication: Waltham, Mass.
First Issue: 2 March 1833
Last Issue: 16 Jan 1836//
Periodicity: Semi-monthly
Editor: S. Bulfinch Emmons
Publisher: S. Bulfinch Emmons
Available From: Amer. Antiquarian Soc.*;
               Boston Pub. Lib.*
Contents:
  Poetry: Original: S. Bulfinch Emmons,
    Samuel G. Bemis, Richard Emmons.
    Selected: Richard Emmons, Southey.
  Prose: Biography. Travel. Familiar
    Essay. Letters.
  Fiction: Sketches. Tales: "Two Yards of
    Jaconet, or a Husband. A Virginia Tale";
    "Ichabod and the Bull"; "The Haunted
    Chamber"; "The Mishaps of Simon Sling-
    stone"; "The Sleigh Ride" [John Neal];
    "The Pride of the Pokanokets"; "A Bee
    Hunt" [W. Irving].
  Miscellaneous: Extracts: from other jour-
    nals. Anecdotes: on various subjects.
    Literary Notices. News: Domestic.

331   TITLES: (1) Holden's Dollar Magazine, of
    Criticisms, Biographies, Sketches, Essays,
    Tales, Reviews, Poetry, etc., etc.
    (2) The Dollar Magazine. [Merged with the
    North American Miscellany.]

Place of Publication: New York
First Issue: Jan 1848
Last Issue: Aug 1851//
Periodicity: Monthly
Editors: Charles W. Holden; Charles F. Briggs
Publishers: William H. Dietz; Fowler &
           Dietz; E.A. & G.L. Duyckinck
Available From: APS; Lib. of Congress.*
              Mott.
Contents:
  Poetry: Original: William Wallace, William
    H. Dietz, Alice Carey, Henry Irving,
    Emily Hermann, Charles W. Holden.
    Selected: Park Benjamin, William Hub-
    bard, Browning, George Moore, William P.
    Mulchinock, John H. Savage, Bayard Tay-
    lor, Henry Vaughan.
  Prose: Biography. Familiar Essay. Criti-
    cism. Book Reviews.
  Fiction: Sketches. Tales: "The 'Pop'
    Visit"; "Smoke"; "The Last Ball at the
    Tuileries"; "Fashions in Feet; or, the
    Tale of the Beautiful To-To"; "Mr.
    Richard Jones and the Polka; or the
    Danger of Delay"; "Albrizzi--A Tale of
    Milan"; "Henry Oswald"; "The Abduction,
    or the Battle of the Red Gun"; "The
    German's Story"; "The Dock-Yard Ghost";
    "The Confession"; "Obed's Altar. A
    Traditionary Story of Connecticut"; "The
    Brother's Revenge; a Legend of Fort Lee";
    "An Escape"; "Recollections of the
    Gifted"; "A Venetian Story"; "A Sunday
    at Dunkstown"; "An Adventure of Kit
    Carson; a Tale of the Sacramento";
    "Crossing the Desert"; "The Croppy's
    Fingers"; "The Coroner's Inquest"; "The
    Widow's Veil"; "Genevieve Galliot"; "The
    Talisman of Affection. The Tale of
    Sakalah, the Caravansary-Keeper"; "The

False Headsman of Cologne"; "The Blue
Captain"; "The Wealthy Union, or Marriage
Without Love"; "The Rescued Maiden";
"Favourite"; "An Irishman's Revenge";
"The Silver Arrow. A Tale of Savoy";
"The Mysterious Huntsman. A Tale of
Illinois"; "Catharine Dermody's Marriage";
"The First Patient"; "Border Bullets";
"Hand and Glove"; "The Slumberers"; "Royal
Clemency"; "The Height of Ugliness";
"Arthur Campbell"; "Miss Moonshine's
Expectations"; "Ethan Brand, or the
Unpardonable Sin" [Hawthorne].
  Miscellaneous: Extracts: from other jour-
    nals; by various authors, Bryant, Dryden.
    Literary Notices.

332   TITLE: The Hudson Mirror, and Columbia
    County Farmer, a Semi-Monthly Journal
    Devoted to Polite Literature, Agriculture,
    the Fine Arts, &c. &c.

Place of Publication: Hudson, N.Y.
First Issue: 4 May 1839
Last Issue: 18 April 1840//?
Periodicity: Semi-monthly
Editor: P. Dean Carrique
Publisher: P. Dean Carrique
Available From: Lib. of Congress; N.Y. Pub.
              Lib.*
Contents:
  Poetry: Original: Lydia H. Sigourney,
    C. Theresa Clarke. Selected: Louis L.
    Noble, Mary Howitt, Felicia Hemans,
    George W. Patten, Hannah F. Gould,
    Thomas Moore, Coleridge, L.E. Landon,
    Barry Cornwall, George Pope Morris,
    Alfred B. Street, Park Benjamin, Thomas
    J. Beach.
  Prose: Travel. Essay. Familiar Essay.
  Fiction: Sketches. Tales: "The Emissary.
    Founded on Fact"; "The Flower-Girl and
    the Porter"; "The Trespasser in Maine:
    Or the Memorable Expulsion of a Speculator
    from Certain Disputed Territory"; "The
    Pirates of Cardanas"; "Little White Hat.
    A German Legend"; "Eloisa, the Beautiful.
    A Russian Tale of Truth"; "The Old Farm-
    House"; "Sir Dowling O'Hartigan"; "Lucy
    Raymond, or the Poor Girl"; "Yankee
    Pedagogues and Dutch Damsels. A Legend
    of the City of Hudson" [James Kirke Pauld-
    ing]; "The Lottery Ticket. A True
    Narrative"; "Alfred the Gipsy"; "Alberto
    Torvi. A Tale"; "Pelayo, and the Mer-
    chant's Daughter" [W. Irving]; "Animal
    Magnetism; or, Love Triumphant Over
    Science"; "The Miser Outwitted. An
    Original Tale of a Man About Town";
    "Isabel Irvington; or, a Leaf from the
    Life of a Coquette."
  Miscellaneous: Extracts: from other jour-
    nals; by various authors; W. Irving,
    Washington, Francis Bacon. Anecdotes:
    on various subjects; Franklin. News:
    Domestic.

333   TITLE: The Hummingbird, or Herald of Taste.

Place of Publication: Newfield, Conn.

First Issue: 11 April 1798
Last Issue: 9 June 1798//
Periodicity: Intended to be weekly
Editor: L. Beach
Publisher: L. Beach
Available From: APS; Amer. Antiquarian Soc.
Mott.

Contents:
Poetry: Original.
Prose: Biography. Familiar Essay.
Miscellaneous: News: Domestic.

334   TITLE: The Huntingdon Literary Museum; and
Monthly Miscellany.

Place of Publication: Huntingdon, Pa.
First Issue: Jan 1810
Last Issue: Dec 1810//
Periodicity: Monthly
Editors: William R. Smith; Moses Canan
Publisher: John M'Cahan
Available From: APS; Amer. Antiquarian Soc.*
Contents:
Poetry: Original: John L. Thompson,
Charles J. Cox, J.N. Barker, William
R. Smith. Selected: Catherine Dermody,
Burns, Thomas Moore, Scott, Thomas
Campbell, Byron.
Prose: Biography: Buonaparte. Travel.
Familiar Essay. Letters.
Fiction: Essay Serials: "The Essayist";
"My Tablets." Sketches. Tale: "Mis-
trust; or, Blanche and Osbright: A
Feudal Romance" [Matthew Gregory (Monk)
Lewis].
Miscellaneous: Extracts: from other jour-
nals; by various authors; Matthew Gregory
[Monk] Lewis, Hester L. Thrale Piozzi,
Mason Locke Weems, Jefferson, W. Irving.
Anecdotes: on various subjects; S. John-
son, Pope, Voltaire, Swift, Addison.
Literary Notices.

335   TITLE: The Idiot, or, (The) Invisible
Rambler.

Place of Publication: Boston
First Issue: 20 Dec 1817
Last Issue: 2 Jan 1819//
Periodicity: Weekly
Editor: "Samuel Simpleton"
Publisher: ?
Available From: Amer. Antiquarian Soc.*
Boston Pub. Lib.
Contents:
Poetry: Original. Selected.
Prose: Familiar Essay. Criticism.
Fiction: Tales: "An Affair of Honour";
"Jack's Return and Marriage"; "The
Indian Preacher"; "Fatal Effects of
Pride"; "The Miser"; "A Scene of Horror
at Naples"; "The Kind Wife."
Miscellaneous: Anecdotes: on various sub-
jects.

336   TITLE: The Idle Man.

Place of Publication: New York

First Issue: 1821
Last Issue: 1822//
Periodicity: ?
Editor: Richard Henry Dana
Publishers: Wiley & Halsted
Available From: APS; Lib. of Congress.*
Mott.

Contents:
Poetry: Original: Bryant.
Prose: Familiar Essay. Criticism: on
Edmund Kean, S. Johnson. Letters.
Fiction: Tales: "Edward and Mary";
"Thomas Thornton"; "Paul Felton."

337   TITLE: The Illinois Monthly Magazine.
[Superseded by The Western Monthly Magazine q.v.]

Place of Publication: Vandalia, Ill.;
Cincinnati
First Issue: Oct 1830
Last Issue: Sept 1832//
Periodicity: Monthly
Editor: James Hall
Publishers: Robert Blackwell & James Hall;
Corey and Fairbank
Available From: APS; Lib. of Congress.*
Mott. Poole.

Contents:
Poetry: Original. Selected: Bryant,
James Ashcroft.
Prose: Biography: Thomas Biddle, Daniel
Boone. Travel. Essay. Familiar Essay.
Criticism. Letters. Book Reviews.
Fiction: Sketches. Tales: "The Mis-
sionaries"; "The Philadelphia Dun"; "The
Village Musician"; "The Intestate, or
Jeremy Smith's Widow"; "Slighted Love.
A Tale"; "Michel de Coucy, a Tale of
Fort Chartres"; "The Pirates: A Sea
Tale"; "The Useful Man"; "My Cousin Lucy
and the Village Teacher"; "Familiarity;
or, the Widow's Wig."
Miscellaneous: Extracts: from other jour-
nals. Anecdotes: on various subjects;
Daniel Boone. Literary Notices.

338   TITLE: The Illustrated Family Magazine; for
the Diffusion of Useful Knowledge. [See
The New England Family Magazine; for the
Diffusion of Useful Knowledge.]

339   TITLES: (1) The Impartial Gazetteer, and
Saturday Evening's Post (2) The New-York
Weekly Museum (3) The Weekly Museum
(4) New-York Weekly Museum, or Polite
Repository of Amusement and Instruction
(5) The Ladies' Weekly Museum, or Polite
Repository of Amusement and Instruction.

Place of Publication: New York
First Issue: 17 May 1788
Last Issue: 25 Oct 1817//
Periodicity: Weekly
Editor: James Oram
Publishers: Harrisson and Purdy; John
Harrisson; James Oram
Available From: APS; Univ. of Chicago Lib.*

Contents:
  Poetry: <u>Original</u>: John Harrisson, R. Faw-
    cett, Samuel Rogers, R.A. Davenport, Mary
    Robinson. <u>Selected</u>: Freneau, Sophia
    Lee, Edmund Waller, E. O'Brien, Mary
    Robinson, William Cowper, Burns, Southey,
    George Dyer, Timothy Dwight, Robert
    Treat Paine.
  Prose: <u>Essay</u>. <u>Familiar Essay</u>.
  Fiction: <u>Essay Serial</u>: "The Moralist."
    <u>Sketches</u>. <u>Tales</u>: "The Grey Mare, the
    Better Horse"; "The Soliloquy of Thirza,
    the Wife of Abel"; "The Reclaimed Hus-
    band"; "Disinterested Love"; "Lindor and
    Lucinda; or, the Necessity of a Good
    Choice in Marriage"; "The Fatal Effects
    of Sudden Joy, an Affecting Story"; "The
    Effects of Discontent"; "The Domestic
    Tornado"; "The Amorous Friar"; "The
    Happy Shipwreck"; "We Are All Good for
    Something. A Story"; "The Life and Ad-
    ventures of a Good-Natured Man"; "The
    Unfortunate Irishman"; "Julia: Or, Ad-
    ventures of a Curate's Daughter"; "Leo-
    cadia"; "Angelica"; "The Magdalen";
    "Armida: Or, the Metamorphosis";
    "Fanny; or, the Fair Foundling"; "The
    Embarrassments of Love"; "The Good
    Uncle"; "Amoria; or, the Unfortunate
    Fair-One"; "The Pilgrim's Story"; "The
    Heir of the House of Oldfield"; "Count
    Hohenlow"; "The Melancholy Man"; "The
    Dangers of Delay"; "The Cornish Curate";
    "Waterman of Besons; a Moral Tale"; "The
    Glebe House; a Tale"; "The Two Castles";
    "Schabraco"; "The Spanish Hermit";
    "Griselidis"; "The Father and Daughter";
    "Justina and Rosina"; "The Eventful
    Journey"; "Edeliza; a Gothic Tale";
    "Constantio; a Tale"; "Idda of Token-
    burg; or the Force of Jealousy"; "The
    Widow; a Tale"; "Winter Quarters";
    "Jessica: Or, an Inn-Keeper's Story";
    "The Misanthrope"; "Eupheme; or, the Nun
    of St. Clare"; "The Duel"; "The Marriage
    Promise"; "The Merchant's Daughter";
    "The Unwilling Imposter"; "The Brothers";
    "The Maid of the Inn, or, the Golden
    Fleece"; "Robert the Brave"; "Louisa.
    A Tale of Truth"; "The Cave of St. Sid-
    well"; "The Treacherous Friend";
    "Immolin"; "St. Herbert"; "Story of
    Seraphina"; "The Victim"; "The Maid of
    Switzerland"; "The Fortune-Hunter."
  Miscellaneous: <u>Extracts</u>: from other jour-
    nals; by various authors. <u>Anecdotes</u>:
    on various subjects: Washington, David
    Hume, Voltaire, Cromwell. <u>Literary
    Notices</u>. <u>News</u>: Foreign and Domestic.

340   TITLES: (1) <u>The Impartial Register</u> (2) <u>The
       Salem Impartial Register</u> (3) <u>Essex Regis-
       ter</u>.

       Place of Publication: Salem, Mass.
       First Issue: 12 May 1800
       Last Issue: 24 March 1819//
       Periodicity: Bi-weekly
       Editors: William Carlton; Warwick Palfray,
         Jr.

Publishers: William Carlton; H. Pool & W.
    Palfray, Jr.
Available From: Amer. Antiquarian Soc.
Contents:
  Poetry: <u>Original</u>. <u>Selected</u>: William
    Jones, Schiller, Gray, Pope, Joel Barlow,
    James Beattie, James Montgomery, William
    Smyth, Jeremy Collier.
  Prose: <u>Travel</u>. <u>Familiar Essay</u>. <u>Letters</u>.
  Fiction: <u>Sketches</u>.
  Miscellaneous: <u>Anecdotes</u>: on various sub-
    jects. <u>Literary Notices</u>. <u>News</u>: Foreign
    and Domestic.

341   TITLE: <u>The Independent Republican: And
       Miscellaneous Magazine</u>.

       Place of Publication: Newburyport, R.I,
       First Issue: [Only one issue published?]
                    Aug 1805//?
       Periodicity: ?
       Editor: ?
       Publisher: Angier March
       Available From: APS; Amer. Antiquarian Soc.
       Contents:
         Poetry: <u>Selected</u>: Charles Churchill,
           William Cowper.
         Prose: <u>Essay</u>: "On the Dread of Thunder";
           "Character of the Hindus."
         Miscellaneous: <u>News</u>: Foreign and Domestic.
       Note: The object of the journal was to
         support and defend the cause of
         Federalism.

342   TITLE: <u>The Inquisitor</u>.

       Place of Publication: Philadelphia
       First Issue: 30 Dec 1818
       Last Issue: 19 Jan 1820//?
       Periodicity: Weekly
       Editor: James McMinn
       Publisher: James McMinn
       Available From: APS; Lib. Co. of Philadelphia
       Contents:
         Poetry: <u>Original</u>. <u>Selected</u>.
         Prose: <u>Familiar Essay</u>.
         Fiction: <u>Tales</u>: "Sophia, or the Dangerous
           Indiscretion, a Tale Founded on Facts";
           "The Female Warrior; or, Fortunio"; "The
           Modern Griselda, or a Lesson to Wives";
           "Henry and Louisa,--An Interesting Tale";
           "The Exile. A Tale"; "Love the Best
           Antidote Against Pride. A Tale"; "The
           Generous Russian; or, Love and Gratitude."
         Miscellaneous: <u>Anecdotes</u>: on various sub-
           jects; Lavater.

343   TITLE: <u>The Instructor</u>.

       Place of Publication: New York
       First Issue: 6 March 1755
       Last Issue: 8 May 1755//
       Periodicity: Weekly
       Editors: J. Parker; W. Weyman
       Publishers: J. Parker; W. Weyman
       Available From: APS; Lib. of Congress.*
                       Mott.

Contents:
  Poetry: Original.
  Prose: Familiar Essay. Letters.
  Fiction: Sketches. Tales: "The Orang-
    Outang. A Fable"; "The Amphisbaena. A
    Fable"; "The Party-Colour'd Shield. A
    Fable."

344 TITLE: The Intellecual Regale, or Ladies'
     Tea Tray.

Place of Publication: Philadelphia
First Issue: 19 Nov 1814
Last Issue: 30 Dec 1815//?
Periodicity: Weekly
Editor: Mrs. Carr
Publisher: Dennis Heartt
Available From: APS; Amer. Antiquarian Soc.
Contents:
  Poetry: Original. Selected: Hannah
    More, Southey.
  Prose: Biography. Essay. Letters.
  Fiction: Essay Serials: "My Common-Place
    Book"; "Ariel"; "Bachelor's Hall";
    "Scrutoire"; "Tea Tray Review." Tales:
    "Edgar and Eliza"; "Clermont Herbert; or
    Presentiment."
  Miscellaneous: Extracts: from other jour-
    nals; by various authors. Anecdotes:
    on various subjects. Literary Notices.
    News: Domestic.

345 TITLE: The Iris, a Semi-Monthly Journal.
     Devoted to Polite Literature: Containing
     Moral and Sentimental Tales, Original
     Communications, News of the Day, History,
     Arts, Biography, Amusing Miscellany,
     Humourous and Historical Anecdotes, Poetry,
     &c. &c.

Place of Publication: Binghamton, N.Y.
First Issue: 4 June 1842
Last Issue: 21 June 1845//?
Periodicity: Semi-monthly
Editor: Charles P. Cooke
Publisher: Charles P. Cooke
Available From: Amer. Antiquarian Soc.;
                Northwestern Univ.,
                Evanston, Ill.
Contents:
  Poetry: Original: J. Broughton, Thomas
    L. Harris, James Lumbard. Selected:
    Charles Fenno Hoffman, Lydia H. Sigour-
    ney.
  Prose: Biography: Addison, Joel Barlow,
    Goldsmith. Essay. Familiar Essay.
  Fiction: Sketches. Tales: "The School
    Mistress"; "Aminadab Button; or, the
    Politician"; "A High Heart in Low
    Stations" [Lydia J. Pierson]; "The
    Broken Miniature"; "Edward Morley; or
    the Reward of Perseverance"; "The Iron
    Shroud, a Tale of Italy"; "Rodrigue
    Dias de Bivar; or, the Spanish Cavalier";
    "Fort Griswold, a Tale of the American
    Revolution"; "Felix Darnley, the Stu-
    dent"; "College Recollections; or, the
    Discontented Student"; "Harry Blake, a
    Story of Circumstantial Evidence";

"Waste Paper; 'Or, Trifles Light as Air"
[Frances S. Osgood]; "The Devil and Tom
Walker" [W. Irving]; "The Huguenot's
Revenge. A Tale of France"; "Fame and
Fashion; or, the Country Boy"; "A Rail-
road Adventure."
Miscellaneous: News: Domestic.

346 TITLE: The Iris and Burlington Gazette.
     [See The Iris, or Semi-Monthly Literary
     and Miscellaneous Register.]

347 TITLES: (1) The Iris and Literary Repository
     (2) The Iris and Literary Souvenir.
     [Supersedes The Iris and New Hampshire
     Literary Record.]

Place of Publication: Manchester, N.H.;
                      Concord, N.H.
First Issue: April 1842
Last Issue: April 1843//
Periodicity: Monthly
Editors: S.H. Napoleon; B. Everette
Publishers: Emerson & Murray; E.D. Boylston
Available From: Amer. Antiquarian Soc.*;
                Yale Univ.*
Contents:
  Poetry: Original. Selected: Byron, Park
    Benjamin, Thomas Haynes Bayly, Wordsworth,
    Nathaniel P. Willis, Frances S. Osgood,
    James T. Fields, E. Lytton Bulwer, Lucy
    Hooper, Frances Brown, Bryant, Caroline
    Norton, E.C. Stedman, L.J. Cist, Mary
    Howitt, George Pope Morris, John
    Sterling, Lydia H. Sigourney, Mrs. Abdy.
  Prose: Familiar Essay.
  Fiction: Sketches. Tales: "General
    Washington and Count Pulaski: Or, the
    Unknown Warrier. A Tale of the American
    Revolution"; "The Deformed Girl"
    [Whittier]; "The White Horseman"; "The
    Young Collegian. A New England Tale";
    "The Maiden, the Chief, and the Warrior.
    A Tale of the American Revolution"; "The
    Countess Montagna; or, Bertha, the
    Spinner"; "The Mask [sic] of the Red
    Death" [Poe]; "The Rescue. A Tale of the
    Revolution"; "Terrible Revenge of Esquo
    the Fearless. An Indian Tale of the
    Connecticut"; "The Ordeal; or, the Tri-
    umph of Natural Affection"; "Running the
    Gauntlet; or, the Blockade of Buenos
    Ayres. A Tale of the Sea"; "The Maiden's
    Escape; or, the Soldier Mendicant. A
    Tale of the American Revolution"; "Gio-
    vana, the Georgian Pirate: Or, the
    Black Dragon. A Tale of the Atlantic";
    "The Broken Miniature"; "Catochus: Or,
    Burying a Man Alive"; "The Gypsy Girl";
    "James Walpole: Or, a Tale of the
    Times."
  Miscellaneous: Extracts: from other jour-
    nals; by various authors. Anecdotes:
    on various subjects. Literary Notices.
  Note: Boasts of being "The Cheapest Monthly
    Magazine in New England" [$1 per annum].

348 TITLE: The Iris; Devoted to Science, Liter-
      ature, and the Arts, Including Medical News.

      Place of Publication: Richmond, Va.
      First Issue: [Only one issue published?]
                    March 1848//?
      Available From: Va. State Lib., Richmond;
                       Tenn. State Lib., Nashville

349 TITLE: The Iris, or Literary Messenger.

      Place of Publication: New York
      First Issue: Nov 1840
      Last Issue: Oct 1841//
      Periodicity: Monthly
      Editors: ?
      Publishers: ?
      Available From: Lib. of Congress*; N.Y.
                       Pub. Lib.*

      Contents:
        Poetry: Original: A.H. Everett, Cornelia
          E. da Ponte. Selected: Edward Hooper.
        Prose: Biography. Essay. Familiar Essay.
          Criticism: on German lit., Dante,
          Chaucer, Burns, Emerson.
        Fiction: Essay Serial: "Metaphysical
          Fragments." Sketches. Tales: "Haroun
          Abulafia. A Tale of Damascus"; "Scenes
          in Paradise"; "Thecla, or the Nun of
          Thebaïs"; "The Ruined Student"; "The
          Lovers. A Tale of the Revolutionary
          War in Ireland"; "The Irish Pedlar";
          "The Might of the Poet and His Reward";
          "The Adept"; "The Walk Among the Lindens";
          "Mary Conover"; "Zoe Mou."
        Miscellaneous: Extracts: by various
          authors. Literary Notices.

350 TITLES: (1) The Iris, or Semi-monthly
      Literary and Miscellaneous Register
      (2) The Iris and Burlington Gazette.

      Place of Publication: Burlington, Vt.
      First Issue: 4 Jan 1828
      Last Issue: 14 April 1829//
      Available From: Univ. of Vt., Burlington*;
                       Boston Pub. Lib.*

351 TITLE: The John-Donkey: A Journal of the
      Present Time and for Pastime.

      Place of Publication: New York; Philadelphia
      First Issue: 1 Jan 1848
      Last Issue: 21 Oct 1848//
      Periodicity: Weekly
      Editors: Thomas Dunn English; George G.
                Foster
      Publishers: George Dexter; G.B. Zieber
      Available From: APS; Harvard Univ.* Mott.
      Contents:
        Poetry: Original. Selected.
        Prose: Familiar Essay. Book Reviews.
        Fiction: Essay Serials: "Our Indian
          Gallery"; "The Alphabet Illustrated";
          "Historical Facts." Sketches. Tale:
          "The Adventures of Don Key Haughty."
        Miscellaneous: Anecdotes: on various sub-
          jects; Poe. News: Domestic.

      Note: Articles were satirical jabs at con-
        temporary events, fads, writers, political
        figures, etc.

352 TITLE: Journal des dames ou, les souvenirs
      d'un vieillard. [Caption Title: Ladies
      Journal. Running title: Variétés
      Littéraires; ou, les souvenirs d'un
      vieillard.]

      Place of Publication: New York
      First Issue: Jan 1810
      Last Issue: Dec 1810//
      Periodicity: Monthly
      Editor: Benjamin Chaigneau
      Publisher: Benjamin Chaigneau
      Available From: APS; Lib of Congress*
      Contents:
        Poetry: Original. Selected.
        Prose: Travel. Essay.
        Fiction: Sketches. Tales: "Les bateliers
          de la Seine"; "Suite de Pytagore, ou, le
          fou de New-York"; "Cela sera, cela doit
          être. Nouvelle historique."
        Miscellaneous: Extracts: from other jour-
          nals; by various authors; Madame de
          Genlis. Anecdotes: on various subjects.
          Literary Notices.

353 TITLE: Journal inutile, ou mélanges politiques
      et littéraires.

      Place of Publication: New York
      First Issue: Nov 1824
      Last Issue: 19 May 1825//?
      Periodicity: Weekly
      Editors: ?
      Publishers: ?
      Available From: APS; Amer. Antiquarian Soc.
      Contents:
        Poetry: Original. Selected: Byron.
        Prose: Biography: Boileau, Voltaire,
          Columbus, Buonaparte, Franklin. Familiar
          Essay. Letters. Book Reviews.
        Fiction: Sketches. Tales: "Les ermites
          en liberté"; "L'entrangère";"Une aventure.
          De ma tante."
        Miscellaneous: Extracts: by various
          authors; Las Casas. Anecdotes: on
          various subjects; Buonaparte, Molière,
          Rousseau.

354 TITLE: Journal of Belles Lettres.

      Place of Publication: Lexington, Ky.
      First Issue: 20 Nov 1819
      Last Issue: 20 Feb 1820//
      Periodicity: Semi-monthly
      Editors: P.D. Mariano; Edward Everett
      Publisher: Thomas Smith
      Available From: APS; Univ. of Chicago
      Contents:
        Prose: Original. Selected.
        Prose: Essay. Criticism.
        Fiction: Sketches. Tale: "Gonnella--A
          Tale by Pietro Fortini."
      Note: Focuses primarily on French and
        Italian literature.

355   TITLE: The Journal of Belles Lettres.
       [Accompanied Waldie's Select Circulating
       Library q.v.]

       Place of Publication: Philadelphia
       First Issue: 25 June 1832
       Last Issue: April 1842//?
       Periodicity: Weekly
       Editors: Adam Waldie; John Sanderson
       Publishers: Adam Waldie; Adam Waldie & Co.
       Available From: APS; Amer. Antiquarian Soc.
       Contents:
         Poetry: Selected: Amelia Opie, Charles
           Churchill, Thomas Campbell, J.G. Lock-
           hart, Wordsworth, J.R. Planche, Shelley,
           Mary Howitt, Mrs. Abdy, L.E. Landon,
           Southey, Elizabeth Barrett, George W.
           Bethune, Robert Rose, Mary Anne Browne,
           Eliza Cook, Burns, Caroline Norton,
           Lydia H. Sigourney, Barry Cornwall,
           Joanna Baillie, Lamartine, William H.
           Burleigh, Richard Nisbett.
         Prose: Biography: Hannah More, Scott,
           Byron, Sir John Suckling, Samuel
           Richardson, Horace Walpole. Travel.
           Essay. Familiar Essay. Criticism.
           Letters. Book Reviews.
         Fiction: Essay Serials: "Notes of a
           Bibliomaniac"; "American Grumbler."
           Sketches. Tales: "The Unlucky Present:
           A Tale"; "Davie Fairbairn"; "Peter
           Simple"; "Japhet, in Search of a
           Father"; "Diary of a Blase"; "The Metro-
           politan Emigrant"; "The Doctor, &c.";
           "You Can't Marry Your Grandmother!";
           "Sir Hurry Skurry"; "Frank Farley"; "The
           Maison de Santé"; "First Love; or,
           Constancy in the Nineteenth Century";
           "The Prima Donna. A Tale"; "The Old
           Gentleman Who Pops About"; "Country
           Lodgings"; "The Painter's Daughter, a
           Tale"; "My Husband's 'Winnings.' A
           Household Incident"; "Neal Malone, an
           Irish Comic Story"; "'Will Nothing Love
           Me?'"; "The Benovolent Madman"; "Mahomet"
           [Carlyle]; "The Diving Bell"; "Peter
           Schlemihl" [Adelbert von Chamisso].
         Miscellaneous: Extracts: from other jour-
           nals; by various authors. Anecdotes:
           on various subjects; Garrick. Literary
           Notices.
       Note: Contains early reprints of the reviews
           and literary notices from such journals
           as The London Literary Gazette, The
           Gentleman's Magazine, Blackwood's,
           Fraser's, and others.

356   TITLE: Judy.

       Place of Publication: New York
       First Issue: 28 Nov 1846
       Last Issue: 20 Feb 1847//?
       Periodicity: Weekly
       Editors: ?
       Publishers: Burgess & Stringer
       Available From: APS; Yale Univ.* Mott.
       Contents:
         Poetry: Original. Selected.
         Prose: Familiar Essay.
         Fiction: Sketches.

       Miscellaneous: News: Domestic.
       Note: A satirical, whimsical journal which
           contains a number of cartoons.

357   TITLE: Juvenile Gazette.

       Place of Publication: Boston
       First Issue: 18 March 1848
       Last Issue: 28 May 1848//?
       Periodicity: Weekly
       Editors: W. Roscoe Deane; G.W. Chapman;
                 G.G. Crocker
       Publishers: Deane, Chapman, & Crocker
       Available From: Boston Pub. Lib.; Amer.
                        Antiquarian Soc.
       Contents:
         Poetry: Original.
         Prose: Essay. Familiar Essay.
         Fiction: Sketches. Tale: "Robert Emmet
           and His Love."
         Miscellaneous: Extracts: from other jour-
           nals. Anecdotes: on various subjects.
           News: Foreign and Domestic.

358   TITLE: Juvenile Gazette.

       Place of Publication: Providence, R.I.
       First Issue: Nov 1819
       Last Issue: Jan 1820//?
       Periodicity: Monthly
       Editors: ?
       Publishers: ?
       Available From: APS; Brown Univ. Lib.*
       Contents:
         Poetry: Original. Selected.
         Prose: Letters.
         Fiction: Sketches.
         Miscellaneous: Extracts: from other jour-
           nals. Anecdotes: on various subjects.

359   TITLE: The Juvenile Gazette; Being an
       Amusing Repository for Youth.

       Place of Publication: Providence, R.I.
       First Issue: 24 Nov 1827
       Last Issue: 15 Nov 1828//
       Periodicity: Weekly
       Editor: Oliver Kendall, Jr.
       Publisher: Oliver Kendall, Jr.
       Available From: Amer. Antiquarian Soc.*;
                        Brown Univ., Providence*
       Contents:
         Fiction: Sketches.
         Miscellaneous: Anecdotes: on various sub-
           jects; S. Johnson, Franklin.
       Note: Motto: "Much in a little."

360   TITLE: Juvenile Key.

       Place of Publication: Brunswick, Me.
       First Issue: 18 Sept 1830
       Last Issue: 27 Aug 1831//?
       Periodicity: Weekly
       Editor: "Oliver Oldwise"
       Publishers: Z.J. & J.W. Griffin
       Available From: Lib. of Congress; Bowdoin
                        Coll., Brunswick, Me.

Contents:
  Poetry: Selected: Thomas Haynes Bayly,
    James Hogg.
  Prose: Biography. Travel. Familiar Essay.
  Fiction: Sketches. Tales: "The Snow-
    Storm"; "The Two Apprentices"; "The
    Hermit of Chantilly"; "The Young
    Shepherdess"; "The Last Friend of the
    Poor Debtor"; "Man of Feeling" [Henry
    Mackenzie]; "Willie the Piper"; "The
    Lonely Inn. A Tale of Alarm."
  Miscellaneous: Extracts: from other jour-
    nals. Anecdotes: on various subjects.
    News: Foreign and Domestic.

361   TITLE: The Juvenile Magazine.

      Place of Publication: Utica, N.Y.
      First Issue: Jan 1827
      Last Issue: Dec 1828//
      Periodicity: Monthly
      Editors: ?
      Publishers: Western Sunday School Union
      Available From: Amer. Antiquarian Soc.*;
                      N.Y. Pub. Lib.
      Contents:
        Poetry: Selected.
        Prose: Biography. Essay. Familiar Essay.
        Fiction: Sketches. Tales: "Harry the
          Apprentice"; "The Boy and His Bible"; "A
          Visit to a Sunday School"; "The Deaf,
          Dumb, and Blind Girl."
        Miscellaneous: Extracts: from other jour-
          nals. Anecdotes: on various subjects.

362   TITLE: Juvenile Magazine; and Youth's
      Monthly Visiter.

      Place of Publication: New York
      First Issue: Jan 1831
      Last Issue: June 1832//?
      Available From: N.Y. Hist. Soc.; Harvard
                      Univ.

363   TITLE: The Juvenile Magazine, Consisting of
      Religious, Moral, and Entertaining Pieces
      in Prose and Verse. Original and Selected.

      Place of Publication: Philadelphia
      First Issue: May 1811
      Last Issue: Aug 1813//?
      Periodicity: Monthly [Irregular]
      Editor: Arthur Donaldson
      Publisher: Arthur Donaldson
      Available From: APS; Boston Pub. Lib.
      Contents:
        Poetry: Original. Selected: James Mont-
          gomery, William Cowper.
        Prose: Biography: John Woolman. Travel.
          Essay. Familiar Essay. Letters.
        Fiction: Sketches.
      Note: Issue three gives an account of
        Donaldson's "School for the People of
        Colour."

364   TITLE: The Juvenile Magazine, or Miscellane-
      ous Repository of Useful Information.

Place of Publication: Philadelphia
First Issue: 1802
Last Issue: 1803//?
Periodicity: Bi-monthly
Editors: Benjamin Johnson; Jacob Johnson
Publishers: Benjamin Johnson; Jacob Johnson
Available From: APS; N.Y. Pub. Lib. Mott.
Contents:
  Poetry: Selected: William Cowper, John
    Cotton, Erasmus Darwin, James Beattie,
    Gray, Wordsworth, S. Johnson, Christopher
    Smart, Coleridge, Southey.
  Prose: Biography: William Cowper, Lavater,
    Washington. Travel. Essay. Familiar
    Essay.
  Fiction: Essay Serials: "The Amateur";
    "The Budget"; "The Moralist." Sketches.
    Tales: "Affecting Story of a Merchant
    and His Dog"; "The Canary Bird"; "The
    Wanderer"; "Amurath, an Eastern Tale";
    "Omar, or the Punishment of Avarice";
    "Hassan; or the Camel Driver"; "The
    Fisherman."
  Miscellaneous: Extracts: from other jour-
    nals; by various authors; Jefferson,
    Hester L. Thrale Piozzi, S. Johnson,
    William Jones. Anecdotes: on various
    subjects; John Locke, S. Johnson, Dryden,
    Erasmus Darwin.

365   TITLE: The Juvenile Miscellany. [Supersedes
      The Juvenile Miscellany q.v. edited by
      Lydia Maria Child.]

      Place of Publication: Boston
      First Issue: Sept 1834
      Last Issue: Dec 1836//?
      Periodicity: Monthly
      Editor: Sarah J. Hale
      Publisher: E.R. Broaders
      Available From: Boston Pub. Lib.; Amer.
                      Antiquarian Soc.

      Contents:
        Poetry: Original.
        Prose: Travel. Essay. Familiar Essay.
          Letters.
        Fiction: Sketches. Tales: "The Balloon";
          "The Wooden Cross"; "The Mother and Son";
          "The Greys."
        Miscellaneous: Anecdotes: on various sub-
          jects.

366   TITLE: The Juvenile Miscellany. For the
      Instruction and Amusement of Youth.
      [Superseded by The Juvenile Miscellany
      (Sarah J. Hale) q.v.]

      Place of Publication: Boston
      First Issue: Sept 1826
      Last Issue: Aug 1834//
      Periodicity: Bi-monthly
      Editor: Lydia Maria Child
      Publishers: John Putnam; Putnam & Hunt;
                  Carter & Hendee; Allen and Tick-
                  nor
      Available From: APS; Lib. of Congress.*
                      Mott.

Contents:
  Poetry: <u>Original</u>. <u>Selected</u>: James G.
    Percival, Thomas Moore, Bryant, Hannah
    F. Gould, Lydia H. Sigourney.
  Prose: <u>Biography</u>: Benjamin West, Franklin,
    John Smith, Penn. <u>Travel</u>. <u>Essay</u>.
    <u>Familiar Essay</u>. <u>Letters</u>.
  Fiction: <u>Essay Serials</u>: "Extracts from a
    Journal"; "American Scenes." <u>Sketches</u>.
    <u>Tales</u>: "Adventure in the Woods"; "Mother
    and Eliza"; "The Dwarf"; "Maria and
    Frances, the Birth Day Present"; "The
    French Orphan, or . . . the New Year's
    Reward"; "Emily Walter"; "The Rural
    Feast"; "The Roses"; "The Lace Workers";
    "John White and Albert Williams, or the
    Lapse of Twenty Years. A Tale"; "Nichols,
    the Little Wool Merchant"; "The Cottage
    Girl"; "Tom Gordon's Party"; "The Little
    Goodwins"; "The Little Savoyard and His
    Dog"; "Ferdinand and Zoe"; "School Hours";
    "The Little Queen"; "Adrian Lee, or a Walk
    at Noon"; "William Burton"; "Lucy Nelson;
    or, the Boy-Girl"; "Billy Bedlow; or, the
    Girl-Boy"; "Spring in the City"; "Ralph
    and Margaret."
  Miscellaneous: <u>Anecdotes</u>: on various sub-
    jects.

367   TITLE: <u>The Juvenile Monthly</u>.

Place of Publication: Amherst, Mass.
First Issue: [Only one issue published?]
              Nov 1829//?
Periodicity: Intended to be monthly
Editors: ?
Publishers: Mt. Pleasant Classical Institu-
             tion
Available From: Amer. Antiquarian Soc.
Contents:
  Poetry: <u>Original</u>. <u>Selected</u>.
  Prose: <u>Familiar Essay</u>. <u>Book Reviews</u>.
  Miscellaneous: <u>Extracts</u>: from other jour-
    nals. <u>News</u>: Foreign.
Note: Contains one essay in French, one in
  Greek. Motto: Look you!--the boy hath
  grown to fifteen winters--And is a
  gossiping with bearded thoughts.

368   TITLE: <u>Juvenile Museum</u>.

Place of Publication: Mount Pleasant, Ohio
First Issue: 16 Sept 1822
Last Issue: 27 Sept 1823//
Available From: Pub. Lib. of Cincinnati*;
                 Oberlin Coll., Oberlin, Ohio*

369   TITLE: <u>The Juvenile Port-Folio, and Literary
      Miscellany; Devoted to the Instruction,
      and Amusement of Youth</u>. [Superseded by
      <u>The Parlour Companion</u> q.v.]

Place of Publication: Philadelphia
First Issue: 17 Oct 1812
Last Issue: 7 Dec 1816//
Periodicity: Weekly
Editor: Thomas G. Condie, Jr.
Publisher: Thomas G. Condie, Jr.

Available From: APS; Hist. Soc. of Pa.*
                 Mott.
Contents:
  Poetry: <u>Original</u>. <u>Selected</u>: Burns, Scott,
    Cervantes, Charles James Fox, Thomas
    Moore, Luis de Camoens, Southey, Byron,
    Anthony Pasquin.
  Prose: <u>Essay</u>. <u>Familiar Essay</u>. <u>Letters</u>.
  Fiction: <u>Essay Serials</u>: "Laconicks";
    "Risibles." <u>Sketches</u>. <u>Tales</u>: "Francis
    and Eloisa"; "Stephen and Fanny"; "Charles
    and Peggy"; "Leonora"; "Maria Manly and
    Mr. Frankly"; "Gregory and Harriet";
    "The Wild Rose of Langollen"; "The
    Bashful Man"; "The Unfortunate Daughter";
    "The Irishman's Cabin"; "The Soldier's
    Wife"; "Maria Arnold"; "The Mad Girl";
    "Marcus and Monimia"; "The Fisherman's
    Cabin"; "Louisa Harcourt"; "Florio and
    Emilina"; "Lucy Watson"; "The Looking
    Glass. A Tale of Former Times";
    "Petulantus and Felicia"; "The Maniac--
    A Fragment"; "The Heir of the House of
    Oldfield"; "Colin and Susan--Or True
    Love Rewarded"; "Old Edwards"; "Hubert"
    A Tale"; "Edward Dudley"; "Miss Williams";
    "The West Indian"; "Pierre. A German
    Tale"; "Charles Clerville"; "Edward St.
    Clair"; "Volkmar.--A Swiss Tale"; "Agnes
    Addison"; "Louisa Stanly."
  Miscellaneous: <u>Extracts</u>: from other jour-
    nals; by various authors; John Locke,
    Voltaire, S. Johnson, Richard Cumberland.
    <u>Anecdotes</u>: on various subjects; Franklin,
    Garrick, Dryden, S. Johnson, Voltaire,
    Thomas Warton.

370   TITLES: (1) <u>Juvenile Rambler; Designed for
      Families and Schools</u> (2) <u>Juvenile Rambler;
      or, Family and School Journal</u>.

Place of Publication: Boston
First Issue: 4 Jan 1832
Last Issue: 25 Dec 1833//
Periodicity: Weekly
Editors: ?
Publishers: Allen and Goddard; Allen &
             Ticknor; Brown & Peirce; Ford
             & Damrell
Available From: Lib. of Congress*; Boston
                 Pub. Lib.*
Contents:
  Poetry: <u>Original</u>. <u>Selected</u>: William
    Cowper, Sarah J. Hale, George Washington
    Light, Anna Letitia Barbauld, Thomas
    Moore, Lydia H. Sigourney, Alaric Watts,
    Hannah F. Gould, Caroline Norton.
  Prose: <u>Biography</u>. <u>Travel</u>. <u>Essay</u>.
    <u>Familiar Essay</u>. <u>Letters</u>.
  Fiction: <u>Essay Serial</u>: "The Dead Bird."
    <u>Sketches</u>. <u>Tales</u>: "The Three Silver
    Trouts"; "Lost Children. A Tale of Fifty
    Years Ago"; "Tom Cringle's Log"
    [Michael Scott].
  Miscellaneous: <u>Extracts</u>: from other jour-
    nals; by various authors. <u>Anecdotes</u>: on
    various subjects; Goldsmith, William
    Cowper. <u>News</u>: Domestic.

AN ANNOTATED BIBLIOGRAPHY OF AMERICAN LITERARY PERIODICALS, 1741 - 1850

371 TITLE: Juvenile Repertory.

Place of Publication: Philadelphia
First Issue: 1828
Last Issue: 1829//?
Available From: Yale Univ.; Trinity Coll.,
 Hartford

372 TITLE: The Juvenile Repository.

Place of Publication: Boston
First Issue: [Only one issue published?]
 July 1811//?
Periodicity: ?
Editors: ?
Publishers: ?
Available From: APS; Amer. Antiquarian Soc.
Contents:
 Poetry: Selected: John Gay.
 Prose: Essay.
 Miscellaneous: Extracts: from other jour-
 nals; by various authors; Mason Locke
 Weems. Anecdotes: Washington.

373 TITLE: The Juvenile Repository.

Place of Publication: Boston
First Issue: 6 July 1833
Last Issue: 1834//?
Periodicity: Weekly
Editors: ?
Publishers: Benjamin H. Greene; Leonard C.
 Bowles; Joseph Dowe
Available From: Amer. Antiquarian Soc.;
 Boston Pub. Lib.
Contents:
 Poetry: Original. Selected.
 Prose: Biography: Hannah More, Penn.
 Familiar Essay. Letters.
 Fiction: Sketches. Tales: "The Quakers,
 and Little Mary"; "The Italian Wanderers;
 or the Tale of Riego and Cora"; "Old
 Dick, the Sailor."
 Miscellaneous: Extracts: from other jour-
 nals; by various authors; Goldsmith.
 Anecdotes: on various subjects; Washing-
 ton, Goldsmith, Franklin, Cotton Mather,
 Shakespeare, Benjamin Rush.

374 TITLE: The Juvenile Repository.

Place of Publication: Providence, R.I.
First Issue: Jan 1830
Last Issue: 27 March 1830//?
Periodicity: Semi-monthly
Editor: Samuel S. Wilson
Publisher: Samuel S. Wilson
Available From: Amer. Antiquarian Soc.
Contents:
 Poetry: Original. Selected.
 Fiction: Sketches. Tales: "The Sisters--
 A Contrast"; "George Gray's Wedding";
 "The Rivals."
 Miscellaneous: News: Domestic.

375 TITLE: Juvenile Repository; Containing
 Lessons and Stories for the Young.

Place of Publication: New York
First Issue: 1842
Last Issue: 1845//?
Available From: Simmons Coll., Boston

376 TITLES: (1) The Kaleidoscope (2) Boston
 Kaleidoscope and Literary Rambler.

Place of Publication: Boston
First Issue: 5 Dec 1818
Last Issue: 13 Nov 1819//
Periodicity: Weekly
Editor: N.H. Wright
Publishers: Hews & Goss; Sylvester T. Goss
Available From: Amer. Antiquarian Soc.*
Contents:
 Poetry: Original: J. Cunningham.
 Selected: John M. Williams, R.S. Coffin.
 Prose: Familiar Essay.
 Fiction: Sketches.
 Miscellaneous: Anecdotes: on various sub-
 jects.

377 TITLE: The Key.

Place of Publication: Fredericktown, Md.
First Issue: 13 Jan 1798
Last Issue: 14 July 1798//
Periodicity: Weekly
Editor: John D. Cary
Publisher: John D. Cary
Available From: APS; Lib. of Congress.*
 Mott.
Contents:
 Poetry: Original. Selected: Southey.
 Prose: Biography: "History of Pocuhunta."
 Essay: "The Origin of Tobacco" [Frank-
 lin]. Familiar Essay: "Of the Employ-
 ment of Time, and of Indolence."
 Letters.
 Fiction: Essay Serial: "The Observer."
 Sketches. Tales: "The Story of Miss
 Braddock"; "The Victim. An Indian
 History"; "The Virtuous Father"; "The
 Simple Husband"; "The Generous Mask.
 A Tale. Imitated from the German";
 "The Flight of Happiness. A Fable";
 "Matilda"; "Sobrina and Flirtirella. A
 True Story."
Note: This is the first periodical published
 in Maryland.

378 TITLES: (1) The Knickerbocker: Or, New-York
 Monthly Magazine (2) Knickerbocker
 Monthly; a National Magazine of Literature,
 Art, Politics, and Society (3) American
 Monthly Knicker-bocker. Devoted to
 Literature, Art, Society, and Politics
 (4) Foederal American Monthly.

Place of Publication: New York

First Issue: Jan 1833
Last Issue: Oct 1865//
Periodicity: Monthly
Editors: Charles Fenno Hoffman; Willis
Gaylord Clark; Samuel Daly Lang-
tree; Timothy Flint; Kinahan
Cornwallis; John Holmes Agnew;
Lewis Gaylord Clark
Publishers: Peabody & Co.; J. Disturnell;
Wiley and Long; John Bisco;
John Allen; Samuel Hueston;
Lewis Gaylord Clark; Clark and
Edson; John A. Gray; J.R. Gil-
more; Morris Phillips; J.H.
Elliot; John Holmes Agnew
Available From: APS; Lib. of Congress.*
Mott. Poole.
Contents:
  Poetry: Original: Willis Gaylord Clark,
    Bryant, Park Benjamin, Charles Fenno
    Hoffman, Nathaniel P. Willis, Oliver
    Wendell Holmes, William Gilmore Simms,
    Fitz-Greene Halleck. Selected: Long-
    fellow, George Lunt, John Galt, J.H.
    Bright, Wordsworth, Joel Barlow, Alfred
    B. Street, Maria Edgeworth, John Waters,
    S.D. Dakin, Hans Von Spiegel, H.W. Rock-
    well, W. Thompson Bacon, John H. Rheyn,
    John G. Saxe, James Kennard, Jr.,
    William Pitt Palmer, Cornelius Webbe,
    Southey, E.C. Linden, J. Alretken,
    Lydia H. Sigourney, Hannah F. Gould,
    G.B. Singleton, Mary Howitt, Coleridge,
    Scott, Milton, Schiller, James G.
    Percival, Felicia Hemans, William B.
    Tappan, Mary Anne Browne, Whittier,
    Thomas Campbell, William Cutter.
  Prose: Biography: Edmund Kean, Scott,
    Byron, S. Johnson, Daniel Webster,
    Gilbert Stuart. Travel. Essay.
    Familiar Essay. Criticism. Letters.
    Book Reviews.
  Fiction: Essay Serials: "Horae Germanicae";
    "Vagaries of a Humorist"; "Excerpts from
    the Common Place Book of a Septuagenarian";
    "My Wife's Book"; "Ollapodianna"; "Odds
    and Ends from the Port Folio of a Penny-
    a-Liner"; "Knickerbockeriana"; "My Grand-
    Father's Port-Folio." Sketches. Tales:
    "Running Against Time. A Tale" [James
    Kirke Paulding]; "Stock-am-eisen--Or, the
    Iron Trunk"; "Amy Dayton"; "The Proselyte.
    A Tale of the Eighteenth Century"; "An-
    drew Bichel, the Butcher of Girls"; "The
    First Steamboat on the La Plata; or, 'The
    Monogamist'"; "The Burning of the Ships.
    A Story of the Revolution"; "The Albrozzi.
    A Tale of Venice"; "A Night in '98";
    "Martha: Or, the Grand Cataract of
    Bogota"; "Violetta and Thoroughgrab. A
    Tale of the West"; "Travels of an Indian
    Princess in the United States"; "Souchong,
    Slamg-Whang, and Bohea: Or the Three
    Editors of China"; "My Friend's Manu-
    script"; "The Patriots of the Tyrol. A
    Tale of the Nineteenth Century--Founded
    on Fact"; "Wilson Conworth"; "The Fate
    of Percy"; "Letters from Palmyra";
    "Francis Mitford"; "Notes of a Surgeon";
    "A Hotel Dinner"; "The Old Town Pump";
    "Love in a Lazzaret"; "The Old Family

Clock. A Tale of the Past"; "The Crayon
  Papers" [W. Irving]; "Mocha Dick: Or,
  the White Whale of the Pacific"; "Sleepy
  Hollow. By Geoffrey Crayon, Gent"
  [W. Irving]; "The Birds of Spring. By
  Geoffrey Crayon, Gent" [W. Irving]; "The
  History of Drusilla Darracott"; "The
  Country Doctor"; "The Day-Dream of a
  Grocer"; "The Quod Correspondence";
  "Edward Alford and His Play-Fellow"; "The
  Hermit of Cetara"; "The Polygon Papers";
  "The Mail-Robber"; "The Legend of Don
  Roderick" [W. Irving]; "Adventures of a
  Yankee Doodle"; "Ned Buntline's Life-
  Yarn"; "The Saint-Leger Papers"; "Mr.
  Manning's Ramble: A Tale of the Past";
  "The Egyptian Letters"; "The Oregon Trail,
  or a Summer Out of Bounds" [Francis
  Parkman, Jr.].
Miscellaneous: Extracts: from other jour-
  nals; by various authors. Anecdotes: on
  various subjects. Literary Notices.
  News: Foreign and Domestic.
Note: Some of the leading contributors were:
  William Leggett, Willis Gaylord Clark,
  W. Irving, Bryant, James Kirke Paulding,
  Charles Fenno Hoffman, Nathaniel P. Willis,
  Fitz-Greene Halleck, Mathew Carey, Ben-
  jamin Rush, William Dunlap, Bayard Taylor,
  William E. Burton, Oliver Wendell Holmes.

379   TITLE: The Ladies' Album. [See American
      Lady's Album and Gentlemen's Parlor
      Miscellany.]

380   TITLE: The Ladies' & Gentlemen's Pocket
      Magazine of Literary & Polite Amusement.
      [See The Lady & Gentleman's Pocket Magazine
      of Literary and Polite Amusement.]

381   TITLES: (1) The Ladies' Companion, a Monthly
      Magazine, Embracing Every Department of
      Literature. Embellished with Original
      Engravings, and Music Arranged for the
      Piano-Forte, Harp and Guitar (2) The
      Ladies' Companion, and Literary Expositor;
      a Monthly Magazine Embracing Every Depart-
      ment of Literature. Embellished with
      Original Engravings, and Music Arranged for
      the Piano Forte, Harp and Guitar.

      Place of Publication: New York
      First Issue: May 1834
      Last Issue: Oct 1844//
      Periodicity: Monthly
      Editors: William W. Snowden; Emma C. Embury;
            Lydia H. Sigourney
      Publisher: William W. Snowden
      Available From: Lib. Co. of Philadelphia
                      Lib. of Congress. Mott.
      Contents:
        Poetry: Original: Grenville Mellen, Park
          Benjamin, Isaac C. Pray, Jr., Mary Anne
          Browne, Lydia H. Sigourney, Ann S.
          Stephens, Seba Smith, Hannah F. Gould,
          Caroline F. Orne, John Pierpont, Char-
          lotte Cushman, Frances S. Osgood, Charles
          Sherry, Horatio Gates, Samuel Woodworth,

James F. Otis, H.T. Tuckerman, Albert
Pike, Rufus Dawes, Robert Hamilton,
William B. Tappan, Mary E. Hewitt,
J.H. Clinch, T.S. Arthur, Emma C.
Embury, William Gilmore Simms, George
Pope Morris, J.N. M'Jilton, Longfellow,
Henry B. Hirst, Epes Sargent, Thomas
Dunn English, Anna Cora Mowatt, William
G. Howard, A.D. Woodbridge, Henfy J.
Bedlow. Selected: James Hogg, Burns,
Dryden, Byron.
Prose: Biography: Felicia Hemans. Essay.
Familiar Essay. Book Reviews.
Fiction: Essay Serials: "Sketches by
Lamp-Light" [John Neal]; "Dots and
Lines"; "Our Library" [Emma C. Embury];
"Sketches in the west"; "Leaves from a
Table-Book" [Nathaniel P. Willis];
"Theatricals." Sketches. Tales: "The
Deluded"; "True Honor--A Tale"; "Here-
ward, the Hunter"; "The Lost Diamond";
"Angling; or, the Story of a Country
Girl" [Seba Smith]; "The First and Second
Wife; or, the Confessions of a Discon-
tended Man" [Emma C. Embury]; "Memat-
tanon; or, Jack of the Feather. An
Indian Tale of Virginia"; "Is't My
Nephew, or Not?"; "Northington, a Tale
of the Seventeenth Century" [Caroline F.
Orne]; "Alfred, the Gipsy"; "The Female
Spy; a Domestic Tale of the Revolutionary
War"; "Love in a Cottage"; "The Charib
Bride; a Legend of Hispaniola"; "Mid-
night in the Wilderness. A Tale of
1688"; "The Queen's Vow. A Tale of
Elizabeth"; "Mary Derwent. A Tale of
the Early Settlers"; "The Gamester's
Fortune"; "A Legend of the Passaic";
"The Haunted Homestead"; "The Chain of
Gold. A Tale of Truth"; "The Unsummoned
Witness"; "The Birgin's Vengeance. A
Tale"; "Correggio"; "Love and Friendship;
or, the Heart's Ordeal"; "Lucy Wieland";
"Alice Copley. A Tale of Queen Mary's
Time"; "Rapin of the Rock; or, the Out-
law of the Ohio. A Tale of the 'Cave-
in-Rock'"; "The Embroidered Mantle";
"The Wife's Duty. A Tale of the
Mississippi"; "Sebastian Bach and His
Family"; "The Jewess of Cairo"; "Biddy
Woodhull; or, the Pretty Hay-Maker. A
Tale"; "The Tie of Honor"; "The Pre-
destined Bachelor"; "Caroline Renton. A
Tale of the Revolution"; "Annette Delancy";
"Anna Leslie"; "A Family of the Street
of Sevres"; "Jem Thalimer's Female Ward;
or the Inconvenience of Having Two
Characters" [Nathaniel P. Willis];
"Arnold; or, the British Spy. A Tale of
Treachery and Treason"; "Flora Lester;
or, Scenes in the Life of a Belle"; "The
Toll-House; or, Romance and Reality";
"The Cousins; or, a Tale of Passion";
"The Romance of Carolina"; "Charles
Willett; a Tale of the Revolution"; "The
Landscape-Garden" [Poe]; "The Ghost Ball"
[Nathaniel P. Willis]; "The Mystery of
Marie Roget" [Poe]; "The Ups and Downs
of Lot Wyman."

Miscellaneous: Extracts: from other journals; by various authors; S. Johnson,
Sterne, Nathaniel P. Willis. Anecdotes:
on various subjects. Literary Notices.

382 TITLES: (1) The Ladies' Garland, Devoted to
Literature, Amusement and Instruction,
Containing Original Essays, Female Bio-
graphy, Historical Narratives, Sketches of
Society, Topographical Descriptions, Moral
Tales, Anecdotes, &c., Poetry, Original
and Selected, &c., &c. (2) The Ladies'
Garland, and Family Magazine (3) The
Ladies' Garland and Dollar Magazine. A
Monthly Journal (4) The Ladies' Garland
and Family Wreath Embracing Tales, Sketches,
Incidents, History, Poetry, Music, etc.

Place of Publication: Philadelphia
First Issue: 15 April 1837
Last Issue: Dec 1850//
Periodicity: Semi-monthly; Monthly
Editors: John Libby; J. Van Court; Samuel
D. Patterson
Publishers: John Libby; J. Van Court;
Samuel D. Patterson
Available From: APS; N.Y. Pub. Lib. Mott.
Contents:
Poetry: Original: Lydia J. Pierson, Lydia
H. Sigourney, Thomas McKellar, J. Burgin,
James Lumbard, Thomas L. Harris, Almira
H. Andrews, James Russell Lowell, Char-
lotte B. Gage, Jaenette M. Browne,
Angeline Cargin, E. Sherman Keeney, J.N.
Terwilliger, Oliver Crane, David Rice,
Ida Vale, H.B. Wildman, E.T. Fletcher,
T.S. Arthur. Selected: Horace Smith,
Jane Taylor, Thomas Haynes Bayly, Bryant,
Eliza Cook, Thomas Moore, Schiller,
Shelley, L.E. Landon, Susan Wilson, Henry
James Bogue, Longfellow, M.L. Gardiner,
Robert Josselyn, M.A. Townsend, Cole-
ridge, Margaret M'Nary, Park Benjamin,
Mary Collins, Caroline Gilman, Charles
Wolfe, E. Yates Reese, Catharine H.
Waterman, George D. Prentice, Caroline
Norton, George W. Patten, Almira Porter,
Mary Howitt, Charles Jeffreys, A.N.
Messenger, Charles Swain, Samuel Wood-
worth, S.E. Southerland, Whittier, Robert
Gilfillan, Oliver Wendell Holmes, Fitz-
Greene Halleck, Richard Howitt, James R.
Ludlow, Henry H. Paul, Emily Hermann,
D.H. Barlow, Barrick, Ralph Hoyt, S.J.
Howe, Charles MacKay, Anna Blackwell,
H.H. Clements, Barry Cornwall, Willis
Gaylord Clark, John Westall, Hannah F.
Gould, William Leggett, James Aldrich,
Lewis J. Cist, W.G.J. Barker, William
Cutter, James Montgomery, Edward Young,
Bernard Barton, Nathaniel P. Willis,
Anna Savage, Elizabeth Barrett.
Prose: Biography. Travel. Essay.
Familiar Essay.
Fiction: Sketches. Tales: "The Stranger's
Grave"; "The Fallen Chief"; "The Lost
Flowers"; "Isola Bella"; "Bishop George
and the Young Preacher"; "The Little

Hunch-Back Girl"; "The Lost Child"; "The Village Pastor's Wife"; "The Charter"; "The Fortunes of the Maid of Arc"; "The Contrast"; "Romantic New England Legend"; "The Blind Boy"; "The Outcast"; "Germantown"; "The Separation"; "The Temptations of Rachel Morrison"; "Judge Crane and the Landlady"; "Estelle"; "A Story of Real Life"; "The Mother and Her Children"; "The Cousins"; "The Sabbath Wreckers"; "The Dead of Separation"; "Grace Wentworth"; "The Locksmith of Philadelphia"; "The Blighted One"; "The Black Veil"; "The Recluse of Nazareth"; "The Wife's Promise"; "The Lover's Talisman"; "The Boar's Back"; "They Say"; "Lucy Austin"; "The Baronet's Bride"; "The First and Last Quarrel"; "The Anaconda"; "The Veteran's Tale"; "The Horse Blanket"; "Cousin Kate"; "Emily Waters"; "The Night Watch"; "The Life Boat"; "A Tale of Real Life"; "The Warning"; "Fanny Grey"; "The Victims of Inebriation"; "The Montreal Merchant"; "The Doale, and the Mother"; "Kate Elliott"; "Louisa;--Or, My First Love"; "The Palsied Heart"; "The Uncouth Friend"; "Louisa Dennison"; "The Death of a Sister"; "The Pocket Bible"; "The Brown Mug"; "The Gold Chain"; "A Tale of a Tea Kettle"; "The Stolen Child"; "Hzynomia"; "Adah.--A Tradition of Albania"; "The Lady of Elm-Wood"; "The Sabbath Day Wedding."
Miscellaneous: Extracts: from other journals; by various authors. Anecdotes: on various subjects. News: Foreign and Domestic.

383   TITLE: The Ladies' Garland, Devoted to Miscellaneous Literature, but Principally Designed for the Edification and Improvement of Females, and to Them Respectfully Dedicated by the Editor.

Place of Publication: Harpers Ferry, Va.
First Issue: 14 Feb 1824
Last Issue: 7 June 1828//
Periodicity: Weekly
Editor: John S. Gallaher
Publisher: John S. Gallaher
Available From: APS; Lib. of Congress
Contents:
  Poetry: Original. Selected: Bernard Barton, Alaric Watts, James Montgomery, James G. Brooks, Thomas Campbell, R.B. Sheridan, William B. Tappan, Scott, Thomas Paine, John Bowring, Joshua Marsden, John Quincy Adams, Edward Everett, Felicia Hemans, Charles Sprague, Byron, Southey, Samuel Rodgers, James G. Percival.
  Prose: Biography. Essay. Familiar Essay.
  Fiction: Sketches. Tales: "The Broken Vow. A Village Tale"; "The Return"; "The Son and Heir"; "A Story for the Irascible"; "The Forrest of Warriors . . . A Tale"; "The Head and Heart"; "The Widow of Zebra"; "Sophia, or the Girl of the Pine Woods"; "Amelie"; "Lucy Mar"; "Friendship

Carried to an Imprudent Length"; "The Shipwreck"; "The Bleeding Heart"; "The Generous Mask, a Tale Initiated from the German"; "The Gamester"; "Eugenia de Mirande. An Interesting Story"; "Love's Victim"; "The Shrieking Ghost"; "Adem dai"; "The Grave-Yard"; "Decision--A Tale"; "Jenny Kelly"; "The Last Herring"; "Ellerslie Cottage"; "The Indian Boy"; "Caleb and Matilda. A Tale of the Revolution"; "The Savoyards. Or, a Journey to Mont Blanc"; "Guilio, a Tale"; "Rosina Vangorden, or the Offspring of a Daughter"; "The Lovers' Quarrel"; "The Wanderer's Return."
Miscellaneous: Extracts: from other journals; by various authors; Schiller, Felicia Hemans, W. Irving, Sidney. Anecdotes: on various subjects. Literary Notices.

384   TITLES: (1) The Ladies' Literary Cabinet, Being a Miscellaneous Repository of Literary Productions, in Prose and Verse (2) The Ladies' Literary Cabinet, Being a Repository of Miscellaneous Literary Productions, Both Original and Selected, in Prose and Verse.

Place of Publication: New York
First Issue: 15 May 1819
Last Issue: 21 Dec 1822//?
Periodicity: Weekly
Editor: Samuel Woodworth
Publishers: Woodworth & Huestis; Nathaniel Smith & Co.
Available From: APS; Amer. Antiquarian Soc. Mott.
Contents:
  Poetry: Original: Samuel Woodworth. Selected: Erasmus Darwin, Goldsmith.
  Prose: Biography. Essay. Familiar Essay. Criticism. Letters. Book Reviews.
  Fiction: Essay Serials: "The Trifler"; "Leisure Hours"; "The Miscellanist"; "The Selector"; "The Essayist." Sketches. Tales: "The Caliph Almanser, or, How to Judge of Men. A Tale"; "Josephine. A Tale of Truth"; "Love and Generosity, a Tale, Founded on Fact"; "Kedar and Amela, an Arabian Tale" "The Happy Pair; an Idyll"; "Martius and Sophia"; "Resignation. An Original Tale" [Samuel Woodworth]; "The Fair Maniac"; "The Wife of a Genius, a True Tale"; "Clarinda; a Tale for Young Ladies"; "Norwegian Tale"; "The Marauder." Novels: "Magnanimity. An Original Novel" [Samuel Woodworth]; "Rural Amusements; or, Rustic Holidays."
  Miscellaneous: Extracts: from other journals; by various authors; Kotzebue, W. Irving, Washington Allston. Anecdotes: on various subjects; Charles Churchill, Maria Edgeworth, Buonaparte, R.B. Sheridan, Franklin, Joseph Dennie, Washington, Lady Mary Wortley Montagu, Goldsmith, Garrick, Swift, S. Johnson, Byron. Literary Notices.

385 TITLES: (1) <u>Ladies' Literary Museum; or
Weekly Repository</u> (2) <u>Lady's and Gentle-
man's Weekly Museum, and Philadelphia
Reporter</u> (3) <u>Lady's and Gentleman's
Weekly Literary Museum and Musical Maga-
zine</u> (4) <u>Literary & Musical Magazine</u>.

Place of Publication: Philadelphia
First Issue: 5 July 1817
Last Issue: 9 June 1820//?
Periodicity: Weekly
Editor: Henry C. Lewis
Publisher: Henry C. Lewis
Available From: APS; Hist. Soc. of Pa.
Contents:
  Poetry: <u>Original</u>. <u>Selected</u>: R.S. Coffin,
    Thomas Campbell, James Montgomery,
    E.T. Pilgrim, Richard Cumberland, Della
    Crusca, Thomas Moore, Henry C. Lewis.
  Prose: <u>Biography</u>: Amelia Opie. <u>Familiar
    Essay</u>. <u>Criticism</u>. <u>Letters</u>.
  Fiction: <u>Essay Serials</u>: "The Olio. By
    Marmaduke Medley, Esq. and Others"; "The
    Humbug Society"; "Musical Sketches."
    <u>Tales</u>: "Othma and Eugenia, or, the
    Village Maniac"; "Alphea . . . A Tale";
    "The Cottager's Wife"; "Zaida--A
    Romance"; "The Legends of Lampidosa";
    "The Adventures of a Night. A Romance";
    "Albert, the Romantic Enthusiast. A
    Tale"; "Westerville and Louisa; or, the
    Temple of Sensibility"; "The Kiss: Or
    Mohamasim the Ass-Driver"; "The Wild
    Boar, and the Crafty and Valiant Welchman.
    A Humorous Tale." <u>Novels</u>: "The White
    Cottage. A Novel"; "Family Events, or a
    Friend in Need. A Novelette"; "The
    Isolated Lovers. A Novel."
  Miscellaneous: <u>Extracts</u>: from other jour-
    nals; by various authors; Kotzebue,
    Goldsmith. <u>Anecdotes</u>: on various sub-
    jects; Swift, Voltaire, Bunyan, Joshua
    Reynolds. <u>Literary Notices</u>. <u>News</u>:
    Domestic.

386 TITLES: (1) <u>The Ladies' Literary Port Folio</u>
(2) <u>The Literary Port Folio</u> [Running title:
Philadelphia Port Folio: A Weekly Journal
of Literature, Science, Art, and the Times.
Absorbed by <u>The Album. And Ladies' Weekly
Gazette</u> q.v.]

Place of Publication: Philadelphia
First Issue: 10 Dec 1828
Last Issue: 9 Dec 1829//
Periodicity: Weekly
Editors: Thomas Cottrell Clarke; Robert
        Morris; Eliakim Littell
Publisher: Eliakim Littell
Available From: Lib. of Congress*; Hist.
        Soc. of Pa.* Mott.
Contents:
  Poetry: <u>Original</u>: Harriet Muzzy, Nathaniel
    P. Willis, Daniel Bryan, Thomas Cottrell
    Clarke, James G. Brooks, Thomas Haynes
    Bayly, Willis Gaylord Clark, Charles
    Swain. <u>Selected</u>: Maria Edgeworth,
    Felicia Hemans, James Montgomery,
    George Wither, James G. Percival,
    Fitz-Greene Halleck, Robert Treat Paine,

William Leggett, Lydia H. Sigourney,
Wordsworth, Mary Anne Browne, Matthew
Gregory [Monk] Lewis, S.G. Goodrich,
Hannah F. Gould, Mary Howitt, Robert
Montgomery, Thomas Pringle, Thomas
Moore, John G. Brainard.
  Prose: <u>Biography</u>: Thomas Moore. <u>Essay</u>.
    <u>Familiar Essay</u>. <u>Criticism</u>. <u>Book Reviews</u>.
  Fiction: <u>Sketches</u>. <u>Tales</u>: "The Ship-
    wreck'd Wanderer"; "Stage Coach Acquaint-
    ance"; "The Zantoete Lovers"; "Lost and
    Won" [Mary Russell Mitford]; "Mary
    Harvey. A Tale of Other Times"; "A Tale
    of the West"; "Polydore Crosey"; "The
    Last of the Moystons"; "The Ten Piastres";
    "The Renegade"; "Cousin Mary" [Mary
    Russell Mitford]; "The Castilian Captive";
    "The Pirates, or, Errors of Public
    Justice"; "Caroline St. Amand"; "The
    First and Last Kiss"; "The Halt on the
    Mountain. A Tale of the Spanish War";
    "The Fisherman's Daughter"; "First and
    Last Love"; "A Tale of Resignation, or,
    the Heart of Gold"; "Walter Errick";
    "The Pride of Woodburn. A Simple Tale";
    "Jack the Shrimp."
  Miscellaneous: <u>Extracts</u>: from other jour-
    nals; by various authors; Shelley, James
    Fenimore Cooper, Thomas Paine.
    <u>Anecdotes</u>: on various subjects.

387 TITLE: <u>Ladies Literary Repository. A Semi-
Monthly of Literature, Science, and the
Fine Arts</u>.

Place of Publication: Lowell, Mass.
First Issue: [Only two issues published?]
        1841//
Available From: Boston Pub. Lib.

388 TITLES: (1) <u>The Ladies' Magazine</u> (2) <u>The
Ladies' Magazine, and Literary Gazette</u>
(3) <u>American Ladies' Magazine; Containing
Tales, Essays, Literary and Historical
Sketches, Poetry, Criticism, Music, and a
Great Variety of Matter Connected with Many
Subjects of Importance and Interest</u>.
[Merged into <u>Godey's Lady's Book</u> q.v.]

Place of Publication: Boston
First Issue: Jan 1828
Last Issue: Dec 1836//
Periodicity: Monthly
Editor: Sarah J. Hale
Publishers: Putnam & Hunt; Marsh, Caper &
        Lyon; James B. Dow
Available From: APS; Lib. of Congress.*
        Mott.
Contents:
  Poetry: <u>Original</u>: Lydia H. Sigourney,
    Hannah F. Gould, Sarah J. Hale.
    <u>Selected</u>: Schiller, William Congreve,
    William Cowper, N.H. Carter, Anna Maria
    Wells, Felicia Hemans, L.M. Francis,
    Lydia H. Sigourney, Stella Phelps, E.F.
    Ellet, Sarah J. Hale, Thomas R. Hofland,
    E.B. Kenrick, Emma Willard, William H.
    Willis, Jane E. Locke, Clement Durgin.

Prose: Biography: Joanna Baillie, Felicia
Hemans. Travel. Essay. Familiar Essay.
Criticism. Letters. Book Reviews.
Fiction: Essay Serials: "Scraps from a
Port-Folio"; "The Manuscript"; "Recollec-
tions"; "Conversations at the Fireside";
"Domestic Sketches." Sketches. Tales:
"The Fair Eckbert"; "The Brother";
"Legend of the White Mountains"; "The
Grave of Moran"; "The Deaf Girl"; "The
Good Match"; "Flirtation"; "The Tea Party";
"Woman's Constancy"; "Alexander Standish;
or, Love in the Olden Times"; "The
Warning"; "The Nocturnal Rescue"; "The
Brownie of Cawdor Castle"; "The Spectre";
"The Two Sister of Scio"; "Clarence, or a
Tale of Our Own Time"; "The First Grave
of the Hamlet"; "Laura Brodlee"; "The
Satin Pelisse"; "Catherine Wells"; "The
Pearl Necklace"; "The Idiot"; "The Dead
Hand"; "The Dark Closet"; "The Deserted
Child"; "The Three Cornelias"; "The
Bachelor's Excuse"; "The Brothers"; "The
Twin Sisters"; "The Prisoner"; "The
Farmer and His Sons"; "A Persian Apologue";
"The Good Goaler"; "Mrs. Morey. A New
Year's Story"; "No Steamboats--A Vision"
[James Fenimore Cooper]; "A Vision of
Human Happiness"; "The Country Cousin";
"Margaret Campbell"; "Alice Goodwin and
Balch the Drover"; "The Distiller's
Family"; "Estelle Aubert"; "The Botanizing
Party"; "Ellen Orne, a Domestic Tale";
"Agnes Staunton"; "The Broken Merchant";
"The New-Year's Gift"; "The Deacon's
Daughter"; "The Gambler's Wife"; "Lost
Beauty"; "Mary Clinton"; "Marriage of
Madame Roland"; "My Friend's Wife";
"Poor Mary.--A Mother's Story"; "The First
Need of Fame"; "The Pickletons"; "The
Deaf and Blind: A Tale of Truth"; "A
Letter from Aunt Lodemia Wilkins"; "A
Lawyer's Revenge"; "The Merchant's Wife";
"Embroidery Versus Turtle-Soup: Or,
Woman in Her Proper Sphere"; "The Fron-
tier House"; "The Two Suitors"; "Ellen
Montford"; "Agnes Montalban; or, the
Ambitious Mother."
Miscellaneous: Extracts: from other
journals; by various authors. Anecdotes:
on various subjects. Literary Notices.

389 TITLE: Ladies' Magazine.

Place of Publication: Savannah, Ga.
First Issue: 13 Feb 1819
Last Issue: 7 Aug 1819//
Available From: Duke Univ., Durham*;
Rutgers Univ., New
Brunswick, N.J.

390 TITLE: The Ladies' Magazine and Album.
[See American Lady's Album and Gentlemen's
Parlor Miscellany.]

391 TITLE: The Ladies' Magazine and Album. Devoted to the Arts, Science, Music, Painting,
Religion and Literature. [See American
Lady's Album and Gentlemen's Parlor Miscellany.]

392 TITLE: The Ladies' Magazine, and Literary
Gazette. [See The Ladies' Magazine.]

393 TITLE: The Ladies' Magazine of Literature,
Fashion and Domestic Economy. [See Miss
Leslie's Magazine; Home Book of Fashion,
Literature and Domestic Economy.]

394 TITLES: (1) The Ladies' Mirror (2) The
Ladies' Mirror. Embracing a Choice Collection of Original and Selected Matter, Adap-
ted to the Different Branches of Polite
Literature. Containing Not an Idea That
Would Tend to "Give virtue scandal, innocence a fear,/Or from the soft-eyed virgin
steal a tear" (3) The Ladies' Mirror, Devoted Exclusively to the Different Branches
of Polite Literature (4) The Ladies' Mirror; Devoted Exclusively to the Different
Branches of Polite Literature--Embracing a
Choice Collection of Original and Selected
Matter (5) The Ladies' Mirror: A Literary
and Miscellaneous Magazine.

Place of Publication: Southbridge, Mass.;
Woonsocket Falls, R.I.
First Issue: 28 Aug 1830
Last Issue: 1 Jan 1834//?
Periodicity: Semi-monthly
Editor: William Northup Sherman
Publishers: George W.H. Fisk; Milton Joslin;
Sherman & Wilder
Available From: Amer. Antiquarian Soc.;
Brown Univ., Providence
Contents:
Poetry: Original. Selected: Harriet
Muzzy, Byron, Thomas Moore, Sarah J. Hale,
Whittier, Mary E. Brooks, Mary Anne Browne,
J.O. Rockwell, Thomas Haynes Bayly. L.E.
Landon, B.B. Thatcher, Thomas Roscoe,
William Leggett, Samuel Woodworth, John
Bowring, Willis Gaylord Clark, Nathaniel
P. Willis, Felicia Hemans, Joseph Rodman
Drake, Bryant, Robert Morris, Park
Benjamin, Caroline Norton, Hannah F.
Gould, James G. Percival, George D.
Prentice, Freneau, Barry Cornwall.
Prose: Biography: W. Irving. Familiar
Essay. Criticism: on W. Irving.
Fiction: Sketches. Tales: "The Forsaken
Girl" [Whittier]; "St. Maur.--A Tale of
Truth" [Lydia H. Sigourney]; "The Confes-
sions of a Suicide" [Whittier]; "Henry
St. Clair" [Whittier]; "The Forged Note;
or Arthur Mowbray"; "Everard Graham";
"The Lace Cravat"; "The Soldier's Bride";
"Waldstein's Mount. A Swiss Tale"; "The

Maniac Criminal"; "William Lawrence"; "A Tale of the Aborigines"; "The Captive Regained. A Tale of the Last War"; "The Keeper of the Prison-Ship Jersey"; "The Veteran's Reward"; "The Inkeeper's Story"; "The Palatine"; "Jean St. Aubin"; "The Jew's Revenge"; "Washington and His Adjutant. A Tale of Other Days"; "The Outlaw of the Pines, a Tale of the Revolution"; "The Robber of the Rhine"; "The Brownie of Cawdor Castle"; "Story of the Young Robber" [W. Irving]; "Musa, or the Reformation" [James Kirke Paulding]; "Azim, an Oriental Tale."
  Miscellaneous: Extracts: from other journals; by various authors. Anecdotes: on various subjects. Literary Notices. News: Foreign and Domestic.

395 TITLE: The Ladies' Mirror: A Literary and Miscellaneous Magazine. [See The Ladies' Mirror.]

396 TITLE: Ladies' Miscellany.

Place of Publication: Salem, Mass.
First Issue: 7 Nov 1828
Last Issue: 30 March 1831//?
Periodicity: Weekly
Editors: ?
Publishers: ?
Available From: Lib. of Congress*; Amer. Antiquarian Soc.*
Contents:
  Poetry: Original. Selected: Nathaniel P. Willis, Felicia Hemans, James Montgomery, John G. Brainard, Fitz-Greene Halleck, Lydia H. Sigourney, Thomas Campbell, Barry Cornwall, Robert Montgomery, Hannah More, John Bowring, William Leggett, James G. Brooks, Whittier, Miss Jewsbury, James Hogg, Edward Fitzgerald, R.H. Wilde, James G. Percival, J.O. Rockwell, Samuel Woodworth, James N. Barker, Emily Taylor, Byron, Thomas Haynes Bayly, Sarah J. Hale, Bernard Barton, Scott, Mary Anne Browne, Timothy Flint, Caroline Norton, L.E. Landon, Hannah F. Gould, B.B. Thatcher, Goethe, Thomas Moore, Jane Taylor, Rufus Dawes.
  Prose: Familiar Essay. Letters.
  Fiction: Sketches. Tales: "The Monument. A Tale of Truth"; "Arthur Mordington"; "The Rose in January"; "The Covenanters. A Scottish Traditionary Tale"; "The Penitents"; "The Pride of the Village" [W. Irving]; "A Tale of the Deserted Isle"; "First and Last Crime"; "Harriet Bruce"; "The First and Last Kiss"; "The Nutshell. A Tale"; "Dora Creswell"; "The Martyr--A Historical Tale"; "Appearances Deceitful" [Kotzebue]; "A Tale of Truth" [Coleridge]; "Cosmo de Marlini. A Venetian Tale"; "Death of a Mother" [Richard Henry Dana]; St. Maur. . . . A Tale of Truth" [Lydia H. Sigourney]; "Henry and William Nelson"; "Expiation"; "The First Born"; "The Rival Mothers"; "Death at the Toilet."

Miscellaneous: Extracts: from other journals; by various authors. Anecdotes: on various subjects. Literary Notices.

397 TITLES: (1) The Ladies' Monitor (2) Lady's Monitor. [Superseded by The New York Journal and Weekly Monitor.]

Place of Publication: New York
First Issue: 8 Aug 1801
Last Issue: 29 May 1802//
Periodicity: Weekly
Editors: Isaac Newton Ralston; Phineas Heard
Publishers: Isaac Newton Ralston; Phineas Heard; Heard and Forman
Available From: APS; Amer. Antiquarian Soc.
Contents:
  Poetry: Original: John Davis. Selected: S. Johnson, Burns, William Hayley, Southey, R.B. Davis, Peter Pindar, Mary Robinson.
  Prose: Biography: David Humphreys, John Trumbull, Hannah More, Chatterton, Mary Wollstonecraft. Travel. Essay: "A Vindication of the Rights of Woman" [Mary Wollstonecraft]. Familiar Essay. Letters.
  Fiction: Essay Serials: "The Monitor"; "The Reflector"; "Gossipiana"; "The Plaintiff." Sketches. Tales: "The Ghost: A Tale. Founded on Fact"; "The Trials of Arden"; "The Witch of the Wold" [Charlotte Smith]. Novels: "The Beggar Girl: A Novel"; "Margaretta; or, the Village Maid"; "A Lesson on Concealment; or, Memoirs of Mary Selwyn" [Charles Brockden Brown].
  Miscellaneous: Extracts: from other journals. Anecdotes: on various subjects. Literary Notices.

398 TITLE: The Ladies Museum.

Place of Publication: Philadelphia
First Issue: 25 Feb 1800
Last Issue: 7 June 1800//
Periodicity: Weekly
Editor: Isaac Newton Ralston
Publisher: Isaac Newton Ralston
Available From: APS; Lib. Co. of Philadelphia.* Mott.
Contents:
  Poetry: Original: John Davis. Selected: John Gifford.
  Prose: Travel.
  Fiction: Sketches. Tales: "Tears of Gratitude"; "Zaydor. An Eastern Tale"; "Alphonso and Marina: An Interesting Spanish Tale"; "Cecilia Wevil. A Moral Tale."
  Miscellaneous: Extracts: from other journals. Anecdotes: on various subjects.
Note: Motto: "The Mind to Improve--And yet Amuse" [Same motto as The Ladies' Monitor q.v.]

399 TITLE: Ladies' Museum, and Western Repository of Belles Lettres.

Place of Publication: Cincinnati
First Issue: 1830
Last Issue: 25 Dec 1830//?
Available From: Western Reserve Hist. Soc.,
    Cleveland

400   TITLE: The Ladies Museum. Being a Repository
    of Miscellaneous Literary Productions, Both
    Original and Selected--In Prose and Verse.

Place of Publication: Providence, R.I.
First Issue: 16 July 1825
Last Issue: 22 July 1826//
Periodicity: Weekly
Editor: Eaton W. Maxcy
Publisher: Eaton W. Maxcy
Available From: APS; Amer. Antiquarian Soc.*
Contents:
    Poetry: Original. Selected: Thomas Moore,
      James G. Percival.
    Prose: Familiar Essay. Letters.
    Fiction: Essay Serial: "Reminiscences."
      Sketches. Tales: "Mandonoch--A Tale";
      "Frederick and Marianne. A Tale--Founded
      on Fact"; "Leucadea and Rodolpho."
    Miscellaneous: Extracts: from other jour-
      nals; by various authors; W. Irving.
      Anecdotes: on various subjects.

401   TITLE: The Ladies' Pearl: A Monthly Maga-
    zine. [See The Ladies' Pearl, and Literary
    Gleaner: A Collection of Tales, Sketches,
    Essays, Anecdotes, and Historical Inci-
    dents.]

402   TITLES: (1) The Ladies' Pearl, and Literary
    Gleaner: A Collection of Tales, Sketches,
    Essays, Anecdotes, and Historical Incidents
    (2) The Ladies' Pearl: A Monthly Magazine
    (3) The Lady's Pearl; a Monthly Magazine,
    Devoted to Moral, Entertaining and Instruc-
    tive Literature (4) The Lady's Pearl.
    Devoted to Moral, Entertaining, and Instruc-
    tive Literature.

Place of Publication: Lowell, Mass.
First Issue: June 1840
Last Issue: July 1843//?
Periodicity: Monthly
Editors: Daniel Wise; Mary A. Fletcher
Publishers: E.A. Rice & Co.; Rice & Wise;
        P.D. & T.S. Edmands
Available From: APS; Amer. Antiquarian Soc.
      Mott.
Contents:
    Poetry: Original: C. Theresa Clarke, Lydia
      H. Sigourney, Caroline F. Orne, Caroline
      L. North, Jane E. Locke, Whittier, William
      B. Tappan, M.L. Gardiner, Charles W.
      Denison. Selected: Hanna F. Gould,
      Lydia H. Sigourney, Joanna Baillie, Burns,
      Mrs. Seba Smith, William Cowper, Felicia
      Hemans, Coleridge, William Leggett,
      Eliza Cook, B. Jonson, Goldsmith, Words-
      worth, Scott, Barry Cornwall, Thomas
      Moore, George Pope Morris, Poe, James
      Montgomery, Schiller.

Prose: Biography: Burns, Hannah More,
    Caroline F. Orne. Essay. Familiar
    Essay.
Fiction: Sketches. Tales: "Athelwold and
    Elfrida, or the Ambitious Beauty"; "The
    Wreckers. A Cornish Tale"; "Alice
    Thornton, or the New Dress"; "The Trans-
    formed: Or, the Goth's Triumph"; "Lady
    Woodley, or the Children's Party"; "The
    Gipsy's Revenge"; "The Sheik's Revenge.
    An Eastern Tale"; "The Valley--The Hills.
    A Tragic Tale"; "The Two Beauties" [T.S.
    Arthur]; "As Good as Any Body"; "The Con-
    trast; or, the Blue Mantilla"; "Sarah
    Forest; or, the Guardian."
Miscellaneous: Extracts: from other jour-
    nals; by various authors; Amos Bronson
    Alcott, John Quincy Adams. Anecdotes:
    on various subjects; Penn, Scott,
    Goldsmith, Buonaparte.

403   TITLE: Ladies' Port Folio, Comprising a
    Variety of Useful and Entertaining Matter,
    Suitable for Both Sexes, and All Ages.

Place of Publication: Boston
First Issue: 1 Jan 1820
Last Issue: 8 July 1820//?
Periodicity: Weekly
Editor: Sylvester T. Goss
Publisher: Sylvester T. Goss
Available From: APS; Amer. Antiquarian Soc.
Contents:
    Poetry: Original. Selected: Southey,
      Byron, Franklin, Burns, Selleck Osborne.
    Prose: Biography. Letters. Book Reviews.
    Fiction: Essay Serials: "Domestic Sketch-
      es"; "The Desultory Contributor."
      Sketches. Tales: "Marcus and Monimia.
      A Tale"; "The Kiss: Or Mohamasim, the
      Ass Driver"; "The Narrative of Omar";
      "The Fair Maniac. A True Story"; "Henry:
      --A Tale"; "Inebriation: A Moral Tale";
      "The Loves of Seid and Sayda"; "Circum-
      stantial Evidence. A Tale"; "The Duel.
      A Tale"; "The Danger of Delay. A Tale,
      Founded on Facts"; "Henry and Emma. A
      Tale"; "The Cavern. A Tale of Other
      Times"; "Edward and Lucy. A Tale."
    Miscellaneous: Extracts: from other jour-
      nals; by various authors; Amelia Opie.
      Anecdotes: on various subjects. Literary
      Notices.

404   TITLE: The Ladies' Repository, and Gatherings
    of the West: A Monthly Periodical Devoted
    to Literature and Religion. [Superseded by
    The National Repository.]

Place of Publication: Cincinnati
First Issue: Jan 1841
Last Issue: Dec 1876//
Periodicity: Monthly
Editor: L.L. Hamline
Publishers: J.F. Wright and L. Swormstedt
Available From: APS; Lib. of Congress.*
      Mott.

Contents:
  Poetry: Original: Cornelia Augusta, George
    Waterman, William Baxter, Lucy Seymour,
    E.H. Hatcher, J.E. Edwards, John T.
    Brame, Lois B. Adams. Selected: Lydia
    H. Sigourney, Wordsworth, Dryden, James
    Hogg.
  Prose: Biography. Travel. Essay.
    Familiar Essay. Criticism.
  Fiction: Sketches.
  Miscellaneous: Extracts: from other
    journals; by various authors. Literary
    Notices.

405   TITLE: Ladies' Visiter.

Place of Publication: Marietta, Pa.
First Issue: 24 May 1819
Last Issue: 18 April 1820//
Periodicity: Monthly
Editor: William Peirce
Publisher: William Peirce
Available From: APS; Hist. Soc. of Pa.*
Contents:
  Poetry: Original. Selected: Scott,
    Goldsmith
  Prose: Biography: William Cowper. Essay.
    Familiar Essay. Letters.
  Fiction: Sketches. Tales: "Love Prefered
    to Fortune. A Sentimental Tale, Founded
    on Fact"; "Grasmere--A Tale"; "The
    Debtor.--A Tale"; "The Reformed Rake . . .
    A Tale."
  Miscellaneous: Extracts: from other jour-
    nals; by various authors; Sterne, Addison,
    Scott, Thomas Moore. Anecdotes: on
    various subjects.

406   TITLE: Ladies Visitor.

Place of Publication: Boston
First Issue: 4 Dec 1806
Last Issue: 28 Feb 1807//
Periodicity: Weekly
Editor: Ebenezer French
Publisher: Ebenezer French
Available From: APS; Lib. of Congress*
Contents:
  Poetry: Original. Poetry: Erasmus Darwin,
    Mary Robinson, Swift, William Shenstone,
    George Colman.
  Prose: Biography. Essay. Familiar Essay.
    Letters.
  Fiction: Essay Serial: "The Visitor."
    Sketches. Tales: "Albert and Emma, an
    Interesting History"; "The Hungry Arab.
    A Tale from the Tohfet Al Mojoilis."
  Miscellaneous: Extracts: from other jour-
    nals. Anecdotes: on various subjects.
    News: Domestic.

407   TITLE: The Ladies' Weekly Museum, or Polite
    Repository of Amusement and Instruction.
    [See The Impartial Gazetteer, and Saturday
    Evening's Post.]

408   TITLE: The Ladies' Wreath, a Magazine Devoted
    to Literature, Industry and Religion.

Place of Publication: New York
First Issue: May 1846
Last Issue: Jan 1862//
Periodicity: Monthly
Editor: Mrs. S.T. Martyn
Publishers: Martyn & Ely; J.C. Burdick;
            Burdick and Scovill
Available From: Amer. Antiquarian Soc.;
            Yale Univ. Mott.
Contents:
  Poetry: Original: M.L. Gardiner, Jane S.
    Woolsey, Anna E. Rodman, George S.
    Burleigh, E.M. Fargo, Miriam F. Hamilton,
    Lena Livingston, Frances P. Laughton,
    Lucy Larcom, Mary E. Linden, Jane Clifton,
    Sarah S. Lowell, Hannah E. Bradbury, Lydia
    H. Sigourney. Selected: Ann S. Stephens,
    Wordsworth, Coleridge, Longfellow, James
    G. Percival, Thomas Hood, Spenser, Frances
    S. Osgood, Lydia H. Sigourney, William D.
    Gallagher.
  Prose: Biography: Mary Russell Mitford,
    Jenny Lind, Catharine Hayes. Essay.
    Familiar Essay. Criticism. Letters.
  Fiction: Sketches. Tales: "Edith";
    "Pietro and Madalena"; "The Morning
    Ramble"; "Poor Kitty Gray, or the Warning
    Vision"; "Alice Reed"; "The Student's
    Dilemma"; "The Hill-Side Grave"; "Broken
    Vows"; "Cousin Leonard"; "The Old Apple
    Tree"; "The Doctor's Wife"; "Love and
    Duty"; "Old Letters; or Aunt Amy's
    Reminiscence"; "Philip Carlton"; "Fruits
    of Sorrow: Or an Old Maid's Story";
    "Omnia Vincit Amor; or Labor"; "The Iron
    Ring. A Romance of an Unromantic Cen-
    tury"; "Alice--A Story of Our Village";
    "Cousin Sybil,--Or, Who Is the Lady?";
    "The Lost Talisman"; "Riches Without
    Wings"; "The Evening Before Marriage";
    "The Yankee Girl."
  Miscellaneous: Anecdotes: on various sub-
    jects. Literary Notices.

409   TITLES: (1) The Lady & Gentleman's Pocket
    Magazine of Literary and Polite Amusement
    (2) The Ladie's & Gentlemen's Pocket Maga-
    zine of Literary & Polite Amusement   (3) The
    Lady's & Gentleman's Pocket Magazine of
    Literary & Polite Amusement.

Place of Publication: New York
First Issue: 15 August 1796
Last Issue: Nov 1796//
Periodicity: Monthly
Editors: J. Fellows; J. Lyon
Publishers: J. Fellows; J. Lyon
Available From: APS; Yale Univ.* Mott.
Contents:
  Poetry: Original. Selected.
  Prose: Biography. Essay: "Hints to Young
    Authors." Familiar Essay.
  Fiction: Sketches. Tale: "A Tale Address-
    ed to the Novel Readers of the Present
    Time."
  Miscellaneous: Literary Notices.

410 TITLE: <u>Lady's and Gentleman's Weekly Literary</u>
<u>Museum and Musical Magazine</u>. [See <u>Ladies'</u>
<u>Literary Museum</u>; or <u>Weekly Repository</u>.]

411 TITLE: <u>Lady's and Gentleman's Weekly Museum,</u>
<u>and Philadelphia Reporter</u>. [See <u>Ladies'</u>
<u>Literary Museum</u>; or <u>Weekly Repository</u>.]

412 TITLE: <u>Lady's Book</u>. [See <u>Godey's Magazine</u>.]

413 TITLE: <u>The Lady's Magazine and Musical</u>
<u>Repository</u>.

Place of Publication: New York
First Issue: Jan 1801
Last Issue: June 1802//
Periodicity: Monthly
Editor: N. Bell
Publishers: G. & R. Waite
Available From: APS; Lib. Co. of Philadel-
　　　　　　　　phia.* Mott.
Contents:
　Poetry: <u>Original</u>. <u>Selected</u>: Robert
　　Bloomfield, S. Johnson, James Thomson,
　　John Davis, Coleridge.
　Prose: <u>Biography</u>: Washington, Kotzebue.
　　<u>Essay</u>. <u>Familiar Essay</u>. <u>Criticism</u>.
　　<u>Letters</u>.
　Fiction: <u>Sketches</u>. <u>Tales</u>: "The Monk of
　　the Grotto"; "The Castle de Warrenne";
　　"The Maid of St. Marino"; "Bromley Melmot";
　　"The Cavern of Strozzi"; "The Generous
　　Sultana. An Arabian Tale"; "The Wooden
　　Leg: An Helvetic Tale"; "The Triumph
　　of Truth. A Tale"; "Hafez and Amina.
　　An Eastern Tale"; "Albert and Laura. A
　　Swiss Tale"; "The Sham Ghost"; "The Tur-
　　ban. A Turkish Tale." <u>Drama</u>: "All
　　Happiness Is Illusion. A Dramatic Anec-
　　dote" [Kotzebue].
　Miscellaneous: <u>Extracts</u>: from other jour-
　　nals; by various authors; Jefferson,
　　Edward Gibbon, Mary Wollstonecraft,
　　Jefferson. <u>Anecdotes</u>: on various sub-
　　jects; Kotzebue. <u>News</u>: Foreign and
　　Domestic.

414 TITLE: <u>The Lady's [Ladies] Magazine; and</u>
<u>Repository of Entertaining Knowledge</u>.

Place of Publication: Philadelphia
First Issue: June 1792
Last Issue: May 1793//
Periodicity: Monthly
Editor: W. Gibbons
Publisher: W. Gibbons
Available From: APS; Hist. Soc. of Pa.*
　　　　　　　　Mott.
Contents:
　Poetry: <u>Selected</u>: William Walsh.
　Prose: <u>Biography</u>. <u>Travel</u>. <u>Essay</u>.
　　<u>Familiar Essay</u>. <u>Criticism</u>: "On the
　　Nature and Essential Qualities of Poetry,
　　as Distinguished from Prose"; "On Female
　　Authorship." <u>Book Reviews</u>.

Fiction: <u>Essay Serials</u>: "The Essayist";
　"The Observer." <u>Sketches</u>. <u>Tales</u>: "The
　Old Soldier. An Oriental Tale"; "Selima.
　An Oriental Tale"; "The Eight Hundred and
　Seventy Ninth Lesson of the Philosopher
　Zumo: Or, the Inordinate Indulgence of
　Parents Severely Chastised. An Eastern
　Tale"; "Nouradin and Fatima. An Eastern
　Tale"; "Selico: An African Tale"; "The
　Misanthrope Reconciled to the World. A
　Tale"; "The Miseries of Going Abroad in
　Quest of Fortune. A Grecian Tale."
Miscellaneous: <u>Literary Notices</u>. <u>News</u>:
　Foreign and Domestic.

415 TITLE: <u>The Lady's Miscellany; or, Weekly</u>
<u>Visitor, and Entertaining Companion for the</u>
<u>Use and Amusement of Both Sexes</u>. [See <u>The</u>
<u>Weekly Visitor, or, Ladies' Miscellany</u>.
<u>Containing, Original and Selected Composi-</u>
<u>tions, in Prose and Verse, Designed Chiefly</u>
<u>to Improve the Minds and Amuse the Leisure</u>
<u>Hours of the Female Parts of Society</u>.]

416 TITLE: <u>Lady's Monitor</u>. [See <u>The Ladies'</u>
<u>Monitor</u>.]

417 TITLE: <u>The Lady's Pearl; a Monthly Magazine,</u>
<u>Devoted to Moral, Entertaining and Instruc-</u>
<u>tive Literature</u>. [See <u>The Ladies' Pearl,</u>
<u>and Literary Gleaner: A Collection of Tales,</u>
<u>Sketches, Essays, Anecdotes, and Historical</u>
<u>Incidents</u>.]

418 TITLE: <u>The Lady's Pearl. Devoted to Moral,</u>
<u>Entertaining, and Instructive Literature</u>.
[See <u>The Ladies' Pearl, and Literary</u>
<u>Gleaner: A Collection of Tales, Sketches,</u>
<u>Essays, Anecdotes, and Historical Incidents</u>.]

419 TITLE: <u>The Lady's Weekly Miscellany</u>. [See
<u>The Weekly Visitor, or, Ladies' Miscellany</u>.
<u>Containing, Original and Selected Composi-</u>
<u>tions, in Prose and Verse, Designed Chiefly</u>
<u>to Improve the Minds and Amuse the Leisure</u>
<u>Hours of the Female Parts of Society</u>.]

420 TITLES: (1) <u>Lady's Western Magazine, and</u>
<u>Garland of the Valley</u> (2) <u>Lady's Western</u>
<u>Magazine</u>.

Place of Publication: Cincinnati; Chicago;
　　　　　　　　　　　　Milwaukee
First Issue: Jan 1849
Last Issue: June 1849//?
Periodicity: Monthly
Editors: Benjamin F. Taylor; J.E. Hurlbut
Publishers: Benjamin F. Taylor; J.E. Hurlbut
Available From: APS; Duke Univ. Mott.
Contents:
　Poetry: <u>Original</u>. <u>Selected</u>: R.H. Stoddard,
　　William H. Bushnell, W.B. Fairchild,
　　Frances A. Fuller, Edwin Heriot, Barry

Cornwall, Benjamin F. Taylor, Thomas
Hood, Oliver Wendell Holmes, Henry A.
Clark.
Prose: Biography. Essay. Familiar Essay.
Fiction: Sketches. Tales: "Laetitia";
"The Comforter"; "The Casket of Jewels
Returned"; "The Dark Lady"; "'What Shall
I Be?' Two Pictures from the Past"; "Ho!
For California"; "The Gold Seekers of
the Sacramento."
Miscellaneous: Extracts: from other jour-
nals; by various authors; E. Lytton
Bulwer, Lamartine. Literary Notices.

421   TITLE: The Lay-Man's Magazine.

Place of Publication: Martinsburgh, Va.
First Issue: 16 Nov 1815
Last Issue: 7 Nov 1816//?
Periodicity: Weekly
Editors: ?
Publishers: ?
Available From: APS; Duke Univ.*
Contents:
Poetry: Original. Selected: James
Montgomery.
Prose: Travel. Familiar Essay. Letters.
Fiction: Sketches. Tales: "The Cottager's
Wife"; "The Dairyman's Daughter, an Auth-
entic and Interesting Narrative"; "A
True Account of a Pious Negro"; "The
Young Cottager."
Miscellaneous: Extracts: from other jour-
nals. Anecdotes: on various subjects;
S. Johnson.

422   TITLE: The Legendary, Consisting of Original
Pieces, Principally Illustrative of American
History, Scenery, and Manners.

Place of Publication: Boston
First Issue: [Only two issues published?]
1828//?
Periodicity: Intended to be Quarterly
Editor: Nathaniel P. Willis
Publisher: S.G. Goodrich
Available From: Conn. Hist. Soc., Hartford*;
Boston Pub. Lib.*
Contents:
Poetry: Original: Joseph H. Nichols,
I. M'Lellan, Jr., J.W. Miller, Robert
Morris, Fitz-Greene Halleck, Willis
Gaylord Clark, Nathaniel P. Willis,
E.P. Blount, William Grigg, William
Cutter, Henry Pickering, S.G. Goodrich,
Grenville Mellen. Selected: Bryant,
Wordsworth, Lydia H. Sigourney.
Prose: Essay. Criticism.
Fiction: Sketches. Tales: "The Church
in the Wilderness"; "The Rapids";
"Romance in Real Life"; "The Palisadoes";
"The Indian Wife"; "The Conscript
Brothers"; "The Murderer's Grave"; "The
Camp Meeting"; "The Schoolmaster"; "The
Siege of Soleure"; "Elizabeth Latimer."
Miscellaneous: Extracts: by various
authors. Literary Notices.

423   TITLE: The Liberator.

Place of Publication: Boston
First Issue: 1 Jan 1831
Last Issue: 29 Dec 1865//
Periodicity: Weekly
Editor: William Lloyd Garrison
Publishers: William Lloyd Garrison; Oliver
Johnson; Isaac Knapp
Available From: APS; Amer. Antiquarian Soc.*
Mott.
Contents:
Poetry: Original. Selected: John G.
Brainard, Bryant, William Cowper, Whittier,
Anna Maria Wells, James Montgomery,
Felicia Hemans, John Bowering, Grenville
Mellen, Thomas Hood, Hannah F. Gould,
T.K. Hervey, Byron, Wordsworth, William
Collins, Coleridge, Abraham Cowley,
James Hogg, Joseph Rodman Drake, Shakes-
peare, B. Jonson, Milton, Pope, Thomas
Campbell, Alonzo Lewis, Scott, Goldsmith,
Nathaniel P. Willis, W. Irving, Southey,
Sidney, Phillis Wheatley, W.J. Snelling,
Leigh Hunt, Bernard Barton, Frances
Whipple, James G. Percival, David
Humphreys, Thomas Carew, Maria W. Stewart,
John Wilson, Barry Cornwall, Willis
Gaylord Clark, Nathaniel H. Carter,
Jane Taylor, Lydia H. Sigourney, Thomas
Haynes Bayly, Chateaubriand, Mary Howitt,
Shelley, Edward Young, John Moore,
Addison, George Herbert, Tennyson.
Prose: Biography: Phillis Wheatley,
Jefferson, Boswell. Travel. Familiar
Essay. Criticism. Letters. Book
Reviews.
Fiction: Essay Serials: "The Family
Circle"; "An Evening at Home." Sketches.
Tales: "Edward and Mary"; "The Rose";
"The Little Dog. A Fable"; "A True Tale
for Children"; "A Bear Story"; "Story of
1973"; "The Coliseum" [Shelley]; "Change
of Situations; or the Excellence of the
Golden Rule"; "Aunt Margery's Talk with
the Young Folks."
Miscellaneous: Extracts: from other jour-
nals; by various authors; Franklin,
Coleridge, Whittier, Hazlitt. Anecdotes:
on various subjects; Hazlitt, Melville,
Burns, William Cowper, Hume, Voltaire,
Franklin, Byron. Literary Notices.
News: Domestic.

424   TITLE: The Liberty Bell.

Place of Publication: Boston
First Issue: 1839
Last Issue: 1858//
Periodicity: Annually
Editors: ?
Publishers: American Anti-Slavery Society;
Massachusetts Anti-Slavery Fair
Available From: APS; Univ. of Pa.*

Contents:
  Poetry: Original: Henrietta Sargent,
    John Pierpont, Mary Clark, Harriet
    Winslow, William Lloyd Garrison, G.S.
    Burleigh, James Russell Lowell, William
    W. Story, David Lee Child, R.R. Madden,
    William Howitt, Emily Taylor, Elizabeth
    Poole, Harriet Martineau, Theodore Par-
    ker, Charles Follen, Mary Howitt, Susan
    Wilson, Maria White, Bernard Barton,
    J.W. Higginson, E.L. Follen, Lydia Maria
    Child, Ann Greene Chapman, Ann Warren
    Weston, Caroline Weston, Maria Weston
    Chapman, J.F. Clarke, J.B. Taylor.
    Selected: Elizabeth Barrett Browning,
    John Bowring, Richard Milnes, Longfellow,
    Andrew Crosse, Allen C. Spooner, Cassius
    M. Clay, Paul Flemming, John Quincy
    Adams.
  Prose: Essay. Familiar Essay.
  Fiction: Sketches. Tales: "Charity
    Bowery"; "Letter to a Student of History";
    "A Morning Walk"; "The Quadroons"; "A
    Day in Kentucky"; "Two Nights in St.
    Domingo"; "Story of a Fugitive"; "Lewis
    Herbert"; "Philip Catesby"; "The Dream
    Within a Dream"; "The Last of the Slaves";
    "Mount Verney"; "A True Tale of the
    South"; "The Insurrection and Its Hero";
    "Old Sambo"; "Annie Gray"; "A Daughter
    of the Riccarees."

425 TITLE: The Literary. A Miscellany for the
     Town.

Place of Publication: New York
First Issue: [Only one issue published]
              15 Nov 1836//
Periodicity: ?
Editor: Evert A. Duyckinck
Publisher: Henderson Greene
Available From: Lib. of Congress; N.Y.
                 Hist. Soc.
Contents:
  Poetry: Original: "Sights in the City"
    [Cornelius Mathews].
  Prose: Familiar Essay: "L'Envoy" [Evert
    A. Duyckinck]; "The Club" [Cornelius
    Mathews]; "The Life of Dr. Braindeath"
    [William A. Jones]. Criticism: "The
    Old Prose Writers" [Evert A. Duyckinck];
    "Mr. George Jones, the American Trage-
    dian" [Russell Trevett].
Note: Only 30 copies printed.

426 TITLE: The Literary Age.

Place of Publication: Philadelphia
First Issue: 7 Dec 1842
Last Issue: 15 March 1843//
Periodicity: Weekly
Editor: Reynell Coates
Publisher: G.W. Ridgway
Available From: Lib. of Congress; Amer.
                 Philosophical Soc.,
                 Philadelphia*
Contents:
  Poetry: Original: Charles F. Sterling,

Reynell Coates. Selected: Bryant,
    Anne C. Lynch, Felicia Hemans, Thomas
    Dunn English, Lamartine.
  Prose: Biography: Lydia H. Sigourney.
    Essay. Familiar Essay. Book Reviews.

  Fiction: Essay Serial: "Reveries of the
    Sanctum." Sketches. Tales: "An Adven-
    ture During the Greek Revolution"; "A
    Rainy Evening"; "A Traitor's Doom."
  Miscellaneous: Extracts: from other jour-
    nals; by various authors; Dickens,
    Franklin. Anecdotes: on various sub-
    jects. Literary Notices. News: Foreign
    and Domestic.

427 TITLE: The Literary American.

Place of Publication: New York
First Issue: 8 July 1848
Last Issue: 24 Aug 1850//?
Periodicity: Weekly
Editor: G.P. Quackenbos
Publisher: A.J. Townsend
Available From: Univ. of Chicago*; N.Y.
                 Hist. Soc.
Contents:
  Poetry: Original: Allie Vernon, J.P.
    Marron, J.M. Knowlton, Anna Saltus,
    Samuel J. Pike, Hannah M. Bryant, G.P.
    Quackenbos, Miron J. Hazeltine, William
    P. Mulchinock, Henry Bradfield, Harriete
    F. Read, Leila Cameron, Charles Russell
    Clarke. Selected: Lydia H. Sigourney,
    William Gilmore Simms.
  Prose: Biography. Travel. Essay.
    Familiar Essay.
  Fiction: Sketches. Tales: "War Life; or,
    the Adventures of a Light Infantry
    Officer"; "The Gamesters: A French Story";
    "Blanche Dudley; or, the Two Wills";
    "The Smuggler's Leap"; "The Child of the
    Islands! Or, the Shipwrecked Gold-
    Seekers"; "One Error; or, Yielding to
    Temptation"; "The Guest of Glenstrae.
    A Highland Tale"; "Jose Maria, the Great
    Spanish Robber"; "The Signal; or, the
    Castle of Salurn"; "An Adventure of
    Cagliostro"; "The Sacrifice. A Tale of
    Duty"; "Help Yourself. A Tale"; "The
    Royal Lover, and the Prime Minister's
    Daughter"; "Reformation; or, 'Better Late
    Than Never'"; "The Brooklyn Belle, a Leaf
    in College Life"; "The Two Draughts; or,
    the Physician of Leipsig"; "Raymond; or,
    the Chance Meeting"; "The Midnight Ride.
    A Tale of the Oregon Fur Trade"; "The
    Silver Chimes; or, the Astrologer of
    Gotham"; "The Duellist's Vow. A Tale for
    the Times."
  Miscellaneous: Extracts: from other jour-
    nals; Bryant. Anecdotes: on various
    subjects; Jefferson, Wordsworth, Swift,
    Goldsmith, Washington, Dickens, Poe,
    Franklin. Literary Notices. News:
    Foreign and Domestic.

428 TITLE: Literary & Musical Magazine. [See
     Ladies' Literary Museum; or Weekly
     Repository.]

429 TITLE: The Literary and Philosophical Repertory: Embracing Discoveries and Improvements in the Physical Sciences; the Liberal and Fine Arts; Essays Moral and Religious; Occasional Notices and Reviews of New Publications; and Articles of Miscellaneous Intelligence.

Place of Publication: Middlebury, Vt.
First Issue: April 1812
Last Issue: May 1817//
Periodicity: Quarterly [Irregular]
Editor: S. Swift
Publisher: S. Swift
Available From: APS; Amer. Antiquarian Soc.*
Contents:
  Poetry: Original: Christopher R. Greene, Sarah Smith. Selected: William Cowper, Pope, Goldsmith, B. Jonson, Henry Kirke White, Dryden, Byron, Charles Dibdin, William Jones, John Cotton, Richard Cumberland, Thomas Moore, Robert Treat Paine, John Howard Payne.
  Prose: Biography: Benjamin Tompson. Travel. Criticism. Letters.
  Fiction: Essay Serial: "The Medley."
  Miscellaneous: Extracts: from other journals; by various authors; Burns.

430 TITLE: The Literary and Scientific Repository, and Critical Review. [Superseded by The United States Magazine and Literary and Political Repository q.v.]

Place of Publication: New York
First Issue: June 1820
Last Issue: May 1822//
Periodicity: Quarterly
Editor: Charles H. Gardner
Publishers: Wiley & Halsted
Available From: APS; Lib. of Congress.* Mott.

Contents:
  Poetry: Original: Fitz-Greene Halleck. Selected: Shelley, Byron.
  Prose: Biography. Letters. Book Reviews.
  Miscellaneous: Extracts: from other journals; by various authors; James Hogg. Literary Notices.
  Note: Critical reviews on the works of Charles Brockden Brown, W. Irving, James Kirke Paulding, John Howard Payne, Shelley, B. Jonson, Colley Cibber, Byron, John Dennis, Sidney, Schiller, Southey, Timothy Dwight, Thomas Campbell, Kotzebue.

431 TITLE: The Literary and Theological Review.

Place of Publication: New York; Boston
First Issue: Jan 1834
Last Issue: Dec 1839//
Periodicity: Quarterly
Editors: Leonard Woods, Jr.; Charles D. Pigeon
Publishers: D. Appleton & Co.; William Pierce; Franklin Knight; Otis, Broaders and Co.; Ezra Collier; Charles D. Pigeon

Available From: APS; Lib. of Congress.* Mott. Poole.
Contents:
  Poetry: Selected: Richard Henry Dana, Robert Montgomery, Goethe.
  Prose: Biography. Travel. Essay: "On the Doctrine of Election"; "Piety of the Seventeenth Century"; "The Fathers of New England." Familiar Essay. Criticism: "American Criticism on American Literature"; "Thoughts on Modern Literature"; "Neglect of the Classics in the Literary Institutions of This Country." Letters. Book Reviews: on William Ellery Channing, E. Lytton Bulwer, Jonathan Edwards, Coleridge, Richard Henry Dana, Goethe, Lamartine, Robert Montgomery, Harriet Martineau, S. Johnson, George Whitefield.
  Miscellaneous: Extracts: by various authors. Literary Notices.
  Note: Leading Contributors: Henry R. Schoolcraft, Edward S. Gould, Calvin E. Stowe, Enoch Pond, Lyman H. Atwater. Although this journal is primarily religious, it is of some literary interest.

432 TITLE: Literary Cabinet.

Place of Publication: New Haven, Conn.
First Issue: 15 Nov 1806
Last Issue: 31 Oct 1807//?
Periodicity: Semi-monthly
Editors: ?
Publishers: O. Steele & Co.
Available From: APS; Boston Pub. Lib.* Mott.
Contents:
  Poetry: Original. Selected: Thomas Campbell.
  Prose: Essay. Familiar Essay. Criticism: on William Cowper. Letters.
  Fiction: Essay Serial: "The Essayist."
  Note: Published by editors from the senior class of Yale College "for the purpose of improving the youth of this College in the art of Writing." The journal includes several rather lengthy essays: "Strictures on Palaephilus" and "Of the Origin and Formation of Yale College."

433 TITLE: The Literary Cabinet, and Western Olive Branch, Devoted to Literature and the Diffusion of Useful Knowledge. [Superseded by The Western Gem and Cabinet of Literature q.v.]

Place of Publication: St. Clairsville, Ohio
First Issue: 16 Feb 1833
Last Issue: 8 Feb 1834//
Periodicity: Bi-monthly
Editor: Thomas Gregg
Publisher: Horton J. Howard
Available From: APS; Western Reserve Hist. Soc., Cleveland

Contents:
  Poetry: Original: George W. Thompson, B.B. Phares. Selected: Whittier, Barry Cornwall, George D. Prentice, Otway Curry, Richard Henry Dana, Hannah F. Gould, R.J. Everett, Lydia H. Sigourney, Fitz-Greene Halleck.

Prose: Biography. Travel. Essay.
Familiar Essay. Book Reviews.
Fiction: Sketches. Tales: "The Lake of
Canandaigua"; "Alquina, or the Mohawk
Chief"; "City Night-Piece" [Goldsmith];
"The Fall of Michilimacinac"; "The
Magdalen"; "The Valley of the Susquehan-
na"; "The Muddy-Brookers"; "The Pirate.
A Tale of the Mexican Gulf"; "The Re-
venge"; "First Love"; "The Lone Indian";
"The Intemperate."
Miscellaneous: Extracts: from other
journals; by various authors; Nathaniel
P. Willis, P.M. Wetmore, William D.
Gallagher, Hannah F. Gould, Beranger.
Literary Notices.

434   TITLES: (1) Literary Cadet, and Saturday
Evening Bulletin (2) Literary Cadet and
Rhode-Island Statesman (3) Cadet and
Statesman.

Place of Publication: Providence, R.I.
First Issue: 22 April 1826
Last Issue: 18 July 1829//?
Periodicity: Weekly; Bi-weekly
Editors: Smith & Parmenter
Publishers: Smith & Parmenter
Available From: Amer. Antiquarian Soc.*;
            N.Y. Pub. Lib.

Contents:
  Poetry: Original: R.S. Coffin, Sumner
  Lincoln Fairfield. Selected: R.S.
  Coffin, William Collins, Thomas Moore,
  Byron, Felicia Hemans, Harriet Muzzy,
  Schiller, Edward Everett, James G.
  Percival, Burns, Bryant, Scott, Thomas
  Campbell, George Croly, L.E. Landon,
  William Falconer, Jane Taylor, George D.
  Prentice, R.H. Wilde, Fitz-Greene
  Halleck, Edmund Waller, Sumner Lincoln
  Fairfield, Mary Russell Mitford,
  Nathaniel P. Willis, Wordsworth, James
  Hogg, Allan Cunningham, Anna Letitia
  Barbauld, Shelley, Thomas Paine, Sarah
  J. Hale, James Montgomery, Barry Corn-
  wall, Anna Maria Wells, Charles Swain,
  Alaric Watts, Robert Montgomery, George
  Wither, Mary Anne Browne, Coleridge,
  P.M. Wetmore, Henry Neele, Louisa P.
  Smith, Goethe.
  Prose: Biography. Letters. Book Reviews.
  Fiction: Sketches. Tales: "Tales of an
  Itinerant"; "Love and Ingratitude"; "The
  Prediction"; "The Lover's Last Visit";
  "The Green Petticoat"; "The Heroic
  Daughter"; "The Mysterious Visitors. A
  Legendary Tale"; "Lucy of the Fold";
  "Travels of a Troglodyte"; "Genevieve";
  "The Veteran's Reward"; "The Fountain";
  "The Twin Flowers"; "The Last of the
  Family"; "The Bridal Robe"; "Edwin and
  Ellen. A Tale--Founded on a Fact"; "Hay
  Carrying"; "Abduction of Miss Turner";
  "Clara Glenmurray"; "Blanch D'Albi";
  "The Stranger Emigrants"; "The Fair
  Maniac"; "The Constant Venetian"; "The
  Serenade; or the Clandestine Marriage";
  "Henry O'Connor"; "Theodore Harland. A

Premium Tale"; "The Village of L"; "Which
Is the Bride? An Old English Tale";
"Highland Widow"; "John Henry Fitz Allen";
"The Village Ball, or Ella's Birth Day";
"The Widow Bewitched"; "The Widow and
Her Son"; "Legend of the White Mountains";
"The Wedding and the Funeral" [Sarah J.
Hale]; "Adelia Montrose"; "North West
Hanna. A Tale of the Pacific Ocean";
"Paul Lorraine" [Nathaniel P. Willis];
"The Sister Victims"; "The Soldier's
Son"; "Canarissa. A Grecian Tale";
"Lorenzo and Angelina"; "Ellen Stanley,
or the Victim of Vanity"; "The Young
Corsair"; "The White Cottage"; "Marian
Godfrey, a Sketch of 1651"; "The Two
Rivals"; "The Coquette"; "Matowissa";
"The Second Wife"; "Dreaming Tim Jarvis";
"The Last of the Boatmen"; "The Election.
A Tale" [Mary Russell Mitford]; "The
Castilian Captive, or the Pacha Per-
plexed"; "Longchamps"; "The Pride of the
Village" [W. Irving]; "Ferdinando Eboli--
A Tale"; "Dora Creswell" [Mary Russell
Mitford]; "The Young Surgeon"; "'The
Fair Eckbert'."
Miscellaneous: Extracts: from other jour-
nals. Anecdotes: on various subjects.
Literary Notices. News: Foreign and
Domestic.

435   TITLE: The Literary Casket: Devoted to
Literature, the Arts, and Sciences.

Place of Publication: Hartford, Conn.
First Issue: 4 March 1826
Last Issue: 3 Feb 1827//
Periodicity: Semi-monthly
Editors: ?
Publishers: Norton & Russell
Available From: APS; Lib. of Congress*
Contents:
  Poetry: Original. Selected: John G.
  Brainard, Felicia Hemans, Scott.
  Prose: Biography: Anna Letitia Barbauld,
  Jefferson. Travel. Essay. Familiar
  Essay. Book Reviews.
  Fiction: Essay Serial: "Censor."
  Sketches. Tales: "The Misanthrope";
  "The Rival Brothers. A Tale of the
  Revolution."
  Miscellaneous: Anecdotes: on various sub-
  jects; R.B. Sheridan, Voltaire. Literary
  Notices.

436   TITLE: The Literary Casket, Devoted to Literature, the Arts, Science, Statistical Information, &c. &c. [See The Literary
Messenger.]

437   TITLE: The Literary Companion.

Place of Publication: New York
First Issue: 16 June 1821
Last Issue: 8 Sept 1821//
Periodicity: Weekly
Editors: George B. Huntley; John T. Huntley

Publishers: G. & J. Huntley
Available From: APS; N.Y. Pub. Lib.*
Contents:
Poetry: Original. Selected: Byron,
Burns, Samuel Rogers, Thomas Moore.
Prose: Biography. Travel. Familiar
Essay. Letters.
Fiction: Essay Serials: "The Lustrum";
"Gossipiana"; "The Reflector." Sketches.
Tales: "The Enthusiast: An Original
Tale"; "War, a Tale"; "The Witch of the
Wold" [Charlotte Smith]; "The Castle
Ruins"; "The Prediction."
Miscellaneous: Extracts: from other
journals; by various authors; Southey.
Anecdotes: on various subjects.
Literary Notices. News: Foreign.

438   TITLE: The Literary Emporium; a Compendium
of Religious, Literary, and Philosophical
Knowledge.

Place of Publication: New York
First Issue: Jan 1845
Last Issue: Jan 1847//
Periodicity: Monthly
Editor: J.K. Wellman
Publisher: J.K. Wellman
Available From: APS; Yale Univ.*
Contents:
Poetry: Original: James Stillman,
John Newman. Selected: George H.
Colton, Lydia H. Sigourney, Whittier,
Rufus Dawes, Felicia Hemans, Robert
Montgomery, Grenville Mellen, Eliza Cook,
Park Benjamin, Nathaniel P. Willis,
Bryant, James G. Percival, William B.
Tappan, Poe, Mrs. Seba Smith, Charles
Swain, James Montgomery, Caroline Norton,
Mary Howitt, Hannah F. Gould, Charles
Grenell, John Waters, Bayard Taylor,
William Wistar.
Prose: Biography. Travel. Essay.
Familiar Essay. Criticism.
Fiction: Essay Serials: "The Finer
Feelings"; "On the Cultivation of the
Mind." Sketches. Tales: "Fashionable
Life, or a Tale of 'Good Society'";
"Circumstantial Testimony"; "My Friend's
Manuscript"; "Mrs. Stewart, or Disci-
pline and Effort"; "The Wife."
Miscellaneous: Extracts: from other
journals; by various authors; W. Irving,
John Inman.

439   TITLES: (1) The Literary Emporium. Devoted
to Useful Intelligence, Original and
Selected Tales, Essays, Poetry, &c. (2)
The New Havener. Devoted to Useful Intel-
ligence, Original and Selected Tales,
Essays, Poetry, &c.

Place of Publication: New Haven, Conn.
First Issue: 16 June 1835
Last Issue: 4 Aug 1838//
Periodicity: Semi-monthly; Weekly
Editor: William Storer, Jr.
Publisher: William Storer, Jr.

Available From: Bowdoin Coll., Brunswick,
Me.; Amer. Antiquarian Soc.
Contents:
Poetry: Original: J.H. Clinch. Selected:
Burns, J.N. M'Jilton, Lydia H. Sigourney,
Henry Kirke White, R. Shelton MacKenzie.
Prose: Biography: Benjamin West. Essay.
Familiar Essay. Letters.
Fiction: Essay Serials: "The Court Room";
"Midnight Broodings." Sketches. Tales:
"Laura Lovel. A Sketch--For Ladies Only";
"Pride and Passion"; "The Mountaineer.
An Original Tale, Founded on Fact"; "My
Friend's Marriage"; "The Red Box. Or,
Scenes at the General Wayne. A Tale";
"Charles Darnley.--A Tale"; "Mr. and Mrs.
Peregrine Pringle"; "The Fatalist"; "The
Mail Robber"; "The Boat Club"; "Veronica,
the Red Haired"; "Mary Bell" [Ann S.
Stephens]; "The Haunted Cave. (A Tale
of the Past)"; "The Motherless Son";
"New Year's Day" [Catharine M. Sedgwick];
"The Cherokee's Threat" [Nathaniel P.
Willis]; "The Murderer's Daughter";
"The Young Fisherman of the Palisades.
A Historic Tale" [Nathan C. Brooks];
"The Negro Insurrection. A Tale of New
Orleans"; "The Broken Miniature."
Miscellaneous: Extracts: from other
journals; by various authors; W. Irving.
Anecdotes: on various subjects. News:
Domestic.

440   TITLES: (1) The Literary Examiner, and
Western Monthly Review (2) The Examiner
and Hesperian.

Place of Publication: Pittsburgh
First Issue: May 1839
Last Issue: May 1840//
Periodicity: Monthly
Editor: E. Burke Fisher
Publishers: Whitney & M'Cord
Available From: APS; Newberry Lib.,
            Chicago.* Mott.
Contents:
Poetry: Original: E. Burke Fisher.
Selected: Edmund H. Sears, Grenville
Mellen, Lewis J. Cist, Mrs. Seba Smith,
Mary Howitt, Frances H. Whipple, Geoffrey
H. Boyle.
Prose: Biography: Daniel Webster, John
Quincy Adams. Essay. Familiar Essay.
Criticism. Book Reviews.
Fiction: Essay Serial: "Sketches of
Village Character." Sketches. Tales:
"Jehoida Hawkins; or the Auto-Biography
of a Persecuted Vagabond"; "Clara
Shelby.--A Tale of the South"; "Eight-
Six: A Story of Shay's Rebellion"; "The
Arab Maiden"; "The Revenge. A Legend of
Tophet"; "Chillicothe: Or, the Golden
Arrow"; "The Reclaimed"; "Ringwood the
Rover: A Tale of Florida"; "Love's
Guerdon. A Tale for the Ladies"; "The
Annals of 'Eighty-Six.' An Historical
Romance."
Miscellaneous: Literary Notices.

441   TITLE: The Literary Focus, a Monthly
            Periodical.

       Place of Publication: Oxford, Ohio
       First Issue: June 1827
       Last Issue: May 1828//
       Periodicity: Monthly
       Editors: The Erodelphian and Union Literary
                 Societies (Miami University)
       Publishers: The Erodelphian and Union
                    Literary Societies (Miami
                    University)
       Available From: APS; Ohio State Hist. Soc.,
                        Columbus*
       Contents:
         Poetry: Original. Selected: Byron,
           Boston Bard, John Bowering, Thomas
           Moore, James Montgomery, Thomas Green
           Fessenden.
         Prose: Biography: LaFayette. Essay.
           Familiar Essay. Criticism. Letters.
         Fiction: Essay Serials: "The Budget";
           "Les Amourettes." Sketches. Tales:
           "'The Hunters of Kentucky' or the Recol-
           lections of an Early Settler"; "The
           Power of Beauty. A Syrian Tale"; "Tale
           of a Chemist"; "The Little Brook & the
           Star."
         Miscellaneous: Extracts: from other
           journals; by various authors; Thomas
           Moore, R.B. Sheridan, S. Johnson.
           Anecdotes: on various subjects;
           Sterne, Franklin. Literary Notices.

442   TITLE: The Literary Gazette.

       Place of Publication: Concord, N.H.
       First Issue: 1 Aug 1834
       Last Issue: 26 June 1835//
       Periodicity: Weekly; Semi-monthly
       Editors: A. Fowler; M. Currier; C.D. Bradley
       Publisher: D.D. Fisk
       Available From: APS; City Lib., Manchester,
                        N.H.*
       Contents:
         Poetry: Original: B.F. Bulfinch, J.H.
           Le Roy. Selected: Byron, Nathaniel P.
           Willis, Hannah F. Gould, Whittier, Thomas
           Moore, Charles Sprague, James G. Percival,
           Thomas Carey, Bryant, William Leggett,
           Lydia H. Sigourney, Hannah More, George
           Pope Morris.
         Prose: Biography: William Roscoe,
           Charles Brockden Brown, Shakespeare.
           Familiar Essay. Book Reviews.
         Fiction: Essay Serials: "Way-side
           Sketches"; "Collectanea." Sketches.
           Tales: "The Bachelor"; "The Partners--
           Or Above and Below. A Tale of Common
           Life"; "The Squatter"; "Tale of a
           Chemist"; "Mary Dyre"; "The Lost One";
           "The Victim."
         Miscellaneous: Extracts: from other
           journals; by various authors; Theodore
           Sedgwick Fay, Nathaniel P. Willis.
           Anecdotes: on various subjects; Gibbon,
           Franklin, Burns, Scott, William Cowper.
           Literary Notices. News: Domestic.

443   TITLE: The Literary Gazette and Quarterly
            Advertiser.

       Place of Publication: Philadelphia
       First Issue: 1841
       Last Issue: 1843//?
       Available From: Univ. of N.C., Chapel Hill*;
                        Boston Pub. Lib.

444   TITLES: (1) The Literary Gazette: Journal
            of Criticism, Science, and the Arts. (2)
            The Literary Gazette: Or, Journal of
            Criticism, Science, and the Arts. Being a
            Collection of Original and Selected Essays.
            [A third series of the Analectic Magazine
            q.v.]

       Place of Publication: Philadelphia
       First Issue: 6 Jan 1821
       Last Issue: 29 Dec 1821//
       Periodicity: Weekly
       Editor: Thomas Isaac Wharton
       Publisher: James Maxwell
       Available From: APS; Amer. Antiquarian Soc.*
                        Mott.
       Contents:
         Poetry: Original. Selected: John Clare,
           Thomas Moore, Thomas Campbell, Shelley,
           George Croly, Byron, Samuel Butler
           ["Hudibras"], James Kirke Paulding.
         Prose: Biography. Travel. Letters.
           Book Reviews.
         Fiction: Essay Serial: "The Camera
           Obscura. By Oliver Optic, Esq."
         Miscellaneous: Extracts: from other jour-
           nals; by various authors; Southey, James
           Hogg, Thomas Campbell. Anecdotes: on
           various subjects; Franklin, Pascal,
           Hogarth, Abraham Cowley, Schiller.
           Literary Notices.

445   TITLE: The Literary Geminae: A Monthly
            Magazine in English and French. [French
            title: Gémeaux littéraires.]

       Place of Publication: Worcester, Mass.
       First Issue: June 1839
       Last Issue: May 1840//
       Periodicity: Monthly
       Editor: Elihu Burritt
       Publisher: Elihu Burritt
       Available From: APS; Amer. Antiquarian Soc.
       Contents:
         Poetry: Original: Lydia H. Sigourney.
           Selected: E. Lytton Bulwer, Mary Howitt,
           Catharine H. Waterman, George D. Prentice,
           Longfellow.
         Prose: Travel. Essay. Familiar Essay.
           Criticism.
         Fiction: Sketches. Tales: "The Rich
           Man"; "The Abencerrage. A Spanish Tale"
           [W. Irving]; "Passages from the Life of
           a Castle-Builder" [W. Irving]; "The Vil-
           lage Death-Bell"; "The 'Dhrame'";
           "Perou-Rou, or the Bellows Mender."
         Miscellaneous: Extracts: from other
           journals; by various authors; Longfellow,
           Edward Everett. Anecdotes: on various
           subjects; S. Johnson.

446   TITLE: Literary Gems.

Place of Publication: New York
First Issue: 10 April 1833
Last Issue: July 1833//?
Periodicity: 3 or 4 times weekly
Editors: ?
Publishers: ?
Available From: APS; N.Y. Hist. Soc.
Contents:
   Poetry: Original. Selected: Thomas
      Moore, W.F. Hawley, Tennyson, Felicia
      Hemans, Lydia H. Sigourney, John
      Bowering, James Montgomery, Goethe.
   Prose: Biography: Daniel Webster.
      Familiar Essay. Criticism.
   Fiction: Essay Serial: "Recollections of
      a Nautical Life." Sketches. Tales:
      "The Water-Spout"; "The Wondrous Tale
      of Alroy"; "The Poor Irish Scholar";
      "Tom Cringle's Log" [Michael Scott];
      "The Veiled Picture"; "The Widow of
      Hebron"; "The Dead Alive"; "The Spectre
      Girl"; "The Hunchback."
   Miscellaneous: Extracts: from other
      journals; by various authors. Anecdotes:
      on various subjects; R.B. Sheridan,
      Franklin.

447   TITLE: The Literary Harvester. A Semi-
       Monthly Journal of Literature, Science,
       and the Fine Arts. Containing Original
       and Selected Tales, Biography, History,
       Sketches of Travels and Adventure,
       Criticism, Moral and Humorous Essays,
       Poetry, Natural Science, News, etc. etc.

Place of Publication: Hartford
First Issue: [?] 1841
Last Issue: 1 Dec 1843//?
Periodicity: Semi-monthly
Editor: German W. Foss
Publisher: German W. Foss
Available From: Lib. of Congress; Amer.
                   Antiquarian Soc.
Contents:
   Poetry: Original: S. Dryden Phelps,
      H. Isabella Snow, T.S. Sperry, German
      W. Foss, J.E. Dawley, Jr., C.D. Stuart,
      W.J. Annable, Rufus Dawes, William
      Warren. Selected: Bryant, Lydia J.
      Pierson, William Comstock, Lydia H.
      Sigourney, William B. Tappan, Whittier,
      Alfred B. Street, M.L. Gardiner, William
      H. Cranston, George Pope Morris.
   Prose: Biography: Frances S. Osgood.
      Essay. Familiar Essay.
   Fiction: Essay Serial: "Rural Sketches."
      Sketches. Tales: "The Doomed Maiden.
      Or the Victim of Superstition"; "Agnes
      Waltham"; "Polly Peablossom's Wedding";
      "The Huguenot's Revenge. A Tale of
      France"; "The Haunted Fountain. A
      Story of the Rhine"; "The Tell-Tale
      Heart" [Poe]; "The Drunkard's Wife";
      "The Stolen Miniature"; "An Inconvenient
      Acquaintance"; "The Stolen Child"; "The
      Hand of Clay. A Thrilling Tale of
      Mystery and Mesmerism" [J.H. Ingraham];

"Death in the Starboard Watch"; "The
Soldier's Lover"; "Norman Jarvis";
"Zephanian Starling. A Real Down East
Story"; "Love and Pistols" [Nathaniel P.
Willis]; "Revenge of Leonard Rosier";
"Love and Whaling. A Lesson to
Coquettes."
   Miscellaneous: Extracts: from other
      journals; by various authors; W. Irving.
      Anecdotes: on various subjects; Charles
      Maturin. Literary Notices.

448   TITLES: (1) The Literary Inquirer: A Semi-
       Monthly Journal, Devoted to Literature and
       Science (2) The Literary Inquirer, and
       Repertory of Literature, Science, and
       General Intelligence.

Place of Publication: Buffalo, N.Y.
First Issue: 1 Jan 1833
Last Issue: 15 Oct 1834//?
Periodicity: Semi-monthly; Weekly
Editor: William Verrinder
Publishers: William Verrinder; S.G. Bacon
Available From: APS; Amer. Antiquarian Soc.
Contents:
   Poetry: Original: George Henry Davis.
      Selected: W.H. Harrison, James
      Montgomery, Charles Swain, John Bowering,
      Felicia Hemans, Sumner Lincoln Fairfield,
      Isaac C. Pray, Jr., Pope, Mary Howitt,
      Barry Cornwall, Lydia H. Sigourney,
      Whittier, L.E. Landon.
   Prose: Biography: Coleridge, James
      Montgomery, Lady Mary Wortley Montagu,
      Southey, Harriet Martineau, Daniel
      Webster, Lope de Vega, Timothy Flint,
      George Wythe. Essay. Familiar Essay.
      Criticism. Letters. Book Reviews.
   Fiction: Sketches. Tales: "The Outlaw
      of the Pines, a Tale of the Revolution";
      "Poor Rosalie"; "A Sporting Adventure in
      Auvergne"; "Stock-am-eisen--Or, the Iron
      Trunk"; "Uncle Anthony's Blunder"; "The
      Valley of the Susquehanna"; "The Revenge
      of the Rejected. A Tale of Mystery";
      "Amy Dayton. A Tale of the Revolution";
      "The Spectre Girl"; "The Dark Maid of
      Illinois"; "The Beautiful Poetess"; "A
      Sketch of Fashionable Life. A Tale";
      "The Ambush. A Tale of the Revolution";
      "The Stolen Daughter"; "The Great Belt";
      "Sir William Deane, or, the Magic of
      Wealth"; "Charles Morsell, or the Elope-
      ment"; "Port Royal"; "The Baronet's
      Bride"; "The Last Indian"; "Gertrude
      Beverly"; "Youth and Womanhood. A Tale
      of Passion"; "Monedo--The Daughter of
      Snow"; "The Cemetry [sic].--A Tale of the
      Revolution"; "The Old and the Young
      Bachelor; or First Love and Last Love";
      "The Wife" [W. Irving]; "The Broken
      Miniature."
   Miscellaneous: Extracts: from other
      journals; by various authors; William
      Cowper, James Montgomery, E. Lytton
      Bulwer, Erasmus, James Kirke Paulding,
      William Dunlap, W. Irving, James G.
      Percival. Anecdotes: on various

subjects; William Cowper, Franklin,
Schiller, Scott, Garrick, Hannah More.
<u>Literary Notices</u>. <u>News</u>: Foreign and
Domestic.

449   TITLE: <u>The Literary Journal</u>.

Place of Publication: Richmond
First Issue: 21 Feb 1835
Last Issue: 28 Nov 1835//?
Available From: N.Y. Hist. Soc.

450   TITLE: <u>The Literary Journal, a Repository
of Polite Literature and the Fine Arts</u>.
[See <u>The Wreath. Devoted to Polite Litera-
ture</u>.]

451   TITLE: <u>The Literary Journal, and Weekly
Register of Science and the Arts</u>.

Place of Publication: Providence, R.I.
First Issue: 8 June 1833
Last Issue: 31 May 1834//
Periodicity: Weekly
Editor: Albert G. Greene
Publishers: Joseph Knowles and Company
Available From: APS; Boston Pub. Lib.*
Contents:
  Poetry: <u>Original</u>: Samuel Bailey, Cynthia
    Taggart, J.O. Rockwell. <u>Selected</u>: R.
    Lovelace, Thomas Carew, Grenville
    Mellen, Lydia H. Sigourney, Felicia
    Hemans, Matthew Gregory [Monk] Lewis,
    James Shirley, L.E. Landon, Coleridge,
    Sir Walter Raleigh, Hartley Coleridge,
    George Wither, B. Jonson, William
    Ingram, Bernard Barton, Robert Southwell,
    Emma C. Embury, Alaric Watts, Sir John
    Suckling.
  Prose: <u>Biography</u>: Roger Williams,
    Schiller, Byron, Burns, William Cowper,
    George Crabbe, Coleridge, Thomas
    Campbell, Wordsworth. <u>Essay</u>. <u>Familiar
    Essay</u>. <u>Criticism</u>. <u>Letters</u>. <u>Book
    Reviews</u>.
  Fiction: <u>Sketches</u>. <u>Tales</u>: "Degalaiphus;
    a Tale of the Fourth Century"; "The
    Haunted Chamber"; "The Ignis Fatuus";
    "Julia; or, the Change of Character";
    "Maria Rosa; or, the Dungeon Rock"; "The
    Red Rose; or, the Value of Time"; "The
    Shark"; "The Young Girls of Paris"; "The
    Blasted Tree"; "The Brothers"; "Port
    Royal"; "The Traveller in Spite of Him-
    self"; "The Trials of a Templar."
  Miscellaneous: <u>Extracts</u>: from other
    journals; by various authors. <u>Anecdotes</u>:
    on various subjects.

452   TITLE: <u>Literary Magazine</u>.

Place of Publication: Boston
First Issue: [Only one issue published]
               1 Jan 1835//
Periodicity: Intended to be monthly
Editor: Isaac McLellan, Jr.

Publisher: E.R. Broaders
Available From: APS; Amer. Antiquarian Soc.
Contents:
  Poetry: <u>Original</u>. <u>Selected</u>: B.B.
    Thatcher.
  Prose: <u>Travel</u>. <u>Familiar Essay</u>.
  Fiction: <u>Sketches</u>. <u>Tales</u>: "The Susseton.
    An Indian Story"; "A Rescue."
  Miscellaneous: <u>Extracts</u>: from other
    journals. <u>Literary Notices</u>.

453   TITLE: <u>The Literary Magazine, and American
Register</u>. [Continued as <u>The American
Register, or General Repository of History,
Politics and Science</u> q.v.]

Place of Publication: Philadelphia
First Issue: Oct 1803
Last Issue: Dec 1807//
Periodicity: Monthly
Editor: Charles Brockden Brown
Publishers: John Conrad and Co.; T. & G.
             Palmer
Available From: APS; Univ. of Pa.* Mott.
Contents:
  Poetry: <u>Original</u>: Alexander Wilson.
    <u>Selected</u>: Luis de Camoens, William
    Cowper, Akenside, John Blair Linn.
  Prose: <u>Biography</u>: Boswell, Erasmus Darwin,
    John Adams, Jefferson, Hamilton, Franklin,
    Burns, Luis de Camoens, Lope de Vega,
    S. Richardson, Schiller. <u>Travel</u>. <u>Essay</u>.
    <u>Familiar Essay</u>. <u>Criticism</u>: on Milton,
    Wordsworth, Goldsmith, Chaucer, Fielding,
    S. Richardson, Spenser, Addison, S.
    Johnson, Pope, Dryden, Gibbon, Southey.
    <u>Letters</u>. <u>Book Reviews</u>.
  Fiction: <u>Essay Serials</u>: "The Traveller";
    "Adversaria"; "The Reflector"; "The
    Melange." <u>Sketches</u>. <u>Tales</u>: "Memoirs
    of Carwin the Biloquist" [Charles
    Brockden Brown]; "History of Philip
    Dellwyn"; "A Student's Diary" [Charles
    Brockden Brown].
  Miscellaneous: <u>Extracts</u>: from other jour-
    nals. <u>Anecdotes</u>: on various subjects;
    Boswell, Edmund Burke, Erasmus Darwin,
    Gray, Boileau, Godwin. <u>Literary Notices</u>.
    <u>News</u>: Foreign and Domestic.

454   TITLES: (1) <u>The Literary Messenger</u> (2) <u>The
Literary Casket, Devoted to Literature, the
Arts, Science, Statistical Information,
&c &c.</u> (3) <u>Western Literary Casket</u> (4)
<u>Western Literary Magazine</u>.

Place of Publication: Pittsburgh
First Issue: June 1840
Last Issue: June 1844//?
Periodicity: Monthly
Editors: Alexander M'Ilwaine; John P. Glass;
        John P. Betker; A.W. Paterson
Publishers: M'Ilwaine & Ivory; William
           Badger
Available From: APS; Univ. of Pittsburgh
Contents:
  Poetry: <u>Original</u>: George H. Thurston,
    William H. Burleigh, Lewis J. Cist,
    J.W.F. White. <u>Selected</u>: Thomas Carew,
    Shelley, Richard Henry Dana.

Prose: Biography: Franklin, W. Irving, Burns, LaFayette, Bolingbroke. Essay. Familiar Essay. Criticism. Letters. Book Reviews.
Fiction: Essay Serials: "Reminiscences of Pittsburgh"; "Prairie Sketches." Sketches. Tales: "The Rescue of Winona"; "An Incident of Other Times"; "Attala; or the Narrative of Choctos"; "Abduhl Bahahman, a Tale; Founded on the History of That Moorish Prince"; "The Widow Woods"; "Henry Wilford, the Revenged"; "The Fielding Family, or a Tale of Poverty and Virtue"; "Genius vs. Wealth, or the Lawyer's History"; "The Young Poet"; "The Prince Pretender"; "The Mystery; or the Fated Husband"; "The Recreant Made Virtuous and Happy"; "Bertardo, the Faithful"; "Tim. Tremont, the Ventriloquist"; "Eutaw Springs, a Tale of the Revolution in the South"; [William Gilmore Simms]; "The Diplomas, or Merit Has Its Own Reward"; "The Robber of the Mountain Pass, or, the Klepht's Revenger"; "The Indian Bride. A Romance of the Pequots"; "The Dauntless, a Traditionary Tale of Western Pennsylvania"; "Hector Randolph. Or, the Conqueror's Triumph"; "The Senator's Doom; or, the Victim and Victor"; "Missolonghi. A Tale of the Greek Revolution"; "Delia Milwood; or, Sketches of Western Peasantry."
Miscellaneous: Extracts: from other journals. Anecdotes: on various subjects; Buonaparte, Smollett, Scott, Isaac Newton. Literary Notices.

455   TITLE: The Literary Mirror.

Place of Publication: Portsmouth, N.H.
First Issue: 20 Feb 1808
Last Issue: 11 Feb 1809//
Periodicity: Weekly
Editor: Stephen Sewall
Publisher: Stephen Sewall
Available From: APS; Boston Pub. Lib.*
Contents:
    Poetry: Original. Selected: Robert Bloomfield, Luis de Camoens, Robert Treat Paine, Milton, Erasmus Darwin, Mary Robinson, R.B. Sheridan, William Collins.
    Prose: Biography: Richard Cumberland. Travel. Familiar Essay. Letters.
    Fiction: Essay Serial: "The Scribbler." Sketches. Tales: "Meletina. A Very Interesting and Pathetic Tale"; "The Wild Rose of Langollen. A Tale."
    Miscellaneous: Extracts: from other journals; by various authors; Richard Cumberland, Goldsmith, Hester L. Thrale Piozzi. Anecdotes: on various subjects; Voltaire, S. Johnson, Shakespeare. Literary Notices.
Note: Motto: Sweet flowers and fruits from fair Parnassus' mount,/And varied knowledge from rich Science fount,/------We hither bring.

456   TITLE: The Literary Miscellany Containing Elegant Selections of the Most Admired Fugitive Pieces, and Extracts from Works of the Greatest Merit, with Originals [of] Prose and Poetry.

Place of Publication: Philadelphia
First Issue: [Undated. 1-2 (nos. 1-16)] 1795//
Periodicity: ?
Editor: T. Stephens
Publisher: W.W. Woodward
Available From: APS; Lib. of Congress*
Contents:
    Poetry: Selected: William Collins, Thomas Holcroft, Chatterton, Gray, John Gay, Marvell.
    Fiction: Tales: "The Dead Ass" [Sterne]; "Edwin and Angelina" [Goldsmith]; "Obidah; or, the Journey of a Day" [S. Johnson]; "The Captive" [Sterne]; "Cololoo" [William Dunlap].

457   TITLE: The Literary Miscellany, Including Dissertations and Essays on Subjects of Literature, Science, and Morals; Biographical and Historical Sketches; Critical Remarks on Language; with Occasional Reviews.

Place of Publication: Cambridge, Mass.
First Issue: 1805
Last Issue: 1806//
Periodicity: Quarterly
Editor: William Hilliard
Publisher: William Hilliard
Available From: APS; Univ. of Mich. Mott.
Contents:
    Poetry: Original. Selected: Marvell.
    Prose: Biography: William Cowper, Erasmus Darwin, S. Johnson. Travel. Familiar Essay. Criticism. Letters. Book Reviews.
    Miscellaneous: Anecdotes: on various subjects; Voltaire.
Note: Contains many critical articles on different areas of literature: on German, Jewish, and classical literature, on the Talmud, English translations of Roman poets, on the present state of English poetry, Milton.

458   TITLE: The Literary Miscellany, or Monthly Review, a Periodical Work.

Place of Publication: New York
First Issue: May 1811
Last Issue: Aug 1811//
Periodicity: Monthly
Editor: Charles N. Baldwin
Publishers: Riley & Adams
Available From: APS; Lib. of Congress
Contents:
    Poetry: Original. Selected: Garrick, Colley Cibber.
    Prose: Biography: Washington. Essay. Familiar Essay. Book Reviews.
    Fiction: Essay Serial: "Essay." Sketches. Tales: "The Hermit. A Tale"; "The Amorous Philosopher. An Arabian Tale"; "Adelaide and Valvaise, or the Triumphs

of Friendship, a Swedish Tale"; "Netley
Abbey: A Gothic Story"; "Thessalonica:
A Roman Story."
Miscellaneous: Extracts: from other
journals. Anecdotes: on various sub-
jects. Literary Notices.

459 TITLES: (1) Literary Miscellany; or, Nation-
al Advertiser (2) Literary Miscellany;
Devoted to Literature, Art, Science and
Discoveries in Medicine and Physiology.

Place of Publication: New York
First Issue: July 1849
Last Issue: 1850//?
Periodicity: Semi-monthly
Editors: ?
Publishers: J. Trow & Co.
Available From: Amer. Antiquarian Soc.
Contents:
Poetry: Selected: Alaric Watts, Oscar
Dunreath.
Prose: Letters.
Fiction: Sketches. Tales: "The Marriage
Crucible. A Thrilling Tale of High and
and Low Life"; "The Duel. A Passage from
History"; "The First Kiss"; "The Foster-
Brother's Revenge."
Miscellaneous: Extracts: from other
journals. Anecdotes: on various sub-
jects. News: Domestic.

460 TITLE: The Literary Museum, a Repository of
the Useful and Entertaining: Including the
Wonders of Nature and Art: Tales of All
Countries and All Ages: Travels: Adventures: Biography, &c. Embellished with
Engravings on Steel, and Music Arranged
for the Piano Forte. [See The World We
Live In. A Semi-Monthly Journal of Useful
and Entertaining Literature.]

461 TITLE: Literary Museum. Devoted to the
Different Branches of Literature, Fine
Arts, &c.

Place of Publication: Geneva, N.Y.
First Issue: 17 March 1834
Last Issue: 30 March 1835//?
Periodicity: Semi-monthly
Editor: H. Fisk
Publishers: Snow & Williams
Available From: Amer. Antiquarian Soc.
Contents:
Poetry: Original. Selected: Lydia H.
Sigourney, Thomas Moore, Joseph Rodman
Drake, Fitz-Greene Halleck, Park Benja-
min, Bryant, T.K. Hervey, Hannah F.
Gould, James G. Percival, Thomas Haynes
Bayly, L.W. Trask, Mary Anne Browne.
Prose: Biography: William Wirt. Essay.
Familiar Essay. Letters.
Fiction: Sketches. Tales: "The Deformed
Girl" [Whittier]; "The Albrozzi--A Tale
of Venice"; "The Claret-Colored Coat";
"The Two Brotherhoods. Or the Robbers";
"The Queen of the Meadow"; "Abaellino,

the Bravo of Venice"; "The Broken Mer-
chant"; "The Stranger's Death-Bed. A
Tale of Fact"; "Will Watch"; "The Part-
ners, or Above and Below."
Miscellaneous: Extracts: from other jour-
nals; by various authors; Chateaubriand,
Lydia H. Sigourney, James Hogg. Literary
Notices.

462 TITLE: The Literary Museum, or Monthly
Magazine.

Place of Publication: West Chester, Pa.
First Issue: Jan 1797
Last Issue: June 1797//
Periodicity: Monthly
Editors: ?
Publishers: Derrick & Sharples
Available From: APS; Amer. Antiquarian Soc.*
Mott.
Contents:
Poetry: Original. Selected: William
Collins, Gray, Peter Pindar, William
Shenstone, Charlotte Smith, Goldsmith.
Prose: Biography. Travel. Essay: "A
New View of the City of Copenhagen, with
Observations on the Character and Manners
of the Danes" [Mary Wollstonecraft].
Familiar Essay. Letters.
Fiction: Sketches. Tales: "Amelia, a
Moral Tale"; "The Apparition, a Tale."
Miscellaneous: News: Foreign and Domestic.

463 TITLE: The Literary Pamphleteer, Containing:
Some Observations on the Best Mode of Promoting the Cause of Literature in the State
of Kentucky: And a Review of the Late
Administration of the Transylvania University.

Place of Publication: Paris, Ky.
First Issue: [Undated. nos. 1-6.] 1823//
Periodicity: ?
Editor: John M'Farland
Publishers: Lyle & Keenon
Available From: APS; Presbyterian Hist.
Soc., Philadelphia*
Contents:
Prose: Essay. Familiar Essay. Book Re-
views.
Note: Although the journal focuses on mat-
ters concerning Transylvania University,
it is of some literary interest, especial-
ly for its book reviews.

464 TITLE: The Literary Pearl and Weekly Village
Messenger.

Place of Publication: Charlton, N.Y.
First Issue: 18 Nov 1840
Last Issue: 13 Feb 1840//
Available From: Harvard Univ.*

465 TITLE: Literary Port Folio. [Running title:
Philadelphia Port Folio: A Weekly Journal
of Literature, Science, Art, and the Times.

Supersedes The Ladies' Literary Port Folio
q.v. United with The Album. And Ladies'
Weekly Gazette q.v. to form The Philadelphia Album and Ladies' Literary Port
Folio.]

Place of Publication: Philadelphia
First Issue: 7 Jan 1830
Last Issue: 1 July 1830//
Periodicity: Weekly
Editors: Eliakim Littell; Thomas Cottrell
        Clarke
Publishers: E. Littell & Brother
Available From: Amer. Antiquarian Soc.*;
                Univ. of Pa.*
Contents:
  Poetry: Selected: Felicia Hemans, James
    Kenney, James Montgomery, Charles Swain,
    Thomas Haynes Bayly, Alaric Watts,
    Francis Jeffrey, Coleridge, Miss Jewsbury,
    Mary Anne Browne, Agnes Strickland, Mary
    Howitt, Robert Montgomery, Thomas Pringle,
    John Clare, Thomas Moore, John G.
    Brainard, Whittier, Bryant, William
    Falconer, J.O. Rockwell.
  Prose: Travel. Essay. Familiar Essay.
    Criticism. Letters. Book Reviews.
  Fiction: Sketches. Tales: "The Desola-
    tion of St. Miniver"; "The Alibi"; "The
    Pride of Woodburn. A Simple Tale";
    "Jack the Shrimp"; "Sir Harry Highflyer:
    A Suicide's Last Carouse"; "The Parthian
    Convert. A Tale of the Primitive
    Christians"; "The Confessions of a
    Suicide"; "The Lovers' Quarrel."
  Miscellaneous: Extracts: from other
    journals; by various authors; Jefferson,
    Cotton Mather. Anecdotes: on various
    subjects; Buonaparte. Literary Notices.
    News: Domestic.

466   TITLE: Literary Recreations.

Place of Publication: Round Hill, Mass.;
                      Northampton, Mass.
First Issue: 24 Jan 1829
Last Issue: 29 Aug 1829//
Periodicity: Weekly
Editors: ?
Publishers: ?
Available From: Lib. of Congress*; N.Y.
                Pub. Lib.
Contents:
  Poetry: Original. Selected.
  Prose: Letters.
  Fiction: Essay Serials: "My Writing
    Desk"; "The Literary Club"; "Scraps by
    a School-Boy." Sketches. Tales:
    "Rivalry. A Tale of the Revolution";
    "The Golden Tooth"; "The White Handker-
    chief--Or the White Lie"; "The Cross
    Road."
  Miscellaneous: Extracts: by various
    authors; Horace Walpole. Anecdotes:
    on various subjects.

467   TITLE: The Literary Register.

Place of Publication: Elyria, Ohio
First Issue: [Only 8 issues published] 1833//
Available From: Western Reserve Hist. Soc.,
                Cleveland

468   TITLE: Literary Register.

Place of Publication: Philadelphia
First Issue: 24 July 1813
Last Issue: 17 Dec 1814//
Periodicity: Weekly
Editor: George Booth
Publisher: John B. Austin
Available From: Hist. Soc of Pa.; Univ. of
                Pa.
Contents:
  Poetry: Original. Selected: Matthew
    Gregory [Monk] Lewis, Swift, Burns, Scott,
    Thomas Moore, Freneau, R.B. Sheridan,
    Peter Pindar, John Blair Linn.
  Prose: Biography: Benjamin Rush. Familiar
    Essay. Letters.
  Fiction: Essay Serials: "The Picture";
    "The Desultory Observer"; "Literary
    Curiosities"; "Meditative Hours"; "Mental
    Museum"; "The Ladies' Toilet"; "The
    Meditator"; "Meditations"; "The Mirror of
    Fashion"; "The Communicator." Sketches.
    Tales: "Tell; or the Cottage of St.
    Gothard"; "Hormona; or, the Grateful
    Slave"; "Ducks and Pease; or, the New-
    castle Rider"; "The Abbey of Clunedale";
    "Murder Will Out"; "The Punishment of
    Family Pride"; "Life of Eugene Aram"
    [E. Lytton Bulwer]; "Amelia Neville; or
    the Disappointment of Envy; and Reward
    of Benevolence"; "The Story of Louisa
    Venoni"; "The Dead Shot; or, the Long
    Pack"; "The Orphans Protected; or, the
    Duty of Relying Upon Providence. A
    Tale"; "Cordelia, or the Heiress of
    Raymond Castle"; "The Duchess of C----";
    "The Young Mother."
  Miscellaneous: Extracts: from other
    journals; by various authors; Swift.
    Anecdotes: on various subjects;
    Shakespeare, Isaac Newton. News:
    Domestic.

469   TITLE: The Literary Register; a Weekly Paper
      Edited by the Professors of Miami University.

Place of Publication: Oxford, Ohio
First Issue: 2 June 1828
Last Issue: 27 June 1829//
Available From: Miami Univ., Oxford*; Ohio
                State Hist. Soc., Columbus

470   TITLE: Literary Repository. A Semi-Monthly
      Journal, Devoted to Polite Literature;
      Embracing Sentimental Tales, Interesting

Adventures, Biography, Traveling Sketches, Extracts from New Publications, Historical Anecdotes, Poetry, &c. &c. [See The Literary Repository. Devoted to Polite Literature; Such as Moral and Sentimental Tales, Original Communications, Biography, Traveling Sketches, Amusing Miscellany, Humorous and Historical Anecdotes, Poetry, &c. &c.]

471   TITLE: The Literary Repository and Scientific and Critical Review.

Place of Publication: New York
First Issue: 1820
Last Issue: 1828//?
Available From: Amer. Museum of Natural Hist., N.Y.; Buffalo and Erie County Pub. Lib., Buffalo

472   TITLES: (1) The Literary Repository. Devoted to Polite Literature; Such as Moral and Sentimental Tales, Original Communications, Biography, Traveling Sketches, Amusing Miscellany, Humorous and Historical Anecdotes, Poetry, &c. &c. (2) Literary Repository. A Semi-Monthly Journal, Devoted to Polite Literature; Embracing Sentimental Tales, Interesting Adventures, Biography, Traveling Sketches, Extracts from New Publications, Historical Anecdotes, Poetry, &c. &c.

Place of Publication: Lowell, Mass.
First Issue: 1 Jan 1840
Last Issue: 12 Dec 1840//?
Periodicity: Semi-monthly
Editor: A.B.F. Hildreth
Publisher: A.B.F. Hildreth
Available From: Newberry Lib., Chicago; Amer. Antiquarian Soc.
Contents:
  Poetry: Original. Selected: Thomas Moore, Wilson Flagg, Henry Kirke White, Nathaniel P. Willis, Hannah F. Gould, George D. Prentice, Charles Fenno Hoffman, William Gaspey, L.E. Landon, Alaric Watts, Lydia H. Sigourney, William Wallace, Emma C. Embury, Henry Neele, Caroline Norton, Coleridge, Mary Howitt, Longfellow, Richard Howitt, Thomas Haynes Bayly.
  Prose: Biography: William Leggett. Familiar Essay.
  Fiction: Sketches. Tales: "The Stranger's Grave"; "The Deed of Separation" [Mrs. Abdy]; "The Manuscript"; "Ups and Downs. A Tale of the Road"; "Charles Elliston"; "The Task; or, How to Win a Mistress. An Affecting Story of the Mountain of the Lovers" [Leigh Hunt]; "A Tale of the Revolution"; "The Old Deacon"; "Cousin Kate; or, the Widow's Wooer" [Emma C. Embury]; "The Three Brides."
  Miscellaneous: Extracts: from other journals; by various authors. Anecdotes: on various subjects.

473   TITLES: (1) Literary Souvenir. A Family Newspaper; Devoted to Polite Literature, Christianity, Science, Morality, Mechanic Arts, and General Intelligence (2) Literary Souvenir. Devoted to Literature, Arts, Sciences, News, etc. (3) Literary Souvenir. A Weekly Journal of Literature, Science, and the Arts. Embellished with Engravings, and Music Arranged for the Pianoforte, Flute, &c. (4) The Literary Souvenir. Devoted to Polite Literature, Useful Knowledge, and General Intelligence.

Place of Publication: Lowell, Mass.; Manchester, N.H.; Boston
First Issue: March 1839
Last Issue: 26 Nov 1842//
Periodicity: Weekly
Editors: A.B.F. Hildreth; S.H. Napoleon; B. Everette; I. Kinsman
Publishers: A.B.F. Hildreth; Emerson & Murray
Available From: Amer. Antiquarian Soc.; Buffalo and Erie County Pub. Lib., Buffalo
Contents:
  Poetry: Original. Selected: Caroline Lee Hentz, L.E. Landon, Nathaniel P. Willis, Milton, Edward J. Porter, Lucy Hooper, Thomas Haynes Bayly, Frances Brown, Byron, James Sheridan Knowles, E. Lytton Bulwer, Caroline F. Orne, Caroline Norton, C. Theresa Clarke, Lewis J. Cist, Alfred L. Smith, George Pope Morris, John Sterling, Bryant.
  Prose: Biography. Familiar Essay.
  Fiction: Essay Serial: "Literary Rain-Drops." Sketches. Tales: "The Belle; or My Aunt Martha"; "A Tale of the Revolution"; "White Thunder; or, the Indian Murder"; "Family Secrets: Or, the Husband Reformed"; "The Vicar's Daughter"; "Eleonora" [Poe]; "Terrible Revenge of Esquo the Fearless. An Indian Tale of the Connecticut"; "The Attorney"; "The Maiden's Escape; or the Soldier Mendicant. A Tale of the American Revolution"; "The Honey Moon"; "The Broken Miniature"; "Giovana, the Georgian Pirate: Or, the Black Dragon. A Tale of the Atlantic"; "The Lady's Slipper"; "Catochus: Or, Burying a Man Alive"; "The Corsican Soldier in America. A Tale of Buonaparte's Wars"; "The Dissecting Room"; "The Iron Shroud. A Tale of Italy."
  Miscellaneous: Extracts: from other journals; by various authors. Anecdotes: on various subjects. Literary Notices. News: Foreign and Domestic.

474   TITLES: (1) The Literary Tablet. Containing Essays in Poetry and Prose, on Morality, History, Biography, the Fine Arts, Agriculture, and General Literature (2) The Literary Tablet; or a General Repository of Various Entertainment, Containing Essays, Original and Selected, in Poetry and Prose (3) The Literary Tablet: Or, a General Repository of Useful Entertainment: Consisting of Essays, Original and Selected, in Poetry and Prose.

Place of Publication: Hanover, N.H.
First Issue: 6 Aug 1803
Last Issue: 5 April 1807//?
Periodicity: Semi-monthly
Editors: Moses Davis; Nicholas Orlando
Publisher: Moses Davis
Available From: APS; Amer. Antiquarian Soc.
Contents:
  Poetry: Original. Selected: William
    Shenstone, Thomas Campbell, S. Johnson,
    William Cowper, Mary Robinson, Robert
    Bloomfield, Pope, Milton, David
    Humphreys, Smollett, Dryden, John Gay,
    Burns, William Gifford, Matthew Prior,
    Hannah More, Southey.
  Prose: Biography: Smollett, Voltaire,
    Pocahontas, William Cowper, Francis
    Bacon, Garrick, Lady Mary Wortley
    Montagu, William Pitt. Essay. Familiar
    Essay. Letters.
  Fiction: Essay Serials: "The Caterer";
    "The Rustic"; "The Observator"; "The
    Archer." Sketches. Tales: "Horatius
    and Alphonso, a Tale"; "The Maid of the
    Hamlet. A Tale"; "The Adventures of
    Scarmentado. A Satyrical Novel."
  Miscellaneous: Extracts: from other
    journals; by various authors; Goldsmith,
    Mary Robinson, Maria Edgeworth, Milton.
    Anecdotes: on various subjects.

475   TITLE: The Literary Tablet. Devoted to the
Cause of Education, Polite Literature,
Moral and Sentimental Tales, Poetry, &c.,
&c.

Place of Publication: New Haven, Conn.
First Issue: 1833
Last Issue: 29 March 1834//
Periodicity: Semi-monthly
Editors: Edwin Peck; G.M. Buckingham
Publishers: Edwin Peck; G.M. Buckingham
Available From: APS; Yale Univ.
Contents:
  Poetry: Original. Selected: Thomas
    Campbell, Harvey D. Little, Charles
    Sprague, Peter Pindar, George Kent,
    Fitz-Greene Halleck, Lydia H. Sigourney.
  Prose: Biography: Davey Crocket. Essay.
    Familiar Essay. Criticism. Letters.
    Book Reviews.
  Fiction: Essay Serial: "Extracts from
    the Diary of a Student." Sketches.
    Tales: "The Child of the Cascade. A
    Western Tale"; "The Magdalen"; "Occa-
    sional Glimpses at a Poet. A Tale of
    Truth"; "Constance and Montrose"; "The
    Ambush. A Tale of the Revolution";
    "The Pride of the Village" [W. Irving];
    "The Heiress of Rock-Hollow"; "Almanza,
    a Moorish Tale."
  Miscellaneous: Extracts: from other
    journals; by various authors; William
    D. Gallagher. Anecdotes: on various
    subjects. Literary Notices. News:
    Domestic.

476   TITLE: The Literary Union: A Journal of
Progress, in Literature and Education,
Religion and Politics, Science and
Agriculture.

Place of Publication: Syracuse, N.Y.
First Issue: 7 April 1849
Last Issue: July 1850//?
Available From: Brown Univ., Providence;
              N.Y. State Lib., Albany

477   TITLE: The Literary Visiter.

Place of Publication: Wilkes-Barre, Pa.
First Issue: 1813
Last Issue: 1815//
Available From: Trinity Coll., Hartford*;
              Wyoming Hist. and Geolog.
              Soc., Wilkes-Barre

478   TITLES: (1) The Literary World. A Gazette
for Authors, Readers, and Publishers (2)
The Literary World; a Journal of Society,
Literature, and Art (3) The Literary
World: A Journal of Science, Literature,
and Art.

Place of Publication: New York
First Issue: 6 Feb 1847
Last Issue: 31 Dec 1853//
Periodicity: Weekly
Editors: Evert A. Duyckinck; Charles Fenno
          Hoffman; George L. Duyckinck
Publishers: Osgood & Co.; Evert A. and
          George L. Duyckinck
Available From: APS; Yale Univ.* Mott.
Contents:
  Poetry: Original: Caroline M. Sawyer,
    R.S. Greeley, William Gilmore Simms,
    Ralph Hoyt, J.B. Taylor, H.T. Tuckerman,
    Mary E. Hewitt, H.J. Bradfield, R.H.
    Stoddard, William G. Dix, E.C. Kinney,
    Thomas Powell, Charles F. Brooks, Emily
    Hermann. Selected: Whittier, W.A.
    Butler, Charles MacKay, Beranger, Emma C.
    Embury, Joanna Baillie, Carl Benson,
    W.H.C. Hosmer, Martin Tupper, Edward
    Marshall, C.M. Farmer, Henry Morford,
    Frances Brown, Emily Hermann, George
    Croly, Lamartine, Poe, Theodore Hook,
    Calderón, Longfellow, Tennyson.
  Prose: Biography. Travel. Essay.
    Familiar Essay. Criticism. Letters.
    Book Reviews.
  Fiction: Essay Serials: "Sketches of
    American Life"; "What Is Talked About";
    "The Colonel's Club." Sketches.
  Miscellaneous: Extracts: from other
    journals; by various authors; Carlyle,
    Beranger, Southey, Leigh Hunt, Milton,
    Horace Smith, Emerson, Ralph Hoyt, William
    Cowper, Alfred B. Street. Literary
    Notices.

479 TITLE: <u>Littell's Dollar Magazine; Consisting of Voyages and Travels, Biography, Tales, Poetry and Miscellany.</u> [Compiled from <u>The Museum of Foreign Literature and Science</u> q.v.]

Place of Publication: Philadelphia
First Issue: Jan 1841
Last Issue: Oct 1841//?
Available From: Newberry Lib., Chicago

480 TITLES: (1) <u>Littell's Living Age</u> (2) <u>The Living Age</u>.

Place of Publication: Boston
First Issue: 11 May 1844
Last Issue: Aug 1941//
Periodicity: Weekly
Editor: Eliakim Littell
Publishers: T.H. Carter & Company; Waite, Peirce & Company; E. Littell & Company; Littell, Son & Company; Littell & Gay
Available From: APS; Lib. of Congress.*
Mott. <u>Poole</u>.
Contents:
  Poetry: <u>Selected</u>: Emerson, Bryant, Fitz-Greene Halleck, Longfellow, Luis de Camoens, William Roscoe, Charles Sprague, J.E. Carpenter, Thomas Haynes Bayly, Lydia H. Sigourney, Schiller, Schlegel, Frances Anne Butler, Thomas Hood, Charles MacKay, Frances Brown, Andrew Winter, Barry Cornwall, W.S. Landor, James Russell Lowell, Richard Howitt, William B. Tappan, John Keble, Thomas Campbell, Poe, Mary Howitt, Scott, Nathaniel P. Willis, Alan Cunningham, Elizabeth Barrett Browning.
  Prose: <u>Biography</u>: William Hazlitt, Southey, Charles James Fox, Frances Brown. <u>Travel</u>. <u>Essay</u>. <u>Criticism</u>. <u>Letters</u>. <u>Book Reviews</u>.
  Fiction: <u>Sketches</u>. <u>Tales</u>: "The Tailor Creditor"; "Our Family: A Domestic Novel"; "The Man of Genius; a Little French Novel"; "Henry Welby, the Hermit of Cripplegate"; "Ten Pounds: A Tale"; "The Love Child"; "Connor M'Gloghlin. A Tale of the Lower Shannon"; "Wine"; "The Curate; or, Hopes"; "La maison maternelle"; "Bridget Pathlaw"; "The Schoolmaster's Dream"; "The Last of the Contrabandieri"; "The Bride of an Hour"; "The Milkman of Walworth"; "Tales of the Colonies"; "Frankland the Barrister"; "Mrs. Mark Luke; or, West Country Exclusives"; "The Story of Martha Guinnis and Her Son"; "The Deformed"; "The Author's Daughter"; "Manner and Matter--A Tale"; "Helmsley Hall"; "The Young Country Clergyman.--A Scottish Story"; "The Next of Kin.--A Memoir"; "A Greek Monk's Tale"; "St. Giles and St. James"; "Capsicum House for Young Ladies"; "The Maiden Aunt"; "The One-Eyed Widow and the Schoolmaster"; "The Intercepted Letters. A Tale of the Bivouac"; "The Story of a Family"; "Feats on the Fiord", "The Cross on the Snow Mountains.--A Scandinavian Tale"; "The Maiden and Married Life of Mary Powell"; "The Modern Vassal"; "Deborah's Diary"; "Lettice Arnold"; "Maurice Tiernay, the Soldier of Fortune"; "The Heirs of Gauntry. A Tale"; "The House of Guise"; "My Novel; or, Varieties in English Life."
  Miscellaneous: <u>Extracts</u>: from other journals. <u>Anecdotes</u>: on various subjects; Dickens, Buonaparte, Shakespeare, Margaret Fuller, S. Johnson. <u>Literary Notices</u>. <u>News</u>: Foreign and Domestic.

481 TITLE: <u>Littell's Saturday Magazine, or, Spirit of the Magazines and Annuals.</u> [Superseded by <u>Littell's Spirit of the Magazines and Annuals</u> q.v.]

Place of Publication: Philadelphia
First Issue: July 1836
Last Issue: Dec 1837//
Available From: Univ. of Minn., Minneapolis*; Univ. of Ariz., Tucson*

482 TITLE: <u>Littell's Spirit of the Magazines and Annuals.</u>

Place of Publication: Philadelphia
First Issue: Jan 1838
Last Issue: 1840//
Available From: Pub. Lib. of Cincinnati*; Univ. of Ariz., Tucson*

483 TITLE: <u>The Little Gentleman</u>.

Place of Publication: New Haven, Conn.
First Issue: 1 Jan 1831
Last Issue: 29 April 1831//
Periodicity: Irregular
Editors: Students of Yale
Publisher: Hezekiah Howe
Available From: Amer. Antiquarian Soc.*; Ohio State Hist. Soc., Columbus*

Contents:
  Poetry: <u>Original</u>.
  Prose: <u>Familiar Essay</u>. <u>Letters</u>.
  Fiction: <u>Essay Serial</u>: "On Matters and Things in General." <u>Tale</u>: "The Gathering."
Note: In a 1933 letter to Clarence Brigham, Andrew Keogh, librarian at Yale University, states: "Kingsley, in his Yale book, page 349 says about it [<u>The Little Gentleman</u>]: 'The year 1831 was apparently a good year for anonymous literary enterprises among the students of the college. A second periodical, whose first number appeared in January of this year, was the <u>Little Gentleman</u>, edited, in part at least, by students of the law department. It was satirical, but not bitter or ill-natured, and afforded amusement to its unknown editors and the town. Its pages made definite allusions to lawyers, and possibly, in one or two instances, to young ladies; but it was a harmless sort of publication, whose importance consisted largely in the secret of its origin.'"

484   TITLE: The Living Age. [See Littell's
       Living Age.]

485   TITLE: The Louisville Literary News-Letter.
       Devoted to News, Science, Literature and
       the Arts.

       Place of Publication: Louisville, Ky.
       First Issue: 1 Dec 1838
       Last Issue: 28 Nov 1840//?
       Available From: Univ. of Chicago*; Univ. of
                        Ky., Lexington

486   TITLES: (1) The Lowell Offering; Repository
       of Original Articles on Various Subjects,
       Written by Factory Operatives (2) The
       Lowell Offering: A Repository of Original
       Articles, Written by Females Employed in the
       Mills (3) The Lowell Offering; a Repository
       of Original Articles, Written Exclusively
       by Females Actively Employed in the Mills
       (4) The Lowell Offering and Magazine.
       Written and Edited by Female Operatives
       (5) The Lowell Offering. Written, Edited
       and Published by Female Operatives in the
       Mills. [Superseded by New England Offer-
       ing.]

       Place of Publication: Lowell, Mass.
       First Issue: Oct 1840
       Last Issue: Dec 1845//
       Periodicity: Monthly
       Editors: Harriet Jane Hanson; Harriot F.
                 Curtis
       Publisher: William Schouler
       Available From: APS; Amer. Antiquarian Soc.*
                        Mott.
       Contents:
         Poetry: Original.
         Prose: Familiar Essay. Letters.
         Fiction: Essay Serials: "Recollections of
           an Old Maid"; "Familiar Sketches"; "Tales
           of Factory Life"; "Album Tributes";
           "Leaves"; "Sketches of the Past"; "Stories
           from the Linn-Side"; "The Portrait
           Gallery"; "Incidents of Adventure";
           "Chapter on Life as It Is." Sketches.
           Tales: "The Sea of Genius"; "Abby's
           Year in Lowell"; "The Wedding Dress";
           "Clara Stanly"; "Prejudice Against Labor";
           "Agnes and Emma"; "Evening Before Pay-
           Day"; "Harriet Greenough"; "The Princess.
           An Oriental Fairy Tale"; "Leisure Hours
           of the Mill Girls"; "The White Mountain
           Sisters"; "The Unsetting Sun"; "A Tale
           of Life as It Is"; "The Village Chronicle";
           "Garfilena. A Hungarian Tale"; "Painting
           and Sculpture. An Italian Tale"; "Truth's
           Pilgrimage."
         Miscellaneous: Literary Notices.

487   TITLE: The Lyceum Reporter and Critical
       Miscellany.

       Place of Publication: New York
       First Issue: 6 May 1842
       Last Issue: 20 August 1842//?
       Available From: N.Y. Hist. Soc.*

488   TITLE: The Magnet and Cincinnati Literary
       Gazette.

       Place of Publication: Cincinnati
       First Issue: 9 June 1827
       Last Issue: 25 Aug 1827//?
       Available From: Kan. State Hist. Soc., Topeka

489   TITLE: The Magnet and Ladies' Literary Gar-
       land.

       Place of Publication: New York
       First Issue: [Only one issue published]
                     May 1830//
       Periodicity: Intended to be monthly
       Editor: A.S. Winterbottom
       Publisher: S.N. Rudkin
       Available From: Amer. Antiquarian Soc.; N.Y.
                        Pub. Lib.
       Contents:
         Poetry: Original. Selected: Bernard Bar-
           ton, Felicia Hemans, Louisa P. Smith.
         Prose: Biography. Travel. Familiar Essay.
           Criticism.
         Fiction: Sketches.
         Miscellaneous: Anecdotes: on various sub-
           jects.

490   TITLE: The Magnolia: Or, Literary Tablet:
       Devoted to Literature, Moral and Sentimental
       Tales, Poetry, &c. &c.

       Place of Publication: Hudson, N.Y.
       First Issue: 5 Oct 1833
       Last Issue: 20 Sept 1834//
       Periodicity: Semi-monthly
       Editor: P. Dean Carrique
       Publisher: P. Dean Carrique
       Available From: APS; Yale Univ.
       Contents:
         Poetry: Original. Selected: Bryant,
           Felicia Hemans, Nathaniel P. Willis,
           Fitz-Greene Halleck, T.K. Hervey, George
           D. Prentice, Byron, Whittier, Willis
           Gaylord Clark, Thomas Haynes Bayly,
           James G. Percival, Robert Montgomery,
           Nathan C. Brooks.
         Prose: Familiar Essay. Letters.
         Fiction: Sketches. Tales: "Haviland
           Hall"; "The Novice, or the Convent Demon";
           "The Veiled Picture. A Tale of the Fine
           Arts"; "Theophilus and Isabella: A Tale
           Founded on Fact"; "The Stolen Daughter";
           "The Flute Player. A Tale"; "The Two
           Rings. A Tale of the Thirteenth Century";
           "The Murdered Lovers. A Tale of the
           Revolution"; "Arthur St. John"; "Amiot
           and Stanley; or a Change of Fortune";
           "The Broken Heart" [W. Irving]; "The
           Physician's Visit"; "The Merchant's
           Daughter."
         Miscellaneous: Anecdotes: on various sub-
           jects. News: Domestic.

491   TITLE: The Magnolia; or, Southern Apalachian.
       A Literary Magazine and Monthly Review.
       [See The Southern Ladies' Book: A Magazine
       of Literature, Science and Arts.]

492 TITLE: The Magnolia: Or Southern Monthly. [See The Southern Ladies' Book: A Magazine of Literature, Science and Arts.]

493 TITLE: The Maine Monthly Magazine. [Formed by the union of The Portland Magazine q.v. and The Eastern Magazine q.v.]

Place of Publication: Bangor; Portland, Me.
First Issue: July 1836
Last Issue: June 1837//
Periodicity: Monthly
Editor: Charles Gilman
Publishers: Duren & Thatcher; Edward Stephens
Available From: APS; Hist. Soc. of Pa.*
          Mott.
Contents:
  Poetry: Original: Jane Locke, Hannah F. Gould, George W. Patten, C.P. Cranch. Selected: J.N. M'Jilton, Lydia H. Sigourney, Thomas Moore, Grenville Mellen, Isaac C. Pray, Jr., Thomas Campbell, Shelley, Park Benjamin.
  Prose: Travel. Familiar Essay. Criticism. Book Reviews.
  Fiction: Essay Serials: "Philosophical Musings"; "Stray Leaves from My Portfolio." Sketches. Tales: "The Ruin"; "My Friend's Marriage"; "A Visit to the Old Homestead"; "My Uncle Ben's Wig"; "The Emigrant"; "A Legend of Monhegan"; "Louisburgh"; "Julia St. Germain. A Tale from Facts"; "The Dark Lake, a Tale of Superstition"; "The Maniac Hermit"; "Simpkinses"; "A Trip Out of Town: Or--Knight of the Long Nine."
  Miscellaneous: Extracts: by various authors. Literary Notices.

494 TITLE: Maine Washingtonian Journal and Temperance Herald. Devoted to Temperance, General News of the Day, Selected Tales, Poetry, Agriculture, Domestic Economy, &c. &c. [See Washingtonian Temperance Journal and Family Reader. Devoted to Temperance, General News of the Day, Selected Tales, Poetry, Agriculture, Domestic Economy, &c. &c.]

495 TITLE: The Manuscript.

Place of Publication: New York
First Issue: [Undated. nos. 1-12] 1827-28//
Periodicity: Monthly
Editor: Elam Bliss
Publishers: G. & C. Carvill; Elam Bliss
Available From: APS; Lib. of Congress
Contents:
  Prose: Familiar Essay.
  Fiction: Tales: "The Sagacious Dog"; "The Visit"; "Mary Linden"; "The Highland Banditti"; "The Country Clergyman"; "The Money Dreamer"; "Tales of the Prison"; "The Legend of Schooley Mountain"; "The Reward of Avarice"; "The Rival Lovers"; "The Faithful Greek."
  Miscellaneous: Extracts: from other journals; by various authors; William Cowper, Thomas Moore.

496 TITLES: (1) Masonic Mirror: And Mechanics' Intelligencer (2) Boston Masonic Mirror (3) Boston Masonic Mirror: Science, Literature and Miscellany.

Place of Publication: Boston
First Issue: 7 Jan 1826
Last Issue: 25 Jan 1834//
Periodicity: Weekly
Editor: Charles W. Moore
Publishers: Moore & Prowse; Moore & Sevey
Available From: APS; Harvard Univ.
Contents:
  Poetry: Original: Stephen Greenleaf, Henry Stone. Selected: Mary Anne Browne, Bryant, James G. Percival, James Hogg, Caroline Goodwin, James G. Brooks, Thomas Campbell, James W. Miller, William Pitt Palmer, Thomas Pringle, Hannah F. Gould, Felicia Hemans, Matthew Gregory [Monk] Lewis, Allan Cunningham, John Bowering, John Nichols, Thomas Marshall, Fitz-Greene Halleck, Thomas Moore, Thomas Haynes Bayly, Thomas Hood, Henry Neele, Miss Jewesbury, Scott, Burns, Caroline Lamb, L.E. Landon, Emma C. Embury, C.E. Horn, Caroline Norton, Grenville Mellen, Hugh Moore.
  Prose: Biography: Defoe. Essay. Familiar Essay. Criticism. Book Reviews.
  Fiction: Sketches. Tales: "The Tiger"; "Fernando, or, the Force of Conscience"; "Eleanor of Gwienne"; "The Guerrilla Chief"; "A Legend of Love"; "Ellen, an American Tale of 1814"; "The Lovers"; "Edgar and Amelia"; "Laurel Hill"; "The Robber's Daughter"; "Palermon"; "The Last Relic"; "Look a Second Time"; "Gideon Grinder"; "The Smuggler"; "The Death Warrant"; "The Ruined Man"; "Going in the Country"; "The Honey Moon"; "The Boa Constrictor and Goat"; "Dancing with a Prince"; "Evelina" [Fanny Burney]; "The Sailor Boy's First Voyage"; "Is He Married?"; "The Righteous Never Forsaken"; "The Last Day of Grace"; "The Hindoo Mother"; "The Wedding Day"; "My Aunt Tabitha"; "The Vision of Cynthia"; "My Cousin Isabel"; "The Stormed Fort"; "Recollections of the Revolution"; "The Silesian Girl"; "Hell Bridge"; "The Last of the Druids"; "The Imprisoned"; "Confessions of a Convict"; "The Goddesses"; "Mariana the Neapolitane"; "The Clepht. A Tale of the Morca"; "The Hour of Fortune"; "The Soldier's Wife"; "A Husking: Or the First and Last Spree"; "Sacrifice of a Hindoo Woman"; "The Twins"; "Hungarian Horse Dealer"; "The Corrupt Judge"; "The Tin Pedler and Sleepy David"; "The Betrothed"; "The Buccaneer"; "Peabody's Leap"; "An African's Revenge" [Eugene Sue].
  Miscellaneous: Anecdotes: on various subjects; R.B. Sheridan, Thomas Paine, Scott, Franklin, John Quincy Adams. Literary Notices. News: Foreign and Domestic.

497 TITLE: The Masonic Miscellany and Ladies' Literary Magazine, a Periodical Publication Devoted to Masonic and General Literature.

Place of Publication: Lexington, Ky.
First Issue: July 1821
Last Issue: June 1823//
Periodicity: Monthly
Editor: William Gibbes Hunt
Publisher: William Gibbes Hunt
Available From: Harvard Univ.; Western
        Reserve Hist. Soc., Cleve-
        land. Mott.
Contents:
  Poetry: Original. Selected.
  Prose: Familiar Essay. Letters.
  Fiction: Sketches. Tales: "The Cypress
    Crown--A Tale"; "Valerius--A Roman Story";
    "The Graves of the Forest"; "The Force
    of Filial Affection. A Moral Tale";
    "Julia and Edward."
  Miscellaneous: Extracts: by various
    authors; W. Irving, Hannah More, James
    Fenimore Cooper. Anecdotes: on various
    subjects; Smollett, S. Johnson.

498   TITLE: The Masonic Olive Branch and Literary
       Portfolio.

Place of Publication: Fredericksburg, Va.
First Issue: 2 Jan 1837
Last Issue: 15 Sept 1837//?
Available From: Huntington Lib., San Marino,
        Calif.*

499   TITLES: (1) The Massachusetts Magazine: Or,
    Monthly Museum of Knowledge and Rational
    Entertainment (2) The Massachusetts Maga-
    zine, or Monthly Museum. Containing the
    Literature, History, Politics, Arts,
    Manners, & Amusements of the Age.

Place of Publication: Boston
First Issue: Jan 1789
Last Issue: Dec 1796//
Periodicity: Monthly
Editors: Thaddeus Mason Harris; William
       Biglow
Publishers: Isaiah Thomas and Company
Available From: Amer. Antiquarian Soc.*;
        Lib. of Congress.* Mott.
Contents:
  Poetry: Original: Thaddeus Mason Harris.
    Selected: William Jones, Hester L. Thrale
    Piozzi, Mather Byles, Charlotte Smith,
    Thomas Paine, S. Johnson, Goldsmith,
    Timothy Dwight, Garrick Franklin, Burns,
    Hannah More, Joel Barlow.
  Prose: Biography. Travel. Essay.
    Familiar Essay. Criticism. Letters.
    Book Reviews.
  Fiction: Essay Serials: "The General
    Observer"; "The Essayist"; "The Occa-
    sional Visitor"; "The Gleanor"; "The
    Mirror"; "The Repository"; "The Memo-
    rialist"; "The Speculator"; "The Inves-
    tigator"; "The Echo"; "The Venator."
    Sketches. Tales: "Florio, an Affecting
    Story"; "Good and Bad News, a Tale";
    "Vanessa: Or, the Feast of Reason";
    "Lindor's Story"; "The Misfortunes of
    Ligrae, a Tale too True"; "Alexis: Or,
    the Cottage in the Woods"; "Melancholy

Tale of Seduction"; "Sacontala: Or, the
    Fatal Ring"; "Ivar and Matilda"; "Rofetta,
    a Tale"; "Sadok, a Tale"; "Walter, a Tale."
  Miscellaneous: Extracts: from other jour-
    nals; by various authors; William Bartram,
    Mary Wollstonecraft, Goldsmith, Sterne,
    Hester L. Thrale Piozzi, Addison, Boswell,
    Fanny Burney, Franklin, B. D'Israeli.
    News: Foreign and Domestic.
Note: Several leading contributors are Joseph
    Dennie, Sarah Wentworth Morton, and
    William Biglow.

500   TITLE: The Massachusetts Quarterly Review.

Place of Publication: Boston
First Issue: Dec 1847
Last Issue: Sept 1850//
Periodicity: Quarterly
Editors: Ralph Waldo Emerson; Theodore
       Parker; James Elliot Cabot
Publishers: Coolidge & Wiley
Available From: Amer. Antiquarian Soc.*;
        Lib. of Congress.* Mott.
        Poole.
Contents:
  Poetry: Original. Selected.
  Prose: Biography. Essay. Criticism: on
    William Prescott, Emerson, William Ellery
    Channing, John Quincy Adams. Book Reviews.
  Miscellaneous: Literary Notices.
Note: Leading contributors: Emerson, Samuel
    G. Howe, George Findlay, James Russell
    Lowell, Richard Hildreth, Theodore Parker.

501   TITLES: (1) The Massachusetts Spy (2) The
    Massachusetts Spy or, Thomas's Boston
    Journal (3) Thomas's Massachusetts Spy or,
    American Oracle of Liberty (4) Thomas's
    Massachusetts Spy or, the Worcester Gazette
    (5) The Worcester Magazine q.v. (6) Thomas's
    Massachusetts Spy or, the Worcester Gazette.

Place of Publication: Boston; Worcester, Mass.
First Issue: 17 July 1770
Last Issue: 11 Oct 1820//
Periodicity: Tri-weekly; Bi-weekly; Weekly
Editors: Isaiah Thomas; Z. Fowle; James
       Elliot
Publishers: Isaiah Thomas; Z. Fowle; James
       Elliot
Available From: Amer. Antiquarian Soc.*
Contents:
  Poetry: Original. Selected.
  Prose: Essay.
  Miscellaneous: Anecdotes: on various sub-
    jects. Literary Notices. News: Foreign
    and Domestic.
Note: Although primarily a newspaper, this
    publication is of literary interest.

502   TITLE: The Massachusetts Watchman, and
       Periodical Journal.

Place of Publication: Palmer, Mass.
First Issue: June 1809
Last Issue: May 1810//?
Periodicity: Monthly

Editor: Ezekiel Terry
Publisher: Ezekial Terry
Available From: APS; N.Y. Hist. Soc.
Contents:
  Poetry: Original. Selected.
  Prose: Biography. Essay. Familiar Essay.
  Fiction: Sketches. Tales: "The Squire
    and the Farmer's Daughter"; "The Cobler
    of Messina."
  Miscellaneous: Extracts: from other jour-
    nals; by various authors. Anecdotes: on
    various subjects; Pope, Swift, Franklin,
    Isaac Newton. News: Domestic.

503   TITLE: Le Médiateur, journal politique et
       littéraire.

Place of Publication: Philadelphia
First Issue: 2 April 1814
Last Issue: 3 Aug 1814//?
Periodicity: Weekly
Editor: C.A.F. Levavasseur
Publisher: J. Desnoues
Available From: Harvard Univ.; Amer.
                Philosophical Soc.,
                Philadelphia*
Contents:
  Poetry: Selected.
  Prose: Familiar Essay. Book Reviews.
  Miscellaneous: Anecdotes: on various sub-
    jects. Literary Notices. News: Foreign.
Note: Devoted largely to the Napoleonic
  struggles.

504   TITLE: The Medley, or Monthly Miscellany.

Place of Publication: Lexington, Ky.
First Issue: Jan 1803
Last Issue: Dec 1803//
Periodicity: Monthly
Editors: ?
Publishers: ?
Available From: APS; Lib. of Congress.*
                Mott.
Contents:
  Poetry: Original. Selected: Thomas Paine.
  Prose: Biography: Charles James Fox,
    Jefferson, William Jones, Samuel Adams.
    Essay. Familiar Essay. Criticism.
    Letters.
  Fiction: Essay Serial: "The Ambulator."
    Sketches. Tales: "History of Mr.
    Allen"; "Abou Taib: An Eastern Tale";
    "Omar; or the Punishment of Avarice";
    "History of Maria Arnold"; "The Story of
    Alcander and Septimus"; "National
    Prejudices Overcome; or the History of
    Sir Oliver George"; "The Vision of Hamid.
    An Eastern Tale." Drama: "Oromasis. A
    Dialogue."
  Miscellaneous: Extracts: from other jour-
    nals; by various authors; Kotzebue,
    Jefferson, Mary Wollstonecraft. Anec-
    dotes: on various subjects.

505   TITLE: The Medly; or, the Saturday's Comical
       Amuse'r.

Place of Publication: Albany
First Issue: 18 Aug 1827
Last Issue: 3 Nov 1837//
Available From: N.Y. Hist. Soc*

506   TITLE: Merrimack Magazine and Ladies'
       Literary Cabinet. [Merged with the
       Merrimack Miscellany q.v.]

Place of Publication: Newburyport, Mass.
First Issue: 17 Aug 1805
Last Issue: 9 Aug 1806//
Periodicity: Weekly
Editors: Whittingham Gilman; John Gilman
Publishers: Whittingham and John Gilman
Available From: APS; Amer. Antiquarian Soc.*
Contents:
  Poetry: Original. Selected: Thomas Dibdin,
    Anthony Pasquin, William Cowper, S. John-
    son, R.B. Sheridan, James Thomson, James
    Beattie, Edmund Waller, Fulke Greville,
    Swift.
  Prose: Biography: Henry Mackenzie. Essay.
    Familiar Essay. Criticism. Letters.
  Fiction: Essay Serial: "Sentimental
    Gleaner." Sketches. Tales: "The Turn-
    pike Gate: A Tale"; "The Kind Uncle: A
    Moral Tale"; "The Twin Brothers. A Tale";
    "The Slaves. A Tale too True"; "The
    Recluse"; "The Pretended Sage. An Arabic
    Tale"; "The Wild Rose of Langollen";
    "The Rigid Father. A Tale"; "Angelina.
    A Tale"; "Florio and Lucilla. A Moral
    Tale"; "Almira and Alonzo"; "Frank Leeson.
    A Singular Tale, Founded on Fact."
    Novels: "William and Mary"; "The Star-
    ling." Drama: "The Father: Or, Ameri-
    can Shandyism" [William Dunlap].
  Miscellaneous: Extracts: from other jour-
    nals. Anecdotes: on various subjects;
    Fenelon, Goldsmith, Washington, Swift,
    Franklin. Literary Notices. News: Do-
    mestic.

507   TITLE: Merrimack Miscellany. [Merged with
       the Merrimack Magazine and Ladies' Literary
       Cabinet q.v.]

Place of Publication: Newburyport, Mass.
First Issue: 8 June 1805
Last Issue: 5 Oct 1805//
Periodicity: Weekly
Editor: William B. Allen
Publisher: William B. Allen
Available From: APS; Amer. Antiquarian Soc.*
Contents:
  Poetry: Original. Selected: Erasmus
    Darwin, William Cowper, Richard Cumber-
    land, Amelia Opie.
  Prose: Biography: David Humphreys, John
    Trumbull, Mary Wollstonecraft, Joel
    Barlow. Letters: Lady Mary Wortley
    Montagu.
  Fiction: Essay Serial: "The Collectanea."
    Sketches. Tale: "The Widow and Her Son.
    A Popular Turkish Tale."
  Miscellaneous: Extracts: from other jour-
    nals. Anecdotes: on various subjects;
    Hogarth, Addison, Earsmus. Literary
    Notices. News: Domestic.

508   TITLE: Merry's Museum and Parley's Magazine.
      [See Robert Merry's Museum.]

509   TITLE: The Methodist Magazine, for the Year
      1797 [and 1798]. Containing Original
      Sermons, Experiences, Letters, and Other
      Religious Pieces; Together with Instructive
      and Useful Extracts, from Different Authors.

      Place of Publication: Philadelphia
      First Issue: Jan 1797
      Last Issue: Dec 1798//
      Periodicity: Monthly
      Editors: ?
      Publishers: Henry Tuckniss; John Dickins
      Available From: APS; Lib. Co. of Philadel-
                       phia.* Mott.
      Contents:
        Poetry: Original. Selected.
        Prose: Biography: of religious figures.
        Travel. Essay: "Thoughts on the Writings
        of Baron Swedenborg" [John Wesley]; "Cu-
        rious Remarks on the Different Degrees of
        Heat Imbibed from the Sun's Rays, by
        Clothes of Different Colours" [Franklin].
        Familiar Essay. Letters.
        Fiction: Sketches.
        Miscellaneous: Extracts: by various
        authors. Anecdotes: on various subjects.

510   TITLES: (1) The Metropolitan; a Miscellany
      of Literature and Science (2) The Washing-
      ton Literary Gazette; a Miscellany of
      Literature, Science, and the Fine Arts.

      Place of Publication: Washington, D.C.
      First Issue: 5 Dec 1832
      Last Issue: 8 Feb 1837//
      Periodicity: Weekly [Irregular]
      Editors: ?
      Publishers: ?
      Available From: Lib. of Congress; N.Y. Pub.
                       Lib.
      Contents:
        Poetry: Original: R.H. Pratt. Selected:
        Southey, James Sheridan Knowles, Felicia
        Hemans, J.W. Simmons, Caroline Norton,
        Barry Cornwall, Thomas Hood.
        Prose: Essay. Familiar Essay. Criticism.
        Letters. Book Reviews.
        Fiction: Essay Serial: "Confessions of an
        Old Bachelor." Sketches. Tales: "Love
        and Authorship"; "A Sea-Scape"; "La
        Sortilega; or, the Charmed Ring"; "The
        Mutiny"; "Tom Fane and I"; "Mirabeau";
        "The Steam Excursion"; "Jacob Faithful";
        "Mr. Clarence Gower: Or, a Peep into a
        'Genteel' Boarding House"; "The Brothers,
        An Authentic Tale of Ireland"; "Japhet
        in Search of a Father"; "Tom Raffles."
        Miscellaneous: Extracts: from other jour-
        nals; by various authors; Nathaniel P.
        Willis. Anecdotes: on various subjects;
        Isaac Newton, Buonaparte. Literary
        Notices. News: Foreign and Domestic.

511   TITLE: The Metropolitan Magazine.

      Place of Publication: New Haven, Conn.
      First Issue: 1833
      Last Issue: 1835//
      Periodicity: Monthly
      Editors: ?
      Publishers: Peck and Newton
      Available From: Lib. of Congress*; Amer.
                       Antiquarian Soc.*
      Contents:
        Poetry: Original: John Francis. Selected:
        Byron, R. Shelton Mackenzie.
        Prose: Biography. Travel. Familiar Essay.
        Fiction: Essay Serials: "The Oxonian";
        "The Pasha of Many Tales." Sketches.
        Tales: "Imprisonment for Debt. A True
        Story"; "Jacob Faithful"; "The Spanish
        Barber"; "Minnie Grey; or, the Shepherd
        of Shingham's Daughter"; "Fortune's
        Frolics"; "Dick Dennett; or, the Sanguine
        Man"; "The Wedding Garment"; "The Spunging
        House"; "Maria Howard. A Tale of Real
        Life"; "Clara; or, Love and Superstition";
        "The Life of a Sub-Editor"; "Japhet, in
        Search of a Father"; "Antonio, the
        Student of Padua."
        Miscellaneous: Literary Notices.

512   TITLE: The Metropolitan Magazine. [American
      Edition.]

      Place of Publication: New York
      First Issue: Jan 1836
      Last Issue: June 1842//
      Periodicity: Monthly
      Editors: Theodore Foster; William Lewer
      Publishers: Theodore Foster; William Lewer
      Available From: Yale Univ.*; Princeton Univ.
      Contents:
        Poetry: Original: R. Shelton Mackenzie,
        L.M. Montagu, Washington Browne, J.B.
        Walker, Nathaniel P. Willis. Selected:
        John Waring, Richard Howitt, G. Douglas
        Thompson, Beranger, E. Lytton Bulwer,
        Schiller, Mary Boyle, R.S. Fisher.
        Prose: Travel. Criticism. Letters.
        Book Reviews.
        Fiction: Essay Serials: "Leaves from My
        Minute-Book"; "Paris in Light and Shade";
        "Ephemera, or Etchings from Life."
        Sketches. Tales: "Diary of a Blasé";
        "Snarleyyow; or, the Dog Friend" [Marryat];
        "The Life of a Sub-Editor; or, a Mid-
        shipman's Cruises"; "'The Bouncing
        Amazon'"; "The Charity Sister. A Tale";
        "The Fortune Hunter. A Tale of Harrogate";
        "The Expiation"; "The Young Pretender.
        A Tale"; "Frank Farley"; "The Life,
        Opinions, and Pensile Adventures of John
        Ketch"; "Ardent Troughton, the Wrecked
        Merchant"; "Mr. Midshipman Easy"
        [Marryat]; "Paleotti. A Tale of Truth";
        "The Prima Donna. A Tale"; "The Floren-
        tine Merchant. A Tale"; "Family Inter-
        ference. A Tale for Young Married People";

"The Maremma"; "The Bench and the Bar"; "The Mariner's Daughter. A Story of the Sea"; "The 'Bit o' Writin'"; "Peggy Canty, the Southern Irisher"; "The Backwoods of America"; "The Impregnable Bachelor"; "The Chiffonier of Paris"; "The Black Silk Dress"; "'What Has Become of Her?' A Tale of Nassau."

513   TITLE: Meyer's British Chronicle, a Universal Review of British Literature, &c.

Place of Publication: New York
First Issue: Jan 1827
Last Issue: 1831//?
Periodicity: Monthly
Editors: ?
Publishers: ?
Available From: Univ. of Calif., Berkeley; Lib. of Congress
Contents:
    Poetry: Selected: Thomas Hood, Thomas Moore, James Montgomery, Felicia Hemans, Allan Cunningham, Robert Montgomery, Coleridge.
    Prose: Biography: Buonaparte. Travel. Essay. Criticism. Book Reviews.
    Fiction: Sketches. Tales: "Captain Maitland's Narrative"; "An Old Sailor's Tale"; "The Fate of the Gamester"; "Life in the British Army"; "The Depôt--the Mess--the Duel."
    Miscellaneous: Extracts: from other journals; by various authors; Scott, Byron, W. Irving, Leigh Hunt. Anecdotes: on various subjects; Scott, R.B. Sheridan, Washington. Literary Notices.

514   TITLE: The Microcosm: A Literary and Religious Magazine. [See The Microcosm: Or the Little World of Home.]

515   TITLE: The Microscope and General Advertiser. [See The Microscope. By Tim Tickler, Jr. Esq.]

516   TITLES: (1) The Microcosm: Or the Little World of Home (2) The Microcosm: A Literary and Religious Magazine.

Place of Publication: New Haven, Conn.
First Issue: July 1834
Last Issue: Oct 1837//
Periodicity: Monthly
Editors: ?
Publishers: Peck & Newton; Whitmore & Buckingham; P.B. Whitmore; L.H. Young
Available From: Amer. Antiquarian Soc.*; Lib. of Congress*
Contents:
    Poetry: Original. Selected: G.E. Daggett, Coleridge, Felicia Hemans, Charles Sprague, James Hall, Bernard Barton, William Cowper, Emma C. Embury, Charles Lamb, Wordsworth, Egerton Brydges, George Herbert, John Davies, John Bowring, James William Miller.

Prose: Essay. Familiar Essay. Criticism: on Felicia Hemans, Wordsworth. Letters. Book Reviews.
Fiction: Essay Serial: "The Little Genius." Sketches. Tales: "Visit to a New Married Couple"; "Mary Heartly; or, the Evils of Protracted Courtship"; "The Wife for a Missionary"; "Edward Fairfield; or, the Influence of Suspicion"; "A Love Letter and Its Consequences"; "The Guardian Angel"; "The History of a Trifler."
Miscellaneous: Extracts: from other journals; by various authors. Anecdotes: on various subjects. Literary Notices.

517   TITLES: (1) The Microscope, and Herald of Fancy (2) The Microscope, and Independent Examiner.

Place of Publication: Albany
First Issue: 10 March 1821
Last Issue: 20 Dec 1827//?
Periodicity: Weekly
Editors: ?
Publishers: ?
Available From: APS; Amer. Antiquarian Soc.
Contents:
    Poetry: Original. Selected.
    Prose: Biography: Byron. Letters. Book Reviews.
    Fiction: Sketches. Tale: "Peter Kraus. The Legend of the Goatherd."
    Miscellaneous: Extracts: from other journals. Anecdotes: on various subjects. Literary Notices. News: Domestic.

518   TITLE: The Microscope, and Independent Examiner. [See The Microscope, and Herald of Fancy.]

519   TITLES: (1) The Microscope. By Tim Tickler, Jr. Esq. (2) The Microscope and General Advertiser.

Place of Publication: Louisville, Ky.; New Albany, Ind.
First Issue: 17 April 1824
Last Issue: 10 Sept 1825//
Periodicity: Weekly
Editor: T.H. Roberts
Publisher: Johnston & Roberts
Available From: APS; Univ. of Chicago
Contents:
    Poetry: Original. Selected: Samuel Woodworth.
    Prose: Letters.
    Fiction: Tales: "Sally's Vindication"; "The Gambler--(A Tale of Truth)"; "The Modern Griselda, or, a Lesson to Wives"; "The Young Robber." Novel: "René, a Novel Translated from the French" [Chateaubriand].
    Miscellaneous: Extracts: by various authors. Anecdotes: on various subjects; William Shenstone, Molière. Literary Notices.
Note: The purpose of this journal was to suppress vice and "to shoot folly as it flies." As a result, the office was

raided and destroyed. Then on 22 September 1824, the paper appeared in New Albany, Ind.

520   TITLE: The Microscope, Edited by a Fraternity of Gentlemen.

Place of Publication: New Haven, Conn.
First Issue: 21 March 1820
Last Issue: 8 Sept 1820//
Periodicity: Bi-weekly
Editors: ?
Publishers: A.H. Maltby & Co.
Available From: APS; Lib. of Congress*
Contents:
  Poetry: Original. Selected: Pope.
  Prose: Essay. Familiar Essay. Criticism. Letters.
  Fiction: Sketches. Tale: "The Affecting History of Gabriel Gap."

521   TITLES: (1) The Middlesex Gazette (2) The Middlesex Gazette, or Federal Adviser.

Place of Publication: Middletown, Conn.
First Issue: 8 Nov 1785
Last Issue: 28 Dec 1820//
Periodicity: Weekly
Editors: ?
Publishers: Woodward & Green; Moses H. Woodward; T. Dunning; T. & J.P. Dunning
Available From: Amer. Antiquarian Soc.*
Contents:
  Poetry: Original. Selected: James Montgomery, Jane Taylor, Dorothy Dubois, Swift, William Cowper, George Crabbe, Joseph Brown Ladd.
  Prose: Biography. Familiar Essay. Book Reviews.
  Fiction: Sketches. Tales: "On the Venality of Servants: An Italian Story"; "Mary"; "Harlequin"; "Look Out!"; "The History of Leonora De Valesco"; "Honesty Is the Best Policy."
  Miscellaneous: Anecdotes: on various subjects; Dryden. News: Foreign and Domestic.

522   TITLES: (1) The Minerva, or Literary, Entertaining, and Scientific Journal: Containing a Variety of Original and Selected Articles, Arranged under the Following Heads: Popular Tales, the Gleaner, the Traveller, the Drama, Biography, Arts and Sciences, Literature, Poetry, etc. (2) The New-York Literary Gazette, and Phi Betta Kappa Repository (3) The New-York Literary Gazette, and American Athenaeum.

Place of Publication: New York
First Issue: 6 April 1822
Last Issue: 3 March 1827//?
Periodicity: Weekly
Editors: George Houston; James G. Brooks; George Bond

Publishers: E. Bliss and E. White; James G. Brooks; James G. Brooks & George Bond
Available From: APS; Lib. of Congress.* Mott.
Contents:
  Poetry: Original. Selected: Felicia Hemans, Francis Quarles, L.E. Landon, Alaric Watts, Barry Cornwall, Charles James Fox, Herbert Knowles, Thomas Moore, Wordsworth, Bernard Barton, John Bowring, Washington Allston, Sumner Lincoln Fairfield, Byron, Nathaniel P. Willis, Coleridge, Thomas Roscoe, James Hogg, John Neal, Charles Lamb, William Gilmore Simms, Allan Cunningham, Joanna Baillie, Herrick, Robert Bloomfield, Shakespeare, Frances Wright, John Clare, William Roscoe, J.R. Sutermeister, Luis de Camoens, Goethe, Shelley, Charles Dibdin.
  Prose: Biography: Schiller, Pope, S. Johnson, John Dennis, William Falconer, Hogarth, Burns, Chatterton, J. Macpherson, Walter Raleigh, Jane Shore, Rousseau, Luis de Camoens, Montesquieu. Travel. Essay. Familiar Essay. Criticism: on Charles Brockden Brown. Letters. Book Reviews.
  Fiction: Essay Serials: "Desultory Thoughts and Sketches"; "Solitary Hours"; "The Pilgrim." Sketches. Tales: "Firouz-Abdel. A Tale of the Upas Tree"; "The Golden Snuff-Box"; "Ver-Vert; or, the Parrot of the Nuns"; "The Conscious Lovers; a Tale of the Drama"; "Ben Pie, or the Indian Murderer: A Tale Founded on Facts"; "The Arab Chief"; "The Hungarian Girl"; "Paul Wilmot"; "Henry Birkenshaw"; "The Bridal Eve"; "Maria Maitland. An English Story"; "The Love-Charm"; "The Bottle-Imp"; "The Grotto of the Heart"; "Dream-Children: A Reverie" [Charles Lamb]; "The Sorcerers, a Legend"; "The Nameless Story"; "The Indian Orphan" [L.E. Landon]; "The King of the Peak, a Derbyshire Tale"; "The Miller of Eldrig"; "The Yorkshire Alehouse"; "Kate of Windiewa's"; "The Mother's Dream"; "The Archer of Ulvescroft"; "The Death of Walter Selby"; "The Dice"; "Iolanda; or the Court of Love"; "The Alchymist of Pisa"; "The Haunted Cellar"; "Omar of Bagdad. A Moral Tale"; "Claudine. A Swiss Tale"; "Nytram, Prince of Paramania: An Oriental Tale"; "The Door in the Wall. An English Modern Tale"; "The Czar and Czarowitz. A Russian Tale"; "Princess Matilda and Prince Morterio. A Saracen Tale"; "The Twin Brothers of Mezzorania. An African Tale"; "The Green Coat, and the Brown Coat. A Tale for Men of Pleasure"; "Edric of the Forest. A Romance"; "The Rival Brothers"; "The Criminal; an English Narrative"; "The Dread of the Supernatural"; "Isabella, or the Picture of a Peer not yet Deceased"; "Perrin; or Rural Probity"; "The Brothers of Dijon"; "Story of Griselda"; "The Black Gondola"; "The Peer and the Village Curate"; "Hormona, or the Grateful Slave";

"The Abbey of Clunedale"; "The Story of
Father Nicholas"; "Story of Flavilla";
"The Midnight Murder"; "Muzio, an
Italian Tale"; "Ottmar. An Eastern
Tale"; "The Royal Taylor. A Tartarian
Tale"; "Theodora: A Moral Tale"; "Janet
Armstrong; an Irish Tale"; "Gustavus
and Adelina"; "Love in the Galleys"; "The
Vicar's Tale"; "Nina, or the Maniac of
Villeneuve"; "Selico and Berissa, an
African Tale"; "The Good Natured Man:
A Tale of the Drama"; "Bathmendi; A
Persian Tale"; "A New Tale of Temper"
[Amelia Opie]; "The Power of Beauty.
A Syrian Tale"; "The Quaker; a Tale of
the Drama"; "Emma the Foundling. A Tale
of the Eleventh Century"; "The Exile of
the Alleghany; or National Gratitude.
An American Tale"; Ishmael and Miriam.
A Tale of the Desert"; "Amelia Neville;
a True Story"; "Angelica: Or the
Munificent Heiress"; "The Recluse";
"Wilson Merton"; "Amurath, an Eastern
Monarch."
Miscellaneous: Extracts: from other jour-
nals; by various authors; William Hayley.
Anecdotes: on various subjects.
Literary Notices. News: Foreign and
Domestic.

523   TITLE: The Minerva; or, Lady's and Gentlemen's Magazine.

Place of Publication: Richmond
First Issue: 11 Sept 1804
Last Issue: ?
Available From: Va. State Lib., Richmond

524   TITLE: The Minerviad: Devoted to Literature
and Amusement, for the Ladies.

Place of Publication: Boston
First Issue: 30 March 1822
Last Issue: 7 Sept 1822//
Periodicity: Semi-monthly
Editor: John R. Parker
Publisher: John R. Parker
Available From: APS; Amer. Antiquarian Soc.*
Contents:
  Poetry: Original. Selected: Amelia Opie.
  Prose: Biography. Familiar Essay. Criti-
    cism: on Byron, Southey.
  Fiction: Essay Serials: "The Plagiary";
    "The Ladies' Friend"; "The Epigrammatist";
    "Mooriana"; "The Ladies' Kaleidoscope";
    "The Physiogomist." Sketches. Tales:
    "The Sorrows of Amelia; or, Deluded
    Innocence. A Tale--Founded on Fact";
    "Adelaide; or, the Lovely Rustic"; "Story
    of Cecilia--A Tale"; "Amelia: Or the
    Sentimental Fair"; "Journey in Quest of
    a Wife."
  Miscellaneous: Extracts: from other jour-
    nals. Anecdotes: on various subjects;
    William Shenstone. Literary Notices.

525   TITLE: The Mirror of Literature, Amusement,
and Instruction. Containing Original
Essays, Historical Narratives, Biographical
Memoirs, Manners & Customs, Sketches, Tales
of Humor, Anecdotes, Gems of Wit, Sentiment,
Poetry, &c.

Place of Publication: Boston
First Issue: ?
Last Issue: 1825//?
Periodicity: Monthly
Editors: ?
Publishers: Perkins, Wait & Co.
Available From: APS; Boston Pub. Lib.
Contents:
  Poetry: Original. Selected: Thomas
    Campbell, Felicia Hemans, Byron,
    Shakespeare, Schiller.
  Prose: Biography: Buonaparte. Travel.
    Essay. Familiar Essay. Criticism: on
    Byron, Milton, Shakespeare, W. Irving,
    Swift, Pope. Book Reviews.
  Fiction: Essay Serials: "Modern Pilgrim-
    ages"; "Table Talk"; "The Family Journal."
    Sketches. Tales: "Harry Halter the
    Highwayman"; "The Lepreghaun, or Gold
    Goblin"; "Rouge et Noir"; "The Village
    Bells"; "Ada Reis: A Tale."
  Miscellaneous: Extracts: from other jour-
    nals. Anecdotes: on various subjects.

526   TITLE: The Mirror of Taste and Dramatic
Censor.

Place of Publication: Philadelphia
First Issue: Jan 1810
Last Issue: Dec 1811//
Periodicity: Monthly
Editor: Stephen Cullen Carpenter
Publishers: Bradford and Inskeep; Thomas
            Barton Zantzinger and Co.
Available From: APS; Univ. of Pa.* Mott.
Contents:
  Poetry: Original. Selected: Thomas Moore,
    Byron, William Holloway, Henry Kirke
    White, Burns, Milton, Herrick, Richard
    Cumberland, Joanna Baillie, John Davis.
  Prose: Biography: J.P. Kemble, Garrick,
    Colley Cibber, Abraham Cowley, William
    Cowper, Lope de Vega, Thomas Cooper,
    Thomas Betterton. Essay. Familiar Essay.
    Criticism. Letters. Book Reviews.
  Fiction: Essay Serial: "Dramaticus."
    Sketches. Drama: "The Foundling of the
    Forest. A Play"; "Man and Wife; or,
    More Secrets Than One: A Comedy";
    "Venoni, or the Novice of St. Marks"; "A
    New Way to Pay Old Debts, a Comedy";
    "Alfonso, King of Castile: A Tragedy
    in Five Acts" [Matthew Gregory (Monk)
    Lewis]; "The Free Knights, or the Edict
    of Charlemagne: A Drama in Three Acts."
  Miscellaneous: Anecdotes: on various sub-
    jects; Voltaire, Garrick, John Gay,
    Thomas Cooper, Addison, Swift, Molière,
    Hannah More, S. Johnson, Lope de Vega,
    Anthony Pasquin. Literary Notices.

527   TITLE: <u>The Mirror of Taste, and Wednesday Morning Family Miscellany</u>.

Place of Publication: Philadelphia
First Issue: 28 March 1832
Last Issue: ?
Available From: Yale Univ.

528   TITLE: <u>Mirror of the Times; Devoted to Odd-Fellowship, Poetry, Miscellany, News of the Day; etc.</u>

Place of Publication: New York
First Issue: 1848
Last Issue: 1851//?
Available From: N.Y. State Lib., Albany; Newberry Lib., Chicago

529   TITLE: <u>Miscellaneous Cabinet</u>.

Place of Publication: Schenectady, N.Y.
First Issue: 12 July 1823
Last Issue: 3 Jan 1824//?
Periodicity: Weekly
Editors: ?
Publishers: ?
Available From: APS; Amer. Antiquarian Soc.
Contents:
  Poetry: <u>Original</u>. <u>Selected</u>: James G. Percival, Joshua Marsden, Gray, Bryant, Thomas Moore, James Montgomery, Samuel Woodworth, Selleck Osborne, Thomas Campbell, Byron.
  Prose: <u>Essay</u>. <u>Familiar Essay</u>. <u>Criticism</u>. <u>Book Reviews</u>.
  Miscellaneous: <u>Anecdotes</u>: on various subjects. <u>Literary Notices</u>. <u>News</u>: Foreign and Domestic.

530   TITLE: <u>The Miscellaneous Magazine</u>.

Place of Publication: Trenton, N.J.
First Issue: Jan 1824
Last Issue: Dec 1824//
Periodicity: Monthly
Editor: P.S. Wiggins
Publisher: P.S. Wiggins
Available From: APS; Lib. of Congress*
Contents:
  Poetry: <u>Original</u>. <u>Selected</u>: James Montgomery, Felicia Hemans.
  Prose: <u>Familiar Essay</u>.
  Fiction: <u>Essay Serial</u>: "The Selector." <u>Sketches</u>. <u>Tales</u>: "Escape from Death-- At Sea" [James Hogg]; "The Broken Heart" [W. Irving].
  Miscellaneous: <u>Extracts</u>: from other journals; by various authors, James Hogg, W. Irving, James Fenimore Cooper. <u>Anecdotes</u>: on various subjects. <u>Literary Notices</u>. <u>News</u>: Foreign and Domestic.

531   TITLES: (1) <u>The Miscellaneous Scrap Book. Devoted to Polite Literature, Such as Moral and Sentimental Tales, Instructive and Amusing Miscellany, Poetry, Anecdotes, &c.</u> (2) <u>Scrap Book</u>.

Place of Publication: Hartford
First Issue: 8 Oct 1834
Last Issue: 23 Jan 1836//?
Periodicity: Bi-weekly; Weekly
Editor: G.W. Kappel
Publisher: G.W. Kappel
Available From: Univ. of Pa.; Princeton Univ.
Contents:
  Poetry: <u>Original</u>: Edwin H. Chapin. <u>Selected</u>: William Cowper, George Crabbe, Scott, Thomas Moore, Felicia Hemans, R. Shelton Mackenzie, James G. Percival, Lydia H. Sigourney, L.E. Landon.
  Prose: <u>Familiar Essay</u>. <u>Letters</u>.
  Fiction: <u>Essay Serials</u>: "Leisure Talk"; "Notes by a Pedagogue." <u>Sketches</u>. <u>Tales</u>: "The History of a Merchant's Widow, and Her Young Family"; "Ben Pie, or the Indian Murderer"; "Sophia, or the Girl of the Pine Woods"; "The Wedding" [Whittier]; "Bachelor Sam"; "Fair Annie MacLeod. A Tale"; "Lafitte or the Baratarian Chief. A Tale"; "The Flute Player. A Tale."
  Miscellaneous: <u>Extracts</u>: from other journals; by various authors; E. Lytton Bulwer. <u>Anecdotes</u>: on various subjects; Patrick Henry, Swift, Penn. <u>News</u>: Domestic.

532   TITLE: <u>The Miscellany</u>.

Place of Publication: New Haven, Conn.
First Issue: 6 Nov 1829
Last Issue: 6 May 1831//
Available From: ?

533   TITLE: <u>The Miscellany</u>.

Place of Publication: Trenton, N.J.
First Issue: 10 June 1805
Last Issue: 2 Dec 1805//?
Periodicity: Weekly
Editors: ?
Publisher: James Oram
Available From: APS; Lib. Co. of Philadelphia*
Contents:
  Poetry: <u>Original</u>. <u>Selected</u>: William Collins, Thomas Moore, Burns, Amelia Opie, S. Johnson's <u>The History of Rasselas, Prince of Abissinia</u>.
  Prose: <u>Travel</u>. <u>Familiar Essay</u>. <u>Criticism</u>. <u>Letters</u>.
  Fiction: <u>Sketches</u>. <u>Tales</u>: "Sambrac the Indian. A Tale"; "Justice Vanquishing the Force of Nature. A Persian Tale"; "Contentment, the Attainment of Happiness. A Tale"; "Adelbert."

Miscellaneous: Extracts: from other journals; by various authors; Lavater.
Anecdotes: on various subjects; Franklin,
S. Johnson, Milton, Isaac Newton, Washington, Addison, Boswell. News: Domestic.

534   TITLES: (1) Miss Leslie's Magazine; Home
Book of Fashion, Literature and Domestic
Economy (2) The Ladies' Magazine of
Literature, Fashion and the Fine Arts
(3) Arthur's Ladies' Magazine of Elegant
Literature and the Fine Arts. [Merged into
Godey's Lady's Book q.v., later Godey's
Magazine.]

Place of Publication: Philadelphia
First Issue: Jan 1843
Last Issue: April 1846//
Periodicity: Monthly
Editors: Eliza Leslie; T.S. Arthur
Publishers: Morton McMichael; E. Ferrett and
Co.
Available From: APS; Lib. of Congress.*
Mott.
Contents:
Poetry: Original: Lydia H. Sigourney,
T.S. Arthur, Nathaniel P. Willis, Long-
fellow, Park Benjamin, James G. Percival.
Selected: Lydia Maria Child, Barry
Cornwall, Sarah J. Hale, William H.
Carpenter, Oliver Wendell Holmes, Lucy
Hooper, Mary Howitt, Wordsworth, Frances
S. Osgood, Charles Fenno Hoffman,
Felicia Hemans, Scott, Albert Pike,
Coleridge, Mary C. Denver, Burns, Joseph
H. Butler, James Hungerford, Bernard
Barton, William Wallace, Sarah H. Whit-
man, W.H. Timrod, James N. Barker, Byron,
Thomas Carew.
Prose: Essay. Familiar Essay. Criticism.
Letters. Book Reviews.
Fiction: Essay Serials: "Birds and Song";
"American Views." Sketches. Tales:
"Jack Ketch. A Temperance Tale"; "Lucy
Heathwood"; "Kate Connor"; "The Russian
Prince"; "Passages from the Diary of a
Late Clergyman"; "The Perplexed Lover";
"The Belle of Red River. A Domestic
Tale of Louisiana"; "The Love of Later
Years"; "The Boarding School Friends";
"John Bicker, the Dry Dominie of
Kilwoody"; "The Wife. A Tale of the
Hard Times"; "The Heiress"; "The Daughter-
in-Law"; "Catharine Bloomer. Or, New
Aims in Life"; "Munificence--A Tale of
Life"; "Heinrich and Blanca: Or, the
Three Brothers."
Miscellaneous: Anecdotes: on various sub-
jects. Literary Notices.

535   TITLE: The Mistletoe. [Superseded by
Wheler's Southern Monthly Magazine.]

Place of Publication: Athens, Ga.
First Issue: Jan 1849
Last Issue: March 1849//
Periodicity: Monthly
Editors: J.W. Burke; T.A. Burke
Publishers: J.W. Burke; T.A. Burke

Available From: APS; N.Y. Pub. Lib.
Contents:
Poetry: Original: C.L. Wheler. Selected:
Whittier, Catharine W. Barber, Edwin
Heriot.
Prose: Familiar Essay.
Fiction: Essay Serial: "Mistletoe Boughs."
Sketches. Tales: "The Intemperate: A
Thrilling Story of the West"; "The Doom
of the Drinker: Or the Infuriated Tiger";
"The Bridal Eve: A Legend of the American
Revolution."
Miscellaneous: Anecdotes: on various sub-
jects.

536   TITLE: The Mohawk Mirror, and Independent
Chronicle: A Semi-Monthly Journal of
Literature and Morals, Intelligence,
Business, Arts, Agriculture and Reform.

Place of Publication: Little Falls, N.Y.
First Issue: Jan 1841
Last Issue: 14 June 1844//
Periodicity: Semi-monthly
Editor: Edward M. Griffing
Publisher: Edward M. Griffing
Available From: Lib. of Congress; N.Y. State
Lib., Albany*
Contents:
Poetry: Original: Jefferson Sutherland,
E.M. Redstone, A.W. Eaton, C.R. Williams,
M.L. Gardiner. Selected: Longfellow,
Thomas Hood, Jesse E. Dow, Barry Corn-
wall, Lydia H. Sigourney, Isaac C. Pray,
Jr., Christopher Smart, Southey, Byron,
Hannah F. Gould, John Quincy Adams,
James T. Fields.
Prose: Biography: George Whitefield.
Letters.
Fiction: Sketches. Tales: "Yankee Punish-
ment of Theft: A Melting Story"; "The
King's Ship"; "The Curs'd House: A
Tale"; "The Turned Head"; "The Love Mar-
riage: Or, Heaven Helps Them That Help
Themselves"; "The Ladies' Fair" [T.S.
Arthur]; "Agnes Sorel de Merivanne: The
Recluse Coquette [Timothy Flint].
Miscellaneous: Extracts: from other jour-
nals; by various authors. Anecdotes: on
various subjects; Chateaubriand.
Literary Notices. News: Foreign and
Domestic.

537   TITLE: The Monitor, Designed to Improve the
Taste, the Understanding, and the Heart.
[Merged into The Guardian q.v., Later The
Guardian and Monitor q.v.]

Place of Publication: Boston
First Issue: Jan 1823
Last Issue: Dec 1824//?
Periodicity: Monthly
Editor: Hervey Wilbur
Publishers: R. Bannister; Cummings, Hilliard,
& Co.
Available From: APS; Borwn Univ., Providence
Contents:
Poetry: Original. Selected: Walter
Raleigh.

Prose: <u>Biography</u>: Martin Luther.
  <u>Familiar Essay</u>. <u>Letters</u>.
Fiction: <u>Sketches</u>. <u>Tales</u>: "An Indian
  Tale"; "Al-Mohdi--An Eastern Tale."
Miscellaneous: <u>Extracts</u>: by various
  authors; Franklin. <u>Anecdotes</u>: on
  various subjects; George Whitefield,
  Isaac Newton, Bolingbroke.

538 TITLES: (1) <u>The Monthly Anthology, and Boston
  Review, Containing Sketches and Reports of
  Philosophy, Religion, History, Arts and
  Manners</u> (2) <u>Monthly Anthology, or Magazine
  of Polite Literature</u> (3) <u>Monthly Anthology,
  or Massachusetts Magazine</u> (4) <u>Monthly
  Anthology, or Boston Review</u>. [Superseded
  by <u>The General Repository and Review</u> q.v.]

Place of Publication: Boston
First Issue: Nov 1803
Last Issue: June 1811//
Periodicity: Monthly
Editors: David Phineas Adams; William Emerson;
  Samuel Cooper Thatcher; William
  Smith Shaw; James Savage; Alexander
  H. Everett
Publishers: Munroe & Francis; B. & J. Homans;
  E. Lincoln; Snelling and Simons;
  Hastings, Etheridge and Bliss;
  T.B. Wait and Company
Available From: APS; Amer. Antiquarian Soc.*
  Mott.
Contents:
  Poetry: <u>Original</u>. <u>Selected</u>: Fessenden,
    B. D'Israeli, Thomas Paine, Anthony
    Pasquin, Dryden, Scott, William Cowper,
    Southey, Pope.
  Prose: <u>Biography</u>: John Blair Linn, Penn,
    John Trumbull, William Collins, Patrick
    Henry, Alexander Hamilton, Richard Bent-
    ley, Rousseau, Charles James Fox, William
    Pitt, George Wither, Erasmus, André
    Michaux, Bolingbroke. <u>Travel</u>. <u>Essay</u>.
    <u>Familiar Essay</u>. <u>Criticism</u>: on Pope,
    S. Johnson, William Cowper, Burns, Gold-
    smith, Franklin, Denham, Parnell, Vol-
    taire, Gray, Swift, Southey, Michael
    Drayton, Dante, Spenser, Shakespeare,
    Chaucer, Donne, Marvell, Sterne, Joel
    Barlow, Milton, Addison. <u>Letters</u>. <u>Book
    Reviews</u>.
  Fiction: <u>Essay Serials</u>: "The Botanist";
    "The Loiterer"; "The Guest"; "The Col-
    lectanea"; "Literary Wanderer"; "The
    Remarker"; "Silva"; "Biographia Americana."
    <u>Sketches</u>. <u>Tales</u>: "Argenis: A Moral and
    Political Romance"; "Story of Cecilia";
    "Edmorin and Ella. An Eastern Tale."
  Miscellaneous: <u>Extracts</u>: from other jour-
    nals; by various authors. <u>Anecdotes</u>:
    on various subjects; S. Johnson, Gold-
    smith, Pope, William Cowper, Franklin,
    Voltaire, Thomas More. <u>Literary Notices</u>.
    <u>News</u>: Domestic.
Note: Leading Contributors: Daniel Webster,
  John Pickering, Andrews Norton, Josiah
  Quincy, Washington Allston, John Quincy
  Adams, Benjamin Silliman.

539 TITLE: <u>Monthly Anthology, or Magazine of
  Polite Literature</u>. [See <u>The Monthly An-
  thology, and Boston Review, Containing
  Sketches and Reports of Philosophy, Religion,
  History, Arts and Manners</u>.]

540 TITLE: <u>Monthly Anthology, or Massachusetts
  Magazine</u>. [See <u>The Monthly Anthology, and
  Boston Review, Containing Sketches and
  Reports of Philosophy, Religion, History,
  Arts and Manners</u>.]

541 TITLE: <u>The Monthly Chronicle of Original
  Literature</u>.

Place of Publication: New York
First Issue: [Only one issue published?]
  July 1839//?
Available From: Boston Athenaeum; N.Y. Hist.
  Soc.

542 TITLE: <u>The Monthly Literary Advertiser</u>.

Place of Publication: New York
First Issue: July 1841
Last Issue: Dec 1841//
Available From: N.Y. Pub. Lib.*

543 TITLE: <u>The Monthly Literary Advertiser</u>.

Place of Publication: Philadelphia
First Issue: Sept 1815
Last Issue: Jan 1817//?
Periodicity: Monthly
Editor: H.C. Carey
Publisher: H.C. Carey
Available From: Amer. Antiquarian Soc.;
  Harvard Univ.
Contents:
  Prose: <u>Book Reviews</u>.
  Miscellaneous: <u>Literary Notices</u>.
Note: Devoted exclusively to literary notices
  and short book reviews.

544 TITLE: <u>The Monthly Magazine</u> (Lancaster, Pa.).
  [See <u>The Gleanor; or, Monthly Magazine</u>.]

545 TITLE: <u>The Monthly Magazine, and American
  Review</u>. [Superseded by <u>The American Review,
  and Literary Journal</u> q.v.]

Place of Publication: New York
First Issue: April 1799
Last Issue: Dec 1800//
Periodicity: Monthly
Editor: Charles Brockden Brown
Publishers: T. & J. Swords
Available From: APS; Hist. Soc. of Pa.*
  Mott.
Contents:
  Poetry: <u>Original</u>: John Davis. <u>Selected</u>:
    William Cowper, Southey.

Prose: <u>Travel</u>. <u>Essay</u>: on Edward Gibbon, Mary Wollstonecraft, Joel Barlow, Timothy Dwight, Kotzebue, John Trumbull, Thomas Paine, Southey, Schiller, Lemuel Hopkins, David Humphreys, Jefferson, William Cowper. <u>Familiar Essay</u>. <u>Criticism</u>. <u>Letters</u>. <u>Book Reviews</u>.
Fiction: <u>Essay Serial</u>: "The Speculatist." <u>Sketches</u>. <u>Tales</u>: "Thessalonica" [Charles Brockden Brown]; "Memoirs of Stephen Calvert" [Charles Brockden Brown]; from <u>Edgar Huntly</u> [Charles Brockden Brown].
Miscellaneous: <u>Anecdotes</u>: on various subjects. <u>Literary Notices</u>.

546   TITLE: <u>The Monthly Magazine and Literary Journal</u>.

Place of Publication: Winchester, Va.
First Issue: May 1812
Last Issue: April 1813//
Periodicity: Monthly
Editor: John Heiskell
Publisher: John Heiskell
Available From: APS; Lib. of Congress*
Contents:
  Poetry: <u>Original</u>. <u>Selected</u>: William Holloway, Charlotte Smith, S. Johnson, Amelia Opie, Thomas Campbell.
  Prose: <u>Biography</u>: David Hume, Captain John Smith, George Frederick Cooke. <u>Familiar Essay</u>. <u>Letters</u>. <u>Book Reviews</u>.
  Fiction: <u>Sketches</u>. <u>Tales</u>: "Clementina: A Narrative"; "The Abbey of Santo Pietra; or, a Father's Vengeance."
  Miscellaneous: <u>Extracts</u>: from other journals; by various authors; Voltaire. <u>Anecdotes</u>: on various subjects; Garrick, Swift, Samuel Foote, Colley Cibber, Cromwell.

547   TITLE: <u>Monthly Magazine of Belles-Lettres and Arts, the Lady's Book</u>. [See <u>Godey's Magazine</u>.]

548   TITLE: <u>The Monthly Magazine of Religion and Literature</u>.

Place of Publication: Gettysburg, Pa.
First Issue: Feb 1840
Last Issue: Jan 1841//
Periodicity: Monthly
Editor: W.M. Reynolds
Publisher: W.M. Reynolds
Available From: Hist. Soc. of Pa.*; Lib. of Congress*
Contents:
  Poetry: <u>Original</u>: Charles West Thomson, Nathan C. Brooks, W.R. Morris.
  Prose: <u>Biography</u>: religious figures, Goethe. <u>Travel</u>. <u>Essay</u>. <u>Criticism</u>: on Goethe. <u>Book Reviews</u>.
  Fiction: <u>Essay Serial</u>: "Stray Thoughts." <u>Sketches</u>. <u>Tale</u>: "Scenes in the Life of a Western Emigrant."
  Miscellaneous: <u>Extracts</u>: from other journals. <u>Literary Notices</u>.

Note: A great emphasis is placed on German religion and literature.

549   TITLE: <u>The Monthly Miscellany; a Religious and Literary Review and Monthly Register of Discoveries and Improvements in the Arts and Sciences Conducted on the Joint Stock Principle</u>.

Place of Publication: Atlanta; Richmond; New Orleans
First Issue: 15 Jan 1849
Last Issue: 16 June 1849//?
Available From: Duke Univ., Durham*

550   TITLE: <u>The Monthly Miscellany, or Vermont Magazine</u>.

Place of Publication: Bennington, Vt.
First Issue: April 1794
Last Issue: Sept 1794//
Periodicity: Monthly
Editor: Anthony Haswell
Publishers: Haswell & Mackay
Available From: APS; N.Y. Hist. Soc.* Mott.
Contents:
  Poetry: <u>Original</u>. <u>Selected</u>: David Humphreys.
  Prose: <u>Essay</u>: "Remarks Concerning the Savages of North America" [Franklin]. <u>Familiar Essay</u>. <u>Letters</u>.
  Fiction: <u>Sketches</u>. <u>Tales</u>: "The Indian Cottage, a Tale Founded on Fact"; "Azakia. A Canadian Story"; "The Beggar and His Dog, a Tale"; "Theodosia. A Tale"; "The Pilgrim's Story"; "Timur--An Eastern Tale."
  Miscellaneous: <u>News</u>: Domestic.

551   TITLE: <u>The Monthly Recorder</u>.

Place of Publication: New York
First Issue: April 1813
Last Issue: Aug 1813//
Periodicity: Monthly
Editors: ?
Publishers: ?
Available From: APS; Amer. Antiquarian Soc.*
Contents:
  Poetry: <u>Original</u>. <u>Selected</u>: William Roscoe, Mary Russell Mitford, Herrick.
  Prose: <u>Biography</u>: William Cliffton, Mary Russell Mitford. <u>Familiar Essay</u>. <u>Letters</u>. <u>Book Reviews</u>.
  Fiction: <u>Sketches</u>. <u>Tales</u>: "The Inquisition"; "Jaques Aymar, or, the Divining Rod"; "Tooti Nameh; or, Tales of a Parrot."
  Miscellaneous: <u>Extracts</u>: from other journals. <u>Anecdotes</u>: on various subjects. <u>Literary Notices</u>. <u>News</u>: Foreign and Domestic.

552   TITLE: <u>The Monthly Register, Magazine, and Review, of the United States</u>. [See <u>The Monthly Review and Literary Miscellany of the United States</u>.]

553   TITLE: <u>The Monthly Repository and Library of Entertaining Knowledge</u>.

Place of Publication: New York
First Issue: June 1830
Last Issue: Sept 1834//
Periodicity: Monthly
Editor: Francis S. Wiggins
Publisher: Francis S. Wiggins
Available From: APS; Yale Univ.
Contents:
   Poetry: <u>Original</u>: Joseph Rusling, Lydia
   H. Sigourney. <u>Selected</u>: Lucretia Maria
   Davidson, Hugh Hutton, John Bowring,
   Felicia Hemans, Thomas Moore, Mary Anne
   Browne, T.K. Hervey, Lydia H. Sigourney,
   Alonzo Lewis, Grenville Mellen, Mary
   Howitt, Mrs. Seba Smith, Thomas Haynes
   Bayly, Wordsworth, Bryant, Charles Sprague,
   Caroline Norton, Byron, James Montgomery,
   Robert Southwell.
   Prose: <u>Biography</u>: Henry Kirke White,
   S. Johnson, Benjamin West, Franklin,
   Patrick Henry, Milton, Walter Raleigh.
   <u>Travel</u>. <u>Essay</u>. <u>Familiar Essay</u>. <u>Criticism</u>. <u>Book Reviews</u>.
   Fiction: <u>Sketches</u>.
   Miscellaneous: <u>Extracts</u>: from other journals; by various authors; Lydia H.
   Sigourney, Goldsmith, W. Irving, James G.
   Percival, John Locke, S. Johnson.
   <u>Anecdotes</u>: on various subjects;
   Washington, Milton. <u>Literary Notices</u>.

554   TITLES: (1) <u>The Monthly Review and Literary Miscellany of the United States</u> (2) <u>The Monthly Register, Magazine, and Review, of the United States</u>.

Place of Publication: Charleston, S.C.; New
            York
First Issue: Jan 1805
Last Issue: Dec 1807//
Periodicity: Monthly
Editors: Stephen C. Carpenter; John Bristed;
          E. Sargeant
Publishers: E. Sargeant; William P. Farrand;
             William P. Farrand and E. Sargeant
Available From: APS; Boston Athenaeum
Contents:
   Poetry: <u>Original</u>. <u>Selected</u>: William
   Cowper, Fessenden, Thomas Moore.
   Prose: <u>Biography</u>. <u>Travel</u>. <u>Essay</u>.
   <u>Familiar Essay</u>. <u>Criticism</u>: A section
   labelled "Literature and Criticism" discusses the dangers of novel reading,
   various writers' works, drama, the state
   of American literature, and "Criticism on
   French Literature" and "Dramatic Criticism." <u>Book Reviews</u>.
   Fiction: <u>Essay Serials</u>: "The Archer";
   "The Wanderer." <u>Sketches</u>. <u>Tales</u>: "Men
   and Women: A Moral Tale"; "Filial Piety
   and Modest Benevolence. A Narrative";
   "Affecting Story of a Merchant and His
   Dog."
   Miscellaneous: <u>Extracts</u>: from other journals; by various authors; Milton, William
   Cowper, Edmund Burke. <u>Anecdotes</u>: on

various subjects; Franklin, S. Johnson,
Boswell, Defoe, Molière, John Dennis,
Pope, Washington. <u>Literary Notices</u>.
<u>News</u>: Domestic.

555   TITLE: <u>The Monthly Rose and Literary Cabinet</u>.

Place of Publication: Boston
First Issue: July 1845
Last Issue: Jan 1850//?
Periodicity: Monthly
Editor: Henry C. Shepard
Publishers: Henry C. Shepard; Benjamin P.
             Lane
Available From: Lib. of Congress; Amer.
                 Antiquarian Soc.
Contents:
   Poetry: <u>Original</u>. <u>Selected</u>: Felicia
   Hemans.
   Prose: <u>Letters</u>.
   Fiction: <u>Sketches</u>. <u>Tales</u>: "The Life &
   Travels of Jack Foster"; "Oregon Twenty."
   Miscellaneous: <u>Extracts</u>: from other journals. <u>Anecdotes</u>: on various subjects.
   <u>Literary Notices</u>.
Note: Contains mostly light-hearted sketches
   and anecdotes.

556   TITLE: <u>The Monthly Traveller, or, Spirit of the Periodical Press. Containing Popular Selections from the Best Foreign and American Publications, Together with Original Notices of the Current Literature of the Times</u>.

Place of Publication: Boston
First Issue: Jan 1830
Last Issue: Dec 1838//?
Periodicity: Monthly
Editors: ?
Publishers: Badger & Porter
Available From: Lib. of Congress; Boston
                 Pub. Lib.
Contents:
   Poetry: <u>Original</u>: Richard Rutherford.
   <u>Selected</u>: L.E. Landon, Mary Anne Browne,
   Fitz-Greene Halleck, Allan Cunningham,
   Felicia Hemans, James Hogg, Wordsworth,
   Robert Morris, Whittier, James G. Percival, T.K. Hervey, Caroline Norton,
   Hannah F. Gould, Thomas Haynes Bayly,
   Lydia H. Sigourney, Park Benjamin,
   Bryant, C.W. Thomson, Washington Allston,
   Emma C. Embury, Miss Jewsbury, Mary
   Howitt, Charles Swain, Robert Montgomery,
   Barry Cornwall, Thomas Hood, John G.
   Brainard, Leigh Hunt, W.O. Peabody,
   Thomas Moore, Shelley, Scott, Elizabeth
   Bogart, Edward C. Pinckney, Charles
   Sprague, Eliza Cook, George W. Patten,
   George Pope Morris, William Wallace,
   Catharine H. Waterman, E. Lytton Bulwer,
   Thomas Campbell, Alonzo Lewis, James
   Montgomery, James T. Fields.
   Prose: <u>Biography</u>. <u>Travel</u>. <u>Essay</u>.
   <u>Familiar Essay</u>. <u>Book Reviews</u>.
   Fiction: <u>Sketches</u>. <u>Tales</u>: "The Smuggler's
   Isle"; "Hansel Monday"; "Ellen Myles";
   "The Fifth Proprietor"; "The Monk"

[George D. Prentice]; "Owney Sullivan"; "Scenes in the Old-Colony"; "Gowannahee . . . . A Tale"; "Rosedale" [Mary Russell Mitford]; "The Rival Brothers. A Tale": "The Cousins" [Mary Russell Mitford]; "Death at the Toilet"; "The Masked Bridegroom"; "The Lottery Ticket"; "The Last of His Tribe"; "A Profligate's Last Month"; "Lelia's Lamp, an Italian Story"; "Legend of the Rose of the Alhambra" [W. Irving]; "The Coliseum" [Shelley]; "Old Matthew, the Mat Seller" [Mary Russell Mitford]; "Old Rosy Posy"; "The Young Robber" [W. Irving]; "Kascambo. A Tale of the Caucasus"; "The Wedding and the First Cup" [Grenville Mellen]; "Woman's Error; or, the Duellists"; "Without a Rival" [Theodore Sedgwick Fay]; "The Flower Girl"; "The School of Reform. A Domestic Tale"; "Rachel Orme"; "The Quadroon--A Tale"; "The Cunning Lunatic"; "Alice Vere"; "The Pirate's Ward. A Legend of the Alleghany"; "Amelia"; "Monos and Diamonos" [E. Lytton Bulwer]; "The Pale Rose of the Squamscot"; "The Angler" [W. Irving]; "David Swan" [Hawthorne]; "True Ordeal of Love" [E. Lytton Bulwer]; "The Broken Miniature."
Miscellaneous: Extracts: from other journals; by various authors. Anecdotes: on various subjects; Buonaparte, Isaac Newton, E. Lytton Bulwer, Walter Raleigh, Scott, Washington, Byron, S. Johnson, Maria Edgeworth. Literary Notices.

557 TITLE: The Monthly Visitor, Devoted to the Dissemination of Popular Literature, Miscellany, &c. [Superseded by The Philadelphia Visitor, Devoted to the Dissemination of Popular Literature, Miscellany, &c. q.v.]

Place of Publication: Philadelphia
First Issue: May 1834
Last Issue: April 1835//
Periodicity: Monthly
Editors: ?
Publishers: ?
Available From: Lib. of Congress*; Lib. Co. of Philadelphia*
Contents:
  Poetry: Original. Selected.
  Prose: Biography: Richard Steele. Familiar Essay. Letters.
  Fiction: Sketches. Tales: "The Mysterious Monk. A Tale"; "Black Dennis"; "The Magdalen. A Tale Founded on Facts"; "The Vow: A Northern Tale"; "The Dashing Lieutenant: Or, More Ways Than One"; Lafitte, the Baratarian Chief. A Tale Founded on Fact"; "The Cavern of Death."
  Miscellaneous: Extracts: from other journals; by various authors. Anecdotes: on various subjects; Colley Cibber, Cromwell.

558 TITLE: The Monument. A Volume Devoted to Polite Literature, Science, and the Fine Arts. [See The Baltimore Monument. A Weekly Journal, Devoted to Polite Literature, Science, and the Fine Arts.]

559 TITLE: Moonshine. By the Lunarian Society. [Merged with The Baltimore Magazine q.v.]

Place of Publication: Baltimore
First Issue: 20 June 1807
Last Issue: 23 July 1807//?
Periodicity: Irregular
Editor: Samuel Jefferis
Publisher: Samuel Jefferis
Available From: APS; Lib. of Congress*
Contents:
  Poetry: Original.
  Fiction: Novel: "The Starling. A Novel in Miniature."
  Miscellaneous: Anecdotes: on various subjects.
Note: Contains articles by Edwin Arion, Timothy Varnish, Vincent Lunardi, Henry Henpeck, Martin Scribbler.

560 TITLE: The Moral and Political Telegraph: Or, Brookfield Advertiser.

Place of Publication: Brookfield, Mass.
First Issue: 6 May 1795
Last Issue: 17 Aug 1796//
Periodicity: Weekly
Editor: Elisha H. Waldo
Publisher: Elisha H. Waldo
Available From: Amer. Antiquarian Soc.*
Contents:
  Poetry: Selected: William Doddridge, Cervantes.
  Prose: Familiar Essay.
  Fiction: Sketches. Tale: "Theodore."
  Miscellaneous: Anecdotes: on various subjects. News: Foreign and Domestic.

561 TITLE: The Moralist.

Place of Publication: New York
First Issue: 27 May 1814
Last Issue: 7 Nov 1814//?
Periodicity: Irregular
Editors: Garrit C. Tunison; Thomas Snowden
Publishers: Tunison & Snowden
Available From: APS; Lib. of Congress*
Contents:
  Prose: Familiar Essay.
  Miscellaneous: Anecdotes: on various subjects. Literary Notices.

562 TITLES: (1) The Mother's Assistant and Young Lady's Friend (2) The Mother's Assistant, Young Ladies' Friend and Family Manual (3) The Mother's Assistant and Fireside Miscellany (4) The Mother's Assistant and Child's Friend.

Place of Publication: Boston
First Issue: July 1842
Last Issue: Dec 1863//?
Periodicity: ?
Editor: William C. Brown
Publisher: William C. Brown
Available From: Lib. of Congress; Amer. Antiquarian Soc.

Contents:
  Poetry: <u>Original</u>: Hodges Reed, W.M. Thayer,
  Rhoda B. Huse. <u>Selected</u>: Thomas Hood,
  George Wither, Charles MacKay, George H.
  Calvert, Mary Howitt, Nathaniel P. Willis,
  Thomas C. Upham, James Montgomery, Giles
  Fletcher, William B. Tappan, Lydia Maria
  Child, Charles Swain.
  Prose: <u>Biography</u>. <u>Essay</u>. <u>Familiar Essay</u>.
  Fiction: <u>Sketches</u>. <u>Tales</u>: "Mary Leonard,
  or the Faithful Friend"; "Be What You
  Would Seem to Be" [Hannah F. Gould];
  "Early Impressions of the Household Altar";
  "A Sister's Influence"; "'Saw Up and Saw
  Down'"; "Elsie Lee"; "Truth Triumphant:
  Or, the Bible Vindicated"; "Woman's
  Mission"; "The Never-Failing Friend";
  "Fading Loveliness."
  Miscellaneous: <u>Anecdotes</u>: on various sub-
  jects; S. Johnson. <u>Literary Notices</u>.

563 TITLES: (1) <u>Mrs. A.S. Colvin's Weekly Messenger, Containing a Variety of Original
  and Selected Articles, on Subjects Interesting to Society</u> (2) <u>Mrs. Colvin's Weekly
  Messenger</u>.

  Place of Publication: Washington, D.C.
  First Issue: 15 June 1822
  Last Issue: 29 March 1828//?
  Periodicity: Weekly
  Editor: Mrs. A.S. Colvin
  Publishers: ?
  Available From: Lib. of Congress; Boston
              Athenaeum
  Contents:
  Poetry: <u>Original</u>: Mrs. A.S. Colvin,
  Ormond Oswald. <u>Selected</u>: James G.
  Percival, James Stuart, Harriet Muzzy,
  R.H. Wilde, Felicia Hemans.
  Prose: <u>Biography</u>. <u>Essay</u>. <u>Familiar
  Essay</u>. <u>Letters</u>. <u>Book Reviews</u>.
  Fiction: <u>Essay Serial</u>: "Authoresses and
  Autographs." <u>Sketches</u>. <u>Tales</u>: "Osman
  and Fatima. A Turkish Story"; "The Sea
  Voyage"; "James Morland, the Cottager";
  "The Highland Widow" [Scott].
  Miscellaneous: <u>Extracts</u>: from other
  journals; by various authors. <u>Anecdotes</u>:
  on various subjects. <u>News</u>: Foreign and
  Domestic.

564 TITLE: <u>The Museum and Literary Repository</u>.
  [See the <u>Western Museum and Belles-Lettres
  Repository</u>.]

565 TITLES: (1) <u>The Museum of Foreign Literature
  and Science</u> (2) <u>The Museum of Foreign
  Literature, Science, and Art</u>. [Supersedes
  <u>The Saturday Magazine</u> (originally <u>The
  Philadelphia Register</u> q.v.). United with
  <u>The American Eclectic</u> q.v. to form <u>The
  Eclectic Museum of Foreign Literature</u> q.v.]

  Place of Publication: Philadelphia; New York
  First Issue: July 1822
  Last Issue: Dec 1842//
  Periodicity: Monthly

Editors: Robert Walsh, Jr.; Eliakim Littell;
              J.J. Smith
Publishers: E. Littell and R. Norris Henry;
              E. Littell and T. Holden;
              E. Littell & E. Bliss & E. White
Available From: APS; Boston Pub. Lib.*
              Mott. <u>Poole</u>.
Contents:
  Poetry: <u>Selected</u>: James Montgomery,
  Wordsworth, Byron, Thomas Randolph,
  Skelton, Tourneur, Thomas Campbell, Donne.
  Prose: <u>Biography</u>. <u>Travel</u>. <u>Familiar Essay</u>.
  <u>Letters</u>. <u>Book Reviews</u>.
  Fiction: <u>Sketches</u>. <u>Tales</u>: "Walter of
  Aquitane--An Historical Romance";
  "Casanova's Adventures in Warsaw"; "The
  Doomed Man"; "The Son and Heir"; "The
  Power of Beauty, a Syrian Tale"; "The
  Twelve Nights"; "Confessions of an English
  Opium Eater" [De Quincey].
  Miscellaneous: <u>Extracts</u>: from other
  journals; by various authors; James
  Montgomery, W. Irving, Southey, De Quincey.
  <u>Anecdotes</u>: on various subjects; R.B.
  Sheridan, Washington, Lady Mary Wortley
  Montagu, John Wilkes, William Coombe.
Note: Contains serialized fiction by Dickens,
  Thackeray, E. Lytton Bulwer, and others.

566 TITLE: <u>Museum of Literature; Being a Selection
  of Choice Articles from the English Reviews
  and Magazines</u>. [See <u>The Daguerreotype: A
  Magazine of Foreign Literature and Science;
  Compiled Chiefly from the Periodical Publications of England, France, and Germany</u>.]

567 TITLES: (1) <u>The Nassau Monthly</u> (2) <u>The
  Nassau Literary Magazine</u>.

  Place of Publication: Princeton, N.J.
  First Issue: Feb 1842
  Last Issue: --
  Periodicity: Monthly
  Editors: the Senior Class at Princeton
  Publisher: John T. Robinson
  Available From: Princeton Univ.*; Lib. of
              Congress
  Contents:
  Poetry: <u>Original</u>. <u>Selected</u>: Novalis,
  Southey, Park Benjamin, Longfellow.
  Prose: <u>Essay</u>. <u>Familiar Essay</u>. <u>Criticism</u>:
  on Milton, Dickens, S. Johnson, Goldsmith,
  Benjamin West, Spenser, Madame de Staël,
  E. Lytton Bulwer, Goethe, William
  Motherwell.
  Fiction: <u>Essay Serial</u>: "College Portraits."
  <u>Sketches</u>.
  Miscellaneous: <u>Anecdotes</u>: on various sub-
  jects. <u>Literary Notices</u>.

568 TITLE: <u>The National Aegis</u>.

  Place of Publication: Worcester, Mass.
  First Issue: 2 Dec 1801
  Last Issue: 1895//?
  Periodicity: Weekly
  Editors: Robert Johnson; Sewall Goodridge;
              Samuel Cotting; Henry Rogers.

Publishers: Robert Johnson; Sewall Goodridge;
             Samuel Cotting; Henry Rogers
Available From: Amer. Antiquarian Soc.
Contents:
  Poetry: Original: Daniel Waldo Lincoln.
    Selected: William White, Thomas Campbell,
    Burns, Dibdin, Scott, William Bay.
  Prose: Biography. Familiar Essay. Letters.
    Book Reviews.
  Fiction: Sketches.
  Miscellaneous: Extracts: from other jour-
    nals; by various authors; Burns, Jeffer-
    son, Franklin. Anecdotes: on various
    subjects. News: Foreign and Domestic.

569 TITLES: (1) The National Atlas and Sunday
     Morning Mail (2) The National Atlas and
     Tuesday Morning Mail (3) The National
     Atlas, and Tuesday Morning Mail. A Weekly
     Periodical for the Parlour.

Place of Publication: Philadelphia
First Issue: 31 July 1836
Last Issue: 23 Jan 1838//
Periodicity: Weekly
Editor: Samuel C. Atkinson
Publisher: Samuel C. Atkinson
Available From: Lib. Co. of Philadelphia*;
                 Lib. of Congress
Contents:
  Poetry: Original. Selected: Byron, James
    Sheridan Knowles, Lydia H. Sigourney,
    Goethe, Bernard Barton, Barry Cornwall,
    Grenville Mellen, Isaac C. Pray, Jr.,
    James Montgomery, Edward Everett, Thomas
    Dunn English, Thomas Haynes Bayly,
    Felicia Hemans, Jane H. Williams.
  Prose: Biography. Travel. Essay.
    Familiar Essay. Letters. Book Reviews.
  Fiction: Essay Serial: "Omnibus Chit-
    Chat." Sketches. Tales: "The Unknown";
    "Love and Constancy"; "Halina Radzivil:
    Or, the Battle of Warsaw"; "The Merchant's
    Clerk"; "Mr. Midshipman Easy"; "The Two
    Students, or Love and Crime"; "The Name-
    less One. A Tale of Florence"; "Marie
    Jeanne"; "The Woodcutter. A Tale of the
    Mississippi"; "Armand de Ligny. A Tale
    of the Sixteenth Century"; "Witch Creek.
    A Romance"; "Merinah. A Tale of the
    Emigrants"; "The Martyrs. A Tale of the
    American Revolution"; "The Baronet's
    Daughter"; "The Tory's Daughter. A Tale
    of the Revolution"; "The Bride of Beer-
    haven; or, the Grandfather's Prophecy";
    "The Alchymist"; "The Houri. A Persian
    Tale"; "The Irish Lieutenant and His
    Double"; "David Swan" [Hawthorne]; "The
    Hero of King's Mountain. A Tale of the
    Revolution"; "The Secret Cell"; "The
    Anaconda. An East-India Tale."
  Miscellaneous: Extracts: from other jour-
    nals; by various authors; W. Irving.
    Anecdotes: on various subjects. Literary
    Notices. News: Foreign and Domestic.

570 TITLE: The National Atlas and Tuesday Morn-
     ing Mail. [See The National Atlas and
     Sunday Morning Mail.]

571 TITLE: The National Gazette.

Place of Publication: Philadelphia
First Issue: 31 Oct 1791
Last Issue: 26 Oct 1793//
Periodicity: Bi-weekly
Editor: Philip Freneau
Publisher: Philip Freneau
Available From: Amer. Antiquarian Soc.
Contents:
  Poetry: Original: Philip Freneau.
  Prose: Essay.
  Fiction: Sketches.
  Miscellaneous: Anecdotes: on various sub-
    jects. Literary Notices. News: Foreign
    and Domestic.

572 TITLE: The National Magazine and Republican
     Review.

Place of Publication: Washington, D.C.
First Issue: Jan 1839
Last Issue: June 1839//
Periodicity: Monthly
Editors: Henry J. Brent; John L. Smith
Publisher: Fulton & Smith
Available From: APS; Yale Univ.*
Contents:
  Poetry: Original: William B. Tappan,
    Thomas Holley Chivers, William B. Fair-
    child, Edward R. Boyle. Selected: George
    Lunt, George Hill, Rufus Dawes.
  Prose: Travel. Essay. Familiar Essay.
    Criticism: "Byron and His Contemporaries."
    Book Reviews.
  Fiction: Essay Serial: "Musings by the
    Hearth." Sketches. Tales: "The Triumph";
    "The Idiot Baron"; "Confessions of a Lover";
    "Joel Jumble. A Tale for Fathers";
    "Cleanthus: A Tale of Humility."
  Miscellaneous: Extracts: from other jour-
    nals. Literary Notices.

573 TITLE: National Magazine; or, a Political,
     Historical, Biographical, and Literary
     Repository. [Continued in Washington, D.C.
     as the National Magazine; or, Cabinet of the
     United States q.v.]

Place of Publication: Richmond, Va.
First Issue: 1 June 1799
Last Issue: 22 Dec 1800//
Periodicity: Semi-quarterly
Editor: James Lyon
Publisher: James Lyon
Available From: APS; Amer. Antiquarian Soc.
Contents:
  Poetry: Original. Selected.
  Prose: Biography: Nathaniel Greene [by
    Mathew Carey], Jefferson, Hamilton,
    Albert Gallatin. Travel. Essay.
    Familiar Essay. Criticism: "On
    Elegiac Poetry" [John Blair Linn].
    Letters: "Extract from Joel Barlow's
    Letter Lately Addressed to the People
    of the United States."
  Fiction: Sketches.
  Miscellaneous: Extracts: by various
    authors; Jefferson, Joel Barlow.

574   TITLE: National Magazine; or, Cabinet of the United States. [Supersedes the National Magazine; or, a Political, Historical, Biographical, and Literary Repository q.v.]

Place of Publication: Washington, D.C.
First Issue: Oct 1801
Last Issue: 11 Jan 1802//
Periodicity: Irregular; Weekly
Editor: Richard Dinsmore
Publisher: Richard Dinsmore
Available From: APS; Harvard Univ.
Contents:
   Poetry: Original. Selected: William Roscoe, Robert Merry.
   Prose: Biography: Burns. Travel. Essay. Letters.
   Fiction: Sketches.
   Miscellaneous: Extracts: by various authors. Anecdotes: on various subjects. Literary Notices. News: Foreign and Domestic.

575   TITLE: The National Magazine, or Lady's Emporium.

Place of Publication: Baltimore
First Issue: Nov 1830
Last Issue: July 1831//
Periodicity: Monthly
Editor: Mary Barney
Publisher: Mary Barney
Available From: APS; Univ. of Texas, Austin*
Contents:
   Poetry: Original. Selected.
   Prose: Biography: Rousseau, Lydia H. Sigourney. Familiar Essay. Criticism. Letters. Book Reviews.
   Fiction: Essay Serials: "The Circulating Library"; "Excerptions: From the Note-Book of an Omnivorous Reader." Sketches. Tales: "The Cave of the Enchantress"; "The Young Italian"; "Auld Lang Syne; the Reminiscences of an Octagenerian. A Tale"; "Fashionable Scandal"; "Haidee; or, a Tale of Southern Life"; "The Campanile"; "The Rival Beauties"; "Gebel Teir; or Mountain of Birds"; "The Last Coffin."
   Miscellaneous: Extracts: from other journals; by various authors. Anecdotes: on various subjects. Literary Notices.

576   TITLES: (1) National Museum, and Weekly Gazette (2) National Museum, and Weekly Gazette of Discoveries, Natural Sciences, and the Arts.

Place of Publication: Baltimore
First Issue: 13 Nov 1813
Last Issue: 12 Nov 1814//
Periodicity: Weekly
Editor: Camill M. Mann
Publisher: Camill M. Mann
Available From: APS; Univ. of Pa.
Contents:
   Poetry: Original. Selected: Milton, Luis de Camoens, Shakespeare, James Thomson, Matthew Prior, Matthew Gregory

[Monk] Lewis, James Montgomery, Goldsmith, William Cowper, William Roscoe.
   Prose: Biography. Familiar Essay.
   Fiction: Sketches.
   Miscellaneous: Extracts: from other journals. Anecdotes: on various subjects; Penn, S. Johnson. News: Foreign and Domestic.

577   TITLE: The National Pilot.

Place of Publication: New Haven, Conn.
First Issue: 6 Sept 1821
Last Issue: 11 Sept 1824//?
Periodicity: Weekly
Editor: Sebastian M. Dutton
Publisher: Sebastian M. Dutton
Available From: APS; Yale Univ.
Contents:
   Poetry: Original. Selected: Thomas Moore, James G. Percival, R.S. Coffin, William B. Tappan, William Roscoe, Lorenzo K. Dow, James M'Henry, Selleck Osborne, James Montgomery, Burns, Luis de Camoens, Joanna Baillie, Peter Pindar, Byron, Thomas Campbell, Barry Cornwall, Felicia Hemans, Richard Lovelace, C.M. Thayer, Henry Neele, Bryant, George O. Borrow.
   Prose: Biography: Hogarth, Chatterton, James Hogg, Gray. Travel. Essay. Familiar Essay. Letters. Book Reviews.
   Fiction: Essay Serial: "Historical Sketches." Sketches. Tales: "The Sport of Fortune. An Anecdote Taken from Real Life"; "Village Tales. The Farm House"; "A True Tale"; "Affecting Tale"; "The Fire Irons--Or Family Quarrels"; "700,000 Ministers!"
   Miscellaneous: Extracts: from other journals; by various authors; Franklin, W. Irving, Thomas Campbell, Jefferson, Hannah More. Anecdotes: Buonaparte, Garrick, George Whitefield, Franklin, Mungo Park, S. Johnson, Swift, Pope, Lady Mary Wortley Montagu, Fisher Ames, Byron. Literary Notices. News: Foreign and Domestic.

578   TITLE: The National Recorder. [See The Philadelphia Register, and National Recorder.]

579   TITLE: The Naturalist and Journal of Natural History, Agriculture, Education, and Literature.

Place of Publication: Nashville, Tenn.
First Issue: Jan 1846
Last Issue: Dec 1846//
Available From: Yale Univ.; Vanderbilt Univ., Nashville

580   TITLE: Neal's Saturday Gazette & Lady's Literary Museum.

Place of Publication: Philadelphia

First Issue: 1844
Last Issue: 27 Dec 1845//?
Available From: Univ. of Minn., Minneapolis;
                Hamilton Coll., Clinton, N.Y.

581   TITLE: The New American Magazine.

      Place of Publication: Woodbridge, N.J.
      First Issue: Jan 1758
      Last Issue: March 1760//
      Periodicity: Monthly
      Editor: Silvanus Americanus [Samuel Nevill]
      Publisher: James Parker
      Available From: APS; Lib. Co. of Philadelphia.
                      Mott.
      Contents:
        Poetry: Original. Selected: Matthew Prior,
          Pope, John Gay, Gray.
        Prose: Travel. Essay: "The History of
          North America." Familiar Essay. Letters.
        Fiction: Essay Serials: "The Occasional
          Writer"; "The Impartial Politician"; "The
          Traveller." Tale: "The Medicine. A
          Tale for the Ladies."
        Miscellaneous: Extracts: by various
          authors; Thomas Paine. News: Foreign
          and Domestic.

582   TITLE: The New England Chronicle: Or, the
      Essex Gazette. [See The Essex Gazette.]

583   TITLES: (1) The New England Family Magazine;
      for the Diffusion of Useful Knowledge (2)
      The Illustrated Family Magazine; for the
      Diffusion of Useful Knowledge.

      Place of Publication: Boston
      First Issue: Feb 1845
      Last Issue: Sept 1846//
      Periodicity: Monthly
      Editor: Robert L. Wade
      Publishers: Bradbury, Soden & Co.
      Available From: APS; Lib. of Congress*
      Contents:
        Poetry: Selected: Thomas Campbell, Robert
          Gilfillan, James G. Percival, Barry
          Cornwall, T.K. Hervey, Coleridge,
          B. Jonson, Samuel Daniel, James Russell
          Lowell, Scott.
        Prose: Biography. Travel. Essay.
          Familiar Essay: "Adventure of Herman
          Melville." Criticism. Book Reviews.
        Fiction: Essay Serials: "Characteristics
          of American Scenery"; "Modern Affecta-
          tions"; "Fireside Chit-Chat." Sketches.
          Tales: "The Field of Culloden"; "The
          Goldmaker's Village"; "The Shot in the
          Eye. A True Story of Texas Border Life";
          "The Blind Squatter"; "The Freaks of
          Fortune"; "Fray Christobal"; "The Frog
          and the Fox"; "Suspicion, or the Last
          Apple"; "The Rifle, a Tale of Arkansas";
          "The Path of Duty--A Tale."
        Miscellaneous: Extracts: from other jour-
          nals; by various authors; W. Irving.
          Anecdotes: on various subjects.

584   TITLES: (1) The New England Farmer, Contain-
      ing Essays, Original and Selected, Relating
      to Agriculture and Domestic Economy, with
      Engravings and the Prices of Country Pro-
      duce (2) The New England Farmer and Horti-
      cultural Journal [subtitle as above] (3)
      The New England Farmer and Gardener's Jour-
      nal [subtitle as above] (4) The New England
      Farmer and Horticultural Register [subtitle
      as above].

      Place of Publication: Boston
      First Issue: 3 Aug 1822
      Last Issue: 24 June 1846//
      Periodicity: Weekly
      Editors: Thomas Green Fessenden; Henry
               Colman; Allen Putnam; Joseph Breck
      Publishers: Thomas W. Shepard; William
               Nichols; John B. Russell; George
               C. Barrett; Joseph Breck
      Available From: Univ. of Calif., Berkeley;
               Yale Univ. Mott.
      Contents:
        Poetry: Original: Fessenden. Selected.
        Prose: Essay. Familiar Essay.
        Fiction: Sketches.
        Miscellaneous: Extracts: from other jour-
          nals. Anecdotes: on various subjects.
          News: Foreign and Domestic.
      Notes: Although largely agricultural in con-
        tent, this journal is interesting because
        of its editor, Fessenden, and for its lead-
        ing contributors: Daniel Webster [the
        Marshfield Farmer], Timothy Pickering, and
        John Lowell.

585   TITLES: (1) New-England Galaxy & Masonic
      Magazine (2) New-England Galaxy and United
      States Literary Advertiser (3) The Galaxy
      (4) The Boston Pearl and Galaxy.

      Place of Publication: Boston
      First Issue: 10 Oct 1817
      Last Issue: 29 March 1839//?
      Periodicity: Weekly
      Editor: Joseph T. Buckingham
      Publisher: Joseph T. Buckingham
      Available From: APS; Amer. Antiquarian Soc.
               Mott.
      Contents:
        Poetry: Original. Selected: Southey,
          Hawkesworth, Herbert Knowles, Joseph R.
          Otis, William Cowper, Joanna Baillie,
          Bryant, Byron, Selleck Osborne, Scott,
          George Buchanan, Felicia Hemans, John
          Quincy Adams, Garrick, Thomas Campbell.
        Prose: Biography: Benjamin West, R.B.
          Sheridan, John Wolcott, William Jones,
          Haydn, DeWitt Clinton. Travel. Familiar
          Essay. Criticism. Letters. Book
          Reviews.
        Fiction: Essay Serials: "The Little
          Preacher"; "From the Shop of Pertinax
          Period & Co."; "The Quizzer"; "The
          Smoker's Corner." Sketches. Tale:
          "Peter Rugg, the Missing Man" [William
          Austin].
        Miscellaneous: Extracts: from other

journals; by various authors. Anecdotes: on various subjects; Swift, Voltaire, Rousseau, Garrick. Literary Notices. News: Foreign and Domestic.

586   TITLE: New-England Galaxy and United States Literary Advertiser. [See New-England Galaxy & Masonic Magazine.]

587   TITLE: New England Literary Herald.

Place of Publication: Boston
First Issue: Sept 1809
Last Issue: Jan 1810//
Periodicity: ?
Editors: ?
Publishers: Farrand, Mallory, & Co.
Available From: APS; Lib. of Congress*
Contents:
Note: Contains only book reviews and literary notices.

588   TITLES: (1) The New-England Magazine (2) The New-England Magazine of Knowledge and Pleasure.

Place of Publication: Boston
First Issue: Aug 1758
Last Issue: March 1759//
Periodicity: Monthly
Editor: Urbanus Filter
Publisher: Benjamin Mecom
Available From: APS; Hist. Soc. of Pa.* Mott.
Contents:
    Poetry: Original. Selected: Swift.
    Prose: Biography: Cromwell. Essay: "On the Use, Abuse, and Liberty of the Press, with a Little Salutary Advice"; "On the Duty of Authors." Familiar Essay. Letters.
Note: Benjamin Mecom also published The Penny Post, Containing Fresh News, Advertisements, Useful Hints, &c. (Philadelphia), which contained primarily poetry and anecdotes.

589   TITLE: The New-England Magazine. [Merged into The American Monthly Magazine q.v.]

Place of Publication: Boston
First Issue: July 1831
Last Issue: Dec 1835//
Periodicity: Monthly
Editors: Joseph T. Buckingham; Edwin Buckingham
Publishers: J.T. and E. Buckingham; J.T. Buckingham; E.R. Broaders
Available From: APS; Univ. of Pa.* Poole.
Contents:
    Poetry: Original: Oliver Wendell Holmes, Hannah F. Gould, I. M'Lellan, Jr., A.D. Woodbridge, George Pope Morris, Whittier, James Sheridan Knowles, H.T. Tuckerman, Walter Severn, Thomas Power. Selected: Byron, Schiller, Park Benjamin, Goethe, Lydia H. Sigourney, Southey, Richard

Henry Dana, George D. Prentice, Dante, Phillis Wheatley, Cynthia Taggart, James G. Percival, Hannah F. Gould, Grenville Mellen, H.T. Tuckerman.
    Prose: Biography: Fitz-Greene Halleck, Bryant, James G. Percival, Charles Sprague, Hannah F. Gould, Edward Everett, Mathew Carey, Daniel Webster. Travel. Essay. Familiar Essay. Criticism. Letters. Book Reviews.
    Fiction: Essay Serials: "The Limping Philosopher"; "Selections from the Papers of an Idler"; "Letters from Ohio"; "Dramatic Reminiscences"; "The Autocrat of the Breakfast Table" [Oliver Wendell Holmes]; "Leaves Torn Out of a Scrap Book"; "My Books"; "The Nervous Man"; "Sketches from Memory. By a Pedestrian." Sketches. Tales: "The Schoolmaster"; "The Mysterious Mustard-Pot, a Tragical Tale"; "The Hermitage of Candu. An Oriental Tale"; "The Clergyman's Daughter"; "The Fair Eckbert"; "A Natick Tale"; "Saul Knapp-- Or the Life of a Yankee"; "Torquemada: A Tale of the Peninsular War"; "The Dead Set. Wherein I Speak of Most Disastrous Chances"; "The Mad-House"; "Passaconaway"; "Shoankah"; "Our Village Gardener"; "The Opium Eater"; "The Vocation"; "Montfort and Isabel. A Tale"; "Margaret Bell's Vow"; "The Issati Converts. A Tale of the Wilderness"; "Reminiscences of a Rogue"; "Uncle Sam and His Boys. A Tale for Theologians"; "Nannie Kon's Bible"; "The Thunder Storm; a Tale of Old Customs"; "My First Dining Out"; "The Bishop and His Cats"; "Reflections of a Jail Bird"; "The Gray Champion" [Hawthorne]; "The Squatter" [John Neal]; "The Rogue in Spite of Himself"; "Will the Wizard" [John Neal]; "Young Goodman Brown" [Hawthorne]; "Wakefield" [Hawthorne]; "The Ambitious Guest" [Hawthorne]; "A Rill from the Town Pump" [Hawthorne]; "The Old Maid in the Winding-Sheet" [Hawthorne]; "The Vision of the Fountain" [Hawthorne]; "The Devil in Manuscript."
    Miscellaneous: Anecdotes: on various subjects. Literary Notices. News: Domestic.

590   TITLE: The New-England Magazine, a Religious and Literary Monthly Miscellany. [See The Worcester Magazine, a Literary and Religious Miscellany.]

591   TITLE: The New England Quarterly Magazine; Comprehending Literature, Morals, and Amusement.

Place of Publication: Boston
First Issue: April, May, June 1802
Last Issue: Oct, Nov, Dec 1802//
Periodicity: Quarterly
Editors: ?
Publisher: Hosea Sprague
Available From: APS; Amer. Antiquarian Soc.* Mott.

Contents:
  Poetry: Original. Selected: Timothy
    Dwight, Richard Cumberland, David
    Humphreys, Amelia Opie, Anna Letitia
    Barbauld, Erasmus Darwin.
  Prose: Biography: Descartes, Lope de Vega,
    Thomas More, Rochefoucauld, Locke, Boileau,
    Voltaire, Adam Smith, Joshua Reynolds,
    Hannah More, John Dennis, Isaac Newton,
    Chatterton, Madame de Staël. Travel.
    Familiar Essay. Criticism: on Pope,
    Southey, Gray, Erasmus Darwin, Goldsmith,
    Voltaire, S. Richardson.
  Fiction: Essay Serial: "The Moral Obser-
    ver." Sketches. Tales: "History of the
    Maid of the Hay Stack"; "Danger of Sport-
    ing with the Affections. Illustrated in
    a Tale."
  Miscellaneous: Anecdotes: Edward Gibbon,
    Rousseau, Voltaire, Milton, S. Johnson,
    Shakespeare.

592 TITLE: The New Hampshire and Vermont Journal:
     Or, the Farmer's Weekly Museum. [See The
     New Hampshire Journal: Or, the Farmer's
     Weekly Museum.]

593 TITLE: The New Hampshire and Vermont Magazine,
     and General Repository.

     Place of Publication: Haverhill, N.H.
     First Issue: July 1797
     Last Issue: Oct 1797//
     Periodicity: Monthly
     Editor: John Moseley Dunham
     Publisher: John Moseley Dunham
     Available From: APS; Lib. of Congress. Mott.
     Contents:
       Poetry: Original.
       Prose: Biography. Essay. Familiar Essay.
       Fiction: Sketches. Tales: "The Duel.--
         A Fragment"; "A Remnant. Or Sequel of a
         Legendary Tale."

594 TITLES: (1) The New Hampshire Journal: Or,
     the Farmer's Weekly Museum (2) The New
     Hampshire and Vermont Journal: Or, the
     Farmer's Weekly Museum (3) Farmer's Museum,
     or Lay Preacher's Gazette (4) Farmer's
     Museum, or Literary Gazette (5) The
     Farmer's Museum.

     Place of Publication: Walpole, N.H.
     First Issue: 11 April 1793
     Last Issue: 15 Oct 1810//
     Periodicity: Weekly
     Editors: Isaiah Thomas; David Carlisle, Jr.;
         Joseph Dennie
     Publishers: Isaiah Thomas; David Carlisle,
         Jr.; David Newhall; Thomas &
         Thomas; Thomas & Thomas and
         Cheever Felch; Cheever Felch
     Available From: Amer. Antiquarian Soc.*
         Mott.

Contents:
  Poetry: Original: Thomas Green Fessenden,
    John Davis. Selected: Peter Pindar,
    Burns, Mary Robinson, Amelia Opie, Thomas
    Moore, James Thomson, William Cowper,
    James Pye.
  Prose: Biography. Familiar Essay.
    Criticism. Letters.
  Fiction: Essay Serial: "The Rural Wanderer."
    Sketches. Tales: "The Sorrows of
    Amelia: Or, Deluded Innocence"; "On Life--
    An Allegorical Vision."
  Miscellaneous: Extracts: by various
    authors; Jefferson. Anecdotes: on various
    subjects; Franklin. Literary Notices.
    News: Foreign and Domestic.
  Note: Several of the leading contributors
    were Royall Tyler, Thomas Green Fessenden,
    Joseph Dennie.

595 TITLE: New-Hampshire Magazine. Devoted to
     Literature, Education, Moral and Religious
     Reading.

     Place of Publication: Manchester, N.H.;
                          Great Falls, N.H.
     First Issue: Aug 1843
     Last Issue: July 1844//
     Periodicity: Monthly
     Editor: E.D. Boylston
     Publisher: E.D. Boylston
     Available From: Amer. Antiquarian Soc.*;
                     Lib. of Congress*
     Contents:
       Poetry: Original: Mary Spaulding, H. Fisk,
         Caroline F. Orne, J.Q.A. Wood, E.P.
         Bowman, David Gilchrist, J.W. Barker,
         D.C. Eddy. Selected: Lydia H. Sigourney,
         Sarah J. Hale, Hannah F. Gould, James G.
         Percival, Nathaniel P. Willis, James
         Russell Lowell, James Montgomery, George
         Kent, E. Lytton Bulwer, Schiller, Whittier,
         Charles James Fox.
       Prose: Biography: Washington Allston,
         Captain John Smith. Essay. Familiar
         Essay.
       Fiction: Sketches. Tales: "The Indian
         Maiden"; "An Eastern Tale"; "The Royal
         George: Or 'Any Port in a Storm'"; "Miss
         Eliza Leslie" [John Neal]; "Cocheco. A
         Tale of the Early Settlers"; "The Haunted
         House. A New-Hampshire Tale"; "The Two
         Maidens" [T.S. Arthur].
       Miscellaneous: Extracts: from other jour-
         nals; by various authors; Bryant, Daniel
         Webster, E. Lytton Bulwer. Anecdotes:
         on various subjects; Washington.

596 TITLE: The New Hampshire Magazine: Or, the
     Monthly Repository of Useful Information.

     Place of Publication: Concord, N.H.
     First Issue: June 1793
     Last Issue: Nov 1793//
     Periodicity: Monthly

Editor: Elijah Russell
Publisher: Elijah Russell
Available From: APS; Univ. of Minn.,
                 Minneapolis.* Mott.
Contents:
  Poetry: Selected: John Gay, John Trumbull.
  Prose: Biography: Walter Raleigh, Isaac
    Newton, Cromwell. Travel: Ledyard,
    William Bartram. Familiar Essay. Letters.
  Fiction: Essay Serials: "The Instructor";
    "The Biographer." Sketches. Tales: "The
    Story of Altamont and Arabella"; "The
    Wretched Tailloh.--An African Story."
  Miscellaneous: News: Foreign and Domestic.

597   TITLE: The New-Hampshire Mercury, and General
      Advertiser.

      Place of Publication: Portsmouth, N.H.
      First Issue: 24 Dec 1784
      Last Issue: 12 March 1788//
      Periodicity: Weekly
      Editor: Robert Gerrish
      Publisher: Robert Gerrish
      Available From: Amer. Antiquarian Soc.*
      Contents:
        Poetry: Original. Selected: John
          Cunningham, W. Woty.
        Prose: Familiar Essay. Letters.
        Fiction: Sketches. Tales: "The Fortunate
          Affliction"; "The Test of Generosity: An
          Apologue"; "The Fair Duellist. A Tale
          from Life"; "The Handsome Wife"; "Edict
          of Penance"; "The Critical Minute: Or
          the Ever Favored too Much."
        Miscellaneous: Extracts: by various
          authors; Jefferson. Anecdotes: on various
          subjects. Literary Notices. News:
          Foreign and Domestic.

598   TITLE: The New-Haven Gazette, and the
      Connecticut Magazine.

      Place of Publication: New Haven, Conn.
      First Issue: 16 Feb 1786
      Last Issue: 18 June 1789//
      Periodicity: Weekly
      Editors: ?
      Publishers: Meigs & Dana
      Available From: APS; Yale Univ. Mott.
      Contents:
        Poetry: Original. Selected: Richard
          Cumberland, William Cowper, S. Johnson,
          Richard Falconer, David Humphreys,
          William Collins, Joel Barlow, Gray,
          Thomas Warton.
        Prose: Biography. Familiar Essay.
          Letters.
        Fiction: Essay Serial: "The Friend."
          Sketches: "Polly Baker" [Franklin].
          Tales: "Tale for the Affluent"; "The
          Rainbow, a Fable"; "The Painters, a
          Fable."
        Miscellaneous: Extracts: by various
          authors; Thomas Paine, Montesquieu,
          Swift, David Humphreys, Adam Smith,
          S. Richardson, Voltaire, Jefferson,
          Goldsmith, Edward Gibbon, Franklin.

Anecdotes: on various subjects; Swift,
Hogarth. Literary Notices. News:
Foreign and Domestic.

599   TITLE: The New Havener. Devoted to Useful
      Intelligence, Original and Selected Tales,
      Essays, Poetry, &c. [See The Literary
      Emporium. Devoted to Useful Intelligence,
      Original and Selected Tales, Essays,
      Poetry, &c.]

600   TITLE: The New-Jersey Magazine, and Monthly
      Advertiser, Containing a Choice of Curious
      and Entertaining Pieces in Prose & Verses,
      with a Collection of the Most Recent Occur-
      rences Received from Europe, the West-Indies
      & North-America, & Several Advertisements.

      Place of Publication: New Brunswick, N.J.
      First Issue: Dec 1786
      Last Issue: Feb 1787//
      Periodicity: Monthly
      Editors: Frederick Quequelle; James Prange.
      Publishers: Frederick Quequelle; James Prange
      Available From: APS; Lib. of Congress. Mott.
      Contents:
        Poetry: Original.
        Prose: Biography: George Whitefield.
          Travel. Familiar Essay. Letters.
          Criticism: "An Account of a Novel Intitled
          Amelia; by Henry Fielding, Esq. To Which
          Are Added Some General Remarks."
        Fiction: Sketches. Tales: "Story of
          Orestes & Almeda"; "Story of Eudosius
          and Clarinda"; "Remarkable Story of Gioto,
          an Italian Painter, and His Crucifix";
          "An Oriental Tale, or the Friendship
          Corrupted."
        Miscellaneous: Anecdotes: on various
          subjects. News: Foreign and Domestic.

601   TITLE: The New Jersey Monthly Magazine.

      Place of Publication: Newark, N.J.
      First Issue: [Only one issue published?]
                   April 1825//?
      Periodicity: Intended to be monthly
      Editors: ?
      Publishers: ?
      Available From: Amer. Antiquarian Soc.
      Contents:
        Poetry: Original.
        Prose: Biography. Travel. Essay.
          Familiar Essay. Letters.
        Fiction: Tales: "Altamont and Arabella";
          "Adam Bell" [James Hogg].
        Miscellaneous: Extracts: from other jour-
          nals; by various authors; Hazlitt.
          Anecdotes: on various subjects.

602   TITLES: (1) The New Mirror, of Literature,
      Amusement, and Instruction: Containing
      Original Papers; Tales of Romance; Sketches
      of Society, Manners, and Every-day Life;
      Domestic and Foreign Correspondence; Wit and
      Humour; Fashion and Gossip; the Fine Arts,

and Literary, Musical and Dramatic Criticism;
Extracts from New Works; Poetry Original and
Selected; the Spirit of the Public Journals;
etc. etc. etc. (2) The Weekly Mirror
(3) New-York Mirror: A Reflex of the News,
Literature, Arts, and Elegancies of Our
Time (4) The American Literary Gazette
and New York Weekly Mirror.

Place of Publication: New York
First Issue: 8 April 1843
Last Issue: 2 Oct 1847//?
Periodicity: Weekly
Editors: George Pope Morris; Nathaniel P.
     Willis; Hiram Fuller
Publishers: Morris, Willis & Fuller;
     H. Fuller
Available From: APS; Lib. of Congress.*
     Mott.
Contents:
  Poetry: Original: Nathaniel P. Willis,
   George Pope Morris, Richard Henry Dana,
   Sarah J. Clarke, C.D. Stuart, Anna Saltus,
   Thomas Dunn English, Owen G. Warren,
   W. Patterson Cantwell, George Howard.
   Selected: James Russell Lowell, Barry
   Cornwall, Henry B. Hirst, Albert Pike,
   Arthur Morrell, Anna Cora Mowatt, Eliza
   Cook, Alaric Watts, William D. Gallagher,
   Frances S. Osgood, Caroline Norton, Leigh
   Hunt, Shelley, Whittier.
  Prose: Biography: Buonaparte. Travel.
   Essay. Familiar Essay. Criticism.
   Letters. Book Reviews.
  Fiction: Essay Serials: "Mirror Reflexes";
   "Chit-Chat of New York"; "Diary of Town
   Trifles"; "Dashes at Life with a Free
   Pencil." Sketches. Tales: "The Gipsy's
   Star. A Tale of the Abruzzo"; "The China
   Pitcher"; "Juliana"; "Light Vervain";
   "The Poet and the Mandarin" [Nathaniel P.
   Willis]; "Hereditary Failings"; "Journal
   of a Poor Vicar"; "The Gold Bubble"; "The
   Poet's Laura"; "Three Visits to the Hotel
   des Invalides"; "Shahatan"; "Tom Tucker";
   "The Discarded"; "The Bracelet"; "The
   Pearl of Geneva"; "The Banker's Wife";
   "The Oath That Was Kept"; "The Yacht. A
   Tale of the English Coast"; "The Princess
   Pauline"; "The Brigand's Wife"; "Citizen
   Regulus"; "A Hint to Husbands; or, a
   Widower's Bequest"; "Donna Sylveria Lopez
   and Her Lovers"; "The Little Frenchman
   and His Water Lots"; "The Panic of Thirty-
   Six. A Story of Wall-Street"; "The Stage
   of Competitors. A Tale of the Road"; "The
   Gentleman from Cahawba and His Drowsy
   Victim"; "Miseries of a Well-Bred Man";
   "How Will It Look?"; "The Bear of Carniola";
   "The Puce-Colored Carp. A Tale"; "The
   Recovered Treasure. An Old English Le-
   gend"; "The Brazilian Bride"; "Mary; or,
   the Blighted Blossom"; "Life at the South.
   A Lyncher's Own Story"; "The Wine Cellar";
   "The Law's Victim" [Dickens]; "The Black
   Prophet"; "The Creole's Courtship";
   "Abelard and Heloise"; "The Young Wife";
   "Mary Eckar. A School for Young Widows.
   An Original Tale"; "1844, or, the Power
   of the 'S.F.' A Tale Developing the
   Secret Action of Parties in the Late

Election Canvass" [Thomas Dunn English];
"The Trippings of Tom Pepper: Or the
Results of Romancing." Novel: "Dombey
and Son" [Dickens].
  Miscellaneous: Extracts: from other jour-
   nals; by various authors; Emerson,
   Nathaniel P. Willis, Dickens, Poe, E.
   Lytton Bulwer, Scott, Coleridge, Thomas
   Hood. Anecdotes: on various subjects.
   Literary Notices. News: Foreign and
   Domestic.

603 TITLE: The New Monthly Magazine and Literary
     Journal. [American Edition] [See also item
     604.]

Place of Publication: Boston; New York;
                 Philadelphia
First Issue: Jan 1821
Last Issue: Dec 1825//?
Periodicity: Monthly
Editor: N. Hale
Publishers: E. Littell; R. Norris Henry;
     Oliver Everett; Cummings,
     Hilliard & Co.
Available From: APS; Hist. Soc. of Pa.*
Contents:
  Poetry: Selected: Thomas Campbell, Joanna
   Baillie, Schiller, Richard Clitheroe,
   Charles Maturin, Byron, R.B. Sheridan,
   William Cowper, H.H. Milman.
  Prose: Biography: Ugo Foscolo, Rousseau.
   Travel. Familiar Essay. Criticism.
   Letters. Book Reviews.
  Fiction: Essay Serials: "Walks in the Gar-
   den"; "Jonathan Kentucky's Journal";
   "Grimm's Ghost"; "Modern Pilgrimages";
   "Table Talk"; "Journal of a Tourist";
   "The Confessional"; "The Months"; "The
   Spirits of the Age"; "The Family Journal";
   "Old Pages and Old Times"; "London Lyrics."
   Sketches. Tales: "The Harp, a Tale";
   "The First Spring: A Winter-Night Story";
   "The Village Bells"; "Ada Reis: A Tale";
   "The Crown of Victory"; "Giulio, a Tale."
  Miscellaneous: Extracts: from various
   authors; Schiller, Quevedo. Anecdotes:
   on various subjects; James Macpherson.

604 TITLE: The New Monthly Magazine and Literary
     Journal. [American Edition--New Series]
     [See also item 603.]

Place of Publication: Boston; New York;
                 Philadelphia
First Issue: Jan 1833
Last Issue: June 1834//
Periodicity: Monthly
Editor: E. Lytton Bulwer
Publishers: Allen and Ticknor; Charles S.
     Francis; Carey and Hart
Available From: APS; Boston Pub. Lib.*
Contents:
  Poetry: Selected: Caroline Norton, Tenny-
   son, Corenlius Webbe, Leigh Hunt, Thomas
   Haynes Bayly, Walter Savage Landor, Mary
   Howitt, Felicia Hemans, L.E. Landon.
  Prose: Biography: Byron, Horace Walpole.
   Essay. Familiar Essay. Criticism.
   Letters. Book Reviews.

Fiction: Essay Serials: "The Modern Platonist"; "Asmodeus at Large"; "Chapters from the Note-Book of a Deceased Lawyer." Tales: "Ixion in Heaven" [B. D'Israeli]; "Life in Death"; "The Veiled Picture. A Tale of the Fine Arts"; "Perran Path. A Cornish Story"; "Fi-Ho-Ti; or the Pleasures of Reputation. A Chinese Tale"; "The Divorcée Devoté"; "Inhabitants of a Country Town"; "The Ruined Laird"; "The Late Mr. Tardy"; "Mrs. John Jones's Picnic"; "Magpie Castle"; "The Gauchos; a Tale of the Pampas"; "The Debtor's Experience"; "An Adventure at St. Helena, in May, 1816." Drama: "Eugene Aram" [E. Lytton Bulwer]; "Dialogues of the Living." Miscellaneous: Extracts: by various authors; William Godwin. Anecdotes: on various subjects. Literary Notices.

605 TITLE: The New Novelists Magazine.

Place of Publication: New York
First Issue: [Only one volume published?] 1837//?
Available From: Univ. of Chicago*; Univ. of Minn., Minneapolis*

606 TITLE: The New Orleans Miscellany: A Monthly Periodical. Devoted to the Interests of Popular Science, and to the Advancement of Southern Literature.

Place of Publication: New Orleans
First Issue: Dec 1847
Last Issue: Feb 1848//?
Periodicity: Monthly
Editor: D. Macaulay
Publisher: D. Macaulay
Available From: APS; La. State Univ.
Contents:
Poetry: Original: John Tomlin, Mary E. Lee, G.P. Quackenbos, George Wyndham. Selected: Charles Sprague, Coleridge.
Prose: Biography. Essay. Familiar Essay. Criticism. Letters. Book Reviews.
Fiction: Essay Serial: "Treasure Trove." Sketches. Tales: "A Scene in Prairie Land; or, the Drama of Human Life"; "The Village Lovers"; "Mary Calvert; a Tale of the Catholic Excitement."
Miscellaneous: Anecdotes: on various subjects. Literary Notices.

607 TITLE: The New Star. A Republican, Miscellaneous, Literary Paper.

Place of Publication: Concord, N.H.
First Issue: 11 April 1797
Last Issue: 3 Oct 1797//
Periodicity: Weekly
Editors: ?
Publishers: Russel & Davis; Apollos Kinsley
Available From: APS; Harvard Univ. Mott.
Contents:
Poetry: Original. Selected: Swift.
Prose: Familiar Essay. Letters.

Fiction: Essay Serials: "The Warning"; "The Friend." Sketches.
Miscellaneous: Extracts: from other journals; by various authors; Joseph Dennie, Addison. Anecdotes: on various subjects.

608 TITLES: (1) The New World, a Weekly Journal of Popular Literature, Science, Music and the Arts, Containing the Newest Works by Celebrated Authors, Sermons by Eminent Divines, Original and Selected Tales and Poetry, &c., &c. (2) The New World. A Weekly Family Journal of Popular Literature, Science, Art and News.

Place of Publication: New York
First Issue: 6 June 1840
Last Issue: 10 May 1845//
Periodicity: Weekly
Editors: Park Benjamin; Henry C. Deming; James Mackay
Publisher: J. Winchester
Available From: Lib. of Congress; Amer. Antiquarian Soc.
Contents:
Poetry: Original: James Aldrich, H.W. Rockwell, E.N. Gamble, Whittier, Anna Cora Mowatt, Park Benjamin, Charlotte Cushman, I. M'Lellan, Jr., Frances S. Osgood, W.C. Richards, Longfellow, H.T. Tuckerman, Lydia H. Sigourney, C.H. Lewis, Edward A. McLaughlin, Caroline M. Sawyer, Mathilda P. Hunt. Selected: L.E. Landon, George Lunt, Mary Howitt, Lydia H. Sigourney, Epes Sargent, Mrs. Abdy, Hannah F. Gould, Frances S. Osgood, Joanna Baillie, Anna Cora Mowatt, Charles Dibdin, Bryant, Lucy Hooper, Longfellow, Tennyson, Thomas Moore, Charles MacKay, Wordsworth, Charles Swain, Caroline Bowles, Beranger, Shakespeare, Bernard Barton, James Montgomery, Park Benjamin, T.B. Macaulay, Keats, Abraham Cowley, Christopher Marlowe, Walter Raleigh, Alfred Tenny, Leigh Hunt, Barry Cornwall, Eliza Cook, Herrick, Shelley, William Beckford.
Prose: Biography: Goldsmith, Bryant, Southey. Travel. Essay. Familiar Essay. Criticism. Letters. Book Reviews.
Fiction: Essay Serials: "Letters from a Pedestrian"; "Reminiscences of an Old Federalist." Sketches. Tales: "Mrs. Bartholomew Winks's 'Pleasure Party'"; "The Country Schoolmaster"; "Beds and Bedrooms" [Leigh Hunt]; "Jane Sinclair; or the Fawn of Spring-Vale" [William Carleton]; "Charles O'Malley, the Irish Dragoon"; "The Duchess of Ferrara. A Tale of the Middle Ages"; "The Deformed"; "Ashore and Afloat"; "Sewell and Hewell; or, the Rival Shopkeepers!"; "The History of Samuel Titmarsh and the Great Hogarty Diamond"; "The Admiral's Daughter"; "The Anointed Eve. A Fairy Tale"; "Jack Hinton, the Guardsman"; "The Miser's Daughter. A Tale" [William Harrison Ainsworth]; "Philip Gangle"; "Carl Stelling: The Painter of Dresden"; "The Shrift on the Raft"; "'Milor Trotter Chigswell'"; "Marion de Lorme. A Tale"; "The One-Handed Lady";

"Jack Shaddock"; "Born to Love Pigs and Chickens" [Nathaniel P. Willis]; "My Grandfather's Dream"; "The Brown Mug" [Mrs. Seba Smith]; "Polly Gray and the Doctors" [Mrs. Seba Smith]; "La Morgue"; "The Lost Pearl"; "The Desert King"; "Cousin Frank" [Catharine Maria Sedgwick]; "The Potter's Daughter of Corinth"; "Vaninka"; "Autobiography of an Orphan Girl"; "Axel and Anna; a Correspondence Between Two Stories of the Same House"; "Laura Willoughby"; "An Adventure in the Life of Mr. Jonas Jenkins"; "Cornelia Bororquia; or, the Victim of the Inquisition"; "Lights and Shades; or, the Life of a Gentleman on Half-Pay"; "John Manesty, the Liverpool Merchant"; "The Two Brothers"; "The Mysterious Prediction. A Legend of Crutched Friars"; "The Witchfinder"; "Physiology of the Polka." Novels: "Master Humphrey's Clock" [Dickens]; "Ten Thousand a Year" [Samuel Warren]; "Barnaby Rudge" [Dickens]; "Guy Fawkes. A Historical Romance" [William Harrison Ainsworth]; "Stanley Thorn"; "The Pic Nic Papers" [Dickens]; "Handy Andy"; "The Chevalier; or, the Twenty-Fourth of August, 1572"; "The Wandering Jew." Drama: "Money: A Comedy in Five Acts" [E. Lytton Bulwer]; "Gulzara, the Persian Slave: A Drama in Five Acts" [Anna Cora Mowatt]; "The Triumph of Lucca. A Tragedy" [L.E. Landon]; "The Royal Poetaster. An Historical Drama in One Act"; "The Rose of Arragon: A Play in Five Acts" [James Sheridan Knowles]; "Edwin the Fair. An Historical Drama."

Miscellaneous: Extracts: from other journals; by various authors; Carlyle, W. Irving, Edward Gibbon, Thomas Campbell, B. D'Israeli, Daniel Webster. Anecdotes: on various subjects; Buonaparte, S. Johnson, James Fenimore Cooper, Chateaubriand, Whittier, Thomas Campbell, Scott, Dickens. Literary Notices. News: Foreign and Domestic.

609   TITLE: The New-York Amulet, and Ladies' Literary and Religious Chronicle.

Place of Publication: New York
First Issue: 9 Jan 1830
Last Issue: 15 March 1831//
Periodicity: Semi-monthly
Editor: Theophilus Fisk
Publisher: Theophilus Fisk
Available From: N.Y. Hist. Soc.*; Amer. Antiquarian Soc.*
Contents:
  Poetry: Original: Park Benjamin, Mary E. Brooks, Sarah Aikin, Elizabeth Bogart, Whittier. Selected: Felicia Hemans, John Bowring, Willis Gaylord Clark, Thomas Moore, Sarah J. Hale, Whittier, Mary Anne Browne, Lydia H. Sigourney, Alaric Watts, Thomas Campbell, Robert Morris, H.S. Ellenwood, Thomas Haynes Bayly, B.B. Thatcher, John G. Brainard.

Prose: Essay. Familiar Essay. Letters.
Fiction: Essay Serials: "The Reflector"; "The Moralist." Sketches. Tales: "The Confessions of a Victim"; "Azim; an Oriental Tale"; "Maria--Or the Victim"; "Everard Graham"; "Deputy Simpkins; or, the Wrong Coach"; "Self Immolation"; "The Duellists. A Tale"; "The Contrast"; "Henry St. Clair" [Whittier]; "The Lottery Ticket"; "The Forged Note; or, Arthur Mowbray. A Tale"; "The Two Mirrors. A Tale of Faery"; "The Sister of Charity. A Mariner's Tale" [Sumner Lincoln Fairfield]; "The Last Friend"; "Morris Williams; or, 'The Enlightened'"; "The Lottery Gambler."
Miscellaneous: Extracts: by various authors; Addison, W. Irving, George Bancroft. Anecdotes: on various subjects. Literary Notices.

610   TITLE: The New-York Cabinet. [See The Cabinet of Literature, Instruction, and Amusement.]

611   TITLE: New York Illustrated Magazine of Literature and Art. [Supersedes The Rover q.v.]

Place of Publication: New York
First Issue: 20 Sept 1845
Last Issue: June 1847//
Periodicity: Weekly
Editor: Lawrence Labree
Publishers: Robinson & Co.; Burgess, Stringer & Co.
Available From: APS; N.Y. Hist. Soc.* Mott.
Contents:
  Poetry: Original: Lawrence Labree, R.H. Stoddard, Joseph H. Butler, George Ten Eyck Sheldon, Robert F. Greeley, Thomas Jeffrey Smith, Jr., E. Oakes Smith. Selected: Park Benjamin, Robert Ingraham, H.H. Clements, C. Donald MacLeod, William Gilmore Simms, Frances S. Osgood, Scott, Charles Maturin, Charles Fenno Hoffman, Sidney Dyer, E. Helfenstein, Wordsworth.
Prose: Biography: Goethe, Colley Cibber, Tennyson, Elizabeth Inchbald. Familiar Essay. Criticism.
Fiction: Essay Serial: "Glimpses of a Soul." Sketches. Tales: "The Last Hour of a Suicide"; "The Maiden of the Rose: Or, Cambridge in 1261"; "Bergeronette"; "Hanging by Proxy. A Tale of New York in 1654"; "The Sisters of South Walsingham"; "The Bowie Knife"; "A Night at Haddon Hall"; "The Smuggler's Bride. A Tale of the Sea"; "King Richard the Third and Lady Anne: An Historical Legend of Crosby Hall"; "Herman the Tiler"; "Natalie Maynard. A Tale of Crime and Clemency"; "The Mysterious Invalid"; "The Fatal Wish"; "Evil May Day"; "Harry Linton, or the Rescue"; "Edith Warren. A Tale of the Revolution"; "The Fatal Secret. A Story of the Revolution"; "The Mercer's Wife"; "Nelly Gray; or Blighted Hopes"; "The Hurdy-Gurdy Girl"; "The Three Students. A Story of

Metropolitan Life"; "The Seamstress. A
Tale of New York City"; "The Scourged
Page"; "Katrina Schuyler. A Sketch of
the Times of Charles the Second" [Theodore
Sedgwick Fay]; "The Maroon. A Legend of
the Caribbees" [William Gilmore Simms];
"Ideal Love" [Charles Fenno Hoffman];
"Courtship of Dombey and Nephew" [Mrs.
Seba Smith]; "The Rescue; a Tale of the
Sixteenth Century"; "The Fatal Phrophecy:
A Tale of the Time of Cortes"; "Little
Mary Thornton, or the Yellow Fever in
New York in 1798"; "Agnes Fairfield. A
Tale of the French Revolution"; "The
Breaking of Swords" [Dickens]; "Iolanda,
--Or the Court of Love. A Tale of the
Fourteenth Century."
  Miscellaneous: Anecdotes: on various sub-
    jects. Literary Notices.

612   TITLE: The New York Literary Gazette.

Place of Publication: New York
First Issue: 2 Feb 1839
Last Issue: 13 July 1839//?
Periodicity: Weekly
Editor: James Aldrich
Publisher: W.V. Oxley
Available From: APS; N.Y. Pub. Lib.
Contents:
  Poetry: Original. Selected: Wordsworth,
    Coleridge, Southey, Tennyson, Goethe,
    Shelley, Fitz-Greene Halleck, Samuel
    Daniel, Rufus Dawes, Thomas Otway,
    Humphrey Davy, Schiller, Lydia H.
    Sigourney, Spenser, Walter Raleigh,
    Elizabeth Barrett, L.E. Landon, Abraham
    Cowley, Barry Cornwall, James Hogg, B.
    Jonson, Thomas Decker, Byron, George
    Chapman, A.J. Moultrie, James Montgomery,
    James Aldrich, William Pitt Palmer,
    Caroline Norton, Richard Crashaw.
  Prose: Familiar Essay. Criticism. Letters.
    Book Reviews.
  Fiction: Essay Serials: "Original Papers
    of the Pantagruel Club"; "Original
    Sketches from My Notebook." Sketches.
    Tales: "The Coliseum. A Fragment"
    [Shelley]; "The Haunted Head"; "The Auto-
    biography of an Old Hat"; "The Valley of
    Servoz. A Savoyard Tale"; "Insurance
    and Assurance"; "The Houri. A Persian
    Tale."
  Miscellaneous: Extracts: from other jour-
    nals; by various authors; B. Jonson,
    Dryden, Emerson, Charles Lamb, Mary
    Wollstonecraft. Anecdotes: on various
    subjects; Wordsworth, Coleridge, George
    Herbert, Buonaparte. Literary Notices.
    News: Domestic.

613   TITLE: The New-York Literary Gazette, and
    American Athenaeum. [See The Minerva, or
    Literary, Entertaining, and Scientific
    Journal: Containing a Variety of Original
    and Selected Articles, Arranged under the
    Following Heads: Popular Tales, the
    Gleaner, the Traveller, the Drama, Biography,
    Arts and Sciences, Literature, Poetry, etc.]

614   TITLE: New York Literary Gazette and Journal
    of Belles Lettres, Fine Arts, Sciences &c.

Place of Publication: New York
First Issue: 1 Sept 1834
Last Issue: 14 March 1835//
Periodicity: Semi-monthly [Irregular]
Editor: A.D. Paterson
Publishers: Swinborne & Paterson
Available From: Lib. of Congress; Boston
                    Pub. Lib.
Contents:
  Poetry: Original.
  Prose: Biography: Thomas Campbell.
    Familiar Essay. Criticism. Book Reviews.
  Fiction: Sketches. Tales: "Macoupin: Or,
    the Talking Potato"; "The Sheep-Stealer";
    "The Church of the Cup of Water."
  Miscellaneous: Literary Notices. News:
    Domestic.
  Note: The journal is composed primarily of
    review articles.

615   TITLE: The New-York Literary Gazette, and Phi
    Betta Kappa Repository. [See The Minerva,
    or Literary, Entertaining, and Scientific
    Journal: Containing a Variety of Original
    and Selected Articles, Arranged under the
    Following Heads: Popular Tales, the Glean-
    er, the Traveller, the Drama, Biography,
    Arts and Sciences, Literature, Poetry, etc.]

616   TITLE: The New-York Literary Journal, and
    Belles-Lettres Repository. [See The Belles-
    Lettres Repository, and Monthly Magazine.]

617   TITLE: The New-York Magazine, and General
    Repository of Useful Knowledge.

Place of Publication: New York
First Issue: May 1814
Last Issue: July 1814//?
Periodicity: Monthly
Editor: James Hardie
Publisher: James Oram
Available From: APS; N.Y. Hist. Soc.*
Contents:
  Poetry: Original. Selected.
  Prose: Biography. Familiar Essay.
    Criticism.
  Miscellaneous: Extracts: by various
    authors; S. Johnson, Joseph Dennie.
    Anecdotes: on various subjects. Literary
    Notices. News: Foreign and Domestic.

618   TITLE: The New-York Magazine; or, Literary
    Repository.

Place of Publication: New York
First Issue: Jan 1790
Last Issue: Dec 1797//
Periodicity: Monthly
Editors: Thomas Swords; James Swords
Publishers: Thomas and James Swords
Available From: APS; Amer. Antiquarian Soc.*
Contents:
  Poetry: Original: Anthony Bleeker, Anna

Eliza Bleeker. Selected: Joel Barlow, Philip Freneau, S. Johnson, Gray, Dryden, Southey, Peter Pindar, Anthony Pasquin, Mary Robinson, Fulke Greville, Della Crusca, Goldsmith, Edward Moore, Harriet Falconer, Chatterton, Pope, Thomas Warton, Robert Southwell.
Prose: Biography. Travel. Criticism. Letters.
Fiction: Essay Serial: "The Drone." Sketches. Tales: "Hafez, an Eastern Tale"; "Fatal Effects of Seduction. A Story Founded on Fact, Veiled Only Under a Fictitious Name"; "The Ambitious Man Punished. A Tale"; "The Unfortunate Mistake. A Tale"; "The Happy Shipwreck: A Tale"; "Thymander and Sobrina; or, the Tortures of Jealousy. A Favorite Story"; "Don Torribio. A Tale"; "Fable of the Two Ears of Corn"; "Arsaces and Ismenia. An Oriental Story"; "The Vine and Oak: A Fable"; "Story of Henry and Anne.--Founded on Fact"; "Ella. A Norwegian Tale"; "Abou Taib: An Eastern Tale"; "Abudah.-- A Tale"; "The Paradise of Schedad.--An Arabian Tale"; "Leander and Adelisa: A Tale"; "The Generous Mask. A Tale"; "The Pyrenean Hermits: A Tale"; "Melai: A Constantinopolitan Tale"; "Firnaz and Mirvan: An Eastern Tale"; "Walter: A Tale"; "Selico: An African Tale"; "Virtue Rewarded. A Pastoral Tale"; "The Tales of an Evening"; "Almoran and Selima. An Oriental Tale"; "Adventure of a Vizar's Daughter: A Tale"; "Ismael: A Moorish Tale"; "The Misfortunes of Ligrae. A Tale too True"; "Sir Gawen: A Tale"; "Edwin and Adela: A Tale"; "The Self-Rival: A Tale"; "The Chevalier Bayard and Madame de Randan--A Tale of the Fifteenth Century"; "Amelia, or the Faithless Briton--An American Tale"; "The Power of Friendship--A Tale"; "The Maid of the Hamlet--A Tale"; "Cleophilia: A Tale"; "The Ruins of Caithness--A Gothic Tale"; "The Basket-Maker. A Peruvian Tale"; "Azakia: A Canadian Story"; "The Duellists:--A French Story"; "Claudine: A Swiss Tale." Novel: "Story of Sarah Phillips.--A Novel."
Miscellaneous: Extracts: from other journals; by various authors. Anecdotes: on various subjects; Franklin, Thomas More. News: Foreign and Domestic.
Note: This journal and The Massachusetts Magazine q.v. were the longest lived magazines of the eighteenth century. Among the leading contributors were Charles Brockden Brown, Elihu Hubbard Smith, Josiah Ogden Hoffman, William Dunlap, Noah Webster, Samuel Latham Mitchell. Among the famous subscribers were George Washington and John Adams.

619   TITLE: The New York Mercury; a Journal of American Literature.

Place of Publication: New York
First Issue: 1838
Last Issue: 1 Jan 1870//?
Available From: Yale Univ.; Univ. of Minn., Minneapolis

620   TITLE: New-York Mirror: A Reflex of the News, Literature, Arts, and Elegancies of Our Time. [See The New Mirror, of Literature, Amusement, and Instruction: Containing Original Papers; Tales of Romance; Sketches of Society, Manners, and Every-day Life; Domestic and Foreign Correspondence; Wit and Humour; Fashion and Gossip; the Fine Arts, and Literary, Musical and Dramatic Criticism; Extracts from New Works; Poetry Original and Selected; the Spirit of the Public Journals; etc. etc. etc.]

621   TITLE: The New York Mirror. A Weekly Journal Devoted to Literature and the Fine Arts. [See The New-York Mirror, and Ladies' Literary Gazette; Being a Repository of Miscellaneous Literary Productions, in Prose and Verse.]

622   TITLES: (1) The New-York Mirror, and Ladies' Literary Gazette; Being a Repository of Miscellaneous Literary Productions, in Prose and Verse (2) The New York Mirror. A Weekly Journal Devoted to Literature and the Fine Arts. [Superseded by The New Mirror, of Literature, Amusement, and Instruction: Containing Original Papers; Tales of Romance; Sketches of Society, Manners, and Every-day Life; Domestic and Foreign Correspondence; Wit and Humour; Fashion and Gossip; the Fine Arts, and Literary, Musical and Dramatic Criticism; Extracts from New Works; Poetry Original and Selected; the Spirit of the Public Journals; etc. etc. etc. q.v.]

Place of Publication: New York
First Issue: 2 Aug 1823
Last Issue: 31 Dec 1842//
Periodicity: Weekly
Editors: Samuel Woodworth; George Pope Morris; Theodore Sedgwick Fay; John Inman; Nathaniel P. Willis; Charles Fenno Hoffman; Epes Sargent; Hiram Fuller
Publishers: George Pope Morris; Hopkins & Morris; Robert S. Williams
Available From: APS; Harvard Univ. Mott.
Contents:
  Poetry: Original: Grenville Mellen, Nathaniel P. Willis, Willis Gaylord Clark, James G. Brooks, Charles Sprague, Bryant, Fitz-Greene Halleck, Thomas Dunn English, Samuel Woodworth. Selected: C.M. Thayer, Henry M. Dobbs, Jr., Thomas Moore, Byron, James G. Percival, Samuel P. Adams, Felicia Hemans, Bryant.
  Prose: Biography: Luis de Camoens, Benjamin Rush, W. Irving, Alexander Hamilton. Travel. Essay. Familiar Essay. Criticism. Letters: Nathaniel P. Willis, Theodore Sedgwick Fay, William Cox. Book Reviews.
  Fiction: Essay Serials: "The Little Genius"; "The Radical" [Theodore Sedgwick Fay]; "Pencillings by the Way" [Nathaniel P. Willis]; "Slipshoddities"; "Diary of Town Trifles"; "More Particularly"; "While We

Hold You by the Button" [Nathaniel P. Willis]. Sketches. Tales: "Whig and Tory. A Tale of the Revolution"; "Caleb and Matilda; an American Tale"; "Oneyo and Marano, an Indian Tale"; "The Broken Vow, a Village Tale"; "Claudius and Rosalie, a Tale of Truth"; "The Refugee. A Tale of the Revolution"; "Edward and Julia"; "Vicissitudes"; "Walter Pennington"; "The Diving Bell"; "Edward and Isabella"; "Elizabeth"; "The Spectre"; "The Wedding Party"; "Virginia St. Victor, an American Tale"; "Harry Ransom, or the Adventures of an Atheist"; "Eugenia de Mirande"; "Friendship and Love"; "Sergeant Jasper. A Tale of the Revolution"; "Sullivan's Island, or the Adventures of a Hermit"; "Imogine, or the History of a Coquette"; "Polydore Crosey"; "Adolphus Granville"; "Green Mountain Life"; "The Will, or the Legal Contest"; "The Widow's Son, or Which Is the Traitor? A Tale of the Revolutionary War"; "The Murderer"; "The Happy Restoration"; "Love Adventures"; "Gipsy of Debretzin"; "The Pale Beauty"; "The Shooting Match"; "Reason and Passion"; "Edward and Mary"; "Tale of the Green Taper"; "Florian and Ellen, or the Lily of the Manor, Founded on Fact"; "Zamire"; "The Exile of the Alleghany, or National Gratitude"; "Walter Moore"; "Eugenia Mornton"; "La chambre d'amour"; "Miss Tassell, or, the Morning Ramble"; "Pierre the Hermit"; "Domestic Applications"; "Citizen and Savage"; "The Stranger, or, the Votary of Folly"; "Brom Von Heighderdonk, the Hartford Physician, a Yankee Story."

Miscellaneous: Extracts: from other journals; by various authors. Anecdotes: on various subjects; S. Johnson, Garrick, Franklin, Fenelon. Literary Notices.

623   TITLE: The New-York Monthly Magazine.

Place of Publication: New York
First Issue: Jan 1824
Last Issue: March 1824//?
Periodicity: Monthly
Editor: James Oram
Publisher: James Oram
Available From: APS; N.Y. State Lib.,
                 Albany.* Mott.

Contents:
  Poetry: Original. Selected: Southey, Byron.
  Prose: Biography. Travel. Familiar Essay. Book Reviews.
  Fiction: Essay Serials: "Critic"; "The Moralist." Sketches. Tales: "The Idrian Miner--An Austrian Tale"; "Real Scenes in the Life of an Actress"; "The Village Bells"; "A Sister's Love."
  Miscellaneous: Extracts: from other journals; by various authors. Anecdotes: on various subjects; B. Jonson, Pope, Franklin.

624   TITLES: (1) New York Polyanthos (2) Polyanthos.

Place of Publication: New York
First Issue: 1836
Last Issue: July 1841//?
Available From: N.Y. Pub. Lib.

625   TITLE: The New-York Review, and Atheneum Magazine. [Supersedes The Atlantic Magazine q.v. and later merged with the United States Literary Gazette (Boston) q.v. to form the United States Review and Literary Gazette q.v.]

Place of Publication: New York
First Issue: June 1825
Last Issue: May 1826//
Periodicity: Monthly
Editors: Henry J. Anderson; William Cullen
          Bryant; Robert C. Sands
Publishers: E. Bliss & E. White
Available From: APS; Lib. of Congress.* Mott.
Contents:
  Poetry: Original: George Bancroft, Richard Henry Dana, Nathaniel P. Willis, Longfellow, Bryant, Fitz-Greene Halleck. Selected: Goethe, Schiller.
  Prose: Biography. Travel. Essay. Familiar Essay. Criticism: on Dante. Letters. Book Reviews: on James Fenimore Cooper, Henry R. Schoolcraft, Daniel Webster, Scott.
  Fiction: Sketches. Tales: "Stories of a Cock and Bull. The Beau's Tale.--A History of Count R----"; "A Nightmare"; "A Pennsylvania Legend."
  Miscellaneous: Extracts: by various authors; Schiller, Byron, James G. Percival. Literary Notices.

626   TITLE: New York State Journal; Devoted to the Affairs of the State Generally and to Literary and Moral Subjects.

Place of Publication: Troy, N.Y.
First Issue: 9 Sept 1835
Last Issue: 7 Sept 1836//?
Available From: N.Y. Pub. Lib.

627   TITLES: (1) The New-York Visiter, and Parlour Companion (2) Visiter and Parlour Companion (3) The Visitor, and Lady's Parlor Magazine (4) The New-York Visitor and Lady's Album.

Place of Publication: New York
First Issue: July 1838
Last Issue: July-Aug 1843//
Periodicity: Monthly
Editor: Joseph W. Harrison
Publisher: Joseph W. Harrison
Available From: Lib. of Congress; N.Y. Pub.
                 Lib.

Contents:
  Poetry: Original: J. Edward Beers, E.D.

Baker, Jr., Maria E. Bisbee, F.J. Otterson. Selected: James Montgomery, Schiller, E. Lytton Bulwer, Thomas Moore, Fitz-Greene Halleck, Miss Jewsbury, Eliza Cook, John Quincy Adams, Ann S. Stephens, Jane H. Williams.
Prose: Biography: Scott. Essay. Familiar Essay.
Fiction: Essay Serial: "American Romance." Sketches. Tales: "Glenalpin; or, the Bandit's Cave"; "Charlotte Margueritte de Montmorenci, Princess of Conde, and Sister of the Great Conde. A Tale of the French Chronicles, Founded on Fact"; "Zicci.--A Tale" [E. Lytton Bulwer]; "The Two Cousins"; "The Pirate's Bride"; "The Picture Gallery"; "The Tutor"; "The Unwedded Bride. A True Story of American Life"; "The Storm Child"; "Adventures on the Moors. A Tale of the Scottish Borders"; "Mary of Mantua"; "Thymander and Sobrina; or, the Tortures of Jealousy"; "The Ransom; or, a Father's Love"; "New Year's Night"; "Grizel Cochrane"; "Adelaide and Valvaise; or, the Triumphs of Friendship.--A Swedish Tale"; "The Profligate, a True Tale"; "Romance of American History. West Point--A Tale of Treason"; "The Wife; or, Woman's Constancy. A Tale of the Trying Times"; "Juliet Rivers; or, a Father's Crime"; "The Son of Annawan"; "The Farmer's Son"; "The Devil's Pulpit, a Legend of Weehawken"; "The Rescue; a Tale of the Revolution"; "Leopoldine and Stephanie; or, the Rival Sisters"; "A Year Among the Yankees"; "The Wanderer of the Deep"; "The Broken Miniature"; "The Maniac"; "Marcella, the Roman Wife"; "Zosinski: A Tale of the Twelfth Century"; "Love and Gooseberries. A Sentimental Story"; "A Tale of Saragossa"; "Isabel de Vere; a Story of Hoboken"; "The Gipsey Chief; or, the Haunted Oak. A Tale of Other Days"; "The Quaker Bride"; "Lucy Pinkham; or, the Romance of Reality"; "Inez Guerara. A Spanish Tale"; "The Devoted"; "The Daughter"; "The Gipsey Mother; or, the Miseries of Enforced Marriage"; "The Broken Cup; or, the Lucky Mischance."
Miscellaneous: Extracts: from other journals; by various authors; Mary Wollstonecraft, Bryant. Anecdotes: on various subjects; Edward Gibbon, Milton, Washington, Franklin, Buonaparte, Penn, Byron. Literary Notices.

628   TITLE: The New-York Visitor and Lady's Album. [See The New-York Visiter, and Parlour Companion.]

629   TITLE: New York Washingtonian and Ladies' Literary Pearl. [See The Pearl: A Ladies' Weekly Literary Gazette. Devoted to the Advocacy of the Various Ladies' Total Abstinence Association.]

630   TITLE: The New-York Weekly Journal.

Place of Publication: New York
First Issue: 5 Oct 1733
Last Issue: 18 March 1751//
Periodicity: Weekly
Editor: John Peter Zenger
Publisher: John Peter Zenger
Available From: Amer. Antiquarian Soc.
Contents:
    Poetry: Original.
    Prose: Essay. Familiar Essay. Letters.
    Fiction: Sketches.
    Miscellaneous: Extracts: by various authors. Literary Notices. News: Foreign and Domestic.

631   TITLE: The New-York Weekly Magazine; or, Miscellaneous Repository: Forming an Interesting Collection of Original and Select Literary Productions in Prose and Verse: Calculated for Instruction and Rational Entertainment--the Promotion of Moral and Useful Knowledge--And to Enlarge and Correct the Understandings of Youth. [Superseded by the Sentimental & Literary Magazine.]

Place of Publication: New York
First Issue: 1 July 1795
Last Issue: 23 Aug 1797//
Periodicity: Weekly
Editors: John Bull; Thomas Burling, Jr.
Publishers: John Bull; Thomas Burling, Jr.; John Tiebout
Available From: APS; Lib. of Congress.* Mott.
Contents:
    Poetry: Original. Selected.
    Prose: Familiar Essay. Letters.
    Fiction: Essay Serials: "The Essayist"; "The Farrago" [Joseph Dennie]. Sketches. Tale: "St. Herbert."
    Miscellaneous: Extracts: from other journals; by various authors. Anecdotes: on various subjects; Swift, Pope, Franklin.

632   TITLE: The New-York Weekly Museum. [See The Impartial Gazetteer, and Saturday Evening's Post.]

633   TITLE: New-York Weekly Museum, or Polite Repository of Amusement and Instruction. [See The Impartial Gazetteer, and Saturday Evening's Post.]

634   TITLE: The New-Yorker, a Weekly Journal of Literature and Intelligence. [Superseded by The New York Weekly Tribune.]

Place of Publication: New York
First Issue: 22 March 1834
Last Issue: 11 Sept 1841//
Periodicity: Weekly
Editors: Horace Greeley; E. Sibbet; J. Winchester; Park Benjamin; Rufus Wilmot Griswold
Publishers: H. Greeley & Co.

Available From: Lib. of Congress.* Mott.
Contents:
  Poetry: <u>Original</u>. <u>Selected</u>: Byron,
    Felicia Hemans, Bernard Barton, Whittier,
    Willis Gaylord Clark, E. Lytton Bulwer,
    Bryant, Henry Neele, Lydia H. Sigourney,
    Hannah F. Gould, Barry Cornwall, Thomas
    Moore, Thomas Campbell, Nathaniel P.
    Willis, Shelley, Fitz-Greene Halleck,
    Thomas Haynes Bayly, Sumner Lincoln Fair-
    field, William Falconer, Caroline Norton,
    William Gilmore Simms, L.E. Landon,
    William H. Burleigh, Wordsworth, Beranger,
    James G. Percival.
  Prose: <u>Biography</u>: William Wirt, Joel
    Barlow, LaFayette, Coleridge, Felicia
    Hemans, Whittier. <u>Travel</u>. <u>Essay</u>.
    <u>Familiar Essay</u>. <u>Criticism</u>. <u>Letters</u>.
    <u>Book Reviews</u>.
  Fiction: <u>Essay Serials</u>: "Passages from My
    Diary"; "Scraps and Sketches"; "Shreds and
    Patches, from the Drawer of a Defunct
    Snip"; "Ollapodiana"; "Recollections of a
    Portrait Painter." <u>Sketches</u>. <u>Tales</u>:
    "The Orphans. A Tale of New-England";
    "The Story of Hester Malpas"; "Jessie
    Gordon"; "The Brothers. A Tale"; "Yankee
    Pedagogues and Dutch Damsels. A Legend
    of the City of Hudson" [James Kirke
    Paulding]; "The Pilgrim of Love"; "Frea
    the Fearless: The Black Bucanier of
    Barbadoes"; "The Ruined Family"; "The
    Citizen and Savage"; "The Lovers of St.
    Clair. A Tale of the French Revolution";
    "Hudusi, the Doubter. An Oriental Tale";
    "The Mad-House of Palermo" [Nathaniel P.
    Willis]; "Tom Fane and I"; "The Wondrous
    Tale of a Little Man in Gosling Green";
    "John W. Robertson. A Tale of a Cent";
    "Euthanasie; a Tale of the Pilgrims";
    "The Deserter"; "The Lunatic" [Nathaniel
    P. Willis]; "The Partners--Or Above and
    Below. A Tale of Common Life"; "Zampieri
    Dominichino. A Tale"; "Souchong, Slang-
    Whang, and Bohea: Or the Three Editors
    of China"; "Frank Wilmot; a Tale"; "The
    Bride of Lindorf"; "A Bell's Biography"
    [Hawthorne].
  Miscellaneous: <u>Extracts</u>: from other jour-
    nals; by various authors. <u>Anecdotes</u>: on
    various subjects. <u>Literary Notices</u>.
    <u>News</u>: Foreign and Domestic.

635   TITLE: <u>News-Gong: A Literary Intelligencer</u>.
      [Supplement to <u>Arcturus</u> q.v.]

      Place of Publication: New York
      First Issue: [Only 3 issues published] 1841//
      Available From: N.Y. Pub. Lib.*

636   TITLE: <u>The Nightingale, or, a Melange de
      Litterature; a Periodical Publication</u>.

      Place of Publication: Boston
      First Issue: 10 May 1796
      Last Issue: 30 July 1796//
      Periodicity: Tri-weekly
      Editors: John Lathrop, Jr.; John Russell

Publishers: John Lathrop, Jr.; John Russell,
    & Co.
Available From: APS; Amer. Antiquarian Soc.*
    Mott.
Contents:
  Poetry: <u>Original</u>: Aaron Hill. <u>Selected</u>:
    Erasmus Darwin, S. Johnson, Peter Pindar,
    Joseph Warton, William Shenstone, Edward
    Young, Shakespeare, Milton.
  Prose: <u>Biography</u>: religious and political
    figures; Joshua Reynolds, Franklin,
    Erasmus Darwin, Pope, Addison. <u>Travel</u>:
    William Bartram. <u>Essay</u>. <u>Familiar Essay</u>.
    <u>Letters</u>.
  Fiction: <u>Essay Serials</u>: "The Theorist";
    "The Philosopher"; "The Microcosm: Or
    Man as He Is"; "The Moralist." <u>Sketches</u>.
    <u>Tales</u>: "The Lady of the Cave"; "The
    Zegris. An Interesting Spanish Novel";
    "The Complaint of Iman; or, the False
    Appearances of Happiness and Misery. An
    Eastern Tale"; "The Sorrows of Amelia, or
    Deluded Innocence. An Historiette
    Founded in Fact"; "The Old Man and His
    Dog. A Tale" [Marmontel]; "Charles and
    Amelia: Or, the Unfortunate Lovers. A
    Tale."
  Miscellaneous: <u>Extracts</u>: by various
    authors; Lavater, William Shenstone.
    <u>Anecdotes</u>: on various subjects; Milton,
    S. Johnson, Franklin. <u>Literary Notices</u>.

637   TITLES: (1) <u>The North American Magazine</u>
      (2) <u>The North American Quarterly Magazine</u>.

      Place of Publication: Philadelphia
      First Issue: Nov 1832
      Last Issue: June 1838//
      Periodicity: Monthly; Quarterly
      Editor: Sumner Lincoln Fairfield
      Publishers: C. Sherman & Co.
      Available From: Lib. of Congress*; Yale
                Univ.* Mott.
      Contents:
        Poetry: <u>Original</u>: Sumner Lincoln Fairfield,
          David Paul Brown, George D. Prentice,
          J.P. Waities. <u>Selected</u>: William D.
          Gallagher, Coleridge, Keats, Otway Curry,
          James Montgomery, Lydia H. Sigourney.
        Prose: <u>Biography</u>: John Howard Payne,
          Francis Hopkinson. <u>Travel</u>. <u>Essay</u>.
          <u>Familiar Essay</u>. <u>Criticism</u>. <u>Letters</u>.
          <u>Book Reviews</u>.
        Fiction: <u>Essay Serials</u>: "Evenings at
          Saint's"; "Table Talk"; "Critical Disser-
          tations." <u>Sketches</u>. <u>Tales</u>: "Sassamon,
          the Traitor and Spy"; "Broker Bullion, or
          Fashionable Life at Saratoga"; "The Pro-
          scribed. A Tale of Scotland"; "The
          Suicide"; "The Beautiful Poetess"; "Life
          in Philadelphia; or, Love, Money, and
          Marriage"; "The Martyrdom of Love. A
          Tale of Actual Occurrences"; "The Confes-
          sions of a Bookworm"; "The Dead Soldier";
          "The Adventures of Bodie Borrowdil Among
          the Literati"; "The Aristocrat, an
          American Tale"; "The Stolen Daughter";
          "The Dead Soldier."

Miscellaneous: Extracts: from other jour-
nals; by various authors; Benjamin Rush.
Anecdotes: on various subjects. Literary
Notices. News: Domestic.

638   TITLE: North American. Or, Weekly Journal
of Politics, Science and Literature.

Place of Publication: Baltimore
First Issue: 19 May 1827
Last Issue: 24 Nov 1827//
Periodicity: Weekly
Editor: Samuel Sands
Publisher: Samuel Sands
Available From: APS; Amer. Antiquarian Soc.*
Contents:
    Poetry: Original. Selected: Thomas Moore,
    Byron, George D. Prentice, Felicia
    Hemans, Alaric Watts, Thomas Hood, L.E.
    Landon, James G. Percival.
    Prose: Biography. Travel. Familiar Essay.
    Criticism. Book Reviews.
    Fiction: Essay Serials: "The American
    Character"; "The Peripatetic." Sketches.
    Tales: "Alice Ford; or, the Days of
    Queen Mary" [Felicia Hemans]; "Nights in
    the Guard-House. Story of Maria de
    Carmo"; "Hope Leslie--Or Early Times in
    Massachusetts" [Catharine M. Sedgwick];
    "Hans Heiling's Rocks--A Bohemian Legend."
    Miscellaneous: Extracts: from other jour-
    nals; by various authors; Scott, James
    Fenimore Cooper. Anecdotes: on various
    subjects. Literary Notices. News:
    Foreign and Domestic.

639   TITLE: The North American Quarterly Magazine.
[See The North American Magazine.]

640   TITLE: The North American Review. [See The
North-American Review and Miscellaneous
Journal.]

641   TITLES: (1) The North-American Review and
Miscellaneous Journal (2) The North
American Review.

Place of Publication: Boston
First Issue: May 1815
Last Issue: Winter 1939-40//
Periodicity: Bi-monthly; Quarterly
Editors: William Tudor; William Cushing;
         Jared Sparks
Publishers: Wells and Lilly; Cummings and
            Hilliard; Oliver Everett;
            Cummings, Hilliard and Company;
            Frederick T. Gray; Gray and
            Bowen; Charles Bowen; Otis,
            Broaders, & Co.; Ferdinand
            Andrews; James Munroe and
            Company; David H. Williams;
            Charles C. Little and James Brown

Available From: APS; Lib. of Congress.*
                Mott. Poole.
Contents:
    Poetry: Original: John Ware, Bryant.
    Selected: Byron, Lydia Huntley, Scott,
    William Cowper, Thomas Moore, John Calcraft,
    Leigh Hunt, Boileau, Goethe, Bryant, James
    Montgomery, James Hogg, James Eastburn,
    James G. Percival, Wordsworth, John G.
    Brainard, Edward C. Pinckney.
    Prose: Biography. Travel. Essay.
    Familiar Essay. Criticism. Letters:
    Jefferson, Franklin, Southey. Book
    Reviews.
    Fiction: Sketches.
    Miscellaneous: Extracts: from other jour-
    nals. Anecdotes: on various subjects;
    Rousseau, Voltaire. Literary Notices.

642   TITLE: The Northern Light; Devoted to Free
Discussion, and to the Diffusion of Useful
Knowledge, Miscellaneous Literature and
General Intelligence.

Place of Publication: Albany
First Issue: April 1841
Last Issue: Sept 1844//
Periodicity: Monthly; Semi-monthly
Editors: John A. Dix; T. Romeyn Beck; Gideon
         Hawley; Amos Dean; Alonzo Potter;
         Thomas W. Olcott; Edward C. Delavan;
         Alfred B. Street; Samuel S. Randall;
         James Hall
Publisher: John A. Dix
Available From: APS; Boston Pub. Lib.*
Contents:
    Poetry: Original: N.T. Rosseter, Alfred
    B. Street, Henry Whiting, Abraham
    Messler, Anna Eliza Gray, Frederick W.
    Cole, C.M. Brosnan, Charles H. Lyon,
    Robert S. Oakley, E.G. Squier, Ezekiel
    Bacon, E.B. O'Callaghan, Henry R. Colcraft,
    Lydia J. Pierson, Jefferson Frazer,
    J. Hunt, Jr., James Matson, Robert
    Neilson. Selected: Henry Wotton, William
    Croswell, Spenser, Abraham Messler,
    B. Jonson, Wordsworth, James G. Percival,
    Hartley Coleridge, Bryant, Burns, Nathan
    C. Brooks, Longfellow.
    Prose: Biography: Henry Wotton, B. Jonson,
    Jefferson, Chaucer. Travel. Essay.
    Familiar Essay. Criticism. Book Reviews.
    Fiction: Essay Serials: "Mems. By a Read-
    ing Man"; "Reapings by a Reader"; "Summer
    Fancies." Sketches. Tales: "The Broken
    Cup"; "The Portrait--A Tale"; "Jenny; or
    the Three Flower Markets of Paris"; "The
    Inn at Cransac"; "Floretta: Or, the First
    Love of Henry IV"; "The Creole Maiden's
    Love"; "The Cross of Honor"; "Tom Trick";
    "Wild Kimball, or the Freshet"; "Mahingah--
    Or the Wolf of the Mahiccanni"; "The
    Pretty Maid of Potsdam"; "Onwawisset, or
    the Two Friends"; "The Power of Popular
    Sanction"; "Sag Harbor Zeb"; "The Abbess
    of Maubuisson"; "The Quaker and the
    Robber."

Miscellaneous: <u>Extracts</u>: from other journals; by various authors; Coleridge. <u>Anecdotes</u>: on various subjects. <u>Literary Notices</u>.
Note: Among the leading contributors were Noah Webster and Horace Greeley.

643 TITLE: <u>The Northwestern Educator and Magazine of Literature and Science</u>.

Place of Publication: Chicago
First Issue: 1847
Last Issue: 1849//
Available From: Cornell Univ., Ithaca; State Hist. Soc. of Wis., Madison

644 TITLE: <u>The Novelist's Magazine, a SemiMonthly Publication; Embracing the Newest and Most Popular Works of Fiction Issued from the British and American Press</u>.

Place of Publication: Philadelphia
First Issue: 1833//
Periodicity: Semi-monthly
Editors: ?
Publishers: C. Alexander & Co.
Available From: Hist. Soc. of Pa.*; N.Y. Pub. Lib.*
Contents:
 Poetry: <u>Selected</u>: Felicia Hemans, James Montgomery.
 Prose: <u>Biography</u>: Madame de Scuderi.
 Fiction: <u>Tales</u>: "The Enchantress"; "The Talisman"; "The Knife"; "Theresa"; "Rebecca"; "Experiments, or, the Lover from Ennui"; "The Upstart. A Tale of Olden Times"; "The Castle of Scharfenstein"; "The Sisters." <u>Novels</u>: "Henry Masterton; or, the Adventures of a Young Cavalier"; "The Adventures of Barney Mahoney"; "Clan-Albin; a National Tale"; "A Marriage in High Life"; "The Mourning Ring"; "A Year and a Day"; "The Youth and Manhood of Cyril Thornton."
 Miscellaneous: <u>Anecdotes</u>: on various subjects.

645 TITLE: <u>The Oasis, a Monthly Magazine, Devoted to Literature, Science and the Arts, Containing Essays, Tales, Poetry, Criticisms, Reviews of New Publications, &c</u>.

Place of Publication: Oswego, N.Y.
First Issue: 12 August 1837
Last Issue: 28 July 1838//
Periodicity: Monthly
Editors: Joseph Neilson; John S. Randall
Publishers: Hull & Henry
Available From: APS; Amer. Antiquarian Soc.*
Contents:
 Poetry: <u>Original</u>. <u>Selected</u>: Felicia Hemans, James Hogg, Scott, Thomas Dunn English.
 Prose: <u>Biography</u>: Scott, Lydia H. Sigourney. <u>Essay</u>. <u>Familiar Essay</u>. <u>Criticism</u>. <u>Letters</u>. <u>Book Reviews</u>.

Fiction: <u>Sketches</u>. <u>Tales</u>: "Snarleyyow; or, the Dog Friend"; "Juba"; "The Daughter in Exile"; "Ernest Maltravers" [E. Lytton Bulwer]; "Our Village Post Office"; "A Night Among the Wolves" [Whittier]; "Edward Merton"; "The Triumph of Pride over Affection"; "R. Sheridan Snicks"; "Catharine Lincoln"; "The Confessions of a Bachelor"; "The Game of Chess"; "A Tale of Passion"; "The Artist of Friula."
Miscellaneous: <u>Extracts</u>: from other journals; by various authors; Nathaniel P. Willis. <u>Anecdotes</u>: on various subjects. <u>Literary Notices</u>.

646 TITLE: <u>The Observer</u>.

Place of Publication: New York
First Issue: 19 Feb 1809
Last Issue: 6 August 1809//
Periodicity: Weekly
Editors: T. Powers; Sinclair; William Elliot
Publishers: T. Powers; Sinclair; William Elliot
Available From: APS; Lib. of Congress*
Contents:
 Poetry: <u>Original</u>. <u>Selected</u>: Sterne, Thomas Campbell, William Shenstone, Burns, Pope, Philip Freneau, Southey, George Crabbe.
 Prose: <u>Essay</u>. <u>Familiar Essay</u>. <u>Letters</u>.
 Fiction: <u>Essay Serial</u>: "The Moralist."
 Miscellaneous: <u>Extracts</u>: from other journals; by various authors; Sterne, Goldsmith, Anna Letitia Barbauld, Burns, Rochefoucauld. <u>Anecdotes</u>: on various subjects. <u>News</u>: Foreign and Domestic.

647 TITLE: <u>The Observer</u>.

Place of Publication: New York
First Issue: 14 Oct 1810
Last Issue: 21 April 1811//?
Periodicity: Weekly
Editors: ?
Publishers: Elliot and Crissy
Available From: APS; N.Y. Hist. Soc.*
Contents:
 Poetry: <u>Original</u>. <u>Selected</u>: Scott, William Roscoe, Thomas Coombe, Chesterfield, S. Johnson, Anna Letitia Barbauld, James Montgomery, John Wolcott, William Somerville, Wordsworth, Southey.
 Prose: <u>Essay</u>. <u>Familiar Essay</u>.
 Fiction: <u>Sketches</u>: "Polly Baker" [Franklin].
 Miscellaneous: <u>Extracts</u>: by various authors. <u>Literary Notices</u>. <u>News</u>: Foreign and Domestic.

648 TITLES: (1) <u>The Observer, and Repertory of Original and Selected Essays, in Verse & Prose, on Topics of Polite Literature, &c</u>. (2) <u>The Observer. By Beatrice Ironside</u>. [Supersedes <u>The Companion and Weekly Miscellany</u> q.v.]

Place of Publication: Baltimore
First Issue: 29 Nov 1806
Last Issue: 26 Dec 1807//
Periodicity: Weekly
Editor: Joseph Robinson
Publisher: Joseph Robinson
Available From: APS; Lib. of Congress.*
            Mott.
Contents:
  Poetry: Original. Selected: Luis de
    Camoens, Amelia Opie, Chatterton, James
    Pye, Ann Radcliffe, Charlotte Smith.
  Prose: Biography: Charles James Fox,
    Voltaire. Travel. Familiar Essay.
    Criticism. Letters. Book Reviews.
  Fiction: Essay Serials: "Lucubrations of
    Benjamin Bickerstaff, Esq"; "From the
    Whim-Whams and Opinions of Launcelot
    Langstaff, Esq."; "The Cameleon"; "The
    Prediction." Sketches. Tales: "African
    Resolution and European Infamy. A True
    Story"; "Reveries of a Recluse"; "On
    Selfishness in Our Enjoyments. An
    Eastern Tale"; "Almoran and Selima. An
    Oriental Tale"; Osmir. An Eastern
    Essay"; "The Most Criminal Not Always the
    Most Unhappy. A Moral Tale"; "Valeria;
    or the Ghost Alive!"
  Miscellaneous: Anecdotes: on various sub-
    jects; S. Johnson.

649   TITLE: The Observer. By Beatrice Ironside.
      [See The Observer, and Repertory of Original
      and Selected Essays, in Verse & Prose, on
      Topics of Polite Literature, &c.]

650   TITLE: The Odd Fellows' Literary Magazine.

      Place of Publication: New York
      First Issue: July 1848
      Last Issue: Jan 1849//?
      Periodicity: Monthly
      Editors: W.K. Cole; C.W. Bryan, James
                Batchellor
      Publisher: Edward Walker
      Available From: Lib. of Congress*; Yale
                Univ.*
      Contents:
        Poetry: Original: Nelson Brown, William
          K. Cole, James Lumbard, Caroline E. Tim-
          low, Viola Wilcox, Charlotte Allen, J.
          Gierlow, Kate St. Clair. Selected:
          Goethe, William Cowper, Shelley, Alfred
          B. Street.
        Prose: Biography. Essay. Familiar Essay.
          Criticism.
        Fiction: Tales: "The Sprig of Laurel";
          "The Three Keys of Human Happiness. An
          Oriental Tale"; "Ahmed the Cobbler";
          "Ferdinand Gerorld, or the Signal of
          Danger"; "Guadeloupe Victoria. A Tale
          of the Mexican Empire"; "Olga--A Russian
          Tale"; "Woman's Wit. Or the Young Mer-
          chant of Bagdad"; "Emma Linden, or Life
          Is not All Dark"; "The Sister of Rem-
          brandt. A Flemish Story"; "The Three
          Ravens; or, Marriage by Compulsion."
        Miscellaneous: Extracts: by various
          authors.

651   TITLE: The Odd Fellows' Magazine, Published
      Quarterly. Comprising a Variety of Subjects
      Which Will Be of Great Utility to the Order,
      and Amusing to Persons Generally.

      Place of Publication: Baltimore
      First Issue: 1 Oct 1825
      Last Issue: 1 Jan 1826//?
      Periodicity: Quarterly
      Editor: John Roach
      Publisher: John Roach
      Available From: APS; N.Y. State Lib., Albany
      Contents:
        Poetry: Original: John Graham, James Wood.
          Selected.
        Prose: Biography. Essay. Familiar Essay.
          Letters.
        Fiction: Tales: "The Siege of Roxburgh.
          Founded on Fact" [James Hogg]; "Albertina;
          a Tale from the German"; "The Hungry Arab.
          A Tale from the Tohfet al Mojailis."
        Miscellaneous: Extracts: by various
          authors. Anecdotes: on various subjects;
          Franklin. Literary Notices.

652   TITLE: The Ohio Miscellaneous Museum.

      Place of Publication: Lebanon, Ohio
      First Issue: Jan 1822
      Last Issue: May 1822//?
      Periodicity: Monthly
      Editors: ?
      Publishers: ?
      Available From: APS; State Hist. Soc. of
                Wis., Madison*
      Contents:
        Poetry: Selected: Selleck Osborne.
        Prose: Biography. Book Reviews.
        Fiction: Tales: "Arthur Fitzroy, or the
          Young Backwoodsman"; "Adventures in
          Havana"; "Emily, the Indian Princess."
        Miscellaneous: Extracts: from other jour-
          nals; by various authors. Anecdotes: on
          various subjects; Franklin. Literary
          Notices. News: Domestic.

653   TITLE: The Olden Time; a Monthly Publication,
      Devoted to the Preservation of Documents
      and Other Authentic Information in Relation
      to the Early Explorations, and the Settle-
      ment and Improvement of the Country Around
      the Head of the Ohio.

      Place of Publication: Pittsburgh
      First Issue: Jan 1846
      Last Issue: Dec 1847//
      Periodicity: Monthly
      Editor: Neville B. Craig
      Publisher: J.W. Cook
      Available From: APS; Hist. Soc of Pa.*
      Contents:
        Prose: Biography. Essay. Familiar Essay.
          Letters.
        Fiction: Sketches.
      Note: Contains many accounts of Indians and
        Indian wars. Although largely historical,
        the journal is of some literary interest.

654 TITLE: The Olio, a Literary and Miscellaneous
     Paper. Containing Biographical Sketches of
     the Most Eminent Naval and Military Char-
     acters in the United States; Extracts from
     History, Travels, Geography, and Novels;
     Poetry, Anecdotes, Bon-Mots, &c. &c. To-
     gether with, a Brief Account of the Passing
     Events of the Day.

     Place of Publication: New York
     First Issue: 27 Jan 1813
     Last Issue: 5 Feb 1814//
     Periodicity: Weekly
     Editor: S. Marks
     Publisher: S. Marks
     Available From: APS; Amer. Antiquarian Soc.*
     Contents:
       Poetry: Original. Selected: Peter Pindar,
         William Ingram, Scott, Thomas Campbell,
         Edward Moore, Edmund Waller, Thomas
         Moore, Byron, Lessing, Burns, Edwin C.
         Holland, John Davis.
       Prose: Biography: Joel Barlow, Benjamin
         Rush. Travel. Familiar Essay. Letters.
       Fiction: Sketches. Tales: "Self-Indul-
         gence: A Tale of the Nineteenth Century";
         "Fanny Mortimer"; "The Daughter; or, a
         Modern Romance"; "Lauretta: A Modern
         Tale" [Marmontel]; "The Shepherdess of
         the Alps: A Tale" [Marmontel]; "The
         Happy Divorce."
       Miscellaneous: Extracts: from other jour-
         nals; by various authors; Goldsmith.
         Anecdotes: on various subjects; Swift,
         George Whitefield, Descartes. News:
         Domestic.

655 TITLE: The Olio; a Literary and Miscellane-
     ous Journal Devoted to the Instruction and
     Amusement of the Junior Class of Society.

     Place of Publication: Cincinnati
     First Issue: 26 May 1821
     Last Issue: 11 May 1822//?
     Available From: Hist. and Philos. Soc. of
                      Ohio, Cincinnati*; Ohio
                      Wesleyan Univ., Delaware

656 TITLE: The Olio, or Rarities of Knowledge.

     Place of Publication: New York
     First Issue: [Undated. nos. 1-50] 1839//?
     Periodicity: Weekly
     Editor: Origen Bacheler
     Publisher: Origen Bacheler
     Available From: Amer. Antiquarian Soc.;
                      Yale Univ.*
     Contents:
       Poetry: Selected: Bryant, James G. Per-
         cival.
       Prose: Travel. Essay. Familiar Essay.
       Fiction: Sketches.
       Miscellaneous: Extracts: from other jour-
         nals. Anecdotes: on various subjects.

657 TITLES: (1) Omnium Gatherum, a Monthly Maga-
     zine, Recording Authentick Accounts of the
     Most Remarkable Productions, Events, and
     Occurrences, in Providence, Nature, and Art
     (2) Omnium Gatherum.

     Place of Publication: Boston
     First Issue: Nov 1809
     Last Issue: Oct 1810//
     Periodicity: Monthly
     Editors: ?
     Publisher: T. Kennard
     Available From: APS; Amer. Antiquarian Soc.*
     Contents:
       Poetry: Original. Selected: Du Bartas,
         Mather Byles, Joseph Green, Charles
         Dibdin, David Humphreys.
       Prose: Biography: Edward Norton. Travel.
         Essay: on the Boston Exchange Coffee-
         House; "Account of a Female Indian."
         Familiar Essay: "London Slang." Letters.
       Fiction: Essay Serials: "The Merry An-
         drew"; "The Juvenile Traveller."
         Sketches. Tale: "Slip Slop."
       Miscellaneous: Extracts: from other jour-
         nals; by various authors. Anecdotes: on
         various subjects; Mather Byles, Jefferson.
         News: Domestic.

658 TITLE: The Opera Glass. Devoted to the Fine
     Arts, Literature, and the Drama.

     Place of Publication: New York
     First Issue: 8 Sept 1828
     Last Issue: 3 Nov 1828//
     Periodicity: Weekly
     Editor: James S. Wallace
     Publisher: James S. Wallace
     Available From: APS; Univ. of Minn.,
                      Minneapolis*

     Contents:
       Poetry: Selected.
       Prose: Familiar Essay. Book Reviews.
       Fiction: Sketches. Tales: "Tales of the
         Wanderer"; "Tale Bearing. An American
         Tale of Real Life."
       Miscellaneous: Anecdotes: on various sub-
         jects. Literary Notices.
     Note: The journal is chatty, gossipy in
       nature; contains reviews of the latest
       theatre productions.

659 TITLE: The Oracle. Moral, Religious and
     Literary.

     Place of Publication: Northampton, Mass.
     First Issue: 6 Jan 1824
     Last Issue: 20 April 1825//
     Periodicity: Semi-monthly
     Editor: H. Ferry
     Publisher: H. Ferry
     Available From: Amer. Antiquarian Soc.;
                      Forbes Pub. Lib., North-
                      hampton, Mass.

Contents:
Poetry: <u>Original</u>. <u>Selected</u>: Robert Montgomery, Luis de Camoens, James G. Percival, Joshua Marsden, R.S. Coffin.
Prose: <u>Biography</u>. <u>Travel</u>. <u>Essay</u>. <u>Familiar Essay</u>.
Fiction: <u>Sketches</u>.
Miscellaneous: <u>Extracts</u>: from other journals; by various authors; Lavater. <u>Anecdotes</u>: on various subjects. <u>News</u>: Domestic.

660   TITLE: <u>The Oracle of the Day</u>.

Place of Publication: Portsmouth, N.H.
First Issue: 4 June 1793
Last Issue: 28 Dec 1799//
Periodicity: Bi-weekly
Editor: Charles Peirce
Publisher: Charles Peirce
Available From: Amer. Antiquarian Soc.
Contents:
Poetry: <u>Original</u>: Maria Champney, H. Fresham. <u>Selected</u>.
Prose: <u>Familiar Essay</u>.
Fiction: <u>Essay Serial</u>: "The Prompter." <u>Sketches</u>. <u>Tale</u>: "Amelia: Or, the Sentimental Fair."
Miscellaneous: <u>Anecdotes</u>: on various subjects. <u>Literary Notices</u>. <u>News</u>: Foreign and Domestic.

661   TITLE: <u>The Ordeal: A Critical Journal of Politicks and Literature</u>.

Place of Publication: Boston
First Issue: 7 Jan 1809
Last Issue: 1 July 1809//
Periodicity: Weekly
Editor: Joseph T. Buckingham
Publisher: Joseph T. Buckingham
Available From: APS; Lib. of Congress.*
                                Mott.
Contents:
Poetry: <u>Original</u>. <u>Selected</u>: Chatterton, Wordsworth, Southey, Erasmus Darwin.
Prose: <u>Biography</u>: Washington. <u>Familiar Essay</u>. <u>Criticism</u>: on Scott, theatre productions. <u>Letters</u>. <u>Book Reviews</u>.
Fiction: <u>Drama</u>: "The Rovers; or, the Double Arrangement"; "Stella."
Miscellaneous: <u>Extracts</u>: from other journals. <u>Anecdotes</u>: on various subjects; Jefferson. <u>Literary Notices</u>.

662   TITLES: (1) <u>The Orion: A Monthly Magazine of Literature, Science, and Art</u> (2) <u>Orion: A Monthly Magazine of Literature and Art</u> (3) <u>The Orion; or, a Southern Monthly: A Magazine of Original Literature and Art</u>.

Place of Publication: Penfield, Ga.; Athens, Ga.
First Issue: March 1842
Last Issue: Aug 1844//
Periodicity: Monthly
Editor: William C. Richards
Publisher: William C. Richards

Available From: APS; Ga. State Lib., Atlanta*
Contents:
Poetry: <u>Original</u>: D.A. Chittenden, William C. Richards. <u>Selected</u>: R.H. Wilde, Hannah F. Gould, Park Benjamin, J.H. Mifflin, Lydia H. Sigourney, Bryant, Felicia Hemans, Luis de Camoens, William Gilmore Simms, Grenville Mellen, James Hungerford, Alfred B. Street, Mary E. Lee, James G. Percival, Goethe, Thomas Hood.
Prose: <u>Biography</u>: Luis de Camoens, Felicia Hemans. <u>Travel</u>. <u>Essay</u>. <u>Familiar Essay</u>. <u>Criticism</u>. <u>Letters</u>. <u>Book Reviews</u>.
Fiction: <u>Essay Serial</u>: "Lights and Shadows of the Heart." <u>Sketches</u>. <u>Tales</u>: "The Trysting Rock: A Tale of Tallulah"; "The Story of Human Love"; "The Miser's Curse"; "Adeline Larnard"; "Alice Seyton"; "The Angel-Bride"; "Margaret Donaldson: Or the Fortune Huntress"; "The Village Postmaster"; "The Smithville Gas Frolic"; "Agnes, a Story of the Revolution"; "Clarence Grahame; or, the Capture of Burgoyne. A Story of the Revolution"; "Major Theophilus Bandbox Bubble, or the Nice Young Man"; "The Phrenologist; or, the Tactics of Doctor Cranium. A Village Story"; "The Fulton Folly, or, the First Steamboat: A Romance of American Biography"; "The Three May Days"; "A Tale of the Saluda"; "The Wood-Cutter's Self"; "Il Capanneto; a Romance of a Summer"; "The Hickory Nut: A Tale."
Miscellaneous: <u>Extracts</u>: from other journals. <u>Anecdotes</u>: on various subjects. <u>Literary Notices</u>.

663   TITLE: <u>The Orion; or, a Southern Monthly: A Magazine of Original Literature and Art</u>. [See <u>The Orion: A Monthly Magazine of Literature, Science, and Art</u>.]

664   TITLES: (1) <u>Orphan's Friend and Literary Repository</u> (2) <u>Baltimore Magazine and Literary Repository</u>.

Place of Publication: Baltimore
First Issue: Nov 1804
Last Issue: April 1805//?
Available From: Enoch Pratt Lib., Baltimore*

665   TITLE: <u>The Pantheon, and Ladies' Literary Museum</u>.

Place of Publication: Westfield, N.Y.
First Issue: 8 June 1830
Last Issue: ?
Available From: Brown Univ., Providence

666   TITLE: <u>The Parent's Gift; or, Youth's Magazine</u>.

Place of Publication: Philadelphia
First Issue: 1830
Last Issue: 1831//?
Available From: Boston Athenaeum

667 TITLES: (1) The Parent's Magazine (2) The Parent's Magazine, and Young People's Friend (3) The Parent's Monitor, and Young People's Friend.

Place of Publication: Gilmanton, N.H.; Concord, N.H.
First Issue: Sept 1840
Last Issue: Sept 1850//?
Periodicity: Monthly
Editors: I. Bird; Mrs. Bird; "An Association of Parents"
Publisher: James Thompson
Available From: Amer. Antiquarian Soc.; Lib of Congress
Contents:
  Poetry: Original. Selected: Hannah F. Gould, Lydia H. Sigourney, Jane Taylor.
  Prose: Biography: Timothy Dwight. Essay. Familiar Essay. Letters.
  Fiction: Essay Serial: "Family Scenes." Sketches.
  Miscellaneous: Extracts: from other journals; by various authors; Amos Bronson Alcott, Willis Gaylord Clark, Lydia H. Sigourney, Catharine M. Sedgwick, Jane Taylor, T.S. Arthur. Anecdotes: on various subjects; Franklin, Buonaparte.

668 TITLE: Parley's Magazine for Children and Youth. [Merged with Robert Merry's Museum q.v.]

Place of Publication: Published simultaneously in New York, Boston, Portland, Philadelphia, Baltimore, Washington, D.C., Richmond, Buffalo, New Orleans
First Issue: 16 March 1833
Last Issue: Dec 1844//
Periodicity: Semi-monthly; Monthly
Editor: Samuel G. Goodrich ["Peter Parley"]
Publishers: Charles S. Francis; Joseph H. Francis; Lilly, Wait, & Co.; Samuel Colman; Colman & Chisholm
Available From: Amer. Antiquarian Soc.; Yale Univ. Mott.
Contents:
  Poetry: Original: Lydia H. Sigourney. Selected: William Howitt, Hannah F. Gould, Barry Cornwall, Mary Howitt, Felicia Hemans, Caroline Norton, Richard Howitt, Miss Jewsbury, H.C. Deakin, Charles Sprague, Lydia H. Sigourney, Miss Pardoe, Grenville Mellen, William Croswell, Eliza Cook, Agnes Strickland.
  Prose: Biography. Travel. Familiar Essay. Letters.
  Fiction: Essay Serials: "Letter from Aunt Newbury"; "Gleanings and Recollections." Sketches. Tales: "The Little Woodcutter"; "The Journal; or, Birthday Gifts"; "Laura Seymour"; "Wanderings of Tom Starboard"; "Mary Wilson. An Original Tale"; "Rambles of Richard Rover"; "Samuel and Henry; a Tale for Brothers and Sisters"; "The

Frolic. An Original Tale"; "The Heroic Soldier"; "Alexander and His Nurse Janet"; "The Tell-Tale"; "Story of Hawkseye, an Indian Chief"; "Wolsey Bridge; or, the Boy Bachelor. A Tale Founded on Fact"; "Lady Lucy's Petition"; "The Tale of a Triangle: Or, Evil Done, That Good Might Come of It" [Mary Howitt]; "The Pretender; or, the Cottage of Glengary."
  Miscellaneous: Extracts: by various authors; W. Irving. Anecdotes: on various subjects; Scott.

669 TITLE: The Parlor Annual, or Young Lady's and Gentleman's Magazine. [See The Youth's Parlor Annual.]

670 TITLE: The Parlour Companion. [Supersedes the Juvenile Portfolio and Literary Miscellany q.v.]

Place of Publication: Philadelphia
First Issue: 4 Jan 1817
Last Issue: 21 Aug 1819//?
Periodicity: Weekly
Editor: Thomas G. Condie, Jr.
Publisher: Thomas G. Condie, Jr.
Available From: APS; Lib. of Congress
Contents:
  Poetry: Original. Selected: Gray, William Roscoe, Anna Seward, Byron, Lessing, Amelia Opie, Timothy Dwight, Boileau, J. Mayne, Richard Cumberland, McDonald Clarke, Edmund Waller, John Suckling, William Strode, Matthew Prior, William Cliffton.
  Prose: Travel. Familiar Essay. Letters.
  Fiction: Essay Serials: "Readings and Reflections"; "The Gatherer"; "The Collector." Sketches. Tales: "The Legacy.--A Tale"; "The Story of Lorraine"; "The Curate"; "Amelia Seldon.--A Tale"; "My Cousin Kate"; "The Liberal Artifice"; "The Governess"; "The Orphan"; "Conscience.--A Tale"; "Clara Hubert"; "The Discovery.--A Historiette"; "Sophy Lefevre"; "The Recluses of Snowden"; "The Fortunate Accident--A Tale"; "Nancy--Or the Eléve of Sensibility"; "The Slave of Suspicion"; "Wallen--A Tale"; "The Story of Abbas"; "Louisa Venomi"; "The Grove of Roses--A Tale"; "Love and Nature--A Tale"; "Motherless Mary"; "The Sisters.--A Tale"; "Amelia De Linval"; "The Pilgrim's Tale"; "The Young Irishman.--A Tale."
  Miscellaneous: Extracts: from other journals; by various authors; Madame de Staël, Joseph Dennie, William Hazlitt, Hester L. Thrale Piozzi. Anecdotes: on various subjects; William Collins, Hogarth, Colley Cibber, Edmund Waller, William Shenstone.

671 TITLE: The Parlour Journal, a Weekly Magazine, Devoted to Literature and the Fine Arts, the Drama, Entertaining and Useful Knowledge, Biographical Sketches, Criticisms

on New Works, &c. Embellished with En-
gravings and Music. [See Peabody's Parlour
Journal. A Weekly Magazine, Dedicated to
High Life, Fashionables, Fashions, Polite
Literature, Criticisms on New Works, the
Fine Arts--the Opera--Theatres--Exhibitions,
etc. Containing General Information upon
Every Subject.]

672 TITLE: The Parlour Magazine, a Weekly Jour-
     nal, Devoted to Literature and the Fine
     Arts, the Drama, &c. &c. [See Peabody's
     Parlour Journal. A Weekly Magazine,
     Dedicated to High Life, Fashionables,
     Fashions, Polite Literature, Criticisms on
     New Works, the Fine Arts--the Opera--
     Theatres--Exhibitions, etc. Containing
     General Information upon Every Subject.]

673 TITLE: The Parlour Magazine, and Literary
     Gazette. A Weekly Journal. Devoted to
     Literature and the Fine Arts, the Drama,
     &c. &c. [See Peabody's Parlour Journal.
     A Weekly Magazine, Dedicated to High Life,
     Fashionables, Fashions, Polite Literature,
     Criticisms on New Works, the Fine Arts--
     the Opera--Theatres--Exhibitions, etc.
     Containing General Information upon Every
     Subject.]

674 TITLE: The Parlour Review, and Journal of
     Music, Literature, and the Fine Arts.

     Place of Publication: Philadelphia
     First Issue: 6 Jan 1838
     Last Issue: 10 March 1838//
     Periodicity: Weekly
     Editor: George Carstensen
     Publisher: George Carstensen
     Available From: APS; N.Y. Pub. Lib.*
     Contents:
       Poetry: Selected: Miss Jewsbury, William
         Roscoe, Victor Hugo.
       Prose: Biography. Essay. Familiar Essay.
       Fiction: Tales: "The Mad Captain"; "Love
         in a Tent"; "The Conscience-Stricken
         Cuirassier"; "The Nuptials"; "An Excellent
         Offer."
       Miscellaneous: Anecdotes: on various sub-
         jects.

675 TITLE: A Parlour-Window Book, for Dull Times.
     [See The Post-Chaise Companion; or, Maga-
     zine of Wit. To Which Is Added, a Number
     of Patriotic and Humorous Songs.]

676 TITLE: The Parterre, a Weekly Magazine,
     Conducted by a Trio.

     Place of Publication: Philadelphia
     First Issue: 15 June 1816
     Last Issue: 28 June 1817//
     Periodicity: Weekly
     Editors: ?
     Publishers: Probasco & Justice
     Available From: APS; Hist. Soc. of Pa.*

Contents:
  Poetry: Original. Selected: Thomas Camp-
    bell, Thomas Moore, James Montgomery,
    Caroline Norton, Erasmus Darwin, William
    Cowper, William Cliffton, James Hogg.
  Prose: Biography: Robert Treat Paine,
    Timothy Dwight, Lady Mary Wortley Montagu.
    Familiar Essay. Criticism. Letters.
  Fiction: Essay Serials: "The Escritoire";
    "The Compiler"; "The Wanderer's Reflec-
    tion"; "Cogitations." Tales: "The History
    of Violentus. A Tale"; "Don Ferdinand de
    Aranda. A Fragment"; "The Bachelor";
    "The Basket of Strawberries"; "The Buffaloe
    Robe. A Tale"; "Albert and Matilda: Or,
    the Friar's Tale"; "The Adventures of
    Will Blair, the Trooper, and His Horse
    Pocket"; "The Unhappy Return. A Tale";
    "The Story of Melissa."
  Miscellaneous: Extracts: from other jour-
    nals; by various authors; S. Johnson,
    Chateaubriand. Anecdotes: on various
    subjects; S. Johnson, Goldsmith, Swift,
    Garrick.

677 TITLE: The Parthenon, or, Literary and
     Scientific Museum.

     Place of Publication: New York
     First Issue: 22 Aug 1827
     Last Issue: 8 Dec 1827//?
     Periodicity: Weekly
     Editor: Samuel Woodworth
     Publishers: Woodworth, Webb, & Co.
     Available From: APS; Newberry Lib., Chicago*
     Contents:
       Poetry: Original. Selected: Milton.
       Prose: Essay. Familiar Essay. Criticism.
         Book Reviews.
       Fiction: Essay Serial: "Desultory
         Thoughts." Tales: "Intolerance. A
         Domestic Tale of the Year 1741"; "The
         Noble Friend"; "Fatal Curiosity. An
         Irish Historical Tale"; "The Midnight
         Murder."
       Miscellaneous: Anecdotes: on various sub-
         jects; Garrick, Dryden, Samuel Foote.
         Literary Notices. News: Domestic.

678 TITLES: (1) The Pastime (2) The Pastime.
     (A Literary Paper).

     Place of Publication: Schenectady, N.Y.
     First Issue: 21 Feb 1807
     Last Issue: 25 June 1808//?
     Periodicity: Weekly
     Editors: ?
     Publishers: Ryer Schermerhorn; E. & E.
                 Hosford
     Available From: APS; N.Y. Hist. Soc.*
     Contents:
       Poetry: Selected: Coleridge, John Blair
         Linn, Southey, Erasmus Darwin, Dryden,
         Robert Treat Paine, Thomas Dermody,
         Thomas Campbell.
       Prose: Biography: Pocahontas, Richard
         Cumberland, Thomas Dermody, Robert Bloom-
         field. Travel. Familiar Essay. Criti-
         cism: "The Genius of Shakespeare and
         Milton Contrasted." Letters.

Fiction: Essay Serial: "The Purveyor."
Sketches. Tale: "Story of Rosalba."
Drama: "Hero and Leander. A Lyrical
Monologue."
Miscellaneous: Extracts: from other jour-
nals. Anecdotes: on various subjects.
Literary Notices.

679   TITLE: The Patriarch; or Family Library
Magazine.

Place of Publication: New York
First Issue: Jan 1841
Last Issue: May 1842//
Periodicity: Monthly
Editors: Rufus William Bailey; William
Cutter; Elihu Burritt
Publisher: George A. Peters
Available From: Amer. Antiquarian Soc.*;
Lib of Congress*
Contents:
Poetry: Original: William Cutter, Lydia
H. Sigourney, Mary S.B. Dana. Selected:
R.C. Trench, Lydia H. Sigourney,
Nathaniel P. Willis.
Prose: Biography: Washington, Hannah
More. Essay. Letters. Book Reviews.
Fiction: Essay Serial: "History of My
Own Generation. By a Quinquagenarian."
Miscellaneous: Extracts: by various
authors; Daniel Webster, Lydia H.
Sigourney. Literary Notices.

680   TITLES: (1) Peabody's Parlour Journal. A
Weekly Magazine, Dedicated to High Life,
Fashionables, Fashions, Polite Literature,
Criticisms on New Works, the Fine Arts--
the Opera--Theatres--Exhibitions, etc.
Containing General Information upon Every
Subject   (2) The Parlour Journal, a Weekly
Magazine, Devoted to Literature and the
Fine Arts, the Drama, Entertaining and
Useful Knowledge, Biographical Sketches,
Criticisms on New Works, &c. Embellished
with Engravings and Music (3) The Parlour
Magazine, a Weekly Journal, Devoted to
Literature and the Fine Arts, the Drama,
&c. &c.   (4) The Parlour Magazine, and
Literary Gazette. A Weekly Journal.
Devoted to Literature and the Fine Arts,
the Drama, &c. &c.

Place of Publication: New York
First Issue: 4 Jan 1834
Last Issue: 31 Oct 1835//
Periodicity: Weekly
Editors: "Several Literary and Fashionable
Characters"
Publishers: Peabody & Co.
Available From: Lib. of Congress; Amer.
Antiquarian Soc.
Contents:
Poetry: Original: J. Harold Halsenbeck.
Selected: Mary Howitt, Robert Montgomery,
Augusta Norton, Scott, Coleridge, William
Falconer, Felicia Hemans, Caroline
Norton, Hannah F. Gould, E. Lytton Bulwer,
Lydia H. Sigourney, Willis Gaylord Clark,
James G. Percival, James Hogg, Barry
Cornwall, Shakespeare, James Sheridan
Knowles, Byron, Bryant, Southey, Thomas

Haynes Bayly, McDonald Clarke, Mary Anne
Browne, Lamartine, Nathaniel P. Willis,
Chateaubriand, John Neal, Thomas Moore,
L.E. Landon, William Gilmore Simms, Words-
worth, Beranger, R.H. Wilde, Joseph
Rodman Drake, Robert Chambers, T.K. Hervey.
Prose: Biography: Fanny Kemble, James
Fenimore Cooper, Coleridge, Goldsmith,
Garrick. Travel. Familiar Essay. Criti-
cism. Letters.
Fiction: Essay Serial: "The Progress of
Humbug." Sketches. Tales: "The Skelton
Hand"; "The Fortune Wooer. A Sketch of
the Nineteenth Century"; "A True Tho'
Tough Yarn About Pat-ty-go-ney, and Other
Matters"; "The Young Heir's Death-Bed"
[Caroline Norton]; "The Maid of Malines,
and the Blind St. Amand"; "Edmond Sparke.
--A Tale"; "Youth and Womanhood. A Tale
of Passion"; "The Dilemma. A Tale";
"Charles Langley"; "Alaric, a Roman Story";
"Transmigration"; "The Freebooter";
"Eustache de Saint Pierre. A Tale of
the Surrender of Calais"; "The Three
Visits"; "Connor O'Flaherty, and the
Fairies"; "'The Wonderful Bottles'";
"Therese.--A Tale"; "The Lovers' Quarrel.
A Tale of the English Chronicles"; "The
Mishaps and Mischances of an Ordinary
Gentleman"; "Nadrine Tracy; or, the Auto-
biography of a Pickpocket"; "Fire Island-
Ana"; "Cruise of a Guinea-Man"; "St. John
of the Island. A Tale of France"; "The
Mate's Love"; "Harry Benson; a Soldier's
Narrative"; "The Adventures of a Cosmo-
polite"; "A Legend of the Priuli";
"Martha; or, the Grand Cataract of
Bogota"; "The Partisan--A Tale of the
Revolution" [William Gilmore Simms]; "My
First Night in a Watchhouse."
Miscellaneous: Extracts: by various
authors; Charles Fenno Hoffman, E. Lytton
Bulwer, Catharine M. Sedgwick, James Hogg,
James Fenimore Cooper. Anecdotes: on
various subjects; Garrick, James Hogg,
W. Irving. Literary Notices.

681   TITLES: (1) The Pearl: A Ladies' Weekly
Literary Gazette. Devoted to the Advocacy
of the Various Ladies' Total Abstinence
Association   (2) New York Washingtonian
and Ladies' Literary Pearl.

Place of Publication: New York
First Issue: 6 June 1846
Last Issue: 27 May 1848//
Periodicity: Weekly
Editor: Virginia R. Allen
Publisher: Francis D. Allen, Jr.
Available From: Lib. of Congress; N.Y. Pub.
Lib.*
Contents:
Poetry: Original: Jacob Carter, Mary
Jane Phelps, James C. Luckey, Charles
H. Cleveland, Thomas Applegate. Selected:
Caroline F. Orne, Sarah J. Clarke,
Barry Cornwall, Alice Carey, Sarah J.
Hale, Lydia H. Sigourney, James G. Per-
cival, William H. Burleigh, Francis C.
Woodworth, Edward Cave.

Fiction: Essay Serial: "Sketches by the Way." Sketches. Tales: "A Country Recollection; or, the Reformed Inebriate"; "The Merchant's Clerk: A Legend of the Old Time in London"; "Fanny Day's Decision"; "Ally Fisher"; "The Neighbor-in-Law" [Lydia Maria Child]; "Elizabeth Fenwicke", "The Cousins" [Mary Russell Mitford]; "Marrying for Love"; "Poor Mary Blake! A Thrilling Story of German Mysticism"; "Things Hardly to Be Believed"; "The Child and His Pumpkins. A Thanksgiving Story"; "Henry Leslie, or, the Lost One Saved from Ruin!"; "The Emperor's Page, or a Midnight Adventure in Paris"; "Rose Lacy; or the Ill-Fated Marriage!"; "Felix Flinder's Night Latch; or, Take Your Wife's Advice!"; "The King's Vision, or, the Lace Cravat!"; "Perrin and Lucette, or the French Cottagers"; "Married in a Jest, or, the Tables Turned on a Practical Joker"; "The Hall of Silence. An Eastern Tale"; "Dumb Love! A Romance of German-Land"; "Thomas, the Watchman; or, the Publican's Silver Dream. A Tale of Boston"; "Sally Lyon's First and Last Visit to the Ale-House" [T.S. Arthur]; "The Husband Tamer"; "Edward Somerville. A Tale of New England"; "Billy Thompson: An Incident of the Revolution"; "The Shawl Buyer"; "The Rumseller's Family" [Nathaniel P. Willis]; "The Cottage Door"; "The Wife's Mistake"; "The Spoiler at Noonday! Or Life in a City Boarding House"; "The Thunderbolt to the Hearth"; "The Hussar's Saddle"; "Wealth and Worth"; "Going to the Dogs" [T.S. Arthur].
Miscellaneous: Extracts: from other journals. Anecdotes: on various subjects. Literary Notices. News: Domestic.

682 TITLE: The Pearl and Literary Gazette. [See The Bouquet: Flowers of Polite Literature.]

683 TITLE: The Pennsylvania Magazine: Or, American Monthly Museum.

Place of Publication: Philadelphia
First Issue: Jan 1775
Last Issue: July 1776//
Periodicity: Monthly
Editors: Robert Aitken; Thomas Paine
Publisher: Robert Aitken
Available From: APS; Hist. Soc. of Pa.*
         Mott.
Contents:
  Poetry: Original: Thomas Paine. Selected: Goldsmith, Allan Cunningham, Phillis Wheatley, Smollett, Thomas Penrose.
  Prose: Biography: foreign political figures; Voltaire. Travel. Essay. Familiar Essay. Letters: Sterne, Penn. Book Reviews.
  Fiction: Essay Serials: "The Old Bachelor"; "The Druid." Sketches.
  Miscellaneous: Extracts: by various authors; Sterne, Penn, S. Johnson, Franklin. Anecdotes: on various

subjects; Thomas Paine. Literary Notices. News: Foreign and Domestic.
Note: The leading contributors were Thomas Paine, John Witherspoon, David Rittenhouse, Benjamin Rush.

684 TITLE: Periodical Sketches by an American Patriot.

Place of Publication: New York
First Issue: [Only one issue published?] Oct 1820//?
Periodicity: ?
Editors: ?
Publishers: A.T. Goodrich & Co.
Available From: APS; N.Y. Pub. Lib.
Contents:
  Prose: Essay: "Sketch of an Indian Irruption into the Town of Shawangunk in the Year 1780."

685 TITLE: Le petit censeur; Critique et littéraire journal français, à New York.

Place of Publication: New York
First Issue: 4 July 1805
Last Issue: 13 Aug 1805//?
Periodicity: Tri-weekly
Editor: C.A. Daudet
Publisher: C.A. Daudet
Available From: APS; N.Y. State Lib., Albany*
Contents:
  Poetry: Original. Selected.
  Prose: Criticism: "Le paradis perdu de Milton"; "Les Beautes Poëtiques d'Young." Letters.
  Miscellaneous: Extracts: from other journals; by various authors; Fenelon, Beaumarchais, Madame de Sévigné. Anecdotes: On various subjects; Franklin. News: Foreign.

686 TITLE: Le petit censeur. Semaine critique & littéraire, française & anglaise.

Place of Publication: Philadelphia
First Issue: 19 Sept 1805
Last Issue: 5 Dec 1805//?
Periodicity: Weekly
Editors: ?
Publishers: ?
Available From: APS; N.Y. Hist. Soc.*
Contents:
  Poetry: Original. Selected: Joseph Dennie, Tasso, Lope de Vega.
  Prose: Biography. Familiar Essay. Criticism: "Of Madame de Sévigné, and the Epistolary Style." Letters. Book Reviews.
  Fiction: Drama: "Les Frondeurs."
  Miscellaneous: Anecdotes: on various subjects. Literary Notices.

687 TITLE: Philadelphia Album, and Ladies' Literary Gazette. [See The Album. And Ladies' Weekly Gazette.]

688 TITLE: The Philadelphia Album and Ladies' Literary Port Folio. [See The Album. And Ladies' Weekly Gazette.]

689 TITLE: The Philadelphia Magazine and Review; or, Monthly Repository of Information and Amusements.

Place of Publication: Philadelphia
First Issue: Jan 1799
Last Issue: June 1799//
Periodicity: Monthly
Editor: Benjamin Davies
Publisher: Benjamin Davies
Available From: APS; Lib. of Congress.*
        Mott.
Contents:
  Poetry: Original. Selected: Richard Cumberland.
  Prose: Letters. Book Reviews: Thomas Holcroft, William Cowper, Von Bülow.
  Miscellaneous: Extracts: by various authors. Anecdotes: on various subjects; Horace Walpole, Franklin. News: Foreign and Domestic.

690 TITLES: (1) Philadelphia Magazine, or Weekly Repository of Polite Literature (2) The Philadelphia Magazine, and Weekly Repertory.

Place of Publication: Philadelphia
First Issue: Jan 1818
Last Issue: 7 Nov 1818//
Periodicity: Weekly
Editors: George Goodman; Joseph R. Chandler
Publishers: G. Goodman & J.R. Chandler; Dennis Heartt
Available From: APS; Hist. Soc. of Pa.*
Contents:
  Poetry: Original. Selected: Peter Pindar, Henry Kirke White, Scott, Robert Treat Paine, Selleck Osborne, Gray, McDonald Clarke, R.S. Coffin.
  Prose: Biography: Matthew Gregory [Monk] Lewis, Hannah More, Benjamin West, Mary Wollstonecraft. Familiar Essay. Letters. Book Reviews.
  Fiction: Essay Serial: "The Pedlar." Sketches. Tales: "Edward and Paulina"; "A Journey in a Diligence"; "Duke Edric; or, the Chieftain's Daughter. A Tale"; "The Recruiting Party. A Tale"; "Griselda. A Pathetic Tale"; "Don Avaranches. A Tale"; "The Pedestrian; or Tales of the Traveller"; "The Parterre"; "The Magic of Love; or, a Wife Metamorphosed"; "Lorenzo, or, the Robber"; "The Stroller's Tale"; "The Deserted Cottage. A Fragment."
  Miscellaneous: Extracts: from other journals; by various authors; Kotzebue, Franklin, B. D'Israeli. Anecdotes: on various subjects; Martin Luther, S. Johnson, Franklin, Fielding, Milton, Colley Cibber, George Whitefield, Garrick. News: Domestic.

691 TITLE: The Philadelphia Minerva. Containing a Variety of Fugitive Pieces, in Prose and Poetry, Original and Selected.

Place of Publication: Philadelphia
First Issue: 7 Feb 1795
Last Issue: 7 July 1798//
Periodicity: Weekly
Editors: ?
Publishers: Woodruff & Turner; Woodruff & Pechin; John Turner; William T. Palmer
Available From: APS; Amer. Antiquarian Soc.
Contents:
  Poetry: Original. Selected: Jane E. Locke, Charlotte Smith, R.B. Sheridan, William Jones, Peter Pindar, Mary Robinson, S. Johnson, Erasmus Darwin, Anna Maria Porter, David Humphreys, Franklin, Christopher Smart, Thomas Dermody.
  Prose: Biography. Essay. Familiar Essay. Letters.
  Fiction: Essay Serials: "The Naturalist"; "The Cynic"; "Roscius"; "The Materialist." Tales: "The Happy Return. A Moral Tale"; "Ardelio's Complaint"; "The Artful Wife. A Moral Tale"; "Hanno: Or, a Tale of West-Indian Cruelty"; "Mahmut and Idris. An Oriental Tale"; "The Chevalier Bayard and Madame de Randan. A Tale of the Fifteenth Century"; "The Suspicious Lover. A Moral Tale"; "Edmund and Maria: Or the Peaceful Villa"; "The Triumph of Sincerity. A Moral Tale"; "The Diamond Pin. A Moral Tale"; "Fanny: Or, the Happy Repentance"; "The Adventures of Alphonso and Alarina; an Interesting Spanish Tale"; "Beauty in Distress. A Pathetic Narrative"; "The School for Libertines: (A Story Founded on Facts)"; "Edward and Egwina. A Tale"; "Sophy Lefevre: Or, the Poor Blind Girl"; "The Honorable Seducer: Or, History of Olivia"; "The Castle of Costanzo. An Italian Story"; "The Heir of the House of Oldfield. A Moral Tale"; "Phebe Smith. A Moral Tale"; "Albert and Almira. A Moral Tale"; "Mortified Ambition. A Moral Tale"; "History of Mr. Wilfort"; "Tarempou and Serinda"; "The New Pygmalion. An Interesting Story"; "Chaubert; the Misanthropist"; "Delphira, or the Benevolent Shepherdess"; "The Horrors of a Monastery. A Tale"; "Two Husbands to One Wife. A Singular Story"; "Virtue Rewarded; or, the History of Fidelia. Founded on Facts"; "Affecting Story of Urbain Grandier"; "The History of Charles Mortimer"; "Caroline: Or, the Seduced American"; "The Fair Hibernian: A Turkish Tale"; "Interesting History of the Baron de Lovzinski"; "Caracaros, Sebastian and Zeredaria. An American Tale"; "The Twin Brothers"; "Love and Generosity: A Tale Founded on Facts"; "Miranda. A Moral Tale"; "Marcus and Monimia. A True Story"; "Amelia: Or the

Faithless Briton"; "Jacquot. A Tale";
"The Reparation. A Tale"; "The Cornish
Curate. A Tale"; "Emilia; or the Un-
forced Repentance"; "The Impressed Sea-
man"; "Drusilla, or, the Fate of Harold.
A Tale of Former Times"; "History of
Maria Feodorovna, a Young Russian Count-
ess"; "The Generous Lady"; "The Friar's
Tale"; "Selico; an African Tale"; "The
Prophetess. An Eastern Tale"; "The Re-
fined Lovers. A Spanish Tale"; "The
Unexpected Discovery. An Oriental Tale";
"Florio and Lucilla; or, the Virtuous
but Fatal Elopement. A Moral Tale."
Miscellaneous: Extracts: by various
authors; Richard Cumberland, Sterne, Mrs.
Inchbald, Ann Radcliffe. Anecdotes: on
various subjects; Samuel Foote, Fanny
Burney, Sidney, Swift, Garrick, Voltaire,
Alaric Watts, Franklin, Cromwell.
Literary Notices. News: Foreign and
Domestic.

692   TITLE: The Philadelphia Monthly Album. And
        Literary Companion.

Place of Publication: Philadelphia
First Issue: July 1840
Last Issue: March 1842//?
Periodicity: Monthly
Editor: William P. Stagers
Publisher: William P. Stagers
Available From: Amer. Antiquarian Soc.;
                Yale Univ.
Contents:
  Poetry: Original: Henry James Bogue, Ben-
    jamin C. Hayes, John Hall, Nicholas J.
    Keefe. Selected: Bryant, Felicia Hemans,
    Robert Montgomery, Nathaniel P. Willis,
    Willis Gaylord Clark, William Leggett,
    George Doane, Thomas Haynes Bayly, Wil-
    liam D. Gallagher, George D. Prentice.
  Prose: Familiar Essay. Criticism.
  Fiction: Essay Serials: "A Cursory Light
    Essay"; "Leaves from a Student's Scrap
    Book." Sketches. Tales: "The Broker's
    Nephew"; "The Arabian Steed" [Thomas
    Haynes Bayly]; "Love in a Hut"; "The
    Lasso, or the Corse Revenge"; "The Wife
    of the Polish Patriot"; "The Unguarded
    Hour"; "The Blind Boy"; "Matthew.--The
    Orphan. A Tale Founded Upon Truth"; "The
    Jew's Revenge"; "The Magic Mirror"; "The
    Parisian Sibyl"; "The First and Second
    Husband"; "Henry St. Clair" [Whittier];
    "The Everlasting Taper"; "Deacon Red-
    wood--The Passionate Father, a Tale
    Founded on Facts of Real Life"; "The Two
    Sisters" [Kotzebue]; "The Burglar's
    Daughter"; "The Foundling of the Dock";
    "Sophy Brentworth"; "The Grape Seed. A
    Moorish Tale"; "The Black Ferry."
  Miscellaneous: Extracts: from other jour-
    nals. Anecdotes: on various subjects;
    Pope, Buonaparte, S. Johnson.

693   TITLE: The Philadelphia Monthly Magazine.
        Devoted to General Literature and the
        Fine Arts.

Place of Publication: Philadelphia
First Issue: Oct 1827
Last Issue: April 1830//
Periodicity: Monthly
Editor: Isaac Clarkson Snowden
Publisher: J. Dobson
Available From: APS; Hist. Soc. of Pa.
Contents:
  Poetry: Original: S.G. Fisher. Selected:
    James G. Percival, Schlegel, Shelley.
  Prose: Biography: Coleridge, Chatterton,
    Schiller. Travel. Essay. Familiar
    Essay. Criticism. Letters. Book Reviews.
  Fiction: Essay Serials: "Vagaries";
    "Progress of Literature in Pennsylvania";
    "The Reconnoiterer"; "The Critic";
    "Thoughts on Fools"; "The Arts and
    Artists." Sketches. Tales: "The Spirit
    of the Reeds"; "Halloran the Pedlar. A
    Tale"; "Jealousy"; "The Story of Hendrick
    Van Buster"; "The Soldier's Daughter";
    "The Schoolmaster of S----"; "Chartiers";
    "La Cuisine"; "The Younger Brother"; "The
    Outlaw of Slimish. A Tale of the United
    Irishmen"; "The Dumb Singular"; "The
    House on the Cliff"; "Haslan and Alkazia.
    A True Story"; "A School for Countrymen";
    "Blind Ike"; "Catharine Bryson";
    "Futurity. A Tale of the Days of Rome";
    "The Ice-Island"; "Stricknadeln; or, the
    Mystery. A Tale"; "The Campaigner's
    Tale"; "The Chamois Hunter. A Tale of
    the Alps"; "The Phantom Players";
    "Retribution. A Tale."
  Miscellaneous: Extracts: by various
    authors; Kotzebue, Leigh Hunt.
    Anecdotes: on various subjects; Swift,
    S. Johnson. Literary Notices.

694   TITLE: The Philadelphia Monthly Magazine, or,
        Universal Repository of Knowledge and
        Entertainment: Consisting of Original
        Pieces, and Selections from Performances
        of Merit, Foreign and Domestic. Calculated
        to Disseminate Useful Knowledge Among All
        Ranks of People, at a Small Expense.

Place of Publication: Philadelphia
First Issue: Jan 1798
Last Issue: Sept 1798//
Periodicity: Monthly
Editors: Thomas Condie; Richard Folwell
Publishers: Thomas Condie; Richard Folwell
Available From: APS; Amer. Antiquarian Soc.*
                Mott.
Contents:
  Poetry: Original. Selected: J. Hopkinson,
    Erasmus Darwin, Robert Merry.
  Prose: Biography: Jeremy Belknap,
    Buonaparte, John Adams, Washington,
    Burns. Travel. Essay. Familiar Essay.
    Criticism. Letters.
  Fiction: Sketches: "Polly Baker" [Frank-
    lin]. Tales: "The Indians; a Tale";
    "The Friar's Tale"; "Rejuvenescence. A
    Tale."
  Miscellaneous: Extracts: from other jour-
    nals. Anecdotes: on various subjects;
    Garrick. Literary Notices. News: Fo-
    reign and Domestic.

Note: Appended is "History of the Pestilence, Commonly Called Yellow Fever, Which Almost Desolated Philadelphia, in the Months of August, September & October, 1798."

695   TITLE: Philadelphia Port Folio: A Weekly Journal of Literature, Science, Art, and the Times. [See The Ladies' Literary Port Folio.]

696   TITLES: (1) The Philadelphia Register, and National Recorder (2) The National Recorder (3) The National Recorder, Containing Essays upon Subjects Connected with Political Economy, Science, Literature, &c.; Papers Read Before the Agricultural Society of Philadelphia; a Record of Passing Events; Selections from Foreign Magazines, &c. &c. (4) The Saturday Magazine: Consisting Principally of Selections from the Most Celebrated British Reviews, Magazines, and Scientific Journals (5) The Saturday Magazine: Containing Miscellaneous Selections from Foreign Magazines. Literary Intelligence. Scientific Notices. Records. Agricultural Papers, Read Before the Agricultural Society of Philadelphia. Variety. Poetry. Being a Continuation of the National Recorder (6) The Saturday Magazine: Being in Great Part a Compilation from the British Reviews, Magazines and Scientific Journals. [Superseded by the Museum of Foreign Literature and Science, later the Museum of Foreign Literature, Science, and Art q.v.]

Place of Publication: Philadelphia
First Issue: 2 Jan 1819
Last Issue: 29 June 1822//
Periodicity: Weekly
Editor: Eliakim Littell
Publishers: Littell & Henry; R. Norris Henry
Available From: APS; Lib. of Congress.*
          Mott.
Contents:
  Poetry: Selected: Thomas Moore, Scott, Wordsworth, Jane Taylor, Christopher Smart, Samuel Woodworth, Leigh Hunt, Bernard Barton, James Montgomery, Southey, William B. Tappan, John Clare, Luis de Camoens, Felicia Hemans, Boileau, James Hogg, Hannah More, Charles Maturin, Thomas Campbell, William Roscoe.
  Prose: Biography: William Pitt, George Crabbe, Southey. Travel. Essay. Familiar Essay. Criticism. Letters. Book Reviews.
  Fiction: Essay Serials: "The Observer"; "Saturday Sermon"; "The Prompter." Sketches. Tales: "The Two Cousins. A Pennsylvania Tale"; "Albert: Or, Christian Virtue Exemplified"; "The Pinch of Snuff"; "The Convict"; "The Auburn Ringlet"; "The Water Lady--A Legend"; "Town and Country"; "The Leper of the City of Aosta; a Tale"; "Theresa. A Fragment.--From Real Life"; "Valerius, a

Roman Story"; "Confessions of an English Opium-Eater: Being an Extract from the Life of a Scholar" [De Quincey]; "Mary Allan: A Tale"; "The Bride of Balachan"; "The Sea Spirit"; "The Rose in January-- A German Tale."
  Miscellaneous: Extracts: from other journals; by various authors. Anecdotes: on various subjects; Washington, Franklin, Pope, Buonaparte, Edward Gibbon, Garrick, Hester L. Thrale Piozzi, Smollett, Sterne, Thomas Browne, Richard Steele. Literary Notices.

697   TITLE: Philadelphia Repertory.

Place of Publication: Philadelphia
First Issue: 5 May 1810
Last Issue: 16 May 1812//
Periodicity: Weekly
Editors: ?
Publishers: Dennis Heartt
Available From: APS; Hist. Soc. of Pa.*
Contents:
  Poetry: Original. Selected: Edward Rushton, Erasmus Darwin, Anthony Pasquin, Selleck Osborne.
  Prose: Biography: John Howard, Robert Treat Paine, Henry Kirke White, Goldsmith, Richard Savage, Milton, Benjamin West, Chatterton, David Rittenhouse, Penn, Captain John Smith, Chateaubriand. Familiar Essay. Letters. Book Reviews.
  Fiction: Essay Serials: "The Contemplator"; "Collector"; "Equitus"; "The Cabinet"; "The Sententious Admonisher"; "Selector"; "Anecdotiana"; "The Invisible Monitor"; "The Moralist." Tales: "The Heiress of Sobeiski. A Romance"; "Castle of Altenheim, or the Mysterious Monk. A Tale." Drama: "Ardennis: Or the Spirit of the Wood. A Tragedy in Five Acts."
  Miscellaneous: Extracts: from other journals; by various authors. Anecdotes: on various subjects; Hogarth, Voltaire, Franklin, S. Johnson, William Cowper, Washington, Dryden, Boswell. Literary Notices. News: Domestic.

698   TITLES: (1) The Philadelphia Repository, and Weekly Register . . . Containing Original Essays, Tales and Novels, Interesting Extracts from New Publications and Works of Merit, Amusing Miscellanies, Remarkable Occurrences, Anecdotes, Bon Mots, Jeu d'esprit, Marriages and Deaths, Poetical Essays, Odes, Sonnets, Songs (a Number of Which Are Set to Music) and Generally, Whatever Is Calculated to Diffuse Interesting and Useful Information, Divert the Fancy, Enlighten the Understanding, Form the Mind, and Mend the Heart (2) The Repository and Ladies' Weekly Museum.

Place of Publication: Philadelphia
First Issue: 15 Nov 1800
Last Issue: 5 April 1806//
Periodicity: Weekly
Editors: David Hogan; John Welwood Scott; Thomas Irwin

Publishers: David Hogan; E. Conrad
Available From: APS; Lib. of Congress.*
        Mott.
Contents:
  Poetry: <u>Original</u>. <u>Selected</u>: Charles Dibdin, Edmund Waller, William Cowper, Swift, Robert Bloomfield, Goldsmith, Hawkesworth, John Blair Linn.
  Prose: <u>Biography</u>: Benedict Arnold, James Beattie. <u>Travel</u>. <u>Familiar Essay</u>. <u>Criticism</u>. <u>Letters</u>.
  Fiction: <u>Essay Serials</u>: "The Commentator"; "The Monitor"; "The Observer"; "The Pedestrian"; "The Trifler"; "The Caterer"; "The Cynic"; "The Enigmatist"; "The Querist"; "The Lucubrator." <u>Sketches</u>. <u>Tales</u>: "Albert, an Original Tale"; "All Is Vanity; a Tale"; "Appearances Deceitful, a Tale"; "Hephestion and Alonzo. An Original Story"; "Lorenzo and Violetta, a Matrimonial Tale"; "Tarempou and Serinda. A Tale"; "Ali and Orasmin; or, the Effects of Envy. An Oriental Tale"; "The Cacique of Ontario. An Indian Tale"; "Zulmira; or, the Inconstant. An Oriental Tale"; "Story of Two Lovers"; "Mistake of Two Lovers"; "Adventures in a Castle. An Original Story"; "The Droll. A Tale"; "The Impostors. A Tale"; "The Ruins"; "Mandonoch. A Tale"; "Edric of the Forest. A Romance"; "Oriander"; "The Nut-Shell. A Tale"; "Romance of the Four Dervishes. A Persian Tale"; "The Adulteress Punished. A Tale"; "The Village Curate; or, As You Like It: A Tale"; "The Schrubbery. A Tale"; "The Maid of Switzerland. A Tale"; "Caracaros and Zedara. An Indian Tale"; "Grimaldi. A True Story"; "Old Nick: A Satirical Story"; "Wolkmar and His Dog." <u>Novels</u>: "The Girl of the Mountains"; "The Beggar Girl"; "Edward Walwin"; "Pierre, a German Novel." <u>Drama</u>: "The Hermit: A Dramatic Trifle."
  Miscellaneous: <u>Extracts</u>: from other journals; by various authors. <u>Anecdotes</u>: on various subjects; Addison, Buonaparte, William Cowper, Swift, Franklin, Goldsmith, S. Johnson, Milton, Pope, Smollett, Sterne, William Collins, Voltaire, Edmund Burke, Dryden, Garrick, Penn. <u>Literary Notices</u>.

699 TITLE: <u>The Philadelphia Visiter: And Parlour Companion. Devoted to Popular and Miscellaneous Literature, Fashions and Music</u>. [See <u>The Philadelphia Visiter, Devoted to the Dissemination of Popular Literature, Miscellany, &c.</u>]

700 TITLES: (1) <u>The Philadelphia Visiter, Devoted to the Dissemination of Popular Literature, Miscellany, &c.</u> (2) <u>The Philadelphia Visiter: And Parlour Companion. Devoted to Popular and Miscellaneous Literature, Fashions and Music</u>. [Supersedes <u>The Monthly Visitor, Devoted to the Dissemination of Popular Literature, Miscellany, &c.</u> q.v.]

Place of Publication: Philadelphia
First Issue: June 1835
Last Issue: 1841//?
Periodicity: Monthly
Editor: H.N. Moore
Publishers: A. Weikel; W.B. Rogers
Available From: Boston Athenaeum; Lib. of Congress
Contents:
  Poetry: <u>Original</u>: Silas Sexton Steele, William D. Baker, Charlotte Cushman, Samuel Rogers, Paul Sobolewski. <u>Selected</u>: Thomas Hood, Selleck Osborne, Felicia Hemans, Thomas Roscoe, Thomas Campbell, Hannah More, Boston Bard, Lydia H. Sigourney, Thomas Haynes Bayly, Byron, Leigh Hunt, Wordsworth, Frances S. Osgood, Grenville Mellen, Scott, B.B. Thatcher.
  Prose: <u>Biography</u>. <u>Essay</u>. <u>Familiar Essay</u>. <u>Letters</u>.
  Fiction: <u>Sketches</u>. <u>Tales</u>: "The Revenge"; "Jerome, the Milane, or, the Henchman of Bourbon"; "The Wife of Seven Husbands"; "Editha, or, the Unnatural Mother"; "The Wooing at Grafton"; "The Only Daughter, or, the Rose of the Isle"; "The Dun"; "The Rings, a Tale of the Field of the Cloth of Gold"; "The Magic Wand"; "Oulon: A Legend of Pennsylvania"; "The First and Last Kiss"; "Ahmed the Cobler. A Persian Tale"; "The Fugitive of the Forest. A Romance"; "The Victim Bride. A Tale of Monadnock"; "Remarkable Adventures of Angelia Madelia"; "The Doomed Bride" [Grenville Mellen]; "Maurice MacCarthy"; "The Brother and Sister. An Italian Story" [Mary Shelley]; "The Exile, or Herbert de Sevrac. A Romance of the Eighteenth Century"; "Davy Jones; or, the Pilot Boat"; "The Unnatural Son"; "Walter Brandon, the Murderer!" "Emma. A Tale"; "The Hermit of the Rock. A Tale of the Seventeenth Century"; "Love Without Hope; or, the Bridal and the Blighted Heart"; "Mary Morris: Or, Leaves from the Diary of a Private Gentleman"; "The Difficulty of Keeping up Appearances"; "Edward Warner; a Tale for the Times"; "Claudine-- A Swiss Tale"; "The Groomsman, a Tale Founded Upon Incidents in Real Life"; "Julia de Lindorf. A Tale of the Guillotine"; "The Village Pastor's Wife"; "The Brazilian Bride"; "Camaralzaman and the Jeweller's Wife. An Oriental Tale"; "The Chiffonier of Paris, a Tale of the Nineteenth Century"; "Leila, or the Seige of Grenada" [E. Lytton Bulwer]; "The Marriage Certificate"; "The Unfaithful"; "An Autobiography. Or Memoirs and Reminiscences of a Young Man"; "The Narrative of John Ward Gibson"; "The Vow" [Charles Maturin]; "The Azamoglan. A Tale of Modern Greece"; "The Royal Professor"; "The Melancholy Stranger"; "The Pirate."
  Miscellaneous: <u>Extracts</u>: from other journals; by various authors; W. Irving, Scott, Coleridge. <u>Anecdotes</u>: on various subjects; Franklin, Swift, S. Johnson, Boswell, Richard Steele, Richard Savage, Garrick, Isaac Newton, Nathaniel P. Willis.

701   TITLE: The Philanthropist.

Place of Publication: Mt. Pleasant, Ohio
First Issue: 12 Sept 1817
Last Issue: 26 Dec 1817//
Periodicity: Weekly
Editors: Charles Osborn; Elisha Bates
Publisher: Elisha Bates
Available From: APS; Western Reserve Hist.
                Soc., Cleveland.* Mott.
Contents:
  Poetry: Selected: William Roscoe,
    Hawkesworth.
  Prose: Familiar Essay. Letters.
  Miscellaneous: Extracts: from other jour-
    nals. Anecdotes: on various subjects;
    John Howard, Hester L. Thrale Piozzi,
    Patrick Henry.

702   TITLE: The Phrenological Magazine and New
York Literary Review.

Place of Publication: Utica, N.Y.
First Issue: [Only one issue published?]
                May 1835//?
Available From: U.S. National Lib. of
                Medecine

703   TITLE: The Pictorial National Library, a
Monthly Miscellany of the Useful and
Entertaining in Science, Art and Literature.
Illustrated with 200 Engravings.

Place of Publication: Boston
First Issue: July 1848
Last Issue: Dec 1849//
Periodicity: Monthly
Editors: ?
Publishers: William Simonds and Company
Available From: Lib. of Congress*; Amer.
                Antiquarian Soc.*
Contents:
  Poetry: Original: Isaac M'Lellan, Jr.,
    Amanda Weston, Caroline F. Orne,
    Cornelia F.L. Bates, J. Eames Rankin,
    Josiah L. Smith, Thomas Wells.
    Selected: B. Jonson, James Montgomery,
    John Neal, Nathaniel P. Willis, Long-
    fellow, T.K. Hervey, Milton, Mrs. Seba
    Smith, W.J. Mickle, Hannah F. Gould,
    Lydia H. Sigourney, John Bowering, Emma
    C. Embury, Thomas Hood.
  Prose: Biography: Daniel Webster,
    Lamartine, John Winthrop, Longfellow,
    Cromwell, Benjamin West, Goldsmith,
    Horace Greeley, Byron, Edmund Burke.
    Travel. Essay. Familiar Essay. Criti-
    cism.
  Fiction: Essay Serials: "Pen and Pencil
    Portraits"; "Things Old." Sketches.
    Tales: "Grizel Cochrane. A Tale of
    Tweedmouth Moor"; "The Greenland Lovers"
    [S. Johnson]; "The Forger. Or, the
    Power of Self-Possession"; "The Black
    Cat" [Poe]; "The Vision of Mirza"
    [Addison]; "The Experience of a Working-
    Man"; "The Envious Brothers; or, the
    Transformation"; "'Petit Caporal;' or,
    the Boy of Milan."

Miscellaneous: Extracts: from other jour-
  nals; by various authors; Scott, Swift.
  Anecdotes: on various subjects; Cromwell,
  Franklin, S. Johnson.

704   TITLE: The Pierian: Or, Youth's Fountain of
Literature and Knowledge.

Place of Publication: New York
First Issue: [Only one issue published?]
                Jan 1843//?
Periodicity: Intended to be monthly
Editor: Anna L. Snelling
Publishers: Saxton & Miles
Available From: N.Y. Pub. Lib.

705   TITLES: (1) The Pioneer. A Literary and
Critical Magazine (2) The Pioneer.

Place of Publication: Boston
First Issue: Jan 1843
Last Issue: March 1843//
Periodicity: Monthly
Editors: James Russell Lowell; Robert Carter
Publishers: Leland & Whiting
Available From: Lib. of Congress*; Amer.
                Antiquarian Soc.* Mott.
Contents:
  Poetry: Original: T.W. Parsons, Jones
    Very, William H. Burleigh, James Russell
    Lowell, W.W. Story, Henry Peters, Whittier.
    Selected: Poe, Elizabeth Barrett.
  Prose: Biography: Aaron Burr. Essay.
    Familiar Essay. Criticism. Book Reviews.
  Fiction: Sketches. Tales: "The Armenian's
    Daughter. A Story of the Great Pestilence
    of Bagdad"; "The Tell-Tale Heart" [Poe];
    "The Hall of Fantasy" [Hawthorne];
    "Dream-Love"; "The Birth-Mark" [Hawthorne].
  Miscellaneous: Literary Notices.

706   TITLE: The Pioneer, Consisting of Essays,
Literary, Moral and Theological.

Place of Publication: Pittsburgh
First Issue: 28 Feb 1812
Last Issue: 8 Oct 1812//
Periodicity: Irregular
Editor: David Graham
Publishers: S. Engles and Co.
Available From: APS; Amer. Antiquarian Soc.*
Contents:
  Poetry: Selected: Pope, Dryden.
  Prose: Biography: Addison. Essay.
    Familiar Essay. Letters.

707   TITLE: The Plumbe Popular Magazine. An
Illustrated Periodical for the Nation.
[See The Popular Magazine: A Journal of
Art and Literature.]

708   TITLE: The Poet's Magazine, a Repository of
Original and Selected American Poetry.

Place of Publication: Albany
First Issue: April 1842

Last Issue: June 1842//
Periodicity: Monthly
Editor: E.G. Squier
Publisher: E.G. Squier
Available From: N.Y. State Lib., Albany*;
              Lib. of Congress
Contents:
   Poetry: Original. Selected: Bryant,
   Longfellow, Amelia B. Welby, Alfred B.
   Street, Lydia J. Pierson, James G. Per-
   cival, Rufus Dawes, Harriet Muzzy,
   William H. Burleigh, C.G. Eastman,
   J.H. Butler, Juliet H. Lewis, Jesse E.
   Dow, Park Benjamin, Mary E. Lee, E.G.
   Squier, R.M. Charlton, J.E. Knight,
   Charles Fenno Hoffman, Lydia H. Sigour-
   ney, James Russell Lowell, Caroline F.
   Orne, William Wallace, Nathan C. Brooks,
   Melzar Gardner, James T. Fields, John
   Todd Brame, W.H.C. Hosmer.

709   TITLES: (1) The Political Censor, or Monthly
      Review of the Most Interesting Political
      Occurrences, Relative to the United States
      of America (2) Porcupine's Political
      Censor, or a Review of Political Occurrences
      Relative to the United States.

      Place of Publication: Philadelphia
      First Issue: March 1796
      Last Issue: March 1797//
      Periodicity: Monthly
      Editor: Peter Porcupine [pseud. of William
              Cobbett]
      Publishers: Benjamin Davies; William
                  Cobbett
      Available From: APS; Amer. Antiquarian Soc.*
                      Mott.
      Contents:
         Prose: Biography: Thomas Paine. Essay:
         "The Age of Reason" [Thomas Paine]; "Mr.
         Noah Webster's Attack on Porcupine."
         Criticism: "On the Poetical Works of
         John Swanwick of Philadelphia." Letters.
         Miscellaneous: Extracts: from other jour-
         nals; by various authors. Literary
         Notices.
      Note: Although this journal is politically
      oriented, it is of literary interest.

710   TITLE: The Political Magazine; and Miscel-
      laneous Repository. Containing Ancient
      and Modern Political and Miscellaneous
      Pieces, Prose and Poetical.

      Place of Publication: Ballston, N.Y.
      First Issue: Oct 1800
      Last Issue: Nov 1800//?
      Periodicity: Monthly
      Editor: William Child
      Publisher: William Child
      Available From: APS; N.Y. State Lib.,
                      Albany*
      Contents:
         Poetry: Original.
         Prose: Biography: Jefferson. Letters.
         Miscellaneous: Extracts: from other jour-
         nals; by various authors; Jefferson.
         Anecdotes: on various subjects; Washing-
         ton.

Note: Although politically oriented, this
      journal is of literary interest.

711   TITLE: The Political Repository: Or, Far-
      mer's Journal.

      Place of Publication: Brookfield, Mass.
      First Issue: 14 Aug 1798
      Last Issue: 4 May 1802//
      Periodicity: Weekly
      Editors: ?
      Publishers: Ebenezer Merriam & Co.
      Available From: Amer. Antiquarian Soc.*
      Contents:
         Poetry: Original. Selected.
         Prose: Biography. Familiar Essay.
         Letters: John Adams.
         Fiction: Sketches. Tales: "The Gamester";
         "The Adelphiad"; "The Turkey"; "Humble
         Confession in a Coalpit"; "Benevolent
         Judge."
         Miscellaneous: Extracts: from other jour-
         nals; by various authors. Anecdotes: on
         various subjects. Literary Notices.
         News: Foreign and Domestic.

712   TITLE: Polyanthos. [See the New York
      Polyanthos.]

713   TITLES: (1) The Polyanthos (2) The Poly-
      anthos. A Monthly Magazine, Consisting of
      Original Performances and Selections from
      Works of Merit.

      Place of Publication: Boston
      First Issue: Dec 1805
      Last Issue: Sept 1814//
      Periodicity: Monthly
      Editor: Joseph T. Buckingham
      Publisher: Joseph T. Buckingham
      Available From: APS; Boston Pub. Lib.* Mott.
      Contents:
         Poetry: Original. Selected: Thomas Wyatt,
         Pope, Thomas Penrose, S. Johnson, Mary
         Russell Mitford, Southey, Lucius M.
         Sargent, Richard Crashaw, Goethe, George
         Buchanan, Timothy Dwight, Thomas Moore,
         William Holloway, Thomas Campbell, Joanna
         Baillie, Burns, Luis de Camoens, Richard
         Savage, Hawkesworth, Robert Treat Paine,
         Thomas Dermody, Gray, Charlotte Smith,
         James Shirley, William Drummond, Robert
         Green, Shakespeare, Thomas Carew, S. John-
         son.
         Prose: Biography: Robert Treat Paine,
         Isaiah Thomas, John Locke, George White-
         field, Franklin, Mather Byles, David
         Humphreys, Jeremy Belknap, T.A. Cooper,
         Richard Cumberland, John Winthrop,
         Samuel Foote, Fennell. Travel. Essay.
         Familiar Essay. Criticism. Letters.
         Book Reviews.
         Fiction: Essay Serials: "The Examiner";
         "Analecta"; "Romance in Real Life"; "The
         Moral Censor"; "The Freebooter"; "Monthly
         Lay Preacher"; "The Contemplator";
         "Trash"; "Mentorian Essays"; "Lucubrations
         of Nehemiah Notional." Sketches. Tales:
         "Story of Maldonata"; "History of Count

Almeida"; "The Fortunate Hindoo"; "Laura
and Manilus"; "Truth. An Indian Tale";
"The Wooden Leg. An Helvetick Tale";
"Jehander, Prince of Ava. An Oriental
Tale"; "Amorvin: A Tale"; "The Partners.
A Tale"; "An Eastern Tale"; "Almamun,
the Miser of Bagdad. A Tale." Drama:
"The Father Outwitted" [Lope de Vega];
"The Opera Dancer: A Dramatick Proverb."
Miscellaneous: Extracts: from other jour-
nals; by various authors; Franklin,
Swift, Chatterton, Chateaubriand,
Voltaire, George Colman, B. D'Israeli,
Owen Felltham, Fenelon, Burns, Goethe,
Anna Letitia Barbauld, Thomas Holcroft,
R.B. Sheridan. Anecdotes: on various
subjects; George Whitefield, Thomas
Wyatt, Garrick, Addison, S. Johnson,
Dryden, Charles Dibdin, R.B. Sheridan,
Voltaire, Spenser, Shakespeare, Gold-
smith, Pope, Franklin, Beaumont and
Fletcher. Literary Notices.

714   TITLES: (1) The Popular Magazine: A Journal of Art and Literature (2) The Plumbe
Popular Magazine. An Illustrated Periodical
for the Nation.

Place of Publication: Philadelphia
First Issue: 31 Oct 1846
Last Issue: Jan 1847//?
Periodicity: Weekly
Editor: Augustine J.H. Duganne
Publisher: The National Publishing Company
Available From: Lib. of Congress; Amer.
                Antiquarian Soc.
Contents:
Poetry: Original. Selected.
Prose: Biography. Essay. Familiar Essay.
   Criticism: on Charles Brockden Brown.
   Book Reviews.
Fiction: Sketches. Tales: "The Criminal
   Assizes. A Romance of the People"; "The
   War of the Pequods"; "The Fall of
   Sejanus"; "The Patrician Gondolier."
Miscellaneous: Literary Notices.

715   TITLE: Porcupine's Political Censor, or a
Review of Political Occurrences Relative
to the United States. [See The Political
Censor, or Monthly Review of the Most
Interesting Political Occurrences, Relative
to the United States of America.]

716   TITLE: The Port Folio, a Monthly Magazine,
Devoted to Useful Science, the Liberal
Arts, Legitimate Criticism, and Polite
Literature, Conducted by Oliver Oldschool,
Esq. Assisted by a Confederacy of Men of
Letters. [See The Port Folio, by Oliver
Oldschool, Esq. Assisted by a Confederacy
of Gentlemen.]

717   TITLE: The Port Folio, and Companion to the
Select Circulating Library. A Semi-Monthly
Publication, on the Basis of Chamber's
Edinburgh Journal: Combining Essays, Ori-
ginal and Selected, on Science, Arts, and
Literature; Biographical Illustrations;
Instructive and Amusing Incidents, Tales,
Music, Poetry, &c. [Running title: Waldie's
Port Folio, and Companion to the Select
Circulating Library. Superseded by Waldie's
Literary Omnibus q.v., later Brown's
Literary Omnibus.]

Place of Publication: Philadelphia
First Issue: 3 Jan 1835
Last Issue: 17 Dec 1836//
Periodicity: Semi-monthly
Editor: Adam Waldie
Publisher: Adam Waldie
Available From: Lib. of Congress*; Amer.
                Antiquarian Soc.*
Contents:
Poetry: Original. Selected: James Hogg,
   L.E. Landon, Mrs. Abdy, William Cowper,
   Felicia Hemans, R.F. Housman, L.J. Montagu,
   Leigh Hunt, Mary Howitt, Matthew Prior,
   Richard Howitt, George Croly, Ebenezer
   Elliott, Bernard Barton, Thomas Moore,
   Charles Swain, Goethe, Barry Cornwall,
   Fitz-Greene Halleck, Joseph Rodman Drake,
   Richard Henry Dana, Nathaniel P. Willis,
   Charles Sprague, John Neal, Thomas Haynes
   Bayly, Lamartine, Robert Montgomery,
   James Montgomery.
Prose: Biography: James Hogg, Jeremy
   Bentham, N.G. Dufief, Sheridan Knowles,
   Charles Lamb, Felicia Hemans. Travel.
   Essay. Familiar Essay. Criticism:
   "Sketches of the Literature of the United
   States" [Timothy Dwight]. Letters. Book
   Reviews.
Fiction: Sketches. Tales: "John MacTag-
   gart, a Highland Story"; "Tale of Grizel
   Cochrane. A Female Mail Robber"; "A Tale
   of the Plague of Edinburgh"; "The Down-
   draught. A Tale"; "Isbel Lucas, a Hero-
   ine of Humble Life"; "F. Smith"; "The Man
   to Win Through the World"; "The Man Who
   Could not Say--No! A Story of Real Life";
   "Gretna Green"; "A Tour on the Prairies"
   [W. Irving]; "The Red Mantle,--A Tale";
   "A Tale of Clydesdale"; "The Little White
   Lady, of Newstead Abbey" [W. Irving]; "My
   Great Grandmother's Harpsichord"; "A
   Gentleman with a Wife in Every Town";
   "Sandy Wright and the Orphan"; "The
   Disasters of Jan Neideltreiber"; "Old
   Maids of Belford Regis"; "My Next Husband";
   "The Story of Vincentio Dellambra"; "The
   Beauty and the Beggar"; "Legend of Count
   Julian and His Family" [W. Irving]; "The
   Hair-Market of Evreux"; "Barba Yorghi, the
   Greek Pilot"; "Barney O'Reirdon, the
   Navigator"; "Diary of a Blasé"; "The
   Huguenot Captain"; "The Last in the Lease";

"The Fickle Lover--A Story for Danglers"; "Arthur Cosway"; "Fanny Fairfield"; "Little Fanny Bethel"; "The Marchioness of Brinvilliers, the Poisoner"; "Harry O'Reardon"; "The Fortune Hunter--A Tale of Harrogate"; "Old Philpotts and His Daughter"; "Captain Gray"; "Mossgate Farm. A Country Story"; "The Turners" [James Hogg]; "O'Shane's Daughter"; "The Young Pretender"; "My Grandfather, a Tale of Bath"; "The Forest Track, a Fact"; "The Bride of Lindorf" [L.E. Landon]; "Les enfans trouvé"; "The Beautiful Incognita"; "The Curate of Langbourn"; "The Mate of the Wild Swan"; "Nina Dalgarooki"; "Emily, a Tale of Paris"; "Izarah, a Tale of the Moors in Spain"; "Rejected Lovers; or, the Juwaub Club"; "The White Muff."
  Miscellaneous: Extracts: from other journals; by various authors; Coleridge. Anecdotes: on various subjects; Byron, Scott, Frances Trollope, Buonaparte. Literary Notices.

718 TITLES: (1) The Port Folio, by Oliver Oldschool, Esq. Assisted by a Confederacy of Gentlemen (2) The Port Folio, a Monthly Magazine, Devoted to Useful Science, the Liberal Arts, Legitimate Criticism, and Polite Literature, Conducted by Oliver Oldschool, Esq. Assisted by a Confederacy of Men of Letters (3) The Port Folio, a Monthly Magazine, Conducted by Joseph Dennie, Esq. (4) The Port Folio, Conducted by Joseph Dennie, Esq. (5) The Port Folio, Conducted by Oliver Oldschool, Esq. (6) The Port Folio, a Monthly Miscellany, Dedicated in Chief to Original Communications in the Popular Departments of Science, Combined with Occasional Criticism, Classical Disquisitions, Miscellaneous Essays, Records of the Progress of the Fine and Useful Arts, with All the Extensive and Variegated Departments of Polite Literature, Merriment, and Wit; to Which Is Added the Proceedings of Congress (7) The Port Folio. By Oliver Oldschool, Esq.

Place of Publication: Philadelphia
First Issue: 3 Jan 1801
Last Issue: Dec 1828//
Periodicity: Weekly; Monthly; Quarterly
Editors: Joseph Dennie; Paul Allen; Nicholas Biddle; Charles Caldwell; Thomas Cooper; Judge Workman; John Elihu Hall
Publishers: Joseph Dennie; Asbury Dickins; Elizabeth Dickins; Bradford and Inskeep; Thomas Silver; Harrison Hall
Available From: APS; Lib. Co. of Philadelphia.* Mott. Poole.
Contents:
  Poetry: Original: Robert H. Rose, John L. Bozman, John Shaw, Edwin C. Holland, Charles J. Ingersoll, H.C. Knight, Richard Nisbett, Alexander Wilson, John Davis. Selected: John Suckling, R.B. Sheridan, Erasmus Darwin, William Cowper, Wordsworth,

Milton, Luis de Camoens, Burns, Thomas Moore, Fessenden, William Gifford, Tasso, Charlotte Smith, Pope, Coleridge, William Shenstone, Philip Freneau, Marvell, Hawkesworth, James Pye, George Colman, Thomas Campbell, James Beattie, Mary Robinson, Amelia Opie, Robert Treat Paine, Gray, S. Johnson, Dryden, Henry Kirke White, Horace Walpole, Shakespeare, James Thomson, Akenside, Scott, George Crabbe, Byron, Maria Edgeworth, Timothy Dwight, Edmund Waller, Davenport, James Montgomery, Leigh Hunt, Richard Alsop, Herrick, Felicia Hemans, B. Jonson, Selleck Osborne.
  Prose: Biography: William Gifford, Boileau, Chatterton, Samuel Butler ["Hudibras"], Edmund Burke, Chaucer, Cervantes, Colley Cibber, Charles Churchill, S. Johnson, Alexander Hamilton, Thomas Parnell, Franklin, John Quincy Adams, Matthew Gregory [Monk] Lewis, R.B. Sheridan, Joseph Dennie, Madame de Staël, Timothy Dwight, Fisher Ames, Benjamin Rush, Benjamin West, William Dunbar, Captain John Smith, Thomas Paine, Voltaire, Rousseau, William Linn, Lindley Murray, Henry Mackenzie, Fenelon, Gray, William Cowper, Richard Glover, Luis de Camoens, Christopher Smart, S. Richardson, Donne, Racine, Thomas Carew, Carlyle, John Blair Linn [by Charles Brockden Brown]. Travel: Von Bülow, John Quincy Adams, Condy Raguet, Joseph Sansom. Essay. Familiar Essay. Criticism. Letters: S. Richardson, Goldsmith, Smollett, Boswell, David Hume, Edmund Burke, Washington, Franklin, William Cowper. Book Reviews.
  Fiction: Essay Serials: "The Olla"; "The Lay Preacher"; "Hortensius"; "The Scribbler"; "The Festoon of Fashion"; "The Barber's Shop"; "The Farrago"; "An Author's Evenings. From the Shop of Messrs. Colon and Spondee" [Joseph Dennie and Royall Tyler]; "The Rural Wanderer"; "The American Lounger"; "The American Observer"; "From the Microcosm"; "The Loiterer"; "The Examiner"; "The Table d'Hote"; "The Beehive"; "An Author's Evenings"; "The Recluse"; "The Salad"; "My Garden"; "The Observer"; "The Adversaria"; "The Album." Sketches. Tales: "The Tripod of Helen. . . . A Tale"; "The Gamesters: A Tale"; "Pierre. A German Tale"; "The Adventures of Scarmentado. A Satirical Novel"; "Story of Amelia Howard"; "The False Prince of Modena"; "Hamet, a Tale"; "Tales of a Parrot. Tooti Nameh"; "The Corsair" [Byron]; "Philadelphia Unroofed"; "San-Yu-Low; or the Three Dedicated Rooms"; "Gabrielle de Vergi; a Tale"; "Agrarius Denterville; or, the Victim of Discontent. A Tale"; "The Solitary Hunter--A Serious Tale of the Indians"; "Jane Olgivie--An Irish Tale"; "Master Robert Shallow: A Romance of Clement's Inn." Novel: "Emily Hammond, an American Novel." Drama: "The Benevolent Cut-Throat: A Play in Seven Acts."

Miscellaneous: <u>Extracts</u>: from other journals; by various authors. <u>Anecdotes</u>: on various subjects; William Cowper, Charles James Fox, Edward Gibbon, Addison, Boileau, Garrick, S. Johnson, Edmund Burke, Rousseau, Smollett, Molière, Burns, Southey, Voltaire, Buonaparte, Goldsmith, Pope, George Whitefield, Washington, Thomas Paine, Milton, Boswell, Erasmus Darwin, Isaac Newton, R.B. Sheridan. <u>Literary Notices</u>. <u>News</u>: Foreign and Domestic.

719   TITLE: <u>The Port Folio, Conducted by Joseph Dennie, Esq.</u> [See <u>The Port Folio, by Oliver Oldschool, Esq. Assisted by a Confederacy of Gentlemen.</u>]

720   TITLES: (1) <u>The Portico, a Repository of Science & Literature</u> (2) <u>The Portico</u>.

Place of Publication: Baltimore
First Issue: Jan 1816
Last Issue: April–May–June 1818//
Periodicity: Monthly
Editors: Tobias Watkins; Stephen Simpson
Publishers: Neale Wills & Company; E.J.
        Coale and Cushing and Jewett
Available From: APS; Amer. Antiquarian Soc.*
        Mott
Contents:
  Poetry: <u>Original</u>: Paul Allen, John Neal, John Pierpont, Rebecca Smith. <u>Selected</u>: Selleck Osborne, Byron, W.L. Bowles, William Cowper, Cottle, Southey, William Shenstone, Richard Cumberland, Charles Churchill.
  Prose: <u>Biography</u>: John Dennis, William Cowper, Scott, Richard Cumberland. <u>Travel</u>. <u>Essay</u>. <u>Familiar Essay</u>. <u>Criticism</u>: on Byron, Scott, Southey, Thomas Moore, Fielding, William Cowper. <u>Letters</u>. <u>Book Reviews</u>: on William Dunlap's life of Charles Brockden Brown.
  Fiction: <u>Essay Serials</u>: "The Club-Room"; "The Swiss Traveller"; "The Pilgrim"; "Omniana"; "The Remains of a Misanthrope"; "Delphian Amusements"; "Delphian Evenings."
  Miscellaneous: <u>Extracts</u>: from other journals. <u>Literary Notices</u>.

721   TITLE: <u>Portland Magazine</u>.

Place of Publication: Portland, Me.
First Issue: 11 May 1805
Last Issue: 8 June 1805//
Periodicity: Weekly
Editor: William Jenks, Jr.
Publisher: William Jenks, Jr.
Available From: APS; Amer. Antiquarian Soc.*
Contents:
  Poetry: <u>Original</u>. <u>Selected</u>.
  Prose: <u>Biography</u>: Pocahontas.
  Fiction: <u>Sketches</u>.
  Miscellaneous: <u>Extracts</u>: from other journals; by various authors; William Cowper. <u>Anecdotes</u>: on various subjects; Swift, R.B. Sheridan. <u>News</u>: Domestic.

722   TITLE: <u>The Portland Magazine, Devoted to Literature</u>. [Merged with <u>The Eastern Magazine</u> q.v. to form <u>The Maine Monthly Magazine</u> q.v.]

Place of Publication: Portland, Me.
First Issue: Oct 1834
Last Issue: June 1836//
Periodicity: Monthly
Editor: Ann S. Stephens
Publisher: Edward Stephens
Available From: APS; Lib. of Congress*
Contents:
  Poetry: <u>Original</u>: William H. Burleigh, William Cutter, R. Shelton Mackenzie, John Neal, Ann S. Stephens, Isaac C. Pray, Jr. <u>Selected</u>: Felicia Hemans, Hannah F. Gould, Willis Gaylord Clark, Whittier, Lydia H. Sigourney, Fanny Kemble, Nathaniel P. Willis, Grenville Mellen.
  Prose: <u>Biography</u>: Madame de Staël, James Fenimore Cooper. <u>Travel</u>. <u>Essay</u>. <u>Familiar Essay</u>. <u>Criticism</u>.
  Fiction: <u>Sketches</u>. <u>Tales</u>: "The Tradesman's Daughter"; "Romance and Reality"; "The Captive Queen's Gift"; "The Bridal, Throne, and Scaffold"; "Sir Henry's Daughter, or the Spy"; "Mary Bell"; "The Diamond Necklace"; "The Jockey Cap."
  Miscellaneous: <u>Extracts</u>: from other journals. <u>Literary Notices</u>.

723   TITLE: <u>Portsmouth Oracle</u>. [See <u>The United States Oracle of the Day</u>.]

724   TITLE: <u>The Portsmouth Weekly Magazine; a Repository of Miscellaneous Literary Matters, in Prose & Verse</u>.

Place of Publication: Portsmouth, N.H.
First Issue: 1 July 1824
Last Issue: 30 June 1825//
Periodicity: Weekly
Editor: John T. Gibbs
Publishers: John T. Gibbs; T.H. Miller
Available From: APS; Amer. Antiquarian Soc.
Contents:
  Poetry: <u>Original</u>. <u>Selected</u>: R.S. Coffin [Boston Bard]; James Montgomery, Washington Allston, Bryant, Herrick, William Cowper, Jane Taylor.
  Prose: <u>Biography</u>: Jane Shore, Lady Jane Grey. <u>Familiar Essay</u>.
  Fiction: <u>Sketches</u>. <u>Tales</u>: "The Ruins--A Fragment"; "Orlando & Lucinda"; "The Twin-Brothers--of Mezzorania. A Tale"; "A Village Tale"; "Herman and Harriet"; "Albudah and Louisa"; "The Barge's Crew"; "The Last Herring."
  Miscellaneous: <u>Extracts</u>: from other journals; by various authors; S. Johnson. <u>Anecdotes</u>: on various subjects; Garrick, S. Johnson, Swift, William Shenstone, John Locke, Horace Walpole, Dante. <u>Literary Notices</u>. <u>News</u>: Domestic.

725 TITLE: The Post-Chaise Companion; or, Magazine of Wit. To Which Is Added, a Number of Patriotic and Humorous Songs. [Volume 1,ii has on the title page: A Parlour-Window Book, for Dull Times.]

Place of Publication: Philadelphia
First Issue: Aug 1820
Last Issue: 22 Jan 1821//?
Periodicity: ?
Editors: ?
Publishers: ?
Available From: Lib. Co. of Philadelphia; N.Y. Pub. Lib.
Contents:
Poetry: Original. Selected: Samuel Woodworth.
Prose: Biography: Edmund Kean. Criticism. Letters.
Fiction: Sketches. Tale: "The Doctrines of Dan Democritus, a Descendant from the Merry Citizen of Abdera."
Miscellaneous: Anecdotes: on various subjects; George Frederick Cooke, S. Johnson, James Thomson, R.B. Sheridan.

726 TITLE: The Poughkeepsie Casket: A Semi-Monthly Literary Journal, Devoted Exclusively to the Different Branches of Polite Literature.

Place of Publication: Poughkeepsie, N.Y.
First Issue: 2 Jan 1836
Last Issue: 2 April 1841//
Periodicity: Semi-monthly
Editors: E.B. Killey; B.J. Lossing; J.H. Selkreg
Publishers: Killey & Lossing
Available From: APS; N.Y. Pub. Lib.*
Contents:
Poetry: Original: Darwin Canfield. Selected: I. D'Israeli, James G. Percival, Grenville Mellen, Lydia H. Sigourney, Thomas Moore, James Montgomery, Nathaniel P. Willis, Selleck Osborne, E. Lytton Bulwer, Hannah F. Gould, Hannah More, Willis Gaylord Clark, Burns, Longfellow, Alfred B. Street, Thomas Hood, Oliver Wendell Holmes, William B. Tappan, Bryant, Park Benjamin, Mary Howitt, Caroline Gilman, Mrs. Seba Smith, Rufus Wilmot Griswold, Frances S. Osgood, Barry Cornwall.
Prose: Biography: Lady Mary Wortley Montagu, Thomas Paine. Travel. Essay. Familiar Essay. Criticism. Letters.
Fiction: Essay Serial: "Flash-Lights." Sketches. Tales: "The Garland of Wit and Love. A Tale of the Reformation"; "A Love Cruise"; "Love and Money. A New-England Tale"; "The Eagle Plume. A Tale of Greece"; "Constance Allerton, or the Mourning Suits"; "Marie Jeanne" [Theodore Sedgwick Fay]; "Three Score and Ten. A Septuagenarian's Story"; "The Unbidden Guest"; "The Young Inebriate: A Tale of the Old Dominion"; "The Physician's Fee"; "Guilletta: Or, the Beautiful Head."

Miscellaneous: Anecdotes: on various subjects; Franklin, James Hogg, Byron, Pope, S. Johnson. News: Domestic.

727 TITLE: The Presbyterian Quarterly and Princeton Review. [See Biblical Repertory. A Collection of Tracts in Biblical Literature.]

728 TITLE: The Princeton Review. [See Biblical Repertory. A Collection of Tracts in Biblical Literature.]

729 TITLE: Quarterly Advertiser, Devoted to Literature and the Fine Arts.

Place of Publication: Boston
First Issue: Jan 1830
Last Issue: Oct 1833//?
Periodicity: Quarterly
Editors: ?
Publishers: ?
Available From: Amer. Antiquarian Soc.*
Contents:
Prose: Book Reviews.
Miscellaneous: Literary Notices.
Note: Consists entirely of literary notices and short book reviews.

730 TITLE: The Ramblers' Magazine, and New-York Theatrical Register: For the Season of 1809-10.

Place of Publication: New York
First Issue: 1809
Last Issue: 1810
Periodicity: Irregular
Editors: ?
Publisher: D. Longworth
Available From: APS; Lib. of Congress.* Mott.
Contents:
Poetry: Original. Selected.
Prose: Biography: of actors and actresses. Familiar Essay. Criticism. Letters.
Fiction: Essay Serial: "The Perambulator."
Miscellaneous: Anecdotes: on various subjects; Jefferson, S. Johnson, Boswell. Literary Notices.

731 TITLE: Record of Genius: A Literary and Miscellaneous Magazine. [See The Record of Genius: A Semi-Monthly Literary and Miscellaneous Magazine. Devoted to Original and Selected Tales, Essays, General Knowledge, Miscellany and Poetry.]

732 TITLES: (1) The Record of Genius: A Semi-Monthly Literary and Miscellaneous Magazine. Devoted to Original and Selected Tales, Essays, General Knowledge, Miscellany and Poetry. [Running title: Record of Genius: A Weekly Literary and Miscellaneous Magazine] (2) Record of Genius: A Literary and Miscellaneous Magazine.

Place of Publication: Utica, N.Y.
First Issue: 16 May 1832
Last Issue: 25 May 1833//?
Periodicity: Weekly; Semi-monthly
Editors: C.W. Everest; C. Corbitt
Publisher: Quartus Graves
Available From: Amer. Antiquarian Soc.;
Yale Univ.*
Contents:
  Poetry: Original. Selected: Felicia
    Hemans, Lydia H. Sigourney, Samuel G.
    Goodrich, Hannah F. Gould, Thomas Moore,
    Whittier, Mary Anne Browne, Chester A.
    Griswold, Willis Gaylord Clark, J.O.
    Rockwell, Fitz-Greene Halleck, James G.
    Percival, L.E. Landon.
  Prose: Biography. Essay. Familiar Essay.
  Fiction: Essay Serials: "Vagaries";
    "Lucubrations"; "Cogitations." Sketches.
    Tales: "A Strange Story"; "Haunelauck.
    Or a Story of the Twentieth Century";
    "The Deformed Girl" [Whittier]; "Effigy";
    "The Maid of the Mountain"; "The Bandit";
    "Lundy's Lane"; "White Tassel"; "The
    Poniard"; "The Bravo"; "History of Uncle
    Sam and His Womankind" [James Kirke
    Paulding]; "The Seal. A Pathetic Story";
    "The Disguise."
  Miscellaneous: Extracts: from other jour-
    nals; by various authors; Shelley,
    Nathaniel P. Willis, Frances Trollope,
    E. Lytton Bulwer. Anecdotes: on various
    subjects; Scott, Byron. News: Domestic.

733   NO ENTRY

734   TITLE: The Red Book.

Place of Publication: Baltimore
First Issue: 23 Oct 1819
Last Issue: 16 March 1821//
Periodicity: Irregular
Editors: Peter Hoffman Cruse; John P.
          Kennedy
Publishers: Peter Hoffman Cruse; John P.
          Kennedy
Available From: Lib. of Congress*; Yale
              Univ.* Mott.
Contents:
  Poetry: Original.
  Prose: Biography. Familiar Essay.
  Fiction: Essay Serials: "From the Tusculum";
    "Market Street Musings"; "From the Obser-
    vatory." Sketches. Tales: "Lady Fashion
    and Lady Good Sense; a Tale"; "The Story
    of Mr. Bronze."
  Miscellaneous: Anecdotes: on various sub-
    jects.
Note: A Note dated 1870 in the Library of
    Congress copy of this journal addressed
    to Mr. Sabin reads: "This is one of the
    rarest of Maryland books (written & printed
    in Baltimore) . . . long out of print &
    probably not a dozen copies in existence
    complete."

735   TITLE: The Reflector.

Place of Publication: Boston
First Issue: [Only one issue published?]
                Sept 1821//?
Periodicity: Intended to be monthly
Editors: ?
Publishers: Wells and Lilly
Available From: APS; Lib. of Congress
Contents:
  Prose: Familiar Essay. Book Reviews.
  Miscellaneous: Literary Notices.

736   TITLE: The Reflector.

Place of Publication: Palmyra, N.Y.
First Issue: 22 Dec 1829
Last Issue: 19 March 1831//?
Periodicity: Weekly
Editors: ?
Publishers: ?
Available From: N.Y. Hist. Soc.; Lib. of
                Congress
Contents:
  Poetry: Original. Selected.
  Prose: Biography. Essay. Familiar Essay.
  Fiction: Sketches.
  Miscellaneous: Anecdotes: on various sub-
    jects. News: Domestic.

737   TITLE: The Religious and Literary Gem, a
        Compendium of Religious, Literary, and
        Philosophical Knowledge. [Absorbed The
        Lady's Pearl.]

Place of Publication: Boston
First Issue: July 1842
Last Issue: Sept 1843//
Periodicity: Monthly
Editor: Charles W. Denison
Publishers: Jonathan K. Wellman; James
        Stringer; Leland & Whiting; Pratt & Co.;
        Pratt, Sears & Co.; Joseph H. Sears

Available From: Amer. Antiquarian Soc.*;
                Lib. of Congress
Contents:
  Poetry: Original: Charles W. Denison,
    Wilson Flagg, C.M. Edwards. Selected:
    Lucy Seymour, Lydia H. Sigourney, Emeline
    S. Smith, Dryden, Francis Quarles, Hannah
    More, James Eastburn, William Cutter,
    George D. Prentice, Joseph L. Chester,
    Bryant, E.F. Ellet, Sarah J. Hale, Charles
    W. Denison, Margaret Robinson, Bernard
    Barton, William B. Tappan.
  Prose: Travel. Essay. Criticism. Letters.
  Fiction: Sketches. Tales: "Fleance: A
    Domestic Story"; "The Factory Girl. An
    Over True Tale"; "The Warning. A Tale of
    Truth"; "The Reclaimed"; "Fashionable Life,
    or a Tale of 'Good Society'"; "My Friend's

Family"; "Leaves from the Journal of a
Poor Vicar in Wiltshire"; "The Hermit.
A Tale of East Rock, Near New Haven,
Conn."
Miscellaneous: Extracts: from other jour-
nals; by various authors; W. Irving,
Horace Greeley.

738   TITLE: The Religious and Literary Repository.

Place of Publication: Annapolis
First Issue: 15 Jan 1820
Last Issue: 23 Dec 1820//
Available From: Enoch Pratt Lib., Baltimore;
                Princeton Theological Seminar-
                ary

739   TITLE: The Religious Monitor, or Theological
Scales: Containing, a Variety of Essays on
Religious and Moral Subjects, Original and
Selected, Interspersed with Sketches of
Biography, Poetry &c. Designed to Open a
Door for a Free and Candid Enquiry After
Religious Truth, for the Promotion of Piety
and Virtue, and the Discouragement of Vice
and Infidelity.

Place of Publication: Danbury, Conn.
First Issue: 7 April 1798
Last Issue: 22 Sept 1798//
Periodicity: Semi-monthly
Editors: ?
Publishers: Douglas & Nichols
Available From: APS; N.Y. Pub. Lib.*
Contents:
  Poetry: Original. Selected.
  Prose: Biography: Jeremy Belknap
  Fiction: Essay Serials: "The Reformer";
    "Every Christian's Assistant"; "Maranatha."
  Miscellaneous: Anecdotes: on various sub-
    jects.

740   TITLE: The Repository and Ladies' Weekly
Museum. [See The Philadelphia Repository,
and Weekly Register . . . Containing Ori-
ginal Essays, Tales and Novels, Interesting
Extracts from New Publications and Works of
Merit, Amusing Miscellanies, Remarkable
Occurrences, Anecdotes, Bon Mots, Jeu
d'esprit, Marriages and Deaths, Poetical
Essays, Odes, Sonnets, Songs (a Number of
Which Are Set to Music) and Generally,
Whatever Is Calculated to Diffuse Interest-
ing and Useful Information, Divert the
Fancy, Enlighten the Understanding, Form the
Mind, and Mend the Heart.]

741   TITLES: (1) The Repository of Modern English
Romance: Comprising All the Best Serial
Novels of the Day, by James, Dickens, Lever,
Ainsworth, Lover, and Other Distinguished
Writers (2) The Repository of Romance, and
Gems of Popular Literature.

Place of Publication: New York
First Issue: Jan 1844

Last Issue: Dec 1845//?
Periodicity: Monthly; Semi-monthly; Monthly
Editors: ?
Publishers: J. Winchester; E. Winchester
Available From: Lib. of Congress; Amer.
                Antiquarian Soc.
Contents:
  Poetry: Selected: Thomas Hood.
  Fiction: Tales: "A Last Confession of Harry
    Lorrequer" [Charles Lever]; "The Witch-
    finder"; "The Three Guardsmen" [Alexandre
    Dumas]; "Arwed Gillenstern. A Swedish
    Historical Tale of the Early Part of the
    18th Century"; "The Deformed. A Tale";
    "Extracts from the Log-Book of a Priva-
    teer's-Man a Hundred Years Ago" [Marryat].
    Novels: "The O'Donoghue; a Tale of Ireland
    Fifty Years Ago" [Charles Lever]; "Saint
    James's: Or, the Court of Queen Anne"
    [William Harrison Ainsworth]; "Arrah Neil;
    or, Times of Old" [G.P.R. James]; "Tom
    Burke of 'Ours'" [Charles Lever]; "Revela-
    tions of London" [William Harrison
    Ainsworth]; "Hortensia; or, the Transfigura-
    tions"; "The Hotel Lambert" [Eugene Sue].
  Miscellaneous: Anecdotes: on various sub-
    jects. Literary Notices.

742   TITLE: The Repository of Romance, and Gems of
Popular Literature. [See The Repository of
Modern English Romance: Comprising All the
Best Serial Novels of the Day, by James,
Dickens, Lever, Ainsworth, Lover, and Other
Distinguished Writers.]

743   TITLES: (1) The Republic of Letters; a Weekly
Republication of Standard Literature (2)
The Republic of Letters; a Republication of
Standard Literature.

Place of Publication: New York
First Issue: 1834
Last Issue: 1836//
Periodicity: Weekly
Editors: William Pearson; Mrs. A.H. Nicholas
Publisher: George Dearborn
Available From: APS; Hist. Soc. of Pa.*
Contents:
  Poetry: Selected: [See Fiction: Literary
    Works].
  Prose: Biography: Franklin, Bolingbroke.
    Essay: [See FICTION: Literary Works].
    Letters: Lady Mary Wortley Montagu [See
    also: FICTION: Literary Works].
  Fiction: Tales: [See Fiction: Literary
    Works]. Literary Works: "The Man of
    Feeling" [Henry Mackenzie]; "The Vicar of
    Wakefield" [Goldsmith]; "Tales of the
    Hall" [George Crabbe]; "Rasselas" [S.
    Johnson]; "The Castle of Otranto" [Horace
    Walpole]; "The Old English Baron" [Clara
    Reeve]; "Lights and Shadows of Scottish
    Life" [John Wilson]; "The Adventures of
    Gil Blas of Santillane" [Le Sage, tr.
    Smollett]; "Julia de Roubigné; a Tale"
    [Henry Mackenzie]; "Zeluco: Various Views
    of Human Nature" [Dr. John Moore]; "Manfred;
    a Dramatic Poem" [Byron]; "Ali's Bride.

A Tale from the Persian" [Thomas Moore];
"The Man of the World" [Henry Mackenzie];
"Gulliver's Travels" [Swift]; "Don Quixote"
[Cervantes, tr. Smollett]; "The Deserted
Village" [Goldsmith]; "Belisarius. A
Tale" [Marmontel]; "Essay on Man" [Pope];
"Il Penseroso" and "L'Allegro" [Milton];
"The Rape of the Lock" [Pope]; "Samson
Agonistes" [Milton]; "Bubbles from the
Brunnens of Nassau, by an Old Man"; "The
Inheritance"; "Letters from England by Don
Manuel Alvarez Espriella" [Southey].

744 TITLE: The Republican Rush-Light. [See The
Rush-Light.]

745 TITLE: The Rhode-Island American, and General
Advertiser. [See The American.]

746 TITLE: The Rhode-Island Literary Repository,
a Monthly Magazine. Containing Biographical
Sketches, Reviews, Dissertations, Literary
Researches, Poetry, Anecdotes, &c.

Place of Publication: Providence, R.I.
First Issue: April 1814
Last Issue: March 1815//
Periodicity: Monthly
Editor: Isaac Bailey
Publishers: Robinson and Howland
Available From: APS; Lib. of Congress*
Contents:
  Poetry: Original. Selected: William
    Cowper, Byron, Abraham Cowley.
  Prose: Biography: Benjamin West, Jeremy
    Taylor, Fisher Ames. Travel. Familiar
    Essay. Letters. Book Reviews.
  Fiction: Essay Serials: "The Babbler";
    "Miscellanea."
  Miscellaneous: Extracts: from other jour-
    nals; by various authors; Chateaubriand.
    Anecdotes: on various subjects; Swift,
    Sidney, Burns, Pope. Literary Notices.

747 TITLE: Richmond Lyceum Journal. Devoted to
the Moral and Intellectual Improvement of
Young Men.

Place of Publication: Richmond
First Issue: April 1838
Last Issue: March 1839//
Periodicity: Monthly
Editors: Members of the Richmond Lyceum
Publishers: Members of the Richmond Lyceum
Available From: Lib. of Congress*; Virginia
                State Lib., Richmond
Contents:
  Poetry: Original. Selected: Lucy Seymour,
    L.E. Landon, Thomas Campbell.
  Prose: Biography. Essay. Familiar Essay.
    Criticism.
  Fiction: Sketches. Tales: "The Broken
    Pitcher"; "The Law Student"; "The Devil
    and His Bride"; "The Poor Rich Man and the
    Rich Poor Man" [Catharine M. Sedgwick];
    "The Three Sisters" [E. Lytton Bulwer].

Miscellaneous: Extracts: from other journals; by various authors; Fenelon.

748 TITLES: (1) Robert Merry's Museum (2) Merry's
Museum and Parley's Magazine. [Merged with
Parley's Magazine for Children and Youth q.v.]

Place of Publication: Boston; New York
First Issue: Feb 1841
Last Issue: Nov 1872//
Periodicity: Monthly
Editors: Robert Merry; Samuel G. Goodrich;
  Louisa M. Alcott
Publishers: I.C. & J.N. Stearns; Bradbury and
  Soden; G.W. & S.O. Post; D. Mac-
  Donald & Co.; S.T. Allen & Co.
Available From: APS; Hist. Soc. of Pa. Mott.
Contents:
  Poetry: Original. Selected: Anna Letitia
    Barbauld, Southey, James Montgomery,
    Frances Child, Felicia Hemans, James
    Thomson, Mary Howitt, H.H. Brownall.
  Prose: Biography: William Ellery Channing,
    Martin Luther, Franklin, John Wesley,
    Fenelon, Philip Sidney, Goldsmith. Essay.
    Familiar Essay. Letters. Book Reviews.
  Fiction: Essay Serials: "Peter Pilgrim's
    Account of His Schoolmates"; "The Old Man
    in the Corner"; "Peeps at Paris." Sketches.
    Tales: "My Own Life and Adventures; by
    Robert Merry"; "The Travels, Adventures,
    and Experiences of Thomas Trotter"; "Story
    of Philip Brusque"; "The Siberian Sable-
    Hunter"; "Inquisitive Jack"; "Dick
    Boldhero"; "Conjugal Affection"; "The Two
    Miss Smiths; or, the Tale of a Turban";
    "'Take Care of Number One'"; "The Story
    of George's Journey."
  Miscellaneous: Anecdotes: on various sub-
    jects; Franklin, Haydn, Patrick Henry,
    S. Johnson, Coleridge.

749 TITLE: Roberts' Semi-Monthly Magazine, for
Town and Country.

Place of Publication: Boston
First Issue: 15 Jan 1841
Last Issue: 1 Jan 1842//
Periodicity: Semi-monthly
Editor: George Roberts
Publisher: George Roberts
Available From: APS; Boston Pub. Lib.*
Contents:
  Poetry: Original. Selected: H.T. Tucker-
    man, Thomas W. Parsons, Samuel Woodworth,
    Alfred B. Street, James T. Fields, J.M.
    M'Lellan, Jr., Thomas Moore, Whittier,
    Alonzo Lewis, William Gilmore Simms,
    Hannah F. Gould, Longfellow, R. Shelton
    Mackenzie, Charles Fenno Hoffman, Robert
    Morris, Mrs. Abdy, Epes Sargent, Caroline
    Norton, Barry Cornwall, E. Lytton Bulwer,
    Anna L. Snelling, Mary Anne Browne.
  Prose: Biography: Bryan Waller Proctor.
    Criticism. Book Reviews.
  Fiction: Sketches. Tales: "The Pawnbroker's
    Window"; "'The Poacher'"; "A Night Excur-
    sion with Martin Zurbano"; "The Sad Bird

of the Adriatic.--A Tale" [H.T. Tuckerman];
"The Wife" [W. Irving]; "Imagination. A
Tale for Young Women" [James Fenimore
Cooper]; "George St. George Julian.--The
Prince"; "Old St. Paul's--An Historical
Romance" [William Harrison Ainsworth];
"The Double Marriage"; "The Criminal
Brothers"; "A Passage in the Life of
Alfieri"; "The Banker's Daughter"; "Heart
--A Tale" [James Fenimore Cooper]; "The
Confessions of a Swindler"; "The Eve of
St. Bartholomew"; "Marquinez and la
Collegiala. A Romance of the Peninsular
War"; "The Young Member's Wife"; "Forty-
one Tons of Indigo; or, the Careful Deal-
er"; "The English Mariner. Three Days
from the Life of Cavendish the Rover";
"The Ancient Regime"; "Eleonora,--A Fable"
[Poe]; "The Lamplighter's Story" [Dickens];
"Nicholas Dunks; or Fried Mackeral for
Dinner"; "Circumstantial Evidence--A Tale";
"The Married Officer--A Tale"; "Peter
Benson, the Miser.--A Tale." Drama: "Old
Maids" [James Sheridan Knowles].
Miscellaneous: Extracts: from other jour-
nals; by various authors; Marryat.

750   TITLE: Roberts's World of Romance. Cheap
       Republication of Novels, Tales, &c.

Place of Publication: Boston
First Issue: [Only five issues published?]
              1840//?
Periodicity: Weekly
Editor: George Roberts
Publisher: George Roberts
Available From: Lib. of Congress
Contents:
  Poetry: Selected: Mrs. Abdy, Mrs. Seba
    Smith, Thomas Moore, Lalla Rookh.
  Prose: Criticism: "Shakespeare and His
    Friends, the 'Golden Age' of Merry
    England."
  Fiction: Tales: "High-Ways and By-Ways,
    or Tales of the Roadside; Picked Up in the
    French Provinces by a Walking Gentleman."

751   TITLE: Robinson's Magazine, a Weekly Reposi-
       tory of Original Papers; and Selections
       from the English Magazines.

Place of Publication: Baltimore
First Issue: 18 July 1815
Last Issue: 26 June 1819//
Periodicity: Weekly
Editor: Joseph Robinson
Publisher: Joseph Robinson
Available From: APS; N.Y. State Lib., Albany*
Contents:
  Poetry: Original. Selected: Burns, Byron,
    John Leyden, William Cowper, Charles
    Phillips, Matthew Gregory [Monk] Lewis,
    John Wolcott, Goethe, James Hogg.
  Prose: Biography: Franklin, James Hogg.
    Travel. Essay. Familiar Essay.
    Criticism. Letters. Book Reviews.

Fiction: Sketches. Tales: "The Revenge
  of Tirinie: A Highland Legend"; "The
  Fudge Family in Paris"; "A Spanish Story";
  "Legends of Lampidosa"; "Pierre Huet; or
  the Square Tower"; "Christian Wolf. A True
  Story"; "The History of the Cashals. A
  Tale"; "The Vampyre; a Tale" [Byron].
Miscellaneous: Extracts: from other jour-
  nals; by various authors. Anecdotes: on
  various subjects; Goldsmith, Franklin,
  Buonaparte, Matthew Prior, R.B. Sheridan.
  Literary Notices.

752   TITLE: The Rose Bud. Devoted to Literature
       and Domestic Intelligence.

Place of Publication: Newark, N.J.
First Issue: 9 May 1840
Last Issue: 5 June 1841//?
Available From: Rutgers Univ., New Brunswick,
                 N.J.; Univ. of Minn.,
                 Minneapolis

753   TITLE: The Rose of the Valley: A Flower of
       the West, that Blooms to Enrich the Mind.
       Devoted to Literature, Instruction, Amuse-
       ment, and Interesting Biography.

Place of Publication: Cincinnati
First Issue: Jan 1839
Last Issue: July 1840//
Periodicity: Monthly
Editor: G.G. Moore
Publisher: G.G. Moore
Available From: APS; Pub. Lib. of Cincinnati
Contents:
  Poetry: Original. Selected: L.E. Landon,
    Charles Dingley, James G. Percival, Lydia
    H. Sigourney, Caroline Norton.
  Prose: Biography. Familiar Essay. Letters.
  Fiction: Sketches. Tales: "In Search of a
    Situation"; "The Repository. A Tale";
    "The Strange Passenger"; "Mariamne";
    "Emily S. and Her Repentant Father"; "The
    Maid of Soleure"; "The Cruel Father"; "The
    Poor Student"; "The Charter, a Tale"; "The
    Widow and Her Infidel Son."
  Miscellaneous: Extracts: from other jour-
    nals; by various authors; James G.
    Percival. Anecdotes: on various subjects;
    Swift.

754   TITLE: The Rover: A Weekly Magazine of Tales,
       Poetry, and Engravings, Also Sketches of
       Travel, History and Biography. [Superseded
       by the New York Illustrated Magazine of
       Literature and Art q.v.]

Place of Publication: New York
First Issue: March 1843
Last Issue: Sept 1845
Periodicity: Weekly
Editors: Mrs. Seba Smith; Lawrence Labree
Publishers: Labree, Dean & Co.; Robinson &
             Co.; S.B. Dean & Co.
Available From: APS; N.Y. State Lib., Albany.*
                 Mott.

Contents:
  Poetry: Original: E.W. Gunning, Anne
    Eliza Ponsonby, Lawrence Labree, C.D.
    Stuart, Augustus Shea, Mrs. Seba Smith,
    Hugh More. Selected: John Bowring,
    William Wallace, Elizabeth Oakes Smith, W.H.
    Carpenter, Bryant, Barry Cornwall,
    Whittier, Robert Montgomery, Fitz-Greene
    Halleck, Thomas Campbell, H.T. Tuckerman,
    Eliza Cook, Thomas Haynes Bayly, Hannah
    F. Gould, James G. Percival, Robert C.
    Sands, Lydia H. Sigourney, Burns, Park
    Benjamin, Thomas Hood, Longfellow, Byron,
    Tennyson, H.H. Clements, Oliver Wendell
    Holmes, Felicia Hemans, Shelley, Arthur
    Morrell, Mary Howitt.
  Prose: Biography: Scott. Travel. Essay.
    Familiar Essay. Letters.
  Fiction: Sketches: Thomas Haynes Bayly,
    Mrs. Seba Smith, Elizabeth Oakes Smith, Emma
    C. Embury, Nathaniel Hawthorne. Tales:
    "The Wandering Jew"; "Lucille: Or, the
    French Harpiste"; "The Brilliant Locket";
    "A Thanksgiving Story"; "The Legend of
    King Robert of Sicily" [Leigh Hunt]; "Kitty
    Dangerous"; "The Tempter. A Tale of
    Jerusalem"; "Circumstantial Evidence. A
    Tale Founded on Fact"; "Hereditary Honors.
    A Tale of Love and Mystery"; "Jeannot and
    Colin" [Voltaire]; "Guido and Isabel; a
    Sicilian Story"; "The Vow, a Northern
    Tale"; "The Green Mountain Boy. A Tale
    of Ticonderoga"; "The Prodigal Son. From
    Tales of the Borders"; "A Tale of an Old
    Highlander" [James Hogg]; "A Tale of Bos-
    ton in Olden Times" [Felicia Hemans];
    "Skenando. The Oneida Chief. An Affect-
    ing and True Tale"; "The Wife of Peter
    Powers. A Tale of the Early Settlers";
    "The Lay of the Laborer" [Thomas Hood];
    "The Peasant Girl of Urbino"; "The Wife"
    [Frances S. Osgood]; "The Bastile" [James
    Sheridan Knowles]; "Hell Gate" [W. Irving];
    "Story of an Earthquake" [Leigh Hunt];
    "Moslem Honor: A Spanish Tale" [W. Irving];
    "Washington's Escape: A Tale of the
    Revolution"; "St. Croix: A Tale of the
    Days of Terror"; "The Stroller's Tale";
    "Zoe. A Tale of the Youth of Julius
    Caesar"; "A Tale of Venice"; "The Yankee
    Ball. A Tale of the American Revolution";
    "The Sisters of the Silver Palace. A
    Tale from the Italian Chronicles"; "Who
    Could Have Believed It? A German Tale";
    "The Two Sisters" [Mary Russell Mitford];
    "The Painter's Tale"; "A Tale of a Tar";
    "A Tale of the Plague in Edinburgh"; "The
    Planter. A West Indian Story"; "The
    Awakened Heart" [Emma C. Embury]; "The
    Colonel and the Devil. An Irish Story";
    "Three Fingered Jack. A West India Story";
    "Moowis, or the Indian Coquette" [Henry
    R. Schoolcraft]; "Too Handsome for Any-
    thing" [E. Lytton Bulwer]; "The Circles
    of Human Wishes" [James Kirke Paulding];
    "The Fair Artist" [Sarah J. Hale]; "The
    Temptation of the Capuchins. A Tale of
    Murcia"; "A Tale of the Little Lake"
    [Lydia J. Pierson]; "The Jew: Or Honesty
    the Best Policy"; "Leap Year; or, Woman's
    Privilege"; "The Revenge of St. Nicholas.

A Tale for the Holidays" [James Kirke
  Paulding]; "Anesquette: A Story of the
  Valley D'aspe"; "A Romance of Paris a
  Thousand Years Ago. The Seige" [Miss
  Jewsbury].
Miscellaneous: Extracts: from other jour-
  nals; by various authors. Anecdotes: on
  various subjects.

755 TITLE: The Royal American Magazine, or
     Universal Repository of Instruction and
     Amusement.

Place of Publication: Boston
First Issue: Jan 1774
Last Issue: March 1775//
Periodicity: Monthly
Editors: Isaiah Thomas; Joseph Greenleaf
Publishers: Isaiah Thomas; Joseph Greenleaf
Available From: APS; Amer. Antiquarian Soc.*
               Mott.
Contents:
  Poetry: Original: Benjamin Pratt. Selected.
  Prose: Travel. Essay. Familiar Essay.
    Letters: Franklin.
  Fiction: Essay Serial: "The Directory of
    Love" [Advice to the lovelorn]. Sketches.
    Tales: "The Thunder Storm. A Moral Tale";
    "The Fortune Hunter. A Modern Tale";
    "Hamet: Or the Insufficiency of Luxury
    to the Atainment of Happiness. A Oriental
    Tale"; "History of Lauretta. A Moral
    Tale"; "The Wife of Ten-Thousand! A
    Moral Tale."
  Miscellaneous: Extracts: from other jour-
    nals; by various authors; Goldsmith.
    Anecdotes: on various subjects. Literary
    Notices. News: Foreign and Domestic.
Note: Beginning with 1,i(1774) is Governor
  Hutchinson's "The History of the Colony
  of Massachusetts-Bay, from the First
  Settlement Thereof in 1628, Until Its
  Incorporation with the Colony of Plimouth,
  Province of Main, &c. by the Charter of
  King William and Queen Mary, in 1691."
  The periodical also contains some political
  cartoons by Paul Revere.

756 TITLE: The Rural Casket.

Place of Publication: Poughkeepsie, N.Y.
First Issue: 5 June 1798
Last Issue: 11 Sept 1798//
Periodicity: Weekly
Editors: ?
Publishers: Power & Southwick
Available From: APS; N.Y. Pub. Lib.*
Contents:
  Poetry: Original. Selected: Southey,
    Peter Pindar, William Cowper.
  Prose: Travel. Essay: "The Origin of
    Despair"; "On Domestic Confidence, and
    Family Distrust." Familiar Essay: "Duty
    of Women"; "On Passion." Letters.
  Fiction: Essay Serial: "The Meddler."
    Tales: "The Sick Widow"; "The Pious
    Theft"; "Phoebe Smith"; "Caroline Courtney."
  Miscellaneous: Extracts: from other jour-
    nals. Anecdotes: on various subjects;

Edmund Burke, Edward Young, S. Johnson.
News: Foreign and Domestic.

757   TITLE: The Rural Magazine.

Place of Publication: Newark, N.J.
First Issue: 17 Feb 1798
Last Issue: 9 Feb 1799//
Periodicity: Weekly
Editor: John H. Williams
Publisher: John H. Williams
Available From: APS; Lib. of Congress.*
                 Mott.
Contents:
    Poetry: Original. Selected: Alaric Watts,
      Hester L. Thrale Piozzi, Peter Pindar,
      Lady Mary Wortley Montagu, Josiah Thomas,
      W.P. Carey, J. Pomfret, S. Johnson,
      Erasmus Darwin, Southey, Timothy Dwight,
      William Cowper, Joel Barlow.
    Prose: Familiar Essay.
    Fiction: Essay Serial: "The Lay Preacher."
      Sketches. Tales: "The Glebe House--A
      Tale"; "Timur--An Eastern Tale"; "History
      of the Family of Monsieur de M----"; "The
      Chimera; a Tale of a Looking-Glass"; "The
      Twin-Brothers of Mezzorania. A Mezzoranian
      Tale"; "Abu-Casem's Slippers; an Arabian
      Tale."
    Miscellaneous: Extracts: from other jour-
      nals; by various authors; Voltaire, Swift,
      Goldsmith, Sterne, Addison, Benjamin
      Rush, Hester L. Thrale Piozzi. Anecdotes:
      on various subjects. Literary Notices.
      News: Domestic.

758   TITLE: The Rural Magazine and Farmer's
       Monthly Museum, Devoted to History, Biogra-
       phy, Agriculture, Manufacture, Miscellany,
       Poetry, and Foreign and Domestic Intelli-
       gence.

Place of Publication: Hartford, Conn.
First Issue: Feb 1819
Last Issue: July 1819//
Periodicity: Monthly
Editor: S. Putnam Waldo
Publishers: J. & W. Russell
Available From: APS; Lib. of Congress*
Contents:
    Poetry: Original. Selected: Francis
      Hopkinson, James Montgomery.
    Prose: Biography: David Humphreys, Ethan
      Allen. Essay. Familiar Essay. Book
      Reviews.
    Fiction: Essay Serial: "The Social Com-
      panion." Sketches.
    Miscellaneous: Extracts: by various
      authors. Anecdotes: on various subjects;
      Washington, Timothy Dwight, Joseph Dennie.
      Literary Notices. News: Foreign and
      Domestic.

759   TITLE: The Rural Magazine, and Literary
       Evening Fire-Side.

Place of Publication: Philadelphia
First Issue: Jan 1820

Last Issue: Dec 1820//
Periodicity: Monthly
Editors: ?
Publishers: Richards & Caleb Johnson
Available From: APS; Lib. of Congress*
Contents:
    Poetry: Original. Selected: Thomas
      Warton, John Leyden, Southey, Selleck
      Osborne, Samuel Bishop, James Montgomery,
      Charles James Fox, John Logan, Allan
      Cunningham, Bernard Barton, Joanna Baillie.
    Prose: Travel. Essay. Familiar Essay.
      Letters.
    Fiction: Essay Serials: "The Desultory
      Remarker"; "The Village Teacher."
    Miscellaneous: Extracts: from other jour-
      nals; by various authors; Franklin,
      Jefferson. News: Foreign and Domestic.

760   TITLE: The Rural Magazine: Or, Vermont
       Repository. Devoted to Literary, Moral,
       Historical, and Political Improvement.

Place of Publication: Rutland, Vt.
First Issue: Jan 1795
Last Issue: Dec 1796//
Periodicity: Monthly
Editor: Samuel Williams
Publishers: S. Williams, & Co.
Available From: APS; Amer. Antiquarian Soc.*
                 Mott.
Contents:
    Poetry: Selected: Joseph Brown Ladd,
      William Blackstone, Philip Doddridge,
      Timothy Dwight, Thomas Rowley, Pope,
      William Jones, Thomas Holcroft, Anna
      Letitia Barbauld.
    Prose: Biography: political figures;
      Nathaniel Greene, Penn, John Winthrop,
      Charles James Fox. Travel. Essay.
      Familiar Essay. Letters: S. Johnson.
    Fiction: Essay Serial: "Moral Disserta-
      tions." Sketches. Tales: "Story of
      Rustan" [Voltaire]; "The Chevalier Bayard
      and Madame de Randan--A Tale of the
      Fifteenth Century"; "The Romantic Daughter:
      Or, a Pleasant Revenge"; "Nahamir; or,
      Providence Justified--A Mahometan Tale";
      "Story of Solyman and Almena. An Eastern
      Tale"; "Elmina; or the Flower that Never
      Fades--A Tale for Young Ladies"; "The
      Basket-Maker--A Peruvian Tale."
    Miscellaneous: Extracts: by various
      authors; Franklin, Voltaire, Thomas Paine,
      Smollett, Mathew Carey, Goldsmith. Anec-
      dotes: Swift, Franklin, Rousseau.

761   TITLES: (1) Rural Repository (2) The Rural
       Repository; or, Semi-Monthly Entertaining and
       Amusing Journal: Containing a Variety of
       Original and Select Articles, Arranged Under
       the Following Heads: Original and Popular
       Tales, Essays, Biography, Traveller, Miscel-
       laneous, Summary, Poetry, etc. (3) The
       Rural Repository, or Bower of Literature; a
       Semi-Monthly Literary and Entertaining Jour-
       nal: Containing a Variety of Original and
       Select Articles, Arranged Under the Follow-
       ing Heads: Popular Tales, Biography,

Traveller, Miscellaneous, Poetry, etc.
(4) The Rural Repository, or Bower of Literature; Devoted Exclusively to Polite Literature, Comprised in the Following Subjects: Original and Select Tales, Essays, American and Foreign Biography, Travels, Notices of New Publications, Original and Select Poetry, Amusing Miscellany, Humorous and Historical Anecdotes, &c. &c. (5) The Rural Repository Devoted to Polite Literature, Such as Moral and Sentimental Tales, Biography, Traveling Sketches, Notices of New Publications, Poetry, Amusing Miscellany, Humorous and Historical Anecdotes, &c. &c. [Running title: Rural Repository, a Semi-Monthly Journal, Devoted to Polite Literature; later, Rural Repository. A Semi-Monthly Journal, Embellished with Engravings.]

Place of Publication: Hudson, N.Y.
First Issue: 12 June 1824
Last Issue: Oct 1851//?
Periodicity: Semi-monthly
Editor: William B. Stoddard
Publisher: William B. Stoddard
Available From: Amer. Antiquarian Soc.;
               N.Y. State Lib., Albany

Contents:
Poetry: Original: William Piatt, Eliza Mason, Mary Emily Jackson, S. Compton Smith, M.A. Dodd, George W. Browne, John C. Lowry, T.C. Worden, C.D. Stuart, A.W. Holden, A.A. Forbes, C. Theresa Clark, E.C. Dickerman, Henrietta Gay, Mary L. Gardiner, Mary J. Stratton, William Russell, Jr., Lydia Jane Pierson, C.F. Coy, Clark W. Bryan, Elizabeth St. John, Charles H. Cleveland, L.D. Webb, Catharine Webb Barber, E.C. Pool, William Ford, J.Q.A. Wood, E. Winchester Reynolds, Lucy Page, L. Casandra Brockbank, Barry Gray. Selected: Byron, Thomas Campbell, Felicia Hemans, R.S. Coffin, James G. Percival, G.F. Richardson, Allan Cunningham, Edward C. Pinckney, Nathaniel P. Willis, James Montgomery, Lydia H. Sigourney, Bryant, Samuel G. Goodrich, Grenville Mellen, Thomas Haynes Bayly, L.E. Landon, Whittier, Mary E. Brooks, Thomas Moore, J.M. M'Lellan, Jr., B.B. Thatcher, James A. Harris, Robert Morris, Charles Sprague, Caroline Norton, Fitz-Greene Halleck, Anna Maria Wells, Emma C. Embury, Fanny Kemble, Hannah F. Gould, John Bowring, Miss Pardoe, Joseph Rodman Drake, Albert Pike, Otway Curry, William Leggett, Mary Anne Browne, George Lunt, E. Lytton Bulwer, Isaac C. Pray, Jr., C.F. Ames, Mrs. Abdy, Sarah J. Hale, Elizabeth Bogart, Walter Colton, Mary Howitt, Lucy Seymour, Longfellow, George D. Prentice, Catharine H. Waterman, William S. Holden, Charles Swain, Selleck Osborne, William H. Burleigh, Thomas Hood, Eliza Cook, Henry Channing, Richard Coe, Jr., Mary L. Gardiner, D.C. Colesworthy, William W. Page, Thomas Dunn English, William Motherwell, James Kirke Paulding, R.H. Wilde.

Prose: Biography: Byron, John Trumbull, Lindley Murray, Jefferson, Roger Williams, Benjamin West, John Quincy Adams, Charles Sprague, James G. Brooks, James G. Percival, Scott, John G. Brainard, Thomas Moore, LaFayette, Felicia Hemans, Catharine M. Sedgwick, Henry Neele, Charles James Fox, Mathew Carey, Arbuthnot, Edward Gibbon, Dryden, Cromwell, Tyrone Power, Dickens, Garrick, Buonaparte, Lydia Maria Child, Sarah J. Hale, John Neal, James Kirke Paulding, Lydia H. Sigourney, Maria Edgeworth. Travel. Essay. Familiar Essay. Criticism. Letters.
Fiction: Essay Serials: "The Lawyer's Port Folio"; "Melanges"; "Sketches by the Wayside"; "Random Gleanings." Sketches. Tales: "The Reparation. A Tale"; "The Witch of the Wold" [Charlotte Smith]; "The Inconstant;--A Tale of the Drama"; "The Woodlands"; "The Midnight Murder"; "The Green Petticoat"; "Lafitte, or the Baratarian Chief. A Tale"; "The Bold Dragoon" [W. Irving]; "Fitzalan"; "The Exile of the Alleghany; or National Gratitude. An American Tale"; "Theodore Roland"; "The Strawberry Girl"; "Winter's Tale"; "Rosina Vangorden, or the Offspring of a Daughter"; "The Heir of Lansdown"; "Ambition, or the Story of William and Catharine"; "Isabella and the Moor: A Spanish Tale"; "Charles and Angelina. Or the Faithful Lovers"; "The Edrian Miner, an Austrian Tale"; "The Magic Dollar. A Tale of Alsace"; "The House on the Moors. A Tale"; "The Deserter"; "The Twin Sisters"; "Emily Glyndale"; "A Pennsylvanian Legend"; "Theodore Harland. A Premium Tale"; "The Happy Meeting"; "The Village Ball. Or Ella's Birth Day"; "The Starry Tower" [Henry Neele]; "Matilda Raymond, or One of My Grandmother's Stories"; "The Black Knight"; "Which Is the Bride? An Old English Tale"; "The Cousins. A Tale"; "The Soldier's Son"; "A New Tale of Temper" [Amelia Opie]; "Rosa St. Herbert, or the Maid of the Inn"; "The Ruse" [Nathaniel P. Willis]; "The Emigrant" [Sarah J. Hale]; "The House on the Cliff"; "The Election. A Tale" [Mary Russell Mitford]; "The Goldsmith of Westcheap"; "The Secrets of the Heart. A Tale"; "The Uneducated Wife"; "Frances, or the Effects of Jealousy"; "Clifton Rock. A Tale of the Year 1676"; "The Vendue"; "The Country Cousin"; "Wakonda, a Tale of the Frontiers"; "The Headsman. A Tale of Doom"; "Arthur of Avoca, or the Mystery of Mysteries"; "Ghost of My Uncle"; "The Irish Princess"; "The Merchant's Daughter"; "The Philadelphia Dun"; "The Triple Marriage"; "The Two Sisters" [Kotzebue]; "The Demon Ship; the Pirate of the Mediterranean"; "The Pearl Necklace"; "The Maniac Criminal"; "Mary Warren"; "The Pioneer; a Tale of the Mohawk"; "Manatonski; or, the Indian's Revenge"; "Ashton Grey"; "The Waggoner"; "Giulietta" [L.E. Landon]; "Two Yards of Jaconet, or a Husband. A Virginia Tale"; "The Rival Brothers; a

Tale of the Revolution"; "The Drover. A Tale"; "Boonesborough"; "The Rose of the Alhambra" [W. Irving]; "Poor Rosalie"; "The Double Marriage. A Tale"; "Lights and Shadows of New England Life"; "The Patriot Mother"; "A Sketch of Fashionable Life; a Tale"; "Timothy Pipkin"; "Kate Bouverie"; "The Intemperate" [Lydia H. Sigourney]; "Gertrude Beverly"; "Abaellino, the Bravo of Venice"; "The New Year's Gifts"; "Julia Gray, or the Orphan"; "The Dissenting Minister"; "The Martyr, a Tale of the American Revolution"; "The Wife of the Susquehannah, a Tale of the Last War"; "Selim and Zaida"; "Catharine"; "Wives of the Colony. A Tale of the Old Dominion"; "The Young Fisherman of the Palisades. A Historical Tale"; "The Thunder Storm. A Tale"; "The Brazilian Bride"; "The Wife. A Tale of America"; "The Melmoth Family"; "The Negro Insurrection. A Tale of New Orleans"; "Laura Lovel. A Sketch--For Ladies Only"; "The Fall of Bexar: A Texian Tale"; "Chase Loring. A Tale of the Revolution"; "The Old Maid's Legacy"; "The Spirit of the Potomac"; "You Can't Marry Your Grandmother"; "Isabel, the Orphan"; "The White Horseman"; "Lydia Ashbaugh, the Witch"; "May Martin, or the Money Diggers. A Green Mountain Tale"; "The Gunsmith of Orleans, or the Dead Woman's Secret"; "The Fatal Cosmetic; or, the Evils of 'White Lies'"; "El Bandelero"; "Ruth Deane; or, the Collegian's Sister"; "Angling; or, the Story of a Country Girl"; "The Price of a Heart"; "The Marriage Certificate"; Kellingham House, a Tale of the Suburbs of London"; "The Godfather"; "The Wordsworth Family. A Domestic Tale of New England"; "The Beggar-Girl of the Pont-des-arts"; "The Game of Chess"; "Mr. Chancy's Cooking Stove"; "Mary Morris, or Leaves from the Diary of a Gentleman"; "Lucy Pinkham; or, the Romance of Reality"; "The Scout: A Tale of the Woods of Maine"; "The Linen-Draper's Assistant"; "The Gipsey Mother; or, the Miseries of Enforced Marriage"; "Cardillac, the Jeweller"; "The Slave; or, Martinique in 1720"; "The Light Keeper"; "The Beautiful Unknown; or, the Dwarf and Massey Finke. A Tale of Philadelphia in Olden Time"; "The Silver Bottle: Or the Adventures of 'Little Marlboro' in Search of His Fortune"; "Nelly, the Rag-Gatherer"; "The Ugly Effie; or the Neglected One and the Pet-Beauty"; "The Magic Purse; or Leaves from the Portfolio of a Monomaniac"; "The Mute Doctor, or the Man with Many Names. A Tale of Passion"; "Sibyl Floyd"; "The Mysterious Stranger. A Tale of Passion, Founded on Fact"; "Kaam; or Daylight, the Arapahoe Half-Breed. A Tale of the Rocky Mountains"; "The Flower Fancier. A Domestic Story"; "Sense and Sympathy"; "Coralinn: A Persian Tale"; "Jacob Jones: Or the Man Who Couldn't Get Along in the World"; "Circumstantial Evidence"; "The Story of the Lucky Doctor"; "Ashburton: Or the Changes of Life"; "Irene Meredith. Or,

the Adventures of a Gold Watch"; "After the Ball; or, the Two Sir Williams"; "Our Village Post Office"; "Janet Allison's Two Rival Beaux"; "The Ruffian Boy. A Tale Founded on Fact"; "'Bear and Forbear'"; "Violet Vinton, or the Daughter's Influence--A Tale of Truth"; "Kuk Wiggins. The Man Who Ran Away from His Name"; "Mary Linton: Or, the World as It Is"; "The Dream, and the Parson's Wife. A Narrative Founded on Fact"; "The Governess"; "The Three Visits: 1705-1806-1840"; "The Dancing Feather, or the Amateur Free-booters."
Miscellaneous: Extracts: from other journals; by various authors. Anecdotes: on various subjects. News: Domestic.

762   TITLE: The Rural Repository, or Bower of Literature; Devoted Exclusively to Polite Literature, Comprised in the Following Subjects: Original and Select Tales, Essays, American and Foreign Biography, Travels, Notices of New Publications, Original and Select Poetry, Amusing Miscellany, Humorous and Historical Anecdotes, &c. &c. [See Rural Repository.]

763   TITLE: The Rural Visiter: A Literary and Miscellaneous Gazette.

Place of Publication: Burlington, N.J.
First Issue: 30 July 1810
Last Issue: 22 July 1811//
Periodicity: Weekly
Editor: ?
Publishers: D. Allinson and Co.
Available From: Univ. of Pa.*; Amer. Antiquarian Soc.*
Contents:
  Poetry: Original. Selected: John Blair Linn, Scott, Thomas Moore, Erasmus Darwin, Pope, Burns, James Montgomery, John Davis, Selleck Osborne, Anthony Pasquin, William Roscoe.
  Prose: Biography. Essay. Familiar Essay. Letters.
  Fiction: Essay Serials: "The Recorder"; "Orchardist"; "Lecturer"; "Mentor"; "Sojourner"; "Rhapsodist." Sketches. Tales: "The Twin Brothers of Mezzorania. A Tale"; "History of Alvira. A Tale of Truth."
  Miscellaneous: Extracts: from other journals; by various authors; David Hume. Anecdotes: on various subjects. News: Foreign and Domestic.

764   TITLES: (1) The Rush-Light (2) The Republican Rush-Light.

Place of Publication: Philadelphia
First Issue: 15 Feb 1800
Last Issue: 30 Aug 1800//?
Periodicity: Irregular
Editor: Peter Porcupine [Pseud. of William Cobbett]

Publisher: William Cobbett
Available From: APS; Lib. of Congress.*
                  Mott.
Contents:
  Poetry: Selected.
  Prose: Biography: Benjamin Rush. Letters.
  Miscellaneous: Anecdotes: Benjamin Rush,
    Noah Webster. Literary Notices.
Note: With volume II, Cobbett, now in England,
    is no longer focusing on Benjamin Rush,
    but on American-English relations.

765   TITLE: Rutgers Literary Miscellany. A Monthly
        Periodical.

Place of Publication: New Brunswick, N.J.
First Issue: Jan 1842
Last Issue: Dec 1842//
Periodicity: Monthly
Editors: Faculty members of Rutgers College
Publisher: Rutgers College
Available From: APS; Rutgers Univ.*
Contents:
  Poetry: Original: Mary L. Gardiner.
    Selected: Hannah F. Gould, Bryant,
    Felicia Hemans, Gray, Alfred B. Street.
  Prose: Biography: Hannah F. Gould, L.E.
    Landon, Bryant. Essay. Familiar Essay.
    Criticism.
  Fiction: Essay Serial: "The Student's
    Miscellanies." Sketches. Tales: "The
    Charm Broken"; "The Green Mountain Home,
    or the Apprentice. A Temperance Tale,
    Founded on Fact."
  Miscellaneous: Anecdotes: on various sub-
    jects. Literary Notices.

766   TITLE: The Salem Impartial Register. [See
        The Impartial Register.]

767   TITLE: Salmagundi, or, the Whim-Whams and
        Opinions of Launcelot Langstaff, & Others.

Place of Publication: New York
First Issue: 24 Jan 1807
Last Issue: 25 Jan 1808//
Periodicity: Irregular
Editor: Washington Irving
Publisher: David Longworth
Available From: APS; Harvard Univ.* Mott.
Contents:
  Poetry: Original: William Irving.
  Prose: Biography: Joseph Dennie. Familiar
    Essay.
  Fiction: Sketches.
Note: Salmagundi is, of course, a satirical
    journal and the model for others of
    its kind. Among the leading contributors
    were James Kirke Paulding, and Washington
    and William Irving.

768   TITLE: Salmagundi. Second Series. By
        Launcelot Langstaff, Esq.

Place of Publication: New York
First Issue: 30 May 1819
Last Issue: 19 Aug 1820//

Periodicity: Semi-monthly
Editor: James Kirke Paulding
Publishers: Haly and Thomas
Available From: APS; Harvard Univ.* Mott.
Contents:
  Poetry: Original.
  Prose: Essay. Familiar Essay. Letters.
  Fiction: Essay Serial: "From My Elbow
    Chair." Sketches. Tales: "The Old
    Ferry House"; "The Legend of Adam Engle-
    bright"; "The Bashaw of Cyprus"; "The
    Philanthropist."

769   TITLE: Sargent's New Monthly Magazine, of
        Literature, Fashion, and the Fine Arts.

Place of Publication: New York
First Issue: Jan 1843
Last Issue: June 1843//
Periodicity: Monthly
Editor: Epes Sargent
Publishers: Sargent & Company
Available From: APS; N.Y. Hist. Soc.*
Contents:
  Poetry: Original: Epes Sargent. Selected:
    Emma F. Allston, C.P. Cranch, Rufus Dawes,
    Frances S. Osgood, Oliver Wendell Holmes,
    Alfred B. Street, Nathaniel P. Willis,
    James G. Percival, Anna Cora Mowatt, Park
    Benjamin, Henry Stanhope Lee, Whittier,
    John Quincy Adams, James Kirke Paulding,
    Charles Fenno Hoffman.
  Prose: Biography. Familiar Essay. Letters.
  Fiction: Essay Serial: "The White Room."
    Tales: "The Blue-Stocking"; "An Incon-
    venient Acquaintance"; "The Old Apple
    Dealer" [Hawthorne]; "The Marquis in
    Petticoats" [Nathaniel P. Willis]; "The
    Antique Ring" [Hawthorne]; "Practitioners
    and Patients"; "A Sketch of Hahnemann and
    His Wife"; "A Matrimonial Mistake."

770   TITLE: Sartain's Union Magazine of Literature
        and Art. [See The Union Magazine of Litera-
        ture and Art.]

771   TITLE: The Satirist. A Journal of Criticism,
        Literature and Fine Arts.

Place of Publication: Albany
First Issue: [Only one issue published?]
              Feb 1842//?
Available From: Boston Pub. Lib.

772   TITLES: (1) The Satirist. By Lodowick
        Lash'em (2) The Boston Satirist; or Weekly
        Museum.

Place of Publication: Boston
First Issue: 16 Jan 1812
Last Issue: 9 May 1812//
Periodicity: Weekly
Editor: James L. Edwards
Publisher: James L. Edwards
Available From: APS; Lib. of Congress.* Mott.
Contents:
  Poetry: Original. Selected.

Prose: <u>Biography</u>. <u>Familiar Essay</u>. <u>Letters</u>.
Fiction: <u>Essay Serial</u>: "The Corrector."
  <u>Sketches</u>.
Miscellaneous: <u>Extracts</u>: from other jour-
  nals. <u>Anecdotes</u>: on various subjects;
  Joseph Dennie. <u>Literary Notices</u>.

773   TITLES: (1) <u>The Saturday Evening Post, an
  Illustrated Weekly Magazine</u> (2) <u>Atkinson's
  Saturday Evening Post</u> (3) <u>Atkinson's Saturday Evening Post, and Bulletin</u> (4) <u>Atkin-
  son's Evening Post, and Philadelphia Saturday News</u>.

Place of Publication: Philadelphia
First Issue: 18 Aug 1821
Last Issue: ?
Periodicity: Weekly
Editors: Thomas Cottrell Clarke; Morton
         McMichael; G.R. Graham; J.S.
         Du Solle; C.J. Peterson
Publishers: Atkinson & Alexander; S.C.
            Atkinson; Du Solle & Graham;
            G.R. Graham & Co.
Available From: APS; Hist. Soc. of Pa.*
                Mott.
Contents:
  Poetry: <u>Original</u>. <u>Selected</u>: R.S. Coffin,
    Thomas Moore, William Cowper, Thomas
    Campbell, Byron, William B. Tappan,
    Goldsmith, Selleck Osborne, Peter Pindar,
    James G. Percival.
  Prose: <u>Biography</u>: Mather Byles. <u>Essay</u>.
    <u>Familiar Essay</u>. <u>Criticism</u>. <u>Letters</u>.
    <u>Book Reviews</u>.
  Fiction: <u>Essay Serials</u>: "The Ladies'
    Friend"; "The Pedlar"; "The Observer";
    "The Miscellanist"; "The Essayist"; "The
    Medley"; "Sketches"; "The Solitaire";
    "The Itinerant"; "The Hogshead of Odd
    Things"; "Idle Hours"; "The Moralist";
    "Collectanea"; "Desultory Sheets."
    <u>Sketches</u>. <u>Tales</u>: "Fanny"; "The Wild
    Rose of the Valley. A Tale"; "The Prus-
    sian Soldier. A Story"; "Miles Colvine";
    "The Idle Man"; "The Grave. A Plain Un-
    varnished Tale"; "Guilt Triumphant over
    Innocence, or the Story of Emma Somerton";
    "The Rainbow"; "The Emigrant; or, the
    Bird of Paradise"; "The Fortunate Duel-
    lists"; "Tales of the Deep"; "Allan
    Campbell, or, the Minstrel Warrior. A
    Tale"; "Greenwich Hospital. A True Tale";
    "St. Andrew's Cross, or, Ada Dirleton. A
    Tale of the Ninth Century"; "The Infant
    Tecumseh. An American Tale"; "The Exile";
    "The Pirate's Bride"; "The Black Profes-
    sor of the Black Art--A True Tale"; "Emma
    Moreton, a West Indian Tale"; "The Wan-
    derer's Legacy, or, the Warlock of
    Rotherglen"; "The Only Daughter, or, the
    Rose of the Isle"; "Love and the Black-
    smith"; "The Indian of the Falls Valley,
    or, the Foundling Maid"; "Furgus Bane;
    or, the Sybel of Linlithglen"; "Albert
    Rollardo. An Original Tale."

Miscellaneous: <u>Extracts</u>: from other journals; by various authors; William Cowper,
  Scott, W. Irving, Franklin, James Fenimore
  Cooper. <u>Anecdotes</u>: on various subjects;
  Franklin, William Cowper, Swift, Chesterfield, Garrick, William Cobbett, Washington, Hogarth, Buonaparte, Byron, Colley
  Cibber. <u>Literary Notices</u>. <u>News</u>: Foreign
  and Domestic.

774   TITLE: <u>The Saturday Magazine: Consisting
  Principally of Selections from the Most
  Celebrated British Reviews, Magazines,
  and Scientific Journals</u>. [See <u>The Philadelphia Register, and National Recorder</u>.]

775   TITLE: <u>The Scourge. By Tim Touchstone, Esq</u>.

Place of Publication: Boston
First Issue: 10 Aug 1811
Last Issue: 28 Dec 1811//
Periodicity: Weekly
Editor: Merrill Butler
Publisher: James L. Edwards
Available From: APS; Amer. Antiquarian Soc.*
                Mott.

Contents:
  Poetry: <u>Original</u>. <u>Selected</u>: Thomas Moore,
    Gilpin.
  Prose: <u>Biography</u>: Buonaparte. <u>Essay</u>.
    <u>Familiar Essay</u>. <u>Letters</u>. <u>Book Reviews</u>.
  Fiction: <u>Essay Serial</u>: "The Observer and
    His Friend." <u>Sketches</u>.
  Miscellaneous: <u>Extracts</u>: from other jour-
    nals. <u>Anecdotes</u>: on various subjects.
    <u>Literary Notices</u>. <u>News</u>: Foreign and
    Domestic.

776   TITLE: <u>Scrap Book</u>. [See <u>The Miscellaneous
  Scrap Book. Devoted to Polite Literature,
  Such as Moral and Sentimental Tales, Instructive and Amusing Miscellany, Poetry, Anecdotes, &c</u>.]

777   TITLE: <u>The Select Circulating Library. Containing the Best Popular Literature, Including Memoirs, Biography, Novels, Tales,
  Travels, Voyages, &c</u>. [Running title:
  <u>Waldie's Select Circulating Library</u>.]

Place of Publication: Philadelphia
First Issue: 1 Oct 1832
Last Issue: April 1842//
Periodicity: Weekly
Editor: Adam Waldie
Publisher: Adam Waldie & Co.
Available From: Amer. Antiquarian Soc.;
                Lib. of Congress.*
Contents:
  Poetry: <u>Selected</u>: Wordsworth, Goldsmith,
    John Leyden, Thomas Haynes Bayly, Leigh
    Hunt, Schiller, Goethe, Bryant, Matthew
    Prior, Lydia H. Sigourney, James Mont-
    gomery, Felicia Hemans, James Hogg,

L.E. Landon, Dryden, Hartley Coleridge, Mrs. Abdy, Nicholas Biddle, Thomas Moore, Richard Howitt, Mary Howitt, Barry Cornwall.
Prose: Biography: Hannah More, William Cowper, Scott, Goldsmith, L.E. Landon. Travel. Criticism. Letters. Book Reviews.
Fiction: Tales: "Waldstein, or the Swedes in Prague"; "Klosterheim, or the Masque"; "The Hill and the Valley. A Politico-Economical Tale"; "The Gentle Recruit"; "Saratoga"; "Wacousta, or, the Prophecy; a Tale of Detroit and Michillimackinac"; "The Black Velvet Bag"; "Shipwreck of the Medusa, Comprising the Suffering of the Picard Family"; "Captain X----."; "Lady Barbara of Carloghie, and the Johnstons of Fairly. A Story of the Dominie"; "The Priors of Lawford"; "The Earthquake of Caraccas, a Tale of Venezuela"; "Arthur St. John"; "My Sister Kate"; "The German's Tale"; "Good Sir Walter"; "The Deaf and Dumb Page"; "Helen, a Tale" [Maria Edgeworth]; "The Curate's Tale, or Practical Joking"; "Jack the Shrimp"; "Bubbles from the Brunnens of Nassau"; "The Three Westminster Boys"; "Freya the Fearless, the Black Buccaneer of Barbadoes"; "High Life"; "The Broken Miniature"; "Alemoor, a Tale"; "The Two Scotch Williams"; "The Little Ferryman"; "The Lace Cap"; "Antonio, the Student of Padua"; "The Fashionable Wife and Unfashionable Husband"; "My Cousin Nicholas, or the Bullwinkles of Underdown Hall"; "The Cliffords of Craven. A Tradition"; "The Cruise of the Midge"; "The Odd-Tempered Man"; "A Tale of Trials; Told to My Children"; "The Pilgrims of Walsingham, or Tales of the Middle Ages"; "Hester"; "The Jordans of Grange, and the Old Maids of Balmogy"; "A Tale of Rosamund Gray and Old Blind Margaret" [Charles Lamb]; "Gilbert Gurney"; "The Widow's Dog"; "Clan-Albin; a National Tale"; "The Merchant's Clerk"; "The Dean of Santiago. A Tale from the Conde Lucanor"; "Schloss Hainfeld; or a Winter in Lower Styria"; "The Saracen, or Matilda and Malek: A Crusade Romance"; "The Great Unknown. A Tale"; "Libertino Genuchi. An Italian Story"; "Vincent Desborough. A Tale"; "The Nuwaub's Daughter"; "The Aristocrat's Wife. A Tale of the French Revolution"; "The City of the Sultan; and Domestic Manners of the Turks in 1836"; "Nat Phin and His Wife"; "Ethel Churchill; or, the Two Brides"; "The Augsburg Goldsmith. A Tale of the Fifteenth Century"; "The Household Wreck"; "The Kuzzilbash. A Tale of Khorasan"; "My Schoolmaster's Daughter. A Tale"; "The Queen's Diamonds"; "The Lace Merchant of Namur"; "Wedding Slippers" [Mary Russell Mitford]; "Yes and No. A Tale of the Day"; "Home; or, the Iron Rule. A Domestic Story"; "The Romance of the Harem"; "Monsieur Durance. The Man of the Two Adventures"; "The Blighted One. A True Tale"; "Maclean and Cameron; or, the Two Merchants"; "The

Contrast"; "The Absent Man"; "The Best Natured Man in the World"; "The Story of Mandrin, the Smuggler Captain"; "The Peasant and the Prince" [Harriet Martineau]; "Confessions of a Maniac"; "Kate Somerville"; "Joseph Rushbrook, or the Poacher." Novels: "Waltham"; "The Black Watch"; "Henry Quatre; or, the Days of the League"; "Crichton. An Historical Romance" [William Harrison Ainsworth]; "Picciola; or, Captivity Captive"; "Night and Morning." Drama: "The Broken Heart"; "Salvator Rosa, or the Portrait of Danae"; "Henriquez"; "The Match"; "The Homicide"; "The Stripling"; "Enthusiasm"; "The Separation."

778   TITLE: The Select Journal of Foreign Periodical Literature.

Place of Publication: Boston
First Issue: Jan 1833
Last Issue: Oct 1834//
Periodicity: Quarterly
Editors: Andrews Norton; Charles Folsom
Publisher: Charles Bowen
Available From: Univ. of Pa.*; Newberry Lib., Chicago.* Mott.
Contents:
  Poetry: Selected: Felicia Hemans, Tennyson, Beranger, Charles Lamb, James Shirley, Alicia LeFanu, Amelia Opie, Mary Howitt.
  Prose: Biography: LaFayette, Hegel, Johann Gottlieb Fichte, William Roscoe. Travel. Essay. Letters. Book Reviews.
  Miscellaneous: Extracts: from other journals.
Note: Primarily book reviews.

779   TITLES: (1) Select Reviews, and Spirit of the Foreign Magazines (2) Select Reviews of Literature, and Spirit of the Foreign Magazines. [Continued as the Analectic Magazine q.v.]

Place of Publication: Philadelphia
First Issue: Jan 1809
Last Issue: Dec 1812//
Periodicity: Monthly
Editors: Enos Bronson; Samuel Ewing
Publishers: Hopkins and Earle; John F. Watson
Available From: APS; Lib. of Congress.* Mott.
Contents:
  Poetry: Original. Selected: Burns, William Cowper, Milton, Peter Pindar, Amelia Opie, Charlotte Smith, William Congreve, Sterne, Southey, Byron, Joseph Blockett, John Poole, Anna Seward, Charles Dibdin, E.A. Elton, Mary Russell Mitford, James Montgomery, William Holloway, Henry Richard Wood, Scott, Chatterton, William Dimond, Joel Barlow.
  Prose: Biography: Richard Cumberland, Joshua Reynolds, Joseph Haydn, Benjamin West, Thomas Paine, Buonaparte, Bolingbroke, Penn. Travel. Essay. Familiar Essay. Criticism. Book Reviews.
  Fiction: Sketches. Tales: "The Kiss: Or, Mohamasim the Ass Driver"; "Story of Melissa."

Miscellaneous: Extracts: from other journals; by various authors; Charlotte Smith.
Anecdotes: on various subjects; Molière,
Isaac Newton, Addison, Steele.
Note: Included are many reviews on all subject areas, but primarily on literary
concerns.

780 TITLE: The Shamrock, or Hibernian Chronicle.

Place of Publication: New York
First Issue: 15 Dec 1810
Last Issue: 30 Jan 1813//
Periodicity: Weekly
Editor: Edward Gillesby
Publishers: Largin & Thompson; Edward
           Gillesby
Available From: Amer. Antiquarian Soc.*
Contents:
  Poetry: Selected: J. M'Creery, Swift,
    Thomas Moore, James Stuart, Hector M'Neil.
  Prose: Biography. Familiar Essay. Letters.
  Miscellaneous: Extracts: by various
    authors. Anecdotes: on various subjects.
    Literary Notices. News: Foreign and
    Domestic.

781 TITLE: Simms' Monthly Magazine. [See The
     Southern and Western Monthly Magazine and
     Review.]

782 TITLE: Smith's Weekly Volume, A Select Cir-
     culating Library for Town and Country, Con-
     taining the Best Popular Literature. [Mer-
     ged into the Anglo-American (New York).]

Place of Publication: Philadelphia
First Issue: 1 Jan 1845
Last Issue: 25 March 1846//
Periodicity: Weekly
Editor: Lloyd P. Smith
Publisher: Lloyd P. Smith
Available From: N.Y. Pub. Lib.*; Lib. of
              Congress*
Contents:
  Poetry: Selected: Eliza Cook, Nicholas
    Biddle, Charles Swain, Longfellow, Edward
    Moxon, Wordsworth, Schiller.
  Prose: Biography: Hannah More, Charlotte
    Smith, Elizabeth Inchbald, Lady Mary
    Wortley Montagu, Anna Letitia Barbauld,
    Anna Seward, Hester L. Thrale Piozzi,
    Fanny Burney, Mary Wollstonecraft, Ann
    Radcliffe, Jane Austen. Travel.
    Familiar Essay. Letters. Book Reviews.
  Fiction: Essay Serial: "Notes of a
    Bibliomaniac." Sketches. Tales: "The
    Three Kingdoms: England, Scotland, Ire-
    land"; "The Master-Passion: A Tale of
    Chamount"; "Texas and the Gulf of
    Mexico; or, Yachting in the New World";
    "Mademoiselle Lenormand; or, the Evils
    of Listening to a Parisian Fortune-Teller";
    "Ireland and the Irish"; "The Eventful
    Life of a Soldier"; "An Eligible Match;
    a Tale of a Country House"; "A Tale of
    Tweeddale"; "The Fresh Water Fisherman;
    a Tale"; "The Lay of the Labourer"

[Thomas Hood]; "The Hussar"; "The Wounded
Spirit; a Tale"; "The Cricket on the Hearth,
a Fairy Tale of Home" [Dickens].
Miscellaneous: Literary Notices.

783 TITLE: Something. Edited by Nemo Nobody, Esq.

Place of Publication: Boston
First Issue: 18 Nov 1809
Last Issue: 12 May 1810//
Periodicity: ?
Editors: ?
Publishers: ?
Available From: APS; Amer. Antiquarian Soc.*
              Mott.
Contents:
  Poetry: Original.
  Prose: Familiar Essay.
  Miscellaneous: Anecdotes: on various sub-
    jects. Literary Notices.

784 TITLE: South-Carolina Weekly Museum, and
     Complete Magazine of Entertainment and
     Intelligence. Containing a Great Variety
     of Original and Selected Essays, on Differ-
     ent Subjects, Poetry, Foreign and Domestic
     Intelligence, &c. &c.

Place of Publication: Charleston, S.C.
First Issue: 1 Jan 1797
Last Issue: July 1798//
Periodicity: Weekly
Editor: T.P. Bowen
Publishers: William Primrose Harrison and Co.
Available From: APS; N.Y. Hist. Soc.*
Contents:
  Poetry: Original. Selected: Thomas
    Penrose, John Scott, Miss Pennington,
    William Ashburnham, Matthew Gregory [Monk]
    Lewis, Burns, George Dyer, Miss Tomlins,
    Charles Lloyd, Helen Maria Williams,
    Robert Merry.
  Prose: Biography. Travel. Essay. Familiar
    Essay. Letters.
  Fiction: Essay Serial: "The Observor."
    Sketches. Tales: "Aucassin and Nicolette";
    "Orasmin and Almira, an Oriental Tale";
    "Remarkable History of the Chevalier
    Bayard"; "The Pyrenean Shepherds: A Frag-
    ment"; "Yonora: An American Indian Tale";
    "Bianca: A True Story"; "The Twin-Brothers
    of Mezzorania. A Mezzoranian Tale";
    "Leonora, or the Contending Families: An
    Heroic Tale"; "Love Triumphant"; "Ibrahim
    and Almira. An Eastern Tale"; "The Wel-
    come Disappointment. A Tale"; "The False
    Alarm. A Moral Story"; "Optimism. A
    Dream"; "Affecting History of St. Andre";
    "Feudal Consuetudes; or, the Superior and
    the Vassal. A Tale"; "The Reparation. A
    Tale"; "The Hermit of the Cavern. A
    Spanish Story"; "Marcus and Monimia."
  Miscellaneous: Extracts: from other jour-
    nals; by various authors; Mary Wollstone-
    craft, Sterne. Anecdotes: Swift, Donne,
    Dryden, Garrick. News: Foreign and
    Domestic.

785   TITLE: The Southern and Western Literary
       Messenger and Review: Devoted to Every
       Department of Literature and the Fine Arts.
       [See The Southern Literary Messenger: De-
       voted to Every Department of Literature and
       the Fine Arts.]

786   TITLE: The Southern and Western Monthly
       Magazine and Review. [Running title:
       Simms' Monthly Magazine. Merged into The
       Southern Literary Messenger q.v.]

       Place of Publication: Charleston, S.C.
       First Issue: Jan 1845
       Last Issue: Dec 1845//
       Periodicity: Monthly
       Editor: William Gilmore Simms
       Publishers: Burges & James
       Available From: APS; N.Y. Pub. Lib.*
       Contents:
         Poetry: Original: Adrian Beaufain, W.
           Gardner Blackwood, Bernard Hilton.
           Selected: Alfred B. Street, Nathaniel P.
           Willis, Schiller, Lydia H. Sigourney,
           Thomas Holley Chivers, J.M. Legare.
         Prose: Biography: Mason Locke Weems,
           Daniel Boone, Byron. Essay. Familiar
           Essay. Criticism. Book Reviews.
         Fiction: Essay Serials: "Time's Wallet";
           "The Epochs and Events of American
           History, as Suited to the Purposes of Art
           in Fiction." Sketches. Tales: "Those
           Old Lunes! Or, Which Is the Madman?";
           "The Last Feast of the Lucumo; or the
           Picture of the 'Grotto del Tifone'";
           "Oakatibbe; or the Choctaw Sampson"; "The
           Marion Family"; "Onslow; or the Protege
           of an Enthusiast. An Historical Tradi-
           tionary Tale of the South"; "The Snake
           of the Cabin"; "Bayard the Chevalier."
         Miscellaneous: Literary Notices.

787   TITLES: (1) The Southern Ladies' Book: A
       Magazine of Literature, Science and Arts
       (2) The Magnolia: Or Southern Monthly
       (3) The Magnolia; or, Southern Apalachian.
       A Literary Magazine and Monthly Review
       (4) The Magnolia; or Southern Monthly.

       Place of Publication: Macon, Ga.; Savannah,
                           Ga.; Charleston, S.C.
       First Issue: Jan 1840
       Last Issue: June 1843//
       Periodicity: Monthly
       Editors: Philip C. Pendleton; George F.
                Pierce; William Gilmore Simms
       Publishers: Philip C. Pendleton; George F.
                   Pierce; Burges & James; P.C.
                   Pendleton, and Burges & James
       Available From: Lib. of Congress; Univ. of
                           South Carolina, Columbia*
       Contents:
         Poetry: Original: Ellen B.H. Freeman,
           Mary E. Lee, Robert M. Charlton, A.B.
           Meek, John Love Lowrie, George W. Patten,
           J.E. Snodgrass, W.C. Richards, Mary
           Gertrude Kyle, James W. Simmons, William
           W. Holden, Edward J. Porter. Selected:
           R.H. Wilde, Goethe, Thomas Holley Chivers,

Charles Maturin, Park Benjamin, James
Hungerford.
         Prose: Biography. Travel. Essay. Familiar
           Essay. Criticism. Letters. Book Reviews.
         Fiction: Essay Serial: "Georgia Scenes."
           Sketches. Tales: "The Hero of the Lakes";
           "Emma and Gerral.--A Story"; "The Spirit
           of Contradiction.--A Tale"; "The Ghost
           Seer"; "The Knights of the Golden Horse-
           Shoe: A Traditionary Tale of the Cocked
           Hat Gentry in the Old Dominion"; "The Ad-
           ventures of the Last of the Abencerage";
           "The Loves of the Driver; a Story of the
           Wigwam" [William Gilmore Simms]; "The
           Conspirators; a Tale of 1790"; "The Last
           Song of the Biloxi. A Tradition of the
           South" [William Gilmore Simms]; "Myra
           Cunningham: A Tale of 1780"; "The Chief
           of the White Feather: A Tale of Florida";
           "Love and Consumption"; "The Clairvoyante:
           A Tale"; "The Peasant Queen. A Swedish
           Chronicle"; "Annihilation. A Romance of
           the Night"; "Castle Dismal; or, the
           Bachelor's Christmas; a Nouvellette"
           [George B. Singleton]; "Henry Herbert.--A
           Tale of the Revolution"; "Rhea Sylva";
           "Sturmer.--A Tale of Mesmerism"; "Turgesius
           --A Historical Romance of the Danish
           Dominion in Ireland"; "Colomba; or the
           Corsican Revenge. A Tale"; "The Bell of
           the Rock."
         Miscellaneous: Extracts: from other jour-
           nals; by various authors; W. Irving,
           Timothy Dwight, William Cowper. Anecdotes:
           on various subjects. Literary Notices.

788   TITLE: Southern Lady's Companion; a Monthly
       Periodical Devoted to Literature and
       Religion.

       Place of Publication: Nashville, Tenn.
       First Issue: 1847
       Last Issue: 1854//?
       Available From: State Hist. Soc. of Wis.,
                           Madison; Univ. of Texas,
                           Austin

789   TITLE: The Southern Lady's Magazine. A
       Monthly Journal, of Literature, Art and
       Science. [Running title: Garland's Lady's
       Magazine.]

       Place of Publication: Baltimore
       First Issue: April 1850
       Last Issue: May 1850//?
       Periodicity: Monthly
       Editors: H.M. Garland, Jr.; Margaret Piggot
       Publisher: H.M. Garland, Jr.
       Available From: Lib. of Congress*
       Contents:
         Poetry: Original. Selected: Southey,
           Alice Carey, Robert Bruce.
         Prose: Familiar Essay.
         Fiction: Sketches. Tales: "A True Tale
           of Hallowe'en"; "Zara; a Sketch of the
           East"; "A Trip over the Allegany Mountains;
           or, the Danger of Convicting on Circum-
           stantial Evidence"; "My Cousin Adele."

Miscellaneous: _Extracts_: from other journals; by various authors. _Anecdotes_: on
various subjects.

790 TITLES: (1) The Southern Literary Journal,
and Monthly Magazine (2) The Southern
Literary Journal, and Magazine of Arts.
[Superseded by _Southron_ (Tuscaloosa, Ala.).]

Place of Publication: Charleston, S.C.
First Issue: Sept 1835
Last Issue: Dec 1838//
Periodicity: Monthly
Editor: Daniel K. Whitaker
Publisher: Bartholomew R. Carroll
Available From: APS; Lib. of Congress.*
              Mott. _Poole_.
Contents:
  Poetry: _Original_: Anna Maria Wells, R.M.
    Charlton, William Gilmore Simms, B.B.
    Thatcher, James W. Simmons, William
    Keenan, John B. White. _Selected_: James
    Hogg, Schiller, Addison, Edward Carroll.
  Prose: _Biography_. _Essay_. _Familiar Essay_.
    Criticism. _Book Reviews_.
  Fiction: _Essay Serial_: "From Our Arm-
    Chair." _Sketches_. _Tales_: "The Maid of
    the Castle"; "A Tale of the Revolution";
    "The Cherokee Embassage"; "The Baron";
    "The Partisan"; "Death of Grierson"; "The
    Banished Lord"; "A Resurrection"; "Christ-
    mas in the Parishes"; "The Birthright of
    April"; "Bryhhilda"; "Ellen Reynolds";
    "A Sudden Cold"; "The Spirit Bridegroom";
    "The Fate of Alcestis"; "The Debut:--
    London"; "Sabrador"; "The Huntsman's Tale";
    "My Man Dick"; "The Pine Woods"; "The
    Nameless City"; "Thle-Cath-Cha; or the
    'Broken Arrow'"; "The Nuptials"; "Another
    Day at Chee-Ita"; "The Conspiracy";
    "Isabel of St. Augustine"; "The Investi-
    ture"; "The Outcast"; "Drogoole, the
    Tailor of Serendib"; "A Tale of Ashley";
    "Ipsistos"; "My First Love"; "The Con-
    script"; "The Outlaw's Daughter"; "Curran
    and the Pig"; "An Old Time Story";
    "Guiletta: Or, the Fair Hand"; "La Pola."
  Miscellaneous: _Extracts_: from other jour-
    nals; by various authors; Keats, Francis
    Bacon. _Anecdotes_: on various subjects;
    Franklin, Francis Bacon. _Literary Notices_.
  Note: One of the leading contributors was
    William Gilmore Simms.

791 TITLES: (1) The Southern Literary Messenger:
Devoted to Every Department of Literature
and the Fine Arts (2) The Southern and
Western Literary Messenger and Review: Devoted to Every Department of Literature and
the Fine Arts.

Place of Publication: Richmond
First Issue: Aug 1834
Last Issue: June 1864//
Periodicity: Monthly
Editors: James E. Heath; Edward V. Sparhawk;
         Thomas W. White; Edgar Allan Poe;
         Benjamin B. Minor; John R. Thompson;
         Matthew F. Maury; George W. Bagby;
         Frank H. Alfriend

Publishers: Thomas W. White; Benjamin B. Minor;
            John R. Thompson; Macfarlane &
            Fergusson; Wedderburn & Alfriend
Available From: APS; Lib. of Congress.*
              Mott. _Poole_.
Contents:
  Poetry: _Original_: Margaret Davidson, Park
    Benjamin, James F. Otis, William B. Fair-
    child, C.W. Everett, L.J. Cist, T.H.
    Shreeve, R.H. Gould, John S. Reid, George
    Wallis, Lydia Jane Pierson, S.J. Howe,
    A.B. Meek, E.B. Hale, Charles Fenno
    Hoffman, William Wallace, Bryant, Jane T.
    Lomax, Mrs. Seba Smith, C.J. Eames, E.C.
    Clemons, William B. Tappan, Henry B. Hirst,
    Mary Hewitt, E.H. Evans, Jane Taylor,
    Lydia H. Sigourney, John C. M'Cabe,
    Henry Thompson, F.W. Thomas, C.M.F. Deems,
    H.T. Tuckerman, S.S. Bradford, W.G.
    Blackwood, Longfellow, Poe, Mary S.B.
    Dana, Philip Pendleton Cooke, Sidney Dyer,
    J.C. Brent, William Gilmore Simms, B.W.
    Huntington, Marian Horton, Nathaniel P.
    Willis, Nathan C. Brooks. _Selected_:
    C.C. Felton, Schiller, Beranger, John
    Kenyon, Longfellow, George B. Singleton,
    Nathan C. Brooks, William Gilmore Simms,
    John C. M'Cabe, John Carroll Brent, R.H.
    Wilde, William Blackstone, Lucy T. Johnson,
    Poe, Timothy Flint, Lindley Murray, James
    Hogg, George Pope Morris, Hugh Blair,
    Mathew Carey, James Thomson, Alex Lacey
    Beard, George Watterston, Giles M'Quiggin,
    M.S. Lovett, Robert M. Bird, Edwin
    Saunders.
  Prose: _Biography_. _Travel_. _Essay_. _Familiar
    Essay_. _Criticism_. _Letters_. _Book Reviews_.
  Fiction: _Essay Serials_: "Glimpses into the
    Biography of a Nameless Traveller";
    "Readings with My Pencil"; "Marginalia"
    [Poe]. _Sketches_. _Tales_: "The Perils of
    Passion"; "Doctor Faw"; "The Governess";
    "Miss Hayley"; "A Couple of Love-Letters";
    "Constance Woodburn: A Tale of Every-Day
    Life"; "Pocahontas, the Indian Princess";
    "The Game of Chess"; "Jack-O'-Lantern:
    A New Light Story"; "The Bachelor's
    Death-Bed"; "Lucile: A Novelette";
    "Francis Armine, a Romance"; "The Adven-
    turess"; "Pelayo: A Romance of the Goth";
    "The Grave in the Forest"; "Dorcas
    Lindsay: Or, the Bachelor's Writing Desk";
    "Alice Richmond"; "Confessions of a Novel
    Reader"; "Transfigured--A Tale from the
    German"; "Sister Agnes: Or, the Doomed
    Vestal of the Hotel Dieu"; "The Predic-
    tion"; "The Magic Rock" [Park Benjamin];
    "The Blighted One"; "The Lover's Talisman;
    or, the Spirit Bride"; "The Missionary--
    A Tale"; "Story of Caliph Stork"; "The
    Return"; "Gertrude Hoffman"; "The Yellow
    Blossom of Glynn"; "The Motherless Daugh-
    ters"; "The German's Daughter"; "The
    Island of Cypress"; "Naked Hearts: Or,
    Confidential Correspondence. A Tale";
    "The Fatherless Daughter"; "Murty O'Hanley";
    "A Tale of the Little Lake"; "Coralinn:
    A Persian Tale"; "Florence Courtland";
    "The Winter Night's Club"; "The Muffled
    Priest"; "The Vow"; "The Enchanted Gifts";
    "Stephano Colonna, or Love and Lore"; "The

Sciote Captive"; "Woman's Influence";
"The Wheel of Life"; "An Over True
Tale"; "The Death Knell"; "Wilful Love";
"The Widow and Her Son"; "Mrs. Sad's
Private Boarding-House"; "The Iron Mask";
The Fortunes of Esther, the Jewess";
"The Speedwell. A Tale"; "John Carper,
the Hunter of Lost River"; "The Noted
Firm. A Tale"; "The Two Country-Houses";
"Where Is She? A Tale"; "The Rector's
Daughter"; "The Crime of Andrew Blair";
"The Captain's Story"; "The Seldens of
Sherwood"; "The Quakeress"; "Cupid's
Sport"; "Lionel Granby"; "Sully: A Tale
of the Blue Ridge"; "Constantine: Or,
the Rejected Throne"; "The Desenter: A
Romance of the American Revolution,
Founded on a Well Authenticated Incident";
"Love and Authorship"; "Misfortune and
Genius: A Tale Founded on Fact"; "The
Maid of Malines"; "Circumstantial Evi-
dence. A Tale Founded on Fact"; "The
Village or Fourth July 183-. A Tale";
"Berenice--A Tale" [Poe]; "A Tale of the
West, Founded on Fact"; "Morella--A Tale"
[Poe]; "Lionizing. A Tale" [Poe]; "Hans
Phaall--A Tale" [Poe]; "The Visionary--
A Tale" [Poe]; "Bon-bon--A Tale" [Poe];
"Loss of Breath. A Tale à la Blackwood"
[Poe]; "MS Found in a Bottle" [Poe];
"Metzengerstein. A Tale in Imitation of
the German" [Poe]; "The Duc de L'omelette"
[Poe]; "Epimanes" [Poe]; "A Tale of
Jerusalem" [Poe]; "Love and Constancy";
"Marco Visconti: A Tale of the Four-
teenth Century"; "Arthur Gordon Pym"
[Poe]; "Young Mortality's Memories";
"The Curse"; "The Spy: A Tale of the
Revolution"; "Olive Etherington";
"Spheeksphobia: Or, the Adventures of
Abel Stingflyer, A.M. A Tragic Tale";
"The Deserter"; "Memoir of the Ambitious
Lawyer": "My First Night in a Watch
House." Novels: "Gertrude"; "Norman
Leslie" [Theodore Sedgwick Fay].
Miscellaneous: Extracts: from other jour-
nals; by various authors; Wordsworth,
Keats, Nathaniel P. Willis, Fitz-Greene
Halleck, L.E. Landon, Leigh Hunt,
Voltaire, Franklin, Goethe. Anecdotes:
on various subjects; Dryden, Coleridge.
Literary Notices.

792　TITLE:　The Southern Quarterly Review.

Place of Publication: New Orleans; Charles-
　　　　　　　　　　　ton, S.C.
First Issue: Jan 1842
Last Issue: Feb 1857//
Periodicity: Quarterly
Editors: Daniel K. Whitaker; J. Milton
　　　　　Clapp; William Gilmore Simms;
　　　　　James H. Thornwell; James D.B.
　　　　　DeBow
Publishers: Daniel K. Whitaker; Burges &
　　　　　　　James; Walker and Richards;
　　　　　　　C. Mortimer; Edward H. Britton
Available From: Amer. Antiquarian Soc.*;
　　　　　　　　　Harvard Univ.* Mott. Poole.

Contents:
　Poetry: Selected: James A. Hillhouse,
　　Longfellow, James G. Percival, Mary S.B.
　　Dana, Lewis Foulk Thomas, Amelia Welby,
　　Cornelius Mathews, Elizabeth Barrett,
　　Byron, Fitz-Greene Halleck, Wordsworth,
　　Philip James Bailey, Richard Henry Dana,
　　Bayard Taylor, Ralph Hoyt.
　Prose: Biography: Thomas More, Byron,
　　Bolingbroke, Cromwell, Southey. Travel.
　　Essay. Familiar Essay. Criticism.
　　Letters. Book Reviews.
　Miscellaneous: Extracts: from other jour-
　　nals; by various authors. Anecdotes: on
　　various subjects. Literary Notices.
　Note: The journal contains review articles
　　on Longfellow, The Dial [q.v.] and trans-
　　cendentalism, Dickens, Macaulay, E. Lytton
　　Bulwer, Washington Allston, Whittier,
　　James G. Percival, Milton, Euguene Sue,
　　Rabelais, Elizabeth Barrett, W. Irving,
　　Hugh Swinton Legaré, Edward Everett,
　　Jonathan Edwards, Rufus Wilmot Griswold,
　　Goethe, Fanny Kemble, William Howitt,
　　William Gilmore Simms, Henry Mackenzie,
　　William Prescott, Carlyle, Chaucer, Words-
　　worth, Browning, Byrant, S. Johnson,
　　Richard Henry Dana, Lamartine, Melville,
　　Shakespeare, H.T. Tuckerman, Nathaniel P.
　　Willis.

793　TITLE:　The Southern Review.

Place of Publication: Charleston, S.C.
First Issue: Feb 1828
Last Issue: Feb 1832//
Periodicity: Quarterly
Editors: Stephen Elliott, Stephen Elliott,
　　　　　Jr.; Hugh Swinton Legaré
Publisher: A.E. Miller
Available From: APS; Lib. of Congress.*
　　　　　　　　　Mott. Poole.

Contents:
　Poetry: Selected: James G. Percival,
　　James Montgomery, Byron, B. Jonson, Samuel
　　Danforth, Benjamin Woodbridge, Michael
　　Wigglesworth, Roger Wolcott, Bryant.
　Prose: Biography. Travel. Essay.
　　Familiar Essay. Criticism. Book Reviews.

794　TITLE:　Southron: Or, Lily of the Valley
　　　　　　　Devoted to Literature, Instruction, Amuse-
　　　　　　　ment, etc.

Place of Publication: Gallatin, Tex.
First Issue: Jan 1841
Last Issue: Dec 1841//?
Available From: La. State Univ., Baton Rouge;
　　　　　　　　　Tenn. State Lib., Nashville

795　TITLE:　South-Western Journal. A Magazine of
　　　　　　　Science, Literature and Miscellany.

Place of Publication: Natchez, Miss.
First Issue: 15 Dec 1837
Last Issue: 30 July 1838//
Periodicity: Semi-monthly
Editor: J.A. Van Hoesen

Publishers: The Jefferson College and
            Washington Lyceum
Available From: Amer. Antiquarian Soc.;
                Amer. Philosophical Soc.,
                Philadelphia*
Contents:
  Poetry: <u>Original</u>: John P. Shannon.
    <u>Selected</u>: Bryant, Joseph Rodman Drake,
    Victor Hugo.
  Prose: <u>Biography</u>: John Quincy Adams.
    <u>Travel</u>. <u>Essay</u>. <u>Familiar Essay</u>. <u>Letters</u>.
    <u>Book Reviews</u>.
  Fiction: <u>Sketches</u>.
  Miscellaneous: <u>Anecdotes</u>: on various sub-
    jects. <u>News</u>: Foreign and Domestic.

796   TITLE: <u>Southwestern Literary and Monthly</u>
      <u>Review</u>. [See the <u>Western Literary Journal</u>
      <u>and Monthly Review</u>.]

797   TITLE: <u>The Souvenir, a Literary Work,</u>
      <u>Embellished with Engravings</u>.

      Place of Publication: Philadelphia
      First Issue: 4 July 1827
      Last Issue: 8 Dec 1830//
      Periodicity: Weekly
      Editor: Philip Price, Jr.
      Publisher: Philip Price, Jr.
      Available From: APS; Hist. Soc. of Pa.
      Contents:
        Poetry: <u>Original</u>. <u>Selected</u>: James
        Beattie, Felicia Hemans, Bryant, Shelley,
        Byron, L.E. Landon, James G. Percival,
        James Kirke Paulding, Amelia Opie, Lydia
        H. Sigourney, James Montgomery, Charles
        Sprague, Thomas Hood, T.K. Hervey, Anna
        Seward, Coleridge, Matthew Gregory [Monk]
        Lewis, John Bowring, Joanna Baillie,
        Emma C. Embury, Grenville Mellen,
        Charles Swain, Nathaniel P. Willis,
        Sarah J. Hale, Wordsworth, William
        Roscoe.
        Prose: <u>Biography</u>: Coleridge, Felicia
        Hemans, Fitz-Greene Halleck, John Quincy
        Adams, Jefferson. <u>Essay</u>. <u>Familiar Essay</u>.
        <u>Book Reviews</u>.
        Fiction: <u>Essay Serial</u>: "Sketches, by a
        Solitary Rambler." <u>Sketches</u>. <u>Tales</u>:
        "The Spectre's Voyage"; "Elphin Irving,
        the Fairies' Cupbearer"; "Annette
        Laranne"; "Miles Colvine"; "Josephine,
        the German Emigrant"; "The Covenanter's
        Marriage Day"; "The Widow's Son, or the
        Story of a Brother-in-Law"; "The Minister's
        Beat"; "Mary Allan"; "Insurance and As-
        surance"; "The Rose in January"; "The
        Married Actress"; "A Roland for an
        Oliver. A Tale of the Revolution"; "A
        Bridal in the Early Settlements";
        "Caroline Hartland"; "Love Will Find a
        Way Out"; "Henry Staunton"; "The Sun
        Dial"; "Emily Clarendon"; "Bebut the
        Ambitious. A Persian Tale"; "The
        Euthanasia. A Story of Modern Greece";
        "The Tapestried Chamber. Or the Lady in
        the Sacque" [Scott]; "The Wife of Seven
        Husbands."

Miscellaneous: <u>Extracts</u>: from other journals; by various authors; Thomas Hood,
  Charles Lamb, James Fenimore Cooper.
  <u>Anecdotes</u>: on various subjects; Swift,
  Pope, Addison, Abraham Cowley, Goldsmith,
  Schiller, Franklin. <u>Literary Notices</u>.
  <u>News</u>: Foreign and Domestic.

798   TITLE: <u>The Souvenir: A Monthly Magazine,</u>
      <u>Devoted to Historical Tales, Historical and</u>
      <u>Biographical Sketches, Antiquarian Re-</u>
      <u>searches, Poetry, and General Miscellany</u>.

      Place of Publication: New York
      First Issue: [Only five issues published]
                   1848//
      Periodicity: Monthly
      Editor: Isaac Wescott
      Publisher: Berford and Company
      Available From: Lib. of Congress; N.Y. State
                      Lib., Albany*
      Contents:
        Poetry: <u>Selected</u>: Ralph Hoyt, Whittier,
        Lydia H. Sigourney, Eliza Cook.
        Prose: <u>Biography</u>. <u>Travel</u>. <u>Familiar Essay</u>.
        Fiction: <u>Essay Serial</u>: "Curiosities of
        the Eighteenth Century." <u>Sketches</u>.
        <u>Tales</u>: "The Fatal Deception. A Tale";
        "Caonabo: Or, the Cazique of Maguano";
        "Frederick and Adelia; or, the Ways of
        Providence"; "The American Deserters.
        A Tale of the Revolution."
        Miscellaneous: <u>Anecdotes</u>: on various sub-
        jects; Washington, Goethe. <u>Literary</u>
        <u>Notices</u>.

799   TITLE: <u>Spectacles</u>.

      Place of Publication: Baltimore
      First Issue: 6 June 1807
      Last Issue: 18 July 1807//
      Periodicity: Weekly
      Editor: Joseph Harmer
      Publisher: Joseph Harmer
      Available From: APS; Amer. Antiquarian Soc.
      Contents:
        Poetry: <u>Original</u>.
        Prose: <u>Familiar Essay</u>. <u>Letters</u>.
        Miscellaneous: <u>Extracts</u>: Hugh Henry
        Brackenridge. <u>Anecdotes</u>: on various
        subjects; Samuel Foote, Garrick.

800   TITLE: <u>The Spirit of '76</u>.

      Place of Publication: Nashville, Tenn.
      First Issue: 25 April 1844
      Last Issue: 26 Aug 1847//
      Available From: Chicago Hist. Soc.; Tenn.
                      State Lib., Nashville

801   TITLE: <u>Spirit of the Forum, and Hudson</u>
      <u>Remarker</u>.

      Place of Publication: Hudson, N.Y.
      First Issue: [Only one issue published?]
                   16 April 1817//?

Periodicity: ?
Editors: an Association of Gentlemen
Publishers: ?
Available From: APS; Lib. of Congress
Contents:
  Poetry: Original.
  Prose: Essay.

802   TITLE: The Spirit of the Pilgrims.

Place of Publication: Boston
First Issue: Jan 1828
Last Issue: Dec 1833//
Periodicity: Monthly
Editors: ?
Publishers: Peirce and Williams
Available From: Lib. of Congress*; Harvard
                Univ.*
Contents:
  Prose: Biography: John Calvin, Coleridge,
  William Cowper, Thomas Paine, Fisher
  Ames, Richard Baxter, Ezra Stiles.
  Travel. Essay: "Death-Bed of Dr. John-
  son"; "Reflections Occasioned by the
  Death of Lord Byron, with Some Account of
  His Character." Familiar Essay. Letters.
  Book Reviews.
  Miscellaneous: Extracts: from other jour-
  nals; by various authors; Mather Byles,
  Washington. Anecdotes: on various sub-
  jects; Cotton Mather, Isaac Newton.
  Literary Notices.
Note: Although the journal is primarily
  religious in content, it is of literary
  interest.

803   TITLE: The Spirit of the Public Journals;
       or, Beauties of the American Newspapers,
       for 1805.

Place of Publication: Baltimore
First Issue: 1805//
Periodicity: Annual
Editor: George Bourne
Publisher: George Dobbin & Murphy
Available From: APS; Amer. Antiquarian Soc.*
Contents:
  Poetry: Selected: John Davis
  Prose: Essay. Familiar Essay.
  Fiction: Sketches. Tale: "Honesty the
  Best Policy."
  Miscellaneous: Extracts: from other jour-
  nals. Anecdotes: on various subjects.
Note: The extracts are from approximately
  90 American newspapers--not from literary
  or miscellaneous journals.

804   TITLE: The Stand.

Place of Publication: Hartford, Conn.
First Issue: 21 Dec 1819
Last Issue: 14 Aug 1820//?
Periodicity: Irregular
Editors: a Society of Young Men
Publishers: ?
Available From: APS; Boston Athenaeum

Contents:
  Poetry: Original. Selected: Burns.
  Prose: Familiar Essay.

805   TITLE: The Standard Library: A Weekly
       Republication of Romance, Biography,
       History, Travels, &c. &c. &c.

Place of Publication: New York
First Issue: 20 Feb 1841
Last Issue: 15 May 1841//?
Periodicity: Weekly
Editors: Francis A. Bonnard; William
          Fitzgerald
Publishers: Bonnard & Fitzgerald; Francis
             A. Bonnard
Available From: Amer. Antiquarian Soc.*
Contents:
  Prose: Essay.
  Fiction: Tales: "Stories of Waterloo";
  "The Subaltern; or, Sketches of the
  Peninsular War, During the Campaigns of
  1813, 1814."

806   TITLE: The Stranger.

Place of Publication: Albany
First Issue: 3 July 1813
Last Issue: 25 June 1814//
Periodicity: Weekly
Editor: John Cook
Publisher: John Cook
Available From: APS; Harvard Univ.*
Contents:
  Poetry: Original. Selected: Thomas Moore,
  Scott, Byron, Thomas Campbell, Erasmus
  Darwin, Southey, Herrick, Keats, Peter
  Pindar, William Robert Spencer, Samuel
  Rogers.
  Prose: Biography: Byron, Madame Du Deffand.
  Travel. Essay. Familiar Essay. Criti-
  cism. Letters. Book Reviews.
  Fiction: Essay Serial: "The Melange."
  Sketches. Tale: "Truth.--An Indian Tale."
  Miscellaneous: Extracts: from other jour-
  nals; by various authors; William Cowper,
  Southey. Anecdotes: on various subjects;
  Cervantes, Daniel Webster, Christopher
  Smart, George Whitefield, S. Johnson,
  Addison. Literary Notices.

807   TITLE: The Student; Devoted to Literature,
       Religion and Education.

Place of Publication: Watertown, N.Y.
First Issue: 1 Aug 1837
Last Issue: 2 July 1838//
Available From: N.Y. State Lib., Albany

808   TITLE: The Subterranean.

Place of Publication: New York
First Issue: 24 May 1845
Last Issue: 22 May 1847//
Periodicity: Weekly

Editor: Mike Walsh
Publisher: Mike Walsh
Available From: APS; N.Y. Pub. Lib.
Contents:
  Poetry: Original: George D. Prentice,
    Henry Kirke White, John G. Brainard,
    Anne C. Lynch, James Montgomery, Eliza
    Cook, Longfellow, H.H. Clements, T.B.
    Read. Selected: Keats, Charles MacKay,
    Byron, Thomas Hood, Thomas Campbell,
    Beranger, John P. Shannon, William Black-
    wood, William J. Snelling, Lydia H.
    Sigourney, Mary L. Gardiner, Alaric Watts.
  Prose: Essay. Familiar Essay. Criticism.
  Fiction: Sketches. Tales: "The Heir of
    Linn"; "Friendship of a Panther, or, a
    Soldier in the Desert"; "The Quaker's
    Daughter. A Story of Old Salem"; "Emma
    Morton. A Tale of Boston and Its En-
    virons"; "The Lieutenant's Tale, or the
    Condemned Soldier's Last Hour. A Tale
    of the Florida War"; "The Young Rebel.
    A Tale of the Carolinas"; "The Judge's
    Charge"; "The Deserted One"; "The Dove
    of the Storm"; "The Last Offer."
  Miscellaneous: Anecdotes: on various sub-
    jects.

809   TITLE: The Sword and Pen, a Journal of
       Literature, Politics and Military Science.

       Place of Publication: New York
       First Issue: 1 Oct 1840
       Last Issue: July 1841//?
       Available From: N.Y. State Lib., Albany;
                       Univ. of Mich., Ann Arbor

810   TITLE: The Tablet. A Miscellaneous Paper,
       Devoted to the Belles Lettres.

       Place of Publication: Boston
       First Issue: 19 May 1795
       Last Issue: 11 Aug 1795//
       Periodicity: Weekly
       Editor: Joseph Dennie
       Publisher: William Spotswood
       Available From: APS; Amer. Antiquarian Soc.*
                       Mott.
       Contents:
         Poetry: Original. Selected: Thomas
           Holcroft, James Pye.
         Prose: Biography: William Drummond, Adam
           Smith, Edmund Burke.
         Fiction: Essay Serials: "The Farrago";
           "From the Shop of Messrs. Colon &
           Spondee" [by Joseph Dennie and Royall
           Tyler. From the Farmer's Weekly Museum
           q.v.]

811   TITLE: The Talisman. [Reissued in 1833 as
       Miscellanies.]

       Place of Publication: New York
       First Issue: 1828
       Last Issue: 1830//
       Periodicity: Annual
       Editor: Francis Herbert
       Publisher: Elam Bliss

Available From: APS; N.Y. Pub. Lib.*
Contents:
  Poetry: Original. Selected.
  Prose: Travel. Familiar Essay.
  Fiction: Tales: "Mr. de Viellcour and His
    Neighbors. A Tale, Moral and Chirographic-
    al"; "Major Edgerton"; "The Legend of the
    Devil's Pulpit"; "The Little Old Man of
    Coblentz"; "Drummond. A Tale of the Dis-
    mal Swamp"; "The Indian Spring"; "The
    Peregrinations of Petrus Mudd"; "The
    Marriage Blunder."

812   TITLE: The Temperance Advocate and Literary
       Repository.

       Place of Publication: Philadelphia
       First Issue: 31 July 1841
       Last Issue: 1 July 1843//?
       Available From: N.Y. Hist. Soc.

813   TITLE: The -----------. By Nonius Nondescript,
       Esq.

       Place of Publication: Washington, D.C.
       First Issue: 18 Feb 1826
       Last Issue: 18 May 1826//?
       Periodicity: Irregular
       Editor: ?
       Publisher: Pishey Thompson
       Available From: APS
       Contents:
         Poetry: Original. Selected: Thomas Moore.
         Prose: Familiar Essay. Letters.
         Fiction: Sketches. Tales: "The Back-
           woodsman in Washington"; "The Birth-Place
           of the Hero."

814   TITLES: (1) The Theatrical Censor. By an
       American (2) The Theatrical Censor. By a
       Citizen.

       Place of Publication: Philadelphia
       First Issue: 9 Dec 1805
       Last Issue: 3 March 1806//
       Periodicity: Bi-weekly
       Editors: John Watts; John Phillips
       Publishers: John Watts; John Phillips
       Available From: APS; Amer. Antiquarian Soc.*
                       Mott.
       Contents:
         Prose: Biography: Fennell. Letters.
       Note: Contains reviews of plays: R. B.
         Sheridan's School for Scandal; Thomas
         Holcroft, George Colman, Shakespeare,
         Colley Cibber, Matthew Gregory [Monk]
         Lewis.

815   TITLE: The Thespian Mirror: A Periodical
       Publication. Comprising a Collection of
       Dramatic Biography, Theatrical Criticism,
       Miscellaneous Literature, Poetry, &c. &c.

       Place of Publication: New York
       First Issue: 28 Dec 1805
       Last Issue: 31 May 1806//
       Periodicity: Weekly [Irregular]

Editor: John Howard Payne
Publisher: Southwick & Hardcastle
Available From: APS; Harvard Univ.* Mott.
Contents:
  Poetry: Original.
  Prose: Biography: Fennell, Thomas Cooper, Garrick.
  Fiction: Tale: "Sophia Woodbine. A Tale of Truth from the MSS. of a Lady."
  Miscellaneous: Anecdotes: on various dramatic subjects; Arbuthnot.
Note: Contains reviews of Nicholas Rowe, Fennell, Thomas Cooper.

816   TITLE: The Thespian Monitor, and Dramatick Miscellany.

Place of Publication: Philadelphia
First Issue: 25 Nov 1809
Last Issue: 16 Dec 1809//?
Periodicity: Weekly
Editor: "Barnaby Bangbar, Esq."
Publisher: Mathew Carey
Available From: APS; Lib. of Congress.
                Mott.
Contents:
  Prose: Biography: Thomas Morton.
  Miscellaneous: Extracts: by various authors and dramatists. Literary Notices.
Note: Contains reviews and synopses of plays by Thomas Morton, Kotzebue, William Dunlap, Thomas Holcroft, George Colman, Shakespeare.

817   TITLE: Thespian Oracle, or Monthly Mirror.

Place of Publication: Philadelphia
First Issue: [Only one issue published]
            Jan 1798//
Periodicity: Intended to be monthly
Editors: ?
Publisher: T.B. Freeman
Available From: APS; Hist. Soc. of Pa.*
Contents:
  Poetry: Original.
  Miscellaneous: Anecdotes: Shakespeare, S. Johnson.

818   TITLE: The Thistle; a Literary Journal.

Place of Publication: Cincinnati
First Issue: [Only one issue published?]
            18 Nov 1822//?
Available From: Hist. and Philosophical Soc.
                of Ohio, Cincinnati; Ohio
                State Hist. Soc., Columbus

819   TITLE: The Thistle. An Original Work, Containing a Great Many Good Things.

Place of Publication: Boston
First Issue: 4 Aug 1807
Last Issue: 1 Sept 1807//?
Periodicity: Semi-monthly
Editor: "Roderic Rover, Esq."
Publishers: Etheridge & Bliss
Available From: APS; Amer. Antiquarian Soc.

Contents:
  Poetry: Original.
  Prose: Familiar Essay: "Uncle Isaac's Ramble" [lighthearted, no consequence articles on various subjects].
  Miscellaneous: Anecdotes: on various subjects.
Note: Motto: "This, That, and T'other; Witticisms and Criticisms."

820   TITLE: Thomas's Massachusetts Spy or, American Oracle of Liberty. [See The Massachusetts Spy.]

821   TITLE: Thomas's Massachusetts Spy or, the Worcester Gazette. [See The Massachusetts Spy.]

822   TITLE: The Tickler.

Place of Publication: Philadelphia
First Issue: 16 Sept 1807
Last Issue: 17 Nov 1813//?
Periodicity: Weekly
Editor: "Toby Scratch'em"
Publisher: George Helmbold, Jr.
Available From: APS; Amer. Antiquarian Soc.
                Mott.
Contents:
  Poetry: Selected: Anthony Pasquin, Leigh Hunt, James Thomson, Fessenden.
  Prose: Biography. Letters.
  Miscellaneous: Extracts: from other journals; by various authors. Anecdotes: on various subjects; Franklin. News: Domestic.

823   TITLES: (1) The Time-Piece, and Literary Companion (2) The Time Piece.

Place of Publication: New York
First Issue: 13 March 1797
Last Issue: 30 Aug 1798//
Periodicity: Tri-weekly
Editors: Philip Freneau; Alexander Menut;
         Matthew L. Davis; Robert Saunders
Publishers: P. Freneau & A. Menut; P. Freneau & M.L. Davis; M.L. Davis & Co.; Robert Saunders
Available From: APS; State Hist. Soc. of
                Wis., Madison.* Mott.
Contents:
  Poetry: Original. Selected: William Roscoe, Mary Robinson, Sterne, William Doddridge.
  Prose: Biography: LaFayette. Travel. Familiar Essay. Letters.
  Fiction: Essay Serial: "The Cluster." Sketches. Tale: "Tomo Cheeki. The Creek Indians in Philadelphia."
  Miscellaneous: Extracts: from other journals; by various authors; Edmund Bruke, Swift, Thomas Campbell, Jefferson, Thomas Paine, Edward Young, Sterne. Anecdotes: on various subjects; S. Johnson, Boswell, George Whitefield, Topham Beauclerk, Dryden, Pope, Thomas Otway, Cromwell,

Edmund Waller, Swift, Milton, Francis Bacon, Thomas Paine. Literary Notices. News: Domestic.

824 TITLE: The Times.

Place of Publication: Boston
First Issue: 12 Dec 1807
Last Issue: 15 Oct 1808//
Periodicity: Weekly
Editors: ?
Publishers: Oliver & Munroe
Available From: Amer. Antiquarian Soc.*
Contents:
  Poetry: Original. Selected: William Cowper.
  Prose: Essay. Familiar Essay.
  Fiction: Sketches. Tales: "Alphonso and Emily"; "Sinclair."
  Miscellaneous: Anecdotes: on various subjects. Literary Notices. News: Foreign and Domestic.

825 TITLE: The Toilet: A Weekly Collection of Literary Pieces, Principally Designed for the Amusement of the Ladies.

Place of Publication: Charleston, S.C.
First Issue: 17 Jan 1801
Last Issue: 7 March 1801//?
Periodicity: Weekly
Editors: ?
Publisher: Samuel Etheridge
Available From: APS; Amer. Antiquarian Soc.*
Contents:
  Poetry: Selected.
  Prose: Biography. Familiar Essay. Criticism. Letters.
  Fiction: Essay Serials: "The Female Observer"; "The Censor"; "Sketch." Sketches.
  Miscellaneous: Extracts: Dryden.

826 TITLE: The Toilet, or Ladies' Cabinet of Literature.

Place of Publication: Providence, R.I.
First Issue: 5 Jan 1828
Last Issue: 17 Jan 1829//?
Periodicity: Weekly
Editor: S.M. Fowler
Publishers: Smith & Parmenter
Available From: Amer. Antiquarian Soc.; Brown Univ., Providence, R.I.*
Contents:
  Poetry: Original. Selected: Felicia Hemans, Francis Quarles, Emma Roberts.
  Fiction: Sketches. Tales: "The New-Zealander. A Tale Founded on Fact"; "Charles Gloster, or the Breath of Slander."
  Miscellaneous: Anecdotes: on various subjects. News: Domestic.

827 TITLE: The Town.

Place of Publication: New York
First Issue: 1 Jan 1807
Last Issue: 12 Jan 1807//?
Periodicity: Irregular--several times weekly
Editors: ?
Publisher: J. Osborn
Available From: APS; N.Y. State Lib., Albany*
Contents:
  Poetry: Original. Selected.
  Prose: Letters: "Roger de Coverley" [Addison].
  Fiction: Essay Serial: "My Scissors."
  Miscellaneous: Literary Notices.
Note: A periodical devoted to the analysis of plays by Goldsmith et al., actors [Thomas Cooper, Garrick], and reviews of plays.

828 TITLES: (1) The Town (2) The Town and American Punch.

Place of Publication: New York
First Issue: 15 Feb 1845
Last Issue: 26 July 1845//?
Periodicity: Weekly
Editors: "The Council of Ten"
Publishers: Andrews, Beaumont & Co.; Ira Oliver Beaumont & Co.
Available From: Lib. of Congress*; Boston Pub. Lib.*
Contents:
  Poetry: Original.
  Prose: Familiar Essay. Letters.
  Miscellaneous: Extracts: from other journals; by various authors; Nathaniel P. Willis. Anecdotes: on various subjects; Park Benjamin, Nathaniel P. Willis, W. Irving, John Neal, Evert Duyckinck, Bryant, Sarah J. Hale, Lydia H. Sigourney, Catharine M. Sedgwick, Beranger, Epes Sargent, Cornelius Mathews, Margaret Fuller.
Note: A satirical, whimsical periodical. "A Weekly Paper of Fun, Frolic and Philosophy."

829 TITLE: The Truth, by J. Ironside.

Place of Publication: New Haven, Conn.
First Issue: Sept 1819
Last Issue: Oct 1819//
Periodicity: Monthly
Editors: ?
Publishers: ?
Available From: APS; Yale Univ.*
Contents:
  Poetry: Original. Selected: Arbuthnot.
  Prose: Familiar Essay.
  Fiction: Essay Serial: "The Round Table." Sketches.

830 TITLE: The Two Worlds: A Weekly Journal of American and European Literature, News, Science and the Fine Arts.

Place of Publication: New York
First Issue: 2 Feb 1850
Last Issue: 26 Oct 1850//?
Periodicity: Weekly
Editors: John J. Bailey; William Rose
          Wallace; Spencer Wallace Cone
Publishers: J.L. Lockwood & Co.; William
          B. Parker
Available From: Amer. Antiquarian Soc.*;
          Harvard Univ.*
Contents:
  Poetry: Original: William Wallace, R.N.
    Cromwell, Marcus H. Trowbridge, J. Webb,
    H.H. Clements. Selected: Mary E. Hewitt,
    Leigh Hunt, Schiller, James Montgomery,
    George Pope Morris, Thomas Campbell.
  Prose: Biography: John Sterling, Thomas
    Hood, Wordsworth, Shelley. Travel.
    Essay. Familiar Essay. Book Reviews.
  Fiction: Essay Serials: "Ramblings of a
    Humorist"; "Leaves from a Note Book."
    Sketches. Tales: "The Margrave";
    "Giuseppe: Founded Upon Facts of Real
    Life"; "The Onyx Ring"; "The Floating
    Beacon"; "The Rival Brothers: Or, the
    Chamois Hunters"; "A Wedding 'Above
    Bleeker'"; "Leonora di Tarento; or the
    Anointers of Milan"; "Julia de Fenes-
    tranges"; "Falkenstein. A Tale of
    Germany"; "Blanche Rose. A Love Story
    of the Twelfth Century"; "The Prima
    Donna of Madrid."
  Miscellaneous: Extracts: from other jour-
    nals. Anecdotes: on various subjects;
    Shakespeare, Carlyle, Goldsmith,
    S. Johnson. Literary Notices. News:
    Foreign and Domestic.

831 TITLES: (1) Uncle Ezekiel's Youth's Cabinet
     (2) Uncle Ezekiel's Youth's Cabinet. A
     Semi-Monthly Journal, Devoted to the
     Interests of Youth (3) Uncle Ezekiel's
     Youth's Cabinet. A Monthly Journal,
     Devoted to the Interests of Youth.

Place of Publication: Concord, N.H.
First Issue: 1844
Last Issue: 15 March 1846//?
Periodicity: Semi-monthly; Monthly
Editor: "Ezekiel Loveyouth"
Publisher: J.F. Witherell
Available From: Amer. Antiquarian Soc.;
          New Hampshire State Lib.,
          Concord
Contents:
  Poetry: Original: C.B.P. Witherell.
    Selected: Frances S. Osgood.
  Prose: Biography: Washington. Essay.
    Letters.
  Fiction: Sketches. Tales: "Brave Bobby
    and His Little Master"; "The Dogs of
    St. Bernard"; "Mark Maxwell: Or I Can
    and I Will"; "Auto-Biography of an Old
    News-Paper"; "Adventures of Jack Fear-
    less."
  Miscellaneous: Anecdotes: on various
    subjects.

832 TITLE: Uncle Jesse's Gazette.

Place of Publication: Concord, N.H.
First Issue: 5 Jan 1848
Last Issue: 6 Dec 1848//?
Available From: Dartmouth Coll., Hanover,
          N.H.

833 TITLE: The Union Herald, Devoted to the
     diffusion of Religious Knowledge, Select
     Miscellany, Literature and General Intel-
     ligence.

Place of Publication: Cazenovia, N.Y.
First Issue: April 1842
Last Issue: ?
Available From: N.Y. State Lib., Albany;
          N.Y. Hist. Soc.

834 TITLES: (1) The Union Magazine of Literature
     and Art (2) Sartain's Union Magazine of
     Literature and Art.

Place of Publication: New York; Philadelphia
First Issue: July 1847
Last Issue: Aug 1852//
Periodicity: Monthly
Editors: Mrs. Caroline M. Kirkland; John S.
          Hart; Reynell Coates; John Sartain
Publishers: Israel Post; John Sartain and
          William Slonaker; John Sartain
          & Co.; James L. DeGraw
Available From: APS; Lib. of Congress.*
          Mott.
Contents:
  Poetry: Original: M.N. McDonald, R.H.
    Stoddard, William Wallace, Edith May,
    Emma C. Embury, Nathaniel P. Willis,
    Elizabeth Emmet, Mary S.B. Dana, Long-
    fellow, Caroline May, James Russell
    Lowell, S.C, Kinney, Mary E. Hewitt,
    Louise O. Hunter, John H. Bryant, H.J.
    Woodman, J. Hagen, D. Ellen Goodman,
    Lydia H. Sigourney, Hannah F. Gould,
    Frances S. Osgood, Francis C. Woodworth,
    Charles Fenno Hoffman, Park Benjamin,
    William Gilmore Simms, H.P. Grattan,
    John G. Saxe, Poe, W.H.C. Hosmer, Anne
    C. Lynch, George S. Burleigh. Selected:
    Lydia H. Sigourney, Hannah F. Gould,
    Frances S. Osgood, Francis C. Woodworth.
  Prose: Essay. Familiar Essay. Criticism.
    Book Reviews.
  Fiction: Essay Serials: "Sight-Seeing in
    Europe" [Mrs. Caroline M. Kirkland];
    "Ktaadn, and the Maine Woods" [Thoreau];
    "Roanoke; or, Where Is Utopia?" [C.H.
    Wiley]. Sketches. Tales: "The Emigrant
    Boy"; "The Tenant for Life"; "The Long
    Chase"; "The Green Mountaineers"; "Meta
    Berghel. Or the Love Dream"; "The City
    Clerk"; "Conquering a Peace"; "The Missing
    Manuscript"; "Lilla Lincoln's Punishment";
    "The Zangen Maiden"; "The Knight's Re-
    turn"; "Love in the Valley of the Juniata";
    "Mike Smiley"; "The Provident Belle";

"The Pilgrim of Love; or, the Biography of a Troubadour"; "The New Englanders"; "The Swamp Ghost at Christmas"; "The Unwilling Bride"; "The Dilemma; or, Cousin Phil's Confessions"; "Lizzy Greene"; "Crescent Beach"; "Jacky Pringle; or, the Poor Sometimes Grateful"; "Utouch and Touchu"; "Table Chat"; "Love and Murder. A Tale of Mystery"; "The Bewildered Savage" [Lydia Maria Child]; "Shawangunk Mountain"; "The Grand House in Our Village"; "The Voice of the Mute"; "The Querxen, Erdmänchen and Fairymen"; "La Fioraja"; "Memory; or the Old Man's Dream" [Emma C. Embury]; "Bachelor's Wives"; "The City of Peace"; "The Seamstress"; "Clara and Lucy"; "Cocheeco. A Tale of the Early Settlement of New Hampshire"; "The Rescue"; "The Shadow and the Light of a Young Man's Soul" [Walt Whitman]; "The Duel"; "Aslog and Orm, or the Giants and Dwarfs' Feast"; "A Country Doctor"; "The Beggar Ship"; "The Lost Children"; "The Alms-House Boy"; "The Music of Our Neighborhood"; "A Village Fourth of July" [Alfred B. Street]; "The Black Rover"; "The Price of Blood"; "The Countess. A Romance"; "The Heron in Ireland"; "An Up-Town Crisis; or, Mrs. Luther Leather's First Friday Morning" [Nathaniel P. Willis]; "Mr. Elworthy's Heirs. A Tale" [Mary Howitt]; "The Fate, or the Lover's Revenge."

835 TITLES: (1) The United States Literary Advertiser, and Publishers' Circular. A Monthly Register of Literature, Fine Arts, &c. (2) United States Literary Advertiser, Publishers' Circular, and Monthly Register of Literature and Art. [Merged into the New-England Galaxy q.v.]

Place of Publication: New York
First Issue: July 1841
Last Issue: July 1843//
Periodicity: Monthly
Editors: J. Langley; H.G. Langley
Publishers: J. & H.G. Langley
Available From: Amer. Antiquarian Soc.; Yale Univ.
Contents:
  Prose: Book Reviews.
  Miscellaneous: Literary Notices.
Note: Consists entirely of literary notices and short book reviews.

836 TITLE: The United States Literary Gazette. [United with the New York Review and Atheneum Magazine q.v. to form the United States Review and Literary Gazette q.v.]

Place of Publication: Boston
First Issue: 1 April 1824
Last Issue: Sept 1826//
Periodicity: Semi-monthly; Monthly
Editors: James G. Carter; Theophilus Parsons
Publishers: Cummings, Hilliard, & Co.; Harrison Gray

Available From: APS; Amer. Antiquarian Soc.* Mott. Poole.
Contents:
  Poetry: Original: John A. Jones, Rufus Dawes, Grenville Mellen, James G. Percival, Richard Henry Dana, Longfellow, Bryant. Selected: Burns, Thomas Moore, Leigh Hunt, Thomas Campbell, Nathaniel P. Willis, Washington Allston, Schiller.
  Prose: Biography. Travel. Essay. Familiar Essay. Criticism. Letters. Book Reviews.
  Fiction: Essay Serials: "The Lay Monastery" [Longfellow]; "The Bachelor." Sketches.
  Miscellaneous: Anecdotes: on various subjects. Literary Notices. News: Foreign and Domestic.

837 TITLE: The United States Magazine. A Repository of History, Politics, and Literature.

Place of Publication: Philadelphia
First Issue: Jan 1779
Last Issue: Dec 1779//
Periodicity: Monthly
Editor: Hugh Henry Brackenridge
Publisher: Francis Bailey
Available From: APS; Lib. Co. of Philadelphia.* Mott.
Contents:
  Poetry: Original: Francis Hopkinson, Philip Freneau. Selected.
  Prose: Essay: "An Oration on the Advantages of American Independence." Familiar Essay. Letters.
  Fiction: Essay Serial: "Political Diary."
  Miscellaneous: News: Foreign and Domestic.
Note: This journal is primarily concerned with politics, wars, and the new government.

838 TITLE: The United States Magazine, and Literary and Political Repository. [Supersedes The Literary and Scientific Repository, and Critical Review.]

Place of Publication: New York
First Issue: [Only one issue published?] Jan 1823//?
Periodicity: Intended to be monthly
Editor: Charles Wiley
Publisher: Charles Wiley
Available From: APS; Lib. of Congress
Contents:
  Poetry: Selected: James M'Henry.
  Prose: Book Reviews.
  Miscellaneous: Literary Notices.

839 TITLE: United States Magazine, or, General Repository of Useful Instruction and Rational Amusement.

Place of Publication: Newark, N.J.
First Issue: April 1794
Last Issue: Aug 1794//
Periodicity: Monthly
Editor: ?
Publisher: John Woods

Available From: APS; Amer. Antiquarian Soc.*
                        Mott.
Contents:
  Poetry: <u>Original</u>. <u>Selected</u>: James
    Thomson, David Humphreys, Peter Pindar.
  Prose: <u>Familiar Essay</u>. <u>Letters</u>.
  Fiction: <u>Sketches</u>.
  Miscellaneous: <u>Anecdotes</u>: on various sub-
    jects. <u>News</u>: Foreign and Domestic.

840   TITLE: <u>United States Oracle, and Portsmouth</u>
        <u>Advertiser</u>. [See <u>The United States Oracle</u>
        <u>of the Day</u>.]

841   TITLES: (1) <u>The United States Oracle of the</u>
        <u>Day</u> (2) <u>United States Oracle, and Ports-</u>
        <u>mouth Advertiser</u> (3) <u>Portsmouth Oracle</u>
        (4) <u>The Portsmouth Oracle</u>.

        Place of Publication: Portsmouth, N.H.
        First Issue: 4 Jan 1800
        Last Issue: 21 Jan 1815//
        Periodicity: Weekly
        Editors: ?
        Publishers: Charles Peirce; William Treadwell
                        & Co.; William Treadwell &
                        Daniel Treadwell; Charles Turell
        Available From: Amer. Antiquarian Soc.*
        Contents:
          Poetry: <u>Original</u>. <u>Selected</u>: Fessenden.
          Prose: <u>Essay</u>. <u>Familiar Essay</u>.
          Fiction: <u>Sketches</u>. <u>Tales</u>: "The Mercy of
            Affliction. An Eastern Story"; "Loss of
            the Lovely Lass."
          Miscellaneous: <u>Anecdotes</u>: on various sub-
            jects. <u>Literary Notices</u>. <u>News</u>: Foreign
            and Domestic.

842   TITLE: <u>The United States Review and Literary</u>
        <u>Gazette</u>. [Formed by the union of the <u>United</u>
        <u>States Literary Gazette</u> q.v. and the <u>New</u>
        <u>York Review and Atheneum Magazine</u> q.v.]

        Place of Publication: Boston; New York
        First Issue: Oct 1826
        Last Issue: Sept 1827//
        Periodicity: Monthly
        Editors: ?
        Publishers: Bowles and Dearborn; G. and C.
                        Carvill
        Available From: APS; Hist. Soc. of Pa.*
        Contents:
          Poetry: <u>Original</u>. <u>Selected</u>: Felicia
            Hemans, Lamartine, Fitz-Greene Halleck.
          Prose: <u>Essay</u>. <u>Letters</u>. <u>Book Reviews</u>.
          Fiction: <u>Tales</u>: "A Border Tradition";
            "The Elopement."
          Miscellaneous: <u>Anecdotes</u>: on various sub-
            jects. <u>Literary Notices</u>.

843   TITLE: <u>The Universal Asylum, and Columbian</u>
        <u>Magazine</u>. [Supersedes <u>The Columbian Maga-</u>
        <u>zine, or Monthly Miscellany</u> q.v.; super-
        seded by <u>The Columbian Museum, or, Univer-</u>
        <u>sal Asylum</u> q.v.]

        Place of Publication: Philadelphia

First Issue: March 1790
Last Issue: Dec 1792//
Periodicity: Monthly
Editors: A Society of Gentlemen
Publisher: William Young
Available From: APS; Hist. Soc. of Pa.*
                    Mott.

Contents:
  Poetry: <u>Original</u>. <u>Selected</u>: Richard
    Savage, James Thomson, Peter Pindar,
    Francis Hopkinson, S. Johnson, Chester-
    field, Thomas Penrose, Helen Maria Williams.
  Prose: <u>Biography</u>: religious and military
    figures, Franklin, Francis Hopkinson,
    Cervantes. <u>Travel</u>: William Bartram.
    <u>Familiar Essay</u>. <u>Criticism</u>. <u>Letters</u>:
    Franklin, Jefferson, John Adams, Thomas
    Paine, Benjamin Rush, Francis Hopkinson,
    Swift. <u>Book Reviews</u>.
  Fiction: <u>Sketches</u>. <u>Tales</u>: "The Story of
    Altamont and Arabella"; "The History of
    Miranda and Cleander: An American Tale";
    "The Flirt. A Moral Tale"; "The Mountain
    Lute"; "Cleophila: A Tale"; "The Self-
    Rival. A Nouvellette."
  Miscellaneous: <u>Extracts</u>: from other jour-
    nals; by various authors; Franklin, Adam
    Smith, Benjamin Rush, Thomas Paine,
    Edmund Burke, S. Johnson, Hester L. Thrale
    Piozzi, Jeremy Belknap. <u>Anecdotes</u>: on
    various subjects; S. Johnson, Sterne,
    Swift, Addison. <u>Literary Notices</u>. <u>News</u>:
    Foreign and Domestic.

844   TITLE: <u>The Universal Medley, Containing</u>
        <u>Selections from the Best English Authors;</u>
        <u>Translations from the Most Esteemed Italian</u>
        <u>and French Writers and a Considerable Por-</u>
        <u>tion of Original Matter</u>.

        Place of Publication: Barnstable, Mass.
        First Issue: 12 Jan 1824
        Last Issue: 1 March 1824//?
        Available From: Harvard Univ.

845   TITLE: <u>The Universalist Palladium and Ladies'</u>
        <u>Amulet, Devoted to the Illustration and De-</u>
        <u>fense of Universalism,--The Cause of Reli-</u>
        <u>gious Freedom--Christian Charity--the Rights</u>
        <u>and Duties of Females, and General Litera-</u>
        <u>ture</u>. [Merged into <u>The Gospel Banner</u>.]

        Place of Publication: Portland, Me.
        First Issue: 9 March 1839
        Last Issue: 12 Feb 1842//
        Periodicity: Semi-monthly
        Editors: an Association of Universalist
                    Clergymen
        Publishers: S.H. Colesworthy; Colesworthy &
                        Fessenden
        Available From: Portland Pub. Lib.*;
                            Amer. Antiquarian Soc.

        Contents:
          Poetry: <u>Original</u>: Leander Hussy, E.W.
            Locke. <u>Selected</u>: James Montgomery,
            Alaric Watts, Felicia Hemans, Ann S.
            Stephens, Thomas Haynes Bayly, Emma C.
            Embury, Longfellow, T.K. Hervey, James
            T. Fields, Sarah J. Hale.

Prose: Biography. Familiar Essay.
Fiction: Essay Serials: "Gleanings by the Way Side"; "Odd Leaves from My Note Book." Sketches. Tales: "The Expiation"; "Everard Graham"; "The Wooing at Grafton"; "The Infidel Converted"; "The Widow's Daughter"; "The Dead-Clearing"; "Gertrude. A Fact" [Whittier]; "Henry St. Clair" [Whittier]; "Lady Viola; or Three Scenes in a Life"; "The Blind Widow and Her Family"; "Pelayo, and the Merchant's Daughter" [W. Irving]; "Noel Ronello. A Tale of the Present Century"; "The Poor Printer, and the Exclusives."
Miscellaneous: Extracts: from other journals; by various authors; W. Irving, John Neal. Anecdotes: on various subjects; Washington. Literary Notices. News: Domestic.

846   TITLE: The Vigil.

Place of Publication: Charleston, S.C.
First Issue: 27 Feb 1798
Last Issue: 3 April 1798//
Periodicity: Weekly
Editors: ?
Publisher: W.P. Young
Available From: APS; Ohio State Univ., Columbus*
Contents:
  Prose: Familiar Essay: Addison-like essays on the pleasures and beauties of summer, thoughts on periodical writers, the characteristics of a "disputant," pleasure and leisure, marriage (especially older women marrying young men), mutability in friendship.

847   TITLE: The Village Museum.

Place of Publication: Cortland Village, N.Y.
First Issue: 9 Oct 1820
Last Issue: 20 Nov 1820//?
Periodicity: Weekly
Editors: ?
Publishers: T.J. Sutherland & D. Hills
Available From: APS; N.Y. Hist. Soc.*
Contents:
  Poetry: Selected: David Humphreys
  Prose: Biography. Travel.
  Fiction: Tale: "The Chieftain's Daughter. A Tale of Past Times."
  Miscellaneous: Extracts: from other journals. Anecdotes: on various subjects.

848   TITLE: The Village Museum.

Place of Publication: York, Pa.
First Issue: Aug 1819
Last Issue: July 1823//
Periodicity: Monthly
Editors: an Association of Young Men
Publishers: P. Hardt; Lewis, Gemmill, & Co.; Gemmill & Lewis
Available From: Lib. of Congress*; Amer. Antiquarian Soc.

Contents:
  Poetry: Original. Selected: Byron, William Jones, Burns, Gray, Charles Dibdin, Barry Cornwall, William B. Tappan, Thomas Moore, Shakespeare, William Cowper, Thomas Campbell, Henry Neele.
  Prose: Biography: Lady Mary Wortley Montagu. Familiar Essay. Criticism. Letters.
  Fiction: Essay Serials: "The Wandering Book-Worm"; "The Loiterer." Sketches. Tales: "The Broken Heart" [W. Irving]; "Irus, a Tale"; "The Castle-Goblin"; "The Progress of Inconstancy. A Tale"; "The Cavalier in France. A Tale of the Seventeenth Century."
  Miscellaneous: Extracts: from other journals; by various authors; W. Irving. Anecdotes: on various subjects; Goldsmith, William Cowper, Dante, Thomas Moore, Swift, Chatterton. News: Domestic.

849   TITLE: The Villager, a Literary Paper.

Place of Publication: Greenwich Village, N.Y.
First Issue: April 1819
Last Issue: June 1819//
Periodicity: Semi-monthly
Editors: ?
Publishers: ?
Available From: APS; Lib. of Congress*
Contents:
  Poetry: Original. Selected: Charlotte Smith, William Collins, Thomas Warton, William Roscoe, Allan Cunningham, Selleck Osborne.
  Prose: Travel. Essay. Familiar Essay. Book Reviews.
  Fiction: Essay Serial: "The Hermit."
  Miscellaneous: Extracts: from other journals; by various authors; Joseph Dennie. Anecdotes: on various subjects. Literary Notices. News: Foreign and Domestic.

850   TITLES: (1) The Virginia Historical Register, and Literary Advertiser (2) The Virginia Historical Register, and Literary Note Book (3) The Virginia Historical Register, and Literary Companion.

Place of Publication: Richmond, Va.
First Issue: Jan 1848
Last Issue: Oct 1853//
Periodicity: Quarterly
Editor: William Maxwell
Publishers: Virginia Historical and Philosophical Society
Available From: Lib. of Congress*; Amer. Antiquarian Soc.*
Contents:
  Poetry: Original. Selected: Coleridge, B. Jonson, Chapman, Middleton, Hartley Coleridge.
  Prose: Biography: Pocahontas. Travel. Essay. Familiar Essay. Letters.
  Fiction: Sketches.
  Miscellaneous: Extracts: from other journals; by various authors; Jefferson, Edmund Burke, William Temple. Anecdotes: on various subjects. News: Domestic.

851   TITLE: The Virginia Literary Museum and
      Journal of Belles Lettres, Arts, Sciences
      &c.

      Place of Publication: Charlottesville, Va.
      First Issue: 17 June 1829
      Last Issue: 9 June 1830//
      Periodicity: Weekly
      Editors: Faculty of the University of Virginia
      Publishers: University of Virginia Press
      Available From: APS; Univ. of Va.,
                         Charlottesville*
      Contents:
        Poetry: Original. Selected.
        Prose: Biography. Essay. Familiar Essay.
          Criticism. Letters. Book Reviews.
        Fiction: Essay Serial: "Jeffersoniana."
          Sketches.
        Miscellaneous: News: Domestic.

852   TITLE: Visiter and Parlour Companion. [See
      The New-York Visiter, and Parlour Compan-
      ion.]

853   TITLE: The Visitor.

      Place of Publication: New Haven, Conn.
      First Issue: 30 Oct 1802
      Last Issue: 25 Oct 1803//
      Periodicity: Weekly
      Editor: J. Walter
      Publisher: J. Walter
      Available From: Lib. of Congress*; Amer.
                         Antiquarian Soc.*
      Contents:
        Poetry: Original. Selected: Thomas Paine,
          William Smyth, William Cowper.
        Prose: Biography: Jeremy Belknap, Cervan-
          tes, Pope. Travel. Familiar Essay.
          Letters.
        Fiction: Essay Serials: "The Invisible
          Wanderer"; "The Censor"; "A Bachelor's
          Evenings"; "The Observer"; "The Connecticut
          Tatler." Sketches. Tale: "Story of
          Belhasar."
        Miscellaneous: Anecdotes: on various sub-
          jects; Buonaparte. Literary Notices.
          News: Foreign and Domestic.

854   TITLE: The Visitor.

      Place of Publication: Richmond, Va.
      First Issue: 11 Feb 1809
      Last Issue: 18 Aug 1810//?
      Periodicity: Semi-monthly; Weekly
      Editors: ?
      Publishers: Lynch & Southgate
      Available From: APS; Lib. of Congress.*
                         Mott.
      Contents:
        Poetry: Original. Selected: Peter Pindar,
          R.W. Spencer, Thomas Campbell, Thomas
          Moore, James Beattie, Swift, Luis de
          Camoens, Anthony Pasquin, Thomas Paine,
          William Carey, James Montgomery.

        Prose: Biography: Pocahontas, Aphra Behn.
          Familiar Essay. Letters.
        Fiction: Essay Serials: "The Poikilorama";
          "The Quizer." Tales: "The Lady Among
          Murderers. A True Story"; "The Storm. An
          Interesting Tale"; "The Dead Shot, or, the
          Long Pack. A Tale" [James Hogg]; "The
          Extraordinary Adventures of a Spanish
          Soldier"; "Pierre. A German Tale"; "Henry
          Fitzowen, a Tale"; "Camire. An American
          Tale"; "Maria Arnold. A Tale--Founded on
          Fact"; "Henry de Montmorency. A Fragment";
          "The Spirit of the Abbey. A Tale";
          "Sophia M----. A True Story"; "The Organ-
          Blower. A Romance in the Modern Style";
          "Agnes Felton. A Tale"; "The Criminal.
          A Tale."
        Miscellaneous: Extracts: from other jour-
          nals; by various authors; Francis Hopkinson,
          Erasmus Darwin. Anecdotes: on various
          subjects. Literary Notices. News:
          Foreign and Domestic.

855   TITLE: The Visitor, and Lady's Parlor Maga-
      zine. [See The New-York Visiter, and
      Parlour Companion.]

856   TITLES: (1) Waldie's Literary Omnibus, News,
      Books Entire, Sketches, Reviews, and Mis-
      cellaneous Intelligence (2) Brown's Literary
      Omnibus. News, Books Entire, Sketches, Re-
      views, Tales, Miscellaneous Intelligence.
      [Merged into The Saturday Evening Post q.v.]

      Place of Publication: Philadelphia
      First Issue: 6 Jan 1837
      Last Issue: 20 July 1838//
      Periodicity: Weekly
      Editors: Adam Waldie; William Brown
      Publishers: Adam Waldie; William Brown
      Available From: APS; Lib. of Congress.* Mott.
      Contents:
        Poetry: Original. Selected: Allan
          Cunningham, Thomas Haynes Bayly, L.E.
          Landon, Mrs. Abdy, Schiller, Thomas Hood,
          Bryant.
        Prose: Biography. Travel. Familiar Essay.
          Criticism. Letters. Book Reviews.
        Fiction: Sketches. Tales: "The Confes-
          sions of an Elderly Gentleman"; "The Es-
          cape. A Narrative" [Kotzebue]; "The
          French Emigrants"; "Henrietta Temple; a
          Love Story"; "The Victims of Society";
          "Mechanics' Children, or Hints to Agrarians";
          "The Three Eras of a Woman's Life"; "Rory
          O'More: A National Romance"; "The Clock-
          maker; or, the Sayings and Doings of
          Samuel Slick, of Slickville" [Thomas
          Chandler Haliburton]; "The Confessions of
          an Elderly Lady"; "Leila; or, the Siege
          of Grenada"; "Aunt Kate's Five Nieces";
          "The 'Genteel' Pigeons. A Household
          Story" [Douglas Jerrold]; "The Hussar";
          "The Robber. A Tale"; "Cahokia, a Legend
          of the Olden Time in Illinois"; "The
          History of a Genius." Novel: "Abel Allnutt.
          A Novel."

Miscellaneous: <u>Anecdotes</u>: on various subjects. <u>Literary Notices</u>. <u>News</u>: Foreign and Domestic.

857   TITLE: <u>Waldie's Port Folio, and Companion to the Select Circulating Library</u>. [See <u>The Port Folio, and Companion to the Select Circulating Library. A Semi-Monthly Publication, on the Basis of Chamber's Edinburgh Journal: Combining Essays, Original and Selected, on Science, Arts, and Literature; Biographical Illustrations; Instructive and Amusing Incidents, Tales, Music, Poetry, &c.</u>]

858   TITLE: <u>Waldie's Select Circulating Library</u>. [See <u>The Select Circulating Library. Containing the Best Popular Literature, Including Memoirs, Biography, Novels, Tales, Travels, Voyages, &c.</u>]

859   TITLE: <u>Walsh's American Review</u>. [See <u>The American Review of History and Politics, and General Repository of Literature and State Papers</u>.]

860   TITLE: <u>The Washington Literary Gazette; a Miscellany of Literature, Science, and the Fine Arts</u>. [See <u>The Metropolitan; a Miscellany of Literature and Science</u>.]

861   TITLE: <u>The Washington Quarterly Magazine of Arts, Science and Literature. With Illustrative Engravings</u>.

Place of Publication: Washington, D.C.
First Issue: July 1823
Last Issue: April 1824//
Periodicity: Quarterly
Editor: Robert Little
Publishers: Pishey Thompson and Davis and Force
Available From: APS; Lib. of Congress*
Contents:
    Poetry: <u>Selected</u>.
    Prose: <u>Essay</u>.
    Miscellaneous: <u>News</u>: Domestic.

862   TITLES: (1) <u>Washingtonian Temperance Journal and Family Reader. Devoted to Temperance, General News of the Day, Selected Tales, Poetry, Agriculture, Domestic Economy, &c. &c.</u> (2) <u>Maine Washingtonian Journal and Temperance Herald. Devoted to Temperance, General News of the Day, Selected Tales, Poetry, Agriculture, Domestic Economy, &c. &c.</u> (3) <u>Washingtonian Journal. Devoted to Temperance, General News of the Day, Selected Tales, Poetry, Agriculture, Domestic Economy, &c. &c.</u>

Place of Publication: Wiscasset, Me.; Portland

First Issue: 13 July 1842
Last Issue: 1846//
Periodicity: Weekly
Editor: Thomas Adams
Publishers: Frederick W. Nichols
Available From: Lib. of Congress
Contents:
    Poetry: <u>Original</u>. <u>Selected</u>: Sarah J. Hale, John Pierpont, Lydia H. Sigourney, Nathaniel P. Willis, William Falconer, George Pope Morris, James Montgomery, Jones Very, James Russell Lowell, F.J. Otterson, Oliver Wendell Holmes, Felicia Hemans, Charles Swain, Hannah F. Gould, D.C. Colesworthy, Thomas Haynes Bayly.
    Prose: <u>Familiar Essay</u>.
    Fiction: <u>Essay Serial</u>: "Recollections of a Washingtonian." <u>Sketches</u>. <u>Tales</u>: "Family Secrets; or, the Husband Reformed"; "The Child and His Pumpkin"; "The Suffering Mother--A Reformed Father"; "The Wife" [W. Irving]; "Mercy O'More, or Love's Rogueries"; "Procrastination"; "The Mask [sic] of the Red Death" [Poe]; "The Drunkard's Daughter"; "The Ordeal; or the Triumph of Natural Affection"; "A Sister's Love; or, the Trials of Grace Falconer"; "A Rosebud Courtship. A Tale of Utopia"; "The Last Warning.--A Tale"; "Elizabeth Gray. The True Hearted Martha Washington"; "Orrin Lacey; or, the Teachings of the Sick Room"; "Charles Bond"; "The Painter's Daughter"; Conrade and Theresa"; "The Lady Clara"; "The Little Drummer or the Price of Military Glory."
    Miscellaneous: <u>Extracts</u>: from other journals; by various authors. <u>Anecdotes</u>: on various subjects. <u>Literary Notices</u>. <u>News</u>: Foreign and Domestic.

863   TITLE: <u>The Wasp. By Robert Rusticoat, Esq</u>.

Place of Publication: Hudson, N.Y.
First Issue: 7 July 1802
Last Issue: 26 Jan 1803//
Periodicity: Irregular
Editor: ?
Publisher: Harry Croswell
Available From: APS; Amer. Antiquarian Soc.*
Contents:
    Poetry: <u>Original</u>.
    Prose: <u>Letters</u>.
    Miscellaneous: <u>Extracts</u>: from other journals. <u>Anecdotes</u>: on various subjects.
Note: Although politically oriented, this journal is of some literary interest.

864   TITLE: <u>The Watervillonian: Devoted to Literature, Morals, Agriculture, News, etc</u>.

Place of Publication: Waterville, Me.
First Issue: 29 May 1841
Last Issue: 30 May 1842//
Periodicity: Weekly
Editor: William Mathews
Publisher: William Mathews
Available From: Lib. of Congress*

Contents:
  Poetry: Original. Selected: Spenser,
    Southey, Thomas Carew, Coleridge, T.K.
    Hervey, Edmund Waller, Byron, Richard
    Henry Dana, William Cowper, Wordsworth,
    Thomas Haynes Bayly, Epes Sargent, Oliver
    Wendell Holmes, R.H. Wilde, Bryant,
    Caroline Lee Hentz, Shelley, William
    Leggett, William Motherwell, Longfellow,
    James Hogg, Fitz-Greene Halleck, L.E.
    Landon.
  Prose: Biography: S. Johnson, Mather
    Byles, Patrick Henry, John Neal. Essay.
    Familiar Essay.
  Fiction: Sketches. Tales: "The First and
    Last Dinner. A Tale of Life"; "The Story
    of La Roche"; "Robert Crane and Hannah
    Oldbug. An Affecting Tale"; "The Bald
    Eagle"; "Martin Franc and the Monk of
    St. Anthony"; "The Blind Boy"; "The
    Spectre Steamer"; "Life of an Old Maid";
    "Hafed's Dream: Or the 'Chance World'";
    "Old Edwards. An English Tale"; "Catch
    a Beau, a Domestic Tale"; "Old Cross-Fire;
    a Story of the North-Western Border"; "The
    Brothers"; "The One Fault, a Tale for
    Husbands and Wives" [Emma C. Embury];
    "The Raft; or the Widow's Two Sons"; "The
    Vice-Legate's Ball"; "The Yankee and the
    Duellist"; "The Cold Hand"; "Losing and
    Winning."
  Miscellaneous: Extracts: from other
    journals; by various authors; William
    Temple, Bolingbroke, Charles Lamb, William
    Ellery Channing. Anecdotes: on various
    subjects. News: Foreign and Domestic.

865   TITLE: The Weekly Magazine of Original Essays,
       Fugitive Pieces, and Interesting Intelli-
       gence.

       Place of Publication: Philadelphia
       First Issue: 3 Feb 1798
       Last Issue: 1 June 1799//
       Periodicity: Weekly
       Editors: James Watters; Ezekiel Forman
       Publishers: James Watters & Co.; Ezekiel
                   Forman
       Available From: APS; Amer. Antiquarian Soc.
                       Mott.
       Contents:
         Poetry: Original: John Davis, Samuel
           Latham Mitchell. Selected: Burns,
           Erasmus Darwin, R.B. Sheridan, Goldsmith,
           William Jones, James Beattie, Lessing,
           Southey, William Doddridge, William
           Shenstone, Edward Rushton, Robert Merry,
           John Gay.
         Prose: Biography: Southey, Hester L.
           Thrale Piozzi, James Pye, Ann Radcliffe,
           Jeremy Belknap, Henry Mackenzie, Franklin,
           Count Rumford. Travel: Volney. Essay.
           Familiar Essay. Criticism: "Character
           and Effects of Modern Novels." Letters.
         Fiction: Essay Serials: "The Man at Home"
           [Charles Brockden Brown]; "The Ubiqui-
           tarian"; "The Schemer"; "The Wanderer."
           Tales: "Tomo Cheeki; the Creek Indians
           in Philadelphia"; "The Sick Widow. A
           Moral Tale"; "The Wishes. An Arabian

Tale"; "Richard Macwill. A Moral Tale";
"The Fatal Effects of False Apologies and
Pretences; a Story"; "The Old Man and His
Dog Trim"; "Amyntas, a Pastoral Tale";
"Omar. A Narrative"; "Sir Gawen. An
Historical Romance"; "Palermon. A Tale."
Novel: "Arthur Mervyn; or, Memoirs of the
Year 1793" [Charles Brockden Brown].
  Miscellaneous: Extracts: from other jour-
    nals; by various authors; Charles Brockden
    Brown's "Sky-Walk." Anecdotes: on various
    subjects; Swift, Edward Gibbon, Franklin,
    S. Johnson. Literary Notices. News:
    Foreign and Domestic.

866   TITLE: The Weekly Mirror. [See The New Mir-
       ror, of Literature, Amusement, and Instruc-
       tion: Containing Original Papers; Tales of
       Romance; Sketches of Society, Manners, and
       Every-day Life; Domestic and Foreign Corres-
       pondence; Wit and Humour; Fashion and Gossip;
       the Fine Arts, and Literary, Musical and
       Dramatic Criticism; Extracts from New Works;
       Poetry Original and Selected; the Spirit of
       the Public Journals; etc. etc. etc.]

867   TITLE: The Weekly Monitor. [Superseded by
       The Evening Fire-Side q.v.]

       Place of Publication: Philadelphia
       First Issue: 16 June 1804
       Last Issue: 8 Dec 1804//
       Periodicity: Weekly
       Editor: Abraham Vickers
       Publisher: Abraham Vickers
       Available From: APS; Lib. of Congress*
       Contents:
         Poetry: Original. Selected: Erasmus
           Darwin, Isaac D'Isareli, R.B. Sheridan,
           Fessenden, S. Johnson, Mary Robinson,
           Thomas Moore.
         Prose: Biography. Essay. Familiar Essay.
           Letters.
         Fiction: Essay Serial: "The Passenger."
         Miscellaneous: Extracts: from other jour-
           nals. Anecdotes: on various subjects;
           S. Johnson. Literary Notices. News:
           Domestic.
         Note: Motto:
           To plan the Labors of Domestic Ease
           Beneath the Sacred Shade of Gentle Pease.
           Pledg'd to No Party's Arbitrary Sway
           I Follow Truth Where E'er It Leads the Way.

868   TITLE: The Weekly Monitor, Entertaining and
       Instructive: Designed to Be Interesting to
       All, But Particularly Intended as a Guide
       to Youth in the Way of Morality and Religion.

       Place of Publication: Boston
       First Issue: 4 June 1817
       Last Issue: 20 Sept 1817//
       Periodicity: Weekly
       Editors: ?
       Publishers: Farnham and Badger
       Available From: APS; Amer. Antiquarian Soc.*

Contents:
Poetry: Original. Selected: William
Doddridge, S. Johnson, William Cowper.
Prose: Biography. Essay. Familiar Essay.
Fiction: Essay Serial: "The Friend to
Youth." Tales: "The Wooden Leg. An
Helvetic Tale"; "Helim the Persian, the
Great Physician. A Tale."
Miscellaneous: Anecdotes: on various sub-
jects.

869 TITLE: The Weekly Museum.

Place of Publication: Baltimore
First Issue: 8 Jan 1797
Last Issue: 28 May 1797//
Available From: Ohio State Univ., Columbus

870 TITLE: The Weekly Museum (New York). [See
The Impartial Gazetteer, and Saturday
Evening's Post.]

871 TITLE: The Weekly Recorder. A Newspaper
Conveying Important Intelligence and Other
Useful Matter, Under the Three General Heads
of Theology, Literature, and National Affairs.

Place of Publication: Chillicothe, Ohio
First Issue: 5 July 1814
Last Issue: 6 Oct 1821//?
Periodicity: Weekly
Editor: John Andrews
Publisher: John Andrews
Available From: APS; Presbyterian Hist. Soc.,
Philadelphia
Contents:
Poetry: Original. Selected: Robert
Montgomery, William Cowper.
Prose: Biography. Essay. Familiar Essay.
Letters. Book Reviews.
Fiction: Essay Serial: "The Presbyterian."
Miscellaneous: Extracts: by various
authors. Anecdotes: on various subjects;
Isaac Newton, Buonaparte, Garrick. Liter-
ary Notices. News: Foreign and Domestic.

872 TITLE: The Weekly Visitant: Moral, Poetical,
Humorous, &c.

Place of Publication: Salem, Mass.
First Issue: 1 Jan 1806
Last Issue: 27 Dec 1806//
Periodicity: Weekly
Editor: Haven Pool
Publisher: Haven Pool
Available From: APS; Amer. Antiquarian Soc.*
Contents:
Poetry: Original. Selected: Southey,
James Thomson, Thomas Moore, Coleridge,
John Davis, Selleck Osborne, Peter Pindar,
Robert Bloomfield, William Holloway, James
Pye, Joseph Story, Luis de Camoens, John
Trumbull, Swift, William Shenstone,
Amelia Opie, Charles Dibdin, William
Cowper.
Prose: Biography: Robert Bloomfield,
William Jones, Mary Robinson. Travel:
Mungo Park. Familiar Essay. Criticism.

Fiction: Essay Serial: "The Social Truant."
Tales: "Robin and Susan"; "The Mercy of
Affliction. An Eastern Tale"; "Love and
Humility. A Roman Romance" [Isaac
D'Israeli]; "The Daughter, or a Modern
Romance"; "Choang and Hansl. A Chinese
Tale" [Goldsmith]; "Elvira. A Fragment."
Novels: "The Zegris. An Interesting
Spanish Novel"; "The Starling. A Novel
in Miniature."
Miscellaneous: Extracts: Robert Burton,
Swift, Rousseau, Joseph Dennie, Goldsmith,
Voltaire, Benjamin Rush. Anecdotes: on
various subjects; Garrick, Benjamin Rush.
News: Domestic.

873 TITLE: The Weekly Visitor. [Combined with
The Lady's Weekly Miscellany q.v. to form
The Lady's Miscellany; or, Weekly Visitor,
and Entertaining Companion for the Use and
Amusement of Both Sexes q.v.]

Place of Publication: New York
First Issue: 12 May 1810
Last Issue: 25 May 1811//
Periodicity: Weekly
Editor: Alexander C. Morton
Publisher: Alexander C. Morton
Available From: APS; N.Y. Pub. Lib.
Contents:
Poetry: Original. Selected: Thomas Moore,
Henry Pope.
Prose: Biography: Thomas Cooper. Familiar
Essay. Letters.
Fiction: Essay Serials: "The Gleanor";
"Invisible Spectator"; "The Advocate";
"The Fragmentist." Tales: "History of
Rinaldo Rinaldini"; "The Big Man in Red; or,
the Martial Maniac"; "The Wedding; or, the
Man in Black"; "The Polish Chieftain";
"The Heiress of Devon"; "Love and Duty"
[Amelia Opie]; "Henry de Montmorency. A
Fragment"; "St. Herbert; or the Victims
of a Prejudice"; "Edmorin and Ella. An
Eastern Tale"; "The Sailor or, the Adven-
tures of a Guinea"; "John Audley, or, the
Adventures of a Night."
Miscellaneous: Extracts: from other jour-
nals. Anecdotes: on various subjects;
George Whitefield, Thomas Cooper, Swift,
Franklin, Washington. News: Domestic.

874 TITLE: The Weekly Visitor.

Place of Publication: Providence, R.I.
First Issue: 11 Oct 1834
Last Issue: 7 March 1835//?
Available From: N.Y. Hist. Soc.

875 TITLE: The Weekly Visitor; or Ladies Miscellany. [Merged with The Ladies Weekly Museum
to form The Weekly Visitor and Ladies'
Museum q.v.]

Place of Publication: New York
First Issue: 10 May 1817
Last Issue: 25 Oct 1817//?
Available From: Yale Univ.

876   TITLES: (1) The Weekly Visitor, or, Ladies'
Miscellany. Containing, Original and
Selected Compositions, in Prose and Verse,
Designed Chiefly to Improve the Minds and
Amuse the Leisure Hours of the Female Parts
of Society (2) The Lady's Weekly Miscellany
(3) The Lady's Miscellany; or, Weekly
Visitor, and Entertaining Companion for the
Use and Amusement of Both Sexes. [See also
The Weekly Visitor.]

Place of Publication: New York
First Issue: 9 Oct 1802
Last Issue: 17 Oct 1812//
Periodicity: Weekly
Editors: ?
Publishers: Ming and Young; John Clough;
           Edward Whitely; M'Carty & White;
           Samuel B. White
Available From: APS; N.Y. Hist. Soc. Mott.
Contents:
  Poetry: Original. Selected: Charles
    Southgate, Thomas Paine, Thomas Moore,
    Burns, Robert Bloomfield, Hester L. Thrale
    Piozzi, Richard Cumberland, Peter Pindar,
    Selleck Osborne, Franklin, Robert Treat
    Paine, Pope, Fessenden, James Montgomery,
    James Kenney, Luis de Camoens, Swift,
    William Holloway, Amelia Opie, Charles
    Dyer, John Blair Linn, Southey, William
    Dunlap, John Suckling, Mary Robinson,
    Goldsmith, William Cowper.
  Prose: Biography: Amelia Opie, S. Johnson,
    William Cowper, Mary Wollstonecraft,
    Hannah More. Travel: Mungo Park,
    William Bartram. Essay. Familiar Essay.
    Criticism. Letters.
  Fiction: Essay Serials: "The Chatterer";
    "The Censor"; "Lucubrations"; "The Spec-
    tator"; "The Lucubrator"; "The Essayist";
    "Glances at Life"; "The Selector."
    Sketches. Tales: "The Nut-Shell. A
    Tale"; "Angelina. A Tale"; "Maria
    Corbin. A Tale"; "Amanda. A Tale
    (Founded on Fact)"; "Richard Macwill. A
    Moral Tale"; "Seduction. A Tale Founded
    on Fact"; "The Indians. A Tale"; "Pierre.
    A German Novel"; "The Conscious Rivals";
    "The Turban. A Turkish Tale"; "The
    Druid. A Tale"; "The Dead Shot; or, the
    Long Pack. A Tale" [James Hogg];
    "Amelia, or the Faithless Briton"; "Don
    Alvaro; a Spanish Tale"; "The Turnpike
    Gate; a Tale"; "The Cavern of Strozzi";
    "Constantia; or, Unexampled Magnanimity.
    A Tale"; "Albert and Emma. An Interesting
    Tale"; "The Spaniard; or, the Pride of
    Birth. A Tale"; "The Witch of the Wold"
    [Charlotte Smith]; "The Robber"; "Selico.
    An African Novel"; "Fatal Effects of
    Seduction. A Tale"; "The Rivals; a
    Pastoral Tale"; "The History of George &
    Charlotte"; "The Slippers. A Turkish
    Tale"; "The Fair Penitent"; "Gostanza and
    Martuccio. A Florentine Tale"; "The Cap-
    tain of Banditti"; "The Friar's Tale";
    "Mirror of Selima"; "Alphonso and Almira;
    or the Noble Forrester. A Sardinian
    Tale"; "The Village Gossip, or, Memoirs
    of a Country Lady"; "The Monk of the
    Grotto"; "Highland Heroism. Or the

Castles of Glencoe and Balloch." Novels:
"The Starling. A Novel in Miniature";
"The Man of Integrity. A Novel"; "Bromley
Melmot; a Novel"; "The Sisters of Rosedale;
or, Modern Adoption. A Novel"; "The Prince
of Brittany"; "De Valcour and Bertha; or,
the Prediction Fulfilled. A Romance";
"Marian and Lydia"; "The Chimney Sweeper.
Or, the School for Levity. A Novel";
"Almedia St. Albans; or, Magnanimity
Rewarded" [Susanna Rowson].
  Miscellaneous: Extracts: from other jour-
    nals; by various authors; Schiller,
    Lavater, Erasmus Darwin, James Beattie,
    Hester L. Thrale Piozzi, Edward Gibbon,
    Burns, Sterne, Swift, Dante, Goldsmith,
    Benjamin Rush, Joseph Dennie. Anecdotes:
    on various subjects; Garrick, George
    Whitefield, Franklin, Buonaparte,
    Goldsmith, S. Johnson, Swift, Sterne.
    News: Foreign and Domestic.
Note: Motto:
      To Wake the Soul by Tender Strokes of Art,
      To Raise the Genius and to Mend the Heart.

877   TITLE: The Western Friend; Devoted to Religion, Morality, Literature, News and Markets.

Place of Publication: Cincinnati
First Issue: 11 Nov 1847
Last Issue: 23 Aug 1849//
Available From: Earlham Coll., Richmond,
               Ind.*; Haverford Coll.,
               Haverford, Pa.

878   TITLE: The Western Garland and People's
Magazine.

Place of Publication: Cincinnati
First Issue: [Undated. nos. 1-12] 1846//
Periodicity: Monthly
Editor: Jno. L. Williams
Publisher: Jno. L. Williams
Available From: Pub. Lib. of Cincinnati*;
               Amer. Antiquarian Soc.*
Contents:
  Poetry: Original: S.S. Lindsay, James W.
    Wales, J.B. Darst, F.W. Cleveland.
    Selected: Hannah F. Gould, Isabel Athel-
    wood, J.H. Clinch, Frances S. Osgood,
    William D. Gallagher, Longfellow.
  Prose: Biography: Madame de Staël. Essay.
    Familiar Essay.
  Fiction: Sketches. Tales: "Crazy Jackson.
    A True Sketch"; "Virtue's Triumph. A
    Narrative Founded on Truth"; "Pat Murphy's
    Fortune"; "The Twin Brothers."
  Miscellaneous: Extracts: from other jour-
    nals. Anecdotes: on various subjects.
    Literary Notices.

879   TITLE: The Western Gem and Cabinet of Literature, Science and News. [Supersedes The
Literary Cabinet, and Western Olive Branch
q.v.]

Place of Publication: St. Clairsville, Ohio
First Issue: [Only one volume published?]
           1834//?

Available From: [The Union List of Serials records no libraries holding this journal.]

880 TITLE: The Western Gleaner, or Repository for Arts, Sciences and Literature.

Place of Publication: Pittsburgh
First Issue: Dec 1813
Last Issue: Sept 1814//?
Periodicity: Monthly
Editors: ?
Publishers: Cramer, Spear and Eichbaum
Available From: APS; Yale Univ.
Contents:
  Poetry: Original. Selected: Byron, Helen Maria Williams, H.H. Brackenridge, James Montgomery, Thomas Campbell, Joanna Baillie, William Leigh Pierce, William Jones, Henry Kirke White.
  Prose: Biography. Essay. Familiar Essay. Letters. Book Reviews.
  Fiction: Essay Serial: "The Listener."
  Miscellaneous: Extracts: from other journals; by various authors; Byron. Anecdotes: on various subjects; Molière, Bolingbroke. Literary Notices.

881 TITLE: The Western Literary and Historical Magazine.

Place of Publication: Louisville, Ky.
First Issue: Jan 1842
Last Issue: Sept 1842//
Available From: State Hist. Soc. of Wis., Madison*

882 TITLE: Western Literary Casket. [See The Literary Messenger.]

883 TITLE: The Western Literary Emporium.

Place of Publication: Cincinnati
First Issue: Jan 1848
Last Issue: April 1849//
Available From: Marietta Coll., Marrietta, Ohio; State Hist. Soc. of Wis., Madison

884 TITLE: The Western Literary Journal, and Monthly Review. [Merged with The Western Monthly Magazine q.v. to form The Western Monthly Magazine, and Literary Journal q.v.]

Place of Publication: Cincinnati
First Issue: June 1836
Last Issue: Nov 1836//
Periodicity: Monthly
Editor: William D. Gallagher
Publishers: Smith and Day
Available From: APS; Lib. of Congress.* Mott.
Contents:
  Poetry: Original: William D. Gallagher. Selected.

Prose: Biography. Essay. Familiar Essay. Book Reviews.
Fiction: Sketches. Tales: "The Deserted Cabin: A Tale of the 'New Purchase'"; "The Ghost of the Bed-Chamber. A Sketch for the Superstitious"; "The Last of the Indian Fighters"; "The Garden-Girl of the Eden-Bank"; "Derrick Vandunk"; "My Uncle's Roast Pig"; "A Celestial Tete-a-tete"; "The Rise and the Fall"; "'Elm Grove.'-- A Story with a Catastrophe"; "Is It Possible?"; "Perseverance: With an Illustration, Drawn from the Life of Tom Towser and His Cousin."
Miscellaneous: Extracts: Schiller, Ingraham, Coleridge. Anecdotes: on various subjects; Byron.

885 TITLE: Western Literary Journal and Monthly Review. [Issued Simultaneously as the Southwestern Literary and Monthly Review (Nashville, Tenn.).]

Place of Publication: Cincinnati
First Issue: Nov 1844
Last Issue: April 1845//
Periodicity: Monthly
Editors: E.Z.C. Judson; L.A. Hine
Publishers: Robinson & Jones
Available From: APS; Carnegie Lib., Pittsburgh*
Contents:
  Poetry: Original: James W. Ward, E.A. Evans, C.B. Gillespie, Otway Curry, T.M. Tweed, Lewis J. Cist. Selected: Emerson Bennett, Amelia B. Welby, J.B. Hickey, Schiller, John Tomlin, William Gilmore Simms.
  Prose: Biography. Essay. Familiar Essay. Book Reviews.
  Fiction: Essay Serials: "Sketches of the Florida War"; "Rocky Mountain Sketches." Sketches. Tales: "The Last of the Bucaneers; a Yarn of the Eighteenth Century"; "The Stranger"; "Killing a Whale"; "A Family History"; "Mary Wilton"; "Bill Mann, Three Sheets in the Wind"; "The Last Chief of the Uchees: A Yarn, Connected with the Early History of Florida"; "One Dollar, or Kindness Rewards Itself"; "The Difference"; "The Bachelor"; "Barney O'Grady: Or the Kilkenny Blacksmith, a Legend of the South of Ireland"; "The Last Sitting"; "The Artist's Love"; "Punishment."
  Miscellaneous: Extracts: from other journals; by various authors; Schiller. Literary Notices.

886 TITLE: Western Literary Magazine. [See The Literary Messenger.]

887 TITLE: The Western Literary Magazine; a Literary Monthly.

Place of Publication: Chicago
First Issue: Oct 1845
Last Issue: Sept 1846//

Available From: Iowa State Traveling Lib.,
Des Moines*

888   TITLE: The Western Literary Magazine and
Journal of Education, Science, Arts and
Morals.

Place of Publication: Detroit
First Issue: April 1849
Last Issue: Sept 1849//?
Available From: Detroit Pub. Lib.; Minn.
Hist. Soc., St. Paul

889   TITLE: The Western Literary Messenger. A
Family Magazine of Literature, Science, Art,
Morality, and General Intelligence.

Place of Publication: Buffalo, N.Y.
First Issue: 1841
Last Issue: April 1857//
Periodicity: Weekly
Editor: J. Clement
Publishers: Jewett, Thomas & Co.; Clement &
Faxon; Chadbourne & Clement
Available From: Lib. of Congress; Amer.
Antiquarian Soc.
Contents:
  Poetry: Original: H.W. Rockwell, Horatio
  Gates, George W. Patten, William O. Butler,
  James Sheridan Knowles, Guy H. Salisbury,
  John Norval, Alice Carey, Phoebe Carey,
  Mariana Hendee, W.H.C. Hosmer, John C.
  Lord, Sylvia G. Foote, J. Clement, Frances
  A. Fuller, R.H. Brown, Thomas Holley
  Chivers. Selected: Lydia H. Sigourney,
  Mary Howitt, William Wallace, George Pope
  Morris, William D. Gallagher, Schiller,
  C.D. Stuart, Beranger, J. Bayard Taylor,
  Elizabeth Oakes Smith, Eliza Cook,
  Nathaniel P. Willis, William Ellery
  Channing, Longfellow, Barry Cornwall,
  Anna Cora Mowatt, Whittier, Mary E.
  Hewitt, William Hubbard, James Russell
  Lowell, Charles G. Eastman, Charles
  MacKay.
  Prose: Sketches. Tales: "The Spy of the
  Mohawk"; "The Retribution; or, the Re-
  venge of Circumstances"; "The Pauper Lad
  of Woodend: Or, a Will and a Way";
  "Bertha. A Story for the Thoughtful";
  "The Quakeress, or a Tale of Fifty Years
  Ago"; "Laura Lyle"; "The Heroic Wife";
  "Nine Years Since"; "The Mysterious Leg";
  "Night of a Railway in Old England"; "The
  Teacher of Music. A Tale of Epidemic";
  "The Crystal Basket; or the Way Mr.
  Hickson Cum to Be a Bachelor"; "A Trip to
  Chicago in the St. Louis"; "The Political
  Campaign;--Or the Club Room"; "The Young
  Forger. From the Note Book of a
  Philadelphia Lawyer"; "Boatswain; or, the
  Faithful Dog."
  Miscellaneous: Extracts: from other jour-
  nals. Anecdotes: on various subjects.
  Literary Notices. News: Foreign and
  Domestic.

890   TITLE: The Western Magazine and Review. [See
The Western Monthly Review.]

891   TITLES: (1) The Western Messenger; Devoted to
Religion and Literature   (2) The Western
Messenger, Devoted to Religion, Life, and
Literature.

Place of Publication: Louisville, Ky.; Boston;
Cincinnati
First Issue: June 1835
Last Issue: April 1841//
Periodicity: Monthly
Editors: Ephraim Peabody; James Freeman
Clarke; William H. Channing; James
H. Perkins; C.P. Cranch
Publishers: Thomas H. Shreve and Co.; Western
Unitarian Association; James
Munroe & Co.; John B. Russell;
James Freeman Clarke; William H.
Channing and James H. Perkins
Available From: APS; Lib. of Congress.*
Mott.
Contents:
  Poetry: Original: Theodore Parker, Ephraim
  Peabody, Elizabeth Peabody, Otway Curry,
  Margaret Fuller, Thomas H. Shreve, Lewis
  Foulk Thomas, Jones Very, C.P. Cranch,
  James Freeman Clarke, Keats, William D.
  Gallagher. Selected: Thomas Hood, Albert
  Pike, John B. Dillon, Felicia Hemans,
  Schiller, Edward C. Pinckney, Winthrop M.
  Praed, Tennyson, Hannah F. Gould, Quevedo,
  Rufus Dawes, George Herbert, Bryant,
  Washington Allston, Henry Vaughan, Charles
  D. Drake, Wordsworth, Byron, Goethe,
  Shelley, Oliver Wendell Holmes, William
  Ellery Channing.
  Prose: Biography. Essay. Familiar Essay.
  Criticism. Letters. Book Reviews.
  Fiction: Sketches. Tales: "Legend of Sir
  Guyon"; "Theodore. Or the Sceptic's
  Progress to Belief"; "Elvira.--A Sketch";
  "A Vision"; "House Warming"; "An Honest
  Lawyer's Fee"; "The Backslider"; "The
  Second Coming"; "New-Year's Day--A Dream";
  "The Race-Course"; "The Suspicious Man";
  "The Stage Driver."
  Miscellaneous: Extracts: from other jour-
  nals; by various authors; Keats. Literary
  Notices.

892   TITLE: Western Minerva, or American Annals of
Knowledge and Literature.

Place of Publication: Lexington, Ky.
First Issue: [Only one issue published]
Jan 1820//
Periodicity: Intended to be Quarterly
Editor: Thomas Smith
Publisher: Thomas Smith
Available From: APS; Acad. of Natural
Sciences, Philadelphia. Mott.
Contents:
  Poetry: Original. Selected: Milton,
  Rousseau.

Prose: Essay. Letters.
Fiction: Essay Serials: "The Sifter"; "The Querist"; "The Monkeys."
Miscellaneous: Extracts: by various authors; Franklin. Literary Notices.

893 TITLE: The Western Miscellany.

Place of Publication: Dayton, Ohio
First Issue: July 1848
Last Issue: June 1849//
Periodicity: Monthly
Editor: B.F. Ellis
Publisher: B.F. Ellis
Available From: APS; Ohio State Hist. Soc., Columbus*
Contents:
Poetry: Selected: Felicia Hemans, Oliver Wendell Holmes.
Prose: Biography. Essay. Familiar Essay.
Fiction: Sketches. Tales: "Catochus"; "A Blue Jacket"; "The Minister's Feast"; "The Maniac Maid.--A Tale of the Tyrol."
Miscellaneous: Extracts: from other journals; by various authors; Franklin, George Lippard, W. Irving. Anecdotes: on various subjects; Addison, Franklin, Milton, S. Johnson.

894 TITLES: (1) The Western Monthly Magazine (2) The Western Monthly Magazine, and Literary Journal. [Supersedes The Illinois Monthly Magazine q.v.]

Place of Publication: Cincinnati
First Issue: Jan 1833
Last Issue: June 1837//
Periodicity: Monthly
Editors: James Hall; Joseph Reese Fry; James B. Marshall; William D. Gallagher
Publishers: Corey and Fairbank; Taylor & Tracy; Flash, Ryder and Co.; Marshall and Gallagher
Available From: APS; Yale Univ.* Mott. Poole.
Contents:
Poetry: Original: Harriet Beecher, Hannah F. Gould, William D. Gallagher, Otway Curry. Selected: Hannah F. Gould, John H. Savage.
Prose: Biography. Travel. Essay. Familiar Essay. Letters. Book Reviews.
Fiction: Essay Serial: "Travels in Hot Weather." Sketches. Tales: "The Spy. A Tale of the Revolution"; "Evening Music at Sea"; "The Black Patriot"; "The Chase"; "The Spectre Hunter, a Legend of the West"; "A New England Sketch" [Harriet Beecher]; "The Blind Artist"; "Aunt Mary"; "The Rustic"; "The Festival at Bluffdale"; "Thanksgiving Day"; "Circumstantial Evidence. A Tale Founded on Fact"; "The Village Pastor's Wife"; "La Rouge, or the Red Tavern"; "The Savoyards."
Miscellaneous: Extracts: from other journals; by various authors; Byron, Caroline Lee Hentz. Literary Notices.

895 TITLE: The Western Monthly Magazine, and Literary Journal. [See The Western Monthly Magazine.]

896 TITLES: (1) The Western Monthly Review (2) The Western Magazine and Review (3) The Western Monthly Review.

Place of Publication: Cincinnati
First Issue: May 1827
Last Issue: June 1830//
Periodicity: Monthly
Editor: Timothy Flint
Publisher: E. Hubbard Flint
Available From: APS; Lib. of Congress.* Mott. Poole.
Contents:
Poetry: Original. Selected: Pope, William Gilmore Simms, Samuel Butler ["Hudibras"].
Prose: Biography. Travel. Essay. Familiar Essay. Criticism. Letters. Book Reviews.
Fiction: Sketches. Tales: "Jemima O'Keefy. --A Sentimental Tale"; "Violetta and Thoroughgrabb. A Tale"; "The Hermit of the Prairies"; "Adventures of Arthur Clenning"; "The Valley of the Shoshonee"; "Agnes Sorel de Merivanne: The Recluse Coquette"; "Col. Plug, the Last of the Boat-Wreckers"; "Paulina, or the Cataract of Tequendama."
Miscellaneous: Extracts: by various authors. Literary Notices.

897 TITLES: (1) Western Museum and Belles-Lettres Repository (2) The Museum and Literary Repository.

Place of Publication: Ithaca, N.Y.
First Issue: 1826
Last Issue: 1828//?
Available From: Cornell Univ., Ithaca

898 TITLE: The Western Quarterly Review.

Place of Publication: Cincinnati
First Issue: Jan 1849
Last Issue: April 1849//
Periodicity: Quarterly
Editor: J.S. Hitchcock
Publisher: J.S. Hitchcock
Available From: APS; Yale Univ.*
Contents:
Poetry: Selected.
Prose: Essay. Familiar Essay. Book Reviews.
Fiction: Sketches.
Miscellaneous: Extracts: by various authors; William D. Gallagher, Sidney Dyer, S. Anna Lewis. Literary Notices.

899 TITLE: Western Recorder.

Place of Publication: Utica, N.Y.
First Issue: 6 Jan 1824
Last Issue: 12 Feb 1833//

Periodicity: Bi-Weekly
Editor: Thomas Hastings
Publishers: Merrell & Hastings; Hastings &
    Tracy
Available From: APS; Amer. Antiquarian Soc.
Contents:
  Poetry: Original: Jane Taylor, Michael
    Bruce. Selected: Bernard Barton, William
    B. Tappan, Sarah J. Hale, Southey, Emily
    Taylor, William Cowper, Anna Letitia
    Barbauld, John G. Brainard, Thomas
    Campbell, John Quincy Adams, James
    Montgomery, Felicia Hemans, Wordsworth,
    Thomas Haynes Bayly, Willis Gaylord Clark.
  Prose: Biography. Travel. Essay.
    Familiar Essay. Letters. Book Reviews.
  Fiction: Sketches.
  Miscellaneous: Extracts: from other jour-
    nals; by various authors. Anecdotes: on
    various subjects; Hannah More, John Adams,
    Penn. Literary Notices. News: Foreign
    and Domestic.

900   TITLE: The Western Review.

Place of Publication: Columbus, Ohio
First Issue: [Only one issue published]
              April 1846//
Periodicity: ?
Editors: ?
Publishers: C.C. & G.R. Hazewell
Available From: APS; Lib. of Congress*
Contents:
  Poetry: Selected.
  Prose: Essay.
  Miscellaneous: Extracts: William D.
    Gallagher. Literary Notices.

901   TITLE: The Western Review and Miscellaneous
    Magazine, a Monthly Publication, Devoted to
    Literature and Science.

Place of Publication: Lexington, Ky.
First Issue: Aug 1819
Last Issue: July 1821//
Periodicity: Monthly
Editor: William Gibbes Hunt
Publisher: William Gibbes Hunt
Available From: APS; Amer. Antiquarian Soc.*
              Mott. Poole.
Contents:
  Poetry: Original: George Beck, Horace
    Holley. Selected: Kleist, Gessner,
    Schlegel, Byron, Madame de Staël, Scott,
    W. Irving, John Trumbull.
  Prose: Biography. Travel. Essay.
    Familiar Essay. Criticism. Letters.
    Book Reviews.
  Fiction: Sketches.
  Miscellaneous: Anecdotes: on various sub-
    jects. Literary Notices.

902   TITLE: Western Shield, and Literary Messen-
    ger. [See The Working-Men's Shield.]

903   TITLE: The Western Spy and Literary Cadet.
    [Subtitle varies.]

Place of Publication: Cincinnati
First Issue: 23 July 1814
Last Issue: 28 Dec 1822//
Available From: State Hist. Soc. of Wis.,
              Madison; Stanford Coll.,
              Stanford, Calif.

904   TITLE: The Whim.

Place of Publication: Philadelphia
First Issue: 14 May 1814
Last Issue: 16 July 1814//?
Periodicity: Weekly
Editor: James Fennell
Publisher: James Fennell
Available From: Hist. Soc. of Pa.;* Harvard
              Univ.
Contents:
  Poetry: Original. Selected: Robert Treat
    Paine, Charles James Fox, Washington
    Allston, William Cowper.
  Prose: Familiar Essay.
  Fiction: Sketches.
  Miscellaneous: Extracts: by various authors;
    Chateaubriand. Anecdotes: on various
    subjects.
Note: The journal claims to be theatrical in
  nature, but there is a smattering of just
  about everything.

905   TITLES: (1) The Worcester Intelligencer: Or,
    Brookfield Advertiser (2) The Worcester
    County Intelligencer: Or, Brookfield
    Advertiser.

Place of Publication: Brookfield, Mass.
First Issue: 7 Oct 1794
Last Issue: 28 April 1795//
Periodicity: Weekly
Editors: Isaiah Thomas; Elisha H. Waldo
Publishers: Isaiah Thomas; Elisha H. Waldo
Available From: Amer. Antiquarian Soc.*
Contents:
  Poetry: Original. Selected.
  Prose: Familiar Essay.
  Fiction: Sketches.
  Miscellaneous: Anecdotes: on various sub-
    jects. Literary Notices. News: Foreign
    and Domestic.

906   TITLES: (1) The Worcester Magazine, a Liter-
    ary and Religious Miscellany (2) The New-
    England Magazine, a Religious and Literary
    Monthly Miscellany.

Place of Publication: Worcester, Mass.
First Issue: 1843
Last Issue: March 1844//?
Periodicity: Monthly
Editors: L. Milton Thayer; L. Augusta Miller;
              S.B. Noyes; Leonard Cox, Jr.
Publishers: William Campbell; R.B. Hancock

Available From: Amer. Antiquarian Soc.*;
                    Newberry Lib., Chicago
Contents:
  Poetry: Original: Charles S. Congden,
    Elbridge G. Robinson, James Bennett,
    S.H. Browne, William Cutter, Lydia H.
    Sigourney, C. Thurber, Charles W.
    Denison, Henry John Sharpe, Horace Smith.
    Selected: Francis Scott Key, Caroline
    Norton, Lydia H. Sigourney.
  Prose: Essay. Familiar Essay.
  Fiction: Sketches. Tales: "The Devil's
    Hand. A Legend of Dedham, Mass."; "Love
    at First Sight"; "Going to Board";
    "Vincezna"; "A Legend of New England";
    "A Tale of Natick"; "Ichabod Crane";
    "A Year at Twenty-One"; "The Blind Boy's
    Return." Drama: "Lights and Shadows
    of Intemperance."

907   TITLE: The Worcester Magazine. Containing
        Politicks, Miscellanies, Poetry, and News.
        [See also The Massachusetts Spy.]

        Place of Publication: Worcester, Mass.
        First Issue: 1st week April 1786
        Last Issue: 4th week March 1788//
        Periodicity: Weekly
        Editor: Isaiah Thomas
        Publisher: Isaiah Thomas
        Available From: APS; Amer. Antiquarian Soc.*
                    Mott.
        Contents:
          Poetry: Original. Selected.
          Prose: Essay: "History of the Late War in
            America."
          Fiction: Essay Serial: "The Worcester
            Speculator." Sketches.
          Miscellaneous: Anecdotes: on various sub-
            jects. Literary Notices. News: Foreign
            and Domestic.

908   TITLE: The Worcester Talisman, a Literary and
        Miscellaneous Journal; Containing Articles
        of Intelligence from Travellers and Voyagers,
        Sketches of Interesting Biography--Popular
        Tales--Original and Selected Poetry--Mis-
        cellaneous Selections and Anecdotes.

        Place of Publication: Worcester, Mass.
        First Issue: 5 April 1828
        Last Issue: 15 Oct 1829//
        Periodicity: Semi-monthly
        Editors: ?
        Publishers: Dorr & Howland
        Available From: Amer. Antiquarian Soc.*;
                     Yale Univ.
        Contents:
          Poetry: Original. Selected: Hannah More,
            Bryant, Barry Cornwall, Alaric Watts,
            Robert Morris, Emory Washburn, Felicia
            Hemans, Susanna Strickland, James G.
            Brooks.
          Prose: Biography: Hannah More. Familiar
            Essay.

Fiction: Sketches. Tales: "The Orphan";
  "The Stage Driver"; "Job Clark";
  "Pequassett"; "The Ice Ship"; "The High-
  lander"; "The Fortunes of Martin Waldeck"
  [Scott]; "Alfred Anson"; "Chivalry of the
  Eighteenth Century"; "A Scene from '76";
  "Mary Benson"; "Hannah Bint" [Mary Russell
  Mitford]; "The Election--A Tale" [Mary
  Russell Mitford].
Miscellaneous: Extracts: from other jour-
  nals; by various authors; W. Irving,
  Bryant. Anecdotes: on various subjects;
  Scott, Byron, Franklin, Boswell, S. Johnson,
  Thomas Paine, William Cobbett. News:
  Domestic.

909   TITLES: (1) The Working-Men's Shield (2)
        Western Shield, and Literary Messenger.

        Place of Publication: Cincinnati
        First Issue: 8 Aug 1832
        Last Issue: 23 Nov 1833//
        Periodicity: Weekly [Irregular]
        Editor: Lewis Foulke Thomas
        Publisher: Richard C. Langdon
        Available From: Lib. of Congress*
        Contents:
          Poetry: Original. Selected: Barry Corn-
            wall, Felicia Hemans, Caroline Norton,
            Emma C. Embury, Charles Swain, Henry Neele,
            Byron, Fanny Kemble, Hannah F. Gould,
            William Motherwell, Miss Pardoe, James
            G. Percival, Thomas Moore, James Shirley,
            James Hogg.
          Prose: Travel. Essay. Familiar Essay.
            Letters.
          Fiction: Essay Serials: "Scenes on the
            Ocean"; "The Rattler"; "Gleanings of a
            Student." Sketches. Tales: "The Berk-
            shire Gold-Finder"; "The Captive Boy";
            "Matilda Usher, a Tale of Other Times";
            "A Scene in the Revolution"; "The City
            of Demons"; "The Haunted Head"; "The
            Phantom Hand"; "Notre Dame"; "The Fisher-
            man of the North Sea"; "The Valley of the
            Susquehanna"; "The Black Napoleon"; "The
            Invalid Pensioner"; "Perran Path. A
            Cornish Story."
          Miscellaneous: Extracts: from other jour-
            nals; by various authors. Anecdotes: on
            various subjects. Literary Notices. News:
            Domestic.

910   TITLES: (1) The World We Live In. A Semi-
        Monthly Journal of Useful and Entertaining
        Literature (2) The Literary Museum, a Re-
        pository of the Useful and Entertaining:
        Including the Wonders of Nature and Art:
        Tales of All Countries and All Ages:
        Travels: Adventures: Biography, &c.
        Embellished with Engravings on Steel, and
        Music Arranged for the Piano Forte.

        Place of Publication: Boston
        First Issue: 6 Jan 1844
        Last Issue: 2 Oct 1847//

Periodicity: Semi-monthly; Annual
Editors: John B. Hall; Andrew J. Loud
Publishers: John B. Hall; R.B. Fitts
Available From: Lib. of Congress*; Brown
Univ., Providence, R.I.
Contents:
  Poetry: Original: Charlotte Allen, Isaac
    M'Lellan, Jr., Ned Buntline, Lizzie Wal-
    cott, John Patch, James H. Brown, Henry
    Cook, John S. Adams. Selected: Robert
    Josselyn, Frances S. Osgood, Jesse E.
    Dow, Martin F. Tupper, Sophia H. Oliver,
    Lydia H. Sigourney, Park Benjamin,
    Charlotte Allen, Longfellow, Emerson,
    J. Gierlow, Catharine W. Barber, James
    Montgomery, Caroline F. Orne, Mary
    Howitt.
  Prose: Familiar Essay. Letters.
  Fiction: Essay Serials: "Epitaphiana: Or,
    Monumental Inscriptions and Churchyard
    Sketches"; "The Collector." Sketches.
    Tales: "Three Adventures Before Midnight";
    "The Widow"; "La Bella Tabaccaia"; "Marshal
    Biron and the Witch of Chefboutonne"; "The
    Left Hand Glove; or Circumstantial Testi-
    mony"; "The Faro Bank"; "The Autumn Storm";
    "The Doomed Family. A Tale of Thrilling
    Interest"; "The First Born"; "The Dream-
    er"; "The Heir Presumptive"; "Ottawa; or
    the History and Legend of Castle Neck";
    "The Hermit of Cumberland"; "Uncle Ned;
    or One Hundred Dollars a Day"; "Eva
    Markland; or, the Capture and Re-Capture";
    "The Neglected Rose-Tree"; "A Night in the
    Gulf of Mexico in an Open Boat" [Ned
    Buntline]. Drama: "Erodia; the Spirit
    of Love and Beauty; or the Law of Love."
  Miscellaneous: Extracts: from other jour-
    nals; by various authors; Horace Greeley,
    Whittier, Theodore Parker. Anecdotes:
    on various subjects. Literary Notices.
  Note: Motto: "We range the earth to gather
    novelty."

911   TITLES: (1) The Wreath. Devoted to Polite
      Literature (2) The Literary Journal, a
      Repository of Polite Literature and the
      Fine Arts.

  Place of Publication: Schenectady, N.Y.;
                        Albany; Troy, N.Y.
  First Issue: 22 Nov 1834
  Last Issue: 6 June 1835//?
  Periodicity: Semi-monthly
  Editor: William H. Burleigh
  Publisher: William H. Burleigh
  Available From: APS; Brown Univ. Providence,
                  R.I.*
  Contents:
    Poetry: Original: Sumner Lincoln Fair-
      field, William H. Burleigh, Charles W.
      Denison, Lydia H. Sigourney. Selected.
    Prose: Biography: Keats. Essay. Familiar
      Essay. Letters.
    Fiction: Sketches. Tales: "Donald Lee";
      "The Captive Queen's Gift"; "The Heiress."

Miscellaneous: Extracts: from other jour-
nals; by various authors; Whittier,
Frances Trollope, Sarah J. Hale. Anec-
dotes: on various subjects; Felicia
Hemans, James Fenimore Cooper, W. Irving.
Literary Notices.

912   TITLE: The Yale Literary Magazine.

  Place of Publication: New Haven, Conn.
  First Issue: Feb 1836
  Last Issue: --
  Periodicity: Monthly
  Editors: The Students of Yale College
  Publishers: Herrick & Noyes; A.H. Maltby;
              T.H. Pease
  Available From: APS; Yale Univ.* Mott.
  Contents:
    Poetry: Original: W.R. Bliss, H.R. Jackson,
      George H. Colton, J.S. Babcock, W. Bacon,
      James Russell Lowell, C. Lyman, H.
      Sherman, W. Learned, C.H. Hall, Guy B.
      Day, William Smith, E. Franklin. Selected:
      Schlegel, Gessner, Schiller, Victor Hugo,
      Tennyson, Oliver Wendell Holmes.
    Prose: Biography. Essay. Familiar Essay.
      Criticism. Book Reviews.
    Fiction: Essay Serials: "The Coffee Club";
      "Papers from the Attic"; "Sea Sketches."
      Sketches. Tales: "The Sciot Girl";
      "Confessions of a Sensitive Man"; "Story
      and Sentiment"; "The Double Disappoint-
      ment"; "The Outlaw and His Daughter";
      "The Sister's Faith"; "The Omnibus"; "A
      Frontier Scene"; "Miss Tabitha Tunk";
      "Dick Versus Dike, or, the Invisible
      Steed"; "The Persecuted"; "The Last Shot.
      A Tale of the Sea"; "Story of a Life";
      "The Victim"; "The Liberators"; "A Tale
      of My Landlord"; "The Antique Infant
      School"; "Lorenzo the Magnificent"; "The
      Doomed"; "The Vassal"; "The Fate of
      Genius"; "Harriet"; "Not Lost, But Gone
      Before"; "Ganymede"; "A Tale of Romance";
      "Jedediah Birch"; "The Mother's Lecture";
      "The Heir of Lichstenstein"; "Almeme";
      "Dekanissora"; "The Coliseum"; "A Scene
      at a Camp-Meeting, or the Consequence of
      a Name"; "The Handsome Stranger"; "Mary.
      A Tale of the Ohio"; "The Serenade";
      "Frank Ashburton; or, the Return"; "The
      Last of the Bodkins"; "The Woodsman";
      "The Witch"; "The Hoaxed"; "Conversano";
      "The Resurrectionists"; "The Two Students";
      "The Young Lawyer"; "Appearance Versus
      Worth. A Tale"; "The Mother's Grave";
      "A Nosegay"; "A Night in Trumbull Gallery";
      "The Pickled Ghost; or, Christmas Eve";
      "The Mexican Volunteer"; "The Vow. A
      Legend of the Iroquois"; "Reason and Fancy.
      An Allegory"; "The Devil's Pulpit"; "The
      Confession; or, a New Way of Fooling a
      Jury"; "Lying-to Under Bare Poles"; "The
      Widow and the Fatherless"; "Outward
      Bound."
    Miscellaneous: Extracts: by various
      authors. Literary Notices.

913 TITLES: (1) <u>The Yankee</u> (2) <u>The Yankee; and</u>
<u>Boston Literary Gazette</u>. [Merged into the
<u>New-England Galaxy & Masonic Magazine</u> q.v.]

Place of Publication: Portland, Me.; Boston
First Issue: 1 Jan 1828
Last Issue: Dec 1829//
Periodicity: Weekly; Monthly
Editors: John Neal; James W. Miller
Publishers: James Adams, Jr.; William S. Wait
Available From: APS; Lib. of Congress*
Contents:
  Poetry: <u>Original</u>. <u>Selected</u>: Grenville
  Mellen, James G. Percival, Longfellow,
  Shelley, John Bowring, George D. Prentice,
  James Montgomery, Richard Henry Dana,
  Nathaniel P. Willis, Joseph H. Nichols,
  Poe, Whittier.
  Prose: <u>Biography</u>: Sumner Lincoln Fairfield,
  John Ledyard, Jeremy Bentham, Byron,
  Daniel Webster. <u>Essay</u>. <u>Familiar Essay</u>.
  <u>Criticism</u>. <u>Letters</u>. <u>Book Reviews</u>.
  Fiction: <u>Essay Serials</u>: "New England as It
  Was"; "New England as It Is"; "Live
  Yankees"; "Discourses"; "Leaves from a
  Journal." <u>Sketches</u>. <u>Tale</u>: "The Second
  Volume."
  Miscellaneous: <u>Extracts</u>: from other jour-
  nals; by various authors; B. D'Israeli.
  <u>Anecdotes</u>: on various subjects; W. Irving,
  Leigh Hunt. <u>Literary Notices</u>. <u>News</u>:
  Domestic.
Note: Motto: "Utility--the Greatest Happiness
  of the Greatest Number."

914 TITLE: <u>The Yankee; and Boston Literary</u>
<u>Gazette</u>. [See <u>The Yankee</u>.]

915 TITLES: (1) <u>The Yankee Miscellany</u> (2) <u>The</u>
<u>Yankee Miscellany, or Boston Monthly Maga-</u>
<u>zine</u>.

Place of Publication: Boston
First Issue: Jan 1839
Last Issue: Dec 1839//
Periodicity: Monthly
Editors: ?
Publishers: Cassady and March; George Oscar
  Bartlett; James Burns
Available From: Amer. Antiquarian Soc.;
  Boston Pub. Lib.*
Contents:
  Poetry: <u>Original</u>: Moses Foster. <u>Selected</u>:
  James T. Fields, Willis Gaylord Clark,
  Frederic S. Hill, Frances S. Osgood,
  Robert Hamilton.
  Prose: <u>Biography</u>: Nathaniel P. Willis.
  <u>Familiar Essay</u>.
  Fiction: <u>Essay Serials</u>: "Yankeana"; "Our
  Light Stand." <u>Sketches</u>. <u>Tales</u>: "The
  Florentine Sculptor. A Tale"; "Marie de
  Lorraine"; "The Gambler's Last Loaf"; "The
  Pirate of the Calaboose"; "The Belles of
  the Mall"; "Eleanor Mallows."
  Miscellaneous: <u>Anecdotes</u>: on various sub-
  jects. <u>Literary Notices</u>.

916 TITLE: <u>The Yankee Miscellany, or Boston</u>
<u>Monthly Magazine</u>. [See <u>The Yankee Mis-</u>
<u>cellany</u>.]

917 TITLE: <u>The Young Ladies' Journal of Litera-</u>
<u>ture and Science</u>.

Place of Publication: Baltimore; Hartford
First Issue: Oct 1830
Last Issue: Nov 1831//
Available From: Harvard Univ.; Univ. of Va.,
  Charlottesville

918 TITLE: <u>The Young Ladies' Mirror, Devoted to</u>
<u>the Different Branches of Polite Literature</u>.

Place of Publication: Geneva, N.Y.
First Issue: 1 Aug 1834
Last Issue: 25 July 1835//
Available From: Syracuse Univ., Syracuse, N.Y.*

919 TITLE: <u>The Young People's Book; or, Magazine</u>
<u>of Useful and Entertaining Knowledge</u>.

Place of Publication: Philadelphia
First Issue: Sept 1841
Last Issue: Aug 1842//?
Periodicity: Monthly
Editor: John Frost
Publisher: Morton M'Michael
Available From: Lib. of Congress; Amer.
  Antiquarian Soc.
Contents:
  Poetry: <u>Original</u>: Henry S. Hagert, Edmund
  Leaf, John B. Longshore, Reynell Coates,
  A.B. Justice, Marion H. Rand, Ellen S.
  Rand. <u>Selected</u>: Sarah J. Hale, Byron.
  Prose: <u>Biography</u>. <u>Travel</u>. <u>Essay</u>.
  <u>Familiar Essay</u>. <u>Letters</u>. <u>Book Reviews</u>.
  Fiction: <u>Essay Serials</u>: "Evenings at My
  Uncle's"; "Evenings at Roseheath."
  <u>Sketches</u>. <u>Tales</u>: "The Ends of Life";
  "The Captive Prince"; "The Two Death Beds:
  Or the Painter and the Queen"; "The Artist,
  the Poet, and the Emperor. An Historical
  Tale"; "The Prodigal's Return"; "The Gem
  of the Sea, or the Approach to Land";
  "The Prince and the Poet"; "The Easter
  Egg; or, the Child's Trial"; "The Black
  Lace Veil."
  Miscellaneous: <u>Extracts</u>: by various
  authors. <u>Anecdotes</u>: on various subjects;
  Washington. <u>Literary Notices</u>.

920 TITLE: <u>Young People's Journal of Science,</u>
<u>Literature, and Art</u>.

Place of Publication: New York; Boston
First Issue: [Only one issue published?]
  Nov 1848//?
Periodicity: Intended to be monthly
Editors: Nathan Brittan; Frances H. Green
Publisher: S.B. Brittan
Available From: Amer. Antiquarian Soc.

Contents:
  Poetry: <u>Original</u>: Fanny Green, C. Chauncey
  Burr.
  Prose: <u>Biography</u>. <u>Essay</u>. <u>Letters</u>.
  Fiction: <u>Sketches</u>.

921   TITLE: <u>Youth's Cabinet</u>.

Place of Publication: Utica, N.Y.
First Issue: 31 March 1815
Last Issue: 21 April 1815//?
Periodicity: Weekly
Editors: ?
Publishers: ?
Available From: APS; Kent State Univ., Kent,
                Ohio*
Contents:
  Poetry: <u>Original</u>. <u>Selected</u>.
  Fiction: <u>Sketches</u>. <u>Tales</u>: "Alfred and
    Dorinda"; "Pastorius: A Nocturnal Tale."
  Miscellaneous: <u>Anecdotes</u>: on various sub-
    jects. <u>News</u>: Domestic.

922   TITLE: <u>The Youth's Cabinet. A Semi-Monthly
       Publication, Designed to Promote the
       Improvement of the Youthful Mind, and to
       Elevate the Character of the Rising
       Generation</u>.

Place of Publication: New York
First Issue: 1843
Last Issue: 1844//?
Periodicity: Semi-monthly
Editors: ?
Publisher: Ralph Hunt
Available From: Hist. Soc. of Pa.
Contents:
  Poetry: <u>Original</u>: Lydia Baxter.
    <u>Selected</u>: Hannah F. Gould, Mary Howitt.
  Prose: <u>Travel</u>. <u>Essay</u>. <u>Familiar Essay</u>.
  Fiction: <u>Essay Serials</u>: "Sketches at
    Sea"; "A Particular Providence"; "Uncle
    William Abroad." <u>Sketches</u>. <u>Tales</u>:
    "Henry and Frances, or a Sister's Love";
    "Celia; or the Way to Be Useful and
    Happy. A Tale of the Present Time."

923   TITLE: <u>The Youth's Cabinet: A Weekly Paper</u>.
       [See <u>Youth's Cabinet, Devoted to Liberty,
       Peace, Temperance, Purity, Truth</u>.]

924   TITLES: (1) <u>Youth's Cabinet, Devoted to
       Liberty, Peace, Temperance, Purity, Truth</u>
       (2) <u>Youth's Cabinet, Devoted to Liberty,
       Peace, Temperance, and Religious, Moral,
       Intellectual, and Physical Education</u>
       (3) <u>Youth's Cabinet. For Families and Sun-
       day Schools</u> (4) <u>The Youth's Cabinet:
       A Weekly Paper</u> (5) <u>Youth's Cabinet. For
       Families and Schools</u>. [Superseded by the
       <u>Youth's Cabinet, a Book of Gems for the
       Mind and the Heart</u>, later <u>Woodworth's
       Youth's Cabinet</u>.]

Place of Publication: Boston: New York
First Issue: 28 April 1837
Last Issue: 1845//
Periodicity: Weekly
Editor: N. Southard
Publishers: N. Southard; Isaac Knapp
Available From: Amer. Antiquarian Soc.;
                Boston Pub. Lib.
Contents:
  Poetry: <u>Original</u>. <u>Selected</u>: Felicia
    Hemans, Hannah F. Gould, Isaac C. Pray,
    Jr., James Montgomery, Lydia H. Sigourney,
    Allan Cunningham, Charles Lamb, Richard
    Howitt, Barry Cornwall, Thomas Moore,
    William B. Tappan, Southey, Bryant,
    Thomas Campbell, Whittier, Henry Kirke
    White, Mary Howitt.
  Prose: <u>Biography</u>. <u>Travel</u>. <u>Essay</u>.
    <u>Letters</u>.
  Fiction: <u>Essay Serials</u>: "Uncle Simon's
    Rambles"; "Uncle William." <u>Sketches</u>.
    <u>Tales</u>: "The Eldest Sister in Childhood";
    "The Contented Mother"; "Isabelle Dudley."
  Miscellaneous: <u>Extracts</u>: from other jour-
    nals; by various authors; Washington.
    <u>Anecdotes</u>: on various subjects; Cromwell,
    Franklin. <u>Literary Notices</u>. <u>News</u>:
    Domestic.

925   TITLE: <u>Youth's Cabinet. For Families and
       Sunday Schools</u>. [See <u>Youth's Cabinet,
       Devoted to Liberty, Peace, Temperance,
       Purity, Truth</u>.]

926   TITLE: <u>The Youth's Companion</u>.

Place of Publication: Boston
First Issue: 16 April 1827
Last Issue: Sept 1929//
Periodicity: Weekly
Editor: Nathaniel Willis
Publisher: Nathaniel Willis
Available From: Lib. of Congress*; Boston
                Pub. Lib.*
Contents:
  Poetry: <u>Original</u>. <u>Selected</u>.
  Prose: <u>Familiar Essay</u>.
  Fiction: <u>Sketches</u>.
  Miscellaneous: <u>Extracts</u>: from other jour-
    nals; by various authors. <u>Anecdotes</u>: on
    various subjects.

927   TITLE: <u>Youths' Guide to Piety and Virtue,
       and Literary Casket</u>.

Place of Publication: Poughkeepsie, N.Y.
First Issue: Sept 1836
Last Issue: Aug 1837//?
Available From: Columbia Univ.*

928   TITLES: (1) <u>Youth's Literary Gazette</u>
       (2) <u>Youth's Miscellany</u>.

Place of Publication: Philadelphia
First Issue: 1 Dec 1832
Last Issue: 22 Nov 1833//
Periodicity: Weekly
Editor: Thomas T. Ash
Publisher: Thomas T. Ash
Available From: Amer. Antiquarian Soc.*;
                N.Y. Pub. Lib.*
Contents:
  Poetry: Original. Selected: Hannah F.
    Gould, Joanna Baillie, Felicia Hemans,
    Bryant, John Bowring, James Montgomery,
    Coleridge, Lydia H. Sigourney, Bernard
    Barton, Nathaniel P. Willis, Bowles.
  Prose: Essay. Letters.
  Fiction: Sketches. Tales: "The Deaf and
    Dumb Boy"; "Flor Silin, the Generous
    Russian Peasant"; "Generosity of the
    Chevalier Bayard"; "Poor Man and His
    Two Sons"; "The Gentleman Beggar"; "The
    Pretty Idiot"; "Osakoi; or, the Faithful
    Subject. A Russian Tale."
  Miscellaneous: Extracts: from other jour-
    nals. Anecdotes: on various subjects.
    Literary Notices.

929   TITLE: The Youth's Literary Messenger, Con-
        taining Tales, Biography, Descriptive
        Geography, Natural History, Philosophy and
        Poetry.

Place of Publication: Philadelphia
First Issue: May 1837
Last Issue: April 1839//
Periodicity: Monthly
Editors: ?
Publishers: ?
Available From: Lib. of Congress*; N.Y.
                Pub. Lib.
Contents:
  Poetry: Original. Selected: Victor Hugo,
    Shakespeare, Thomas Campbell, James
    Beattie, Rousseau.
  Prose: Biography: Henry Kirke White,
    Charles Goldoni, Mary Russell Mitford,
    Fenelon. Travel. Essay. Familiar Essay.
    Letters.
  Fiction: Essay Serial: "The Flower Gar-
    den." Sketches. Tales: "A Night in
    Philadelphia"; "The School-Fellows";
    "Jane Cameron, or the Want of the One
    Thing Needful"; "'Tis Time Enough Yet,'
    or Scenes from the Life of a Procrastina-
    tor"; "The Hunter's Tale"; "Baruch--Or
    the Fountain of Happiness; an Eastern
    Tale"; "The Lost Child"; "Early Recollec-
    tions, or the History of Jessie McDonald";
    "The Yellow Balsam, or a Legend of the
    Riesengebirge"; "The Spoilt Child"; "The
    Stepmother, or Prejudice Vanquished";
    "The Fisherman's Daughter, or the Two
    Vials"; "The Cousins, or the Fruits of
    Education"; "The Two Painters. A Floren-
    tine Story."

Miscellaneous: Extracts: from other
  journals; by various authors. Anecdotes:
  on various subjects; Buonaparte, Sidney.

930   TITLE: Youth's Lyceum.

Place of Publication: New Lisbon, Ohio
First Issue: April 1837
Last Issue: Sept 1837//?
Available From: Ohio State Hist. Soc.,
                Columbus*

931   TITLE: Youth's Lyceum. And Literary Gazette.

Place of Publication: Xenia, Ohio
First Issue: 1834
Last Issue: 11 May 1836//?
Periodicity: Irregular
Editors: ?
Publishers: Youth's Lyceum
Available From: Amer. Antiquarian Soc.
Contents:
  Poetry: Original. Selected.
  Prose: Familiar Essay.
  Fiction: Sketches.
  Miscellaneous: Anecdotes: on various sub-
    jects. Literary Notices. News: Domes-
    tic.

932   TITLE: Youth's Magazine.

Place of Publication: Cincinnati
First Issue: 30 Sept 1834
Last Issue: June 1838//?
Available From: Trinity Coll., Hartford;
                Hist. and Philosophical Soc.
                of Ohio, Cincinnati

933   TITLE: The Youth's Magazine; a Monthly
        Miscellany.

Place of Publication: New York
First Issue: May 1838
Last Issue: April 1841//?
Periodicity: Monthly
Editors: ?
Publishers: T. Mason and G. Lane
Available From: Wesleyan Univ., Middletown,
                Conn.*; Drew Univ., Madison,
                N.J.*
Contents:
  Poetry: Original. Selected: Southey.
  Prose: Biography. Travel. Essay.
    Familiar Essay. Letters.
  Fiction: Sketches.
  Miscellaneous: Extracts: from other jour-
    nals; by various authors. Anecdotes: on
    various subjects; John Wesley, George
    Whitefield, John Bunyan, S. Johnson,
    Jefferson.

934 TITLE: Youth's Magazine: Or, Spirit of the Juvenile Miscellany.

Place of Publication: Boston
First Issue: Jan 1830
Last Issue: Dec 1830//?
Periodicity: Monthly
Editors: ?
Publishers: Putnam & Hunt
Available From: Amer. Antiquarian Soc.;
                Boston Pub. Lib.
Contents:
  Poetry: Selected.
  Prose: Biography: John Elliot. Familiar
    Essay.
  Fiction: Sketches. Tales: "My Mother's
    Gold Ring"; "Ferdinand and Zoe"; "The
    Irish Emigrants"; "Willie, the Blind
    Piper, and His Sister Jeannie"; "School
    Hours"; "Industry and Idleness."
  Miscellaneous: Literary Notices.

935 TITLE: The Youth's Medallion.

Place of Publication: Boston
First Issue: 17 April 1841
Last Issue: 10 Dec 1842//
Periodicity: Semi-monthly
Editors: ?
Publishers: Sleeper, Dix & Rogers; Sleeper
  & Rogers
Available From: Amer. Antiquarian Soc.*;
                N.Y. Hist. Soc.
Contents:
  Poetry: Original. Selected: Barry
    Cornwall, Lydia H. Sigourney, Byron,
    Hannah F. Gould, Charles Sprague,
    Bernard Barton, Southey, James
    Montgomery, William Howitt, Charles
    Swain, Mary Howitt, Longfellow, George
    Pope Morris, Thomas Haynes Bayly,
    Whittier, Joanna Baillie.
  Prose: Biography: Benjamin West. Travel.
    Familiar Essay.
  Fiction: Sketches. Tales: "Jack Shadow";
    "Albert Barry, the Yankee Sailor Boy";
    "Amos Jones, or the Boy Who Went to Sea
    in Spite of Himself"; "The Tea-Rose"
    [Harriet Beecher Stowe].
  Miscellaneous: Extracts: from other
    journals; by various authors. Anecdotes:
    on various subjects; S. Johnson,
    Washington.

936 TITLE: Youth's Mental Casket, and Literary
    Star.

Place of Publication: Jersey City, N.J.
First Issue: 1839
Last Issue: Feb 1842//?
Periodicity: Monthly
Editors: Luther Pratt; A.W. Blakesley

Publishers: Pratt & Blakesley
Available From: Amer. Antiquarian Soc.;
                N.Y. Hist. Soc.
Contents:
  Poetry: Original. Selected.
  Prose: Essay. Familiar Essay.
  Fiction: Sketches. Tale: "Augustin and
    Clara. A Moral Tale."
  Miscellaneous: Extracts: from other jour-
    nals; by various authors. News: Domes-
    tic.

937 TITLE: Youth's Miscellany. [See Youth's
    Literary Gazette.]

938 TITLE: Youth's Monitor.

Place of Publication: Portland, Me.
First Issue: 6 June 1840
Last Issue: 21 May 1842//
Available From: N.Y. Hist. Soc.*;
                Me. Hist. Soc., Portland

939 TITLE: The Youth's Parlor Annual. [Running
    title: The Parlor Annual, or Young Lady's
    and Gentleman's Magazine. Merged into The
    Parlor Annual and Christian Family Magazine,
    later the Family Circle and Parlor Annual.]

Place of Publication: New York
First Issue: May 1844
Last Issue: April 1845//
Periodicity: Monthly
Editor: D. Newell
Publisher: D. Newell
Available From: Amer. Antiquarian Soc.*;
                N.Y. Pub. Lib.*
Contents:
  Poetry: Original: E.S. Hawley, Henry M.
    Parsons, Caroline Gilman, A.B. Whelpley,
    M.J. Hulslander, Isabella O. Shaw.
    Selected: Lydia H. Sigourney, Emma C.
    Embury, Coleridge, Nathaniel P. Willis.
  Prose: Biography. Travel. Essay.
    Familiar Essay. Letters.
  Fiction: Sketches. Tales: "An Affecting
    Tale of Truth. A Warning Voice" [Lydia
    Maria Child]; "Amy Woodleigh"; "The Sea-
    Captain's Wife"; "Alice, a Story of Our
    Village"; "The Last Lament"; "The Stricken
    Widow. Death's Empire Complete"; "The
    Heart's Touchstone"; "After the Masquer-
    ade. Deep Regret, Sincere Repentance";
    "The Forsaken."
  Miscellaneous: Extracts: from other jour-
    nals; by various authors; Horace Greeley,
    Daniel Webster. Anecdotes: on various
    subjects; Buonaparte, Washington.

940 TITLE: The Zodiac, a Monthly Periodical.
    Devoted to Science, Literature and the Arts.

Place of Publication: Albany
First Issue: June 1835
Last Issue: Jan 1837//
Periodicity: Monthly
Editor: ?
Publisher: E. Perry
Available From: APS; Amer. Antiquarian Soc.*
Contents:
  Poetry: <u>Original</u>: A.D. Woodbridge, Lydia
    H. Sigourney. <u>Selected</u>: Robert Chambers,
    James Hogg, Bryant, Schiller.
  Prose: <u>Biography</u>: James Hogg, Tallyrand.
    <u>Essay</u>. <u>Familiar Essay</u>. <u>Criticism</u>.
    <u>Letters</u>.
  Fiction: <u>Essay Serials:</u> "The Power of the
    Press"; "Notes of a Pedestrian." <u>Sketch-</u>
    <u>es</u>. <u>Tales</u>: "Tales of Fathers and Daugh-
    ters"; "The Red Box, or, Scenes at the
    General Wayne."
  Miscellaneous: <u>Extracts</u>: from other
    journals. <u>Anecdotes</u>: on various sub-
    jects; Buonaparte.

Chronological Index of Periodicals

1719

21 December   <u>The Boston Gazette</u> (Boston)
                17 September 1798

1733

5 October   <u>The New-York Weekly Journal</u> (New York)
              18 March 1751

1741

January   <u>The American Magazine</u> (Philadelphia)
             March 1741

January   <u>The General Magazine, and Historical</u>
             <u>Chronicle</u> (Philadelphia) June 1741

1743

2 March   <u>The Boston Weekly Magazine</u> (Boston)
             16 March 1743

5 March   <u>The Christian History</u> (Boston)
             23 February 1745

September   <u>The American Magazine and Historical</u>
             <u>Chronicle</u> (Boston) December 1746

1755

6 March   <u>The Instructor</u> (New York) 8 May 1755

1757

October   <u>The American Magazine and Monthly</u>
             <u>Chronicle for the British Colonies</u>
             (Philadelphia) October 1758

1758

January   <u>The New American Magazine</u> (Woodbridge,
             N.J.) March 1760

August   <u>The New-England Magazine</u> (Boston)
             March 1759

1767

21 December   <u>The Boston Chronicle</u> (Boston)
                21 June 1770

1768

2 August   <u>The Essex Gazette</u> (Salem, Mass.)
             28 March 1776

1769

January   <u>The American Magazine or General</u>
             <u>Repository</u> (Philadelphia)
             September 1769

1770

17 July   <u>The Massachusetts Spy</u> (Boston;
             Worcester, Mass.) 11 October 1820

1773

4 December   <u>The Essex Journal and Merrimack Packet</u>
             (Newbury-Port, Mass.) 2 April 1794

1774

January   The Royal American Magazine (Boston)
           March 1775

1775

January   The Pennsylvania Magazine (Philadelphia)
           July 1776

1779

January   The United States Magazine
           (Philadelphia) December 1779

1781

20 October   The Boston Evening-Post (Boston;
           Worcester, Mass.) 8 October 1789

1783

October   The Boston Magazine (Boston)
           November–December 1786

1784

May   The Gentleman and Lady's Town and
           Country Magazine (Boston)
           January 1785

12 July   The American Mercury (Hartford)
           26 December 1820

24 December   The New-Hampshire Mercury, and General
           Advertiser (Portsmouth, N.H.)
           12 March 1788

1785

10 August   The Carlisle Gazette, and the Western
           Repository of Knowledge (Carlisle,
           Pa.) 23 October 1817

October   The American Monitor (Boston) Only one
           issue published

8 November   The Middlesex Gazette (Middletown,
           Conn.) 28 December 1820

1786

16 February   The New-Haven Gazette, and the Con-
           necticut Magazine (New Haven,
           Conn.) 18 June 1789

1st week   The Worcester Magazine (Worcester,
April   Mass.) 4th week March 1788

September   The Columbian Magazine or Monthly
           Miscellany (Philadelphia)
           February 1790

December   The New-Jersey Magazine, and Monthly
           Advertiser (New Brunswick, N.J.)
           February 1787

1787

January   The American Museum (Philadelphia)
           December 1792

December   The American Magazine (New York)
           November 1788

1788

17 May   The Impartial Gazetteer, and Saturday
           Evening's Post (New York)
           25 October 1817

15 September   The Herald of Freedom, and the Federal
           Advertiser (Boston) 28 June 1793

1789

January   The Massachusetts Magazine (Boston)
           December 1796

February   The Gentlemen and Ladies Town and
           Country Magazine (Boston)
           August 1790

April–May   The Christian's, Scholar's, and
           Farmer's Magazine (Elizabethtown,
           N.J.) February–March 1791

1790

January   The New-York Magazine (New York)
           December 1797

6 January   The Concord Herald, and New Hampshire
           Intelligencer (Concord, N.H.)
           30 October 1805

March   The Universal Asylum, and Columbian
           Magazine (Philadelphia)
           December 1792

1791

31 October   The National Gazette (Philadelphia)
            26 October 1793

1792

6 January   The American Apollo (Boston)
            25 December 1794
June   The Lady's [Ladies] Magazine
            (Philadelphia) May 1793

1793

January   The Columbian Museum, or, Universal
            Asylum (Philadelphia) Only one
            issue published
11 April   The New Hampshire Journal: Or, the
            Farmer's Weekly Museum (Walpole,
            N.H.) 15 October 1810
June   The New Hampshire Magazine (Concord,
            N.H.) November 1793
4 June   The Oracle of the Day (Portsmouth,
            N.H.) 28 December 1799

1794

April   The Monthly Miscellany, or Vermont
            Magazine (Bennington, Vt.)
            September 1794
April   United States Magazine, or, General
            Repository (Newark, N.J.)
            August 1794
7 October   The Worcester Intelligencer: Or,
            Brookfield Advertiser (Brookfield,
            Mass.) 28 April 1795
20 October   Federal Orrery (Boston) 31 October 1796
No date   Alter et idem, a New Review (Reading,
            Pa.) Only one issue published

1795

January   The American Monthly Review; or,
            Literary Journal (Philadelphia)
            December 1795
January   The Rural Magazine: Or, Vermont
            Repository (Rutland, Vt.)
            December 1796
7 February   The Philadelphia Minerva (Philadelphia)
            7 July 1798
6 May   The Moral and Political Telegraph
            (Brookfield, Mass.) 17 August 1796
19 May   The Tablet. A Miscellaneous Paper
            (Boston) 11 August 1795
1 July   The Courier (Boston) 30 December 1795

1 July   The New-York Weekly Magazine; or, Mis-
            cellaneous Repository (New York)
            23 August 1797
No date   The Literary Miscellany (Philadelphia)
            Sixteen issues published

1796

March   The Political Censor (Philadelphia)
            March 1797
10 May   The Nightingale (Boston) 30 July 1796
15 August   The Lady & Gentleman's Pocket Magazine
            of Literary and Polite Amusement
            (New York) November 1796
5 October   The Centenial of Freedom (Newark, N.J.)
            No date 1909

1797

January   The Literary Museum, or Monthly
            Magazine (West Chester, Pa.)
            June 1797
January   The Methodist Magazine (Philadelphia)
            December 1798
1 January   South-Carolina Weekly Museum
            (Charleston, S.C.) July 1798
2 January   The American Universal Magazine
            (Philadelphia) 7 March 1798
8 January   The Weekly Museum (Baltimore)
            28 May 1797
13 March   The Time-Piece, and Literary Companion
            (New York) 30 August 1798
11 April   The New Star (Concord, N.H.)
            3 October 1797
July   The New Hampshire and Vermont Magazine
            (Haverhill, N.H.) October 1797
3 July   The American Moral & Sentimental
            Magazine (New York) 21 May 1798

1798

January   The Philadelphia Monthly Magazine
            (Philadelphia) September 1798
January   Thespian Oracle, or Monthly Mirror
            (Philadelphia) Only one issue
            published
13 January   The Key (Fredericktown, Md.) 14 July
            ·1798
3 February   The Weekly Magazine of Original Essays,
            Fugitive Pieces, and Interesting
            Intelligence (Philadelphia)
            1 June 1799
17 February   The Rural Magazine (Newark, N.J.)
            9 February 1799
23 February   The Green Mountain Patriot (Peacham,
            Vt.) 27 January 1810
27 February   The Vigil (Charleston, S.C.)
            3 April 1798
7 April   The Religious Monitor, or Theological
            Scales (Danbury, Conn.)
            22 September 1798

11 April	The Hummingbird, or Herald of Taste (Newfield, Conn.) 9 June 1798
June	The General Magazine, and Impartial Review (Baltimore) July 1798
5 June	The Rural Casket (Poughkeepsie, N.Y.) 11 September 1798
14 July	The Dessert to the True American (Philadelphia) 19 August 1799
14 August	The Political Repository: Or, Farmer's Journal (Brookfield, Mass.) 4 May 1802

1799

January	The Philadelphia Magazine and Review (Philadelphia) June 1799
2 February	The Franklin Minerva (Chambersburg, Pa.) 18 January 1800
April	The Monthly Magazine, and American Review (New York) December 1800
1 June	National Magazine (Richmond, Va.) 22 December 1800
No date	Cheap Repository (Philadelphia) No date 1800

1800

January	The Columbian Phenix and Boston Review (Boston) July 1800
4 January	The United States Oracle of the Day (Portsmouth, N.H.) 21 January 1815
15 February	The Rush-Light (Philadelphia) 30 August 1800
25 February	The Ladies Museum (Philadelphia) 7 June 1800
26 April	The Baltimore Weekly Magazine (Baltimore) 27 May 1801
12 May	The Impartial Register (Salem, Mass.) 24 March 1819
October	The Political Magazine; and Miscellaneous Repository (Ballston, N.Y.) Nov 1800
November	Child of Pallas (Baltimore) January 1801
15 November	The Philadelphia Repository, and Weekly Register (Philadelphia) 5 April 1806

1801

January	The American Review and Literary Journal (New York) October-November-December 1802
January	The Connecticut Magazine (Bridgeport Conn.) June 1801
January	The Lady's Magazine and Musical Repository (New York) June 1802
3 January	The Port Folio (Philadelphia) December 1828
17 January	The Toilet (Charleston, S.C.) 7 March 1801

8 August	The Ladies' Monitor (New York) 29 May 1802
October	National Magazine; or, Cabinet of the United States (Washington, D.C.) 11 January 1802
2 December	The National Aegis (Worcester, Mass.) No date 1895

1802

5 January	The Balance, and Columbian Repository (Hudson, N.Y.; Albany) 29 December 1809
April-May-June	The New England Quarterly Magazine (Boston) October-November-December 1802
May-June	The Georgia Analytical Repository (Savannah) March-April 1803
7 July	The Wasp. By Robert Rusticoat, Esq. (Hudson, N.Y.) 26 January 1803
July	Connecticut Republican Magazine (Suffield, Conn.) No date 1803
9 October	The Weekly Visitor, or, Ladies' Miscellany (New York) 17 October 1812
30 October	The Boston Weekly Magazine (Boston) 26 April 1806
30 October	The Visitor (New Haven, Conn.) 25 October 1803
No date	The Juvenile Magazine (Philadelphia) No date 1803

1803

January	The Medley, or Monthly Miscellany (Lexington, Ky.) December 1803
22 June	The Hive (Lancaster, Pa.) 12 June 1805
6 August	The Literary Tablet (Hanover, N.H.) 5 April 1807
30 August	The Hive (Northampton, Mass.) 25 December 1804
8 September	The Eastern Argus (Portland, Me.) 1921
October	The Literary Magazine, and American Register (Philadelphia) December 1807
November	The Monthly Anthology, and Boston Review (Boston) June 1811

1804

4 January	The Democrat (Boston) 2 June 1809
28 March	The Corrector. By Toby Tickler, Esq. (New York) 26 April 1804
16 June	The Weekly Monitor (Philadelphia) 8 December 1804
11 September	The Minerva; or, Lady's and Gentlemen's Magazine (Richmond) ?
November	Orphan's Friend and Literary Repository (Baltimore) April 1805
3 November	The Companion and Weekly Miscellany (Baltimore) 25 October 1806
15 December	The Evening Fire-Side (Philadelphia) 27 December 1806

1805

January	The Monthly Review and Literary Miscellany of the United States (Charleston, S.C.; New York) December 1807
16 February	The Apollo (Wilmington, Del.) 24 August 1805
11 May	Portland Magazine (Portland, Me.) 8 June 1805
8 June	Merrimack Miscellany (Newburyport, Mass.) 5 October 1805
10 June	The Miscellany (Trenton, N.J.) 2 December 1805
4 July	Le petit censeur (New York) 13 August 1805
August	The Independent Republican (Newburyport, R.I.) Only one issue published
17 August	Merrimack Magazine and Ladies' Literary Cabinet (Newburyport, Mass.) 9 August 1806
19 September	Le petit censeur (Philadelphia) 5 December 1805
16 October	The Fly; or Juvenile Miscellany (Boston) 2 April 1806
December	The Polyanthos (Boston) September 1814
9 December	The Theatrical Censor (Philadelphia) 3 March 1806
28 December	The Thespian Mirror (New York) 31 May 1806
No date	The Literary Miscellany (Cambridge, Mass.) No date 1806
No date	The Spirit of the Public Journals (Baltimore) Annual 1805

1806

1 January	The Weekly Visitant (Salem, Mass.) 27 December 1806
3 May	The Emerald, or, Miscellany of Literature (Boston) 15 October 1808
9 August	The Charleston Spectator, and Ladies' Literary Port Folio (Charleston, S.C.) 5 December 1806
15 November	Literary Cabinet (New Haven, Conn.) 31 October 1807
29 November	The Observer, and Repertory of Original and Selected Essays (Baltimore) 26 December 1807
4 December	Ladies Visitor (Boston) 28 February 1807

1807

1 January	The Town (New York) 12 January 1807
24 January	American Gleanor and Virginia Magazine (Richmond) 26 December 1807
24 January	Salmagundi (New York) 25 January 1808
February	The Fool. By Thomas Brainless, Esq. (Salem, Mass.) April 1807
21 February	The Pastime (Schenectady, N.Y.) 25 June 1808

July	The Baltimore Magazine (Baltimore) Only one issue published
6 June	Spectacles (Baltimore) 18 July 1807
20 June	Moonshine. By the Lunarian Society (Baltimore) 23 July 1807
4 August	The Thistle (Boston) 1 September 1807
16 September	The Tickler (Philadelphia) 17 November 1813
12 December	The Times (Boston) 15 October 1808
No date	The American Register (Philadelphia) No date 1810
No date	Annales philosophiques, politiques et litteraires (Philadelphia) Only one issue published
No date	The Barber's Shop Kept by Sir David Razor (Salem, Mass.) Only four issues published 1808

1808

7 January	The Eye: by Obadiah Optic (Philadelphia) 29 December 1808
20 February	The Literary Mirror (Portsmouth, N.H.) 11 February 1809
16 June	Abracadabra; or the Conceits of A, B & C (Portland, Me.) ?
September	The Gleanor; or, Monthly Magazine (Lancaster, Pa.) November 1809
21 October	The American (Providence, R.I.) 29 December 1820
22 October	Boston Mirror (Boston) 21 July 1810

1809

January	Select Reviews, and Spirit of the Foreign Magazines (Philadelphia) December 1812
7 January	The Ordeal (Boston) 1 July 1809
11 February	The Visitor (Richmond) 18 August 1810
19 February	The Observer (New York) 6 August 1809
June	The Massachusetts Watchman, and Periodical Journal (Palmer, Mass.) May 1810
2 August	The American Watchman; and, Delaware Republican (Wilmington, Del.) 21 July 1820
September	New England Literary Herald (Boston) January 1810
7 October	L'hémisphère, journal français (Philadelphia) 28 September 1811
November	Omnium Gatherum (Boston) October 1810
18 November	Something. Edited by Nemo Nobody, Esq. (Boston) 12 May 1810
25 November	The Thespian Monitor, and Dramatick Miscellany (Philadelphia) 16 December 1809
No date	The American Magazine of Wonders, and Marvellous Chronicle (New York) Only two volumes published 1809
No date	The Ramblers' Magazine (New York) No date 1810

CHRONOLOGICAL INDEX OF PERIODICALS

1810

January	The Huntingdon Literary Museum (Huntingdon, Pa.) December 1810
January	Journal des dames (New York) December 1810
January	The Mirror of Taste and Dramatic Censor (Philadelphia) December 1811
5 May	Philadelphia Repertory (Philadelphia) 16 May 1812
12 May	The Weekly Visitor (New York) 25 May 1811
19 May	The Hive (Lancaster, Pa.) 11 December 1810
21 May	The Constitutionalist (Exeter, N.H.) 14 June 1814
14 July	The Harvard Lyceum (Cambridge, Mass.) 9 March 1811
30 July	The Rural Visiter (Burlington, N.J.) 22 July 1811
14 October	The Observer (New York) 21 April 1811
3 November	The Emerald. By Peter Pleasant, & Co. (Baltimore) 2 March 1811
15 December	The Shamrock, or Hibernian Chronicle (New York) 30 January 1813

1811

January	The American Review of History and Politics (Philadelphia) October 1812
January	The Baltimore Repertory (Baltimore) June 1811
5 January	The Cabinet; a Repository of Polite Literature (Boston) 23 March 1811
April	Free-Masons Magazine and General Miscellany (Philadelphia) March 1823
May	The Juvenile Magazine (Philadelphia) August 1813
May	The Literary Miscellany, or Monthly Review (New York) August 1811
24 May	The Floriad (Schenectady, N.Y.) 6 December 1811
July	The Juvenile Repository (Boston) Only one issue published
21 September	The Cynick, By Growler Gruff, Esquire (Philadelphia) 12 December 1811
10 August	The Scourge. By Tim Touchstone, Esq. (Boston) 28 December 1811
19 October	The Comet (Boston) 11 January 1812
7 December	The Casket. By Charles Candid (Hudson, N.Y.) 30 May 1812

1812

January	The General Repository and Review (Cambridge, Mass.) October 1813
January	The Halcyon Luminary, and Theological Repository (New York) December 1812
16 January	The Satirist. By Lodowick Lash'em (Boston) 9 May 1812
28 February	The Pioneer (Pittsburgh) 8 October 1812

April	The Literary and Philosophical Repertory (Middlebury, Vt.) May 1817
May	The Monthly Magazine and Literary Journal (Winchester, Va.) April 1813
17 October	The Juvenile Port-Folio, and Literary Miscellany (Philadelphia) 7 December 1816

1813

January	The Analectic Magazine (Philadelphia) December 1821
27 January	The Olio, a Literary and Miscellaneous Paper (New York) 5 February 1814
April	The Monthly Recorder (New York) August 1813
3 July	The Stranger (Albany) 25 June 1814
24 July	Literary Register (Philadelphia) 17 December 1814
13 November	National Museum, and Weekly Gazette (Baltimore) 12 November 1814
December	The Western Gleaner (Pittsburgh) September 1814
No date	The Literary Visiter (Wilkes-Barre, Pa.) No date 1815

1814

1 January	The Boston Spectator (Boston) 25 February 1815
12 February	The Athenæum (New Haven, Conn.) 6 August 1814
April	The Rhode-Island Literary Repository (Providence, R.I.) March 1815
2 April	Le Médiateur, journal politique et littéraire (Philadelphia) 3 August 1814
May	The New-York Magazine, and General Repository of Useful Knowledge (New York) July 1814
14 May	The Whim (Philadelphia) 16 July 1814
27 May	The Moralist (New York) 7 November 1814
5 July	The Weekly Recorder (Chillicothe, Ohio) 6 October 1821
23 July	The Western Spy and Literary Cadet (Cincinnati) 28 December 1822
19 November	The Intellectual Regale. Or Ladies' Tea Tray (Philadelphia) 30 December 1815

1815

31 March	Youth's Cabinet (Utica, N.Y.) 21 April 1815
15 April	L'Abeille américaine (Philadelphia) 9 July 1818
May	The North-American Review and Miscellaneous Journal (Boston) Winter 1939-40

June   The American Magazine (Albany) May 1816
July   The Friend (Albany) June 1816
18 July   Robinson's Magazine (Baltimore)
                  26 June 1819
September   The Monthly Literary Advertiser
                  (Philadelphia) January 1817
16 November   The Lay-Man's Magazine (Martinsburgh,
                  Va.) 7 November 1816

1816

January   The Portico, a Repository of Science &
                  Literature (Baltimore) April-May-
                  June 1818
13 May   The Aeronaut (New York) No date 1822
3 June   The Country Courier (New York)
                  24 March 1817
15 June   The Parterre (Philadelphia) 28 June
                  1817
July   The Alleghany Magazine (Meadville, Pa.)
                  June 1817
12 October   The Boston Weekly Magazine (Boston)
                  25 December 1824

1817

January   The Atheneum; Or, Spirit of the English
                  Magazines (Boston) March 1833
4 January   The Parlour Companion (Philadelphia)
                  21 August 1819
22 January   The Christian Journal, and Literary
                  Register (New York) December 1830
16 April   Spirit of the Forum, and Hudson Re-
                  marker (Hudson, N.Y.) Only one
                  issue published
May   The American Monthly Magazine and
                  Critical Review (New York) April
                  1819
10 May   The Weekly Visitor; or Ladies Miscel-
                  lany (New York) 25 October 1817
4 June   The Weekly Monitor (Boston)
                  20 September 1817
5 July   Ladies' Literary Museum; or Weekly
                  Repository (Philadelphia)
                  9 June 1820
12 September The Philanthropist (Mt. Pleasant, Ohio)
                  26 December 1817
10 October   New-England Galaxy & Masonic Magazine
                  (Boston) 29 March 1839
20 December   The Idiot, or, (The) Invisible Rambler
                  (Boston) 2 January 1819
No date   The American Register (Philadelphia)
                  Only two issues published

1818

January   Philadelphia Magazine (Philadelphia)
                  7 November 1818
7 February   The Academician (New York)
                  29 January 1820
5 December   The Kaleidoscope (Boston)
                  13 November 1819

30 December   The Inquisitor (Philadelphia)
                  19 January 1820

1819

January   The Collegian, or American Students'
                  Magazine (New York) February 1819
January   The Guardian, or, Youth's Religious
                  Instructor (New Haven, Conn.)
                  December 1898
2 January   The Philadelphia Register, and Nation-
                  al Recorder (Philadelphia)
                  29 June 1822
February   The Rural Magazine and Farmer's
                  Monthly Museum (Hartford, Conn.)
                  July 1819
13 February   Ladies' Magazine (Savannah, Ga.)
                  7 August 1819
April   The Villager, a Literary Paper
                  (Greenwich Village, N.Y.)
                  June 1819
May   The Belles-Lettres Repository, and
                  Monthly Magazine (New York)
                  April 1821
15 May   The Ladies' Literary Cabinet (New
                  York) 21 December 1822
24 May   Ladies' Visiter (Marietta, Pa.)
                  18 April 1820
30 May   Salmagundi. Second Series (New York)
                  19 August 1820
16 June   Columbian Telescope & Literary Com-
                  piler (Alexandria, D.C.)
                  20 May 1820
August   The Village Museum (York, Pa.)
                  July 1823
August   The Western Review and Miscellaneous
                  Magazine (Lexington, Ky.)
                  July 1821
September   The Truth, by J. Ironside (New Haven,
                  Conn.) October 1819
23 October   The Red Book (Baltimore) 16 March 1821
November   Juvenile Gazette (Providence, R.I.)
                  January 1820
20 November   Journal of Belles Lettres (Lexington,
                  Ky.) 20 February 1820
21 December   The Stand (Hartford, Conn.)
                  14 August 1820

1820

January   The Rural Magazine, and Literary
                  Evening Fire-Side (Philadelphia)
                  December 1820
January   Western Minerva (Lexington, Ky.)
                  Only one issue published
1 January   Ladies' Port Folio (Boston)
                  8 July 1820
15 January   The Religious and Literary Repository
                  (Annapolis) 23 December 1820
29 January   The Critic. By Geoffrey Juvenal, Esq.
                  (Philadelphia) 10 May 1820
February   The Club-Room (Boston) July 1820
21 March   The Microscope, Edited by a Fraternity
                  of Gentlemen (New Haven, Conn.)
                  8 September 1820

1 April   The American Critic, and General Review (Washington, D.C.) 29 April 1820

1 April   Euterpeiad or, Musical Intelligencer (Boston) June 1823

June   The Literary and Scientific Repository, and Critical Review (New York) May 1822

August   The Post-Chaise Companion (Philadelphia) 22 January 1821

September   The American Masonic Register (New York) June 1823

October   Periodical Sketches by an American Patriot (New York) Only one issue published

1 October   American Academy of Language and Belles Lettres (New York) January 1822

9 October   The Village Museum (Cortland Village, N.Y.) 20 November 1820

No date   The Literary Repository and Scientific and Critical Review (New York) No date 1828

1821

January   The New Monthly Magazine and Literary Journal (Boston; New York; Philadelphia) December 1825

6 January   The Literary Gazette (Philadelphia) 29 December 1821

10 March   The Microscope, and Herald of Fancy (Albany) 29 December 1827

26 May   The Olio (Cincinnati) 11 May 1822

16 June   The Literary Companion (New York) 8 September 1821

July   The Masonic Miscellany and Ladies' Literary Magazine (Lexington, Ky.) June 1823

18 August   The Saturday Evening Post (Philadelphia) No date

September   The Christian Intelligencer (Portland; Gardiner, Me.) 30 December 1836

September   The Reflector (Boston) Only one issue published

6 September   The National Pilot (New Haven, Conn.) 11 September 1824

No date   The Idle Man (New York) No date 1822

1822

January   Collections, Topographical, Historical and Biographical (Concord, N.H.) No date 1824

January   The Ohio Miscellaneous Museum (Lebanon, Ohio) May 1822

2 February   The Columbian Star (Washington, D.C.) 2 May 1829

30 March   The Minerviad (Boston) 7 September 1822

6 April   The Columbian Observer (Philadelphia) 8 August 1825

6 April   The Minerva (New York) 3 March 1827

1 May   The Dawn, a Semi-Monthly Magazine (Wilmington, Del.) 1 November 1822

14 May   Christian Philanthropist (New Bedford, Mass.) 13 May 1823

15 June   Mrs. A. S. Colvin's Weekly Messenger (Washington, D.C.) 29 March 1828

22 June   The Albion (New York) 31 December 1876

July   The Museum of Foreign Literature and Science (Philadelphia; New York) December 1842

3 August   The New England Farmer (Boston) 24 June 1846

29 August   The Gridiron (Dayton, Ohio) 8 May 1823

16 September   Juvenile Museum (Mount Pleasant, Ohio) 27 September 1823

1 October   The Diana, and Ladies' Spectator (Boston) 26 October 1822

19 October   The City Firefly and Humorous Repository (Boston) 25 February 1823

18 November   The Thistle; a Literary Journal (Cincinnati) Only one issue published

No date   Eccentricities of Literature and Life (Boston) No date 1822

1823

January   The Monitor (Boston) December 1824

January   The United States Magazine (New York) Only one issue published

July 1823   The Washington Quarterly Magazine of Arts, Science and Literature (Washington, D.C.) April 1824

12 July   Miscellaneous Cabinet (Schenectady, N.Y.) 3 January 1824

15 July   The Evangelical Repertory (Boston) 15 June 1824

2 August   The New-York Mirror, and Ladies' Literary Gazette (New York) 31 December 1842

No date   The Literary Pamphleteer (Paris, Ky.) No date 1823

1824

January   The American Monthly Magazine (Philadelphia) December 1824

January   The Miscellaneous Magazine (Trenton, N.J.) December 1824

January   The New-York Monthly Magazine (New York) March 1824

1 January   The Cincinnati Literary Gazette (Cincinnati) 29 October 1825

6 January   The Oracle (Northampton, Mass.) 20 April 1825

6 January   Western Recorder (Utica, N.Y.) 12 February 1833

12 January   The Universal Medley (Barnstable, Mass.) 1 March 1824

14 February   The Ladies' Garland (Harpers Ferry, Va.) 7 June 1828

1 April   The United States Literary Gazette (Boston) September 1826

17 April   The Microscope. By Tim Tickler, Jr. Esq. (Louisville, Ky.; New Albany, Ind.) 10 September 1825

May   The Atlantic Magazine (New York) April 1825

12 June   Rural Repository (Hudson, N.Y.) October 1851

1 July   The Portsmouth Weekly Magazine (Portsmouth, N.H.) 30 June 1825

November   Journal inutile (New York) 19 May 1825

1825

January   Biblical Repertory (New York; Princeton; Philadelphia; Pittsburgh) November–December 1888

1 January   The Friendly Visitor (New York) 28 December 1825

April   The New Jersey Monthly Magazine (Newark, N.J.) Only one issue published

21 April   The American Athenæum (New York) 2 March 1826

June   Boston Monthly Magazine (Boston) July 1826

June   The Garland (Auburn, N.Y.) August 1825

June   The New-York Review, and Atheneum Magazine (New York) May 1826

16 July   The Ladies Museum (Providence, R.I.) 22 July 1826

1 October   The Odd Fellows' Magazine (Baltimore) 1 January 1826

1826

January   The Casket (Philadelphia) December 1858

7 January   The Boston Spectator, and Ladies' Album (Boston) 29 December 1827

7 January   Masonic Mirror (Boston) 25 January 1834

18 February   The ----------. By Nonius Nondescript, Esq. (Washington, D.C.) 18 May 1826

4 March   The Literary Casket (Hartford, Conn.) 3 February 1827

22 April   Literary Cadet, and Saturday Evening Bulletin (Providence, R.I.) 18 July 1829

2 June   The Canal of Intelligence (Norwich, Conn.) 18 November 1829

7 June   The Album. And Ladies' Weekly Gazette (Philadelphia) 27 December 1834

19 June   The Candid Examiner (Montrose, Pa.) 18 June 1827

September   The Juvenile Miscellany (Boston) August 1834

October   The United States Review and Literary Gazette (Boston; New York) September 1827

No date   Western Museum and Belles-Lettres Repository (Ithaca, N.Y.) No date 1828

1827

January   The Juvenile Magazine (Utica, N.Y.) December 1828

January   Meyer's British Chronicle (New York) No date 1831

15 January   The Boston Lyceum (Boston) November 1827

3 February   American Masonic Record, and Albany Saturday Magazine (Albany) No date 1832

March   The American Quarterly Review (Philadelphia) December 1837

March   The Harvard Register (Cambridge, Mass.) February 1828

14 April   The Ariel. And Ladies' Literary Gazette (Philadelphia) 24 November 1832

16 April   The Youth's Companion (Boston) September 1929

May   The Western Monthly Review (Cincinnati) June 1830

19 May   North American (Baltimore) 24 November 1827

June   The Literary Focus (Oxford, Ohio) May 1828

9 June   The Magnet and Cincinnati Literary Gazette (Cincinnati) 25 August 1827

4 July   The Souvenir, a Literary Work 8 December 1830

15 August   The Christian, and Literary Register (New York) 1 September 1827

18 August   The Medly; or, the Saturday's Comical Amuse'r (Albany) 3 November 1837

22 August   The Parthenon, or, Literary and Scientific Museum (New York) 8 December 1827

21 September   Eclectic Recorder (New York) 29 March 1828

October   The Philadelphia Monthly Magazine (Philadelphia) April 1830

13 October   The Friend. A Religious and Literary Journal (Philadelphia) June 1955

24 November   The Juvenile Gazette (Providence, R.I.) 15 November 1828

No date   The Manuscript (New York) No date 1828

1928

January   The Ladies' Magazine (Boston) December 1836

January   The Spirit of the Pilgrims (Boston) December 1833

1 January   The Yankee (Portland, Me.; Boston) December 1829

4 January   The Iris, or Semi-monthly Literary and Miscellaneous Register (Burlington, Vt.) 14 April 1829

5 January	The Bower of Taste (Boston) 24 May 1830
5 January	The Toilet, or Ladies' Cabinet of Literature (Providence, R.I.) 17 January 1829
February	The Southern Review (Charleston, S.C.) February 1832
16 February	Boston Literary Gazette (Boston) 9 August 1828
29 March	The Emerald and Baltimore Literary Gazette (Baltimore) 11 April 1829
April	The Amaranth; or Masonic Garland (Boston) October 1829
5 April	The Worcester Talisman (Worcester, Mass.) 15 October 1829
24 April	The Bachelors' Journal (Boston) 18 September 1828
2 June	The Literary Register (Oxford, Ohio) 27 June 1829
8 September	The Opera Glass (New York) 3 November 1828
16 September	The Cabinet of Literature, Instruction, and Amusement (New York) June 1831
20 September	The Atlas. A Select Literary and Historical Journal (New York) 26 October 1833
27 September	The Hive (Salem, Mass.) 20 September 1830
1 November	The Critic (New York) 20 June 1829
7 November	Ladies' Miscellany (Salem, Mass.) 30 March 1831
10 December	The Ladies' Literary Port Folio (Philadelphia) 9 December 1829
No date	Juvenile Repertory (Philadelphia) No date 1829
No date	The Legendary (Boston) Only two issues published 1828
No date	The Talisman (New York) No date 1830

1829

24 January	The Dramatic Mirror (Boston) 8 December 1829
24 January	Literary Recreations (Round Hill, Mass.; Northampton, Mass.) 29 August 1829
April	The American Monthly Magazine (Boston) July 1831
17 June	The Virginia Literary Museum (Charlottesville, Va.) 9 June 1830
November	The Juvenile Monthly (Amherst, Mass.) Only one issue published
6 November	The Miscellany (New Haven, Conn.) 6 May 1831
14 November	The Essayist (Boston) September 1833
12 December	The Cabinet (Taunton, Mass.) 3 December 1831
22 December	The Reflector (Palmyra, N.Y.) 19 March 1831

1830

January	Classical Journal, and Scholars' Review (Boston) December 1830
January	The Juvenile Repository (Providence, R.I.) 27 March 1830
January	The Monthly Traveller (Boston) December 1838
January	Quarterly Advertiser (Boston) October 1833
January	Youth's Magazine (Boston) December 1830
7 January	Literary Port Folio (Philadelphia) 1 July 1830
9 January	The New-York Amulet (New York) 15 March 1831
15 April	The Euterpeiad (New York) 1 November 1831
May	The Magnet and Ladies' Literary Garland (New York) Only one issue published
June	The Monthly Repository and Library of Entertaining Knowledge (New York) September 1834
June	The Pantheon, and Ladies' Literary Museum (Westfield, N.Y.) ?
15 June	Amateur, a Journal of Literature and the Fine Arts (Boston) December 1831
1 July	Godey's Magazine (Philadelphia) August 1898
28 August	The Ladies' Mirror (Southbridge, Mass.; Woonsocket Falls, R.I.) 1 January 1834
18 September	Juvenile Key (Brunswick, Me.) 27 August 1831
October	The Illinois Monthly Magazine (Vandalia, Ill.; Cincinnati) September 1832
October	The Young Ladies' Journal of Literature and Science (Baltimore; Hartford) November 1831
November	The National Magazine, or Lady's Emporium (Baltimore) July 1831
No date	Ladies' Museum, and Western Repository of Belles Lettres (Cincinnati) 25 December 1830
No date	The Parent's Gift; or, Youth's Magazine (Philadelphia) No date 1831

1831

January	Juvenile Magazine; and Youth's Monthly Visiter (New York) June 1832
1 January	The Liberator (Boston) 29 December 1865
1 January	The Little Gentleman (New Haven, Conn.) 29 April 1831

14 May	The Herald of Literature and Science (Detroit) September 1831
11 June	The Bouquet (Hartford; Boston) 14 September 1836
July	Academic Pioneer and Guardian of Education (Cincinnati) December 1832
July	The New-England Magazine (Boston) December 1835
3 September	Albany Literary Gazette (Albany) 7 April 1832
1 October	The Cincinnati Mirror and Ladies' Parterre (Cincinnati) 17 September 1836
No date	Biblical Repository and Classical Review (New York) No date 1850
No date	Family Pioneer & Juvenile Key (Brunswick, Me.) 7 May 1836

1832

January	The American Monthly Review (Boston) December 1833
January	The Green Mountain Repository (Burlington, Vt.) December 1832
4 January	Juvenile Rambler (Boston) 25 December 1833
28 March	The Mirror of Taste (Philadelphia) ?
19 April	The Comet (New York) 28 July 1833
1 May	The Boston Literary Magazine (Boston) April 1833
16 May	The Record of Genius (Utica, N.Y.) 25 May 1833
25 June	The Journal of Belles Lettres (Philadelphia) April 1842
July	American Lyceum (Boston) July 1833
14 July	The Amaranth, or Literary Port Folio (East Bridgwater, Mass.; Boston) 13 February 1836
8 August	The Working-Men's Shield (Cincinnati) 23 November 1833
1 October	The Select Circulating Library (Philadelphia) April 1842
November	The North American Magazine (Philadelphia) June 1838
1 December	Youth's Literary Gazette (Philadelphia) 22 November 1833
5 December	The Metropolitan (Washington, D.C.) 8 February 1837
No date	The Child's Cabinet (New Haven, Conn.) Only one issue published

1833

January	The Dollar Magazine (Philadelphia) December 1833
January	The Knickerbocker (New York) October 1865
January	The New Monthly Magazine and Literary Journal (Boston; New York; Philadelphia) June 1834
January	The Select Journal of Foreign Periodical Literature (Boston) October 1834

January	The Western Monthly Magazine (Cincinnati) June 1837
1 January	The Literary Inquirer (Buffalo, N.Y.) 15 October 1834
16 February	The Literary Cabinet, and Western Olive Branch (St. Clairsville, Ohio) 8 February 1834
March	The American Monthly Magazine (New York) October 1838
2 March	The Hive (Waltham, Mass.) 16 January 1836
16 March	Parley's Magazine for Children and Youth (New York; Boston; Portland; Philadelphia; Baltimore; Washington, D.C.; Richmond; Buffalo; New Orleans) December 1844
10 April	Literary Gems (New York) July 1833
20 April	The Family Magazine (New York) May 1841
8 June	The Literary Journal (Providence, R.I.) 31 May 1834
July	The American Quarterly Observer (Boston) October 1834
6 July	The Juvenile Repository (Boston) No date 1834
1 September	The Cabinet of Literature, and Monthly Miscellany (New York) Only one issue published
1 September	The Guardian (New York) 15 November 1833
5 October	The Magnolia: Or, Literary Tablet (Hudson, N.Y.) 20 September 1834
No date	The Literary Register (Elyria, Ohio) Only eight issues published
No date	The Literary Tablet (New Haven, Conn.) 29 March 1834
No date	The Metropolitan Magazine (New Haven, Conn.) No date 1835
No date	The Novelist's Magazine (Philadelphia) No date 1833

1834

January	The Literary and Theological Review (New York; Boston) December 1839
4 January	Peabody's Parlour Journal (New York) 31 October 1835
7 January	The Child's Newspaper (Cincinnati) 2 September 1834
17 March	Literary Museum (Geneva, N.Y.) 30 March 1835
22 March	The New-Yorker, a Weekly Journal of Literature and Intelligence (New York) 11 September 1841
May	The Ladies' Companion (New York) October 1844
May	The Monthly Visitor (Philadelphia) April 1835
7 June	Baltimore Athenæum (Baltimore) 18 June 1836
July	The Microcosm: Or the Little World of Home (New Haven, Conn.) October 1837
August	The Southern Literary Messenger (Richmond) June 1864

1 August   The Literary Gazette (Concord, N.H.)
         26 June 1835

1 August   The Young Ladies' Mirror (Geneva, N.Y.)
         25 July 1835

23 August   The Cabinet of Entertainment (Boston;
         Salem, Mass.) No date 1835

September   The American Magazine of Useful and
         Entertaining Knowledge (Boston)
         September 1837

September   The Juvenile Miscellany (Boston)
         December 1836

1 September   New York Literary Gazette (New York)
         14 March 1835

30 September   Youth's Magazine (Cincinnati) June 1838

October   The Portland Magazine (Portland, Me.)
         June 1836

8 October   The Miscellaneous Scrap Book (Hartford)
         23 January 1836

11 October   The Weekly Visitor (Providence, R.I.)
         7 March 1835

22 November   The Wreath (Schenectady, N.Y.; Albany;
         Troy, N.Y.) 6 June 1835

6 December   The Champagne Club (Washington, D.C.)
         7 March 1835

No date   The Republic of Letters (New York)
         No date 1836

No date   The Western Gem and Cabinet of Litera-
         ture, Science and News
         (St. Clairsville, Ohio)
         Only one volume published 1834

No date   Youth's Lyceum. And Literary Gazette
         (Xenia, Ohio) 11 May 1836

1835

1 January   Literary Magazine (Boston) Only one
         issue published

3 January   The Port Folio, and Companion to the
         Select Circulating Library
         (Philadelphia) 17 December 1836

15 January   The Family Minstrel (New York)
         15 January 1836

21 February   The Literary Journal (Richmond)
         28 November 1835

18 April   Albany Bouquet (Albany) 19 September
         1835

May   The Phrenological Magazine and New York
         Literary Review (Utica, N.Y.)
         Only one issue published

June   The Philadelphia Visiter (Philadelphia)
         No date 1841

June   The Western Messenger (Louisville, Ky.;
         Boston; Cincinnati) April 1841

June   The Zodiac (Albany) January 1837

16 June   The Literary Emporium (New Haven,
         Conn.) 4 August 1838

July   The Eastern Magazine (Bangor, Me.)
         June 1836

September   The Southern Literary Journal
         (Charleston, S.C.) December 1838

9 September   New York State Journal (Troy, N.Y.)
         7 September 1836

1 October   Carey's Library of Choice Literature
         (Philadelphia) 26 March 1836

No date   Boston Mirror and Literary Chronicle
         (Boston) No date 1835

1836

January   The Metropolitan Magazine (New York)
         June 1842

2 January   The Poughkeepsie Casket (Poughkeepsie,
         N.Y.) 2 April 1841

23 January   The Garland (Union Mills, N.Y.)
         7 January 1837

February   The Yale Literary Magazine (New Haven,
         Conn.) To date

June   The Western Literary Journal, and
         Monthly Review (Cincinnati)
         November 1836

July   The Every Body's Album (Philadelphia)
         June 1837

July   Littell's Saturday Magazine
         (Philadelphia) December 1837

July   The Maine Monthly Magazine (Bangor;
         Portland, Me.) June 1837

31 July   The National Atlas and Sunday Morning
         Mail (Philadelphia) 23 January 1838

September   Youths' Guide to Piety and Virtue, and
         Literary Casket (Poughkeepsie, N.Y.)
         August 1837

8 October   The Baltimore Monument (Baltimore)
         29 September 1838

15 November   The Literary. A Miscellany for the Town
         Only one issue published

No date   Boston Book (Boston) No date 1850

No date   New York Polyanthos (New York) July
         1841

1837

2 January   The Masonic Olive Branch and Literary
         Portfolio (Fredericksburg, Va.)
         15 September 1837

6 January   Waldie's Literary Omnibus (Philadelphia)
         20 July 1838

7 January   The Eglantine (Boston) 23 September
         1837

April   Youth's Lyceum (New Lisbon, Ohio)
         September 1837

15 April   The Ladies' Garland (Philadelphia)
         December 1850

28 April   Youth's Cabinet (Boston; New York)
         No date 1845

May   The Youth's Literary Messenger
         (Philadelphia) April 1839

1 June   The Bangor Journal of Literature,
         Science, Morals, and Religion
         (Bangor, Me.) 24 May 1838

July   The Gentleman's Magazine (Philadelphia)
         December 1840

1 August   The Student (Watertown, N.Y.)
         2 July 1838

12 August   The Oasis (Oswego, N.Y.) 28 July 1838

15 December   South-Western Journal (Natchez, Miss.)
         30 July 1838

No date   The New Novelists Magazine (New York)
         Only one volume published

1838

January	The Boston Quarterly Review (Boston) October 1842
January	Littell's Spirit of the Magazines and Annuals (Philadelphia) No date 1840
6 January	The Parlour Review (Philadelphia) 10 March 1838
April	Richmond Lyceum Journal (Richmond) March 1839
2 April	The Friends' Intelligencer (New York) 1 July 1839
May	The Hesperian (Columbus, Ohio; Cincinnati) November 1839
May	The Youth's Magazine (New York) April 1841
5 May	Augusta Mirror (Augusta, Ga.) 18 December 1841
July	The New-York Visiter, and Parlour Companion (New York) July-August 1843
September	The American Museum of Science, Literature, and the Arts (Baltimore) June 1839
8 September	Boston Weekly Magazine (Boston) 11 September 1841
October	The Baltimore Literary Monument (Baltimore) October 1839
17 November	Companion for Youth (New Haven, Conn.) 11 May 1839
1 December	The Louisville Literary News-Letter (Louisville, Ky.) 28 November 1840
8 December	The Expositor (New York) 20 July 1839
No date	The Child's Companion (Skaneateles, N.Y.) No date 1839
No date	The New York Mercury (New York) 1 January 1870

1839

January	The National Magazine and Republican Review (Washington, D.C.) June 1839
January	The Rose of the Valley (Cincinnati) July 1840
January	The Yankee Miscellany (Boston) December 1839
2 February	The New York Literary Gazette (New York) 13 July 1839
March	Literary Souvenir (Lowell, Mass.; Manchester, N.H.; Boston) 26 November 1842
9 March	The Universalist Palladium and Ladies' Amulet (Portland, Me.) 12 February 1842
16 March	The Corsair (New York) 7 March 1840
May	The Literary Examiner, and Western Monthly Review (Pittsburgh) May 1840
4 May	The Hudson Mirror, and Columbia County Farmer (Hudson, N.Y.) 18 April 1840
June	The Literary Geminae (Worcester, Mass.) May 1840

July	The Monthly Chronicle of Original Literature (New York) Only one issue published
August	The American Masonic Register (Albany) October 1847
No date	The Liberty Bell (Boston) No date 1858
No date	The Olio, or Rarities of Knowledge (New York) No date 1839
No date	Youth's Mental Casket, and Literary Star (Jersey City, N.J.) February 1842

1840

January	The Evergreen (New York) June 1841
January	The Southern Ladies' Book (Macon, Ga.; Savannah, Ga.; Charleston, S.C.) June 1843
1 January	The Literary Repository (Lowell, Mass.) 12 December 1840
February	The Monthly Magazine of Religion and Literature (Gettysburg, Pa.) January 1841
9 May	The Rose Bud (Newark, N.J.) 5 June 1841
June	The Ladies' Pearl, and Literary Gleaner (Lowell, Mass.) July 1843
June	The Literary Messenger (Pittsburgh) June 1844
6 June	The New World (New York) 10 May 1845
6 June	Youth's Monitor (Portland, Me.) 21 May 1842
July	The Dial (Boston) April 1844.
July	The Philadelphia Monthly Album (Philadelphia) March 1842
September	The Parent's Magazine (Gilmanton, N.H.; Concord, N.H.) September 1850
October	The Lowell Offering (Lowell, Mass.) December 1845
1 October	The Sword and Pen (New York) July 1841
November	Extra Equator (Bloomington, Ind.) March 1841
November	The Iris, or Literary Messenger (New York) October 1841
18 November	The Literary Pearl and Weekly Village Messenger (Charlton, N.Y.) 13 February 1840
December	Arcturus (New York) May 1842
No date	Roberts's World of Romance (Boston) Only five issues published

1841

January	Amaranth (New Brunswick, N.J.) December 1843
January	The American Eclectic (Boston; New York) November 1842
January	The Dollar Magazine (New York) December 1842
January	The Ladies' Repository (Cincinnati) December 1876
January	Littell's Dollar Magazine (Philadelphia) October 1841

January   The Mohawk Mirror, and Independent Chronicle (Little Falls, N.Y.) 14 June 1844

January   The Patriarch; or Family Library Magazine (New York) May 1842

January   Southron (Gallatin, Tex.) December 1841

15 January   Roberts' Semi-Monthly Magazine, for Town and Country (Boston) 1 January 1842

February   Robert Merry's Museum (Boston; New York) November 1872

20 February   The Standard Library (New York) 15 May 1841

April   The Northern Light (Albany) September 1844

17 April   The Youth's Medallion (Boston) 10 December 1842

29 May   The Watervillonian (Waterville, Me.) 30 May 1842

July   The American Magazine, and Repository of Useful Literature (Albany) April 1842

July   The Monthly Literary Advertiser (New York) December 1841

July   The United States Literary Advertiser, and Publishers' Circular (New York) July 1843

31 July   The Temperance Advocate and Literary Repository (Philadelphia) 1 July 1843

14 August   The Dramatic Mirror and Literary Companion (New York; Philadelphia) 7 May 1842

September   The Young People's Book (Philadelphia) August 1842

9 October   Boston Notion (Boston) 9 March 1844

6 November   Amaranth, Devoted to Literature, and to the Interests of Literary Societies (New York) ?

No date   Ballou's Dollar Monthly Magazine (Boston) No date 1893

No date   Every Body's Book; or, Something for All (New York) ?

No date   Ladies Literary Repository (Lowell, Mass.) Only two issues published

No date   The Literary Gazette and Quarterly Advertiser (Philadelphia) No date 1843

No date   The Literary Harvester (Hartford) 1 December 1843

No date   News-Gong: A Literary Intelligencer (New York) Only three issues published

No date   The Western Literary Messenger (Buffalo, N.Y.) April 1857

January   The Southern Quarterly Review (New Orleans; Charleston, S.C.) February 1857

January   The Western Literary and Historical Magazine (Louisville, Ky.) September 1842

1 January   Brother Jonathan (New York) 23 December 1843

22 January   Every Youth's Gazette (New York) 31 December 1842

February   The Nassau Monthly (Princeton, N.J.) To date

February   The Satirist (Albany) Only one issue published

1 February   The Comet (Washington City) 15 August 1842

March   The Orion (Penfield, Ga.; Athens, Ga.) August 1844

April   The Baltimore Monthly Visitor (Baltimore) Only one issue published

April   The Iris and Literary Repository (Manchester, N.H.; Concord, N.H.) April 1843

April   The Poet's Magazine (Albany) June 1842

April   The Union Herald (Cazenovia, N.Y.) ?

6 May   The Lyceum Reporter and Critical Miscellany (New York) 20 August 1842

June   Garland of the West, and Wisconsin Monthly Magazine (Southport, Wis.) November 1842

4 June   The Iris, a Semi-Monthly Journal (Binghamton, N.Y.) 21 June 1845

July   The Mother's Assistant and Young Lady's Friend (Boston) December 1863

July   The Religious and Literary Gem (Boston) September 1843

9 July   Chicora; or, Messenger of the South (Charleston, S.C.) 24 September 1842

13 July   Washingtonian Temperance Journal and Family Reader (Wiscasset, Me.; Portland) No date 1846

20 July   The Episcopal Family Monitor (New York) 6 November 1843

September   The Artist; a Monthly Lady's Book (New York) May 1843

September   Campbell's Foreign Monthly Magazine (Philadelphia) August 1844

November   Boys' and Girls' Literary Boquet (Philadelphia) June 1846

7 December   The Literary Age (Philadelphia) 15 March 1843

No date   Flag of Our Union (Philadelphia) No date 1853

No date   Juvenile Repository (New York) No date 1845

1842

January   The American Pioneer (Chillicothe, Ohio; Cincinnati) October 1843

January   The Boston Miscellany of Literature and Fashion (Boston; New York) February 1843

January   Rutgers Literary Miscellany (New Brunswick, N.J.) December 1842

1843

January   American Lady's Album and Gentlemen's Parlor Miscellany (Boston) June 1853

January   Boys' and Girls' Magazine (Boston) December 1843

January	The Eclectic Museum of Foreign Literature, Science and Art (New York; Philadelphia) January 1844
January	The Green Mountain Gem (Bradford, Vt.) No date 1849
January	Miss Leslie's Magazine (Philadelphia) April 1846
January	The Pierian (New York) Only one issue published
January	The Pioneer. A Literary and Critical Magazine (Boston) March 1843
January	Sargent's New Monthly Magazine (New York) June 1843
February	Anglo-American Magazine (Boston) July 1843
February	Bibliotheca Sacra (New York; Andover, Mass.; Oberlin, Ohio) ?
March	The Rover (New York) September 1845
8 April	The New Mirror, of Literature, Amusement, and Instruction (New York) 2 October 1847
29 April	The Anglo-American (New York) 13 November 1847
August	New-Hampshire Magazine (Manchester, N.H.; Great Falls, N.H.) July 1844
October	The Child's Friend (Boston) December 1858
No date	The Worcester Magazine, a Literary and Religious Miscellany (Worcester, Mass.) March 1844
No date	The Youth's Cabinet (New York) No date 1844

1844

January	Brownson's Quarterly Review (Boston) October 1875
January	The Columbian Lady's and Gentleman's Magazine (New York) February 1849
January	The Eclectic Magazine of Foreign Literature, Science and Art (New York) June 1907
January	The Repository of Modern English Romance (New York) December 1845
6 January	The World We Live In (Boston) 2 October 1847
25 April	The Spirit of '76 (Nashville, Tenn.) 26 August 1847
May	The Youth's Parlor Annual (New York) April 1845
11 May	Littell's Living Age (Boston) August 1941
September	The Gavel (Albany) No date 1848
November	Western Literary Journal and Monthly Review (Cincinnati) April 1845
2 November	Albany Religious Spectator (Albany) 25 October 1845
No date	Neal's Saturday Gazette & Lady's Literary Museum (Philadelphia) 27 December 1845
No date	Uncle Ezekiel's Youth's Cabinet (Concord, N.H.) 15 March 1846

1845

January	The American Review (New York) December 1852
January	The Literary Emporium (New York) January 1847
January	The Southern and Western Monthly Magazine and Review (Charleston, S.C.) December 1845
1 January	Smith's Weekly Volume (Philadelphia) 25 March 1846
4 January	The Broadway Journal (New York) 3 January 1846
February	The New England Family Magazine (Boston) September 1846
8 February	Dwight's American Magazine, and Family Newspaper (New York) July 1851
15 February	The Town (New York) 26 July 1845
March	The Antiquarian, and General Review (Schenectady, N.Y.; Lansingburgh, N.Y.) February 1849
March	The Aristidean (New York) December 1845
24 May	Alleghanian (New York) 28 June 1845
24 May	The Subterranean (New York) 22 May 1847
July	The Monthly Rose and Literary Cabinet (Boston) January 1850
20 September	New York Illustrated Magazine of Literature and Art (New York) June 1847
October	The Western Literary Magazine (Chicago) September 1846
No date	The Christian Family Magazine (Cincinnati) Only one issue published

1846

January	The Calvary Token and Literary Souvenir (Auburn, N.Y.) December 1846
January	The Naturalist (Nashville, Tenn.) December 1846
January	The Olden Time (Pittsburgh) December 1847
April	The Western Review (Columbus, Ohio) Only one issue published
15 April	The Casket (Cincinnati) 7 October 1846
May	The Ladies' Wreath (New York) January 1862
6 June	The Pearl: A Ladies' Weekly Literary Gazette (New York) 27 May 1848
31 October	The Popular Magazine (Philadelphia) January 1847
28 November	Judy (New York) 20 February 1847
No date	The Western Garland and People's Magazine (Cincinnati) No date 1846

1847

January	The Christian Observatory (Boston) April 1850
January	The Herald of Truth (Cincinnati) July 1848
9 January	The Genesee Olio (Rochester, N.Y.) 27 December 1849
1 February	The Crystal Fount (Baltimore) 1 August 1848
6 February	The Literary World (New York) 31 December 1853
20 February	The Amaranth (Ashland, Ohio) 11 December 1847
June	The American Eagle Magazine (New York) July 1847
July	The American Literary Magazine (Albany; Hartford) August 1849
July	The Union Magazine of Literature and Art (New York; Philadelphia) August 1852
7 August	The Daguerreotype (Boston) 14 April 1849
11 November	The Western Friend (Cincinnati) 23 August 1849
December	The Massachusetts Quarterly Review (Boston) September 1850
December	The New Orleans Miscellany (New Orleans) February 1848
No date	The Northwestern Educator and Magazine of Literature and Science (Chicago) No date 1849
No date	Southern Lady's Companion (Nashville, Tenn.) No date 1854

1848

January	The Boys' and Girls' Magazine, and Fireside Companion (Boston) December 1857
January	Boys' and Girls' Penny Journal (Philadelphia) No date 1853
January	Holden's Dollar Magazine (New York) August 1851
January	The Virginia Historical Register, and Literary Advertiser (Richmond, Va.) October 1853
January	The Western Literary Emporium (Cincinnati) April 1849
1 January	The John-Donkey (New York; Philadelphia) 21 October 1848
5 January	Uncle Jesse's Gazette (Concord, N.H.) 6 December 1848
March	The Iris (Richmond, Va.) Only one issue published
18 March	Juvenile Gazette (Boston) 28 May 1848
July	The Odd Fellows' Literary Magazine (New York) January 1849
July	The Pictorial National Library (Boston) December 1849

July	The Western Miscellany (Dayton, Ohio) June 1849
8 July	The Literary American (New York) 24 August 1850
November	Young People's Journal of Science, Literature, and Art (New York; Boston) Only one issue published
No date	Mirror of the Times (New York) No date 1851
No date	The Souvenir (New York) Only five issues published

1849

January	The American Metropolitan Magazine (New York) February 1849
January	Lady's Western Magazine, and Garland of the Valley (Cincinnati; Chicago; Milwaukee) June 1849
January	The Mistletoe (Athens, Ga.) March 1849
January	The Western Quarterly Review (Cincinnati) April 1849
15 January	The Monthly Miscellany (Atlanta; Richmond; New Orleans) 16 June 1849
April	The Aonidean Magazine and Review (New York) Only one issue published
April	The Western Literary Magazine and Journal of Education, Science, Arts and Morals (Detroit) September 1849
7 April	The Literary Union (Syracuse, N.Y.) July 1850
June	American People's Journal of Science, Literature, and Art (New York) Feb 1850
July	Literary Miscellany; or, National Advertiser (New York) No date 1850
December	The Family Favorite and Temperance Journal (Adrian, Mich.) September 1850

1850

2 February	The Two Worlds (New York) 26 October 1850
April	The Southern Lady's Magazine (Baltimore) May 1850
May	The American Expositor (Mount Vernon, Ohio) Only one issue published
1 May	The Chandelier (Boston) 18 May 1850

Geographical Index of Periodicals

CONNECTICUT

BRIDGEPORT

The Connecticut Magazine

DANBURY

The Religious Monitor

HARTFORD

The American Literary Magazine
The American Mercury
The Bouquet
The Literary Casket
The Literary Harvester
The Miscellaneous Scrap Book
The Rural Magazine and Farmer's Monthly Museum
The Stand
The Young Ladies' Journal of Literature and Science

MIDDLETOWN

The Middlesex Gazette

NEWFIELD

The Hummingbird

NEW HAVEN

The Athenaeum
The Child's Cabinet
Companion for Youth
The Guardian
Literary Cabinet
The Literary Emporium
The Literary Tablet
The Little Gentleman
The Metropolitan Magazine
The Microcosm
The Microscope
The Miscellany

The National Pilot
The New-Haven Gazette, and the Connecticut Magazine
The Truth
The Visitor
The Yale Literary Magazine

NORWICH

The Canal of Intelligence

SUFFIELD

Connecticut Republican Magazine

DELAWARE

WILMINGTON

The American Watchman; and, Delaware Republican
The Apollo
The Dawn

DISTRICT OF COLUMBIA

ALEXANDRIA

Columbian Telescope & Literary Compiler

WASHINGTON

The American Critic, and General Review
The Champagne Club
The Columbian Star
The Comet
The Metropolitan
Mrs. A. S. Colvin's Weekly Messenger
The National Magazine and Republican Review
National Magazine
Parley's Magazine for Children and Youth
The ------------.
The Washington Quarterly Magazine of Arts, Science
    and Literature

GEORGIA

ATHENS

The Mistletoe
The Orion

ATLANTA

The Monthly Miscellany

AUGUSTA

Augusta Mirror

MACON

The Southern Ladies' Book

PENFIELD

The Orion

SAVANNAH

The Georgia Analytical Repository
Ladies' Magazine
The Southern Ladies' Book

ILLINOIS

CHICAGO

Lady's Western Magazine, and Garland of the Valley
The Northwestern Educator and Magazine of Literature
    and Science
The Western Literary Magazine

VANDALIA

The Illinois Monthly Magazine

INDIANA

BLOOMINGTON

Extra Equator

NEW ALBANY

The Microscope

KENTUCKY

LEXINGTON

Journal of Belles Lettres
The Masonic Miscellany and Ladies' Literary Magazine
The Medley
Western Minerva
The Western Review and Miscellaneous Magazine

LOUISVILLE

The Louisville Literary News-Letter
The Microscope
The Western Literary and Historical Magazine
The Western Messenger

PARIS

The Literary Pamphleteer

LOUISIANA

NEW ORLEANS

The Monthly Miscellany
The New Orleans Miscellany
Parley's Magazine for Children and Youth
The Southern Quarterly Review

MAINE

BANGOR

The Bangor Journal of Literature, Science, Morals,
    and Religion
The Eastern Magazine
The Maine Monthly Magazine

BRUNSWICK

Family Pioneer & Juvenile Key
Juvenile Key

GARDINER

The Christian Intelligencer

PORTLAND

Abracadabra
The Eastern Argus
The Maine Monthly Magazine

Parley's Magazine for Children and Youth
Portland Magazine
The Portland Magazine, Devoted to Literature
The Universalist Palladium and Ladies' Amulet
Washingtonian Temperance Journal and Family Reader
The Yankee
Youth's Monitor

WATERVILLE

The Watervillonian

WISCASSET

Washingtonian Temperance Journal and Family Reader

MARYLAND

ANNAPOLIS

The Religious and Literary Repository

BALTIMORE

The American Museum of Science, Literature, and the
     Arts
Baltimore Athenæum, and Young Men's Paper
The Baltimore Literary Monument
The Baltimore Magazine
The Baltimore Monthly Visitor
The Baltimore Monument
The Baltimore Repertory, of Papers on Literary
     and Other Topics
The Baltimore Weekly Magazine
Child of Pallas
The Companion and Weekly Miscellany
The Crystal Fount
The Emerald and Baltimore Literary Gazette
The Emerald
The General Magazine, and Impartial Review, of
     Knowledge and Entertainment
Moonshine
The National Magazine
National Museum, and Weekly Gazette
North American
The Observer, and Repertory of Original and Selected
     Essays, in Verse & Prose
The Odd Fellows' Magazine
Orphan's Friend and Literary Repository
Parley's Magazine for Children and Youth
The Portico, a Repository of Science & Literature
The Red Book
Robinson's Magazine
The Southern Lady's Magazine
Spectacles
The Spirit of the Public Journals
The Weekly Museum
The Young Ladies' Journal of Literature and Science

FREDERICKTOWN

The Key

MASSACHUSETTS

AMHERST

The Juvenile Monthly

ANDOVER

Bibliotheca Sacra

BARNSTABLE

The Universal Medley

BOSTON

The Amaranth
Amateur
The American Apollo
The American Eclectic
American Lady's Album and Gentlemen's Parlor
     Miscellany
American Lyceum
The American Magazine and Historical Chronicle
The American Magazine of Useful and Entertaining
     Knowledge
The American Monitor
The American Monthly Magazine
The American Monthly Review
The American Quarterly Observer
Anglo-American Magazine
The Atheneum
The Bachelors' Journal
Ballou's Dollar Monthly Magazine
Boston Book
The Boston Chronicle
The Boston Evening-Post
The Boston Gazette
Boston Literary Gazette
The Boston Literary Magazine
The Boston Lyceum
The Boston Magazine
Boston Mirror
Boston Mirror and Literary Chronicle
The Boston Miscellany of Literature and Fashion
Boston Monthly Magazine
Boston Notion
The Boston Quarterly Review
The Boston Spectator, and Ladies' Album
The Boston Spectator
The Boston Weekly Magazine (2 March 1743-16 March
     1743)
Boston Weekly Magazine (8 Sept 1838-11 Sept 1841)
The Boston Weekly Magazine (30 Oct 1802-26 April
     1806)
The Boston Weekly Magazine (12 Oct 1816-25 Dec 1824)
The Bouquet
The Bower of Taste
Boys' and Girls' Magazine
The Boys' and Girls' Magazine, and Fireside Companion
Brownson's Quarterly Review
The Cabinet
The Cabinet of Entertainment, and Weekly Visiter
The Chandelier

Merrimack Magazine and Ladies' Literary Cabinet
Merrimack Miscellany

NORTHAMPTON

The Hive
Literary Recreations
The Oracle

PALMER

The Massachusetts Watchman, and Periodical Journal

ROUND HILL

Literary Recreations

SALEM

The Barber's Shop Kept by Sir David Razor
The Cabinet of Entertainment, and Weekly Visiter
The Essex Gazette
The Fool
The Hive
The Impartial Register
Ladies' Miscellany
The Weekly Visitant

SOUTHBRIDGE

The Ladies' Mirror

TAUNTON

The Cabinet

WALTHAM

The Hive

WORCESTER

The Literary Geminae
The Boston Evening-Post
The Massachusetts Spy
The National Aegis
The Worcester Magazine (1843–March 1844)
The Worcester Magazine (April 1786–March 1788)
The Worcester Talisman

MICHIGAN

ADRIAN

The Family Favorite and Temperance Journal

DETROIT

The Herald of Literature and Science
The Western Literary Magazine and Journal of Education, Science, Arts and Morals

MISSISSIPPI

NATCHEZ

South-Western Journal

NEW HAMPSHIRE

CONCORD

Collections, Topographical, Historical and Biograph-
ical, Relating Principally to New-Hampshire
The Concord Herald, and New Hampshire Intelligencer
The Iris and Literary Repository
The Literary Gazette
The New Hampshire Magazine
The New Star
The Parent's Magazine
Uncle Ezekiel's Youth's Cabinet
Uncle Jesse's Gazette

EXETER

The Constitutionalist

GILMANTON

The Parent's Magazine

GREAT FALLS

New-Hampshire Magazine

HANOVER

The Literary Tablet

HAVERHILL

The New Hampshire and Vermont Magazine, and General
Repository

MANCHESTER

The Iris and Literary Repository
Literary Souvenir
New-Hampshire Magazine

PORTSMOUTH

The Literary Mirror
The New-Hampshire Mercury, and General Advertiser
The Oracle of the Day
The Portsmouth Weekly Magazine
The United States Oracle of the Day

WALPOLE

The New Hampshire Journal

NEW JERSEY

BURLINGTON

The Rural Visiter

ELIZABETHTOWN

The Christian's, Scholar's, and Farmer's Magazine

JERSEY CITY

Youth's Mental Casket, and Literary Star

NEWARK

The Centinel of Freedom
The New Jersey Monthly Magazine
The Rose Bud
The Rural Magazine
United States Magazine

NEW BRUNSWICK

Amaranth
The New-Jersey Magazine, and Monthly Advertiser
Rutgers Literary Miscellany

PRINCETON

Biblical Repertory
The Nassau Monthly

TRENTON

The Miscellaneous Magazine
The Miscellany

WOODBRIDGE

The New American Magazine

NEW YORK

ALBANY

Albany Bouquet
Albany Literary Gazette
Albany Religious Spectator
The American Magazine
The American Magazine, and Repository of Useful
   Literature
American Masonic Record, and Albany Saturday Magazine
The American Masonic Register
The Balance, and Columbian Repository
The Friend
The Gavel
The Medly
The Microscope, and Herald of Fancy
The Northern Light
The Poet's Magazine
The Satirist
The Stranger
The Wreath
The Zodiac

AUBURN

The Calvary Token and Literary Souvenir
The Garland

BALLSTON

The Political Magazine

BINGHAMTON

The Iris

BUFFALO

The Literary Inquirer
Parley's Magazine for Children and Youth
The Western Literary Messenger

CAZENOVIA

The Union Herald

CHARLTON

The Literary Pearl and Weekly Village Messenger

CORTLAND VILLAGE

The Village Museum

TROY

New York State Journal
The Wreath

UNION MILLS

The Garland

UTICA

The Juvenile Magazine
The Phrenological Magazine and New York Literary
    Review
The Record of Genius
Western Recorder
Youth's Cabinet

WATERTOWN

The Student

WESTFIELD

The Pantheon, and Ladies' Literary Museum

OHIO

ASHLAND

The Amaranth

CHILLICOTHE

The American Pioneer
The Weekly Recorder

CINCINNATI

Academic Pioneer and Guardian of Education
The American Pioneer
The Casket
The Child's Newspaper
The Christian Family Magazine
The Cincinnati Literary Gazette
The Cincinnati Mirror and Ladies' Parterre
The Herald of Truth
The Hesperian
Ladies' Museum, and Western Repository of Belles
    Lettres
The Ladies' Repository, and Gatherings of the West
Lady's Western Magazine, and Garland of the Valley
The Magnet and Cincinnati Literary Gazette
The Olio
The Rose of the Valley
The Thistle
The Western Friend
The Western Garland and People's Magazine
The Western Literary Emporium
The Western Literary Journal, and Monthly Review

Western Literary Journal and Monthly Review
The Western Messenger
The Western Monthly Magazine
The Western Monthly Review
The Western Quarterly Review
The Western Spy and Literary Cadet
The Working-Men's Shield
Youth's Magazine

COLUMBUS

The Hesperian
The Western Review

DAYTON

The Gridiron
The Western Miscellany

ELYRIA

The Literary Register

LEBANON

The Ohio Miscellaneous Museum

MOUNT PLEASANT

Juvenile Museum
The Philanthropist

MOUNT VERNON

The American Expositor

NEW LISBON

Youth's Lyceum

OBERLIN

Bibliotheca Sacra

OXFORD

The Literary Focus
The Literary Register

ST. CLAIRSVILLE

The Literary Cabinet, and Western Olive Branch
The Western Gem and Cabinet of Literature, Science
    and News

XENIA

Youth's Lyceum

OREGON

PORTLAND

The Christian Intelligencer

PENNSYLVANIA

CARLISLE

The Carlisle Gazette, and the Western Repository of
    Knowledge

CHAMBERSBURG

The Franklin Minerva

GETTYSBURG

The Monthly Magazine of Religion and Literature

HUNTINGDON

The Huntingdon Literary Museum

LANCASTER

The Gleanor
The Hive (22 June 1803–12 June 1805)
The Hive (19 May 1810–11 Dec 1810)

MARIETTA

Ladies' Visiter

MEADVILLE

The Alleghany Magazine

MONTROSE

The Candid Examiner

PHILADELPHIA

L'Abeille américaine, journal, historique, politique
    et littéraire
The Album. And Ladies' Weekly Gazette
The American Magazine and Monthly Chronicle for the
    British Colonies
The American Magazine (Jan 1741–March 1741)
The American Magazine (Jan 1769–Sept 1769)
The American Monthly Magazine
The American Monthly Review
The American Museum
The American Quarterly Review
The American Register (1807–1810)
The American Register (1817)

The American Review of History and Politics, and
    General Repository of Literature and State Papers
The American Universal Magazine
The Analectic Magazine
Annales philosophiques, politiques et litteraires
The Ariel. And Ladies' Literary Gazette
Biblical Repertory
Boys' and Girls' Literary Boquet
Boys' and Girls' Penny Journal
Campbell's Foreign Monthly Magazine
Carey's Library of Choice Literature
The Casket
Cheap Repository
The Columbian Magazine
The Columbian Museum
The Columbian Observer
The Critic
The Cynick
The Dessert to the True American
The Dollar Magazine
The Dramtic Mirror and Literary Companion
The Eclectic Museum of Foreign Literature, Science
    and Art
The Evening Fire-Side
The Every Body's Album
The Eye
Flag of Our Union
Free-Masons Magazine and General Miscellany
The Friend
The General Magazine, and Historical Chronicle
The Gentleman's Magazine
Godey's Magazine
L'hémisphère, journal français
The Inquisitor
The Intellectual Regale
The John-Donkey
The Journal of Belles Lettres
The Juvenile Magazine (May 1811–Aug 1813)
The Juvenile Magazine (1802–1803)
The Juvenile Port-Folio, and Literary Miscellany
Juvenile Repertory
The Ladies' Garland
Ladies' Literary Museum
The Ladies' Literary Port Folio
The Ladies Museum
The Lady's [Ladies] Magazine
The Literary Age
The Literary Gazette and Quarterly Advertiser
The Literary Gazette
The Literary Magazine, and American Register
The Literary Miscellany
Literary Port Folio
Literary Register
Littell's Dollar Magazine
Littell's Saturday Magazine
Littell's Spirit of the Magazines and Annuals
Le Médiateur, journal politique et littéraire
The Methodist Magazine
The Mirror of Taste and Dramatic Censor
The Mirror of Taste, and Wednesday Morning Family
    Miscellany
Miss Leslie's Magazine
The Monthly Literary Advertiser
The Monthly Visitor
The Museum of Foreign Literature and Science
The National Atlas and Sunday Morning Mail
The National Gazette
Neal's Saturday Gazette & Lady's Literary Museum
The New Monthly Magazine and Literary Journal
    [American Edition]

The New Monthly Magazine and Literary Journal
  [American Edition--New Series]
The North American Magazine
The Novelist's Magazine
The Parent's Gift
Parley's Magazine for Children and Youth
The Parlour Companion
The Parlour Review, and Journal of Music, Literature,
  and the Fine Arts
The Parterre
The Pennsylvania Magazine
Le petit censeur
The Philadelphia Magazine and Review
Philadelphia Magazine
The Philadelphia Minerva
The Philadelphia Monthly Album
The Philadelphia Monthly Magazine (Oct 1827–April
  1830)
The Philadelphia Monthly Magazine (Jan 1798–Sept
  1798)
The Philadelphia Register, and National Recorder
Philadelphia Repertory
The Philadelphia Repository
The Philadelphia Visiter
The Political Censor
The Popular Magazine
The Port Folio (3 Jan 1835–17 Dec 1836)
The Port Folio (3 Jan 1810–Dec 1828)
The Post-Chaise Companion
The Rural Magazine, and Literary Evening Fire-Side
The Rush-Light
The Saturday Evening Post
The Select Circulating Library
Select Reviews, and Spirit of the Foreign Magazines
Smith's Weekly Volume
The Souvenir
The Temperance Advocate and Literary Repository
The Theatrical Censor
The Thespian Monitor, and Dramatick Miscellany
Thespian Oracle, or Monthly Mirror
The Tickler
The Union Magazine of Literature and Art
The United States Magazine
The Universal Asylum, and Columbian Magazine
Waldie's Literary Omnibus
The Weekly Magazine
The Weekly Monitor
The Whim
The Young People's Book
Youth's Literary Gazette
The Youth's Literary Messenger

PITTSBURGH

Biblical Repertory
The Literary Examiner, and Western Monthly Review
The Literary Messenger
The Olden Time
The Pioneer
The Western Gleaner

READING

Alter et idem, a New Review

WEST CHESTER

The Literary Museum

WILKES-BARRE

The Literary Visiter

YORK

The Village Museum

RHODE ISLAND

NEWBURYPORT

The Independent Republican

PROVIDENCE

The American
Juvenile Gazette (Nov 1819–Jan 1820)
The Juvenile Gazette (24 Nov 1827–15 Nov 1828)
The Juvenile Repository
The Ladies Museum
Literary Cadet, and Saturday Evening Bulletin
The Literary Journal, and Weekly Register of Science
  and the Arts
The Rhode-Island Literary Repository
The Toilet
The Weekly Visitor

WOONSOCKET FALLS

The Ladies' Mirror

SOUTH CAROLINA

CHARLESTON

The Charleston Spectator, and Ladies' Literary Port
  Folio
Chicora
The Monthly Review and Literary Miscellany of the
  United States
South-Carolina Weekly Museum
The Southern and Western Monthly Magazine and Review
The Southern Ladies' Book
The Southern Literary Journal, and Monthly Magazine
The Southern Quarterly Review
The Southern Review
The Toilet
The Vigil

TENNESSEE

NASHVILLE

The Naturalist and Journal of Natural History,
    Agriculture, Education, and Literature
Southern Lady's Companion
The Spirit of '76

TEXAS

GALLATIN

Southron

VERMONT

BENNINGTON

The Monthly Miscellany

BRADFORD

The Green Mountain Gem

BURLINGTON

The Green Mountain Repository
The Iris

MIDDLEBURY

The Literary and Philosophical Repertory

PEACHAM

The Green Mountain Patriot

RUTLAND

The Rural Magazine

VIRGINIA

CHARLOTTESVILLE

The Virginia Literary Museum and Journal of Belles
    Lettres, Arts, Sciences & c.

FREDERICKSBURG

The Masonic Olive Branch and Literary Portfolio

HARPERS FERRY

The Ladies' Garland

MARTINSBURGH

The Lay-Man's Magazine

RICHMOND

American Gleanor and Virginia Magazine
The Iris
The Literary Journal
The Minerva
The Monthly Miscellany
National Magazine
Parley's Magazine for Children and Youth
Richmond Lyceum Journal
The Southern Literary Messenger
The Virginia Historical Register
The Visitor

WINCHESTER

The Monthly Magazine and Literary Journal

WISCONSIN

MILWAUKEE

Lady's Western Magazine, and Garland of the Valley

SOUTHPORT

Garland of the West, and Wisconsin Monthly Magazine

Index of Editors and Publishers

The main bibliography contains the names of editors and publishers as they appear in the periodicals. In the following index, the names have been regularized and are listed in alphabetical order, followed by the item number(s) in which they appear.

A

Aaron Pennington & Daniel Dodge, 177
Adam Waldie & Co., 355, 777
Adams, David Phineas, 538
Adams, James, Jr., 913
Adams, N., 193
Adams, Thomas, 862
Agnew, John Holmes, 29, 116, 245, 246, 378
A. Hanna & H. Greene, 294
A. H. Maltby & Co., 520
Aitken, Robert, 683
Albro, J. A., 193
Alcott, Amos Bronson, 233
Alcott, Louisa M., 748
Alden, Timothy, 12
Aldrich, James, 612
Alexander, Charles, 262, 298
Alfriend, Frank H., 791
Allen and Goddard, 370
Allen and Ticknor, 366, 370, 604
Allen, Francis D., Jr., 681
Allen, John, 378
Allen, Merrill and Wardwell, 117
Allen, Paul, 718
Allen, Virginia R., 681
Allen, William B., 507
Anderson & Meehan, 209
Anderson, Henry J., 97, 625
Anderson, John, 312
Andrews, Beaumont & Co., 828
Andrews, Ferdinand, 641
Andrews, John, 871
Andrews, Loring, 322
Andrews, Samuel G., 100, 147
A. R. Crain & Co., 163
Armstrong, Samuel T., 143, 251
Arthur, T. S., 104, 105, 109, 534
Ash, Thomas T., 928
A. T. Goodrich & Co., 114, 684
Atkinson & Alexander, 176, 773
Atkinson, Samuel C., 176, 569, 773
Atkinson, Thomas, 12
Atwater, Lyman H., 115
Austin, John B., 468
Aydelotte, B. P., 187

B

Babcock, Elisha, 52
Bacheler, Origen, 270, 656
Bacon, S. G., 448
Badger & Porter, 556
Badger, Thomas, Jr., 258
Badger, William, 454
Bagby, George W., 791
Bailey, Francis, 837
Bailey, Isaac, 746
Bailey, John J., 830
Bailey, Lydia, 70
Bailey, Rufus William, 679
Baillie & Co., 175
Baldwin, Charles N., 4, 458
Ball, Josiah, 278
Ballou, M. M., 103
Bancroft, Monson, 57
B. & J. Homans, 538
Bannister, R., 537
Barlett, John S., 9
Barlow and Babcock, 52
Barney, Mary, 575
Barrett, George C., 584
Barrett, William, 297
Bartlett, George Oscar, 915
Batchellor, James, 650
Bates, Elisha, 701
Beach, L., 333
Beals, E. C., 219
Beck, T. Romeyn, 642
Beecher, E., 193
Belcher & Armstrong, 143, 251
Belcher, Joshua, 143, 251
Belknap and Hall, 24
Bell, N., 413
Bement, C. N., 174
Benjamin Edes & Son, 121
Benjamin, Park, 57, 91, 156, 264, 608, 634
Bennett, Emerson, 175
Berford and Company, 798
Betker, John P., 454
Biddle, Nicholas, 718
Bidwell, Walter Hilliard, 116, 245
Biglow, Horatio, 59

C

E. J. Coale and Cushing and Jewett, 720
E. J. Goodrich, 117
Ela, David H., 142
E. L. Carey & A. Hart, 171
E. L. Garvin & Co., 80
E. Littell & E. Bliss & E. White, 565
E. Littell & Brother, 465
E. Littell & Company, 480
E. Littell and R. Norris Henry, 565
E. Littell and T. Holden, 236, 565
Eliot, John, 126
Elliot and Crissy, 647
Elliot, James, 501
Elliot, J. H., 378
Elliott, Stephen, 793
Elliott, Stephen, Jr., 793
Elliot, William, 646
Embury, Emma C., 176, 381
Emerson & Murray, 345, 473
Emerson, Ralph Waldo, 233, 500
Emerson, William, 538
Emmons, S. Bulfinch, 330
English, Thomas Dunn, 89, 351
Etheridge & Bliss, 819
Etheridge, Samuel, 825
Evans, Charles, 284
Everest, C. W., 732
Everett, Alexander H., 538
Everett, Edward, 319, 354
Everett, Oliver, 603, 641
Everette, B., 345, 473
Evert A. and George L. Duyckinck, 331, 478
Ewing, Samuel, 779

F

Fairfield, Sumner Lincoln, 637
Farley & Goss, 310
Farmer, J., 202
Farnham and Badger, 868`
Farrand and Nicholas, 75
Farrand, Mallory, & Co., 587
Farrand, William P., 554
Fay, Theodore Sedgwick, 622
Felch, Cheever, 594
Fellows, J., 409
Fennell, James, 904
Ferry, H., 659
Fessenden, Thomas Green, 584
Fish, George W. H., 394
Fisher, E. Burke, 440
Fisk, D. D., 442
Fisk, H., 461
Fisk, Theophilus, 609
Fithian, Charles, 154
Fitts, R. B., 910
Fitzgerald, William, 805
Flash, Ryder, & Co., 197, 894
Fletcher, Cleaveland, 191
Fletcher, Mary A., 402
Flint, E. Hubbard, 896
Flint, Timothy, 378, 896
Follen, Eliza L., 186
Folsom, Charles, 778
Folwell, Richard, 694
Foote, John P., 196
Ford & Damrell, 370

Forman, Ezekiel, 865
Forrester, Mark, 153
Foss, German W., 447
Foster, George G., 351
Foster, Theodore, 512
Fowle, Z., 501
Fowler, A., 442
Fowler & Dietz, 331
Fowler, S. M., 826
Francis, Charles S., 604, 668
Francis, Joseph H., 668
Franklin, Benjamin, 293
Franklin, James, 121
Fraser, Donald, 45
Freeman, Edmund, 322
Freeman, James, 126
Freeman, T. B., 817
French, Ebenezer, 406
Freneau, Philip, 571, 823
Frost, John, 919
Fr. Pustet & Co., 157
Fry, Joseph Reese, 894
Fuller, E. Q., 269
Fuller, Hiram, 602, 622
Fuller, Margaret, 233
Fulton & Smith, 572

G

Gallagher, William D., 197, 325, 884, 894
Gallaher, John S., 383
Gamage, G. A., 290
G. and C. Carvill, 115, 495, 842
G. and G. and H. Carvill, 57
G. & J. Huntley, 437
G. & R. Waite, 413
Gardenier, Barent, 222
Gardner, Charles H., 430
Gardner, Melzar, 146
Garlank, H. M., Jr., 789
Garrison, William Lloyd, 423
Gemmill & Lewis, 848
George Bond & Co., 25
George Dobbin & Murphy, 803
George L. Curry and Company, 86
George Washington Light & Co., 253
Gerrish, Robert, 597
Gervase Godard & Co., 302
G. Goodman & J. R. Chandler, 690
Gibbons, W., 414
Gibbs, John T., 724
Gilbert & Dean, 143
Gilbert, Samuel, 143
Gillesby, Edward, 780
Gilman, Charles, 493
Gilman, Whittingham, 506
Gilmore, J. R., 378
Glass, John P., 454
Godard, Gervase, 302
Godey, Louis A., 303
Goodman, George, 690
Goodrich, Samuel G. ["Peter Parley"], 123, 422, 668, 748
Goodridge, Sewall, 568
Goss, Sylvester T., 376, 403
Gould, Stephen, 177
Graham, David, 706

Index of Editors and Publishers

Graham, George R., 176, 298, 773
Graves, Quartus, 732
Gray and Bowen, 641
Gray, Frederick T., 641
Gray, Harrison, 836
Gray, John A., 378
Gray, John Chipman, 319
Greear, William, 326, 327
Greeley, Horace, 634
Green, Fanny, 67
Green, Frances H., 920
Green, T., 121
Greene, Albert G., 451
Greene, Benjamin H., 136, 157, 373
Greene, Henderson, 425
Greenleaf and Freeman, 126
Greenleaf, Joseph, 755
Greenleaf, Oliver C., 251
Greenwood, Grace, 303
Gregg, Thomas, 433
G. R. Graham & Co., 773
Gridley, Jeremiah, 40
Griffin, Joseph, 272
Griffing, Edward M., 536
Griswold, Rufus Wilmot, 156, 176, 634
G. W. & S. O. Post, 748

H

Hale, Nathan, Jr., 130
Hale, N., 603
Hale, Sarah J., 303, 365, 388
Hall, Harrison, 718
Hall, James, 337, 642, 894
Hall, John B., 142, 910
Hall, John Elihu, 718
Hall, Samuel, 254
Haly and Thomas, 768
Hamilton, William, 327
Hamline, L. L., 404
Hancock, R. B., 906
Hanson, Harriet Jane, 486
Hardie, James, 617
Harding, Jesper, 10
Hardt, P., 848
Harmer, Joseph, 799
Harper, G. K., 281
Harris, Thaddeus Mason, 499
Harris, Thomas L., 67, 292
Harrison, Joseph W., 627
Harrisson and Purdy, 339
Harrisson, John, 339
Hart, John S., 834
Hastings & Tracy, 899
Hastings, Etheridge and Bliss, 538
Hastings, Thomas, 899
Haswell & MacKay, 550
Haswell, Anthony, 550
Hawkins, David, Jr., 22
Hawkins, Joseph, 208
Hawley, Gideon, 642
Hawley, William A., 146
Heard and Forman, 397
Heard, Phineas, 397
Heartt, Dennis, 344, 690, 697
Heath, James E., 791
Heinkell, John, 546

Helmbold, George, Jr., 822
Henry, R. Norris, 603, 696
Herbert, Francis, 811
Herbert, Henry William, 57
Herrick & Noyes, 912
Hews & Goss, 376
Hildreth, A. B. F., 309, 472, 473
Hill & Moore, 202
Hilliard and Brown, 60, 320
Hilliard and Metcalf, 295, 319
Hilliard, Gray, and Co., 60
Hilliard, William, 457
Hill, Peter, 57
Hine, Lucius A., 324, 885
Hitchcock, J. S., 898
Hobart, John Henry, 192
Hodge, Charles, 115
Hoff, J., 180
Hoffman, Charles Fenno, 57, 378, 478, 622, 769
Hoffman, Lewis G., 50
Hogan, David, 698
Holcombe, Henry, 301
Holden, Charles W., 331
Holley, Orville Luther, 59
Hope, M. B., 115
Hopkins and Earle, 779
Hopkins & Morris, 622
Hopkinson, Francis, 205
Hough, George, 216
Houston, George, 522
Howard, Horton J., 433
Howe, Hezekiah, 483
Howel, John, 322
Hoyt, Ralph, 164
Hoyt, William, 300
H. Pool & W. Palfray, Jr., 340
Hueston, Samuel, 378
Hull & Henry, 645
Hunt, Freeman, 44
Hunt, Ralph, 922
Hunt, William Gibbes, 497, 901
Huntley, George B., 437
Huntley, John T., 437
Hurlbut, Joseph, E., 146, 420

I

I. C. & J. N. Stearns, 748
Ingraham & Andrews, 147
Ingraham and Hewes, 138
Inman, John, 204, 622
Ira Oliver Beaumont & Co., 828
Irving, Washington, 79, 767
Irwin, Thomas, 698
Isaiah Thomas and Company, 499
Ives, S. B., 329
Ives, W., 329

J

Jabez Parkhurst & Samuel Pennington, 177
James G. Brooks & George Bond, 522
James Kay, Jun. & Co., 115
James Munroe and Co., 60, 233, 641, 891

217

V

Van Benthuysen & Wood, 313
Van Court, J., 382
Van Hoesen, J. A., 795
Verrinder, William, 448
Vickers, Abraham, 867
Vosburgh, Abraham, 222

W

Wade, Robert L., 583
Wait, William S., 913
Waite, Peirce & Company, 480
Waldie, Adam, 70, 355, 717, 777, 856
Waldo, Elisha H., 560, 905
Waldo, S. Putnam, 758
Walker and Richards, 792
Walker, Edward, 650
Wallace, James S., 658
Wallace, William Ross, 830
Walsh, Mike, 808
Walsh, Robert, 57, 70, 71, 72, 75, 565
Walter, Ellwood, 88
Walter, J., 853
Walton, Joseph, 284
W. & S. B. Ives, 329
Ware, Katharine A., 147
Warner & Hanna, 183
Watkins, Tobias, 720
Watson & Co., 176
Watson, Henry O., 155
Watson, John F., 779
Watson, J. V., 269
Watters, James, 865
Watts, John, 814
Webbe, John, 46
Webster, Noah, 43
Wedderburn & Alfriend, 791
Weeden and Barrett, 297
Weeden, Job, 297
Weeks, Jordan & Co., 233
Weikel, A., 700
Weld, H. Hastings, 156, 237
Wellman, Jonathan K., 438, 737
Wells and Lilly, 641, 735
Wescott, Isaac, 798
West, Robert A., 204
Weyman, W., 343
Wharton, Thomas Isaac, 79, 444
Whelpley, James D., 73
Whipple & Damrell, 29
Whitaker, Daniel K., 194, 790, 792
White, Samuel B., 876
White, Thomas W., 791
Whitely, Edward, 876
Whiting, N., 316
Whitmore & Buckingham, 516
Whitmore, P. B., 516
Whitney & M'Cord, 440
Whittemore, J. M., 229
Whittingham and John Gilman, 506
Wiggins, Francis S., 553
Wiggins, P. S., 530
Wilbur, Hervey, 537

Wiley & Halsted, 336, 430
Wiley and Long, 378
Wiley and Putnam, 73, 117
Wiley, Charles, 838
Wiley, J., 57
Willard, Sidney, 60
William and Thomas Bradford, 47
William H. Channing and James H. Perkins, 891
William P. Farrand and E. Sargeant, 554
William Primrose Harrison and Co., 784
William Simonds and Company, 703
William Treadwell & Co., 841
William Treadwell & Daniel Treadwell, 841
Williams, E. D., 227
Williams, David H., 641
Williams, Jno. L., 878
Williams, John H., 757
Williams, John S., 68
Williams, Robert S., 622
Williams, Samuel, 760
Williams, Thomas, 91
Willis and Francis Douglas, 242
Willis, Nathaniel, 242, 926
Willis, Nathaniel P., 56, 221, 237, 422, 602, 622
Wilson & Company, 156, 237
Wilson, James, 77
Wilson, Lewis, 230
Wilson, Samuel S., 374
Winchester, E., 741
Winchester, J., 261, 264, 608, 634, 741
Winterbottom, A. S., 489
Wise, Daniel, 402
Witherell, J. F., 831
Wood and Stratton, 197
Wood, Barnabas, 42
Wood, John S., 42
Woodbridge, Moore & Co., 193
Woodruff & Pechin, 691
Woodruff & Turner, 691
Woods, John, 839
Woods, Leonard, Jr., 431
Woodward & Green, 521
Woodward, Moses H., 521
Woodward, W. W., 456
Woodworth & Huestis, 384
Woodworth, Samuel, 317, 384, 622, 677
Woodworth, Webb, & Co., 677
Workman, Judge, 718
Wright, John, 27
Wright, N. H., 376
W. Tuttle & Co., 177

Y

Young & Uhlhorn, 215
Young, L. H., 215, 516
Young, William, 843
Young, W. P., 846

Z

Zenger, John Peter, 630
Zieber, G. B., 351
Z. J. & J. W. Griffin, 360

Index of Names

The following index is an alphabetical list of the literary figures and those of literary interest whose names appear in the main body of the bibliography. Here, as in the INDEX OF EDITORS AND PUBLISHERS, any name discrepancies have been regularized and are followed by the item number(s) in which these names appear.

A

Abdy, Mrs. Maria, Poetry 271, 347, 355, 608, 717, 749, 750, 761, 777, 856; Tale 472
Adams, Abigail, Biography 234
Adams, John, Anecdote 899; Biography 126, 453, 694; Letters 711, 843
Adams, John Quincy, Addresses and orations 136; Anecdotes 191, 309, 496; Biographies 37, 164, 176, 217, 264, 311, 440, 718, 761, 795, 797; Contributor 538; Criticism 500; Extract 402; Letters 231; Poetry 35, 99, 153, 264, 270, 383, 424, 536, 585, 627, 769, 899; Travel 718
Adams, John S., Poetry 910
Adams, Lois B., Poetry 404
Adams, Samuel, Biography 504
Adams, Samuel P., Poetry 622
Addison, Joseph, Anecdotes 88, 144, 180, 183, 260, 334, 506, 507, 533, 698, 713, 718, 779, 797, 806, 843, 893; Biography 168, 195, 303, 345, 636, 706; Criticism 538; Extracts 163, 405, 499, 607, 609, 757; Letters 827; Poetry 88, 140, 423, 790; Sketch 126; Tale 703
Aikin, Sarah, Poetry 609
Ainsworth, William Harrison, Novels 608, 741, 777; Tales 156, 261, 608, 749
Akenside, Mark, Poetry 453, 718
Alcott, Amos Bronson, Essays 112, 136; Extracts 233, 402, 667
Aldrich, James, Poetry 91, 155, 176, 186, 264, 284, 382, 608, 612
Alexander, J. W., Poetry 284
Alexander, William, Poetry 303
Allen, Charlotte, Poetry 35, 650, 910
Allen, Ethan, Biography 758
Allen, Paul, Poetry 720
Allen, William Butler, Poetry 73
Allibone, Thomas, Subscriber 65
Allston, Emma F., Poetry 769
Allston, Washington, Biography 595; Contributor 538; Extracts 114, 384; Poetry 57, 91, 139, 146, 249, 525, 556, 724, 836, 891, 904; Review 792
Allyn, Vincent G., Poetry 18
Alretken, J., Poetry 378
Alsop, Richard, Poetry 718
Ames, C. F., Poetry 761

Ames, Fisher, Anecdotes 577; Biographies 44, 241, 718, 746, 802
Andersen, Hans Christian, Biography 80; Poetry 245; Tale 245
Andrews, Almira H., Poetry 382
Annable, W. J., Poetry 447
Anster, John, Poetry 237
Applegate, Thomas, Poetry 681
Aquinas, Saint Thomas, Anecdote 283
Arbuthnot, Dr. John, Anecdote 208; Biography 761; Poetry 829
Arnold, Benedict, Biography 698
Arnold, S. G., Poetry 284
Arthur, T. S., Extract 667; Poetry 104, 105, 109, 152, 154, 381, 382, 534; Tales 35, 152, 154, 402, 536, 595, 681
Ashburnham, William, Poetry 784
Ashcroft, James, Poetry 337
Athelwood, Isabel, Poetry 878
Atwater, Lyman H., Contributor 431
Auchinleck, Elizabeth, Poetry 246
Augusta, Cornelia, Poetry 404
Austen, Jane, Biography 782
Austin, William, Tale 585

B

Babcock, J. S., Poetry 73, 912
Bacon, Ezekiel, Poetry 642
Bacon, Francis, Anecdotes 790, 823; Biographies 195, 474; Extracts 332, 790
Bacon, William Thompson, Poetry 64, 73, 136, 142, 221, 378, 912
Bailey, Philip James, Poetry 792
Bailey, Samuel, Poetry 451
Baillie, Joanna, Biography 388; Drama 171; Poetry 9, 70, 79, 88, 114, 161, 194, 355, 402, 478, 522, 526, 577, 585, 603, 608, 713, 759, 797, 880, 928, 935
Baird, Charles W., Poetry 176
Baker, E. D., Jr., Poetry 627
Baker, William D., Poetry 700
Ball, William, Poetry 176
Bancroft, George, Essay 136; Extract 609; Poetry 625

Barbauld, Anna Letitia, Biographies 435, 782;
  Extracts 646, 713; Poetry 138, 192, 209, 295,
  370, 434, 591, 647, 760, 889; Tale 748
Barber, Catharine Webb, Poetry 535, 761, 910
Barber, Elizabeth G., Poetry 37
Barber, William, Poetry 73
Barker, James N., Poetry 334, 396, 534
Barker, J. W., Poetry 595
Barker, W. G. J., Poetry 382
Barlow, D. H., Poetry 382
Barlow, Joel, Anecdotes 93, 277; Biographies 146,
  345, 507, 634, 654; Criticism 538; Essay 545;
  Extract 573; Letters 573; Poetry 43, 205, 340,
  378, 499, 598, 618, 757, 779
Barrett, Charles Bird, Poetry 176
Barrett, Elizabeth, Poetry 176, 245, 355, 382, 424,
  480, 612, 705, 792; Review 792
Barrett, Joseph Hartwell, Poetry 73
Barrington, E. H., Poetry 245
Barton, Bernard, Poetry 48, 88, 138, 146, 164, 176,
  177, 187, 197, 237, 247, 257, 271, 284, 311,
  382, 383, 396, 423, 424, 451, 489, 516, 522,
  534, 569, 608, 634, 696, 717, 737, 759, 899,
  928, 935
Bartram, William, Extract 499; Travel 24, 62, 596,
  636, 843, 876
Bates, Cornelia, F. L., Poetry 703
Baxter, Lydia, Poetry 922
Baxter, Richard, Biography 802
Baxter, William, Poetry 404
Bay, William, Poetry 568
Bayly, Thomas Haynes, Extract 303; Poetry 10, 15,
  19, 48, 88, 98, 146, 154, 164, 176, 261, 303,
  345, 360, 382, 386, 394, 396, 423, 461, 465, 472,
  473, 480, 490, 496, 553, 556, 569, 604, 609, 634,
  680, 692, 700, 717, 754, 761, 777, 845, 856, 862,
  864, 899, 935; Sketch 754; Tales 272, 692
Beach, Thomas J., Poetry 332
Beard, Alex Lacey, Poetry 791
Beattie, James, Biographies 251, 260, 698; Extract
  876; Poetry 270, 327, 340, 364, 506, 718, 797,
  854, 865, 929
Beauclerk, Topham, Anecdote 823
Beaufain, Adrian, Poetry 786
Beaumarchais, Extract 685
Beaumont, Francis, Anecdote 713; Poetry 48
Beckford, William, Poetry 608
Beck, George, Poetry 901
Beckett, G. L., Poetry 227
Beddoes, Thomas Lovell, Drama 9
Bedlow, Henry J., Poetry 381
Beecher, Harriet. See Stowe, Harriet Beecher.
Beers, J. Edward, Poetry 627
Behn, Aphra, Biography 854
Belknap, Jeremy, Extract 843; Biographies 202, 694,
  713, 739, 853, 865; Tale 205
Bemis, Samuel G., Poetry 330
Benjamin, Park, Anecdotes 142, 828; Poetry 42, 53,
  56, 57, 60, 91, 105, 130, 146, 155, 176, 204,
  261, 264, 270, 271, 284, 298, 309, 325, 331,
  332, 345, 378, 381, 382, 394, 438, 461, 493,
  534, 556, 567, 589, 608, 609, 611, 662, 708,
  726, 754, 769, 787, 791, 834, 910; Tale 791
Bennett, Emerson, Poetry 175, 324, 885
Bennett, James, Poetry 906
Bennett, W. C., Poetry 186
Benson, Carl, Poetry 478
Bentham, Jeremy, Biography 168, 538, 717, 913
Béranger, Pierre Jean de, Anecdote 828; Extracts
  433, 478; Poetry 1, 80, 98, 270, 478, 512, 608,
  634, 680, 778, 791, 808, 889

Beresford, Robert, Poetry 262
Bethune, George W., Poetry 355
Betterton, Thomas, Biography 526
Bickerstaff, Isaac, Jr., Biography 300
Biddle, Nicholas, Poetry 777, 782
Biddle, Thomas, Biography 337
Biglow, William, Contributor 499
Bird, Robert M., Extract 325; Poetry 791
Bisbee, Maria E., Poetry 627
Bishop, Samuel, Poetry 759
Blackstone, William, Poetry 138, 760, 791
Blackwell, Anna, Poetry 204, 382
Blackwood, William Gardner, Poetry 786, 791, 808
Blair, Hugh, Poetry 791
Blake, William, Poetry 152
Bleeker, Anna Eliza, Poetry 618
Bleeker, Anthony, Poetry 618
Bliss, W. R., Poetry 912
Blockett, Joseph, Poetry 779
Bloomfield, Robert, Biographies 326, 678, 872;
  Extract 303; Poetry 180, 242, 328, 413, 455, 474,
  522, 698, 872, 876
Blount, E. P., Poetry 422
Boethius, Anicius Manlius Severinus, Biography 251
Bogart, Elizabeth, Poetry 10, 164, 556, 609, 761
Bogue, Henry James, Poetry 35, 382, 692
Boileau, Nicolas, Anecdotes 453, 718; Biographies
  251, 353, 591, 718; Poetry 641, 670, 696
Bolingbroke, Henry St. John, Anecdotes 537, 880;
  Biographies 75, 454, 538, 743, 779, 792;
  Extract 864
Bolling, Robert, Poetry 205
Boone, Daniel, Anecdote 337; Biographies 44, 337,
  786
Borrow, George O., Poetry 577
Boston Bard. See Coffin, R. S.
Boswell, James, Anecdotes 142, 194, 262, 453, 533,
  554, 697, 700, 718, 730, 823, 908; Biographies
  423, 453; Extracts 183, 499; Letters 718
Boucher, Thomas L., Poetry 324
Bowring, John, Poetry 44, 48, 88, 98, 100, 138, 146,
  176, 247, 284, 383, 394, 396, 423, 424, 441, 446,
  448, 496, 516, 522, 553, 609, 703, 754, 761, 797,
  913, 928
Bowles, Caroline, Extract 303; Poetry 88, 608
Bowles, William L., Poetry 164, 234, 303, 720, 928
Bowman, E. P., Poetry 595
Boyle, Edward R., Poetry 572
Boyle, Geoffrey H., Poetry 440
Boyle, Mary, Poetry 512
Boyle, Robert, Biography 40
Boz. See Dickens, Charles.
Bozman, John L., Poetry 718
Brackenridge, Hugh Henry, Criticism 79; Extract 799;
  Poetry 31, 312, 880
Bradbury, Hannah E., Poetry 408
Bradfield, Henry J., Poetry 53, 427, 478
Bradford, S. S., Poetry 791
Bradford, William, Biography 193
Brainard, John G., Biographies 146, 761; Poetry 10,
  44, 48, 88, 97, 146, 154, 241, 253, 270, 284,
  386, 396, 423, 435, 465, 556, 609, 641, 808,
  899
Brame, John Todd, Poetry 404, 708
Brent, John Carroll, Poetry 791
Brewster, William, Biography 193
Bridgesson, Hugh, Poetry 73
Bright, J. H., Poetry 378
Bristed, C. A., Poetry 73
Brockbank, L. Casandra, Poetry 761

English, Thomas Dunn, Poetry 155, 156, 176, 298, 381, 426, 569, 602, 622, 645, 761; Tale 602
Erasmus, Desiderius, Anecdote 507; Biography 538; Extract 448
Evans, E. A., Poetry 885
Evans, E. H., Poetry 791
Everett, Alexander H., Article 136; Poetry 130, 349
Everett, C. W., Poetry 791
Everett, Edward, Biography 589; Contributor 295; Extracts 309, 445; Poetry 383, 434, 569; Review 792; Tale 130
Everett, R. J., Poetry 433

F

Fairchild, William B., Poetry 420, 572, 791
Fairfield, James G., Poetry 58
Fairfield, Sumner Lincoln, Biographies 225, 913; Extract 164; Poetry 10, 18, 60, 88, 125, 146, 147, 164, 225, 257, 309, 434, 448, 522, 634, 637, 911; Tale 609
Falconer, Harriet, Poetry 618
Falconer, Richard, Poetry 598
Falconer, William, Biography 522; Poetry 37, 176, 196, 434, 465, 634, 680, 862
Fargo, E. M., Poetry 408
Farmer, C. M., Poetry 478
Fawcett, R., Poetry 339
Fay, Theodore Sedgwick, Essay Serial 622; Extracts 18, 442; Letters 622; Novel 791; Poetry 204; Tales 262, 556, 611, 726
Felltham, Owen, Extract 713
Felton, C. C., Poetry 791
Fénelon, François de Salignac de la Mothe-, Anecdotes 35, 59, 283, 506, 622; Biographies 718, 929; Extracts 685, 713, 748
Fennell, James, Anecdote 210; Biographies 713, 814, 815; Review 815
Fessenden, Thomas Green, Contributor 594; Poetry 48, 441, 538, 554, 584, 594, 718, 822, 841, 867, 876
Fields, James T., Poetry 130, 142, 152, 269, 309, 347, 536, 556, 708, 749, 845, 915
Fichte, Johann Gottlieb, Biography 778
Fielding, Henry, Anecdote 690; Criticism 453, 600, 720
Findlay, George, Contributor 500
Fisher, E. Burke, Poetry 440
Fisher, R. S., Poetry 512
Fisher, S. G., Poetry 693
Fisk, H., Poetry 595
Fisk, W. H., Poetry 168
Fithian, Charles, Poetry 154
Fitzgerald, Edward M., Poetry 261, 303, 396
Flagg, Wilson, Poetry 142, 472, 737
Flemming, Paul, Poetry 424
Fletcher, E. T., Poetry 382
Fletcher, Giles, Poetry 562
Fletcher, John, Anecdote, 713
Flint, Timothy, Biography 448; Poetry 270, 396, 791; Tale 536
Follen, Charles, Poetry 424
Follen, Eliza L., Poetry 186, 424
Foote, Samuel, Anecdotes 546, 677, 691, 799; Biography 713; Drama 110
Foote, Sylvia G., Poetry 889
Forbes, A. A., Poetry 761
Ford, William, Poetry 761

Forrester, Nilla, Poetry 153
Foscolo, Ugo, Biography 603
Foss, German W., Poetry 447
Foster, Moses, Poetry 915
Fox, Charles James, Anecdote 718; Biographies 480, 504, 538, 648, 760, 761; Poetry 369, 522, 595, 759, 904
Francis, John, Poetry 511
Francis, L. M., Poetry 388
Franklin, Benjamin, Anecdotes 1, 10, 49, 50, 77, 79, 109, 114, 138, 144, 146, 161, 176, 194, 213, 227, 247, 272, 282, 309, 312, 329, 332, 359, 369, 373, 384, 423, 427, 441, 442, 444, 446, 448, 496, 502, 506, 533, 538, 554, 577, 594, 618, 622, 623, 627, 631, 636, 651, 652, 667, 685, 689, 690, 691, 696, 697, 698, 700, 703, 713, 726, 748, 751, 760, 773, 790, 797, 822, 865, 873, 876, 893, 908, 924; Biographies 6, 44, 60, 61, 65, 76, 126, 142, 152, 176, 184, 195, 197, 221, 329, 353, 366, 453, 454, 553, 636, 713, 718, 743, 748, 751, 843, 865; Criticism 538; Essay 321, 377, 509, 550; Extracts 31, 39, 60, 68, 77, 138, 174, 191, 214, 222, 229, 248, 285, 317, 423, 426, 499, 537, 568, 577, 598, 683, 690, 713, 759, 760, 773, 843, 892, 893; Familiar Essay 121; Letters 112, 641, 718, 755, 843; Poetry 208, 403, 499, 691, 876; Sketches 598, 647, 694; Subscriber 65
Franklin, E., Poetry 912
Fraser, William, Poetry 176
Frazer, Jefferson, Poetry 642
Freeman, Ellen B. H., Poetry 787
French, R. C., Poetry 284
Freneau, Philip, Poetry 65, 216, 339, 394, 468, 571, 618, 646, 718, 837
Fresham, H., Poetry 660
Frieze, J., Poetry 191
Fuller, Frances A., Poetry 420, 889
Fuller, Margaret, Anecdotes 480, 828; Articles 136; Contributor 233; Poetry 233, 891
Fuller, Marietta V., Poetry 15

G

Gage, Charlotte B., Poetry 382
Gage, Frances D., Poetry 324
Gallagher, William D., Extracts 433, 475, 898, 900; Poetry 18, 155, 197, 284, 324, 325, 408, 602, 637, 692, 878, 884, 889, 891, 894
Gallatin, Albert, Biography 573
Galt, John, Poetry 378
Gamage, G. A., Poetry 48
Gamble, E. N., Poetry 608
Gardiner, Mary L., Poetry 8, 42, 292, 382, 402, 408, 447, 536, 761, 765, 808
Gardner, J. B., Poetry 197
Gardner, Melzar, Poetry 708
Garrick, David, Anecdotes 88, 160, 176, 183, 209, 244, 282, 309, 312, 326, 328, 355, 369, 384, 448, 526, 546, 577, 585, 622, 676, 677, 680, 690, 691, 694, 696, 698, 700, 713, 718, 724, 773, 784, 799, 871, 872, 876; Biographies 79, 474, 526, 680, 761, 815; Drama 827; Poetry 196, 382, 458, 499, 585
Garrison, William Lloyd, Poetry 424
Gaspey, William, Poetry 472
Gates, Horatio, Poetry 381, 889
Gay, Henrietta, Poetry 761

Gay, John, Anecdote 526; Poetry 282, 372, 456, 474, 581, 596, 865
Gellert, C. F., Poetry 246
Genlis, Madame de, Extract 352; Tale 93
Gessner, Johann Matthias, Poetry 901, 912
Gibbon, Edward, Anecdotes 139, 442, 591, 627, 696, 718, 865; Biographies 43, 197, 761; Criticism 79, 453; Essay 545; Extracts 413, 598, 608, 876
Gierlow, J., Poetry 650, 910
Gifford, John, Poetry 398
Gifford, William, Biography 718; Poetry 474, 718
Gilchrist, David, Poetry 595
Gilfillan, Robert, Poetry 245, 382, 583
Gillespie, C. B., Poetry 175, 885
Gilman, Caroline, Poetry 382, 726, 939
Gilpin, William, Poetry 775
Glover, Richard, Biography 718
Godfrey, Thomas, Jr., Biography 320; Poetry 41
Godwin, Mary Wollstonecraft. See Wollstonecraft, Mary.
Godwin, William, Anecdote 453; Extracts 31, 604
Goethe, Johann Wolfgang von, Anecdotes 57, 233, 798; Biographies 138, 548, 611; Book Reviews 61, 431; Criticism 75, 548, 567; Extracts 88, 229, 233, 270, 713; Poetry 48, 109, 176, 186, 221, 396, 431, 434, 446, 522, 569, 589, 612, 625, 641, 650, 662, 713, 717, 751, 777, 787, 891; Letters 104; Review 792; Tale 186
Goldoni, Charles, Biography 929
Goldsmith, Oliver, Anecdotes 80, 138, 183, 251, 283, 319, 326, 370, 373, 384, 402, 427, 506, 538, 676, 698, 713, 718, 751, 797, 830, 848, 876; Biographies 10, 79, 210, 345, 608, 680, 697, 703, 748, 777; Criticism 139, 321, 453, 538, 567, 591; Drama 827; Extracts 1, 174, 176, 312, 373, 385, 455, 474, 499, 553, 598, 646, 654, 755, 757, 760, 872, 876; Letters 718; Poetry 6, 77, 109, 143, 174, 212, 384, 402, 405, 423, 429, 462, 499, 576, 618, 683, 698, 743, 773, 777, 865, 876; Tales 128, 146, 456, 743, 872
Goodman, D. Ellen, Poetry 204, 834
Goodrich, C. A., Poetry 44
Goodrich, J. W., Poetry 6
Goodrich, Samuel G., Poetry 48, 146, 147, 164, 386, 422, 732, 761
Goodwin, Caroline, Poetry 496
Goodwin, H. M., Poetry 73
Gott, Nathaniel, Poetry 177
Gough, Benjamin, Poetry 284
Gould, Hannah F., Biography 589; Contributor 431; Extract 433; Poetry 6, 8, 18, 44, 48, 53, 60, 64, 88, 98, 105, 109, 124, 146, 152, 154, 156, 175, 176, 187, 197, 200, 241, 243, 245, 253, 257, 270, 284, 303, 309, 332, 366, 370, 378, 381, 382, 386, 388, 396, 402, 423, 433, 438, 442, 461, 472, 493, 496, 536, 556, 589, 595, 608, 634, 662, 667, 668, 680, 703, 722, 726, 732, 749, 754, 761, 765, 834, 862, 878, 891, 894, 909, 922, 924, 928, 935; Tale 562
Gould, R. H., Poetry 791
Graham, John, Poetry 651
Graham, Lily, Poetry 37
Grahame, James, Poetry 19
Granger, L., Poetry 15
Grattan, H. P., Poetry 204, 834
Gray, Anna Eliza, Poetry 642
Gray, Barry, Poetry 761

Gray, Thomas, Anecdotes 329, 453; Biographies 577, 718; Criticism 538, 591; Extract 303; Poetry 10, 205, 271, 300, 340, 364, 456, 462, 529, 581, 598, 618, 670, 690, 713, 718, 765, 848
Greeley, Horace, Anecdote 156; Biographies 309, 703; Contributor 57, 642; Extracts 737, 910, 939; Poetry 270
Greeley, Robert F., Poetry 611
Greeley, R. S., Poetry 478
Green, Fanny, Poetry 67, 920
Green, Joseph, Poetry 657
Green, Robert, Poetry 713
Greene, Christopher R., Poetry 429
Greene, Nathaniel, Biographies 218, 573, 760; Poetry 205
Greenleaf, Stephen, Poetry 496
Grenell, Charles, Poetry 438
Greville, Fulke, Poetry 506, 618
Grey, Lady Jane, Biographies 326, 724
Grigg, William, Poetry 422
Griswold, Chester A., Poetry 732
Griswold, Rufus Wilmot, Poetry 726; Review 792
Gunning, E. W., Poetry 754

H

Hagen, J., Poetry 834
Hagert, Henry S., Poetry 919
Hale, E. B., Poetry 156, 791
Hale, Edward Everett, Tale 130
Hale, Nathan, Biography 311
Hale, Sarah J., Anecdote 828; Biography 761; Extracts 60, 911; Poetry 48, 105, 124, 125, 138, 154, 155, 197, 264, 270, 303, 309, 370, 388, 394, 396, 434, 534, 595, 609, 681, 737, 761, 797, 845, 862, 899, 919; Tales 35, 309, 434, 754, 761
Haliburton, Thomas Chandler, Tale 856
Hall, C. H., Poetry 912
Hall, James, Poetry 516
Hall, John, Poetry 692
Halleck, Fitz-Greene, Biographies 303, 589, 797; Extract 791; Poetry 10, 48, 70, 88, 146, 164, 197, 204, 225, 270, 378, 382, 386, 396, 422, 430, 433, 434, 461, 475, 480, 490, 496, 556, 612, 622, 625, 627, 634, 717, 732, 754, 761, 792, 842, 864
Halsenbeck, J. Harold, Poetry 680
Hamersley, William J., Poetry 153
Hamilton, Alexander, Biographies 453, 538, 573, 622, 718; Subscriber 65
Hamilton, Miriam F., Poetry 408
Hamilton, Robert, Poetry 176, 381, 915
Hanaford, J. H., Poetry 35
Handel, George Frederick, Anecdotes 128, 183, 208; Biographies 261, 271, 317
Hardenberg, Friedrich von, Poetry 567
Harrington, Richard, Poetry 298
Harris, James A., Poetry 761
Harris, Joseph, Poetry 8
Harris, Thaddeus Mason, Poetry 499
Harris, Thomas L., Poetry 8, 67, 292, 345, 382
Harrison, W. H., Poetry 448
Harrisson, John, Poetry 339
Haslet, A., Poetry 191
Hatcher, E. H., Poetry 404

INDEX OF NAMES

M

Macaulay, Thomas Babington, Criticism 115; Poetry 73, 168, 261, 608; Review 792
M'Cabe, John C., Poetry 18, 104, 791
M'Creery, J., Poetry 780
McDonald, M. N., Poetry 834
M'Donald, Sarah, Poetry 8
M'Henry, James, Poetry 10, 58, 70, 303, 577, 838
Machiavelli, Nicollò, Criticism 117
McIlvaine, J. H., Poetry 298
M'Jilton, John N., Poetry 105, 109, 176, 197, 381, 439, 493; Tale 99
Mackay, Charles, Poetry 245, 246, 264, 269, 382, 478, 480, 562, 608, 808
McKellar, Thomas, Poetry 382
Mackenzie, Henry, Biographies 506, 718, 865; Review 792; Tales 360, 743
Mackenzie, R. Shelton, Poetry 439, 511, 512, 531, 722, 749
McLaughlin, Edward A., Poetry 608
M'Lellan, Isaac, Jr., Poetry 253, 422, 589, 608, 703, 910
M'Lellan, J. M., Jr., Poetry 749, 761
MacLeod, C. Donald, Poetry 156, 611
M'Nary, Margaret, Poetry 382
M'Neil, Hector, Poetry 780
Macpherson, James, Anecdote 603; Biographies 146, 522
M'Quiggin, Giles, Poetry 109, 791
Madden, R. R., Poetry 424
Madison, James, Biography 302; Subscriber 65
Malcom, Joss, Poetry 191
Mandell, D. J., Poetry 191
Mandeville, Bernard de, Criticism 59
Mann, Mary H., Poetry 142
Manson, J. B., Poetry 245
Marlowe, Christopher, Poetry 608
Marmontel, Jean François, Tales 636, 654, 743
Marron, J. P., Poetry 427
Marryat, Frederick, Extract 749; Tales 512, 714
Marsden, Joshua, Poetry 383, 529, 659
Marshall, Edward, Poetry 478
Marshall, Thomas, Poetry 496
Martin, Margaret, Poetry 99
Martineau, Harriet, Book Review 431; Extract 60; Poetry 186, 424; Tale 777
Marvell, Andrew, Biography 76; Criticism 538; Poetry 290, 456, 457, 718
Marvell, Ik. See Mitchell, Donald Grant.
Marvin, W. F., Poetry 176
Mason, Eliza, Poetry 761
Mason, Myron L., Poetry 37
Mather, Cotton, Anecdotes 373, 802; Biography 225; Extracts 190, 465
Mathews, Cornelius, Anecdote 828; Familiar Essay 425; Illustrations 86; Poetry 425, 792
Mathews, Helen, Poetry 298
Matson, James, Poetry 642
Maturin, Charles Robert, Anecdote 447; Biography 114; Extract 114; Poetry 603, 611, 696, 787; Tale 700
May, Caroline, Poetry 834
May, Edith, Poetry 834
Mayne, J., Poetry 670
Meek, Alexander Beaufort, Poetry 155, 787, 791

Mellen, Grenville, Poetry 48, 57, 60, 64, 70, 146, 152, 176, 191, 243, 270, 284, 298, 381, 422, 423, 438, 440, 451, 493, 496, 553, 569, 589, 622, 662, 668, 700, 722, 726, 761, 797, 836, 913; Tales 272, 556, 700
Melville, Herman, Anecdote 423; Book Reviews 116, 193; Extract 80; Review 792
Merry, Robert, Poetry 322, 574, 694, 784, 865; Tale 748
Messenger, A. N., Poetry 382
Messler, Abraham, Poetry 642
Michaux, André, Biography 538
Mickle, W. J., Poetry 703
Middleton, Thomas, Poetry 850
Mifflin, J. Houston, Poetry 298, 662
Mifflin, Maria, Poetry 154
Miller, James William, Poetry 422, 496, 516
Miller, John, Poetry 100
Milman, H. H., Poetry 603
Milnes, Richard M., Poetry 261, 424
Milton, John, Anecdotes 44, 139, 164, 183, 309, 533, 553, 591, 627, 636, 690, 698, 718, 823, 893; Biographies 309, 553, 697; Criticism 194, 295, 457, 525, 538, 567, 678, 685; Extracts 131, 284, 303, 474, 478, 554; Poetry 69, 144, 195, 295, 317, 378, 423, 453, 455, 473, 526, 576, 636, 677, 703, 718, 743, 779, 892; Review 792
Mitchell, Donald Grant, Tale 73
Mitchell, Samuel Latham, Contributor 618; Poetry 865
Mitford, Mary Russell, Biographies 408, 551, 929; Poetry 139, 211, 264, 434, 551, 713, 779; Tales 386, 434, 556, 681, 754, 761, 777, 908
Moffet, John Newland, Poetry 105
Moir, D. M., Poetry 186
Molière (Jean Baptiste Poquelin), Anecdotes 353, 519, 526, 554, 718, 779, 880; Biography 76
Montagu, Lady Mary Wortley, Anecdotes 384, 565, 577; Biographies 448, 474, 676, 726, 782, 848; Letters 260, 507; Poetry 104, 241, 757
Montagu, L. J., Poetry 717
Montagu, L. M., Poetry 512
Montesquieu, Charles Louis de Secondat de, Anecdote 79; Biography 522; Extracts 283, 598
Montgomery, James, Anecdote 88; Biography 448; Extracts 303, 448, 565; Poetry 18, 19, 42, 44, 48, 57, 88, 93, 98, 105, 138, 139, 144, 154, 174, 176, 184, 192, 196, 209, 225, 247, 257, 264, 270, 272, 284, 285, 290, 298, 302, 310, 316, 317, 340, 363, 382, 383, 385, 386, 396, 402, 421, 423, 434, 438, 441, 446, 448, 465, 513, 521, 529, 530, 553, 556, 562, 565, 569, 576, 577, 595, 608, 612, 627, 637, 641, 644, 647, 676, 696, 703, 717, 718, 724, 726, 748, 758, 759, 761, 763, 777, 779, 793, 797, 808, 830, 845, 854, 862, 876, 880, 899, 910, 913, 924, 928, 935
Montgomery, Robert, Biography 202; Book Review 431; Poetry 10, 48, 164, 176, 386, 396, 431, 434, 438, 465, 490, 513, 556, 659, 680, 692, 717, 754, 871
Moore, Dr. John, Novel 743
Moore, Edward, Poetry 618, 654
Moore, George, Poetry 331
Moore, Hugh, Poetry 496
Moore, John, Poetry 423
Moore, John S., Poetry 227
Moore, Thomas, Anecdotes 175, 251, 848; Biographies 386, 761; Criticism 59, 79, 194, 295, 320, 720; Extracts 303, 405, 441, 495; Poetry 9, 37, 44, 48, 49, 77, 88, 93, 98, 105, 114, 123, 128, 139,

234

N

O

P

Q

317, 334, 369, 378, 383, 396, 402, 405, 423, 434,
435, 468, 480, 496, 531, 534, 538, 556, 568, 583,
585, 611, 641, 645, 647, 654, 680, 690, 696, 700,
718, 763, 779, 806, 901; Tales 88, 176, 563, 797,
908
Scuderi, Madame de, Biography 644
Sears, Edmund H., Poetry 440
Seaton, Oneida, Poetry 153
Sedgwick, Catharine Maria, Anecdote 828; Biography
761; Extract 667; Poetry 154, 176; Tales 53,
152, 439, 608, 638, 747
Severn, Walter, Poetry 589
Sévigné, Marie de Rabutin-Chantal, Madame de,
Biography 110; Criticism 686; Extract 685
Sewall, Samuel, Extract 190
Seward, Anna, Biography 782; Poetry 670; 779, 797
Seymour, Lucy, Poetry 105, 109, 404, 737, 747, 761
Shaftesbury, Anthony Ashley Cooper, first earl of,
Sketch 126
Shakespeare, William, Anecdotes 142, 262, 373, 455,
468, 480, 591, 713, 817, 830; Biographies 101,
146, 442; Criticism 79, 93, 139, 525, 538, 678;
Extract 303; Poetry 9, 25, 85, 88, 117, 212, 233,
242, 249, 282, 326, 423, 522, 525, 576, 608, 636,
680, 713, 718, 848, 929; Reviews 792, 814, 816
Shannon, John P., Poetry 795, 808
Sharman, Edward, Poetry 177
Sharp, Benjamin, Poetry 68
Sharpe, Henry John, Poetry 906
Shaw, Isabella O., Poetry 939
Shaw, John, Poetry 718
Shea, Augustus, Poetry 754
Sheldon, E. M., Poetry 42
Sheldon, George Ten Eyck, Poetry 611
Shelley, Mary Godwin, Tales 176, 700
Shelley, Percy Bysshe, Biographies 48, 309, 830;
Criticism 116, 227, 430; Extracts 303, 386, 732;
Poetry 10, 48, 56, 57, 123, 136, 146, 212, 221,
243, 253, 324, 355, 382, 423, 430, 434, 444, 454,
493, 522, 556, 602, 608, 612, 650, 693, 754, 797,
864, 891, 913; Tales 423, 556, 612
Shenstone, William, Anecdotes 326, 519, 524, 670,
724; Extracts 321, 636; Poetry 214, 406, 462, 474,
636, 646, 718, 720, 865, 872
Shepard, Isaac Fitzgerald, Poetry 142, 204
Sheridan, Richard Brinsley, Anecdotes 48, 93, 144,
384, 435, 446, 496, 513, 565, 713, 718, 721,
725, 751; Biographies 43, 93, 109, 144, 192, 197,
221, 251, 585, 718; Criticism 320; Extracts 441,
713; Poetry 79, 138, 383, 455, 468, 506, 603,
691, 718, 867, 865; Review 814
Sherman, H., Poetry 912
Sherry, Charles, Poetry 381
Shippen, Joseph, Poetry 41
Shirley, James, Poetry 44, 451, 713, 778, 909
Shoemaker, William L., Poetry 227
Shore, Jane, Biography 144, 522, 724; Criticism
251
Shreve, Thomas H., Poetry 791, 891
Sidney, Sir, Philip, Anecdotes 691, 746, 929;
Biography 748; Criticism 430; Extract 383;
Poetry 9, 423
Sigourney, Lydia H., Anecdote 828; Biographies 426,
575, 645, 761; Criticism 37; Extracts 461, 553,
667, 679; Poetry 8, 10, 15, 18, 37, 42, 44, 48,
56, 57, 64, 70, 91, 98, 104, 105, 124, 142, 146,
147, 152, 154, 176, 184, 191, 204, 225, 227, 237,
241, 243, 246, 257, 264, 270, 271, 272, 284, 303,
309, 325, 332, 345, 347, 355, 366, 370, 378, 381,
382, 386, 388, 396, 402, 404, 408, 422, 423, 427,
433, 438, 439, 442, 445, 446, 447, 448, 451, 461,

472, 475, 480, 493, 531, 534, 536, 553, 556, 569,
589, 595, 608, 609, 612, 634, 637, 641, 662, 667,
668, 679, 680, 681, 700, 703, 708, 722, 726, 732,
737, 753, 754, 761, 777, 786, 791, 797, 798, 808,
834, 862, 889, 906, 910, 911, 924, 928, 935, 939,
940; Tales 394, 396, 761
Sill, Joseph, Poetry 298
Silliman, Benjamin, Contributor 538
Simes, Louisa, Poetry 18
Simmons, James W., Poetry 510, 787, 790
Simms, William Gilmore, Contributor 790; Poetry 57,
64, 73, 98, 155, 325, 378, 381, 427, 478, 522,
611, 634, 662, 680, 749, 790, 791, 834, 885, 896;
Review 792; Tales 53, 454, 611, 680, 787
Singleton, George B., Poetry 57, 378, 791; Tale 787
Skelton, John, Poetry 565
Small, James M., Poetry 154
Smart, Christopher, Anecdotes 329, 806; Biography
718; Poetry 93, 364, 536, 691, 696
Smith, Adam, Biographies 591, 810; Extracts 598, 843
Smith, Alfred L., Poetry 473
Smith, Captain John, Biographies 43, 44, 329, 366,
546, 595, 697, 718; Letters 43
Smith, Charlotte, Biography 782; Extracts 313, 779;
Poetry 76, 101, 110, 196, 234, 462, 499, 546,
648, 691, 713, 718, 779, 849; Tales 397, 761,
876
Smith, Elihu Hubbard, Contributor 618
Smith, Elizabeth Oakes. See Smith, Mrs. Seba.
Smith, Emeline S., Poetry 737
Smith, Horace, Extract 478; Poetry 245, 382, 906
Smith, Josiah L., Poetry 703
Smith, L. M., Poetry 227
Smith, Louisa P., Poetry 270, 434, 489
Smith, Rebecca, Poetry 720
Smith, Sarah, Poetry 429
Smith, S. Compton, Poetry 761
Smith, Mrs. Seba, Poetry 91, 99, 130, 156, 176, 204,
381, 402, 438, 440, 553, 611, 703, 726, 750, 754,
791, 889; Sketch 754; Tales 91, 298, 608, 611
Smith, Thomas Jeffrey, Jr., Poetry 611
Smith; William, Poetry 912
Smith, William R., Poetry 334
Smollett, Tobias George, Anecdotes 79, 251, 311, 454,
497, 696, 698, 718; Biography 474; Extract 760;
Letters 718; Novel 743; Poetry 214, 474, 683
Smyth, William, Poetry 340, 853
Snelling, Anna L., Poetry 749
Snelling, William J., Poetry 48, 423, 808
Snodgrass, Augustus, Poetry 204
Snodgrass, J. Evans, Poetry 64, 227, 787
Snow, H. Isabella, Poetry 447
Sobolewski, Paul, Poetry 700
Somerville, William, Poetry 647
Sotheby, William, Poetry 75
Southerland, S. E., Poetry 382
Southey, Robert, Anecdote 718; Biographies 10, 93,
302, 448, 480, 608, 696, 792, 865; Book Review
116; Criticism 79, 97, 192, 430, 453, 524, 538,
591, 720; Essay 545; Extracts 303, 325, 437, 444,
478, 565, 806; Letters 641, 743; Poetry 76, 77,
79, 93, 97, 101, 139, 164, 170, 174, 192, 196,
209, 245, 264, 284, 310, 313, 326, 330, 339,
344, 355, 364, 369, 377, 378, 383, 397, 403,
423, 474, 510, 536, 538, 545, 567, 585, 589,
612, 618, 623, 646, 647, 661, 678, 680, 696,
713, 720, 756, 757, 759, 779, 789, 806, 864,
865, 872, 876, 899, 924, 933, 935; Tale 748
Southgate, Charles, Poetry 876
Southwell, Robert, Poetry 285, 451, 553, 618

X– Y–Z

Index of Tales, Novels, and Drama

A work appearing in more than one periodical but with varying internal punctuation is listed only once in this index. A tale appearing in more than one periodical that is occasionally followed by "A Tale," is, similarly, listed only once. Works appearing in more than one periodical with varying sub-titles are listed separately. When some variation in the spelling of words occurs within titles of the same work ("The Mask of the Red Death" and "The Masque of the Red Death"), those titles are combined in this index.

F

G

"Gabrielle de Vergi; a Tale" 718
"The Galanti-Show; or, Laughter and Learning All the Year Round" 81
"The Gallery of a Misanthrope" 57
"The Gambler" 249
"The Gambler--(A Tale of Truth)" 519
"The Gambler's Last Loaf" 915
"The Gambler's Wife" 388
"The Game of Chess" 645, 761, 791
"The Gamester" 181, 383, 711
"The Gamesters: A French Story" 427
"The Gamesters: A Tale" 718
"The Gamester's Daughter" 64, 142
"The Gamester's Fortune" 381
"Ganymede" 912
"The Garden-Girl of the Eden-Bank" 884
"Garfilena. A Hungarian Tale" 486
"The Garland of Wit and Love. A Tale of the Reformation" 726
"Gaspar Scriblerus" 64
"The Gathering" 483
"The Gauchos; a Tale of the Pampas" 604
"Gebel Teir; or Mountain of Birds" 575
"The Gem of the Sea, or the Approach to Land" 919
"General Washington and Count Pulaski: Or, the Unknown Warrior. A Tale of the American Revolution" 345
"The Generosity of the Chevalier Bayard" 928
"The Generous Lady" 691
"The Generous Mask. A Tale" 618
"The Generous Mask. A Tale. Imitated from the German" 377, 383
"The Generous Russian; or, Love and Gratitude" 342
"The Generous Stranger" 176
"The Generous Sultana. An Arabian Tale" 413
"Genevieve" 434
"Genevieve Galliot" 331
"Genius vs. Wealth, or the Lawyer's History" 454
"The 'Genteel' Pigeons. A Household Story" [Douglas Jerrold] 856
"The Gentleman Beggar" 928
"The Gentleman from Cahawba and His Drowsy Victim" 602
"A Gentleman with a Wife in Every Town" 717
"The Gentle Recruit" 777
"George Gray's Wedding" 374
"George Harvest: Parson and Comedian" 312
"George St. George Julian" 261
"George St. George Julian.--The Prince" 749
"The German Gibbet" 100
"The German Jew" 248
"The German's Daughter" 791
"The German's Story" 331
"The German's Story, or the Tale of Hiram Heltzenpacker" 58
"The German's Tale" 777
"Germantown" 382
"Gertrude" 791
"Gertrude. A Fact" [Whittier] 845
"Gertrude Beverly" 10, 197, 448, 761
"Gertrude de Wart, or, Fidelity Until Death" 138
"Gertrude Hoffman" 791
"Gertrude of Wyoming" [Thomas Campbell] 277
"The Ghost: A Tale. Founded on Fact" 397
"The Ghost. A Village Story" 176
"The Ghost Ball" [Nathaniel P. Willis] 381

"The Ghostly Funeral" 73
"The Ghost of Granny Hogins" 48
"Ghost of My Uncle" 761
"The Ghost of the Bed-Chamber. A Sketch for the Superstitious" 884
"The Ghost-Seer" [Schiller] 56, 787
"Ghost Stories" 73
"Gideon Grinder" 496
"Gilbert Gurney" 777
"Giovana, the Georgian Pirate: Or, the Black Dragon. A Tale of the Atlantic" 345, 473
"The Gipsey Chief; or, the Haunted Oak. A Tale of Other Days" 627
"The Gipsey Mother; or, the Miseries of Enforced Marriage" 627, 761
"Gipsy of Debretzin" 622
"The Gipsy's Revenge" 402
"The Gipsy's Ride" [Nathaniel P. Willis] 272
"The Gipsy's Star. A Tale of the Abruzzo" 602
"The Girl of the Cane Brake" 197
"The Girl of the Mountains" 698
"Giulietta" [L. E. Landon] 761
"Giulio, a Tale" 603
"Giuseppe: Founded Upon Facts of Real Life" 830
"The Glebe House; a Tale" 339, 757
"Glenalpin; or, the Bandit's Cave" 627
"Glenorran: Or, the Picture Gallery" 109
"The Glenroys" 237
"Glicera" 234
"The Goal Chaplain: Or a Dark Page from Life's Volume" 81
"The Goblet" 261
"The Goddesses" 496
"The Godfather" 761
"Going in the Country" 496
"Going to Board" 906
"Going to the Dogs" [T. S. Arthur] 681
"The Gold Bubble" 602
"The Gold Chain" 382
"The Golden Locket: A Tale of the Nineteenth Century. Founded on Facts" 35
"The Golden Snuff-Box" 522
"The Golden Speculation" 53
"The Golden Tooth" 466
"The Goldmaker's Village" 583
"The Gold Pen" 37
"The Gold Seekers of the Sacramento" 420
"The Goldsmith of Padua" 48
"The Goldsmith of Westcheap" 761
"Gonnella--A Tale by Pietro Fortini" 354
"Gonzalez the Fated One, or the Gipsey's Prediction" 248
"Good and Bad News, a Tale" 499
"The Good Goaler" 388
"Good Little Violet" 186
"The Good Match" 388
"The Good Natured Man: A Tale of the Drama" 522
"Good Sir Walter" 777
"The Good Uncle" 339
"Gossip and Mischief" 245
"Gostanza and Martuccio. A Florentine Tale" 876
"The Governess" 670, 761, 791
"Gowannahee. . . . A Tale" 556
"Grace Falkiner" 142
"Grace Kennedy--A Tale" 10, 236
"Grace Lindin. Four Ages in the Life of an American" 204
"Grace Mills" 186
"Grace Wentworth" 382
"The Grand House in Our Village" 834

J

"Jack Fallon, and Jack's Pet" 89
"Jack Hinton, the Guardsman" 156, 608
"Jack Ketch. A Temperance Tale" 534
"Jack Long; or, Lynch-Law and Vengence" [Charles Wilkins Webber] 73
"Jack-O'-Lantern: A New Light Story" 791
"Jack Shaddock" 608
"Jack Shadow" 935
"Jack's Return and Marriage" 335
"Jack the Shrimp" 164, 386, 465, 777
"Jack Waller's Story" 221
"Jacky Pringle; or, the Poor Sometimes Grateful" 834
"Jacob Faithful" 510, 511
"Jacob Jones; or, the Juvenile Delinquent" 53
"Jacob Jones: Or the Man Who Couldn't Get Along in the World" 761
"Jacquot. A Tale" 691
"James Morland, the Cottager" 563
"James Walpole: Or, a Tale of the Times" 345
"Jane Allison's Two Rival Beaux" 761
"Jane Bond. A True Narrative" 316
"Jane Cameron, or the Want of the One Thing Needful" 929
"Jane Ogilvie--An Irish Tale" 718
"Jane Sinclair; or the Fawn of Spring-Vale" [William Carleton] 608
"Janet Armstrong; an Irish Tale" 522
"Janet Melville; or, too Late" 186
"Japhet, in Search of a Father" 355, 510, 511
"Jaques Aymar, or, the Divining Rod" 551
"A Jar of Honey from Mount Hybla" [Leigh Hunt] 168
"Jeanie Stevenson. A Tale of the Dominie" 303
"Jealousy" 693
"Jeannot and Colin. A Tale" [Voltaire] 326, 754
"Jean St. Aubin" 394
"Jedediah Birch" 912
"Jehander, Prince of Ava. An Oriental Tale" 713
"Jehoida Hawkins; or the Auto-Biography of a Persecuted Vagabond" 440
"Jemima O'Keefy. A Sentimental Tale" 88, 896
"Jem Thalimer's Female Ward; or the Inconvenience of Having Two Characters" [Nathaniel P. Willis] 381
"Jenny Kelly" 383
"Jenny; or the Three Flower Markets of Paris" 642
"Jerome Chabert. Or, a Night in the Adriatic" 81
"Jerome, the Milane, or, the Henchman of Bourbon" 700
"The Jerseyman's Story, or the Tale of Isaac Doone, of Brunswick" 58
"Jesse of Dumblane" 88
"Jessica: Or, an Inn-Keeper's Story" 339
"Jessie Gordon" 634
"The Jester and His Child" 298
"The Jeweller's Wife" 81
"The Jewels of Cornelia" 58
"The Jew of Hamah" 292
"The Jew: Or Honesty the Best Policy" 754
"The Jewess of Cairo" 381
"The Jew's Revenge" 394, 692
"Jimmy Charcoal.--Fall of the Carbonari" 262
"Job Clark" 908
"The Jockey Cap" 722
"Joe Hodges" 109
"Joe Oldoak's Revenge" 80
"Joel Jumble. A Tale for Fathers" 572
"John Audley, or, the Adventures of a Night" 873
"John Carper, the Hunter of Lost River" 791
"John Bicker, the Dry Dominie of Kilwoody" 534
"John Henry Fitz Allen" 434
"John MacTaggart, a Highland Story" 717
"John Manesty, the Liverpool Merchant" 608
"John Tarleton. A Tale of New England" 303
"John the Leper. A Tale" 186
"John White and Albert Williams, or the Lapse of Twenty Years. A Tale" 366
"John W. Robertson. A Tale of a Cent" 634
"Johnny Leonard and His Mother" 153
"John's Alive! Or the Bride of a Ghost. Being a True History of True Love" 99
"The Jordans of Grange, and the Old Maids of Balmogy" 777
"Jose Maria, the Great Spanish Robber" 427
"Josephine. A Tale of Truth" 384
"Josephine, the German Emigrant" 797
"Joseph Rushbrook, or the Poacher" 777
"Journal of a Poor Vicar" 602
"The Journal of Julius Rodman, Being an Account of the First Passage Across the Rocky Mountains of North America Ever Achieved by a Civilized Man" [Poe] 298
"The Journal; or, Birthday Gifts" 668
"A Journey in a Diligence" 690
"Journey in Quest of a Wife" 524
"Juba" 645
"The Jubilee of Genius" 131
"Judge Crane and the Landlady" 382
"The Judge's Charge" 808
"Julia and Edward" 497
"Julia de Fenestranges" 830
"Julia de Lindorf. A Tale of the Guillotine" 700
"Julia de Roubigné; a Tale" [Henry Mackenzie] 743
"Julia Gray, or the Orphan" 761
"Juliana" 602
"Julian and Leonor" 262
"Julia: Or, Adventures of a Curate's Daughter" 339
"Julia; or, the Change of Character" 451
"Julia, or the Penitent Daughter" 65
"Julia St. Germain. A Tale from Facts" 493
"Juliet Rivers; or, a Father's Crime" 627
"Julietta; or, the Beautiful Head" 73
"Julius and Maria" 180
"Jumbo and Zairee" 272
"The Juryman Mason" 50
"Justice Vanquishing the Force of Nature. A Persian Tale" 533
"Justina and Rosina" 339
"Justina, or the Will; a Domestic Story" 258
"Justine. A French Tale" 91

K

"Kaam; or Daylight, the Arapahoe Half-Breed. A Tale of the Rocky Mountains" 761
"Kascambo. A Tale of the Caucasus" 303, 556
"Kate Bouverie" 761
"Kate Connor" 534
"Kate Darlington. A Tale of Merry England" 15
"Kate Elliott" 382
"Kate of Windiewa's" 522
"Kate Somerville" 777
"Katrina Schuyler. A Sketch of the Times of Charles the Second" [Theodore Sedgwick Fay] 611
"Kedar and Amela, an Arabian Tale" 384
"The Keeper of the Prison-Ship Jersey" 18, 394
"The Keeping-Room of an Inn; or, Judge Beler's Ghost" 229

M

INDEX OF TALES, NOVELS, AND DRAMA

W

Other Reference Works in Literature
Published by G. K. Hall & Co.

John and William Bartram, William Byrd II,
and St. John de Crèvecoeur:
A Reference Guide
Rose Marie Cutting
6 x 9. xxiii, 174 pp.   ISBN 0-8161-1176-6 $19.00

A Chaucer Dictionary
Proper Names and Allusions, Excluding
Place Names
Bert Dillon
6 x 9. xvii, 266 pp.   ISBN 0-8161-1112-X $25.00

A Bibliography of Chaucer, 1964-1973
Lorrayne Y. Baird
6 x 9. xviii, 287 pp.   ISBN 0-8161-8005-9 $22.00

Folger Shakespeare Library: Catalog of the
Shakespeare Collection
Washington, D.C.
7 x 10. 2 vols. v, 697 pp. iii, 369 pp.
ISBN 0-8161-1009-3 $45.00

A Bibliography of Writings By and About
John Ford and Cyril Tourneur
Kenneth Tucker
6 x 9. xviii, 134 pp.   ISBN 0-8161-7834-8 $15.00

The Critical Reception of Robert Frost
Peter Van Egmond
6 x 9. xiv, 319 pp.   ISBN 0-8161-1105-7 $20.00

Early Puritan Writers: William Bradford,
John Cotton, Thomas Hooker, Edward
Johnson, Richard Mather, Thomas Shepard:
A Reference Guide
Edward J. Gallagher and Thomas Werge
6 x 9. xvi, 207 pp.   ISBN 0-8161-1196-0 $20.00

Seventeenth-Century American Poetry:
A Reference Guide
William J. Scheick and JoElla Doggett
6 x 9. xiv, 208 pp.   ISBN 0-8161-7983-2 $15.00

Roger Williams: A Reference Guide
Wallace Coyle
6 x 9. xiv, 102 pp.   ISBN 0-8161-7986-7 $12.00

Katherine Anne Porter and
Carson McCullers:
A Reference Guide
Robert F. Kiernan
6 x 9. xiv, 194 pp.   ISBN 0-8161-7806-2 $19.00

Sylvia Plath and Anne Sexton:
A Reference Guide
Cameron Northouse and Thomas P. Walsh
5⅜ x 8. vii, 143 pp.   ISBN 0-8161-1146-4 $9.50

Ernest Hemingway: A Reference Guide
Linda Welshimer Wagner
6 x 9. xxii, 383 pp.   ISBN 0-8161-7976-X $22.00

Prices subject to change without notice